W9-BCR-888

Second Edition

Advertising Research:

THEORY AND PRACTICE

Joel J. Davis
School of Journalism & Media Studies,
San Diego State University

Prentice Hall
Boston   Columbus   Indianapolis   New York   San Francisco   Upper Saddle River
Amsterdam   Cape Town   Dubai   London   Madrid   Milan   Munich   Paris   Montreal   Toronto
Delhi   Mexico City   Sao Paulo   Sydney   Hong Kong   Seoul   Singapore   Taipei   Tokyo

Editorial Director: Sally Yagan
Editor in Chief: Eric Svendsen
Acquisitions Editor: Melissa Sabella
Editorial Project Manager: Meeta Pendharkar
Editorial Assistant: Elisabeth Scarpa
Director of Marketing: Patrice Lumumba Jones
Senior Marketing Manager: Anne Fahlgren
Marketing Assistant: Melinda Jensen
Senior Managing Editor: Judy Leale
Project Manager: Debbie Ryan
Production Project Manager: Clara Bartunek
Art Director: Jayne Conte

Cover Designer: Bruce Kenselaar
Manager, Cover Visual Research & Permissions: Karen Sanatar
Cover Art: Fotolia
Media Editor: Denise Vaughn
Media Project Manager: Lisa Rinaldi
Full-Service Project Management: Vishal Gaudhar, Aptara®, Inc.
Composition: Aptara/Falls Church
Printer/Binder: Courier/Westford
Cover Printer: Lehigh-Phoenix Color/Hagerstown
Text Font: Garamond

Photo Credits: Scott Maxwell / LuMaxArt/Shutterstock pp. 89, 92, 95, 97; Asiavasmuncky / Dreamstime.com, p. 89; © Tondafoto | Dreamstime.com, p. 132; Wavebreakmedia Ltd/Dreamstime, p. 132; © miskolin/Fotolia, p. 147; © Koele | Dreamstime.com, p. 158; Photograph by Gil Lora, p. 158; © Py2000 | Dreamstime.com, p. 195; © Sunil281 | Dreamstime.com, p. 252; Iofoto | Dreamstime.com, p. 272; © Gibsonff | Dreamstime.com, p. 277; © Taolmor | Dreamstime.com, p. 277; © Moreauxjer | Dreamstime.com, p. 277; © Palto | Dreamstime.com, p. 328; Kar/Shutterstock, pp. 332, 333; © Vicza | Dreamstime.com, p. 472; © Rhambley | Dreamstime.com, p. 472; © Kurhan | Dreamstime.com, p. 472; Yuri Arcurs/Shutterstock, pp. 490, 491, 492; © Cookelma | Dreamstime.com, p. 642; © Armonn | Dreamstime.com, p. 642; © Anthonyata | Dreamstime.com, p. 642; © Kaarsten | Dreamstime.com, p. 642; © Nyul | Dreamstime.com, p. 272.

Microsoft® and Windows® are registered trademarks of the Microsoft Corporation in the U.S.A. and other countries. Screen shots and icons reprinted with permission from the Microsoft Corporation. This book is not sponsored or endorsed by or affiliated with the Microsoft Corporation.

Library of Congress Cataloging-in-Publication Data
Davis, Joel
  Advertising research : theory and practice/Joel J. Davis.—2nd ed.
    p. cm.
  Includes bibliographical references and index.
  ISBN-13: 978-0-13-212832-2 (alk. paper)
  ISBN-10: 0-13-212832-2 (alk. paper)
  1. Advertising--Research. I. Title.
  HF5814.D38 2012
  659.1072--dc22

                                  2011007121

10 9 8 7 6 5 4 3 2

Prentice Hall
is an imprint of

PEARSON

www.pearsonhighered.com

ISBN 10:   0-13-212832-2
ISBN 13: 978-0-13-212832-2

To Danna, Kyle, and McKenna—My world would be a much more lonely, and much less fun, place without you

BRIEF CONTENTS

CONTENTS

Chapter 7   Analysis of Qualitative Data   173

PART V Applied Topics

PREFACE TO THE SECOND EDITION

Advertising was on the cusp of a metamorphosis when the first edition of *Advertising Research: Theory and Practice* was published. Most recognized that advertising was undergoing significant change but, in retrospect, predictions of the future were nowhere near as breathtaking as the developments we have witnessed. Few predicted the essential importance of online advertising. The recognized value of social networks, consumer-generated media, mobile advertising, in-video game advertising, and viral video was still to come. Many did, however, acknowledge the increasing need for well-designed, insightful research to help advertisers make decisions regarding the best use of these emerging advertising options. This book is an attempt to help students better understand how research performs this role: helping advertisers best make decisions with regard to strategy, target audiences, and creative in an increasingly complex consumer and media environment.

CHANGES TO THE TEXT

This book covers many of the same topics as the first edition, but it is more than just an update. While all of the carry-over chapters from the first edition have been significantly rewritten, new chapters have been added to respond to recent developments in advertisers' behaviors as well as changes and advancements in research design and methodology. Some of the original chapters that addressed issues now of secondary importance to advertisers have been dropped.

This edition shows marked differences from the first edition in four areas.

First, the text itself has been completely rewritten and edited to increase clarity. Students over the years have commented on the "density" and "formality" of the first edition. This text, without sacrificing important content, makes a conscious effort to communicate this content in a way that is much more student-friendly. The text also contains significantly more examples and elaborated discussion versus the first edition. Beyond the revisions to the written text, this edition takes a more visual approach to communicating key concepts. Almost all graphics and visuals from the first edition have been revised to better illustrate key points, and a significant number of new graphics have been added.

Second, all of the research examples have been updated with an eye toward increasing not only currency but also student relevance. New research has not simply been substituted for older research. Rather new research that relates to topics of student interest—social media, online advertising, viral video, video game advertising, and e-mail advertising—has been combined with contemporary examples from traditional media. Along these same lines, brands, products, and situations more likely to be of interest to students have been substituted for many of the examples used in the first edition.

Third, new developments in methodology have been addressed. The manner by which research information is collected has changed over the past decade, with increasing amounts of research being conducted online. In response, the text extends traditional topics such as sampling, question writing, and questionnaire design to online research. In addition, entirely new sections have been added to address online research ethics and online qualitative research. Beyond this, new methodological approaches have been developed since the first edition. Chapters 8 and 9, for example, go beyond cursory discussions of observation research to provide an in-depth discussion of new observational techniques that use computers to observe human behavior (especially in the online environment) and biometric observation that uses eye tracking, physiological measures, and brain waves to explore consumers' responses to advertising. Finally, recent developments in brand mapping, segmentation, advertising testing, and advertising optimization via multivariate research are also addressed.

Fourth, to assist student learning, review questions and application exercises have been completely rewritten. The review questions ask students to locate or recall information presented in a chapter. The application exercises are designed to encourage student engagement with chapter content. Many of the application exercises do not have a single correct answer, but rather are written in a way that encourages students to identify and then evaluate the strengths and weaknesses of potential actions and resulting decisions. Additionally, the application exercises that accompany the supplemental readings encourage students to critically evaluate real research projects.

TO THE STUDENT

Many students enter a research class believing the following:

- Learning about research is useless and unnecessary unless you want to be a researcher.
- Research is the same as number crunching; research and statistics are one and the same.
- Research is the antithesis of creative.

Over the course of a semester, I try to show my students that each of these statements is, in fact, false. This text is my attempt to convince you of the same.

Research Touches Everyone

As an advertising professional, you will encounter and use research in one of two ways. If you decide to become a research specialist, you will be responsible for the planning, execution, analysis, and presentation of research findings. It will be your job to provide the information others need to make the best advertising- and marketing-related decisions. However, if you decide to take a different position, you will be a research user. You will use the information gathered by others to help you make better decisions and to help you do your job more efficiently and successfully.

In short, regardless of the type of position you take, you will either be a user or a creator of research. *Advertising Research: Theory and Practice* will help you in both capacities. This text will teach you how to use and design research. You will also learn how to evaluate the soundness of information gathered by research, how to evaluate the appropriateness of various research techniques for different information needs, and how to interpret and apply research findings. Most important, you will learn that better advertising decision making occurs when you are able to support your professional judgment with research insights.

Research Is Not the Same As Number Crunching

Not all research is numeric. Focus groups and similar forms of research do not even use numbers to summarize the research findings. Quantitative research, on the other hand, entails numeric calculations and, when appropriate, the application of statistical techniques. However, these are only the tools one uses to find out what the numbers *mean and imply* for the decisions that need to be made. *The value of research lies not in number crunching but in interpretation.* Computers can quickly do the math. However, computers cannot tell us what the numbers mean nor what their implications are for the decisions that must be made. Thinking, insightful people are needed to bring meaning to the numbers. As a consequence, successful advertising researchers are not necessarily those who are good at math. Successful advertising researchers are those individuals who are good at thinking, finding patterns, and explaining what a finding means as opposed to what it says.

This edition of *Advertising Research: Theory and Practice* emphasizes the interpretation of research. It views numeric analyses as a means to the discovery of insights, rather than an end in themselves. This is seen in both the text itself and in the research reported in the online supplemental readings. You will see that numeric analyses are absent in many of these research studies and in others only basic math is used to analyze the data. In all cases, however, it is the interpretation of the data that provides the value of the research.

The Best Research Is Creative Research

The planning, conduct, analysis, and presentation of research are creative processes. As you read the text and the supplemental readings, you will see that it takes a great deal of creativity to clearly identify a research problem, design the most appropriate research, create the most useful questionnaire or interview guide, and analyze and present the findings in a way that maximizes the usefulness of those findings to decision makers. It is easy to design bad research. It is easy to present research findings that decision makers ignore because the findings are viewed as simplistic or irrelevant. Creative research is much more difficult to design, interpret, and present, but the findings and insights provided by creative research are welcomed and valued. *Advertising Research: Theory and Practice* provides you with the knowledge and skills that you need to be a creative research end user or designer. Each chapter, as well as the supplemental readings, provides numerous examples of the creative side of research.

Reading the Text

Every attempt has been made to make the information in *Advertising Research: Theory and Practice* useful, accessible, and understandable. Nevertheless, some content is by its very nature difficult to understand. With this in mind, it is recommended that you begin each chapter at its end. Read the review questions before you read the chapter. This will help you identify key terms and concepts. Then read the application exercises. This will help you understand the type of situations to which the chapter content is applicable. Then read the chapter. Finally, answer the review questions and any application exercises that you are assigned. Your postreading performance on the review questions and application exercises will help you distinguish between concepts you have successfully learned and those that you need to review. Finally, conclude each chapter with relevant online supplemental readings. This will help you most clearly see how chapter content applies to real world situations.

TO THE INSTRUCTOR

Advertising Research: Theory and Practice is divided into five parts. This organization of the text, coupled with its breadth of coverage, provides a great deal of instructor flexibility with regard to which topics are covered over the course of a semester and the order in which topics are presented. Additionally, the reports and presentations provided in the online supplemental readings allow instructors to develop multiple assignments to reflect their own course priorities.

Parts I and II provide an introduction to issues related to all research. The discussion in Part I provides a framework for the planning and conduct of research (Chapter 1) and introduces students to ethical considerations in research, paying particular attention to research ethics in an online environment (Chapter 2). Section II discusses sources of information in research: secondary information (Chapter 3), and samples and sampling (Chapter 4).

Part III focuses on qualitative research. Chapter 5 provides a detailed discussion of approaches to the collection of qualitative data, introducing the student to a broad range of qualitative data collection techniques including qualitative interviewing, projective techniques, repertory grid, and laddering. Chapter 6 discusses the planning and conduct of focus groups, while Chapter 7 provides detailed guidance for the analysis of qualitative data.

The nine chapters in Part IV compliment the qualitative discussion with a focus on quantitative research. The section begins with two chapters on observation research. Chapter 8 discusses human and automated observation of consumer behavior, with significant discussion focused on relating the observation of online behaviors to advertising decision making. Chapter 9 explores the increasing use of biometric research by advertising decision makers and discusses eye tracking, brain wave analysis and combined physiological approaches. Chapters 11 through 13 focus on data collection. After a discussion of measurement and related issues (Chapter 11), the discussion continues with a focus on how to phrase and construct survey questions (Chapter 12) and questionnaire design (Chapter 13). The discussion of experimentation (Chapter 14) is followed by two chapters that address quantitative data analysis through descriptive and inferential statistics (Chapters 15 and 16).

Part V, the concluding section, focuses on topics of specific interest to advertisers and advertising researchers. Topics include segmentation (Chapter 17), brand mapping including perceptual mapping (Chapter 18), concept and communication testing (Chapter 19), and post-production advertising testing and optimization (Chapter 20). The section concludes with a discussion of how to best prepare and present research findings (Chapter 21).

TEACHING AIDS

PowerPoint Presentations (0132128349)

A comprehensive set of PowerPoint slides that can be used by instructors for class presentations or by students for lecture preview or review is available.

Instructor's Manual (0132128330)

A complete instructor's manual, prepared by the author, can be used to prepare lecture or class presentations, find answers to the end of chapter application exercises and even to design the course syllabus.

Test Item File (0132835746)

The test bank for the 2nd edition contains over 50 questions for each chapter. Questions are provided in multiple-choice and true/false format. Page numbers corresponding to answers to the questions are provided for each question.

This Test Item File supports Association to Advance Collegiate Schools of Business (AACSB) International Accreditation. Questions in the Test Item File were prepared with the AACSB learning standards in mind. Where appropriate, the answer line of each question indicates a category within which the question falls.[1] This AACSB reference helps instructors identify those test questions that support their learning goals.

WHAT Is the AACSB?   AACSB is a not-for-profit corporation of educational institutions, corporations, and other organizations devoted to the promotion and improvement of higher education in business administration and accounting. A collegiate institution offering degrees in business administration or accounting may volunteer for AACSB accreditation review. The AACSB makes initial accreditation decisions and conducts periodic reviews to promote continuous quality improvement in management education. Pearson Education is a proud member of the AACSB and is pleased to provide advice to help you apply AACSB Learning Standards to any of your courses.

What Are AACSB Learning Standards?   One of the criteria for AACSB accreditation is the quality of the curricula. Although no specific courses are required, the AACSB expects a curriculum to include learning experiences in such areas as:

- Communication abilities
- Ethical understanding and reasoning abilities
- Analytical skills
- Use of information technology
- Dynamics of the global economy
- Multicultural and diversity understanding
- Reflective thinking skills

These seven categories are AACSB Learning Standards. While all of these categories are (to a greater or lesser extent) applicable to instruction in advertising research, the several that focus on ethics, reasoning, analytical, and thinking skills directly reflect the text's orientation regarding the interpretation and applied use of research. Questions that test

---

[1] Please note that not all test questions will indicate an AACSB category

skills relevant to these standards are tagged with the appropriate standard. For example, a question testing the moral questions associated with conducting research with children would receive the Ethical understanding and reasoning abilities tag.

How Can I Use These Tags? Tagged questions help you measure whether students are grasping the course content that aligns with AACSB categories. In addition, the tagged questions may help to identify potential applications of these skills. This, in turn, may suggest enrichment activities or other educational experiences to help students achieve these goals.

TestGen Test Generating Software

Pearson Prentice Hall's test-generating software is available from the Instructor Resource Center Online (www.pearsonhighered.com).

- PC/Mac compatible; preloaded with all of the Test Item File questions
- Manually or randomly view test bank questions and drag and drop to create a test
- Add or modify test bank questions using the built-in Question Editor
- Print up to 25 variations of a single test and deliver the test on a local are network using the built-in QuizMaster feature

Companion Website Featuring Supplemental Readings (0132576600)

At http://www.pearsonhighered.com/davis, instructors and students can click on the Companion Website link to access the supplemental readings for this text.

The one universal comment most commonly heard from both students and their instructors is "show us how this applies to the real world." This text, more so than any other research text, responds to this comment with its supplemental readings. The Companion Website for *Advertising Research: Theory and Practice* is home to excerpts from actual research as well as complete research reports and presentations. These materials illustrate how the concepts discussed in the text are applied in real world settings in the United States, Canada, England, and Australia. Many of these reports are proprietary, and we greatly appreciate the willingness of the report owners to allow us to showcase their work. The application exercises accompanying these materials encourage students to apply chapter content as they interact with and critically evaluate these real world materials. (The application exercises also provide an excellent start for class discussion.) The online availability of these materials allows instructors to customize and focus class discussion and assignments on specific areas of instructional interest. The supplemental readings are discussed at the end of each appropriate chapter in the section labeled "Applying Chapter Concepts." Application exercises related to the supplemental readings follow those for chapter content.

Three chapters in Parts I and II provide online supplemental readings. Chapter 1 presents materials relevant to the Centers for Disease Control and Prevention VERB communication campaign. The materials illustrate how research plays an important role throughout the advertising planning process. Chapter 3 presents an example of a presentation that primarily relies on secondary research. The presentation provides an excellent model for how to organize, interpret, and draw implications from secondary research. Chapter 4 provides five case studies drawn from the Pew Research Center that illustrate how sampling plans for different research studies are customized to respond to a research project's unique information needs.

Chapter 6 presents the supplemental readings for the qualitative chapters. The readings relate to the planning and results of focus groups designed to provide insights for an advertising campaign designed to reduce the incidence of individuals driving while drowsy. The screener, moderator's guides, advertising concepts, and focus group results are all provided.

Supplemental readings are provided for five of the quantitatively oriented chapters in Part IV.

- Chapter 8 contains two examples of observation research. The social media program designed by Amnesty International to reduce violence against women uses automated observation to evaluate the success of the campaign while the Video Consumer Mapping Study reports the results of the human observation research study of consumers' media usage.

- Chapter 9 presents the results of different applications of biometric research: Tobii Technology provides several case studies that illustrate the use and application of eye tracking research to advertising testing, Etre provides its application of eye tracking to Web site analysis, One to One Insight provides its research report "Emotion, Engagement and Internet Video," and Mindscope provides the results of an fMRI advertising test.

- Chapter 12 presents the results of two research studies with a focus on the questions used for data collection. The Razorfish Digital Brand Experience Report/2009 is designed to provide an in-depth understanding of how the evolving digital environment is changing the way that consumers interact with brands. The Cossette 2009 Social Media Study is designed to gather insights on consumers who use social media, specifically, to provide an in-depth understanding of social media penetration as well a social media users' motivations, behaviors, and attitudes.

- Chapter 13 provides three examples of actual questionnaires to support and extend the text's discussion of question writing and questionnaire design.

- Chapter 14 provides two examples of advertising-related experiments. The first study reprints the Executive Summary from the groundbreaking Interactive Advertising Bureau's "Online Advertising Effectiveness Study." The second study is provided by Massive Incorporated and reports the results of an in-video game advertising test.

Finally, four of the Part V chapters contain supplemental readings.

- Chapter 17 contains two segmentation studies. The Pew Internet & American Life segmentation of information and communication technology users illustrates how segmentation research is planned and analyzed, with particular attention to how segments are formed and described. Dan Pankraz's presentation "Generation C—A

Look Into Their World" provides an example of an in-depth analysis of a single segment and illustrates that this analysis can be as creative and compelling as the topic (or in this case, segment) that is being described.

- Chapter 19 presents the results of two advertising pretesting studies conducted by Health Canada. The first study is a communication test of advertising designed to encourage healthy eating, while the second study tests advertising designed to alert individuals to the danger of secondhand smoke.

- Chapter 20 presents two examples of post-production advertising research. Mapes and Ross has provided a topline copy testing report while a full report of advertising campaign evaluation (the National Tobacco Youth Campaign) has been provided by the Australian Department of Health and Ageing.

- Chapter 21 presents Feed Company's report of its "Viral Video Marketing Survey." This report, similar to reports provided in prior chapters, provides a model for excellence in data presentation.

ACKNOWLEDGMENTS

Many individuals and organizations contributed to the second edition of *Advertising Research: Theory and Practice.*

With regard to the text's content, my students over the years have all made a contribution. They were never hesitant to point out when material was too dense, unintelligible, abstract, or just plain boring. I've tried to revise the text to increase the chance that future students will have a different, more positive, reaction. Additionally, the team at Pearson Higher Education also worked hard to create a student-friendly text. Not only were these individuals a pleasure to work with, their professional judgment and assistance was invaluable. Of special note were Melissa Sabella, James Heine, Meeta Pendharkar, Clara Bartunek, and Kierra Bloom.

The educational value of the text has been immeasurably increased by the willingness of individuals and companies to share their work. I'd like to especially thank Amnesty International UK, Applied Marketing Research, Nick Armitage, Australian Department of Health and Ageing, Catalyst Research, Chocolate Communications, Cossette, Enquiro Search Solutions, Etre Limited, eSpares Ltd., Feed Company, Forrester Research, General Electric, HCD Research, Health Canada, Impact Research, Interactive Advertising Bureau, 1st2c Ltd., Luckie and Company, Mediamark Research Intelligence, The Nielsen Company, Dan Pankraz, SocialMedia8, Dr. Jeffrey Stanton, Pew Research Centers, Razorfish, Scout Labs, and Strategic Business Insights. Beyond these companies and individuals, I'm especially grateful to five individuals who not only provided proprietary materials but also unselfishly gave their time to help me better understand new developments: Barbara Barclay at Tobii, Tony Bazerghi at Mapes and Ross, Devin Hubbard at MindSign Neuromarketing, Jeremi Karnell at One to One Insight, and Jack Koch at Massive Incorporated. I would also like to thank three individuals who assisted in the development of this text through their careful and thoughtful reviews:

Edmund Hershberger	Southern Illinois University, Edwardsville
John Stipe	Grand Valley State University
Kevin R. Wise	University of Missouri

Finally, it is the rare book that is written without personal support. Fortunately, several individuals provided the encouragement and support necessary to keep me motivated and on track. Members of my family (Danna, Kyle, and McKenna) and our unofficial Irish family (Michael and Noirin O'Connell) were always there with a word of encouragement and to point out the glass was more full than empty. Mairead Travers spent many a Thursday evening asking "What's the new page count?" for which I am grateful. Finally, much of this book was written in Kinsale, Ireland. If you are ever visiting and need a place to think, eat, or drink, I'd recommend the gracious hospitality of Anthony Collins and Anne Gavin at the White Lady Hotel.

CHAPTER 1

The Nature and Process of Advertising Research

It used to be easy to define "advertising." An advertisement was, for example, a television commercial, a magazine print ad, a billboard, or a radio spot. While these forms of advertising remain important, the range of options available to advertisers has greatly expanded over the past decade. Advertisers faced with rapidly increasing options realize that informed, successful decisions require credible and creative insights into the consumer, media options, and the competitive environment. Insights that can only come from well-designed research. This chapter introduces you to advertising research.

***

When you are done reading this chapter, you should have a better understanding of:

- the areas in which research helps advertisers make better decisions
- the characteristics and contributions of companies who participate in the design, conduct, and analysis of advertising research
- how the sequential use of different research techniques leads to more successful advertising planning and decision making
- the sequence of steps underlying successful advertising research and the types of decisions made at each step.

Thomas here is little debate that advertising has changed over the past decade. Today's advertisers can take advantage of a broad range of traditional and new media options: television, radio, YouTube, Facebook, Twitter, paid search, mobile, and video game placement, to name just a few. Research techniques and options have also changed. New technologies and techniques allow deeper insights into consumers' attitudes and behaviors. What has not changed (and what has likely increased) is the *need* for research to guide and inform decision making. Regardless of the selected media option or advertising approach, the appropriate use of research greatly increases an advertiser's chances of success. Simply put, research helps advertisers make better informed decisions, and better informed decisions lead to more effective, successful advertising.

Research makes a contribution throughout the entire advertising planning process and typically focuses on four main areas of information needs. These areas, shown in Figure 1.1, are discussed in the next section. However, before this more detailed discussion takes place, several important aspects of the figure should be noted.

- ***Paths are very flexible.*** Advertisers can use research sequentially to address multiple areas of concern prior to making a decision, or they can use research to help them make better decisions in one particular area.

- ***Feedback and revision is an important part of the process.*** Insights gathered from one area of research can be used to guide, inform, and revise decisions reached earlier or in other areas.

- ***An advertiser can enter the process at any point.*** If, for example, elements of the marketplace and consumer are unchanged from prior planning periods, then an advertiser may want to focus research efforts only in the areas of creative development and media.

The next section of this chapter addresses each component of Figure 1.1.

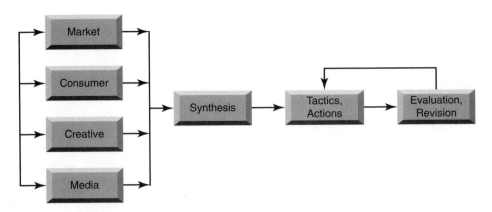

FIGURE 1.1   Overview of the Advertising Research Planning Process

THE CONTRIBUTIONS OF ADVERTISING RESEARCH

The Market

Successful advertising planning always builds upon a research-driven analysis of the marketplace. This research identifies and provides detail on relevant current and potential future issues and trends. It helps those in the planning process better understand the forces shaping the marketplace and how these forces may affect their own and their competitors' brands and advertising efforts. Research in this area typically addresses global, "big issue" questions, such as:

- What are key trends? To what extent do these trends affect product and advertising success? Are these trends likely to continue or shift? In what ways can our products and advertising capitalize on these trends? In what ways will the market be different next year versus this year?

- What is the competitive environment? Who are the category leaders? What brands are currently our primary and secondary competition? With what brands do we want to compete? What activities are representative of the category as a whole and of our particular competitors? How do the activities of our competitors compare to our own with regard to innovation and success?

- What new technologies are (or will soon be) available for advertising planning, execution, and placement? How successful have been recently introduced technologies?

- What are current and future problems and opportunities with regard to advertising planning?

Answers to these types of questions can come from several sources. Advertisers may decide to conduct proprietary research in order to address their own unique situation, or market analyses may be purchased from companies that specialize in this form of research.

The Consumer

Effective advertising, regardless of the medium in which it appears, flows from a thorough understanding of the target audience consumer. There are three dimensions of target audience analysis, all of which are better understood when research is utilized.

One dimension relates to general consumer trends. Questions addressed by research in this area may include:

- What changes in consumer lifestyles have accelerated or slowed over the past five years? How might these trends affect perceptions and use of the product or responses to the advertising?

- What changes in consumer attitudes, beliefs, and priorities have accelerated or slowed over the past five years? How might changes in these trends affect perceptions and use of the product and responses to the advertising?

The rise of social media as an advertising platform illustrates the importance of answering these types of questions. Advertisers who first noticed this trend were in much stronger positions to capitalize on this development.

Beyond a focus on patterns in lifestyle, attitude, and behavior changes, research also helps advertisers better understand consumers' attitudes in specific areas related to advertising planning and tactics. Research can, for example, provide insights into consumers' willingness to provide personal information in exchange for exposure to more relevant advertising[1] or it can assess consumers' receptivity to advertising placed in video games[2] or on social networking sites.

The second dimension of target audience analysis specifically focuses on the relationship between consumers and the advertised product or service. Here, questions addressed by research include:

- What segments of consumers exist, and what are the strengths/weaknesses/potential of each segment with regard to the advertised product or service?
- Within each segment, what are consumer characteristics with regard to demographics, behaviors, psychographics, and lifestyle? How do these characteristics relate to advertising decision making?
- What are opportunities within each segment based on consumers' purchase patterns, brand trial, and brand loyalty?

Questions such as these are typically answered by segmentation research (see Chapter 17). This type of research divides the total population of consumers into distinct groups, where each group differs (versus other groups) with regard to important attitudes or behaviors. This division of consumers into smaller groups allows advertisers to better understand the tactics and approaches that are most likely to be successful for each group. Figure 1.2 presents an illustration of consumer segmentation, in this case Forrester Research's segmentation based on involvement with social technologies.[3] Note that while the segmentation provides important insights into the characteristics of different groups, the advertiser must determine the best way to apply this information to advertising planning.

Once segments have been identified, research is used to increase the understanding how different segments of consumers perceive the advertiser's and competitors' brands or to better understand the behaviors and attitudes of different segments as these characteristics relate to the advertiser's goals and plans. This knowledge can, for example, helps an advertiser determine whether it is best to reinforce attitudes within one segment of the population or change current attitudes toward the brand within a different segment. Here, when there is a focus on the brand, research helps to answer the following types of questions:

- What are current perceptions of the brand? Are these perceptions in the brand's best interest?
- How do brand perceptions differ among users and nonusers? What is the source or basis of these perceptions? How firmly held are these perceptions?
- What benefits does the target audience seek from products in this category? To what extent is our brand seen as delivering these benefits?
- Are there benefits that our brand offers that other brands do not? Are these benefits *currently* important to our target? Are these benefits *potentially* important to the target? Can these benefits be made important to the target?

Research also helps an advertiser understand how consumers interact with brands and products. Research can help an advertiser understand whether a consumer's decision

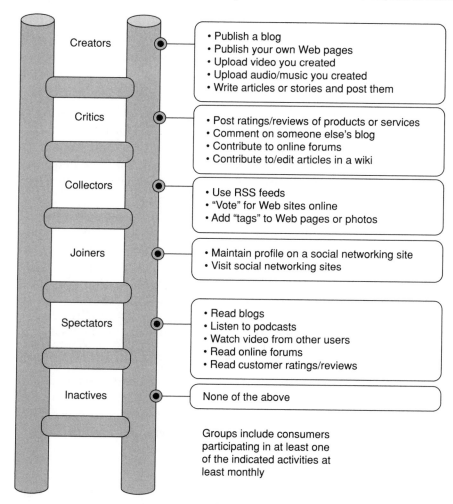

Creators
- Publish a blog
- Publish your own Web pages
- Upload video you created
- Upload audio/music you created
- Write articles or stories and post them

Critics
- Post ratings/reviews of products or services
- Comment on someone else's blog
- Contribute to online forums
- Contribute to/edit articles in a wiki

Collectors
- Use RSS feeds
- "Vote" for Web sites online
- Add "tags" to Web pages or photos

Joiners
- Maintain profile on a social networking site
- Visit social networking sites

Spectators
- Read blogs
- Listen to podcasts
- Watch video from other users
- Read online forums
- Read customer ratings/reviews

Inactives
None of the above

Groups include consumers
participating in at least one
of the indicated activities at
least monthly

FIGURE 1.2   Forrester Research Social Technologies Segmentation

to purchase the product is more rational or emotional, whether or not a great deal of thought or consideration underlies brand selection, and the extent to which consumers perceive the choice of a particular brand as making a statement about themselves. These types of research-based insights provide direction for strategic and creative development, especially for the selection of essential message and creative tone.

A parallel set of questions is addressed by research when the advertising relates to non-brand activities, for example, anti-drug and antismoking advertising, cancer prevention, water conservation, or reducing carbon footprints. These questions include:

- What are current perceptions of our issue? Are these perceptions in the issue's best interest? Are these perceptions primarily emotional or rational? To what extent are these perceptions factually correct?

- How do the basis and content of perceptions differ among those who are positive, negative, and neutral? What is the source or basis of these perceptions? How firmly held are these perceptions?

• What benefits can we offer the target? Are there different benefits for different groups of individuals?

- What are the obstacles or barriers to moving consumers in the desired direction?

Creative

An analysis of the marketplace, consumer, and product or issue typically leads to a determination of positioning—a descriptive statement of the agency's and client's view of the marketplace niche that they believe the product or issue can most successfully fill.[4] Sometimes a positioning is determined based entirely on judgment, but more frequently research is conducted to evaluate the strongest from among a set of positionings. (Chapter 19 provides a detailed discussion of this type of research.)

Once a positioning is selected, the creative team must then translate the positioning into compelling and motivating advertising. An initial step in this creative development process is the identification of the essential message—the advertising's communication goal. Similar to positioning research, essential message research can help an advertiser identify the strongest of several considered messages. Once the essential message is identified and agreed on, research often plays an important role in the evaluation and selection of the creative itself. Here, different approaches to the advertising may be tested in order to identify each approach's strengths and weaknesses or to select the "winning" approach. (Research related to creative decisions is presented in Chapters 19 and 20).

As with the other areas of information need, research designed to provide insights into creative development is not limited to traditional advertising, but rather contributes across a broad range of new media environments. Thus, while research can help to identify the strongest of three proposed television commercials, it can also help to determine the best wording for a paid search ad or the best creative to use in video game placement.

Research not only makes a contribution during the creative development process, it also plays an important role with regard to finished creative in two main areas. First, research helps advertisers determine advertising success. Here, tracking studies can be used to monitor changes in attitudes, beliefs, and behaviors after the campaign has begun to appear. This type of research can be conducted by those involved in the campaign itself or by others external to the campaign who are interested in assessing campaign effectiveness. Milward Brown's Dynamic Tracking™ is an example of this type of research. This research collects feedback from consumers before, during, and after key periods of advertising activity. In doing so, Dynamic Tracking tells advertisers whether their advertising plan has worked by identifying

- whether consumers are aware of a brand's campaign;
- which elements are recalled most strongly;
- whether the media budget is being deployed efficiently;
- whether the intended message is coming across;
- and how the total communications mix is affecting consumers' relationships with the brand.[5]

Second, advertising research plays a key role in demonstrating that the claims put forth in an advertisement are not deceptive as defined by the FTC (Federal Trade Commission) or the FDA (Food and Drug Administration). Both regulatory agencies require that all product claims be supported by credible, well-designed research, that is

> "tests, analyses, research, studies, or other evidence based on the expertise of professionals in the relevant area, that has been conducted and evaluated in an objective manner by persons qualified to do so, using procedures generally accepted in the profession to yield accurate and reliable results."[6]

Advertisers who lack this support face fines and the possibility of having to run corrective advertising. (The role of research in supporting advertising claims is discussed in Chapter 20.)

Media Analysis and Placement

As seen, research addresses a broad range of issues during advertising planning and creative development. The use of research to reach an informed decision tends to increase the likelihood that appropriate insights into the marketplace will be drawn and that the strongest creative approach will be selected. However, even if the correct decisions are made in the prior areas, advertising that is not placed where the target has a high likelihood to see or hear it has little chance of affecting and motivating the target. Unseen or unheard advertising simply cannot work. Thus, one important form of advertising research, media research, helps advertisers and media specialists answer questions such as the following:

- How much are competitors spending on their advertising? How do these levels of spending affect our product or service's budget recommendations?
- Where, if anywhere, should the advertising be concentrated? Should equal emphasis be given to all areas of the country, or should the focus and concentration of spending be in specific geographic areas?
- When and how should advertising be scheduled?
- What is the optimal way to use different media?[7]
- What is the best mix of traditional and new media for accomplishing the product or service's advertising objectives?[8]

Synthesis

Research conducted in each of the prior areas provides important insights. However, in order for an advertiser to make the most informed decision, it is necessary to synthesize learning and insight from each area. The synthesis of research information is a critical step in the advertising planning process because it allows an advertiser to better see the interrelationships among diverse types of sources of information. A well-constructed synthesis is one that clearly presents key research information in a way that allows the advertiser to understand not only the "what" but the "why" of interrelated research findings and insights. Examples of this type of synthesis are:

- Key Trends in Mobile Content Usage and Mobile Advertising[9]
- Making Integrated Campaigns Work: How a Search Marketing Mindset Can Drive the ROI of Display Advertising[10]
- Marketing to Teens and Tweens[11]

Tactics, Actions, Evaluation, and Revision

The synthesis of research findings leads to tactics and actions. The advertising is created, and a commitment is made to media placement. The advertising is "live" and placed in front of the target audience. As discussed earlier, an integral part of this stage is evaluation—the use of research to monitor and assess how well tactics and actions are actually working. An advertiser using paid search, for example, would monitor click-though and conversion rates while an advertiser using customized landing pages might monitor the return on investment generated by alternative pages. An advertiser using television as the core campaign medium might track and monitor levels of awareness and attitude change generated by the campaign. These types of ongoing evaluative research lead to any necessary revisions in the campaign, allowing an advertiser to increase success through the elimination or modification of weaker tactics and the placement of greater emphasis on relatively stronger tactics.

WHO CONDUCTS RESEARCH?

Different types of individuals and organizations contribute to the collection and analysis of research information. These individuals and organizations can be distinguished on the basis of their ultimate involvement in research-based decisions.

Information Users

Individuals with direct responsibility for brand- and advertising-related decisions are the ultimate end users of research. These individuals are typically involved in all stages of the research project, from problem definition and research design through analysis and implications of research results.

Two types of individuals are typically involved in the research process on the client side: brand managers and research specialists. Brand managers are responsible for the marketing and advertising of a particular brand. These individuals, in conjunction with others at their company, use research to help them make decisions related to the product itself (e.g., product formulation, pricing, distribution), product marketing and advertising, and the product's current and potential consumers. Most clients also have an internal research department. Individuals in this department are responsible for coordinating, gathering, analyzing, and disseminating information on all aspects of the marketing activities for one or more of the company's brands and products. The client's research department is involved with a broad range of product and consumer research, the development of advertising campaigns, and the tracking of advertising effectiveness.

Individuals in all advertising agency departments use research to help them make better decisions. In most full-service agencies, research is conducted and analyzed by an internal research department. Smaller agencies may use their account or media personnel as their internal researchers, or they may hire research consultants on an as-needed basis. In both cases, agency researchers, the counterparts of the client's research department, serve two main functions:

- They respond to the ongoing informational needs of agency account management, media, and creative departments by planning, conducting, and analyzing original research as well as by examining and analyzing research conducted by other companies.

- They work closely with the client's research department to make certain that pertinent research conducted by the client is disseminated, with a point of view, to the appropriate agency personnel.

In addition to client-specific research, advertising agency research departments may also conduct research designed to foster a better understanding of consumers or current "hot topics" in advertising and media planning. These research studies may, for example, track changes in consumer attitudes, as in the DDB Lifestyle Study[12] or the Young & Rubicam Brand Asset Valuator.[13]

Research Specialists

No matter how brilliant or experienced a client or agency researcher is, there are still times when assistance is needed in the design or execution of a specific research project. In these cases, a client or agency may turn to a custom research supplier. Individuals who work at these companies are research specialists hired on a project-by-project basis. These specialists may assist in any phase of research: the conceptualization of the research problem, research design and methodology, data analysis, and data interpretation. Other custom research suppliers specialize in particular areas of research (e.g., testing and evaluation of the advertising creative, product positioning, product naming, package design) and in different types of research (e.g., focus groups, research among minorities and children, brainstorming, and new product development). This type of research assistance is typically proprietary, that is, a single client pays the custom research supplier and only that client receives the results of the research.

Related to the custom research supplier is the syndicated research firm. These firms provide expertise in a particular area, but rather than perform proprietary customized research and consultation, they collect and sell the same information to all companies that pay the subscription fee. Advertising agencies are generally interested in four types of syndicated information: media ratings, target audience media usage and demographics, advertising expenditures, and consumer trends.

Media and Consulting Companies

One result of a highly competitive media marketplace is the increased need for media companies to demonstrate their special ability to efficiently and effectively place advertisers' messages in front of the desired target audience. As a result, many media companies invest a significant amount of funds in research designed to increase advertisers' knowledge of their specific medium's strengths and to provide direction for the best use of their medium. Media companies assume that the better an advertiser understands its particular medium, the more positive the advertiser will be toward that medium. DoubleClick is a good example of how media companies use research to increase advertiser knowledge.

> DoubleClick describes itself as "A provider of digital marketing technology and services. The world's top marketers, publishers and agencies utilize DoubleClick's expertise in ad serving, rich media, video, search and affiliate marketing to help them make the most of the digital medium. From its position at the nerve center of digital marketing, DoubleClick provides superior insights and insider knowledge to its customers."[14]

Research provides advertisers with a reason to believe this positioning. Recent research issued by DoubleClick includes Creative Insights on Rich Media, Video Ad Benchmarks: Average Campaign Performance Metrics, Influencing the Influencers: How Online Advertising and Media Impact Word of Mouth, and the multi-year Consumer Touchpoints Series.[15]

Beyond research conducted by the media company itself, media companies may commission or support external research relevant to the medium. Google in collaboration with the WPP Group, for example, has committed nearly $5 million for funded research.[16]

Trade Associations

Trade associations are organizations that are founded and funded by businesses that operate in a specific industry. The purpose of a media-related trade association is to provide a consistent face of the medium to advertisers and the public and to provide information that can facilitate deeper (and hopefully more positive) understanding of that medium. One way in which such understanding is facilitated is through research.[17]

The Interactive Advertising Bureau (IAB) is an excellent example of how a trade association uses research to help advertisers better understand the medium. The IAB describes its role and mission as

> "dedicated to providing thought leadership, incisive research and public policy advocacy on behalf of its membership and the interactive industry. Our mission is to help drive the growth of the interactive marketplace."[18]

Research commissioned and provided by the IAB addresses contemporary issues facing advertisers interested in using new media, for example, banner advertising, advertising in digital media, multimedia advertising planning, and mobile and search marketing.[19]

Field Services

The actual collection of data is typically performed by field services, data collection specialists who collect data on a subcontract basis for agency and client research departments. (Many of these services also provide consultant services with regard to research design and analysis.) Field services perform the data collection function because it is not economically feasible for agencies and their clients to support the number of specialized personnel required to perform these and related tasks. Some field services perform a wide range of data collection activities while others specialize in specific areas, such as pharmaceutical research, mystery shoppers, voter research, or telephone interviewing.

Applied Marketing Research[20] is an excellent example of a full-service field service. This company's approach to supporting advertising and marketing research is reflected in its mission statement:

> Our mission is to provide our clients with insightful and usable information for making marketing decisions. We will accomplish this by employing innovative methods whenever possible; by finding new and innovative ways to apply traditional methods; and by always being responsive to our clients' needs for reliable and valid information that is delivered on time and on budget.

The full range of services provided by Applied Marketing Research is described below, and is also reflected in its corporate print ad (see Figure 1.3).

> *Study Design.* We work with our clients to ensure that we understand how the information will be used to make marketing decisions; we establish relevant research objectives based on those information needs; and we design projects that will meet the research objectives. We provide the following research services to meet your needs: telephone, mail and Internet surveys, focus groups and in-depth interviews, in-home usage tests.

> *Data-Collection Design.* Depending on the nature of the research objectives, we design the appropriate questionnaires or discussion guides for gathering the information needed for decision making.

> *Project Management.* Project managers will monitor the progress of the project to ensure that it is completed on time, on budget, and with the quality our clients expect.

> *Analysis.* In order to dig beneath the surface and determine what the results really mean, Applied uses a variety of simple and sophisticated analytical techniques.

> *Reporting and Consulting.* Applied Marketing Research can provide reports ranging in depth from simple "toplines" and PowerPoint presentations to full management reports including detailed findings, an "executive summary" of the important findings, and our "conclusions and recommendations" based on the study results.

THE PROCESS OF ADVERTISING RESEARCH

Advertising planning and research is a continuous process. Information and insights acquired from one research project or in one area of focus often lead to the identification of ways where additional research can be beneficial. Within this context of ongoing research, specific information needs are satisfied by specific research projects.

The design and conduct of a successful advertising research project passes through three broad stages:

- *Preliminary discussions and agreements* involve identification of a communications or marketing problem or opportunity, justification for the research itself, and specification of informational needs.

EXPERTISE TO MEET YOUR CHALLENGE!

Thorough studies that meet our specification and timeframe—that is what working with Applied Marketing Research is all about. Generally we turn proposals in 24 hours. So call on us for thorough, speedy research.

- In-home product testing
- Web-based survey research using advanced techniques (conjoint, discrete choice, max-diff, Hierarchical Bayes)
- Online tabulations, analysis, chart exports, and real-time data reporting
- Advanced in-house multivariate and statistical analysis
- Certified focus group moderator with expertise in online focus groups, projective techniques and perception analyzer methods
- Bi-lingual Spanish interviewing and moderating
- Executive in-depth interviews
- Reports formatted to meet your company style preferences
- Mixed-mode survey capabilities (combining mail, phone, and on-line data collection)
- State of the art CATI system with predictive dialing
- Four offices nationwide

 APPLIED MARKETING RESEARCH, INC.

WEB SITE: **www.appliedmr.com**
E-MAIL ADDRESS: **d.phipps@appliedmr.com**

KANSAS CITY OFFICE	NEW YORK OFFICE
420 W. 98th Street	244 Fifth Avenue, #243K
Kansas City, MO 64114	New York, NY 1001
1 (816) 442-1010	**1 (212) 717-5104**
ATLANTA OFFICE	NORTHERN CALIFORNIA OFFICE
3645 Marketplace Blvd., Suite 130-301,	101A Hickey Blvd., Suite 118
East Point, GA 30344	South San Francisco, CA 94080
1 (770)9 17-8621	**1 (650) 997-4646**

FIGURE 1.3   Applied Marketing Research Print Ad

- *Planning and data collection* operationalizes agreements reached in the prior stage. As a result, activities carried out in this stage relate to the planning and conduct of the research. During this stage, decisions are reached with regard to the most appropriate type of research to use, study cost and timing, determination of how and from whom (or where) the data will be obtained, and questionnaire and other material preparation. At the end of this stage, the research is initiated and data is collected.

- *Application* involves activities carried out after the data is collected. Data is analyzed, results are reported, and decisions are made based on implications drawn from the data.

The following sections discuss the characteristics of each step in the research process.

Preliminary Discussions and Agreements

The end product of this first broad stage of the research process is a problem statement that contains three elements: (1) a description of the problem or opportunity motivating the research, (2) an explanation as to why research is appropriate for providing the information needed to solve the problem or capitalize on the opportunity, and (3) a statement of specific information that is needed to determine the best way to resolve the problem or capitalize on the opportunity. Each of these components of the problem statement is developed in the sequence shown in Figure 1.4.

Problem Definition

Problem definition is the first and most important step in the research process. Decisions reached later in the research planning process, such as the types of information needed and the best manner in which to obtain this information, are all affected by how the

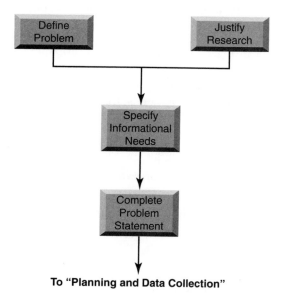

To "Planning and Data Collection"

FIGURE 1.4   Steps in the Development of the Research Problem Statement

problem motivating the research is initially formulated. Unless the research problem is properly defined and focused on the real problem facing the agency or client, the information produced by the research is unlikely to have any value to decision makers. It is critical, therefore, that the description of the problem motivating the research be clear, concise, and properly focused.

There are three general types of advertising-related problems and informational needs. Each requires a slightly different type of problem definition.

The first type of problem statement relates to the selection of alternatives and evaluation of alternative actions. Some problems arise when an advertiser or client is faced with evaluating the relative "goodness" of alternative choices or courses of action. In these situations, the problem definition clearly lists each alternative action under consideration, the reasons for the actions, and the decisions to be reached based on the research findings, for example:

> The Creative Department has written three alternative executions for the new Toyota campaign. These executions are labeled "Fast Car," "Value," and "Still The Best." Only one execution will be produced. We need to conduct research in order to determine the single execution that should be selected and taken forward into production.

> The company is considering changing the design of the product's package. The existing package places the deodorant within a cardboard container, while the proposed new packaging shrink wraps the product so that it can stand on the shelf without additional packaging. It is believed that this new packaging will have greater consumer appeal, will increase positive perceptions of the product, and will improve levels of purchase intent. Research is needed to help us understand the effect of this design change in these areas as compared to the effect and impact of the current packaging so that a decision on product packaging can be made.

The second type of problem statement relates to problems and opportunities. Some research begins with the feeling or knowledge that there is a problem or opportunity in the marketplace. In this case, the statement of the research problem typically begins as a vague statement of beliefs or information needs, for example: "Our sales are down. It's the advertising's fault. Find out what's going on. Fast!" In these situations, the problem definition arises out of a series of questions designed to focus on the problem and reduce the ambiguity of the initial problem statement. The questions in this example might include:

- On what basis are you calculating sales trends? Are you calculating sales based on dollar amounts, units sold, or some other criterion?
- What time periods are you using to determine the sales trend?
- What leads you to believe that the advertising is the root cause of observed sales trends?
- What changes, if any, have been made in your advertising program over the indicated time period? Have there been any shifts in strategy, creative approach, or media spending?

- What changes, if any, have been made in your marketing program over the indicated time period? Have there been any changes in, for example, pricing, product formulation, or distribution?

- What competitive activities have occurred in the indicated time period that might have affected your sales? Have there been any shifts in competitive advertising or marketing activities?

The answers to these questions provide the basis for writing a problem definition that clearly states the reasons why a problem or opportunity is believed to exist and the reasons believed to be the cause of the problem or opportunity, for example:

> Our sales in calendar year 2011 (as measured in units sold) are down 15% versus 2010. Monitoring of our own and competitive activities in the marketplace does not reveal any significant changes in marketplace factors that might affect our sales, for example, new product introductions, pricing, distribution, changes in advertising strategy, or changes in advertising spending. As a consequence, we believe that it is reasonable to assume that the underlying cause of sales declines is consumer-related. Research is needed to determine which consumer factors, such as product awareness and perceptions, product satisfaction, advertising awareness and advertising impact, may be responsible for the declining sales trend.

The third type of problem statement responds to a need to broaden knowledge and understanding of the consumer, product, or marketing environment. This type of problem definition reflects the agency's or client's need for information that will make them better, smarter marketers or advertisers. Problem statements that respond to this type of information need explicitly address the types of information really needed, why this information is needed, and how the information collected by the research will be used, for example:

> The client has initiated their 2011–2012 strategic planning process. One important part of their strategic planning process is an examination of consumer attitudinal and lifestyle trends that may have an impact on the identification and evaluation of strategic alternatives. The client is interested in consumer trends that may have an impact on the proposed repositioning of their All Natural Potato Chip line of products. Research is therefore recommended to explore and determine the potential effects of the following consumer trends for the repositioning: attitudes toward healthy eating, attitudes toward snack foods, attitudes and perceptions of "health"-positioned products (especially in the snack food category), behavioral changes in diet with particular emphasis on the consumption of snack foods, behavioral acceptance and rejection of "health"-positioned products (especially in the snack food category).

Justifying the Need for Research

Problem definitions reflect the difference between what is known and what needs to be known to reduce uncertainty and increase confidence in decisions reached. However, not all decisions require research. When faced with the selection of one of three creative executions, for example, judgment alone can be used to select the one that should be produced. The question, then, is when should judgment alone be used and when should judgment be supported by research?

The appropriateness of research can be evaluated through a cost-value analysis. In general, the justification for research increases when

- the value of the information obtained (in terms of assisting in the decision making process) exceeds the cost to acquire the information, or
- the cost implications of making the wrong decision increases.

Specifying Informational Needs

The final step in completing the problem statement requires the specification of informational needs, that is, (1) identifying the information that responds to the problem definition and (2) best helps the decision maker evaluate the strengths and weaknesses of various decision options and courses of action. The specification of informational needs is extremely important. Specified informational needs become the focus and core of the research questionnaire or interview.

The specification of informational needs is also important from another perspective. Prior to additional research planning, it is important that those who initiate the request for research agree with the statement of informational needs. If this agreement is not obtained in advance of the research, a researcher runs the risk of conducting research that is seen as incomplete or unresponsive to the agency's or client's needs. Consider the Toyota problem definition presented earlier. While this statement clearly defines the problem, it is vague as to what information will be used to evaluate the executions and to select the "winning" execution. The specification of informational needs for this problem definition might read:

> The commercials will be evaluated in four areas: communication of the main idea, reactions to main message communication (believability, uniqueness, and relevance), effect on product perceptions (competitive value, styling, performance, and handling), and reactions to the execution (likeability, uniqueness, relevance).

This statement of informational needs gives management the opportunity to agree or disagree that the criteria listed are an appropriate basis for commercial evaluation and selection.

The Complete Problem Statement

The end result of this initial stage in the research process is a well-defined and focused problem statement that contains three elements: a problem definition, a justification for the research, and the specification of informational needs. An example of a complete problem statement follows.

> The agency is unsure which of two product benefits to emphasize in the new advertising campaign. Alternative benefits are "unsurpassed cleaning ability" and "environmental safety." Benefit research is needed to help identify the

one product benefit that should be the focus of the new advertising campaign. The research will evaluate each benefit in terms of communication, believability, uniqueness and personal relevance; purchase interest and purchase intent; and anticipated product purchase frequency, reasons for purchase intent, and frequency of purchase. Primary, proprietary research is needed to provide this information as the required information is unavailable from any other source. Research is a justified response to this problem given the importance of the decision to be made. The benefit selected will become the focus of the upcoming $5 MM advertising campaign. Basing this decision purely on judgment severely limits confidence that the proper decision has been made and, as a result, the maximum return on advertising investment has been realized.

Planning and Data Collection

Activities conducted in this middle stage of the research process relate to the actual planning and conduct of the research. The specific activities conducted in this phase are: (1) identify the appropriate type of research, (2) address sampling and data collection issues, (3) determine data collection method, (4) set the research budget and timing, (5) prepare, distribute, and obtain approval of the research proposal, (6) prepare the questionnaire and other support materials, (7) conduct the research, and (8) prepare the data for analysis. The sequence and interrelationship of these events are shown in Figure 1.5.

Identify the Appropriate Type of Research

At this point, a researcher is faced with two decisions: should the research use secondary or primary data, and if primary, is qualitative or quantitative research more appropriate?

SECONDARY OR PRIMARY RESEARCH.   The problem definition and identified informational needs determine the approach and types of information which the research will collect. A researcher typically has two options: secondary research and primary research.

Secondary research examines data gathered for a research need other than the current one. This research already exists in printed or electronic form. Sources of secondary research information include internal agency or client records, government agencies, trade associations, information brokers, marketing and advertising research companies, specialized and general interest books, magazines, and academic journals. (Secondary research is discussed in greater detail in Chapter 3.) Primary research involves the collection of original, often proprietary, data specifically collected for the identified problem and generally entails some form of target audience interviewing or observation. The selection of primary versus secondary research is determined by the specific problem addressed by the research and the types of information required for decision making.

Some informational needs can be thoroughly satisfied by secondary research, for example, levels of competitive advertising spending and consumer demographic trends. Information on advertising spending is available through syndicated sources, while ample data on demographic trends have been gathered by governmental agencies and analyzed by general interest and specialized magazines, journals, and books. Some research informational needs can only be satisfied by primary research, for example, the identification

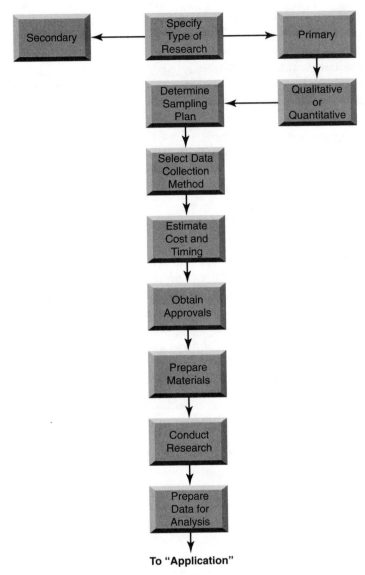

FIGURE 1.5   Steps in Research Planning and Data Collection

of the strongest of three creative approaches or reactions to a specific new product concept. No information likely exists anywhere that will satisfy this type of unique informational need. Finally, some problem statements are best addressed by a combination of secondary and primary research. In these cases, an analysis of secondary information is performed first, for example, a general analysis of consumer demographic and lifestyle trends. Insights from this analysis are then used to refine the original problem statement; for example, specific trends can be isolated and then quantitatively explored in primary research to determine the applicability and effects of these trends on the client's product, service, or communications program.

Different events occur following the selection of a primary or secondary research approach to data collection. As shown in Figure 1.5, when secondary research is conducted, there are no intervening steps between the selection of this approach and the collection of the secondary information (although, infrequently, a research proposal is prepared for secondary research projects). However, before primary research can be conducted, a number of additional steps must take place.

QUALITATIVE VERSUS QUANTITATIVE RESEARCH.   Once primary research is selected as the most appropriate means for obtaining the desired information, a researcher must then determine the primary research approach that provides the type of information that best meets informational needs and provides desired insights. A researcher has two options: qualitative research and quantitative research.

Qualitative research primarily uses open-ended, probing questions (i.e., questions without a prespecified set of answers) to encourage consumers to discuss and share their thoughts and feelings on a particular subject. As a result, qualitative research is most appropriate when one needs

- background information in a particular area when little is already known;
- information to assist in problem formulation or the development of research hypotheses;
- a thorough understanding of the underlying relationship between consumers' feelings, attitudes, and beliefs and their behaviors, especially when information on this relationship cannot be obtained through direct, structured, primarily closed-ended questioning.

Common forms of qualitative research include in-depth individual interviews and focus groups. (Qualitative research is discussed in greater detail in Chapters 5 through 7.)

Quantitative research is best used when generalizability to a larger population is important, when the determination of statistically reliable, quantifiable differences between groups is important, and when statistical analysis of the data is required. Quantitative research encompasses three types of research techniques: observation, physiological measurement, and survey research.

- *Observation research* is the recording of objects, events, situations, or people's behaviors. Observations can take place in either a natural or contrived situation where the presence of the observer may or may not be known.
- *Physiological research* entails the direct measurement of an individual's physical responses to stimuli such as an advertisement. Physiological research measures voluntary (such as eye movements) and involuntary responses (such as brain waves and galvanic skin response).
- *Survey research* is the most common form of quantitative research. It is the systematic collection of information from respondents through the use of questionnaires. Surveys are most commonly administered over the telephone, through the mail, over the Internet, or in person-to-person interviews.

(Quantitative research and analysis is discussed in greater detail in Chapters 8 through 16.)

Qualitative and quantitative research have the same relationship to each other as do secondary and primary research. Qualitative research can be the sole response to an informational need, or it can be used to acquire insights that contribute to a refinement of the problem statement as a precursor to quantitative research. Consider the need for your local metropolitan transit line to increase ridership. The transit line decides that one means to accomplish this goal is to commit funds to an advertising campaign. But they do not know what idea should serve as the core communication of this campaign. Consumer insights are clearly needed. In cases such as these, qualitative research is an appropriate first step:

> Prior to a quantitative survey of the target audience you conduct a series of focus groups where, among other things, you ask participants to describe their commuting and other transportation habits and to explain why they have adapted these habits. One respondent says: "I don't care if I'm trapped in traffic for an hour or two. I love the freedom my car gives me. There's just so much freedom when I drive myself." This remark is important because you did not consider "freedom" as one of the areas that would be explored in the quantitative phase of the research. When the focus groups are completed, "freedom" and other issues not previously considered are used to refine the problem statement for the next phase of (quantitative) research.[21]

Sampling and Data Collection

The sampling plan specifies how study participants will be selected. There are two sampling options: probability sampling and non-probability sampling.

- A *probability sample* is a sample in which each individual or household comprising the universe from which the sample is drawn has a known chance or probability of being selected for inclusion in the research. The selection of specific individuals from this universe is done purely by chance, for example, through the use of a table of random numbers. When probability sampling is used, selection of individuals for survey participation continues until the required number of individuals has been selected and interviewed. The primary advantage of probability sampling lies in the ability to generalize findings to the population from which the sample was drawn. Probability samples, for example, are often used in national opinion polls because of the important need to generalize the findings to the total population.

- A *nonprobability sample* is a sample of individuals who are not selected strictly by chance from the universe of all individuals, but rather are selected in some less random, often more purposeful way. Here, the selection of individuals for study participation can be conducted on the basis of convenience or judgment.

The sampling option selected is determined by a number of factors: the objectives of the research, the research budget, urgency in knowing the results of the research, and the need for generalizability to larger or broader populations. The vast majority of research conducted by advertising agencies uses nonprobability sampling primarily because the procedures associated with probability sampling make them too expensive and time-consuming for most advertising-related research needs. (Sampling techniques and sampling options are discussed in Chapter 4.)

Selection of Data Collection Method

Once the sampling plan is chosen, you then determine the specific method by which identified respondents will be interviewed. There are four primary approaches to respondent interviewing: in-person face to face, by telephone, through printed mail surveys, or through mediated electronic media (for instance, surveys conducted online or through a mobile device). Qualitative research almost always utilizes some form of in-person face-to-face interview. Quantitative research may use any data collection format. Each approach is associated with a unique set of advantages and disadvantages. The data collection method selected will be determined by the types and sensitivity of information required, the complexity of the questionnaire, the research budget, and timing constraints.

Determine the Research Budget and Timing

Cost and timing estimates can be determined before or after the prior steps in the research design process. In the best of all cases, cost and timing estimates follow the prior steps. First, a researcher identifies the most appropriate way to meet informational needs and then determines the cost and amount of time necessary to plan the research, collect and analyze the data, and then present the findings and implications. In this case, budget and timing estimates can be accomplished through the Program Evaluation and Review Technique (PERT):

1. Prepare a list of all activities that need to be completed from the time the study is approved until the results are presented.
2. Arrange listed items in time sequence, paying particular attention to tasks that need to be addressed or completed simultaneously.
3. Determine the amount of time needed to complete each item.
4. Determine the longest "path"—the maximum amount of time required to complete all tasks. This is the amount of time required for the complete research study.
5. Determine the estimated cost of each listed task. Add individual task costs together to determine the total research budget.

Time and money, however, are limited commodities in the advertising business, and as a consequence, cost and timing estimates may precede decisions related to sampling and data collection. A researcher may be told "You have $2,000 and 10 days to get me what I need to know." In such cases, the researcher must decide whether appropriate, useful, valid research can be performed within the time and budget constraints or whether research conducted within the imposed constraints is likely to be worse than no research at all. The latter conclusion should lead to the decision not to conduct the proposed research, but to instead find alternative ways to meet informational needs.

Prepare, Distribute, and Obtain Approval of Research Proposal

The decisions reached in the prior steps are summarized in a written proposal presented to management and other end users of the research. The research proposal consists of several parts.

- *Executive Summary*. A brief synopsis of the key points from each of the more detailed sections in the proposal.

- *Background*. A brief statement of the situational factors and informational needs that led to the decision to conduct the research plus a discussion of any factors that may have influenced subsequent decisions in the research process, for example, budget or time constraints.

- *Problem Statement*. A full problem statement containing a detailed, focused description of the problem(s) motivating the research, a rationale for why research is the recommended approach (as opposed to the sole use of judgment), and a description of the specific types of information the research will provide.

- *Methodology*. A clear, nontechnical description of the research design explaining how the research will be conducted. The data collection method, types of data to be collected, measurement instruments, and analytical procedures should all be discussed.

- *Cost*. A statement of the funds allocated to the research and a detailed breakdown of how this money will be spent.

- *Timing*. A statement of how long the research will take from the time of final approval and a breakdown of the amount of time needed for key components of the research.

- *Appendices*. Any statistical or other detailed information necessary for a complete understanding of the research. The material in this section is typically of a technical nature and is of interest either to those in management who need more detailed information or to those individuals who need to completely understand the research but did not participate in the discussions that led to the research.

The research proposal provides one last opportunity for management to contribute their thoughts to the research process.

Prepare Research Materials

Once the primary research project is approved, the creation of all necessary research materials begins. The questionnaire or interview guide is created, and any necessary directions are written for research companies assisting in the research, such as field services or tabulation houses. If the research requires stimulus materials such as storyboards, animatics, or product concepts, these are also developed at this time.

Conduct the Research

The next to last step in this stage of the research process is data collection. The appropriate sources are consulted, and written documents are obtained in secondary research. Interviews or other forms of observation take place in primary research.

Prepare Information for Analysis

Raw, unorganized information is hard to work with. Thus, this stage of the research process organizes and prepares the data so that it can be analyzed in the application stage. The way in which raw information is organized depends on its source and characteristics.

Secondary information is organized in much the same way that you organize information for a term paper or similar report. The information obtained from personal and written sources is read, categories of information are developed, and then related information is grouped together into the appropriate categories. Qualitative information is organized in a similar manner. Here, however, the sources of the information are the verbal and written records of the interviews with the individuals participating in the research. Primary, quantitative information is typically edited and translated into a computer data file prior to analysis. Editing involves examining the responses recorded on the questionnaires for omissions, appropriateness, and consistency. Therefore, the editing process is important, because it increases the quality of the data. The personal computer and user-friendly statistical programs have greatly increased the ease with which computer data analysis can take place. However, before a computer can be used, the codes representing each individual's responses to the survey questions must be input and stored in a data file.

APPLICATION

This final stage of the research process focuses on what has been learned and the implications of this learning for decision making. The specific activities conducted in this stage are: (1) data analysis, (2) presentation of findings, and (3) application of the findings to decision making.

Data Analysis

Raw data is useless; only data that has been thoroughly analyzed is of any value to decision makers. Thus, one of the major roles of the researcher is to examine, organize, and if appropriate, statistically test the data so that meaningful conclusions and insights can be drawn. The specific types of analytical procedures carried out are determined by the type of data collected.

The analysis of secondary and qualitative information generally requires synthesis. Analysis of these types of data is similar to the process of putting together a jigsaw puzzle without knowing what the finished puzzle will look like. In both cases, individual pieces (of the puzzle or information) need to be pieced together to determine important patterns and trends so that, eventually, the "big picture" is revealed and understood. Quantitative data analysis generally involves data manipulation, summarization, and statistical testing. Analysis may involve descriptive statistics such as percents and frequencies or inferential statistics such as correlation, tests of mean differences, and chi-square.

Present the Results

Next, findings and conclusions drawn from data analysis are presented to management. This presentation can be oral, written, or both (an oral presentation is typically followed by a written report).

Regardless of the way in which results are communicated, the report must be management-oriented. Many research reports are written from the researcher's perspective.

These reports are a complicated and often convoluted description of research methodology and highly technical descriptions of the statistical techniques that were used as part of data analysis. Table after table is presented without organization or interpretation. In these circumstances, the needs of management are not met. A report written from the management perspective clearly and concisely answers management's most basic questions: "What does this information mean?" "What do I know now that I didn't know before?" and "What have I learned so that I can better evaluate my decision alternatives?" (Chapter 21 contains a detailed discussion of how to present research results.)

Decision Making

The last and one of the most important steps in the research process is using the findings to influence decision making. When a research presentation receives the response "That's nice. Thanks." it is certain that the research has wasted the agency's time, personnel resources, and money. The research process should end with a management response of "The research has certainly helped us to better understand the strengths and weaknesses of each of our options. Let's use these findings to evaluate each option one more time before we reach our decision." When a researcher receives this response, he or she should be congratulated for designing and presenting an important, valuable piece of research.

APPLYING CHAPTER CONCEPTS

The VERB campaign was a national, multicultural, social marketing campaign coordinated by the U.S. Department of Health and Human Services' Centers for Disease Control and Prevention (CDC). The campaign combined paid advertising, marketing strategies, and partnership efforts in an effort to increase physical activity and displace or replace unhealthy, risky behaviors.[22] The campaign ran from 2002 to 2006.

Tweens, defined as youth aged 9 to 13, were the primary target for the campaign. Within this age group, four demographically defined groups were selected for special targeting: African-Americans, Native Americans, Asian-American and Pacific Islander, and Hispanic Latino. Beyond the youth target, important secondary audiences were parents and adult influencers, including teachers, youth leaders, physical education and health professionals, pediatricians, health care providers, coaches, and others. The goals of the VERB campaign were to

- increase knowledge and improve attitudes and beliefs about tweens' regular participation in physical activity;
- increase parental and influencer support and encouragement of tweens' participation in physical activity;
- heighten awareness of options and opportunities for tween participation in physical activity;
- facilitate opportunities for tweens to participate in regular physical activity;
- increase and maintain the number of tweens who regularly participate in physical activity.

The campaign was very successful in achieving these goals. Awareness of the campaign was very high, and tweens who were aware of the campaign engaged in more physical activity sessions than those who were not aware of the campaign.[23]

The VERB campaign is an excellent example of this chapter's concepts and discussion put into action, illustrating the steps through which research planning passes and how research informs all aspects of advertising decision making, from initial secondary research to target audience identification, message and media selection, creative development, and the assessment of campaign effectiveness. Three types of information on the VERB campaign are provided in the online supplemental readings. The paper by Wong et al. provides the background on VERB. The paper presents an overview of the program and describes how advertising and marketing principles and research were applied to program planning and strategic design. The paper by Berkowitz et al. further illustrates the role of research throughout the lifespan of the program and illustrates the various roles and contributions of research to advertising planning. This paper presents a detailed discussion of how research was used in VERB's planning, execution, and assessment phases. Each area of research's contribution to advertising planning and decision making discussed throughout this chapter is evident in the VERB campaign. Finally, examples of VERB advertising are also provided.[24]

SUMMARY

Research informs advertisers' judgment in four primary areas:

- *Marketplace*—addressing issues such as key trends, the competitive environment, technological advances and impacts, and current and future problems and opportunities.

- *Consumer*—addressing issues related to consumer trends, lifestyles, attitudes, and behaviors, and issues relevant to the brand-consumer relationship.

- *Creative*—helping to determine the most relevant and motivating brand positioning, and the translation of this positioning into persuasive messages and executions.

- *Media*—providing insights into how and where competitive brands are advertising.

The use of research in these areas helps advertisers make more informed decisions, thereby increasing their chances for advertising success.

Research is primarily conducted by information users (e.g., individuals at the agency and client), research specialists, media and consulting companies, and trade associations. Field services assist these people and organizations in the design and collection of research.

A systematic approach to research consists of following a number of steps nested within three broad stages of planning:

- The first stage, *preliminary discussions and agreements*, lays the foundation for the research by culminating in a problem statement. This statement, the result of this stage's initial planning steps, describes the problem or opportunity facing the agency or client that is motivating the research, explains why research appropriate for providing the information needed to solve the problem or capitalize on the opportunity, and explicitly identifies the advertiser's informational needs.

- Activities carried out in the second state of research planning, *planning and data collection*, relate to the planning and conduct of the research. These activities entail: identifying the appropriate type of research; addressing sampling and data collection issues; setting the research budget and timing; preparing, distributing, and obtaining approval of the research proposal; preparing the questionnaire and other support materials; conducting the research; and preparing the data for analysis.

- The final stage of the research process, *application*, focuses on what has been learned and the implications of this learning for decision making. The activities conducted in this stage are: data analysis, presentation of the findings, and application of the findings to decision making.

Review Questions

1. What is the primary goal of advertising research?
2. In *marketplace analyses*, what aspects are studied? What types of questions are addressed?
3. What are the three dimensions of *target audience analyses?*
4. Briefly describe *segmentation research* and its value to advertisers.
5. What is meant by a product's *positioning?*
6. What contributions can research make regarding finished *creative?* Why are these areas important to an advertising campaign?
7. *Media research* is useful for answering what types of questions? Why is this form of research especially important?
8. What is *evaluative research?* How is this type of research used by advertisers?
9. What types of individuals are involved on the client side of the research process? What functions do their counterpart, *agency researchers*, serve?
10. What is a *custom research supplier?* What phases of research can they be involved in?
11. Identify the differences between *propriety* and *syndicated* research. Provide examples of the latter.
12. What purpose do *media companies* serve? On what basic assumption do they function?
13. Briefly explain what a *trade association* is and its central purpose.
14. What group of individuals is responsible for the actual collection of data? What services do they provide?
15. Name and describe the three stages of advertising research.

16. What end product is created by the first stage of the research process? What three elements does this product contain?
17. List and characterize the three main types of advertising-related problems.
18. What form of analysis is used to assess the appropriateness of research? When does the justification increase?
19. Why is *specifying informational needs* important to completing the problem statement? What purpose does this step serve for management?
20. What are the eight steps comprising the second stage of the research process?
21. Identify the differences between *secondary* and *primary* research. In what situation is each form most appropriate?
22. When conducting primary research, which two options are available for obtaining the desired information? Describe both research types and when each should be used.
23. What is the difference between *probability* and *nonprobability* sampling? When should each be used?
24. What are the four primary approaches to respondent interviewing in research? What form is most commonly utilized by qualitative research?
25. How can cost and timing estimates best be determined?
26. What function does the *research proposal* serve, and what are its main components?
27. What three activities comprise the final stage of the research process? Describe the importance of each step and its main elements?

Application Exercises

Application exercises 1 through 6 relate to concepts raised and discussed in this chapter.

1. Examine recent print or online issues of *Advertising Age, Adweek, Branding*, or other related advertising industry publication. Find an instance of research being used to better understand: (a) the competitive marketplace, (b) current or potential consumers, (c) the strengths and weaknesses of advertising creative, and (d) media usage or placement. For each instance (a to d), discuss the nature of the research conducted and how the research was used to inform decision making. Provide a full reference to each article.

2. You have been asked to create a mobile advertising campaign for Netflix, which wants to target adults aged 55 and older. Prepare a list of 10 questions you believe should be addressed via research before the work on the actual campaign begins. (The questions can pertain to any of the four areas shown in Figure 1.1 and discussed on pages 3 to 7). Provide a rationale for why each question is relevant, important, and a basis for sound decision making.

3. Read each of the following problem statements. Using the criteria presented earlier in the chapter, decide if the statement is acceptable as written. If the statement is not acceptably written, then (a) identify the problem or problems with the statement, (b) list the types of questions you would ask to clarify the problem statement, and (c) rewrite the statement to make it acceptably written (speculating as to the types of answers you would receive to your questions).

   Account Management has identified three potential ways in which we can position our product: extra gentle, extra cleaning ability, and better value. We need research to identify the best positioning.

   We have received mixed reactions to our advertising. We need to conduct research to determine the strengths and weaknesses of our advertising among our important target of influential opinion leaders. Based on their reactions, modifications to the advertising will be implemented.

   The client's new consultant has encouraged us to show the product for longer periods of time in the television advertising. He said that this would make for more effective advertising. We need to develop some new advertising with longer product shots and then get our target audience's reactions to this advertising. Then, we'll know if the consultant is right.

4. A 2009 KFC promotion offered coupons for two free pieces of the new grilled chicken, a biscuit and a side order. Unfortunately, the promotion did not go as planned, as many angry customers were turned away for having "invalid" coupons, very long lines prevented others (including paying customers) from ordering, some locations stopped accepting any coupons, and thousands of individuals were unable (after multiple attempts) to even download the coupon. The promotion was stopped well short of its planned ending date. (You can read more about the promotion by typing "KFC grilled promotion" in Google or other search engine.) Imagine that you are a researcher assigned to determine how consumers' attitudes toward KFC changed as a result of this promotion. Write a complete problem statement for this research.

5. Tom's Lo-Cost Save-More Pharmacies, located in middle- to small-sized towns throughout the United States, has hired your agency to develop the new $3 million advertising campaign. Tom's Pharmacies had tremendous growth throughout the early 2000s but growth has slowed over the past several years. Advertising spending has remained consistent at about $3 million. Sales last year were flat. Unfortunately, the company does not have a good understanding of why this slowing has occurred. They do, however, see the new advertising campaign as the way to reverse this trend.

   Think about the discussion of primary and secondary research and the differences between qualitative and quantitative information. Think about how each of these approaches can be used independently or in sequence. Then, write a memo to William Masterly, the CEO of Tom's

Pharmacies, describing the research that you recommend be conducted prior to the development of the advertising creative. Your recommendation can consist of a single piece of research or a sequence of related research steps, each step being informed by the prior steps. Be certain to: (a) fully explain how each step or steps of recommended research will contribute to the creative development process, (b) provide a justification for your selection of information type (primary or secondary) and research approach (qualitative or quantitative) at each stage. Your recommendation should reflect your best thinking, and as a consequence, you should not be concerned at this point with budget or timing.

6. Twister's Pizza is a chain of pizza restaurants specializing in unique pizzas, such as oven-roasted Middle Eastern Vegetarian Pizza and Parisian Sourdough. Sales, after an initial peak soon after opening, have dropped steadily over the past several months. The drop in sales coincided with the termination of Twister's television campaign.

The agency is pleased that Twister's has observed the simultaneous occurrence of these two events and is ready to begin a new wave of advertising. The same commercials used in the initial wave of advertising will be used in the new wave. The agency and Twister's believe that this new wave of advertising should reverse the steadily declining sales trend.

You have been hired by Twister's to provide an independent point of view. Do you support the decision to begin airing the new campaign without any research? If so, support your recommendation. If you do not support the decision, specifically describe the unmet information need(s) that you think research should address and then, for each information need, specify: (a) why you think collecting information to meet that need is important and (b) the approach you would take to collect the information.

Application exercises 7 through 10 relate to the VERB campaign provided in the online supplemental readings.

7. The VERB campaign ended in 2006. Imagine that the CDC wants to restart the campaign, again directed toward tweens. What research would you recommend be conducted prior to the start of the new campaign? Provide a rationale for your recommendation.

8. Imagine that the CDC not only wants to restart the campaign, but also wants to expand the campaign to target individuals aged 14 to 17. What research would you recommend be conducted prior to the start of this expanded campaign? Provide a rationale for your recommendation.

9. Chapter 1 described how multiple research projects can take place sequentially, with the learnings from one project informing and influencing decisions make regarding subsequent projects. Based on the readings, create a flow chart of the research underlying the development and evaluation of the original VERB campaign.

10. In your opinion, was all of the research conducted for the original VERB campaign absolutely necessary? Were there any circumstances in which "informed judgment" could have replaced the research findings? Support your point of view with a well-reasoned rationale.

Endnotes

1. See Steve Smith (2009). "Will Trade My Info for Better Ads." Behavioral Insider at http://www.mediapost.com/publications/?fa=Articles.showArticle&art_aid=105252.
2. See Massive (2008). "Massive Inc. Hosts First In-Game Advertising Upfront Event" at http://www.massiveincorporated.com/press/12.03c.08.htm.
3. See Forrester Research (2009). "Groundswell" at http://www.forrester.com/Groundswell/ladder.html.
4. See, for example, Al Reis and Jack Trout (2000). *Positioning: The Battle for Your Mind* (New York, NY: McGraw-Hill) and Subroto Sengupta (2005). *Brand Positioning* (New York, NY: McGraw-Hill).
5. Milward Brown IMS (undated). "Brand Advertising Tracking" at http://www.imsl.ie/what-we-do/brand-advertising-tracking.asp.
6. Food and Drug Administration (2004). "Guidance for Industry Substantiation for Dietary

Supplement Claims Made Under Section 403(r) (6) of the Federal Food, Drug, and Cosmetic Act" at http://www.cfsan.fda.gov/~dms/dsclmgui.html.

7. Research conducted by Millward Brown and Dynamic Logic is an example of research that provides guidance on how to use a particular medium to its best advantage, in this case digital video. This research found that ad length was an important influence on consumer response: 15 seconds appears to be an optimal length for digital video creative in the pre-roll position. 5-second spots had trouble conveying a message, while 30-second spots risked turning off a viewer waiting to watch something else. 30-second spots did do well, however, at conveying a complex or emotionally resonant message. The full presentation of the Video Ad Effectiveness Study is at http://http://www.iab.net/media/file/DV_Effectiveness_Study.ppt.

8. The Cross Media Optimization Research studies (XMOS) conducted by the Interactive Advertising Bureau are excellent examples of research that helps advertisers answer this type of question. Information on this research is at http://www.iab.net/about_the_iab/recent_press_releases/press_release_archive/press_release/4725.

9. Kevin Muoio (2009). "Key Trends in Mobile Content Usage and Mobile Advertising" at http://www.comscore.com/Press_Events/Presentations_Whitepapers/2009/Key_Trends_in_Mobile_Content_Usage_Mobile_Advertising.

10. Eli Goodman and Keith Wilson (2009). "Making Integrated Campaigns Work: How a Search Marketing Mindset Can Drive the ROI of Display Advertising" at http://www.comscore.com/Press_Events/Presentations_Whitepapers/2009/Making_Integrated_Campaigns_Work_How_a_Search_Marketing_Mindset_Can_Drive_the_ROI_of_Display_Advertising.

11. Paul Gillin (2009). "Marketing to Teens and Tweens" at http://www.slideshare.net/pgillin/marketing-to-teens-and-tweens.

12. See Delbert Hawkins, David Mothersbaugh, and Roger Best (2009). *Consumer Behavior with DDB LifeStyle Study Data Disk* (New York: NY: McGraw-Hill).

13. See Brand Asset Valuator at http://www.brandassetvaluator.com.au/.

14. DoubleClick (undated). "About Us" at http://www.doubleclick.com/about/about_us.aspx.

15. These and other research reports are available from DoubleClick at http://www.doubleclick.com/insight/research/index.aspx.

16. A list of funded topics can be found at http://www.wpp.com/wpp/press/press/default.htm?guid=%7Be0af399a-8450-408c-8ba8-c35d31dae88c%7D.

17. Media-specific research can be found on individual trade association Web sites, for example: *Yellow Pages* (Yellow Pages Association at http://www.ypassociation.org/), *Radio* (Radio Advertising Bureau at http://www.rab.com/), *Newspaper* (Newspaper Association of America at http://www.naa.org/), *Television* (Television Bureau of Advertising at http://www.tvb.org/), *Magazines* (Magazine Publishers of America at http://www.magazine.org/home/), *Direct Marketing* (Direct Marketing Association at http://www.the-dma.org/), *Outdoor* (Outdoor Advertising Association of America at http://www.oaaa.org/), *Word of Mouth* (Word of Mouth Marketing Association at http://womma.org/).

18. Interactive Advertising Bureau at http://www.iab.net/insights_research.

19. IAB research studies and reports can be found at http://www.iab.net/insights_research/530422.

20. The Applied Marketing Research Web site is http://www.appliedmr.com.

21. Adopted from Glen M. Broom and David M. Dozier (1990). *Using Research in Public Relations* (New York, NY: Prentice-Hall).

22. The primary Web site for the VERB campaign is http://www.cdc.gov/YouthCampaign/.

23. For detailed findings, see Marian Huhman (2006). "Promoting Physical Activity Among Tweens: Evaluation Results of CDC's VERB Campaign" available at http://www.kff.org/entmedia/upload/-Promoting-Physical-Activity-Among-Tweens-Evaluation-Results-of-CDC-s-VERB-Campaign-Marian-Huhman.pdf. See also Marian Huffman, Lance D. Potter, Faye L. Wong, et al. (2005). "Effects of a Mass Media Campaign to Increase Physical Activity Among Children: Year-1 Results of the VERB Campaign." *Pediatrics* 116(2):277–284.

24. Additional examples of VERB advertising, including television and radio, can be found at http://www.cdc.gov/youthcampaign/advertising/index.htm.

CHAPTER 2

Research Ethics

The advertising community forgives most honest mistakes. What it does not forgive and what you must absolutely avoid are ethical lapses in judgment or action. You must conduct yourself and your research in ways that meet the highest ethical standards. When your actions do not meet these standards, you hurt yourself, your company, the advertising profession, and potentially the broader society at large. This chapter will help you understand how to maintain high ethical principles in the planning, conduct, analysis, and presentation of advertising research.

***

When you are done reading this chapter, you should have a better understanding of:

- the three aspects of ethical behavior: autonomy, nonmaleficence, and beneficence
- ethical standards regarding interactions with research participants, management, research suppliers, and society as a whole
- special considerations related to research conducted with children and online communities.

Ethics are moral principles that help determine when a course of action is either right or wrong. While this definition is straightforward, it has at times been difficult to put into practice as advertisers and researchers grapple with the question of "If it's to my advantage, and if there is no legal violation, why shouldn't I do it?" Consider the following situations:

- John writes a survey that takes 30 minutes to complete. He informs potential respondents of this at the start of the survey. However, as the research progresses, John finds that because of the length of the survey it is increasingly difficult to recruit participants, driving up the cost of the research. John asks: "What's the harm if I start to tell people the survey length is only 10 minutes?"

- Mary conducts a survey among McDonald's franchisees. In order to increase the chances of obtaining honest responses, she promises the franchisees that all their answers will be confidential. Nevertheless, Mary places a secret code on each questionnaire so that the franchisee can later be identified, should she or the client want to know who provided positive and negative responses. Mary asks: "What's the harm? Why shouldn't I place the code if it helps us better understand the results and improve our long-term planning?"

- Carey, the agency researcher, conducts research to determine consumers' reactions to the client's latest advertising campaign. Carey remembers that the selection of the campaign's spokesperson was a controversial decision, with the client only grudgingly going along with the agency recommendation. The results show that consumers are very positive toward the campaign with one exception: they absolutely hate the spokesperson. Cary asks: "Since overall reactions are so positive, why don't I eliminate from the full report the survey questions that explore reactions to the spokesperson? Why bring up a controversial issue that everyone agrees is settled?"

Situations and questions such as these are commonly faced by researchers. In order to help researchers identify the most appropriate course of action in these and other situations, codes of ethics have been written to provide guidance for decision-making. While these codes of ethics have been written from different perspectives, they nevertheless share a common core set of beliefs.[1]

Research codes of ethics incorporate the principles of autonomy, nonmaleficence, and beneficence.[2] *Autonomy*, often referred to as the principle of self-determination, means that all individuals involved in the research have free deliberation and decision power regarding their participation in the research. While the principle of autonomy certainly applies to research subjects, we will see later in this chapter that it also applies to those involved in the support and approval of the research. *Nonmaleficence* states that it is wrong to intentionally inflict harm on others. *Beneficence* states that one has a positive obligation to remove existing harms, to confer benefits, and to minimize risks whenever and wherever possible.

The remainder of this chapter discusses how each of these principles provides the foundation for ethical research decision making as an advertising researcher interacts with four important groups:

- individuals who participate in the research,
- management who supports the research and uses the information,

- research suppliers who provide consultation and assistance, and
- society as a whole, which is often affected by the reporting and use of information collected.

ETHICS AND INDIVIDUAL RESPONDENTS

The principles of autonomy, nonmaleficence, and beneficence apply to the interactions of researchers and respondents, the individuals who provide the raw information for the vast majority of primary research studies. These principles are reflected in the following guidelines:

- a respondent's decision whether or not to participate in a research study should be an informed decision;
- a respondent may not be mistreated in any way;
- a respondent has an absolute right to confidentiality and privacy unless he or she explicitly agrees otherwise.

Informed Decisions and Informed Consent

Informed consent is required whenever a researcher explicitly asks an individual for information, for example, through questions on a survey or through physiological measures such as eye tracking. Informed consent is required in these circumstances because *private information* (e.g., attitudes, opinions, beliefs, and behaviors) is being collected. The specific medium through which the information is being collected (e.g., telephone, Internet, in-person interviews) does not affect the need to obtain informed consent prior to data collection.

Potential research participants must be provided detailed information in three broad areas if they are to be able to make an informed decision regarding participation.[3]

The first area relates to the context for the research. Here, potential participants must be explicitly told: (1) that they are being asked to participate in a research study, (2) who is conducting the research, (3) the purpose of the research, (4) and who to contact if they have questions about the research. It is important to note, however, that there is some latitude with regard to the second and third points: communicating the research sponsor and purpose. A full and detailed explanation of study goals, sponsorship, and approach may have the potential to bias a respondent, for example, stating that Exxon is conducting a study about the environment. As a consequence, the vast majority of advertising research incorporates some deception. As long as this deception is minimal, causes no harm, and is justifiable by the research design and information needs, it is considered acceptable. A researcher might, for example, say that the research is being conducted by "ABC Marketing Research Company" as opposed to "Exxon Oil."

The second area of informed consent relates to the voluntary nature of participation. Respondents must understand that participation is entirely voluntary and that refusal to participate will not involve any penalty or loss of benefits.[4] Additionally, respondents must be informed that they can discontinue participation at any time, again without penalty or loss of benefits (e.g., being paid an incentive for participating in the research). Discontinuation is always a problem for researchers. During the course of an interview, a respondent may change his or her mind regarding willingness to continue for any number of reasons: lost interest, confusion, poor rapport with the interviewer, or the increasing length of the interview. Given the investment of time (and as a consequence, money) in a partially completed interview, interviewers have an understandable reluctance to terminate the interview. However, regardless of the reason why, a respondent always has the right to end the interview at any time *without* the need to explain why or to be pressured into continuing. It is unethical to design or conduct a research study in a way that prevents a respondent from exercising his or her right to withdraw or refuse to answer at *any stage* during the interview. Any request of the respondent to end the interview must be granted.

The third area of informed consent relates to the characteristics of the research itself. Here a potential participant must be told: (1) what they will have to do to participate (e.g., answer questions of a personal nature, taste products, or watch advertising), (2) how long the interview will take, (3) what will be done with the data (especially noting how confidentiality and privacy will be addressed) and, if applicable, (4) any commitments beyond the initial interview. For example, as part of a research study you show respondents shampoo advertising and then give them a "free" sample of the shampoo's new formulation to take home as a "thank you" for participating in the research. Your intent is to contact respondents in a week to obtain their reactions to the new formulation. It would be a violation of ethical principles if both portions of the research are not explicitly addressed in the informed consent document.

Once all of the information required for an informed consent document has been determined, the informed consent form itself is written. The document should be clearly written and easy to understand, adhering to the following guidelines:[5]

- Words are familiar to the reader. Any scientific, medical, or legal words are clearly defined.
- Words and terminology are consistent throughout the document.
- Sentences are short, simple, and direct.
- Line length is limited to 30–50 characters and spaces.
- Paragraphs are short with one idea per paragraph.
- Verbs are in active voice.
- Personal pronouns are used to increase personal identification.
- Each idea is clear and logically sequenced.
- Study purpose is presented early in the text.
- Titles, subtitles, and other headers help to clarify organization of text.
- Headers are simple and close to text.
- Left margins are justified. Right margins are ragged.
- Upper and lower case letters are used.
- Style and font of print is easy to read.
- No large blocks of print.

A sample informed consent form is shown in Figure 2.1. Note how the form adheres to the prior guidelines and how explicit consent is requested at the very end.

Thank you for learning about our research.

What is the research about?

You are invited to participate in a research study conducted by HTR Associates, an independent marketing research company. The purpose of this research is to obtain attitudes toward three new approaches to automotive advertising. By talking with people like you, we hope to learn what people like and dislike about advertising for these types of products.

What do you have to do?

As a participant you will view three commercials on your computer and then answer from six to nine questions after each commercial. At the end of the survey we will also ask you for some demographic information.

The entire survey, including viewing the commercials, should take between 10 and 15 minutes.

How will the information be used?

Your opinions are important, and will be considered by the advertiser as s/he decides on a final approach to the advertising.

Are your answers confidential?

All your answers are confidential and no personally identifiable information will be associated with your answers. Your identity will not be revealed to any individuals. The data collected in this research will be stored in a locked facility.

Is your participation voluntary?

Your participation in this research study is absolutely voluntary. You may choose not to participate and you may stop your participation at any time, even after you have begun the research.

More information? Questions?

If you have any questions or concerns about this study or if any problems arise, please contact the research manager, Susan McKenna, at 555-666-8765 or susan.mckenna@htrassociates.com. You can contact Susan and then come back to the survey, if you want.

Consent

Please press the "Agree" button below if you decide to participate in the research, If you do not wish to participate, please press the "Decline" button below.

FIGURE 2.1 Sample Informed Consent Document

Mistreatment

Ethical research practice requires that participants not be mistreated during any phases of the research. The following types of situations should be avoided:

- frequent, repeated attempts by the interviewer or research company to conduct the interview or attempts to conduct the interview at the researcher's convenience (e.g., phone calls during the supper hour);
- overly long surveys not being accurately described as such. It is unethical to recruit respondents by misrepresenting the length of the interview. A researcher has an obligation to provide a reasonably accurate estimate of the interview length;
- asking personal questions for "information's sake."

Confidentiality and Privacy

Respondents' expectations that their responses will be treated confidentially are absolute unless they are *explicitly* informed that confidentiality will not be maintained and a written acknowledgement to this effect is signed. Except in this latter case, any violation of confidentiality, no matter how minor you perceive that violation, is a severe breach of ethical research standards. The CASRO code of ethics provides specific guidelines for the maintenance of respondent confidentiality:

- Survey Research Organizations' staff or personnel should not use or discuss respondent-identifiable data or information for other than legitimate internal research purposes.

- The Survey Research Organization has the responsibility for insuring that subcontractors (e.g., interviewers, coding, and tabulation organizations) and consultants are aware of and agree to maintain and respect respondent confidentiality whenever the identity of respondents or respondent-identifiable information is disclosed to such entities.

- Before permitting clients or others to have access to completed questionnaires, respondent names and other respondent-identifying information (e.g., telephone numbers) should be deleted.

- Invisible identifiers on mail questionnaires that connect respondent answers to particular respondents should not be used. Visible identification numbers may be used but should be accompanied by an explanation that such identifiers are for control purposes only and that respondent confidentiality will not be compromised.[6]

Closely related to confidentiality is privacy. Respondents must be informed of any data collection methods that might violate their expectation of privacy. Electronic equipment such as taping, recording, photographing, one-way viewing rooms, and computer cookies may only be used after explicitly informing respondents.

RESPONSIBILITIES TO RESPONDENTS: SPECIAL POPULATIONS

The prior guidelines apply to all respondents. Nevertheless, three groups of respondents merit additional considerations.

Research with Children

A great deal of advertising is directed toward children, and, as a consequence, a great deal of research is conducted with children. The guidelines for ethical behavior discussed earlier in this section apply to both children and adults, but the way in which each guideline is applied differs for each group. How, for example, do you obtain informed consent from a child or make certain that the child understands that he or she may stop participation at any time (after all, they can't tell their schoolteacher they don't want to do their class work)? Special care must be made to protect the interests of child participants, specifically:

- *The child's rights supersede the investigator's rights.* The rights of child research participants are greater than a researcher's need for information. A research design must be evaluated in terms of how well the rights and needs of the child are protected.

- *There may be no physical or psychological harm.*
- *There must be informed written consent of the child's primary caretaker.* Informed consent requires that the caretaker be given accurate information on the professional training and competence of the researcher, the purpose and conduct of the research, the nature of any deception involved in the research, and how the information collected by the research will be used.
- *There may be no coercion to participate.* The rights of parents and children to decline participation must be respected. Parents should be given the explicit opportunity to refuse participation. The child should also be given the right to refuse participation. No counter arguments, incentives, or coercion should be used in an effort to change the child's mind.
- *No diagnostic or other information on the child's participation should be offered.* An advertising researcher is not a clinical psychologist or child development specialist. As a consequence, he or she should not offer interpretations of the child's behavior based on the child's responses to the research stimuli. Comments such as "Out of all the advertising we showed Jerry, he most liked advertising for new guns and soldiers. He was *really* smiling as those guns were shown. He really seems to be into violence." are clearly inappropriate. .
- *Principles apply even if the child or his family is paid for participation.* Payment in money or gifts does not annul any of the prior principles.

Research in Online Communities

As discussed earlier, informed consent is an integral part of ethical research practice. Even so, informed consent is not required for all research situations. Informed consent is not required for the collection/analysis of information or behaviors that are in the public domain or which are conducted in public spaces (i.e., in places where there is no expectation of privacy).[7] With this in mind, consider the following:[8]

- Ford conducts research to determine how people are responding to its newly redesigned Focus and to determine what types of responses can be used to counter negative perceptions. The research entails monitoring automotive chat rooms, recording the comments for later analysis, and then having an employee respond to negative comments using one of three predetermined responses. The effectiveness of each response in changing negative perceptions is evaluated and recorded in order to identify the response that best changes negative attitudes and beliefs. The employee participates in chat conversations under the name "OldCarMan" (not as a Ford employee) and individuals in the chat room are not informed that they are part of a research study and that their conversations are being monitored. (Clearly, informing individuals in the chat room would ruin the research.)
- Astro Drugs wants to find out how the advertising for its new breast cancer drug is being received by women who have been diagnosed with breast cancer. Astro hires a research company to monitor support group forums on breast cancer sites and record all mentions of their drug and advertising for later analysis. The contexts for

the comments, typically these womens' emotions associated with a breast cancer diagnosis, are also recorded. Forum members are never told that their comments are being read and recorded. Once the research is complete, Astro Drugs will use the insights collected to help in identifying the direction for its new advertising campaign. If appropriate, Astro may also use some of the womens' comments in its advertising, although individuals would not be named.

There is no clear answer as to whether each of the prior research actions is ethical. The determination rests upon whether or not forums or similar locations are considered private or public space. Frankel and Siang[9] provide insights into reaching a point of view:

> Some researchers interpret cyberspace to be part of the public domain since newsgroups, listservs, IRCs [and similar forums and locations] they observe are as accessible to anyone as a television or newspaper interview. These researchers believe that the responsibility falls on the disseminators of the messages to filter out what they might consider revealing or private information. Hence, they adopt the position that this type of research should be exempt from the informed consent requirement.
>
> Other scholars disagree with this interpretation, arguing that researchers have an ethical responsibility to understand how the diverse forums of the Internet work and how the users of these forums form expectations about what and where they are communicating. They see the greatest risk for cyberspace participants occurring in the situation where members remain unaware that their messages are being analyzed until the results of the research are published. Moreover, if the results are published in such a way that members of a virtual community can identify their community as the one studied without their knowledge, psychological harm may result. These scholars argue that even though the information is public, communicants may perceive a degree of privacy in their communications.

Given these differing perspectives, it is not surprising that Ess concludes that "doing the right thing, for the right reason, in the right way, at the right time remains a matter of judgment."[10] Our judgment is to recommend the most conservative approach: to treat all of the Internet as private space unless there is no explicit expectation of privacy, such as in blog postings.[11] This approach would require all individuals to provide consent and "opt-in" prior to participation in a research study. Bruckman provides support for this approach in noting that "a frequent mistake made by Internet researchers is, when faced with tradeoff between the needs of subjects and integrity of research, to give priority to the integrity of the research. On further reflection, it should be obvious that this reasoning is faulty—the rights of subjects come first."[12]

Research in Virtual Worlds

One step beyond online communities are virtual worlds such as Second Life.[13] These places are

> a computer-based simulated environment intended for its users to inhabit and interact via avatars. These avatars are usually depicted as textual, two-dimensional,

or three-dimensional graphical representations. The computer accesses a computer-simulated world and presents perceptual stimuli to the user, who in turn can manipulate elements of the modeled world and thus experiences telepresence to a certain degree. Such modeled worlds may appear similar to the real world or instead depict fantasy worlds. The model world may simulate rules based on the real world or some hybrid fantasy world. Communication between users has ranged from text, graphical icons, visual gesture, sound, and rarely, forms using touch, voice command, and balance senses."[14]

Given brands and advertisers entries into these worlds,[15] it is not surprising that attempts to conduct research among virtual world populations soon followed.[16] Jeffrey Stanton, in response to the unique characteristics and challenges of conducting virtual world research, created a "bill of rights" for virtual world respondents. His recommendations are presented in Figure 2.2.[17]

The right to know that I am a subject.

If you obtain data from me in a virtual world for research purposes, I have a right to know that I am in your study.

The right to know you as a researcher.

If I am a subject, you the researcher must represent yourself accurately so that I can confirm your identity. (Although this obligation need not compel the researcher to use a photorealistic avatar, the subject must receive sufficient information to trace the avatar back to a specific person.)

The right to know who approved your study.

Before participating in your study, I have the right to know what ethics body, if any, reviewed your research design.

The right to learn the risks.

You must warn me if the study includes psychologically distressing material, if there is a risk that my avatar or I may be identified, if there may be a tangible or intangible costs to participation, or if other risks to me or my avatar exist.

The right to learn the benefits.

I want to know why my avatar's participation in the study is desirable, even if the benefits to me are indirect.

The right to know why my avatar was chosen.

If researchers contacted my avatar, I want to know how they got my avatar's name and what makes my avatar eligible to participate.

The right to participate as my avatar.

If you recruit me for your virtual world study, I have the right to respond to your study in the identity and role I have selected for my avatar. (In short, researchers should rarely admonish an avatar to "respond as you would in real life.")

FIGURE 2.2   Virtual World Respondent's Bill of Rights

The right to protect my group.

If you are studying my social group, I have the right to protect the integrity and continued existence of my group. (In principle, if members of the group object to the researcher's presence or use of the group for research, those members should have veto power. In practice, it may be impractical for researchers to obtain active consent from every member of a large group, or from a group that has inactive members.)

The right to teleport.

When participating in your study, I reserve the right to teleport out of the research situation if I am uncomfortable with any of the procedures or questions.

The right to debriefing.

If you use deception or disguise of purpose in the study, I deserve to learn about it afterwards.

The right to be left alone.

Following my avatar's participation in your study, whether I completed it or not, I have the right to not be contacted again by the researchers.

FIGURE 2.2 (*continued*)

RESPONSIBILITIES TO CLIENTS

Every advertising research study has a client. The client may be internal (i.e., other departments within the advertising agency) or external (e.g., the company that employs the agency). Similar to informed consent for research subjects, a client's participation in and support of the research should be completely voluntary, and the agreement to conduct research should be taken only after he or she is fully informed of the costs, benefits, procedures, and expected business value of the proposed research. Beyond this, your dealings with both internal and eternal clients require adherence to the ethical principles discussed earlier, as reflected in the following guidelines:

- Research recommendations should be appropriate. Research should be recommended only when it is the best means for satisfying the client's information needs. When research is recommended, it is important to use the research technique best suited to collecting the highest quality information in the most efficient manner.

- All information gathered throughout the research process should be treated in a confidential and proprietary manner.

- All findings should be presented in a straightforward, truthful, and nonmisleading manner.

- Clients should be kept informed of all changes or departures from agreed upon methodology, cost, or timing estimates.

Appropriate Research

Most researchers love to do research. They enjoy the challenge of identifying problems and developing creative ways to find information that helps solve these problems. As a consequence, at times researchers have a tendency to excessively recommend research.

Ethical standards require that recommendations to conduct research be supportable by valid arguments. Research should only be recommended when it has a high likelihood of providing valid, useful information that contributes to the decision making process *and* when the economic consequences of making a wrong decision outweigh the cost of conducting the research.

A second aspect of appropriateness relates to research methodology. Clients are rarely sophisticated researchers and therefore rely on a researcher's expertise to recommend the methodology that has the greatest potential for collecting reliable, useful information in a timely and cost-efficient manner. You must make certain that your recommendations meet these criteria. If, for example, four focus groups are sufficient, it is unfair to the client and unethical on your part to recommend eight or 12 groups just because the additional groups "would be interesting." Similarly, if a convenience sample of 200 respondents can provide the required information, it is unethical to recommend a national probability sample of 1,000 individuals. Finally, because any particular research problem can be addressed by several approaches, one sign of ethical professionalism is, whenever appropriate, to develop several reasonable approaches to a particular problem and then discuss the relative advantages of each with the client. Then, express a point of view on which approach you consider to be the most appropriate. A client may not always agree with your recommendation, but you have acted ethically in (we assume) fairly presenting the strengths and weaknesses of viable alternatives.

Confidential and Proprietary

Maintaining the confidentiality of information and treating information in a proprietary manner are extremely important. Confidentiality requirements apply to all information obtained as part of the research process, that is, information acquired through conversations with the client and other involved individuals, information acquired through examination of the client's written documents, and information collected by the research project itself. All client-provided information and information generated as a result of the examination of this information remain the proprietary property of the client and should never be revealed without the client's permission.

Presentation of Findings

The presentation of data and findings must be straightforward and not misleading. The failure to completely report all relevant data or attempts to manipulate the data to create false impressions are clear violations of ethical standards. Misleading reporting generally takes one of two forms.

One form of misleading data presentation occurs when there is a failure to include all information necessary to evaluate presented data and findings. Data and findings can only be fairly evaluated and applied to the decision-making process when *all* pertinent information is available for examination. Therefore, when presenting research findings, the exclusion of "bad" data is ethically prohibited as are partial or summary presentations without accompanying detail. The following hypothetical example illustrates this principle:

> Two finished commercials are tested. It is decided that the commercial that has the most positive effect on purchase intent will receive the greater amount of media support in the commercial rotation. The research shows that the two commercials

have identical purchase intent scores on a 5-point scale. However, the percent showing strong purchase intent is much higher for Commercial A versus Commercial B, as shown in the following table.

	Commercial A	Commercial B
Average purchase intent	3.2	3.2
Percentage of respondents "strongly agreeing" that they were likely to purchase the product after viewing the commercial	45%	10%

Based on this presentation of the findings, the researcher concludes that Commercial A (which, in fact is the researcher's favorite) is the stronger commercial and should be given the majority of media support. Unfortunately, this decision may not be as simple as this and may, in fact, be wrong. In reality, the commercials had very different effects on purchase intent as shown by the complete data table:

Purchase Intent Scale	Commercial A	Commercial B
Average Purchase Intent	3.2	3.2
% Strongly agree positive	45	10
% Slightly agree positive	0	40
% Neither agree nor disagree	20	10
% Slightly agree negative	0	40
% Strongly agree negative	35	0

The incomplete reporting of the full findings masked real and important differences in the pattern of response to the two commercials. Commercial A tended to polarize the sample. The majority of people who saw this commercial were either strongly positive or strongly negative. On the other hand, *no* individual who saw Commercial B had a strong negative reaction. Additionally, in terms of *total positive* agreement, more people who saw Commercial B (50% versus 45%) agreed that they were interested in purchasing the product. Overall, Commercial B may be the better commercial to support.

The line charts shown in Figure 2.3 also illustrate the misleading effect of excluding critical data. Both charts present the trend in advertising awareness between 2000 and 2010. The data presentation in the top chart supports the conclusion that awareness is positive and growing. When all data is provided in the bottom chart, it can be seen that this conclusion is quite false.

A second form of misleading data reporting occurs when impressions left by data presentation are not, in reality, justified by the data. This can occur when data is manipulated to create incorrect conclusions, for example, when inappropriate scales are used on tables or charts. The charts shown in Figure 2.4 compare preference for three social networking sites. In fact, preference is about equal for all three sites (see top pie chart), yet the use of small scale increments (in the bar chart) and 3D perspective (in both the

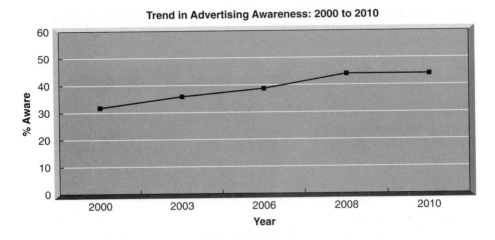

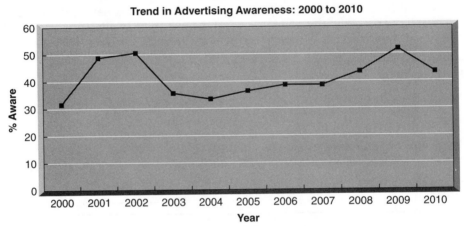

FIGURE 2.3   Misleading Data Presentation Due to Data Omission

bar and lower pie chart) makes it appear that preference for MySpace far exceeds the remaining two sites.

It is important to note that a researcher's obligation to present properly analyzed and interpreted research findings does not end with the written or oral presentation of the findings. The Association for Institutional Research describes the long-term need to ensure proper interpretation as follows:

> The . . . researcher shall make efforts to anticipate and prevent misunderstandings and misuse of reports . . . by careful presentation and documentation in original reports, and by diligent follow-up contact with . . . users of those reports. If a . . . research report has been altered, intentionally or inadvertently, to the degree that its meaning has been substantially distorted, the . . . researcher shall make reasonable attempts to correct such distortions and/or to insist that . . . authorship be removed from the product.[18]

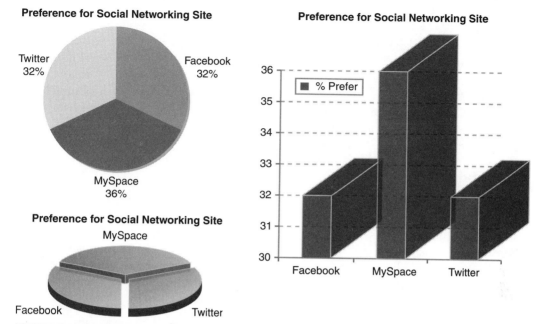

FIGURE 2.4 Misleading Data Presentation Due to Visual Manipulation

Project Changes

Many research projects are executed as planned. Here, the methodological approach collects the desired information, and cost and timing estimates are accurate. Some projects, however, can encounter problems once data collection has begun. These problems can be related to unforeseen difficulty with contacting and recruiting target respondents, the questionnaire taking longer to administer than indicated in pilot tests, or the field service being unable to collect the data as quickly as indicated in its bid letter. None of these types of problems are particularly disastrous for a research study. However, what is disastrous (and unethical) is responding to research-related problems by altering study design, cost or timing *without* informing the client. It is unethical (as well as unprofessional) to make any changes in research design without client consultation. Moreover, the client must be promptly informed of the cost or timing implications of any changes to the research study.

RESPONSIBILITIES TO RESEARCH COMPANIES

Marketing research organizations are businesses that provide support throughout the research process. These firms may provide assistance in study design and data analysis, or may employ the individuals that create the questionnaire, conduct interviews, or otherwise supervise data collection. Ethical considerations require that you refrain from the following behaviors:

- issuing calls for bids or proposals when a supplier has already been selected (pre-selection),
- using the proposal process to obtain free advice, and
- making false promises to obtain lower costs.

Pre-selection

As an advertising researcher, you will interact with a great number of research companies. Some companies will be enjoyable and stimulating to work with, while others will not. When presented with the choice of which company to select for a particular project, there is nothing wrong in selecting a company that in the past has demonstrated high levels of professionalism and expertise and with which you have established a good working relationship. It is unethical, however, to predetermine prior to the bid process which company will receive the project and then issue a call for bids and proposals only to satisfy corporate requirements.

Free Advise

Researchers and research companies deal with ideas; their products are their original thoughts, insights, methodologies, and expertise. As a result, we strongly caution against soliciting detailed proposals in order to "pick the brains" of those with expertise in cases where you have no intention to award the project to one of the companies that has submitted a proposal. Furthermore, we caution against using the recommendations and techniques submitted as part of the proposal process without appropriate compensation. Proper ethical procedures for soliciting bids and proposals require the following:

- A company should be informed that its proposal is one of several being solicited.
- Technical ideas and methodological recommendations must be treated confidentially. No technique or recommendation can be taken from one proposal for use by another organization without prior permission.
- All unaccepted proposals remain the property of the originating organization unless appropriate payment has been made.

False Promises

An unethical practice closely related to the idea of "free advice" is making false promises to reduce the cost of conducting a research study. It is unethical to falsely say to a research supplier, "If you give us a break on the cost of this research, I know that I can throw a lot of business your way later in the year."

RESPONSIBILITIES TO SOCIETY

> *It is my responsibility, as a researcher, to listen for the voice of the people and make it heard. Research serves its highest purpose when it speaks for the citizen or the consumer, when it brings the wants and wishes and ideas of people to light, not for manipulation or exploitation, but for translation into needed products and laws and services.*[19]

This pledge should act as a guiding principle for every project you initiate and for every project for which you report results. Putting this pledge into practice by adhering to the principles of nonmaleficence and beneficence requires the following:

- data and findings reported for public use should be complete;
- data and findings reported for public use should be properly interpreted;

- data reported for public use will be based on sound, objective research judgment;
- research will not be used as a guise for marketing or sales efforts.

Complete Data and Findings

Earlier we discussed that an important ethical responsibility to clients is the full and complete reporting of data and findings. This responsibility is equally important when preparing data for public use. A researcher who withholds negative or damaging information from public release of research is no different than the manufacturer who fails to disclose potentially damaging information about a product. Both mislead through deception and misinformation.

Proper Interpretation

As discussed earlier, misleading reporting occurs when data presentation leads individuals to draw conclusions that are not justified by the actual data. Misleading data presentation on a societal level occurs most frequently when the data is manipulated to provide support for an advocacy position. Consider the following:

> (From a radio report) The demographics of Plainville are certainly changing. It's not the town it once was, that's for certain. Over the past two years the ethnic composition of Plainville has shown phenomenal increases. The percent of African-Americans in town has increased nearly 400% while the number of Hispanics has increased nearly 700%. And these trends show no sign of slowing.

The radio report is clearly alarmist. It leaves the impression that African-Americans and Hispanics are taking over the town. A much different impression would have been communicated if the actual data were reported: that the percentage of the total population accounted for by African-Americans rose from 0.5% to 2% while the percentage accounted for by Hispanics rose from 0.2% to 1.4%.

Sound, Objective Research

Advertising or marketing research that is not conducted in a sound manner tarnishes the entire research industry and has the potential to harm the public. This type of research typically uses biased samples in order to maximize the likelihood of obtaining desired results. Ethical violations would occur, for example, when conducting preference research among those who are already favorable toward your product or conducting research in markets that do not represent normal or ordinary market conditions.

Research Is Not a Guise for Other Activities

In recent years, there has been a rise in the number of mailings and telephone calls that use research as a pretext for accomplishing nonresearch objectives such as sales, fund

W🦏rld Species Defense Associ🐘tion

5567 Two Twin Oaks River Drive   *Ramona, New York 10021*

Dear Animal Lover:

We need your opinions to help us plan next year's activities. Can you please answer the three questions below?

1. Do you think that the indiscriminate and senseless slaughter of
    innocent whales needs to end immediately?

    Yes, stop the killing now   ≪ ≫
    No   ≪ ≫

2. Concerned individuals believe that poisoning of gophers and other
    ground animals as a means of population control is inhumane because
    this causes the animals to die a painful death over several days. Do
    you think this kind of poisoning should be outlawed?

    Yes, stop the agony now   ≪ ≫
    No   ≪ ≫

3. Recent legislative changes have raised the limits to the amount of
    filth, sludge and slime that corporations can dump into the ocean,
    threatening the survival of thousands of aquatic animals. Should these
    laws be altered to stop the deaths in our oceans?

    Yes, change the laws now   ≪ ≫
    No   ≪ ≫

If you answered "yes" to the prior questions then you share our concerns. We can work together to make our planet a better place for all who share it. But, unfortunately, this work requires the financial support of caring, concerned individuals like you.

Can we count on you to help us? Please visit our web site at www.wsdassn.net to help us help those who can't help themselves. Any donation will be greatly appreciated.

Sincerely,

Jane Morgan

FIGURE 2.5   Illustration of Unethical Use of Research as a Guise for Marketing Activities

solicitation, or the creation of a database. A respondent will interpret a lead-in of "I'm taking a survey and am interested in your opinions" as an indication that the goal is the collection of information. Using this type of approach for other reasons is both deceptive and a clear violation of ethical standards. The "survey questionnaire" shown in Figure 2.5 illustrates what to avoid in this regard.

SUMMARY

As a member of the advertising profession, you have the responsibility to adhere to the ethical principles of *autonomy* (giving decision-making authority to respondents), *beneficence* (remove harm and bestow benefits), and *nonmaleficence* (do no harm). You must adhere to these principles as you interact with four groups of individuals: research respondents, internal and external clients, research support companies, and the public. Ethical standards and behaviors that you should follow in your professional relationships with each of these groups are:

Research Respondents:
The decision to participate must be an informed one. Informed consent must accurately describe the context for the research, the voluntary nature of the research, and the characteristics or demands of the research.

Mistreatment must be avoided during all phases of the research.

The decision to end participation must be respected.

Deceptions must cause no harm and be justifiable given the research design and information needs.

Special care must be taken when conducting research with unique/special populations, such as children, in online communities or in virtual worlds.

The right to confidentiality and privacy is absolute.

Research Clients:
Methodological recommendations must be appropriate.

All information is confidential and proprietary.

Findings must be presented honestly, objectively, and in a nonmisleading manner.

Research Companies:
There must be no false calls for proposals or use of the proposal process to obtain free advice.

No false promises should be given.

Society:
Data and findings must be complete, not misleading and properly interpreted and reported.

Collected data will represent sound, objective research.

Research should not be used as a pretext for sales, fundraising, or database creation efforts.

Review Questions

1. Define the ethical principles of *autonomy*, *nonmaleficence*, and *beneficence*.

2. What guidelines describe how a researcher should interact with study respondents?

3. In what circumstances is *informed consent* required? What is meant by this term?

4. What areas need to be addressed by the researcher in order for the participant to be able to make an informed decision regarding participation?

5. When writing an informed consent document, what guidelines should be adhered to?

6. How can a research study be planned to minimize or eliminate respondent mistreatment?

7. What is meant by "A respondent has an absolute right to confidentiality and privacy"? When is it acceptable for a researcher *not* to maintain confidentiality?

8. Identify five considerations necessary for protecting the interests of child participants.

9. Under what circumstances is informed consent *not* necessary?

10. What are special considerations for conducting research in virtual worlds?

11. What guidelines govern a researcher's interactions with his or her internal and external clients?

12. Briefly describe two aspects of *appropriateness* that should be considered when recommending research.

13. With regard to research clients, how can a researcher *maintain confidentiality* and treat information in a *proprietary manner*?

14. What guidelines are important to keep in mind when presenting data to one's client? What forms of data presentation could be misleading?

15. What is the ethical way to handle changes in research design, cost, or timing once the study has been approved?

16. List and explain the three ethical guidelines governing a researcher's interactions with marketing research organizations.

17. What ethical guidelines govern a researcher's responsibility toward society? Briefly describe each of these principles?

Application Exercises[20]

1. Each of the situations described in parts "a" to "j" represents a type of practice that some researchers have engaged in or have approved. Read each situation and prepare a point of view that either defends or criticizes that action. Be certain to provide support for your point of view.

   a. The Melvin Harris Corporation is the parent company of Pizza-to-Go, a chain of franchised Pizza Restaurants. Melvin Harris asks you to conduct a survey of its franchisees. You and Melvin agree that, in order to obtain the most honest answers, strict confidentiality of respondents and their responses must be maintained. You then prepare the questionnaires for mailing. In order to know who has responded to the first mailing (so that a second mailing can be sent to nonresponders), you place an identification code on the questionnaires. After the study is complete, you present the results to Melvin. One question on the survey asked each franchisee to rate the leadership ability of Melvin Harris. Twenty-five percent of the sample rated Melvin Harris' leadership ability "excellent." Melvin asks for the names of those who provided the "excellent" rating in order to give them a more substantial Christmas bonus.

   b. You conduct personal interviews with target audience women in a mall. As part of the interview, each woman tries and comments on your client's shampoo. At the end of the interview, you give each woman a free bottle of the shampoo as a "thanks for participating gift." You do not tell each woman that they will be called back in a week to be re-interviewed after they have used the product at home.

   c. You have constructed a 30-minute telephone interview. During the first week of interviewing, potential respondents were told of the interview length. Unfortunately, fewer individuals than anticipated have agreed to be interviewed. You change the introduction to the survey to say: "This is an important survey. It will take a relatively short amount of time."

   d. You are interviewing a number of doctors on their drug prescribing behaviors. A number of doctors say that they will participate only if you send them the results of the study. You agree to send them the results, even though you have no intention of doing so.

   e. You are conducting a series of focus groups. You explain that the client and other interested parties are seated behind the one-way mirror and that the responses will be tape-recorded. You do not mention that the groups are being filmed from behind the mirror.

   f. You are in a bind. You have been asked to design a research study in an area in which you do not have a great deal of expertise. You decide to solicit a number of proposals from customized research companies, take the best ideas from each, and then rebid the job and award the job to the lowest bidder.

g. Your client has decided that telemarketing has the potential to be a successful way to market his product, an expensive but very well-made and effective water purifier. He says that this product is really only useful to those households that drink more than two gallons of water per day. He does not wish to take advantage by selling the product to those who really do not have the need. (He wants to feel good about each sale.) So, he needs to identify just the right people. Your client asks you to evaluate the telemarketing script that he has written:

Hello. My name is _____ and I am calling from WaterCo. Inc. I'm taking just a brief survey of Escondito residents to determine their satisfaction with the municipal drinking water. Can you please tell me . . .

1. Your age (FILL IN) _____
2. The number of people in your household (FILL IN) _____
3. Are you currently satisfied with the quality of the tap water used for drinking in your household?
   YES _____   NO _____
4. Do you currently have an in-tap water purification system?
   YES _____   NO _____
5. Does your family drink, on average, at least two gallons of water per day?
   YES _____   NO _____

IF "NO" TO "QUESTIONS 3 AND 4, AND "YES" TO" QUESTION 5, ARRANGE A TIME FOR AN IN-HOME DEMONSTRATION.

h. The executives of the GIBA Company are very difficult to reach by telephone. However, this is the way that you must reach them to successfully conduct your research. In order to get past each executive's secretary, you say, "I have been referred to (name of executive) to discuss an important, but personal matter."

i. You have noticed that many people are hanging up before the end of a complex 15-minute interview. You offer those who wish to hang up $5 for completing the interview. You offer no money to those who do not state a desire to terminate.

j. You need to obtain copies of competitive advertising and (hopefully) media plans. You call your competitors and ask for the information under the guise of a student working on a class assignment.

2. Richard Fedman has just joined the SSDR Advertising Agency as an Associate Research Director. Richard will supervise research on the Tico Fast Food account. Richard's prior position was a Research Supervisor at another agency where he worked on the Mexicale Foods Account, a competitor of Tico Fast Food. Think about each of the following situations in which Richard might find himself. What course of action would you suggest Richard take in each situation ("a" through "c")?

   a. In a meeting with Tico's management, Todd Kilgore, a Senior Vice President of Development, says that Tico needs to begin to capitalize on consumers' desire to eat healthy. He suggests that Richard plan and conduct a research study to determine the appeal of health-positioned Mexican fast food. Richard knows the answer without doing the research. He conducted the exact same study for Mexicale prior to leaving the company. He knows that consumers are very interested in this type of product, and that based on the research, Mexicale is planning on revising its menu. Should Richard share this knowledge with Todd?

   b. Richard learned a unique and accurate way to identify consumers' taste preferences while working on the Mexicale account. Tico now wants to conduct taste tests of its products. Should Richard describe and recommend this methodology to Tico?

   c. Richard is a very creative researcher. While working at his prior agency, he developed a method for obtaining very meaningful insights into consumers' reactions to advertising. One of SSDR's clients is about to conduct this type of research. Should Richard share this new methodology with SSDR's clients?

3. Examine consumer-oriented publications such as *USA Today, Time,* and *Newsweek,* or more demographically focused publications such as *Gentleman's Quarterly, Redbook,* or *Sassy.* Find a discussion of survey results. Evaluate whether the results and conclusions presented in the article meet the standards of ethical data presentation.

4. Each of the situations described in parts "a" through "c" relates to the ethics of data presentation. Read each situation and then determine if the relevant chart shown in Figure 2.6 satisfies or violates ethical standards for data presentation.

% Change (Index) Versus Prior Year

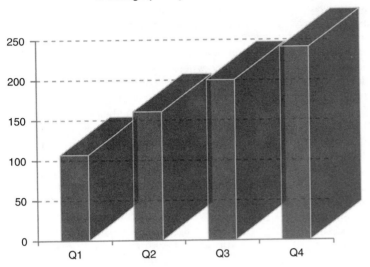

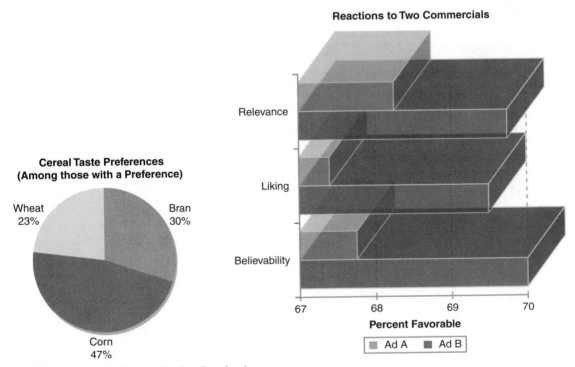

FIGURE 2.6   Graphs for Application Exercise 4

Be certain to explain and defend your point of view.

a. The AABB Agency conducts quarterly research to measure awareness levels of its client's advertising. The percentage of individuals from among the total sample who say that they are aware of the advertising within each quarter is shown in the columns labeled "2009" and "2010" in the table below.

Quarter	2009	2010	Index
Q1 (Jan. to March)	14%	15%	107
Q2 (April to June)	10	16	160
Q3 (July to Sept.)	7	14	200
Q4 (Oct. to Dec.)	5	12	240

An agency researcher takes this data and computes the index for each quarter. An index over 100 indicates that awareness in 2010 was higher than the same quarter in 2009. For example, dividing 15 by 14 in Q1 results in an index of 107, meaning that awareness in 2010 was 7% higher. The 200 index in Q3 indicates that 2010 awareness was double that of the same quarter in 2009. The researcher then concludes that the trend in advertising awareness is very positive, as reflected in the top chart in Figure 2.6. Is the conclusion and chart correct?

b. The client research team conducts a survey to determine the cereal taste preferences of adults aged 25 to 39. They obtain the results shown in the table below.

Cereal Main Ingredient	Percent of Sample
Prefer wheat	10%
Prefer corn	16
Prefer oats	11
No preference	63
Total	**100%**

The research team repercents the data to obtain preferences among only those who express a preference. The pie chart in Figure 2.6 presents this data. Is this chart acceptable?

c. Two commercials are tested. Three key measures of the test are "commercial believability," "commercial liking," and "personal relevance." The percentage of individuals viewing each commercial and providing a positive rating (e.g., agreeing that the commercial was believable) on each measure for that commercial is shown on the right-hand bar chart in Figure 2.6. Is this chart acceptable?

5. Visit an online blog and online discussion group. Provide a point of view that classifies each site as either a public or private space. Defend and justify your point of view.

6. Read the virtual world's bill of rights in Figure 2.2. Write a comparable document that presents the bill of rights for individuals who participate in online communities.

7. You are hired as the Research Director for a national wild animal conservancy. The conservancy wants to put pressure on congress to preserve more land as animal preserves. You conduct research among the members of the conservancy and find that 93% of the members support the increased preservation of land for animal preserves. These individuals agreed with the statement: "The increased preservation of natural lands is an important goal for the United States." The conservancy wants to send a letter to all members of congress announcing the results of this study. The introduction of the letter would report the following:

We've worked for more natural preserves. We know that this is important. And so do the American people. Over 90% of Americans agree that increasing the preservation of land is an important national goal.

The remainder of the letter discusses the conservancy but not the research. Would you approve of this use and communication of the results?

Endnotes

1. The discussion in this chapter draws on the following: National Institutes of Health (1979). *The Belmont Report* at: http://ohsr.od.nih.gov/ guidelines/belmont.html; Council of American Survey Research Organizations (2009). *Code of Standards and Ethics for Survey Research*

at: http://www.casro.org/codeofstandards.cfm); National Bioethics Advisory Commission (2001). *Ethical and Policy Issues in Research Involving Human Participants* at http://bioethics.georgetown.edu/nbac/human/oversumm.html.

2. See Thomas Wasse and Thomas Lengyel (undated). *How IRB's Can Put the Belmont Report into Practice* at http://www.alliance1.org/Research/articlearchive/Belmont-Report_final.pdf for extended discussion of autonomy and maleficence.

3. This discussion draws from U.S. Department of Health and Human Services (1998). *Informed Consent Checklist* at http://www.hhs.gov/ohrp/humansubjects/assurance/consentckls.htm; Friends Research Institute (undated). *Informed Consent Checklist* available at http://www.friendsresearch.org/IRB_Forms/Reviewer-Informed ConsentChecklist.doc. See also Centers for Disease Control and Prevention (1998). *Consent for CDC Research* at casr.ou.edu/hiv/consent_letters.pdf.

4. This aspect of informed consent becomes relevant, for example, when individuals are solicited to participate in a research study and are told that a prize drawing is being used as an incentive. All individuals who read and respond to the informed consent form should be entered into the drawing.

5. National Cancer Institute (2006). *Appendix 3: Checklist for Easy-to-Read Informed Consent Documents* at http:// www.cancer.gov/clinical-trials/understanding/simplification-of-informed-consent-docs/page5#appendix3.

6. Council of American Survey Research Organizations, op. cit.

7. American Psychological Association (2002). *Ethical Principles of Psychologists and Code of Conduct* at apa.org/ethics/code2002.html.

8. These examples are fictitious and for illustrative purposes only.

9. Mark S. Frankel and Sanyin Siang (1999). "Ethical and Legal Aspects of Human Subjects Research on the Internet" at http://www.aaas.org/spp/dspp/sfrl/projects/inters/main.htm.

10. Charles Ess (undated). "Internet Research Ethics" at http://www.nyu.edu/projects/nissenbaum/ethics_ess.html.

11. For more detailed discussion, see Gunther Eysenbach and Jeremy Wyatt (2002). "Using the Internet for Surveys and Health Research." *Journal of Medical Internet Research* at http://www.jmir.org/2002/2/e13.HTML; Jan Colvin and Jane Lanigan (2005). "Ethical Issues and Best Practice for Internet Research." *Journal of Family and Consumer Sciences* September: 34-39; Gunther Eysenbach and James E. Till (2001). "Ethical Issues in Qualitative Research on Internet Communities." *British Medical Journal* November 10: 1103-1105; Dag Elgesem (2002). "What Is Special about the Ethical Issues in Online Research?" *Ethics and Information Technology* 4: 195–203.

12. Amy Bruckman (2002). "Ethical Guidelines for Research Online (version 4/4/02) at http://www.cc.gatech.edu/~asb/ethics.

13. For an extensive listing of virtual worlds, see Virtual Worlds Review (undated) at http://www.virtualworldsreview.com/info/categories.shtml.

14. Wikipedia (undated). Virtual Worlds at http://en.wikipedia.org/wiki/Virtual_worlds.

15. For additional insights into advertisers and marketers use of virtual worlds, see Terra Nova (2004). "Advertising and Branding in Virtual Worlds" at http://terranova.blogs.com/terra_nova/2004/04/advertising_and.html; Betsy Book (2004). "These bodies are FREE, so get one NOW!": Advertising & Branding in Social Virtual Worlds" at http://www.virtualworldsreview.com/papers/adbrand.pdf.

16. See, for example, the *Journal of Virtual Worlds Research* at http://jvwresearch.org; Business Communicators of Second Life (undated) "Nine Questions on Virtual World Market Research" at http://freshtakes.typepad.com/sl_communicators/2008/01/nine-questions.html; Reena Jana (2007). "Mining Virtual Worlds for Market Research" at http://www.businessweek.com/innovate/content/aug2007/id20070813_140822.htm.

17. Jeffrey Stanton (2009). "Social Research Ethics for Virtual Worlds" at Slideshare (http://www.slideshare.net).

18. Code of Ethics of the Association of Institutional Research at http://www.airweb.org/?page=140.

19. Portion of the pledge of the New York Chapter of the American Marketing Association.

20. All situations are hypothetical and data is for illustrative purposes only.

CHAPTER 3

Secondary Research

Advertisers can use either primary or secondary research to help them make better decisions. Primary research collects original information through projects specifically designed to satisfy a current informational need. Secondary research consists of information that has been previously gathered by others for purposes other than the specific project at hand.

***

When you are done reading this chapter, you should have a better understanding of how to:

- identify the characteristics of secondary research information and the differences between secondary information and secondary sources
- identify and evaluate the appropriate uses of secondary research information
- describe the advantages and limitations of secondary research information
- understand how to best use search engines for information search
- identify secondary sources that provide ongoing insights and information relevant to advertising decision making.

This chapter is divided into three main sections. The first section provides an introduction to the characteristics and uses of secondary research as well as guidelines for evaluating the "goodness" of both online and offline sources of secondary information. Next, we present guidance for efficiently identifying secondary information relevant to a specific information need, with a focus on search and search engine techniques. Third, we identify secondary information sources that help advertisers stay informed on a continuing basis.

AN INTRODUCTION TO SECONDARY RESEARCH

Secondary research information is information that has been collected and analyzed by others for a purpose other than specifically responding to a current information need. This contrasts with primary research that is conducted by (or on behalf of) an information user to specifically satisfy that individual's informational need. Secondary research is therefore distinguished from primary research on the basis of two criteria:

- The *individual responsible for planning and conducting the research.* In primary research, the project's researcher is responsible for problem definition, sample design, data collection, data analysis, and the presentation of results. The involvement of a secondary researcher begins after these tasks have been completed. A secondary researcher does not have any control over what information was collected, the method by which the information was collected, or the procedures used to initially analyze the data.

- The *circumstances under which the research was conducted.* In primary research, methodological design and questionnaire content are developed to specifically satisfy the original end users' informational needs. Thus, data coding, organization, and analysis reflect the needs of the individuals who initially requested the research. A researcher using secondary research information must adapt and translate the data from its original use to the secondary researcher's new (and often different) needs.

The U.S. census illustrates how a research study and the information it gathers can be either primary or secondary depending on the circumstances under which the research was initially planned, conducted, and utilized. The census is conducted on behalf of the federal government to help it make decisions related to, among other things, state representation in the House of Representatives and the apportionment of federal funds. In this context, the census is primary research. The initial end users of the information provide direction in the design and conduct of research to make certain that the collected information meets their specific informational needs. An advertiser or marketer, however, could examine census information to better understand shifts in demography so that he or she could identify opportunities for new products or line extensions. In this latter context, census information is being used as secondary research. The advertiser is adapting data collected by others to respond to his or her own informational needs, which are different from the needs that initially motivated the collection of information.

Secondary Information Versus Secondary Sources

It is important to distinguish the concepts of "primary and secondary information" from the concepts of "primary and secondary sources." As just discussed, the terms *primary* and *secondary* information refer to (1) the individual or organization initially responsible for the research and (2) the circumstances under which the research was initially conducted. The U.S. census is primary information when used by the Federal Government; census data is secondary information when used by others. *Primary and secondary sources* refer to the involvement of the information's source in the conduct of the research. A primary source is the individual or organization that originated the information; a secondary source is the individual or organization that provides the information after obtaining it from the original source. The U.S. government, for example, is a primary source for census data, while a newspaper or magazine that reprints and/or interprets selected portions of the census is a secondary source.

The distinction between primary and secondary sources is important because, from an information user's perspective, the two sources are not interchangeable or equally acceptable. The following are three important reasons why one should, whenever possible, obtain information from its primary source:

- ***Completeness.*** A primary source is more complete because it presents the full set of findings in an unabridged form. Bias can occur whenever a secondary source selects and presents portions of the data in an abridged form.
- ***Accuracy.*** Primary sources are considered to be more accurate than secondary sources because of the potential for secondary sources to misinterpret the information or to present the information in a biased or misleading manner. Additionally, secondary sources often omit important footnotes or key textual elements (which were presented by the primary source), thereby changing the meaning and interpretation of the data.
- ***Quality.*** Primary sources will generally describe the methodology through which the data was collected. An examination of this methodology lets a researcher evaluate information quality. Detailed methodological descriptions are typically not provided by secondary sources.

The Uses of Secondary Research

Secondary research contributes to advertising decision making in three primary ways. Information obtained from secondary research can

- directly answer an advertiser's informational needs,
- provide important insights prior to the conduct of primary research,
- contribute to questionnaire development.

DIRECTLY ANSWER INFORMATIONAL NEEDS. In some instances, information obtained from secondary research can completely satisfy and resolve an advertiser's or marketer's informational needs, thereby eliminating the need for any primary research. This can be accomplished in one of two ways.

First, secondary information can provide required information without the need for further analysis or manipulation, for example:

- A media planner might wish to identify cities in which there is an above average concentration of 18- to 34-year olds who have an annual income under $30,000. Similarly, an advertiser might wish to understand population growth or decline in the country's largest metropolitan areas or among specific demographic groups. Both types of information could be obtained from the census or other demographic source. No manipulation of the data is required in order the answer the informational need.

- Advertisers might want to monitor trends and developments in the categories in which their brands compete. A snack food advertiser, for example, could stay current by reading the trend reports compiled by others, such as that shown in Figure 3.1.[1] Again, the information can be used "as is" without further manipulation.

Second, secondary information that cannot answer an informational need in its original form can often satisfy that need if it is manipulated. Manipulation of secondary data might occur when an informational need requires categories different than those used in the secondary data. An advertiser might request demographic trends in the following age groups: under 17 to 30, 31 to 49, 50 to 60, 61 to 75, and 76 and older. Because these are nonstandard age groupings, a researcher would have to create them by combining data from smaller age groupings. Data manipulation might also occur when the secondary research contains the appropriate data but the data is in a form different than that required to meet the advertiser's or marketer's informational need. An advertiser might wish to determine the percentage change in a competitor's advertising expenditures over the prior five years. However, because secondary sources typically report advertising expenditures in terms of dollars, dollar expenditures would need to be changed to percentages in order to respond to the advertiser's request.

The prior examples illustrate how secondary research can answer narrowly focused questions. There are times, however, when an informational need is only satisfied by a synthesis of information from multiple secondary information sources. This latter type of secondary research might address questions such as: "What are the trends in advertisers' use of social media?" or "What are trends and developments in mobile advertising?" A useful and insightful answer to this type of broader, more complex question requires that one conduct a thorough search of the available secondary information, synthesize the findings from various sources, and then provide a point of view on the meaning and implications of the findings. Synthesis and the drawing of implications is essential; a report of secondary findings without accompanying analysis and interpretation will fail to completely satisfy an informational need and, as a consequence, will provide an incomplete basis for subsequent decision making. The two reports provided in the online supplemental readings are excellent models of this type of secondary analysis.

PROVIDE IMPORTANT INSIGHTS PRIOR TO PRIMARY RESEARCH.   Secondary research information can help to clarify, redefine, or refocus a planned primary research study. "An examination of secondary sources provides insights into what is and is not known, the limitations of previous research, the shortcomings of methodologies employed and

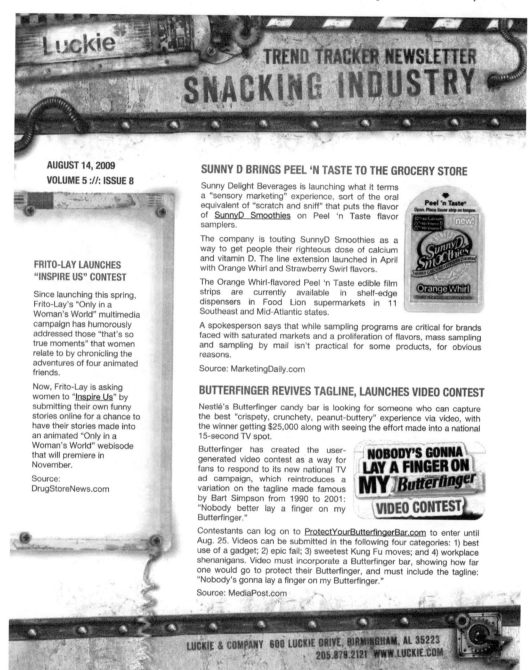

TREND TRACKER NEWSLETTER
SNACKING INDUSTRY

Luckie

AUGUST 14, 2009
VOLUME 5 ://: ISSUE 8

FRITO-LAY LAUNCHES "INSPIRE US" CONTEST

Since launching this spring, Frito-Lay's "Only in a Woman's World" multimedia campaign has humorously addressed those "that's so true moments" that women relate to by chronicling the adventures of four animated friends.

Now, Frito-Lay is asking women to "Inspire Us" by submitting their own funny stories online for a chance to have their stories made into an animated "Only in a Woman's World" webisode that will premiere in November.

Source:
DrugStoreNews.com

SUNNY D BRINGS PEEL 'N TASTE TO THE GROCERY STORE

Sunny Delight Beverages is launching what it terms a "sensory marketing" experience, sort of the oral equivalent of "scratch and sniff" that puts the flavor of SunnyD Smoothies on Peel 'n Taste flavor samplers.

The company is touting SunnyD Smoothies as a way to get people their righteous dose of calcium and vitamin D. The line extension launched in April with Orange Whirl and Strawberry Swirl flavors.

The Orange Whirl-flavored Peel 'n Taste edible film strips are currently available in shelf-edge dispensers in Food Lion supermarkets in 11 Southeast and Mid-Atlantic states.

A spokesperson says that while sampling programs are critical for brands faced with saturated markets and a proliferation of flavors, mass sampling and sampling by mail isn't practical for some products, for obvious reasons.

Source: MarketingDaily.com

BUTTERFINGER REVIVES TAGLINE, LAUNCHES VIDEO CONTEST

Nestlé's Butterfinger candy bar is looking for someone who can capture the best "crispety, crunchety, peanut-buttery" experience via video, with the winner getting $25,000 along with seeing the effort made into a national 15-second TV spot.

Butterfinger has created the user-generated video contest as a way for fans to respond to its new national TV ad campaign, which reintroduces a variation on the tagline made famous by Bart Simpson from 1990 to 2001: "Nobody better lay a finger on my Butterfinger."

NOBODY'S GONNA LAY A FINGER ON MY Butterfinger VIDEO CONTEST

Contestants can log on to ProtectYourButterfingerBar.com to enter until Aug. 25. Videos can be submitted in the following four categories: 1) best use of a gadget; 2) epic fail; 3) sweetest Kung Fu moves; and 4) workplace shenanigans. Video must incorporate a Butterfinger bar, showing how far one would go to protect their Butterfinger, and must include the tagline: "Nobody's gonna lay a finger on my Butterfinger."

Source: MediaPost.com

LUCKIE & COMPANY 600 LUCKIE DRIVE, BIRMINGHAM, AL 35223
205.879.2121 WWW.LUCKIE.COM

FIGURE 3.1   Excerpt from August, 2009 Snacking Trend Report

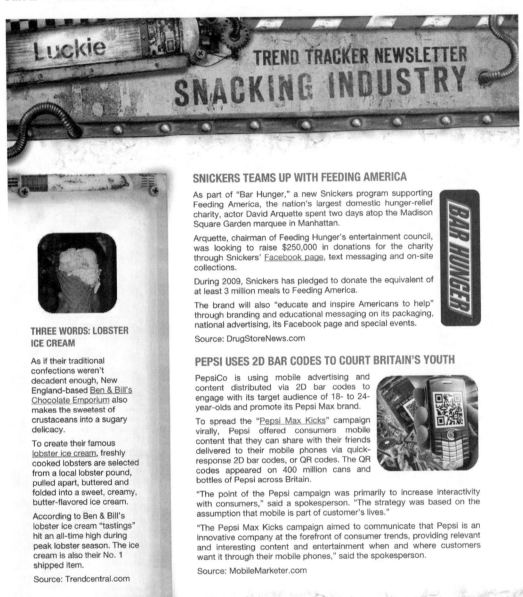

SNICKERS TEAMS UP WITH FEEDING AMERICA

As part of "Bar Hunger," a new Snickers program supporting Feeding America, the nation's largest domestic hunger-relief charity, actor David Arquette spent two days atop the Madison Square Garden marquee in Manhattan.

Arquette, chairman of Feeding Hunger's entertainment council, was looking to raise $250,000 in donations for the charity through Snickers' Facebook page, text messaging and on-site collections.

During 2009, Snickers has pledged to donate the equivalent of at least 3 million meals to Feeding America.

The brand will also "educate and inspire Americans to help" through branding and educational messaging on its packaging, national advertising, its Facebook page and special events.

Source: DrugStoreNews.com

PEPSI USES 2D BAR CODES TO COURT BRITAIN'S YOUTH

PepsiCo is using mobile advertising and content distributed via 2D bar codes to engage with its target audience of 18- to 24-year-olds and promote its Pepsi Max brand.

To spread the "Pepsi Max Kicks" campaign virally, Pepsi offered consumers mobile content that they can share with their friends delivered to their mobile phones via quick-response 2D bar codes, or QR codes. The QR codes appeared on 400 million cans and bottles of Pepsi across Britain.

"The point of the Pepsi campaign was primarily to increase interactivity with consumers," said a spokesperson. "The strategy was based on the assumption that mobile is part of customer's lives."

"The Pepsi Max Kicks campaign aimed to communicate that Pepsi is an innovative company at the forefront of consumer trends, providing relevant and interesting content and entertainment when and where customers want it through their mobile phones," said the spokesperson.

Source: MobileMarketer.com

THREE WORDS: LOBSTER ICE CREAM

As if their traditional confections weren't decadent enough, New England-based Ben & Bill's Chocolate Emporium also makes the sweetest of crustaceans into a sugary delicacy.

To create their famous lobster ice cream, freshly cooked lobsters are selected from a local lobster pound, pulled apart, buttered and folded into a sweet, creamy, butter-flavored ice cream.

According to Ben & Bill's lobster ice cream "tastings" hit an all-time high during peak lobster season. The ice cream is also their No. 1 shipped item.

Source: Trendcentral.com

FOR MORE INFORMATION, PLEASE CONTACT DAVID STUTTS AT DAVID.STUTTS@LUCKIE.COM

FIGURE 3.1 *(continued)*

the generalizability of earlier conclusions."[2] As a result, an examination of relevant secondary research conducted early in the research planning process can improve subsequent primary research in several ways. Secondary research information can

- answer some of the questions originally addressed in the primary research study, making the exploration of these areas unnecessary.
- provide insights that lead to unforeseen, additional areas to explore in the primary research study. Conversely, secondary research may provide insights that discourage the planned exploration of certain areas in primary research.
- cause a change in research hypotheses, resulting in changes in research design or questionnaire content.

CONTRIBUTE TO QUESTIONNAIRE DEVELOPMENT. Secondary research can contribute to improved questionnaire design in two ways. First, secondary research can alert a researcher to problems that might be encountered in the planned primary research, resulting in changes to the form of the questionnaire. A researcher, for example, might have decided to use a number of open-ended questions to probe consumers' attitudes. However, a review of prior research on the same topic might indicate that this type of question works poorly because consumers are unable to verbalize their attitudes. As a consequence, closed-ended versus the originally planned open-ended questions would be used.

Second, secondary research can provide examples of ways to probe and explore specific areas addressed in primary research. A researcher can examine secondary sources to identify specific measures that prior researchers have used. The most relevant and reliable measures can then be modified for use in the planned research study. A researcher who wishes to probe reactions to advertising could save a great deal of time and effort by using measures developed by other researchers rather than starting from scratch.

Advantages of Secondary Research

Secondary research, versus primary research, is typically more efficient in terms of money and time. In general, it is typically much less expensive to use secondary research information than to conduct primary research to collect comparable information. This is almost always true, even when the secondary information must be purchased. Additionally, beyond the absolute cost of obtaining the information, secondary information saves money by helping a researcher focus on real and meaningful gaps in knowledge.

Secondary research saves time because of differences in the rate of information acquisition. It may only take a week, for example, to determine competitors' marketing strategies via an analysis of secondary sources. An analysis of competitors' marketing strategies via primary research might take several months, if such research could be successfully accomplished at all. As a consequence, when insights (particularly quantitative insights) are needed quickly, the only practical alternative is to consult secondary sources. Moreover, "if stringent budget and time constraints are imposed on primary research, secondary research may provide higher quality data then could be obtained with a new research project."[3]

Finally, there are circumstances in which secondary research is the only type of available information. It would be time and cost prohibitive, for example, for a single advertiser or marketer to conduct research similar to the U.S. census or to monitor advertising expenditures of all national advertisers.

Limitations of Secondary Research

In spite of the advantages of secondary research information, the use of this type of information poses dangers to the uninformed or uncritical user. Users of secondary research must clearly understand the limitations of secondary information with regard to availability, relevance, and sufficiency.

AVAILABILITY.   Secondary information cannot be used in some instances simply because it is not available. There may be a lack of secondary information because of

- the uniqueness and specificity of the informational need (e.g., determining consumers' responses to advertising concepts or obtaining taste test preferences to alternative product formulations), or
- the proprietary nature of the desired information (e.g., consumers' responses to competitors' new line extensions).

Informational needs must be met by primary data whenever secondary information is unavailable.

RELEVANCE.   Secondary research best satisfies an advertiser's informational need when it is relevant. The extent to which secondary research information is relevant in a particular circumstance is determined by the correspondence between the advertiser's informational needs and the characteristics of the secondary information with regard to: units of measurement, units of analysis, and timeliness of data collection.

The relevance of secondary information increases when there is a high correspondence between the *units of measurement* used in the secondary research and the advertiser's or marketer's desired units of measurement. An example would be an automobile manufacturer who wishes to track competitors' monthly advertising expenditures. Secondary information that reports dollars spent per month displays an exact correspondence and would therefore be very relevant. Secondary sources that report spending in terms of other units, such as advertising dollars per auto sold or advertising dollars as a percent of gross margin, would be less relevant.

The relevance of secondary information also increases when there is a high correspondence between how an advertiser or marketer defines the *unit of analysis* and how the unit of analysis is defined by the secondary information source. An advertiser may be interested in identifying the average amount of children's cereal purchased per month in households with children aged five to ten. Secondary information that exactly corresponds to this definition would be more relevant than secondary information with different units of analysis, for example, research that uses a different

- category definition (i.e., all cereal purchases versus just children's cereal),
- time period (i.e., per week, every three months), or
- target definition (i.e., households with any child under the age of 12).

Finally, the relevance of secondary information increases with its recency. Most informational needs require current data. Thus, the relevance and usefulness of a secondary information source declines as the data ages.

SUFFICIENCY. Secondary data may be available and relevant but still may not sufficiently satisfy identified informational needs. A shampoo advertiser, for example, might wish to identify the best selling shampoos and brand share of shampoos among men aged 25 to 54 and women aged 25 to 49. While secondary information may be able to supply overall brand share, it may not be able to report brand shares among these specific gender and age groups. When secondary information is insufficient, an advertiser may either conduct primary research or (more dangerously) make a decision based on available but incomplete data.

Evaluating the "Goodness" of Secondary Information

There is typically little problem in locating secondary information. However, before using this information it is necessary to evaluate its source. The criteria discussed in this section help you assess the "goodness" and resulting value of both online and print secondary information sources.[4]

AUTHOR AND SOURCE. Secondary information is only of value when it is created by unbiased, qualified individuals. The following questions help assess author and source characteristics.

- Are one or more authors credited with producing the work? Are they clearly identified?
- Are the credentials of the author(s) available? If so, do the author(s) appear to have relevant training and expertise? Is a biography and description of credentials provided?
- Have the author(s) produced other similar works? How have these works been received and reviewed?
- Are the author(s) affiliated with any organization that might bias their perspective?
- Is it clear who is sponsoring the author(s); that is, what is the credibility of the publisher or Web site owner? Is the publisher/Web site owner free of bias?
- Is there a way to contact the author to verify any details of the source material?
- If you conduct a search for the author and source, what types of descriptors appear?
- If a Web site, what can be inferred from the site's URL? Is it commercial (.com), an organization (.org), or educational institution (.edu)? Is the URL domestic or foreign?

ACCURACY

- Has the page or publication provided external sources to verify presented information through footnotes, bibliographies, or links to external (and trustworthy) locations?
- Has the page or publication been reviewed by external sources?
- Is original data presented whenever possible to support arguments or conclusions? Does supporting data appear to be unaltered and not fabricated?
- Do facts or data appear to be unfairly manipulated to support a point of view? Does the presentation of data appear to be complete and not "cherry-picked?"

- If data is presented in table or graph form, are the tables and graphs clearly and appropriately labeled?
- If data is presented, was the underlying methodology appropriate and unbiased?

CURRENCY

- Is it clear when the material was prepared? Are the underlying data, conclusions, or arguments current enough to have value?
- If the source is a Web site, can it be determined when the material was last updated, revised, or edited? Are external links functional and current?

OBJECTIVITY

- Can opinion be clearly distinguished from fact? Does the source attempt to make this distinction clear within the body of the source material?
- What is the underlying purpose of the source material, that is, to inform or to support an advocacy position? If there are multiple sources from one author or organization, what is the overall tone and perspective?
- If a Web site, what types of pages *link to* the source? What can be inferred from these links about the objectivity of the site with the desired source material?

LOCATING SECONDARY INFORMATION

There are three main sources of secondary information: offline print, non-indexed online sources, and online indexed sources.[5] This section focuses on the latter two sources,[6] paying particular attention to techniques that maximize the relevance and value of online search.

Non-indexed Online Sources

Slideshare and Scribd are resources that are typically poorly indexed in the search engines.[7] Both sites are repositories for PowerPoint presentations, Word documents, and other written materials contributed by individuals, advertising agencies, and research and other companies. While the range of materials on both sites is very large, both sites allow quick and efficient access to materials likely to be of interest to advertisers and marketers, especially when the secondary information need relates to advertising and marketing in new media. A search for "advertising and social media," for example, locates the following documents:[8] *Creating Engaging Advertising for Social Media, Advertising—the Social Media Bit, The Social Media Marketing Disconnect, Social Media and the Future of Advertising, Social Advertising Best Practices, Social Media and Advertising,* and *A Different Perspective on Social Media Advertising.* The majority of materials available at both sites are available for download.

Many agencies also use LexisNexis or other similar databases to locate material unlikely to be indexed by the search engines. LexisNexis "offers a widely used, searchable archive of content from newspapers, magazines, legal documents and other printed sources. LexisNexis describes itself as the 'world's largest collection of public records, unpublished opinions, forms, legal, news, and business information'"[9]

Indexed Online Sources: Search Strategies

It is estimated that there are over 45 billion pages on the World Wide Web. As a result, there are typically thousands, if not millions, of responses to almost any search request. (A search for advertising and social media, for example, returned over 29 million listings.) Search engines such as Google, Yahoo! and Bing can certainly help you find information. The goal for any search, however, is to efficiently find the most relevant information. The use of a systematic search strategy increases the probability that search results are relevant and useful. This section provides one such strategy.[10]

STEP ONE: STATE YOUR INFORMATION NEED   Imagine that your agency has been asked to compete for the Yoplait yogurt account and that the agency has no experience in this product category. Secondary research can help the agency quickly learn about category trends, Yoplait and competitive brand activities, approaches to advertising and promotion, as well as other areas of activity that will ultimately influence advertising strategy and creative development. You have been assigned the task of preparing a briefing regarding trends and developments in the yogurt category.

The first step in developing a search strategy is to express your information need in the form of one or more questions. In this case, the key question is:

What are the current trends in the yogurt category?

STEP TWO: ELIMINATE UNNECESSARY WORDS.   This step reduces the verbiage in each search question by eliminating everything that is unrelated to the question's core idea, in this case:

What are the current trends in the yogurt category?

~~What are the~~ current trends ~~in the~~ yogurt ~~category~~

STEP THREE: EXPAND INITIAL SEARCH PHRASES.   Two things need to be accomplished in this step. First, you increase the chances of searching the breadth of available information by adding synonyms to your search terms. Thus, it is often beneficial to use a thesaurus to expand each initial search phrase. Second, keep in mind that adding an "s" to a search term (such as trends) often provides different results than the singular form (such as trend).[11] As a result, in this example, the initial search phrases use both forms of keywords, each of which is paired with all alternative synonyms

trends yogurt

trend yogurt

developments yogurt

development yogurt

advances yogurt

advance yogurt

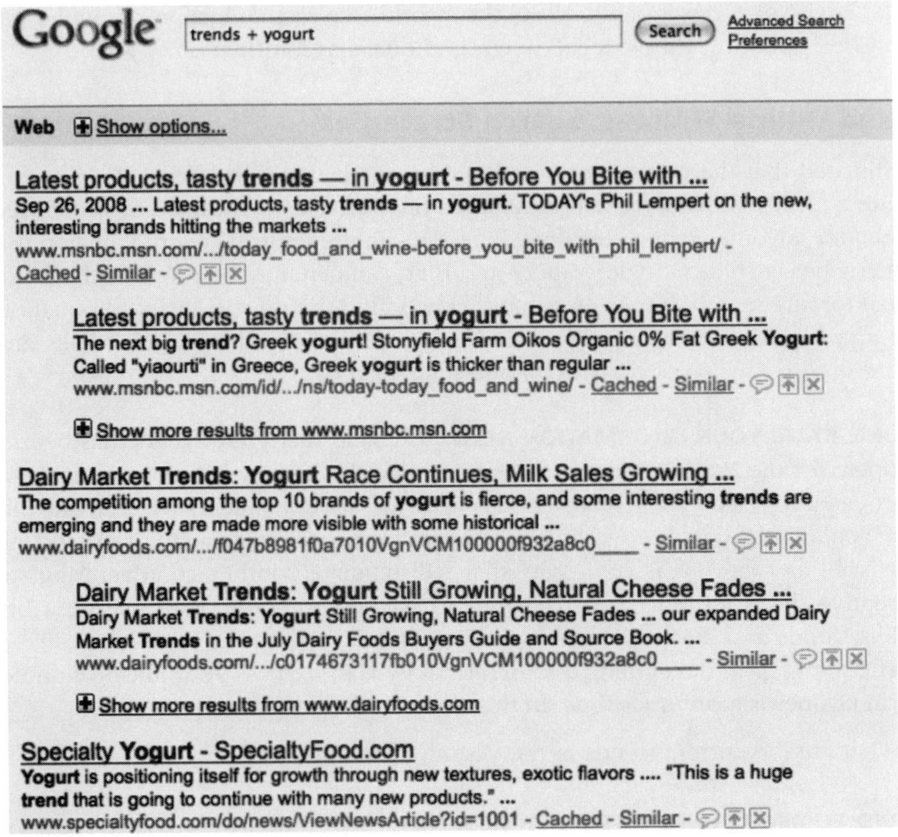

FIGURE 3.2 Google Search Results for "trends + yogurt" and "trend + yogurt"

Note that when using multiple words in a search phrase, you can reduce order effects and increase the number of relevant results by adding a "+" sign between individual words. Thus, the phrase **trends yogurt** is typed into a search engine as **trends + yogurt**. Figures 3.2 and 3.3 illustrate the value of expanding the initial search phrase. Figure 3.2 (on this and the next page) shows the different results returned by Google for **trends + yogurt** and **trend + yogurt**. Figure 3.3 (page 66) shows the additional relevant results for the synonym **phrase developments + yogurt**.

STEP FOUR: CONDUCT THE SEARCH ON SEVERAL SEARCH ENGINES.   Each search engine has its own strengths and weaknesses. Some are better for some types of information searches versus others. As a result, initial searches should be conducted on all three major search engines: Google, Yahoo! and Bing. Figure 3.4 (pages 67 and 68) shows the importance of this as it presents the search results for **trend + yogurt** on Yahoo! and Bing. (Compare these to the Google results for the same search shown in Figure 3.2) Note that while there is some overlap, each search engine makes an independent contribution to locating relevant secondary information sources.

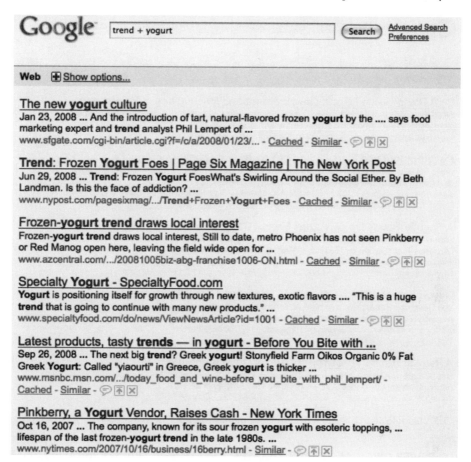

FIGURE 3.2 *(continued)*

STEP FIVE: SYSTEMATICALLY READ KEY FINDINGS AND REFLECT ON RESULTS. Common sense indicates that you will read and explore at least some search results as they occur. However, you will be more efficient in your task of identifying appropriate secondary information if you read these sources systematically, noting the answers to the following types of questions:

- Which search engine(s) produced the best results?
- Which search phrases produced the best results?
- Did some search phrases work better on some search engines versus others?
- Were some search phrases overly broad, producing too many irrelevant results?
- Were some search phrases too narrow, producing too few relevant search results?
- Do any relevant sources use words or phrases that should be used in additional searches?

Your answers to each of these questions influence your actions in the next step.

FIGURE 3.3   Google Search Results for "developments + yogurt"

STEP SIX: REVISE ORIGINAL SEARCH PHRASES; CREATE NEW SEARCH PHRASES; RE-SEARCH ON MOST PRODUCTIVE SEARCH ENGINES.   This step puts into action your answers to the prior questions. Original search phrases are revised, and new search phrases are used on the search engines that provided the best results in Step Four. The following techniques can assist in the revision process and are appropriate to all three major search engines.[12] If the goal is to

- *search for a specific phrase,* enclose it in quotation marks, for example **"yogurt advertising"**;

- *narrow your search by eliminating materials that contain a certain word,* use the minus sign. For example, if you want to search for sites that discuss yogurt developments outside of advertising, you could use the search phrase **"yogurt trend"-advertising**;

- *narrow your search to look for specific types of resources,* you can specify the desired resource type in the search phrase. A search for PDF documents would be **yogurt trends filetype:pdf** while a search for Powerpoint documents would be **yogurt trends filetype:ppt**;

- *expand your search by letting the search engine determine and use synonyms for key search terms,* use the "~" symbol. If, for example, you wanted Google to apply synonyms for the term "trends," your search phrase would be **yogurt - trends**;

- *expand your search by increasing the range of acceptable terms,* connect the search terms with "OR" (in capital letters). The search phrase **yogurt OR yoghurt** would deliver documents with either spelling;

- *focus on and search one individual site* and when there is no site search function available, add the URL of the site to the search phrase. Imagine, for example, that you want to search the entire Dairy Foods Web site using Google. Your search phrase would be **"internet marketing" site:www.diaryfoods.com**. (Note that while this approach can be used to replace a site's internal search engine, we recommend you use a site's internal search engine whenever available);

- *focus on Web sites that use a key term,* use the "inurl" or "intitle" command as the search phrase. If, for example, you wanted to find all Web sites that had the term "yogurt" in their URL, your search phrase would be **inurl:yogurt**. If you wanted to find all Web sites that use the term "yogurt" in a page title, your search phrase would be **intitle:yogurt**.

STEP SEVEN: SEARCH DEEPER, FOLLOW KEY LINKS AND REFERENCES.   Secondary information search is very much like a game of dominoes where one piece of information

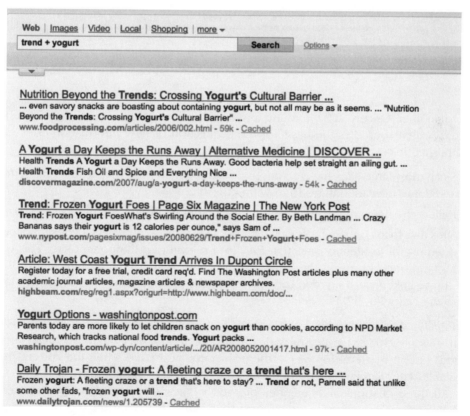

FIGURE 3.4   Yahoo! and bing Search Results for "trend + yogurt"

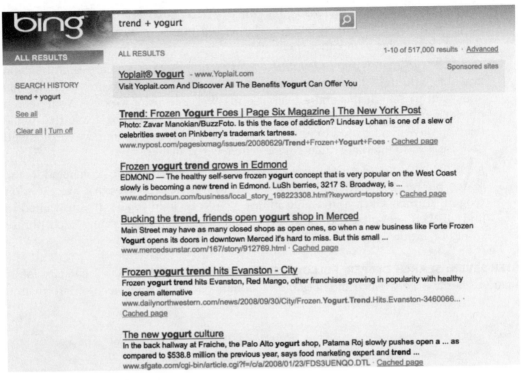

FIGURE 3.4 (continued)

leads to another. Once you have found a relevant and informative secondary information source, use that source as the basis for the acquisition of new information. This can be accomplished in several ways.[13]

- Since most large sites have an internal search engine, use that search engine to find additional relevant articles from within the site.
- Follow the links in relevant documents to other external sources.
- Sites that focus on similar issues typically link to each other. As a consequence, it is often useful to identify sites that *link to* a relevant and important site. This can be accomplished by using the "link" operator in a search engine request. The search phrase link: www.dairyfood.com, for example, provides a listing of all sites linking to the Dairy Food Web site.

Finally, search engines provide ways to simultaneously expand and focus your search. Google, for example, provides several options after each search result. The "Cached" option is useful for seeing the prior form of a page when the current page is unavailable. The "Similar" option provides additional pages similar in focus to the current page. All three of the search engines provide suggestions for related search phrases. These links provide access to documents that may have been missed by the original search phrase.

Beyond the General Search Engines

Search engines are your initial means for identifying appropriate Internet-based secondary research information. Google, however, provides three additional resources.

Blog Search applies Google search technology to blogs.[14] Google notes that "Blog Search indexes blogs by their site feeds, which are checked frequently for new content. This means that Blog Search results for a given blog will update with new content much faster than standard Web searches. Also, because of the structured data within site feeds, it is possible to find precise posts and date ranges with much greater accuracy." While you will need to rigorously evaluate information obtained from blogs, this source nevertheless has the potential to provide important insights. Figure 3.5 displays the Google Blog Search results for **trends + yogurt**.

Google Scholar[15] provides a simple way to broadly search for scholarly literature, although we have found that the academic databases described earlier are a better choice when available. Scholar's search engine allows you to search across many disciplines and sources: peer-reviewed papers, theses, books, abstracts and articles, from academic publishers, professional societies, preprint repositories, universities and other scholarly organizations.

Google Book Search[16] works similarly to Web search. A search on Google Book Search retrieves books with content that contains a match for your search terms. If the book is out of copyright, or the publisher has given Google permission, you will be able to see a preview of the book, and in some cases the entire text. If the book is in the public domain, you can download a PDF copy.

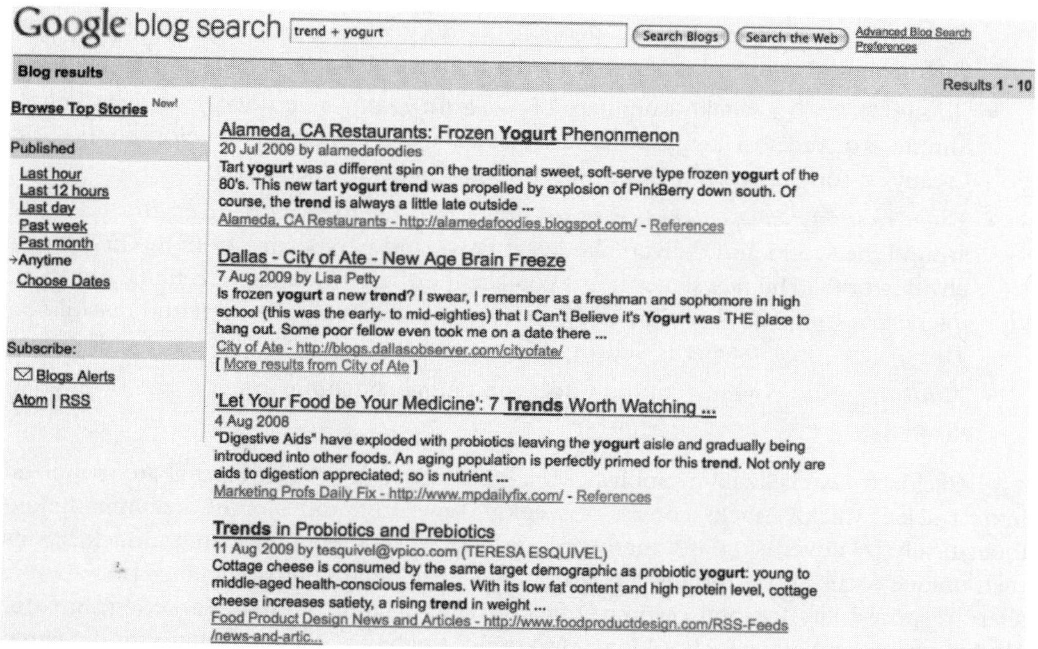

FIGURE 3.5 Google blog search results for "trend + yogurt"

STAYING CURRENT

The prior section provided guidance for locating information in response to a specific information need. Successful advertisers and marketers, however, also use secondary information sources to stay current on a continuing basis. This section provides suggestions for accomplishing this.

E-mail Newsletters

A wide range of organizations publish newsletters. These newsletters either provide a recap of current developments (with links to original sources) or present original analyses and perspectives. The goal, given the great number of newsletters available, is to identify those whose content is most relevant and of interest on a continuing basis. The following are a good place to start, and all subscriptions (which can be obtained on the Web sites indicated) are free of charge.

Newsletter Publishers

Advertising Age (www.adage.com) publishes 12 newsletters related to advertising-related trends and developments. These newsletters include:

- *Ad Age Daily* is a daily newsletter that highlights the most important daily news from *Advertising Age*.
- *Ad Age Digital* is a weekly newsletter that focuses on new forms of digital media and their effect on how marketers engage consumers.
- *Ad Age MediaWorks* provides daily coverage of media developments in broadcast TV, cable, radio, print pages, Web sites, video on demand, broadband, mobile, videogames, iPods, and other new media options.
- *Ad Age Video* is a weekly summary of *Advertising Age* video coverage including 3-Minute Ad Age (an analysis of the week's most important developments) and Creativity Top 5 (a review of the week's most innovative creative work).
- The *Creativity Newsletter* showcases "must-see creative work from the U.S. and around the world and delivers the latest news and perspective from the brand creativity world." The newsletter helps you see the "best TV spots, web films, print ads, interactive campaigns, design and other work from across platform and discipline." The *Creativity Newsletter* is delivered four times a week.
- *Madison+Vine* covers "cutting-edge campaigns pushing the content commerce envelope."

Clickz (www.clickz.com) publishes a large number of newsletters that are organized into "Tracks." ClickZ Tracks consist of weekly, biweekly, and monthly columns linked thematically by advertising and marketing discipline. Each column within a track has its own unique focus and is usually written by one author, although sometimes two authors share responsibility for one column. Clickz Tracks include: E-mail Marketing, Smarter Marketing, Advertising Technology, Marketing Analytics, Media Buying, and Search Engine Marketing.

Mediapost (www.mediapost.com) publishes 24 daily and weekly newsletters all with original content. Some of these newsletters focus on a narrowly defined area, while others provide perspectives on specific demographic or behavioral groups. Mediapost publications fall into the following groups:

- Online media, marketing and advertising newsletters include *Behavioral Insider, Email Insider, Gaming Insider, Just an Online Minute, Metrics Insider, Mobile Insider, Notes From the Digital Frontier, Online Media Daily, Online Publishing Insider, Online Spin, Performance Insider, Search Insider, Social Media Insider, Video Insider.*

- Traditional media planning and buying newsletters include *Magazine Rack, Media Creativity, Media Daily News, Media Technology Futures, Research Brief, TV Board, TV Watch.*

- Brand and product marketing newsletters include *Engage: Boomers, Engage: GenY, Engage: Hispanics, Engage: Moms, Marketing Daily, Marketing: Green, Marketing: Sports.*

NARROWLY FOCUSED NEWSLETTERS. A subscription to eMarketer (www.emarketer.com) provides the latest analyses of online-related advertising and market trends. Two new articles, each with a research foundation, are e-mailed each business day. A subscription to eMarketer also provides the option of receiving eMarketer FYI that provides webinar and event announcements, whitepaper offers, best practices guides, and research briefs.

Harvard Business School's *Working Knowledge* newsletter (hbswk.hbs.edu) offers cutting-edge research and ideas from Harvard Business School faculty. Areas of focus include strategy, leadership and management, organizations, and social enterprise. Recent papers include: *Do Friends Influence Purchases on a Social Network?, Connecting with Consumers Using Deep Metaphors,* and *The Next Marketing Challenge: Selling to "Simplifiers".*

IAB Smartbrief is a publication of the Interactive Advertising Bureau (www.iab.net). It is a daily e-mail newsletter focusing on interactive media specifically designed for advertising, marketing, and media executives. *Smartbrief* editors select key articles from hundreds of publications, create a brief summary of each, and then provide links back to the original sources.

Iconowatch is a weekly newsletter published by Iconoculture (www.iconoculture.com), a cultural trend research company. The company describes itself as "the voice of cultural trends—illuminating not only what's important to consumers worldwide, but also why it's happening and where it's heading."

Marketing Charts (www.marketingcharts.com) presents the results of recent advertising- and marketing-related research from companies such as Nielsen-Online, Harris Interactive, TNS Media Intelligence, and various marketing and advertising research companies. Marketing Charts always provides links to more extensive data and discussion.

The *McKinsey Quarterly* is a print and online business journal produced by the global consulting firm McKinsey & Company (www.mckinsey.com). The *Quarterly's* goal is to "offer new ways of thinking about business management in the private, public, and nonprofit sectors. We aim to help business people run their businesses more productively, more competitively, and more creatively." Of particular interest to advertisers and marketers are articles focused on strategy, technology, and marketing.

Whitepapers, Research Reports, Webinars, and Presentations

Whitepapers and research reports typically present perspectives and research findings related to a company's or organization's area of focus and expertise. These papers serve the dual benefit of keeping advertisers and marketers informed about new ideas and research findings while at the same time promoting the company or organization. Webinars and presentations are a more visual way in which companies present research and perspective. Here, a recorded in-person presentation (webinar) or the slides used in a presentation are made available for viewing. The best way to identify these resources is to locate and visit the Web sites of companies whose focus and expertise aligns with the secondary information needs. The following companies are a good place to start. (Note that all mentioned resources, plus others from each company, are available free of charge.)

ONLINE, DIGITAL, AND EMERGING MEDIA.   Not surprisingly, many of the companies providing whitepapers and related materials focus on online, digital, and emerging media such as social network, video game, and mobile advertising. Leading companies in this area include the following.

Doubleclick (www.doubleclick.com) describes itself as a "provider of digital marketing technology and services. The world's top marketers, publishers and agencies utilize DoubleClick's expertise in ad serving, rich media, video, search and affiliate marketing to help them make the most of the digital medium. From its position at the nerve center of digital marketing, DoubleClick provides superior insights and insider knowledge to its customers." Doubleclick provides a number of important papers that help advertisers and marketers better understand online consumer behavior and the role of advertising in influencing this behavior. Doubleclick's more recent research reports include: *The Brand Value of Rich Media and Video Ads, Creative Insights on Rich Media, Influencing the Influencers: How Online Advertising and Media Impact Word of Mouth,* and *Best Practices for Optimizing Web Advertising Effectiveness*[17]. Beyond these focused reports, Doubleclick also provides the Touchpoint series. This series of four reports provides significant insights into what influences consumer's purchase decisions, online and offline, across a broad range of product and service categories. The latest report (Toughpoints IV) can be read independently of the other reports for a view of current trends, or it can be read after the Touchpoint I, II, and III reports to obtain insights into longer-term consumer trends.

comScore (www.comscore.com) measures the digital world through a combination of behavioral and survey measures. Recent comScore whitepapers include *Making Integrated Campaigns Work: How a Search Marketing Mindset Can Drive the ROI of Display Advertising, How Online Advertising Works: Whither The Click?* and *Consumer Packaged Goods: Internet Advertising Proven to Increase Offline Sales.*

Coremetrics (www.coremetrics.com) is a leading provider of online marketing and business optimization solutions. Recent Coremetrics whitepapers include *Contextual Marketing: Increasing Campaign Effectiveness by Meeting Customer Expectations for Relevant, Targeted Messaging, Optimizing Your Marketing Mix in a Down Economy,* and *Increasing Email Marketing Relevance.*

Dynamic Logic (www.dynamiclogic.com/na/) focuses on marketing effectiveness research. Recent research reports and perspectives include *Targeting Online Ads: Aim for the Bulls-eye or Focus on Hitting the Target, Research Trends Suggest Web Users Are Growing More Accepting of Over-Content Ads,* and *First Look At Mobile Performance: Early Research.*

Enquiro (www.enquiro.com) specializes in business-to-business search marketing, employing a range of research methodologies to provide insights into search behaviors. Recent Enquiro whitepapers include *Building Business Online: Your Digital Persuasion Portfolio, Maximizing Online: Leveraging Your Online Touch Points, Integrated Persuasion: Online and Offline, Mapping the BuyerSphere,* and *Barriers on a Search Results Page.*

The Interactive Advertising Bureau (www.iab.net) is the trade association for online advertising. The IAB is composed of more than 375 leading media and technology companies that are responsible for selling 86% of online advertising in the United States. The IAB Web site provides whitepapers and research reports for both IAB commissioned and member conducted research. You can browse through the extensive research library beginning at http://www.iab.net/insights_research.

Microsoft's Atlas Institute (www.atlassolutions.com/institute_marketinginsights. aspx) publishers Digital Marketing Insights (DMIs), a series of publications by digital marketing experts that help the Institute's customers improve their digital marketing effectiveness. Many of these findings are also made available to the digital marketing industry through whitepapers, podcasts, and webinars. Each DMI is designed to help advertisers more successfully build value with their customers throughout the customer lifecycle: from awareness to acquisition and from retention to growth. One specific Institute goal is to help advertisers better understand the contribution of each advertising exposure to brand purchase behavior or attitude change. DMIs related to this topic include *The Long Road to Conversion: The Digital Purchase Funnel* and *Measuring ROI Beyond The Last Ad.*

Nielsen-Online (www.nielsen-online.com) provides whitepapers, presentations, and webinars across a broad number of online areas, including audience measurement, consumer-generated media, Internet marketing, online advertising, competitive analysis, and industry practices. Some recent Nielsen-Online webinars and papers include *Riding the Wave of Social Networking: Insights and Tactics for Publishers, Marketers and Agencies,,* and *From Customer Satisfaction to Brand Advocacy: The New Building Blocks of Competitive Advantage in the Age of Consumer Control.*

TNS Global is one of the world's leading market research groups providing market insights to a global community of clients. TNS whitepapers typically focus on "big issues" of interest to global marketers and advertisers, as indicated in recent whitepapers:

- *Digital Life, Digital World* tries to capture how the Internet fits into the lives of residents from 16 countries across the world. The report addresses questions such as how digital are consumers' lives. How do they use the Internet? Is a digital life the same as a social life, or does a social life today require a complementary digital life?

- *Harnessing Influence (Social Media)* focuses on the use of social media for advertising, marketing, and branding efforts. The report addresses the question of whether social media use for commercial purposes is just a "bubble" or a phenomenon of lasting importance.

BROADER CONSUMER FOCUS. Chapter One described advertisers' need to understand the broader social trends that provide the context for their advertising efforts. One excellent source of this type of information is the Pew Research Center. The Center is a nonpartisan "fact tank" that provides information on the issues, attitudes, and trends shaping America and the world. Different components of the Center focus on different things, for example, journalism, politics, religion, and the Internet. Of particular interest to advertisers and marketers is the research conducted by the Pew Internet & American Life Project. This research provides insights into three broad areas:

- Activities and pursuits including blogs, music, social networking, video, and work.
- Demographics including the digital divide, families, seniors, and teens.
- Technology and media including broadband, cloud computing, Internet, mobile, new media ecology, and web 2.0.

FOCUS ON A SPECIFIC MEDIUM.   Chapter One discussed how media trade organizations conduct research to inform advertisers about their medium and to proactively position their medium against competitive media. The results of this research is typically posted and made available without charge on the organization's Web site.[18] Representative examples of this type of research include:

- *How America Shops and Spends* and *An Engaged Audience for Advertising and News* (Newspaper Association of America)
- *Engagement, Emotions, and the Power of Radio: A New Study of How Radio Affects Consumer Emotions* and *Radio and the Internet: Powerful Complements for Advertisers* (Radio Advertising Bureau)
- *Measuring Media Efficiently: Assessing ROI Throughout the Purchase Funnel* and *AudienceLab Study of Public Place Engagement* (Magazine Publishers of America)
- *Outdoor Advertising: The Brand Communication Medium and Successful Out of Home Strategies* (Outdoor Advertising Association of America)
- *How the Web is Changing the Way Companies Listen to Their Customers, Integrating Social Media into Your Existing Marketing Plan* and *Finding Passion Points/Creating a Sustainable Social Interaction Model* (Word of Mouth Marketing Association)

APPLYING CHAPTER CONCEPTS

This chapter discussed how secondary research can answer both narrowly and broadly framed questions. An example of the former type of question is "How many people have an account on Facebook and MySpace?" while the latter type of question might be "What are individuals' overall reactions to mobile advertising?" Narrowly framed questions are typically answerable through diligent research. The successful response to a broadly framed question is, however, more than simply collecting and reporting relevant data. Successful responses to broadly framed questions require both considerable research *and* the successful synthesis of information from different sources. Here, data is integrated in a way that allows decision makers to understand how the data fits together to form a pattern and what the implications of that pattern are for upcoming decisions.

The social media trends presentation shown in this chapter's online supplemental readings is an excellent example of a broadly focused, well-synthesized secondary analysis. This presentation seeks to answer the question: "What are the international trends in the growth and usage of social media?" As you read through the presentation, notice how the author has been selective in the data provided, how the sequence of topics allows for knowledge and understanding to build, and how the data is integrated and synthesized to allow the reader to understand key trends and (most important) implications.

SUMMARY

Secondary research information is information that has been collected and analyzed by others for a purpose other than specifically responding to a current informational need. This contrasts with primary research that is conducted by (or on behalf of) an information user to specifically satisfy that individual's informational need. Secondary research is therefore distinguished from primary research on the basis of two criteria: (1) the individual responsible for planning and conducting the research and (2) the circumstances under which the research was conducted. Secondary research contributes to advertising and marketing decision making in three ways. Information obtained from secondary research can directly answer an advertiser's or marketer's informational needs, provide important insights prior to the conduct of primary research, and/or contribute to questionnaire development. Secondary information may be obtained from one of two sources: primary (the individual or company that initially collected the data or prepared the report) and secondary (those who have reprinted or reinterpreted the original data).

Secondary research has two advantages over comparable primary research. Secondary research tends to be more efficient in terms of time and money. Secondary research has several potential limitations. These limitations relate to information availability, relevance, and sufficiency. The "goodness" of secondary information can be evaluated with regard to source accuracy, currency, and objectivity.

A great diversity of external sources exist to answer advertisers' questions and informational needs. Some sources can be located through systematic use of search engines, while other sources are newsletters, whitepapers, presentations, and webinars provided by newsletter publishers, trade organizations, and independent companies.

Review Questions

1. What criteria differentiate primary from secondary research?

2. What is the difference between *secondary information* and *secondary sources?*

3. What are the reasons why a primary source is preferred over a secondary source?

4. Should a researcher ever reanalyze, combine, or manipulate information from secondary sources? Why or why not?

5. What are the main ways in which secondary research contributes to primary research?

6. What are the principal advantages of secondary research versus primary research?

7. What are the principal limitations of secondary research versus primary research?

8. What specific criteria can be used to evaluate the "goodness" of secondary information?

9. Name two sources for finding non-indexed online sources.
10. What are the eight steps that comprise a systematic search strategy? Provide a one- or two-sentence summary of each step.

11. What is a blog search? What is a scholar search?
12. Describe how newsletters, whitepapers, and webinars provide secondary information.

Application Exercises

Application exercises 1 through 6 relate to concepts raised and discussed in this chapter.

1. Select one of the following product categories. Provide 20 references to specific secondary sources that you would use to help you better understand category and brand sales trends, brand share, competitive marketing or advertising activities, and category-specific consumer attitudes and purchase behaviors. For each individual source, provide a complete reference and a brief description of why you believe the source is relevant. Use a range of types of sources. Potential product categories are as follows
   - coffee
   - pain relievers
   - ice cream
   - dog food
   - toothpaste
   - cell phones
   - portable music players
   - bottled water
2. Select one of the categories from Exercise 1. Your goal for the category is to determine new product and packaging developments. Using the suggestions for indexed search on pages 63 to 68, follow each step, keeping notes on your activities and problems/successes. Prepare a short paper that summarizes what you found with regard to search strategies.
3. Each of the following questions can be answered through a review of secondary research. Select one question and (a) write a one- to two-paragraph answer to the question and (b) provide at least 10 references to the sources that you used to answer the question.
   - Is there a relationship between commercial liking and commercial persuasiveness? That is, are consumers more likely to be persuaded in situations where they like a commercial versus situations where they do not like the commercial?
   - What are the most successful strategies for e-mail campaigns?
   - How successful are banner ads in promoting positive brand attitudes?
   - Is mobile advertising effective?
   - When a celebrity spokesperson is used in a commercial, do perceptions of the spokesperson affect product perceptions?
   - How do video game players respond to in-game advertising?
   - What techniques work best for using social networking sites as a marketing tool?
4. Each of the following statements addresses a common advertising-related stereotype or generalization. Select one statement. Use relevant secondary information to determine the truth of each selected statement. For each selected statement, (a) write a one- to two-paragraph response that presents your point of view on the truth or falseness of the statement and (b) provide at least five references to the sources that you used to answer the question.
   - Exposure to children's advertising (by children) makes children more materialistic.
   - There is more sex in advertising today than there was 10 or 20 years ago.
   - The vast majority of ads that stress a product's "environmental benefits" are deceptive.
   - Advertising perpetuates unfavorable racial, ethnic, and gender stereotypes.
5. Select one of the questions from Exercise 3 or statements from Exercise 4. Then, using the evaluation criteria discussed on pages 61 to 62, find a source that would be considered acceptable and one that would be considered unacceptable. Write a short paper that defends your evaluation of each source, incorporating into your paper your answers to the questions discussed on pages 61 to 62.
6. Visit two of the companies discussed on pages 70 to 74. Download and read one paper or other

resource from each company. Then, write a short paper that (a) summarizes the paper you read and (b) provides your point of view regarding why you think the information in the paper is or is not important to advertisers.

Application exercises 7 through 9 relate to the social media trends presentation provided in the online supplemental readings.

7. A portion of the presentation focuses on the United States. It is likely that the dynamics of and trends within the United States have

changed since the original presentation was written. Update and expand this section of the presentation using current data and information.

8. In your opinion, have any new social media trends occurred since the presentation was written? Prepare a brief paper discussing these trends. Be certain to list all of the secondary references used to inform your discussion.

9. Imagine that your client wants you to draw implications of this presentation for a planned social media advertising campaign. Prepare a short paper that addresses this request.

Endnotes

1. The material shown in Figure 3.1 is produced by Luckie (http://www.luckie.com), which also produces trend reports for the banking, telecom, and tourism marketplaces. We strongly recommend a visit to the corporate Web site.

2. David W. Stewart and Michael A. Kamins (1993). *Secondary Research: Information Sources and Methods* (Newbury Park, CA: Sage Publications).

3. Stewart and Kamins, op. cit.

4. This section draws on the following sources: University of British Columbia Library (2009). "Criteria for Evaluating Internet Resources" at http://www.library.ubc.ca/home/evaluating; University of British Columbia Library (2008). "Criteria for Evaluating Print Resources" at http://www.library.ubc.ca/scieng/PrintEval. html; University of California Berkeley Library (2009). "Evaluating Web Pages: Techniques to Apply & Questions to Ask" at http://www.lib. berkeley.edu/TeachingLib/Guides/Internet/ Evaluate.html; Robert Harris (2007). "Evaluating Internet Research Sources" at http://www. virtualsalt.com/evalu8it.htm.

5. Materials located in client files are often cited as a source of secondary information. These sources are technically only secondary to the agency as they are primary information to the client. As such, we do not include them in this discussion. Indexing refers to appearance on the major search engines, such as Google, Bing, and Yahoo!

6. Since most advertising and marketing resources have migrated online, we avoid providing lists of business-related printed materials.

7. Slideshare is located at http://www.slideshare.net and Scribd is located at http://www.scribd.com.

8. The first four documents are available at Slideshare, while the last three are available at Scribd.

9. Wikipedia (undated). "LexisNexis" at http://en. wikipedia.org/wiki/LexisNexis.

10. The initial steps in this discussion are adapted from IRIS (undated). "From Idea to Search Statement" at http://www.clark.edu/Library/ iris/find/search_strategies/search_strategies_p2. shtml.

11. Google search allows for the use of the "*" sign as a replacement for one or more letters. The search phrase **yogurt + trend*** should obtain the same results as **yogurt + trend, yogurt + trends,** and **yogurt + trending**. This may or may not be the case, however, depending upon the specific search. As a result, when there are not too many variations (such as trend and trends), we suggest you search for each phrase individually (as discussed in the text) and not use the "*" sign.

12. The techniques listed are the ones most commonly used. For a complete list of search techniques see Google Guide at http://www. googleguide.com/advanced_operators.html.

13. As the number of sites and documents increases so does the probability of losing some valuable resources. We suggest that you make extensive use of bookmarks during search as well as downloading and/or printing key documents as they occur. However, even when this is done, Google History provides excellent backup for locating prior visited sites. Google History allows you to view and search across the full text of the pages you've visited, including Google searches, Web pages, images, videos, and news stories. You can also manage your Web activity and remove items from your Web history at any time. More information on Google History can be found at http:// www.google.com/support/accounts/bin/topic. py?topic=14148&hl=en.

14. Google Blog Search is located at http:// blogsearch.google.com.

15. Google Scholar is located at http://scholar. google.com.

16. Google Book Search is available at books. google.com.

17. A complete listing of all (and access to) Doubleclick research reports can be found at http://www.doubleclick.com/insight/research/ index.aspx.

18. Media-specific research can be found at the following locations: Radio Ad Lab Studies (http:// www.rab.com/public/rael/rael.cfm), Newspaper Association of America (http://www.naa.org/ TrendsandNumbers/Research.aspx), Magazine Publishers of America (http://www.magazine. org/research/index.aspx), Outdoor Advertising Association of America (http://www.oaaa. org/marketingresources/research.aspx), and Word of Mouth Marketing Association (http:// womma.org/downloads/).

CHAPTER 4

Sampling

A sample is a group of items or individuals selected from a larger population. While all samples are generally useful, not all samples allow a researcher to generalize findings and insights to the broader population from which the sample was drawn. As a result, some types of samples are more appropriate for satisfying certain informational needs than others.

***

When you are done reading this chapter, you should have a better understanding of how to:

- make well-considered and appropriate sampling decisions
- describe the role of sample definition and sample frames in the sampling process
- explain the difference between probability and nonprobability sampling
- identify the strengths and weaknesses of different forms of probability and nonprobability sampling
- determine sample size.

Primary research collects original, typically proprietary information to meet an advertiser's or marketer's informational needs. Primary research is used when secondary research is either nonexistent, unreliable, or too costly. In these circumstances, advertisers may select either qualitative or quantitative research to satisfy their informational needs, and they may use either observational, survey, or physiological methods to collect the necessary data. The remainder of this text discusses the range of primary research approaches, methods and applications.

All primary research entails some form of sampling where a researcher selects people or objects from a population of interest for further study. The quality of research insights and the confidence one has in generalizing these insights to the larger population are directly related to decisions made with regard to sampling. A superior research design using a well-constructed data collection instrument will nevertheless provide useless data if the sample is poorly or inappropriately selected. Good research requires good sampling. As a result, this chapter provides a detailed discussion of sampling and the sampling process.

AN OVERVIEW OF SAMPLING

Sampling is a common process you engage in every day: when you listen to a few tracks from a new band in order to decide if you want to learn and hear more or when you read several reviews of a movie (from among all the movie review sites) in order to decide if you want to see it. When you sample, in these cases and in advertising research, you select and examine members of a larger population in order to learn something new and, in most cases, to draw conclusions about the larger population of which the sampled items are members. The things you sample can be inanimate objects such as music, reviews, examples of competitive advertising, or more commonly, animate objects such as people. Consider the following:

> Every semester Dr. Newson teaches a class entitled "Trends in Social Media." This semester there are 30 students registered for her class. Both John and Mary are considering taking the class next semester, but each wants to make an informed decision prior to enrolling. John shows up to Dr. Newson's class and talks with 10 of the 14 students attending that day. Only about half are enthusiastic and John decides not to take the class next semester. Mary shows up to Dr. Newson's class on final exam day, the day all students in the class had to attend. Mary talks with every third student on his or her way out (10 students in all out of the 30 registered and attending that day). These students are generally quite positive and Mary decides to take the class next semester. It turns out that the class in the upcoming semester was a wonderful experience.

Although John and Mary interviewed equivalent numbers of students, they nevertheless obtained different insights into Dr. Newson's class. This was because they used different sampling approaches. John used *convenience sampling*, in which he interviewed some of the students who just happened to be in class on a particular day. Mary used *random sampling*, on a day in which *every* student in the class had an equal chance of being spoken to. John discovered that how you sample does make a difference; only random sampling allows you to make valid generalizations about the population from which the sample was drawn.

The first part of this chapter focuses on sampling considerations and approaches for quantitative advertising research, beginning with a discussion of random sampling. The latter portion of the chapter discusses special considerations for sampling in qualitative research.

RANDOM SAMPLING AND QUANTITATIVE RESEARCH

Random sampling is most associated with quantitative research. This form of sampling (also known as probability sampling) has a very basic definition: a random sample is one where the researcher ensures that each member of the population of interest has an equal probability of being selected. The decisions related to random sample selection are shown in Figure 4.1. The remainder of this section follows the flow of the figure. First, we discuss how to determine the nature of the surveyed population, that is, whether a sample or a census should be used. Next, we discuss target population definition. This discussion is followed by an exploration of probability sampling, specifically the selection of the sample frame, the different types of probability samples, and how to determine appropriate sample size. The next section of the text (beginning on page 102) discusses an alternative sampling method, nonprobability sampling.

Sample or Census

The first step in the random sampling process determines whether to use a sample or a census. A decision to take a sample results in a subset of the population of interest participating in the research. A decision to take a census results in an attempt to include every member of the population of interest in the research.

A sample, rather than a census, is used in the vast majority of research situations. When dealing with large populations, such as adults aged 18 and older or purchasers of a particular product, the time and cost involved in a census—examining or surveying all members of the target population—exceeds the value of any information or insights obtained from the research. Additionally, even if funds and time were available, a census of the population might still be impossible. There may simply be too many people to ever talk with or some members of the target population may be unreachable. Fortunately, as you will see later in this chapter, there is rarely ever a need to take a census. A well-selected sample can provide information comparable to that of a full census.

There are some situations, however, when a census is preferable. A census is preferable to a sample when

- the population of interest is small and identifiable, or
- sampling might eliminate important cases from the study, or
- credibility requires the consideration of all members of the target population.

The following two examples illustrate situations in which a census is preferable.

A chain of restaurants has 35 franchisees. The chain, which has just begun a new advertising campaign, wishes to determine its franchisees' reactions to the campaign. A census would likely be used. The sample of franchisees is small, all

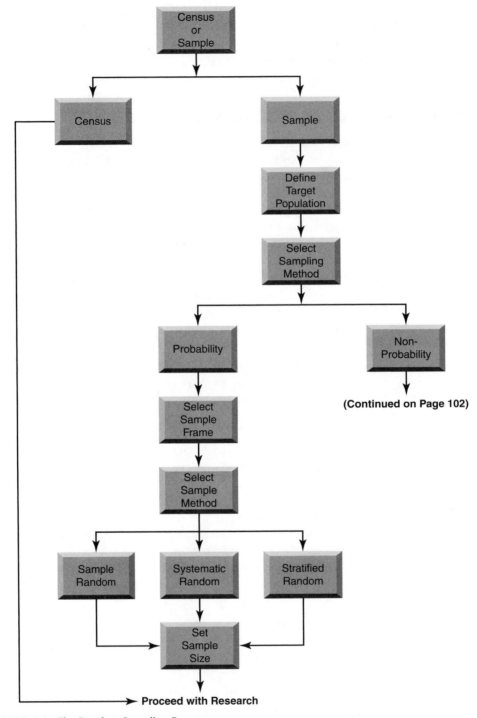

FIGURE 4.1   The Random Sampling Process

franchisees' opinions would be heard and the study would be more credible than a sample because all the franchisees participated (i.e., no one can say "Well, the results are wrong. Just look at who was interviewed. They didn't ask me!")

An advertising agency is about to begin strategic planning for its client Silhouette Shampoo. Silhouette competes most directly with Suave. As part of the planning process, the agency wants to conduct a review and analysis of Suave's advertising. A census would be used. The amount of Suave's advertising is relatively small and can be easily located. In addition, the research findings would have much more credibility if the analysis reflected an examination of all of Suave's advertising.

Define Target Population

The next step in the sampling process requires that you define the target population by explicitly specifying the characteristics of the group of individuals or things in which you are interested. This is a critical step for all forms of advertising research and is therefore required for all types of samples. The adequacy of a target population definition is evaluated in terms of how well the definition (1) unambiguously describes the group of interest and (2) serves to differentiate those things or individuals who are of interest from those who are not.

TARGET DEFINITION AND AN INANIMATE POPULATION.   Imagine a brainstorming session in which account executives and creatives are trying to identify new benefits and competitive positionings for their client, a manufacturer of ibuprofen-based pain relievers. One of the creatives says: "Low price is always an important benefit. Especially when we can relate it to value. So, can we make the claim that our product is the lowest priced name brand pain reliever?" It is agreed that research will be conducted to determine the viability of this claim. The agency researcher says that she will "obtain a random sample of the retail prices of the leading brands of pain relievers in stores across the United States."

Ambiguity and incompleteness make this target population definition inadequate. Consider each of the key components of the proposed target definition:

- *Retail price*. Does this refer to the regular selling price or a sale price? Is the retail price the manufacturer's recommended price, perhaps as marked on the package, or the actual price at which the outlet normally sells the product?

- *Leading brands*. On what basis will leading brands be identified and selected? Is "leading brand" defined on the basis of sales, distribution, advertising expenditures, or consumer awareness?

- *Stores*. What types of stores will be sampled? Any store that sells pain relievers? Drug stores only? Drug stores and grocery stores only? What about convenience or other types of stores?

- *Pain relievers*. Any product designed to relieve any type of pain? Ibuprofen-based products only? Any product containing aspirin, acetaminophen, or ibuprofen? What about combination products, for example, ibuprofen plus antihistamine?

- *Across the United States*. Where across the United States? In every city? In major metropolitan areas? In cities over or under a certain size?

Every combination of answers to the prior questions leads to a different definition of the target population. The "right" target population definition is the one that all involved in the research agree unambiguously defines the target population of interest and best responds to the informational need motivating the research. In this example, the research team might decide to refine the prior target population definition as follows:

The research will determine the average price of leading brands of pain relievers where:

- *Price* refers to the usual selling price as indicated on the item's shelf tag,

- *Pain relievers* refer to any aspirin, acetaminophen- or ibuprofen-based product specifically sold to relieve headache or muscle pain, and the product cannot contain any additional ingredients beyond aspirin, acetaminophen, or ibuprofen.

- *Leading brands* are defined as the five top selling brands of pain relievers (as defined previously) based on 2010 unit sales.

- *Grocery and drug stores* will be the venue for research as these stores account for 92% of relevant sales. Grocery store refers to any store whose merchandise primarily consists of food items. This includes traditional grocery stores and includes some warehouse stores. Drug store refers to any store not included in the prior definition that dispenses prescription medicine.

- The research will take place in 12 cities. *Twelve cities* refer to four cities among the top 10 cities as measured in the 2010 population census, four cities among those ranked 11 to 20, and four cities among those ranked 21 to 30. These cities account for 89% of relevant sales. Within each group, cities will be randomly selected.

Finally, prices of the following sized packages will be sampled: 100 and 250 regular tablet and 30 tablet gelcap. These are the leading sizes based on unit sales.

As can be seen, this target population definition explicitly and unambiguously (with explanation and justification from external sources) defines the target population.

TARGET DEFINITION AND A HUMAN POPULATION.   Populations of individuals are typically defined in some combination of demographic, geographic, and behavioral criteria.

- The *demographic component* of the target population definition specifies relevant age, gender, income, or other related characteristics of the population of interest.

- The *geographic component* specifies the geographic area(s) in which the target population resides. The geographic area can, for example, reflect where a particular product has distribution, where the advertising campaign has aired, or the particular cities or states where the target audience resides.

- The *behavioral component* specifies relevant category- or product-related behaviors. Here, for example, the population of interest can be defined in terms of purchase patterns (i.e., "brand loyalists," defined as individuals whose three of the past four purchases were of the same brand), category participation (i.e., have taken three or more cruises in the past 10 years), or purchase frequency (i.e., have purchased four six-packs of imported beer within the past two weeks).

Consider the following hypothetical circumstance. Imagine that within the past four months, Marvel Comics has added five additional pages of advertising to its series of X-Men comics. These pages have been added on a test basis and were only included in comics sent to retail outlets and subscribing homes that are within the Chicago city limits. Marvel now wants to use research to explore reactions to the additional in-comic advertising. Five researchers each present a different definition of the target population which should be used as the basis for the research, as follows:

Sample definition A:	Purchasers of Marvel X-Men comic books.
Sample definition B:	Subscribers to Marvel X-Men comics.
Sample definition C:	Readers of Marvel X-Men comic books.
Sample definition D:	Individuals who have read any Marvel X-Men comic book within the past 30 days.
Sample definition E:	Men and women between the ages of 10 and 17 who have read at least three new issues of Marvel X-Men comics within the past four months.

All five definitions are inadequate because they fail to note Chicago as the geographic boundary of the test area. Additionally, referring back to the criteria presented earlier, each definition fails to (1) clearly identify and define the individuals who would provide the most relevant information on issues motivating the research and (2) separate individuals of interest from those not of interest.

- *Definitions A and B are too broad.* A "purchaser" of a comic book is not necessarily the reader of the comic. Similarly, a subscriber is not necessarily the reader (e.g., if the parent subscribes to the comic on behalf of the child.) Since, it is the reader's opinions that are of interest, these definitions are unacceptable.

- *Definitions C and D are vague and ambiguous.* In these definitions, a "reader" is anyone who has ever read an X-Men comic. This includes those who have read the most recent issues and those who read an issue four years ago but not since. Similarly, "any X-Men comics within the past 30 days" does not necessarily mean that the comic read is one of the more recent issues. "Any X-Men comic" can refer to a recent issue or an issue that is 10 or more years old. These definitions are inadequate because Marvel is interested in responses to advertising in recent issues. The term, "individuals," is also vague. Will the survey include men (only), women (only) or both men and women?

- *Definition E solves many problems of the prior definitions, but still has problems.* This definition defines a reader in terms of recent reading ("last four months") and the three of four issues criterion helps to assure that the reader has adequate experience with the test issues. However, the age boundaries make this definition unacceptable. This sample definition would bias the survey because older individuals meeting the readership criterion are excluded from the study. (The younger age boundary is reasonable as children younger than 10 are unlikely to be able to answer the survey questions.)

A more acceptable target population definition might be:

> Men and women over the age of seven who have read at least three new issues of Marvel X-Men comics within the past four months. These individuals will either (a) obtain their comics by subscription and reside within the Chicago city limits or (b) be non-subscribers but purchase the minimum of three new issues of X-Men comics all from retail outlets found within the Chicago city limits.

POPULATION TARGET DEFINITIONS AND RESEARCH FINDINGS.   The quality and validity of generalizations drawn from a research study are greatly influenced by its target definition. After all, because different target definitions exclude and include different individuals, the data collected from different groups of individuals is also likely to vary. Two studies designed to study the same thing, but with different target definitions, are likely to have quite different results.

A recent study by the Pew Research Center[1] provides a striking example of the relationship between target definition and research findings. The Pew Center compared its own and Gallup's target definitions of "Muslim" and the resulting effect of these definitions on estimates of Muslim American demographics. The two target definitions that differed with respect to languages spoken and method of contact were:

Pew Research: Nationally representative probability sample; speaks English, Arabic, Urdu, Farsi; reachable via landlines

Gallup: Nationally representative probability sample, speaks English, Spanish; reachable by landlines and cell phones

Demographic Characteristic	Gallup (%)	Pew Total (%)	Pew: Interview Language English (%)	Pew: Interview Language Farsi, Urdu, Arabic (%)
Education				
HS or less	37	53	46	83
Some college	23	23	27	3
College grad	40	24	27	14
Employment Status				
Employed	70	57	64	25
Not employed	30	43	36	75
Race				
White	28	37	33	57
Black	35	24	27	8
Asian	18	20	20	19
Other	19	19	20	16
Age				
18 to 29	36	30	31	20
30 to 44	37	37	37	36
45 to 64	23	28	28	34
65 and older	4	5	4	10

FIGURE 4.2   The Relationship Between Target Population Definition and Research Findings

The demographic characteristics estimated by each approach are shown in Figure 4.2. Note how variations in the language-spoken component of the target definition result in significant differences in demographic estimates.

Select Sampling Method

Once the target population is defined, the next step determines which of two types of sampling methods will be used to identify items or individuals for study inclusion. As discussed earlier, a probability sample is a sample in which each individual, household, or item (generally called a sample element) comprising the universe from which the sample is drawn has an equal probability of being selected for inclusion in the research. The selection of sample elements is done purely by chance, for example, with a table of random numbers, coin flips, or through random digit dialing. When a probability sample is used, the selection of elements from the sample universe continues until the required number of elements has been selected and observed or interviewed. A nonprobability sample is a sample of elements that is not selected strictly by chance from the universe of all individuals, but is rather selected in some less random, more purposeful way. Here, the selection of elements for study inclusion may be made on the basis of convenience or judgment.

The choice of a sampling method is influenced by several factors: the type of generalization required, the researcher's need to minimize sampling error, study timing, and cost. The relative advantages and disadvantages of probability and nonprobability samples mirror each other in these areas.

- *Probability samples* (discussed in the remainder of this section) let a researcher estimate sampling error, calculate reliability, statistically determine the sample size required for a specified degree of confidence, and most important, confidently generalize the findings to the sample universe. In a probability sample, each individual in the target population has an equal chance of participating in the research.
- *Nonprobability samples* (discussed beginning on page 102) are quick and inexpensive to obtain. Research conducted among nonprobability samples is easy to design and carry out. However, a researcher using a nonprobabilty sample cannot calculate sampling error or reliability and has very limited confidence in generalizing the findings the sample universe.

Sample Frame

The sample frame provides the detail on *where* members of the target population will come from by specifying the method used to identify the households, individuals, or other elements specified in the target population definition. You can take one of two approaches to specifying the sample frame. You can either construct or obtain a list to represent the target population or, when lists are incomplete or unavailable, you can specify a procedure such as random digit dialing.

The adequacy of a sample frame is evaluated in terms of how well the frame represents the target population. A perfect sampling frame is identical to the target population; that is, the sample frame contains every population element once and only once, and only population elements are contained in the sampling frame. As might be expected,

---

Perfect Registration

You are a manufacturer of paper goods who wishes to conduct a survey of attitudes and purchasing behaviors among your current clients. The target population is defined as companies that have purchased at least $100 worth of goods within the past three months. The names of all clients meeting these criteria are selected from the company's database and are placed on a separate list (the sample frame) from which study participants will be selected.

Over-registration: Sample Frame Larger Than Target Population

You have just completed a six-month advertising test in metropolitan Atlanta and wish to determine levels of advertising and product awareness as well as brand perceptions. You decide to use random digit dialing among prefixes that are identified as "Atlanta." There are two over-registration problems. First, because of the way telephone companies assign telephone prefixes, not all telephones with an Atlanta prefix actually are in metropolitan Atlanta. Second, the research should be conducted among individuals who have lived in metropolitan Atlanta for at least six months, the time of the advertising test. Random digit dialing will not discriminate between those who have and have not resided for the required amount of time in Atlanta. A screener can be used to adjust the sample frame to better correspond with the target population.

Under-registration: Sample Frame Smaller Than Target Population

You want to assess teachers' reactions to corporate-sponsored educational materials. You select a list of members of the American Federation of Teachers as the sample frame. This frame suffers from under-registration because not all teachers are members of the Federation.

You want to conduct a telephone survey of individuals residing in New York. One potential sample frame might be the telephone book. However, this sample frame is incomplete and suffers from under-registration because a telephone book does not contain individuals with unlisted telephone numbers.

FIGURE 4.3   Registration and Sample Frame Descriptions

perfect sample frames are rare in actual practice. Typically, sample frames will either over-register or under-register the target population. A sample frame that consists of all the elements in the target population plus additional elements suffers from over-registration. An over-registered sample frame is too broad. A sample frame that contains fewer elements than the target population suffers from under-registration. An under-registered sample frame is too narrow and excludes elements from the target population. Examples of sample frames having over- and under-registration as well as perfect registration are provided in Figure 4.3.

Over- and under-registration, if left unaccounted for, can cause significant bias. Over-registration can be reduced by modifying the sample plan or by using a supplemental questionnaire (called a screener) to eliminate individuals not in the target population. Under-registration can be reduced by modifying the sample frame through updating or some other procedure that adds omitted units.

Types of Probability Sampling

Once you know the characteristics of the target population and how the population will be identified, you next need to determine the specific probability sampling procedure by which individuals are selected for study inclusion (see Figure 4.1). The three most common forms of probability sampling used in advertising research are simple random, systematic random, and stratified random samples.[2]

SIMPLE RANDOM SAMPLES.   Simple random samples are frequently used in advertising research. Here, each member of the population has an equal chance of being selected for inclusion in the research. You can think of random sampling as a drawing where the name of each member of the population is placed on a ticket and then placed into a drum. Individual names are selected from the drum. Every name in the drum has an equal chance of being selected. In practice, random number tables or random digit dialing is often used to select a random sample. A visual representation of random sampling is shown in Photo 4.1.

In practice, simple random sampling works as follows: Imagine that you are interested in estimating how much time individuals aged 18 to 24 spend on social networking

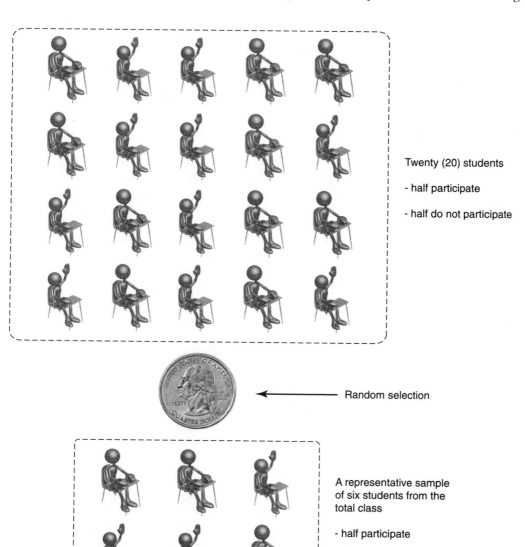

Twenty (20) students

- half participate

- half do not participate

Random selection

A representative sample
of six students from the
total class

- half participate

- half do not participate

PHOTO 4.1 Illustration of Simple Random Sampling

Individual Number	Gender	Education	Average Number of Hours with Social Media
1	Male	High School	3.7
2	Male	High School	3.4
3	Male	High School	6.0
4	Male	High School	1.1
5	Male	College	3.7
6	Male	College	4.1
7	Male	College	2.5
8	Female	High School	2.5
9	Female	High School	4.5
10	Female	High School	1.6
11	Female	High School	4.9
12	Female	College	7.3
13	Female	College	1.8
14	Female	College	4.8
15	Female	College	1.1
16	Female	College	1.6
17	Female	College	2.1
18	Female	College	1.6
19	Female	College	3.7
20	Female	College	6.2

FIGURE 4.4   Target Universe Comprised 18 to 24 Year Olds

sites in a typical day, where "typical day" is defined as "the previous 24 hours." Assume that the entire universe of 18- to 24-year olds is shown in Figure 4.4. If we were to interview every individual in this target universe, we would find that the average number of hours spent in the prior 24 hours was 3.4.

Now, instead of conducting the census of this population, a researcher might use random digit dialing for both landlines and cell phones to contact individuals in this sample universe and ask them to provide the required information.[3] Different samples of five individuals each, the identification number of individuals in each sample, and the average number of hours spent on social networking sites are shown in the table below.

Sample	Individuals	Average Number of Hours
1	3, 4, 7, 13, 14	3.2
2	11, 12, 15, 17, 19	3.8
3	9, 10, 12, 15, 19	3.6
4	1, 8, 9, 15, 20	3.6
5	2, 10, 16, 19, 20	3.3

As can be seen, a simple random sample can provide an accurate estimate of the entire population without having to survey the entire population. While there is some expected variation across samples, different random samples from the universe shown in Figure 4.4 provide estimates comparable to the population as a whole. By randomly selecting individuals from the sample universe, we can accurately estimate the behaviors of the entire target population. In this situation, a simple random sample satisfies the two characteristics of good sampling described earlier in this chapter: it is efficient, and it provides reliable generalizations about the population from which the sample is taken.

SYSTEMATIC RANDOM SAMPLES.   A variation of a simple random sample is a systematic random sample. Systematic random samples typically provide data identical to simple random samples with the added advantage of simplicity—no table of random numbers or coin toss is needed, and sample size can be firmly specified.

Similar to a simple random sample, a systematic sample begins with a sample frame, after which the following steps are taken:

- Count the number of elements on the list.
- Determine the desired sample size.
- Compute a skip interval.
- Select a random place on the list to start.
- Select each element at the appropriate skip interval.

This process is illustrated in Photo 4.2.

Refer again to the universe shown in Figure 4.4. Imagine that we require a final sample size of 5. The skip interval would be four (calculated as 20 ÷ 5). The sample would be drawn by beginning at a random place on the list, perhaps at individual number 7 and then selecting every fourth person from this point on (individuals 11, 15, 19, and 3). As shown in the table below, while there is some variation, a systematic sample accurately estimates the overall population average.

Sample	Individuals	Average Number of Hours
1	2, 6, 10, 14, 18	3.1
2	7, 11, 15, 19, 3	3.6
3	1, 5, 9, 13, 17	3.2

SIMPLE AND SYSTEMATIC SAMPLES: ONLINE SELECTION.   The prior discussion of simple and systematic samples assumed that a sample frame was available and that random sampling could be used to select individuals from the identified source, either through explicit selection or through techniques such as random digit dialing. There are times, however, that the sample frame reflects a set of behaviors and, as a result, not all individuals in the sample frame are known. We might, for example, want to randomly sample the opinions of all individuals to a Web site. True random samples can be obtained in these situations, but only if care is used. Consider the following situation:

Books-4-All has redesigned its home page and seeks to obtain visitors' reactions to this redesign. The new home page goes "live" online at noon on May 17. Books-4-All wishes to interview a random sample of visitors to the new page and will conduct around the clock interviewing for the next week. Books-4-All has two options. First, it can obtain a simple random sample. It can use software that "flips" a virtual coin for each visit, inviting those whose flip comes up "heads" to participate in the research. Alternatively, Books-4-All can obtain a systematic random sample, using software that will sequentially count visits, inviting the person on every 10th visit to participate in the research.

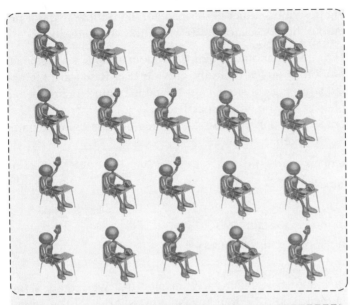

(1) Define desired sample size
   - in this example: 5

(2) Divide total number in
   sample by desired size
   - in this example: 20 ÷ 5 or 4

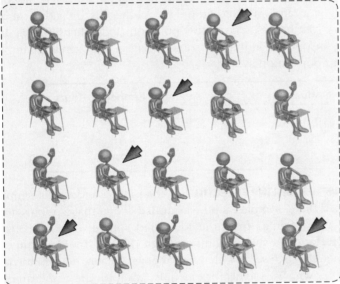

(3) Select starting point
   - in this case Student #4

(4) Start with Student #4 and
   select every 4th student

PHOTO 4.2   Illustration of Systematic Random Sampling

Either of Books-4-All's approaches to respondent selection would obtain a sample, but neither sample would be a true random sample. Remember that in a true random sample every individual has an *equal* chance for selection. Assume that Books-4-All will have 1,000 total visits—not visitors—during the week of the survey. Below are the chances of five individuals being selected in the research when the number of site visits varies across individual:

Joan visits the site 1 time.   Joan's chance for selection is 1 ÷ 1000 or .1%.
Jeff visits the site 10 times.   Jeff's chance for selection is 10 ÷ 1000 or 1%.
Dean visits the site 50 times.   Dean's chance for selection is 50 ÷ 1000 or 5%.

Joan, Jeff, and Dean have unequal chances for selection. The most essential component of random sampling will be violated unless something is done. Books-4-All must devise a scheme in which the basic characteristics of random selection are not violated. The problem can be solved by ensuring that each individual has only one chance to be selected regardless of the number of visits. Books-4-All could, for example, place a cookie on each visitor's computer during their first visit. The cookie would eliminate the respondent from consideration in the study should there be subsequent visits.

In sum, sample frames based on behaviors can provide a rich and appropriate source of data. A researcher using this approach, however, must make certain that the sampling method used to sample from this frame does not violate the basic tenets of random sampling.

STRATIFIED RANDOM SAMPLES.   In the prior examples, simple and systematic random sampling techniques worked well. They were efficient and provided reliable generalizations about the total population. However, these forms of sampling worked well only because the universe was relatively homogeneous with respect to what was being measured. There was little variation among subpopulations that comprised the total sample. The overall average of 3.4 hours did not significantly vary in response to the two subgroup characteristics (gender and education) as shown in the following table:

Sample Group	Average Number of Hours
Male	3.5
Female	3.4
High School Education	3.5
College Education	3.4

Simple and systematic random samples provide fewer reliable generalizations about the total population when significant differences among population subgroups are suspected. The data shown in Figure 4.5 shows the amount of time spent on social networking sites for a new target universe, this time with respondents' age noted. (Again, assume these 20 individuals comprise the entire universe. The distribution of ages in this universe reflects that of the overall U.S. population.)

The table below shows the average time estimates for random samples of five drawn from this universe. As can be seen, there is now a wide variation in the estimates provided, and a researcher has little direction for deciding which one is "right."

Sample	Average Number of Hours
1	3.0
2	1.0
3	2.3
4	.7
5	2.5

Stratified random sampling is a better choice versus simple and systematic random sampling whenever you have a situation where you think there is a large variation in what you are studying due to specific respondent characteristics. In this example, given

Individual Number	Age	Average Number of Hours with Social Media
1	18	2.2
2	22	4.6
3	25	2.1
4	27	3.1
5	32	2.8
6	33	1.5
7	37	1.5
8	38	1.1
9	40	2.2
10	42	.8
11	43	1.0
12	47	.5
13	50	.5
14	55	2.0
15	57	1.0
16	61	.2
17	64	.0
18	73	.0
19	77	.1
20	81	.0

FIGURE 4.5 Target Universe Comprised Individuals Aged 18 Years and Older

that you might suspect that age is related to time spent on social networking sites, you might decide to stratify the sample, that is, divide individuals in the target universe into classes (or strata) and *then* randomly sample from each strata individually. Each stratum is treated and sampled as if it were an independent universe.

Stratified sampling is accomplished a four-step process, as illustrated in Photo 4.3 and described below for the social media usage universe:

- First, *one or more classification criteria that define the strata are identified*. These classification criteria should define independent strata that do not overlap. The classification criterion for the age groups might be:

   Strata 1   Individuals aged 18 to 24
   Strata 2   Individuals aged 25 to 34
   Strata 3   Individuals aged 35 to 49
   Strata 4   Individuals aged 50 and older

- Second, each element in the sample frame is assigned to one and only one stratum. For example, individuals aged 38 would be assigned to Strata 3.

- Third, the total sample size is determined. Assume that for this example we want a final sample size of 1,000.

- Fourth, independent random samples (using either simple or systematic sampling methods) are selected from *each stratum* in a way that results in the total sample size being achieved.

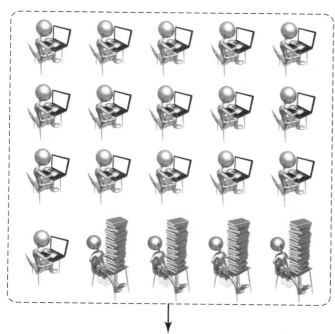

(1) Assign individuals to strata
  - in this example there are two strata: students who read their assignments on their computer (Strata 1), students who read their assignments in books (Strata 2)

(2) Define size of strata
  - in this example Strata 1 is 80% of the total (16 ÷ 20), Strata 2 is 20% (4 ÷ 20)

(3) Define desired final sample size
  - in this example final sample is eight individuals

Proportionate sampling results in a sample with about the same percentage in each strata as in the original sample

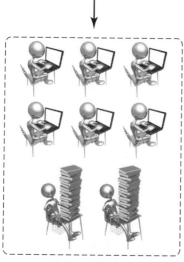

75% from Strata 1
25% from Strata 2

PHOTO 4.3 Proportionate Stratified Random Sampling

The fourth step, sampling from each stratum in order to achieve the desired final sample size, presents two options regarding the *number* of elements selected from each stratum. Either proportionate or disproportionate sampling may be used.

Proportionate stratified sampling selects individuals in proportion to their stratum's size within the total target population. The U.S. census provides that percentage of the adult population falling into each of the four identified strata, as shown below:

Strata 1	Individuals aged 18 to 24	11%
Strata 2	Individuals aged 25 to 34	17%
Strata 3	Individuals aged 35 to 49	29%
Strata 4	Individuals aged 50 and older	43%

Once the proportionate size of each strata is determined, this percentage is multiplied by the desired final sample size for the research, in this case 1,000. The result of this computation represents the number of people to sample from each stratum (now using either random or systematic random sampling). Thus, in this example, sample sizes for each stratum would be:

Strata 1	Individuals aged 18 to 24	11%	Sample size = 110 (.11 × 1,000)
Strata 2	Individuals aged 25 to 34	17%	Sample size = 170 (.17 × 1,000)
Strata 3	Individuals aged 35 to 49	29%	Sample size = 290 (.29 × 1,000)
Strata 4	Individuals aged 50 and older	43%	Sample size = 430 (.43 × 1,000)

Problems arise with proportionate stratified sampling when some strata are small, and as a result, there may not be sufficient numbers of observations or interviews in these smaller strata to permit reliable data analysis. In these cases, disproportionate stratified sampling is used.

Disproportionate stratified sampling, shown in Photo 4.4, selects a predetermined number of elements from each stratum despite the relative size of those strata. Selection is based on analytical considerations, that is, the sample size required for reliable data analysis, as opposed to the size of the stratum within the total universe. When disproportionate stratified sampling is used, the data obtained from an individual stratum must be weighted to compensate for stratum size differentials in the actual sample universe before total sample findings are reported.

Sample Size in Random Samples

Confidence in the generalizations drawn from a random sample is directly affected by sample size. Generally, larger samples permit greater confidence in population estimates and generalizations.

The concept of confidence in sample estimates and generalizations is expressed in terms of the confidence interval and the confidence level. A *confidence interval* is an estimate, plus or minus, of the value of the population estimate; it states the range in which we believe the true population estimate lies. For example, it is common to read that "80% of all adults surveyed agree that there need to be major changes to the income tax code. The confidence interval is ±2%." This means that the true percentage of adults agreeing with the statement probably lies between 78% and 82%. The *confidence level* is the mathematical expression of our confidence that the population estimate lies within the confidence interval.

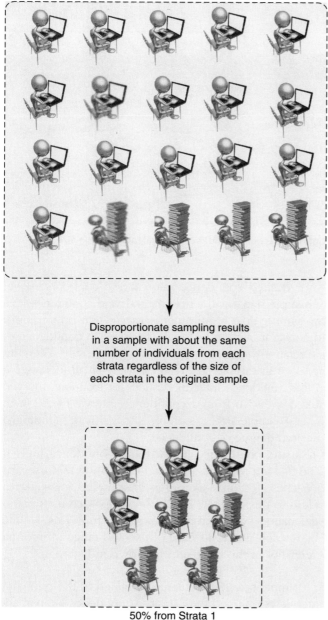

(1) Assign individuals to strata
  - in this example there are two strata: students who read their assignments on their computer (Strata 1), students who read their assignments in books (Strata 2)

(2) Define size of strata
  - in this example Strata 1 is 80% of the total (16 ÷ 20), Strata 2 is 20% (4 ÷ 20)

(3) Define desired final sample size
  - in this example final sample is eight individuals

Disproportionate sampling results in a sample with about the same number of individuals from each strata regardless of the size of each strata in the original sample

50% from Strata 1
50% from Strata 2

PHOTO 4.4   Disproportionate Stratified Random Sampling

For example, a confidence level of 95% means that there is a 95% probability that the population estimate from the research lies within the identified confidence interval.

Sample size is determined in light of confidence intervals and confidence levels. Greater precision in either or both levels requires larger sample sizes. Thus, the most important step in sample size determination occurs when you explicitly state during the

Confidence Level	(±) Confidence Interval	Sample Size
99	8	256
99	5	643
99	2	3,435
99	1	9,068
95	8	149
95	5	377
95	2	2,144
95	1	6,849
90	8	106
90	5	267
90	2	1,560
90	1	5,055

FIGURE 4.6   Relationship Between Confidence Level, Confidence Interval, and Sample Size

planning stages of the research your desired confidence interval and confidence level. The relationship between required sample size, confidence interval, and confidence level is shown in Figure 4.6. Note how sample size requirements vary when one criterion changes while the others are held constant. As can be seen, increases in confidence do not increase in a linear, one-to-one relationship with increases in sample size. There are diminishing returns; very large increases in sample size result in only small increases in confidence level and decreases in the confidence interval. Notice, for example, the very large increase in sample size required to move from a confidence interval of ±2 to an interval of ±1. The goal in determining sample size, therefore, is to estimate the minimal sample size that will provide the desired degree of confidence.

There are two approaches to using confidence interval and confidence level to determine required sample size. The first approach is a manual calculation that uses formulae grounded in statistical theory. These formulae as well as their underlying statistical theory are described in the addendum to this chapter. The second approach uses one of the numerous online sample size calculators. While all perform similar functions, we recommend the calculator provided by Raosoft due to its ease of use and range of information automatically provided.[4] A screenshot of this calculator is shown in Figure 4.7.

ESTIMATE NUMBER OF CONTACTS.   Sample size requirements identified in the prior step reflect the number of completed interviews required for a desired confidence interval and confidence level. A research fact of life, however, is that not all individuals contacted will agree to participate in the research and not all who agree will actually complete the survey or other data gathering instrument. As a result, the number of people contacted is always greater than the final desired sample size. The number of required contacts is determined by the following formula: where DSS is the desired final sample size, ATP represents an estimate of the percentage of the target population who will agree to participate, and CS represents the percentage of those agreeing who will provide complete survey responses:

$$\text{Required number of contacts} = \text{DSS} \div (\text{ATP} \times \text{CS})$$

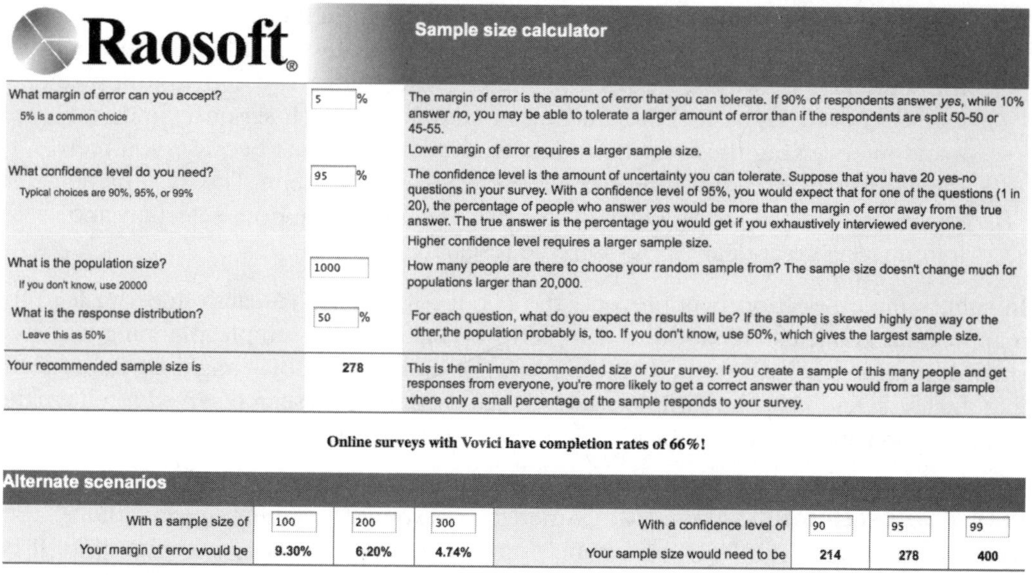

FIGURE 4.7 Raosoft Sample Size Calculator

For example, if the desired final sample size is 500, the percentage agreeing to participate is estimated to be 70% and the expected completion rate is 90%, then the total number of contacts would need to be 893 individuals, calculated as:

$$\text{Required number of contacts} = 500 \div (.7 \times .9)$$
$$= 500 \div (.56)$$
$$= 892.9$$
$$= 893$$

Sample Selection Bias in Probability Samples

Sample bias occurs when members of the population of interest are selected in violation of the basic principle of random sampling, that is, where each observation has an equal chance of being selected for inclusion in the sample. The use of telephone books as the source of numbers for a telephone survey is, for example, likely to lead to sample bias. Even if random sampling is used to select the names and numbers from the telephone book, the sample is still biased because those who do not have listed numbers are systematically excluded from the research. These individuals can never be selected. Additional examples of sample selection bias are represented in the following scenarios.

Imagine that you wish to select a random sample of students from your university. You make a conscientious effort to interview every tenth student who enters the cafeteria. You chose the cafeteria because most students go there at least once during the day. However, because different types of students visit the cafeteria with different frequencies, and not all visit at least once, the sample would be biased.

Now imagine that the entire student body is gathered in the stadium to watch the championship football game. You decide to interview a random sample of the students. However, you avoid interviewing those dressed in "hippie clothes" because you feel they might not take the research seriously and you avoid interviewing those in the fraternity and sorority seats because you feel their opinions are not indicative of the "average" student. The systematic exclusion of these individuals violates the principle of random selection and introduces a great deal of bias into the research.[5]

In sum, sample selection bias prevents the conduct of sound research and can lead to inappropriate conclusions about a sampled population. The sample planning process should therefore include an explicit discussion of how sample bias might be introduced into the study and how the sampling techniques used in the research served to eliminate identified potential sources of bias.

BIAS AND TELEPHONE SAMPLING. Amercians, especially younger individuals, are increasingly adapting cell phones as their only form of telephone communication. It is now estimated that about 15% of the population is now a cell phone-only household with this number even higher among certain segments: about 31% of those aged 18–24 and 20% of Hispanics are now cell-only.

Recent research demonstrates that the implications of this situation for population sampling differ across survey topics. The Pew Center for the People & the Press notes that:

> Surveys that rely only on landline interviews are more likely to produce biased estimates if the segment of the public unreachable on a landline differs substantially from the landline public. If the cell-only respondents are not very different from the landline respondents, the survey estimates will not be biased by the absence of the cell-only group. For example, the landline survey finds that 54% of Americans favor bringing troops home from Iraq; among the cell-only respondents, 55% favor a U.S. troop withdrawal. Thus the overall survey estimate is unaffected when the cell-only respondents are blended in. One way to consider the impact of adding cell-only interviews to a survey is to ask the question: How different would the cell-only have to be for the total survey estimates to be affected by their inclusion?[6]

Thus, when cell phone users are believed to be similar to landline users, adding a separate cell phone sample may not be necessary. Pew has found, for example, that "on key political measures such as presidential approval, Iraq policy, presidential primary voter preference, and party affiliation, respondents reached on cell phones hold attitudes that are very similar to those reached on landline telephones. Analysis of two separate nationwide studies shows that including interviews conducted by cell phone does not substantially change any key survey findings."[7]

Cell phone-only samples need to be added to a landline sample, however, when separate analyses of cell phone-only individuals are of interest or when cell phone users are believed to be dissimilar in attitude or behavior from the overall population. This occurs, for example, when examining the use of technology. The Pew Internet & American Life Project, for example, found that cell phone users are more likely than those in a landline sample to

- live in households earning less than $50,000
- have no education beyond high school
- be students
- be white or African-American
- be childless
- have a broadband connection at home.

Furthermore, in terms of online activities, cell users are more likely to be content creators and bloggers. They are also more likely to have downloaded songs and videos, watched video-sharing sites such as YouTube, and consumed news online. In cases such as this, adding a cell phone sample is very important.[8] Pew describes the process of merging landline and cell phone samples as follows:

> The design of the landline sample ensures representation of both listed and unlisted numbers (including those not yet listed) by using random digit dialing. This method uses random generation of the last two digits of telephone numbers selected on the basis of the area code, telephone exchange, and bank number. A bank is defined as 100 contiguous telephone numbers, for example 800-555-1200 to 800-555-1299. The telephone exchanges are selected to be proportionally stratified by county and by telephone exchange within the county. That is, the number of telephone numbers randomly sampled from within a given county is proportional to that county's share of telephone numbers in the U.S. Only banks of telephone numbers containing three or more listed residential numbers are selected.
>
> The cell phone sample is drawn through systematic sampling from dedicated wireless banks of 100 contiguous numbers and shared service banks with no directory-listed landline numbers (to ensure that the cell phone sample does not include banks that are also included in the landline sample). The sample is designed to be representative both geographically and by large and small wireless carriers.[9]

BIAS AND ONLINE PANELS.   Researchers are increasingly turning to online panels as their source of respondents. When using panels, a researcher identifies target population characteristics and the desired sample size, and then the appropriate number of individuals with the specified characteristics is randomly selected from the panel for participation in the research. The underlying assumption of panel use is that panel characteristics mirror that of the broader U. S. population.

Many research companies offer online panels for research.[10] Not all panels provide equal data quality, however, as panels differ with regard to how the panel was formed, the demographics of panel members, and the extent to which the research company has verified the representativeness of panel composition. E-rewards provides a set of excellent insights for evaluating panel quality, which are adapted below:[11]

- Invitation-only panels are preferred over "opt-in" panels because this recruitment technique helps to reduce "self-selection" bias.
- Panels should aggressively and continuously identify "professional respondents" and immediately expel these individuals from the panel.
- All panel members' demographic and other defining information should be verified.
- Panel demographic composition should be verified, and the panel itself should mirror the general U.S. adult population. Researchers should not have to resort to weighting results to compensate for the lack of panel representativeness.
- Panel response rates should be monitored and be made accessible to all researchers contemplating use of the panel. Consistently unresponsive panel members should be eliminated from the panel.
- The quality of information provided by panel members should be continuously monitored. Panel members who consistently provide poor information (e.g., by providing the same choice for all questions or completing surveys in too short a time frame) should be eliminated from the panel.

NONPROBABILITY SAMPLING AND QUANTITATIVE RESEARCH

The previous section discussed three types of probability samples: simple random, systematic random, and stratified random. Each of these forms of sampling obtains probability samples because all elements in the defined universe have an equal chance of being selected. However, in spite of its advantages, not all advertising research uses probability sampling. Some informational needs do not require the precision and generalizability of probability samples, while other needs cannot justify the associated time and expense. In these cases, other forms of selection labeled nonprobability sampling are selected. The major forms of nonprobability sampling in quantitative research are convenience, judgment, quota, and snowball. The sampling process for nonprobability sampling is shown in Figure 4.8.

Convenience Sampling

Convenience sampling is just what the name implies: study participants are selected because they are convenient and accessible. Interviewing friends, associates, or individuals walking down the street or through the mall are forms of this type of sampling. Convenience sampling, as might be expected, is uncomplicated, quick, and low cost.

Convenience sampling has great potential to provide unreliable and biased information and, therefore, should only be used when there is absolutely no need to generalize the attitudes and behaviors of the convenience sample to the broader population. This is because there is never any assurance that the characteristics of the convenience sample are in any way representative of the larger universe. As a result, it is only appropriate to use convenience sampling for exploratory research or for quick,

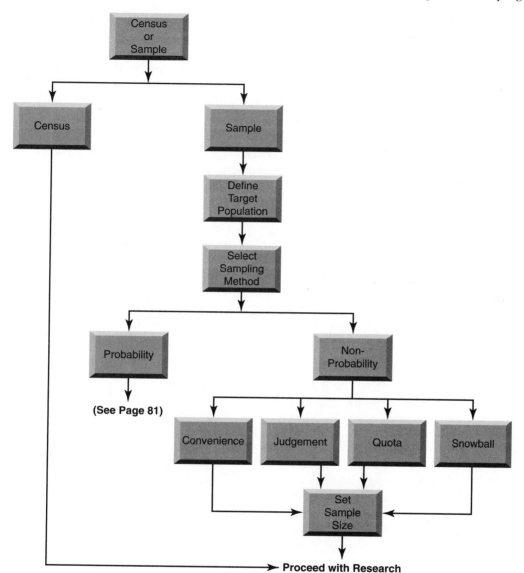

FIGURE 4.8 The Sampling Process and Forms of Nonprobability Sampling

nongeneralizable information relevant to a specific research need, such as question-naire pretesting.

Judgment Sampling

Judgment sampling selects individuals from the target population based on an expert's judgment of who might be the best to interview. The expert may be the researcher, others at the agency, the client, or a specialist with particular expertise. A storekeeper, for example, may decide to sample what he considers the "typical" customers of his business.

One's confidence in the results of research conducted with judgment samples is directly proportionate to the expert's expertise used to identify and select the sample. The greater the expertise, the more likely the results can be trusted, although generalization to the broader population of interest always remains a problem. For example, an expert may believe that the most appropriate target for a college savings program are parents with children aged 10 to 17. If this judgment is correct, then the insights gathered from these interviews will be useful. If the expert's judgment is wrong, however, then research conducted among these individuals is likely to provide misleading direction for future planning. Judgment samples are recommended only when there is absolute confidence in the expert's opinion or, similar to convenience sampling, when only preliminary, exploratory information is required.

Quota Sampling

Quota sampling is an extended form of judgment sampling. It attempts to ensure that demographic or other characteristics of interest are represented in the sample in the same proportion as they are in the target population. Quota samples are obtained through the following five steps:

1. Determine the defining characteristics of the key subgroups.
2. Determine the percent of the total population represented by each defining characteristic.
3. Determine the percent of the total population represented by each quota cell.
4. Translate the percent into a sample size.
5. Sample the population.

Figure 4.9 illustrates the outcome of following the prior steps. First, the universe was divided based on gender and education. Second, the percent of the total population represented by each characteristic is determined and placed in the margins of the table. Third, because the two characteristics are assumed to be independent, the percent of the total sample represented by each cell is calculated by multiplying the appropriate marginal values. For example, the percent of men with less than a high school education is the product of 0.21 (the percent of the total population that has less than a high school education) and 0.48 (the percent of the total population that are men). Fourth, the total sample of 400 individuals is allocated on a percentage basis. In this example, 40 men allocated to the "Less than High School group" are found by multiplying the .1 in this cell in the top chart by the sample size of 400. The total sample of 400 permits sufficient size in each quota cell for subgroup analysis. Were this not the case, total sample size would have to be increased. Finally the sample is selected so that each cell's quota is filled.

Snowball Sampling

Snowball sampling uses current study participants to help recruit future participants from among their friends and acquaintances. Thus, the sample group grows like a rolling snowball. Snowball sampling is typically used for very small, hard-to-reach, or highly specialized populations of individuals; populations where access is facilitated through

Percent of the target population falling into each quota cell

	Education				
Gender	Less Than High School	High School	Some College	College and Above	Total %
Men	10	17	11	10	**48**
Women	11	18	12	11	**52**
Total %	**21**	**35**	**23**	**21**	**100**

Sample size for each cell, given a total sample of 400

	Education				
Gender	Less Than High School	High School	Some College	College and Above	Total
Men	40	68	44	40	**192**
Women	44	72	48	44	**208**
Total	**84**	**140**	**92**	**84**	**400**

FIGURE 4.9   Quota Sampling

personal introductions. Because sample members are not selected from a sampling frame, snowball samples are subject to numerous biases. For example, people who have many friends are more likely to be recruited into the sample. In addition, since snowball sampling relies on referrals from initial participants to generate additional participants, any biasing characteristics of initial respondents are likely to affect all future participants. This reflects the fact that people tend to associate with others like themselves. This increases the chance of correlations and other relationships being found in the study that do not apply to the wider population of which participants are members.

Sample Size in Nonprobability Samples

The nature of nonprobability samples precludes the use of statistical techniques to determine confidence intervals and associated sample size. As a result, sample sizes in nonprobability research typically reflect some form of judgment. Some forms of judgment, however, are better than others.

Unaided judgment is the most arbitrary approach to nonprobability sample size determination. Here, the client or researcher simply says: "A sample of 50 (or 100 or 1,000) will do. This is a good number. One that I feel comfortable with." While the researcher or client may "feel comfortable" with sample sizes selected in this way, there is no assurance that the sample is sufficient to satisfy informational needs. Consequently, this approach should be avoided.

What is the budget? A second approach reflects budget considerations. The amount of funds available for sampling is divided by the cost per sample unit (e.g., the cost to interview one individual) and the result is used to set the sample size. At $10 per interview, for example, a budget of $1,000 dictates a sample size of 100. This approach should also be avoided.

Buying the largest sample size that you can afford has a high potential to produce samples that are either too large or too small given the research's informational needs.

Frame of reference is a more reasonable approach to nonprobability sample size determination, where sample decisions follow the practices of others. Here, you would first determine the sample sizes others have used for similar types of research and would then select samples of comparable size. The strength of this approach lies in the fact that there is often merit in historical precedence. A weakness, however, is that you may not know the validity of the rationale underlying initial decisions of sample size.

Analytical requirements is probably the best method for determining nonprobability sample size. It is recommended that the total number of individuals or observations in major study subgroups total at least 100 while there be a minimum of 20 to 50 individuals in minor analytical groups.

SAMPLE SELECTION AND QUALITATIVE RESEARCH

Purposive sampling is the most common form of qualitative sampling. In this approach, a researcher starts with a specific purpose or information need in mind, and the sample is then selected to include only those people who *in the judgment of the researcher* will be able to provide information relevant to satisfying the information need. Hopefully, individuals selected will represent "information-rich cases for study in depth. Information-rich cases are those from which one can learn a great deal about issues of central importance to the purpose of the research."[12]

The types of individuals selected for the purposive sample are determined by the researcher's judgments, approach, goals, and information needs. Patton[13] notes that a qualitative researcher has a great deal of latitude in identifying and selecting appropriate individuals. Imagine that a researcher wants to explore *why* individuals use Twitter. The most common options and approaches would include sampling

- *extreme or deviant cases* where individuals who are "outliers" are selected. Here, a researcher looks at what rarely happens in order to better understand what usually happens.[14] Twitter users sending more than 200 messages a day would likely fall into this group.

- *typical cases* where "average" or "typical" individuals are selected. Interviewing of individuals in this group is typically most productive after insights from interviews with the prior group are completed. This group might be comprised of individuals who send around four Twitter messages per day (as this is the reported average).

- *highly intense or passionate individuals* who may not be extreme in their behaviors but are highly involved in the area being explored. This group could include Twitter users who, regardless of the number of messages sent, strongly believe that "I couldn't live without my Twitter."

- *confirming or disconfirming cases* where the attitudes or behaviors of individuals selected either support or negate the researcher's pre-existing perspective. This group could include those whose primary motivation for Twitter use is "Because it helps me feel more important" (the researcher's belief) and those who use Twitter for any number of other reasons.

Importantly, these approaches are not mutually exclusive. As opposed to quantitative research where sample characteristics are unchanging from the start of the research, a qualitative researcher has a great deal of flexibility with regard to the sample. A researcher can start the research process with one type of case and then, depending upon what is learned, move to interviews with individuals who possess a different set of characteristics. This approach, interviewing a broad heterogeneous sample of individuals, allows the researcher to acquire insights that cut across a wide variety of individuals and that allow for maximum contrast across cases with differing characteristics. In addition, sample characteristics may change as the research progresses, as a researcher's knowledge increases, and new insights and potential areas for exploration are uncovered.[15]

Sample Size

Sample size in qualitative research is estimated at the start of the research, but the actual number of participants is guided by information gain: interviewing continues as long as the budget permits a researcher to learn new things and gain new insights. The "adequacy of sample size in qualitative research is relative, a matter of judging a sample neither small nor large per se, but rather too small or too large for the intended purposes of"[16] what needs to be learned. A sample of 10, for example, may be adequate if nothing new is being learned from additional interviews, while a sample of 30 may be too small if each new interview provides additional insights. Thus, "determining an adequate sample size in qualitative research is ultimately a matter of judgment and experience in evaluating the quality of the information collected . . . and the intended research outcomes."[17]

APPLYING CHAPTER CONCEPTS

This chapter introduced the procedures underlying both random and nonrandom sampling and provided guidance on the appropriate use of each sampling technique. While the procedures discussed remain constant across different research situations, the details of each sampling plan are selected to specifically respond to the research's goals and informational needs.

The chapter's online supplemental readings provide overviews of and sampling plans for six studies conducted by the Pew Research Center.[18] Note how each study's sampling plan directly responds to the goals and informational needs of the research and how the plans overall move from the relatively simple (in the Parent and Teen Survey) to the complex (particularly the last three studies). It is recommended that you read the topic and overview of each study and then, before reading the Pew approach to sampling, think about the sampling plan that you would recommend. Once this is done, read Pew's approach to sampling.[19]

SUMMARY

The sampling process involves the selection and examination of the elements of a population for drawing conclusions about the larger population of which these elements are members. A good sample is efficient and provides reliable generalizations about the larger population.

All sampling begins with a definition of the target population, the group of elements about which you wish to make inferences and draw generalizations. A well-defined target population unambiguously describes the group of interest and clearly differentiates those things or individuals who are of interest from those who are not.

A determination of the sampling method occurs next. Given the informational needs motivating the research, and the time and financial considerations, either a probability or nonprobability sampling technique will be selected. A probability sample is when each individual, household, or item comprising the universe from which the sample is drawn has an equal chance, or probability, of being selected for inclusion in the research. The selection of sample elements is done purely by chance. A nonprobability sample is when the elements are not selected strictly by chance from the universe of all individuals, but are rather selected in some less random, often more purposeful way.

Probability Sampling

Probability sampling techniques require an additional three planning steps. First, a sample frame must be determined. A sample frame specifies the method you will use to identify the households, individuals, or other elements specified in the target population definition. You can take one of two approaches to specifying the sample frame. You can either construct or obtain a list to represent the target population, or when a list is incomplete or unavailable you can specify a procedure such as random digit dialing for identifying and contacting target individuals. Once a sample frame is selected, it is compared to the target population. A perfect sample frame is identical to the target population; that is, the sample frame contains every population element once and only once, and only population elements are contained in the sampling frame. Typically, however, sample frames are either too broad (over-registration) or too narrow (under-registration). In these latter instances, modifications in the sampling plan can be made to take into account the sample frame's characteristics.

Second, a specific probability sampling technique is selected. The most common forms of probability sampling are simple random samples, systematic random samples, and stratified random samples. Simple and systematic random sampling work well when the target population displays little variability among demographic, geographic, or behavioral subgroups. When wide variability is thought to exist, stratified random sampling (using either proportionate or disproportionate sample selection) is recommended.

Third, statistical techniques are used to determine the most appropriate balance between required sample size and confidence intervals, that is, the range of measurement error.

Nonprobability Sampling

The most common forms of nonprobability sampling are convenience sampling, judgment sampling, quota sampling, and purposive sampling. Convenience sampling should be used with great caution. It is only appropriate to use a convenience sample for exploratory research or for quick, nongeneralizable information relevant to a specific research need, such as questionnaire pretesting. Judgment sampling should also be used with caution, and only when there is great confidence in the judgment of the expert making the sample recommendation.

Sample size is determined based on analytical requirements and reflects the minimum number of observations required for each major and minor analytical subgroup.

Review Questions

1. What is a *random sample?* In what circumstances is a *census* preferable to a *sample?*
2. What are the two characteristics of a well-written target population definition?
3. On what basis are populations of individuals typically defined? Briefly describe each component, providing an appropriate example.
4. Identify the differences between a *probability* and a *nonprobability* sample. What are the relative advantages and disadvantages of each?
5. What type of information is provided by a *sample frame?* Identify two approaches to specifying this frame.
6. How is the adequacy of a *sample frame* evaluated?
7. What are *over-* and *under-registration?* How can each be addressed if identified early in the sample design process?
8. List the three most common forms of probability sampling used in advertising research.
9. How do *simple random samples* work in practice? What benefits do they offer?
10. What is a *systematic random sample?* How is this sample type similar and dissimilar to a *simple random sample?*
11. When using a sample frame based on behaviors, what extra cautions must a researcher take in order to comply with the principles of random sampling?
12. When does a *simple* or *systematic random sample* provide accurate estimates of the target population? When are these estimates more questionable and perhaps less reliable?
13. What is a *stratified random sample?* When is this type of sampling method most appropriate?
14. Explain the four steps used in *stratified sampling* to select the desired sample.
15. What is the difference between *proportionate* and *disproportionate* stratified random sampling? Under what types of conditions is each most appropriate?
16. What are *confidence intervals* and *confidence levels?*
17. Describe the relationship between *confidence intervals, confidence levels,* and *sample size.*
18. Once sample size requirements have been identified, how can the actual *required number of contacts* be calculated?
19. When does *sample selection bias* occur in probability samples? How should the planning process best address this potential bias?
20. What insights can be used to more accurately address online panel quality and reduce biases?
21. Identify the four major forms of *nonprobability sampling* in quantitative research.
22. Briefly explain *convenience* and *judgment samples.* How are they similar and dissimilar? Under what types of circumstances should each be used?
23. What is a *quota sample?* How is this type of sample selected?
24. What is *snowball sampling?* When is this type of sampling typically utilized, and what potential biases does it present?
25. In nonprobability sampling, what types of judgments may come into play? What are the positive and negative aspects to these approaches?
26. Qualitative research commonly uses *purposive sampling.* Explain the principle of this sampling method and how individuals are chosen.
27. How is the *sample size* in qualitative research determined? How is this approach different than that of quantitative research?

Application Exercises

Application exercises 1 through 6 relate to concepts raised and discussed in this chapter.

1. The local chapter of the Arthritis Foundation is preparing for its annual fund-raiser. It is recommended that to better target this year's efforts, research on donor characteristics from last year's fund-raiser be examined. Specifically, the research must describe the demographics of last year's donors. Time is of the essence. Two lists are available. First, a list of the names and addresses of all 11,000 individuals who donated from the last year is stored in the chapter's archives. The file summary of this list

shows that the percent of all last year's donors who donated at various levels is

Supporter (under $25)   39%
Bronze Club ($25-$99)   11
Silver Club ($100-$500)   45
Gold Club ($1,000 or more)   5

It would take about 10 days to retrieve this list. A second list is also available. This list, stored in the chairman's files, lists the first 150 and last 300 donors from the past year.

You have been asked to recommend a sampling plan. Present your recommendations for sampling this population, and provide a discussion of the strengths and weaknesses (if any) of your recommendation. Be certain that your discussion addresses target population definition, sampling method, sample frame (if appropriate), specific sampling approach, and sample size.

2. Tom's Buns N' Burger is a national chain of hamburger restaurants. Tom's wants to conduct research to determine consumers' reactions to its newly revised menu. During the week of March 4, it gives each customer a coupon for a free hamburger and drink. However, the coupon is not valid until the customer calls an 800 number, answers some survey questions, and obtains a validation code. Tom's will use the information it gathers to plan future revisions to its menu.

Comment on Tom's sample plan. Do you agree that the plan is appropriate? Why or why not? If you do not feel that it is appropriate, propose, describe, and justify an alternative sampling plan. Be certain to address all applicable elements as shown in Figure 4.1.

3. The *Weekly World Reporter* conducts weekly surveys to determine the best-selling video games. A description of its methodology follows:

Interviews are conducted with a national sample of 100 discount stores, 250 toy stores, 50 warehouse stores, and 50 video mail order companies.

Interviews with retail outlets are conducted in each of the 50 states on a disproportionate basis, that is, two discount stores, five toy stores, and one warehouse store are surveyed in each state. All stores are in the second largest city in each state. Specific stores within each city are identified by using the city's newspaper. Stores that advertise (and which as a result are assumed to be larger stores) are selected to be interviewed.

Mail order companies are selected from among all mail order advertisers in the current month's Nintendo magazine.

Interviews are conducted by telephone. The individual who answers the phone is asked "What are your five highest-selling games in the past week?" The highest-selling game is awarded five points, the next best selling four points, and so on. Points are then summed among all outlets.

Comment on this sampling plan. Do you agree that the plan is appropriate? Why or why not? If you do not feel that it is appropriate, propose, describe, and justify an alternative sampling plan. Be certain to address all applicable elements as shown in Figure 4.1.

4. Imagine that you are a research consultant. A client comes to you and says that his company has just developed a new financial planning program to help parents plan and save for their child's college education. The plan is structured to help parents start with a minimum of investment and build up the balance without undue pressure on the family's monthly budget. No research has ever been done for this client for this product. All you and the client's researcher have to go on are assumptions that you think are correct.

The client recommends that research be conducted to determine the reactions to various ways in which the program can be marketed and advertised. The client sends you a recommendation for who should be included in the study. The recommendation reads as follows:

I recommend that we conduct a telephone study among parents. Further, because the study is an attempt to assess these parents' interest in programs to help them get an early start in planning for their children's college education I recommend that the interviews, for the sake of efficiency, be conducted among those I feel would most likely be interested in, and have the resources for, participation in such a college planning program, namely those households with small children with total household incomes more than $45,000 per year. We can purchase a comprehensive list of households meeting these criteria from a list supplier and then randomly sample from the list.

Respond to the target universe and sample frame recommendations. Would you accept them as presented, or would you suggest any revisions or modifications? Describe and justify any recommended modifications or revisions.

5. Assume that Family Magazine is one of the country's leading women's magazines and has a national circulation of more than 7,000,000 per copy. Its readers are primarily women. The editors of the magazine decide that they want to do a study of the views and attitudes of the American woman. Specifically, they want the research to be a definitive study and report national trends. They will call this study "The American Woman: What She Thinks and Feels." To collect data for the study, the editors hire an independent research company to write the questionnaire. The editors then take the questionnaire and insert it in one issue of the magazine. The questionnaire is a self-mailer. Readers can indicate their opinions (anonymously) and then return the questionnaire postpaid. Response is exceptional. Nearly 200,000 readers return a questionnaire. The research company analyzes the data, and editors print the results.

Assess the acceptability or unacceptability of this method of data collection given the aims and goals of the magazine's editors.

6. Your client Tastee-Good Ice Cream is ready to bring its new ice cream to market. This ice cream will provide all the flavor and richness of other premium ice creams (such as Hagen-Daas) without fat, calories, or artificial ingredients or sweeteners. The agency has been asked to think of some ways to advertise this product. The creative staff has, after an extensive review of consumer research, created three different creative approaches. Each approach has been turned into a sample commercial. Note, however, that while the creative approaches (i.e., commercials) are different, the intent of all three commercials is the same. The commercials are designed to make women with specific characteristics try the ice cream.

You need to know which creative approach, as represented in the three commercials, is the one that should be selected for production. Each commercial needs to be tested among the target audience in finished form. The target audience has been defined in terms

of demographic, psychographic, and brand specific characteristics as follows:

All of the women we want to talk to must
- be between the ages of 25 and 34,
- live in a household with an annual income of between $40,000 and $50,000,
- be concerned about their weight,
- view ice cream as an indulgence or a treat,
- not be price-conscious when it comes to the price that they pay for packaged ice cream.

Moreover, these women may or may not currently be regular eaters of ice cream. In addition to satisfying all of the previously mentioned characteristics, they must also satisfy one of the following:

- If they eat packaged ice cream regularly, then they must usually eat premium ice cream. (Note, the word "premium" is a trade word, consumers may not use that word to describe the higher-end ice creams.)
- If they do eat packaged ice cream regularly, then it does not matter what type of packaged ice cream they eat. However, the main reason they are not regular eaters of ice cream must be that they are concerned about the perceived negative effects of ice cream on their weight or health.

It is very important that we understand the views of these women in a way that provides a high degree of confidence in the insights and generalizations drawn from the interviews. To respond to the agency's needs, please do the following. First, comment on the adequacy of the target population definition. Feel free to modify the target definition to eliminate problems associated with the lack of clarity. Second, recommend a sampling approach and, if needed, the sample frame. Third, recommend and justify a specific sampling technique. Finally, present your recommendations in terms of sample size.

Application exercises 7 through 11 relate to the Pew research studies provided in the online supplemental readings.

7. The Parent and Teen Survey on Gaming and Civic Engagement used a landline-only sample, while the Values Project research used both landline and cell phone samples. Comment on the potential use of an additional cell phone

sample for the Parent and Teen Survey. Do you recommend the addition of a cell phone-only sample? What would be the advantages? The disadvantages? Regardless of your recommendation, revise the Pew sample plan to include a cell phone sample.

8. The Values Study uses a sampling plan where (for the landline interviews) the interviewer first asks to speak with "the youngest male, 18 years of age or older, who is now at home." If there is no eligible male at home, interviewers ask to speak with "the youngest female, 18 years of age or older, who is now at home." The rationale for this approach is that it improves participation among young people who are often more difficult to interview than older people because of their lifestyles.

   First, comment on this sampling approach. Do you agree with the rationale, or do you feel that it introduces any form of bias into the survey? What is your rationale for your point of view? Second, propose two alternative methods for identifying respondents. Discuss the strengths and weaknesses of each of your proposed plans. Would you select either of your proposed sampling plans over the plan described in the case study?

9. The Digital Footprint study used a mixed-mode approach where random digit dialing was used to collect the quantitative data and the Internet was used for the collection of the qualitative data related to the search for personal information. Clearly, the Internet was the only way to collect the latter information. Consider, however, the use of the random digit dialing for the collection of the quantitative data. Do you believe that the Internet, rather than telephones, should have been used to collect the quantitative data? Why? What are the strengths and weaknesses of an Internet versus telephone mode of data collection for this type of data? Which approach produces less bias? Finally, prepare a detailed sampling plan that explains how data would be collected if one decided to use the Internet for data collection.

10. The Journalism Self-Censorship study was conducted in 2000 and therefore relied on materials created several years ago. For the time period, the sampling plan was close to ideal. Imagine, however, that the Pew Research Center now wants to revisit this topic Clearly the original sampling plan is no longer relevant, especially since it does not contain any mention of online sources. Additionally, the definitions of "journalist" and "news source" have changed since 2000, again because of online developments. With these developments in mind, prepare a detailed sampling plan for the new research study. Be certain to include enough detail (as in the original plan) to allow others to evaluate the acceptability of the plan. Once the plan is completed, prepare a short paper that provides a rationale for the specific decisions represented in the plan, especially noting the reasons for modification to the original plan.

11. The America's Place in the World Study (similar to the Journalism Self-Censorship study) was conducted over a decade ago, before the significant growth of the Internet. As a result, the types of "influentials" noted in the study have likely changed. Imagine that the Pew Research Center wants to update this study recognizing that the definition and sources of "influentials" have changed since the first study was conducted. With these issues in mind, present a detailed sampling plan for the new research study. Be certain to include enough detail (as in the original plan) to allow others to evaluate the acceptability of the plan. Once the plan is completed, prepare a short paper that provides a rationale for the specific decisions represented in the plan, especially noting the reasons for modifications to the original plan.

Theory Underlying Sample Size Determination

As discussed earlier in the chapter, sample size is determined in light of confidence intervals and confidence levels. Greater precision in either or both levels requires larger sample sizes. The calculation to determine sample size, however, depends upon whether your key measures are proportions or averages.

SAMPLE SIZE WHEN THE ESTIMATE IS A PROPORTION

When the research results are expected to be reported as proportions (e.g., "83% of the sample agrees that . . ."), then a table such as that shown in Figure 4.10 may be used to determine the appropriate sample size. (All the information presented in this table is

Sample Size	Expected Level of Response									
	5% or 95%	10% or 90%	15% or 85%	20% or 80%	25% or 75%	30% or 70%	35% or 65%	40% or 60%	45% or 55%	50%
100	4.4	6.0	7.1	8.0	8.7	9.2	9.5	9.8	9.9	10.0
200	3.1	4.7	5.0	5.7	6.1	6.5	6.7	6.9	7.0	7.2
300	2.5	3.5	4.2	4.6	5.0	5.3	5.5	5.7	5.7	5.8
400	2.2	3.0	3.6	4.0	4.3	4.6	4.8	4.9	5.0	5.0
500	1.9	2.7	3.2	3.6	3.9	4.1	4.3	4.4	4.5	4.5
600	1.8	2.5	2.9	3.3	3.5	3.7	3.9	4.0	4.0	4.1
700	1.6	2.3	2.7	3.0	3.3	3.5	3.6	3.7	3.8	3.8
800	1.5	2.2	2.5	2.8	3.1	3.2	3.4	3.5	3.5	3.5
900	1.4	2.0	2.4	2.7	2.9	3.1	3.2	3.3	3.3	3.3
1,000	1.4	1.9	2.3	2.5	2.7	2.9	3.0	3.1	3.1	3.2
1,500	1.1	1.5	1.8	2.0	2.2	2.4	2.5	2.5	2.6	2.6
2,000	1.0	1.3	1.6	1.8	1.9	2.0	2.1	2.2	2.2	2.2
3,000	.8	1.1	1.3	1.5	1.6	1.7	1.7	1.8	1.8	1.8
5,000	.6	.8	1.0	1.1	1.2	1.3	1.3	1.4	1.4	1.4

FIGURE 4.10 Confidence Intervals for Various Sample Sizes and Expected Level of Response (Confidence Level = 95%)

based on a 95% confidence level.) To use this table, you need to have some estimate of the sample's level of response. For example, assume that there are three agree/disagree key questions on a study and that you expect 10% of the sample to agree with one question, 20% to agree with the second, and 85% to agree with the third. Additionally, assume that you want to have a small confidence interval, no more than ±3% for any of the three independent questions. The table shown in Figure 4.10 indicates that a confidence interval of no more than ±3% for an expected response level of:

- 10% requires a sample of 400,
- 20% requires a sample of 700, and
- 85% requires a sample of about 600.

Given these parameters, a sample of about 700 is needed (the largest of the three required sample sizes). If there is doubt as to the level of response, then the use of a 50% estimate for level of response or agreement is appropriate.

There are times, however, when you will want to set a confidence level different than that provided in the table in Figure 4.10. In these cases, sample size can be determined through the formula:

$$sample\ size = \left(\frac{z}{e}\right)^2 \times p \times (1 - p)$$

where p represents the anticipated level of response, z represents the z score for a specific confidence level, and e represents the desired confidence interval. Z scores for specific confidence levels are as follows:

Confidence Level	**Z Score**
99%	2.57
95%	1.96
90%	1.64

Imagine that you ask a group of respondents "Are you aware of advertising for Microsoft Zune?" and you anticipate the proportion saying "yes" to be 35%. Additionally, you want to be 99% confident that the actual proportion estimated by the research is within ±2%. The required sample size for these desired levels of confidence would be:

$$sample\ size = \left(\frac{z}{e}\right)^2 \times p \times (1 - p)$$

$$sample\ size = \left(\frac{2.57}{.02}\right)^2 \times .35 \times (1 - .35)$$

$$sample\ size = (128.5)^2 \times .35 \times (.65)$$

$$sample\ size = 3757$$

The sample size is large because the confidence level and confidence interval demand a high level of precision. Sample size drops dramatically, however, when the confidence interval is raised to ±4% and the confidence level is lowered to 95%:

$$sample\ size = \left(\frac{z}{e}\right)^2 \times p \times (1 - p)$$

$$sample\ size = \left(\frac{1.96}{.04}\right)^2 \times .35 \times (1 - .35)$$

$$sample\ size = (49)^2 \times .35 \times (.65)$$

$$sample\ size = 546$$

The table in Figure 4.10 also illustrates this relationship between confidence intervals and sample size. As can be seen, when we hold the confidence level constant, it takes a fourfold increase in sample size to reduce the confidence interval by half. For example, at the 20% level of expected response, a sample of 100 provides a confidence interval of ±8%, a sample of 400 provides a confidence interval of ±4%, and a sample of about 1,600 provides a confidence interval of about ±2%. The relationship between accuracy (as reflected in smaller confidence intervals) and sample size is illustrated in Figure 4.11. As can be seen, large increases in accuracy are achieved by small increases in sample size up to sample sizes of about 1,000. However, increases in accuracy slow significantly at sample sizes of more than 1,000. This is why most consumer, marketing, and advertising research studies rarely exceed a sample of 1,000 individuals.[20]

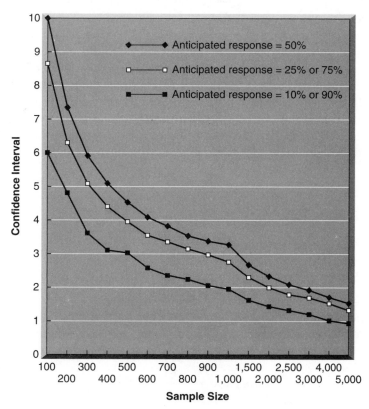

FIGURE 4.11 Relationship Between Sample Size and Confidence Intervals

SAMPLE SIZE WHEN THE ESTIMATE IS A MEAN

Sample sizes for estimates that are means or averages can also be computed. In these cases, an estimate of the range of response is required in addition to the specification of a confidence level and confidence interval. (The range of response is expressed as a "standard deviation." See Chapter 16 for a detailed discussion of the computation and interpretation of this measure.) Because population standard deviations are rarely known, it is typically estimated in one of three ways:

1. Estimate the standard deviation from a prior, similar study conducted among the same population, or
2. Conduct a small pilot study, use the standard deviation from the pilot study as the estimate of the population standard deviation, or
3. Divide the range of response by 4; that is, add the values of the two most extreme response options, and then divide the sum by 4.

Once the standard deviation is estimated and the confidence interval and confidence level are determined, sample size can be estimated through the formula:

$$sample\ size = \frac{z^2 \times s^2}{e^2}$$

where, as in the previous formula, z represents the z score for a specific confidence level (taken from the table shown earlier) and e represents the desired confidence interval. The new term in this equation, s, represents the estimate of the population standard deviation.

Consider an example similar to the one just discussed. Imagine that you ask a group of respondents, "On a scale of one to five, please rate the believability of IBM office product advertising?" You want to be 95% confident that the average rating estimated by the research is within plus or minus .2 points of the true population average. You estimate the sample standard deviation to be 1.5, derived by adding the extremes of the rating scale and dividing by 4 (i.e., $5 + 1 \div 4 = 1.5$). The required sample size for these desired levels of confidence would be 216, calculated as

$$sample\ size = \frac{z^2 \times s^2}{e^2}$$

$$sample\ size = \frac{1.96^2 \times 1.5^2}{.2^2}$$

$$sample\ size = \frac{3.84 \times 2.25}{.04}$$

$$sample\ size = 216$$

As with the prior formula, changes to the confidence level and confidence interval result in changes to required sample size. For example, the required sample size increases significantly if we raise the confidence level to 99% and lower the confidence interval to .1:

$$sample\ size = \frac{z^2 \times s^2}{e^2}$$

$$sample\ size = \frac{2.56^2 \times 1.5^2}{.1^2}$$

$$sample\ size = \frac{6.55 \times 2.25}{.01}$$

$$sample\ size = 1474$$

In sum, the relationship between sample size and accuracy in the survey results is an important consideration when attempting to balance sample size and confidence. When evaluating alternative sample sizes, you need to ask: "Is the increased cost of precision justified by the increased costs of data collection? For example, is a reduction in the confidence level from ±3% to ±1.5% justified given a quadrupled increase in the cost of interviewing?"

Endnotes

1. Pew Research Center (2009). "Why Surveys of Muslim Americans Differ" at http://pew research.org/pubs/1144/muslim-americans-pew-research-survey-gallup.

2. A fourth sampling method is cluster sampling, which is primarily used for research with data collection needs that require personal, at-home interviews. Cluster sampling is appropriate to this form of data collection because it shifts data collection to groups of sampling units rather than individual sampling units. Cluster sampling works as follows: First, the universe described in the sample universe definition is divided into groups, or clusters where every element of the universe is contained in one and only one cluster. Second, clusters are examined for internal representativness. Each cluster should be a "miniuniverse"; that is, the characteristics of the cluster should mirror the characteristics of the total universe. Third, clusters are examined for external comparability. Clusters should be equivalent to each other with regard to important characteristics. Fourth, one or more of the clusters is selected to represent the total universe. Fifth, simple, systematic, or stratified sampling is used to select elements within the cluster. For further discussion of cluster sampling, see Stat Trek, "Statistics Tutorial: Cluster Sampling" at http://stattrek.com/Lesson6/CLS.aspx?Tutorial=Stat.

3. The sample frame for this example, individuals aged 18 to 24 with either a land line or cell phone, is likely to provide good representation of the total universe as the vast majority of 18- to 24-year olds will have one of these telephone connections.

4. The Raosoft sample size calculator is located at http://www.raosoft.com/samplesize.html. Other calculators can be found typing "sample size calculator" in any search engine.

5. These examples are adapted from Earl Babbie (1986). *The Practice of Social Research* (4th Edition) (Belmont, CA: Wadsworth Publishing Company).

6. Pew Center for the People & the Press (2008). "The Impact Of "Cell-Only" On Public Opinion Polling" at http://peoplepress.org/report/391/.

7. Pew Center, op. cit.

8. Lee Rainie (2008). "Polling in the Age of the Cell Phone" at http://www.pewinternet.org/Commentary/2008/June/Polling-in-the-age-of-the-cell-phone.aspx.

9. Pew Center for People & the Press (undated). "About Our Survey Methodology in Detail" at http://peoplepress.org/methodology/about/.

10. See Green Book (2009) for a listing at http://www.greenbook.org/market-research-firms.cfm/online-panels.

11. E-rewards (2009). "What Defines Online Panel Quality" at http://www.e-rewardsresearch.com/downloads/WhatDefinesOnlinePanelQual.pdf. All of the points noted apply to the e-Rewards panel. In addition, Knowledge Networks provides additional insight into panel evaluation and verification at http://www.knowledgenetworks.com/ganp/reviewer-info.html.

12. M. Q. Patton (1990). *Qualitative Evaluation and Research Methods (2nd ed.)* (Newbury Park, CA: Sage Publications).

13. Patton, op. cit.

14. R. Gomm, G. Needham and A. Bullman (2000). *Evaluating Research in Health and Social Care* (London, England: Sage Publications).

15. See Imelda T. Coyne (1997). "Sampling in Qualitative Research. Purposeful and Theoretical Sampling; Merging or Clear Boundaries?" *Journal of Advanced Nursing* 26: 623-630.

16. Margarete Sandelowski (1995). "Sample Size in Qualitative Research," *Research in Nursing & Health* 18: 179–183.

17. Sandelowski, op. cit.

18. See http://pewresearch.org/.

19. All footnoted material in these readings is directly taken or edited from Pew Center source material and is quoted and reproduced with permission of the Pew Research Center. Specific sources are provided in footnotes.

20. When the target population exceeds about 20,000 individuals, then the relationship between sample size and confidence interval becomes independent of the size of the target population. A sample of 1,000 will provide the same confidence interval regardless of whether the target population consists of 20,000, 1,000.000, or 10,000,000 individuals.

CHAPTER 5

Collecting Qualitative Insights

Qualitative research, typically characterized by small sample sizes and probing open-ended questions, helps researchers to get "beneath the surface" by providing feelings, textures, a sense of intensity, and a degree of nuance beyond the numeric descriptions provided by quantitative research. This chapter focuses on qualitative research techniques and begins with a discussion of the characteristics of qualitative research. This is followed by a discussion of the three primary types of questions/techniques used to collect qualitative data. The chapter concludes with direction for the planning and conduct of the qualitative interview.

***

When you are done reading this chapter, you should have a better understanding of:

- the advantages and disadvantages of different approaches to qualitative research and the collection of qualitative information
- the characteristics and appropriate use of direct, projective, and process interviewing techniques
- how to plan for and carry out the qualitative interview, including when and how to probe for additional insights

Qualitative advertising research typically entails the intensive interviewing of a small number of individuals to acquire detailed, in-depth insights into their attitudes, beliefs, motivations, and lifestyles.[1] The goal is to provide a better understanding *why* individuals act as they do rather than numeric descriptions of *what* people do and think. Thus, qualitative research focuses on discovering the nature or structure of attitudes and motivations rather than their frequency or distribution.

The characteristics and goals of qualitative research make it especially well-suited for satisfying a broad range of advertising informational needs. Qualitative research is appropriate whenever there is a need to

- understand the underlying relationship between consumers' feelings, attitudes, beliefs, and their behaviors, especially when information on this relationship cannot be obtained through direct, structured, primarily closed-ended questioning;
- obtain preliminary or background information when little is currently known;
- listen to consumers express their ideas in their own words and/or have first-hand observation of consumers' responses;
- complement quantitative research, either in the preliminary or in the post-research stages.[2] In this regard, qualitative research can help to
  - better define and understand a marketing or advertising problem before quantitative research is conducted;
  - develop hypotheses before the planning and initiation of quantitative research;
  - evaluate the appropriateness of a proposed quantitative research design or sampling plan, for example, when determining the inclusion or exclusion of consumers with certain demographic or behavioral characteristics;
  - obtain insights into audiences of interest to facilitate the creation of quantitative scales or other question types;[3]
  - pilot test questionnaires or similar forms of survey research instruments;
  - amplify, explain, or further explore points emerging from a quantitative study without having to repeat the quantitative study.

Qualitative research works well in each of the prior situations because of its ability to let researchers "get close to the data," to see and hear consumers express their thoughts in their own words. The insights that occur from seeing and hearing the consumer are often a missing component of the numeric summaries reported in quantitative research. Goldman and McDonald point out that:

> Although qualitative research does not tell you how widely distributed an attitude or motivation might be, it does tell you—and in ways surveys cannot— from where those attitudes arise, how they are structured, and what broader significance they may have for consumer behavior. The rich qualitative insights that spring from close inspection of individuals can never be duplicated by large-scale surveys which view the market from a more distant vantage point.[4]

The ability to see and hear consumers is important. Not only does this provide for deeper insights, it also allows researchers to draw insights and explanations from respondents themselves, rather than having to predetermine areas of response or importance.

Finally, compared with quantitative research, qualitative research is (a) often quicker and less costly, especially for satisfying informational needs that do not require numeric, statistically projectable data and (b) more flexible. Qualitative research permits the research team to change course in the middle of a research study. A researcher can, for example, modify the sequence of questions, change question wording, or add new areas to explore.

It is important to note, however, that qualitative research also has limitations that make it an unacceptable procedure for satisfying some forms of advertising-related informational needs. First, and perhaps most important, generalizations obtained from qualitative research are severely limited. In fact, a researcher can confidently generalize the results of a quantitative study *only* to those individuals who participated in that study. There is no assurance that the small number of individuals who participated in the research is in any way representative of the larger population from which they were drawn. Given this limitation, the results of qualitative research should be treated as directional rather than definitive. Second, the small sample sizes used in qualitative research prevent the numeric description of findings. Thus, qualitative research should be avoided when numeric descriptions of population characteristics are required. Third, the interpretation of qualitative research data is more subjective than the interpretation of quantitative data because the basis of qualitative analysis is individuals' comments and verbal responses as opposed to numeric ratings or rankings. As a result, qualitative research should not be used when a nonsubjective and detached description of findings is required.

PERSONAL AND FOCUS GROUP INTERVIEWS

The most common approaches to qualitative advertising research are personal and focus group interviews.

Personal Interviews

Personal interviews (also known as one-on-one, depth, or in-depth interviews) typically take between 30 and 60 minutes and consist of a private, face-to-face conversation between a trained qualitative interviewer and a respondent. Given the time and expense associated with this form of qualitative research, most studies utilizing personal interviews have samples of between 5 and 15 individuals.

A personal interview is a free-flowing, yet structured, conversation between the interviewer and the respondent. While the interviewer and the respondent know the specific topics to be addressed during the interview, the interviewer is free to pursue each topic in different ways with different respondents. Moreover, during the interview, the interviewer is free to create questions and to probe responses that seem interesting and relevant to the goals and informational needs motivating the research. Thus, within a specific research study, the informational goals of each personal interview remain constant although the actual structure of the interviews typically varies among respondents. (The last section of this chapter provides additional insight into the qualitative interview.)

Personal interviews are appropriate for situations in which extensive, detailed probing of attitudes, behaviors, motivations, or needs are required. This is because in the personal interview setting, a respondent is free to express his or her ideas without fear of comment or evaluation from others, as in a focus group. In addition, a personal interview eliminates the potential for group pressure or social norms to alter or discourage honesty in response.

Focus Groups and Minigroups

Focus groups and minigroups are the focused discussion of a *group* of individuals led by a trained moderator. The moderator's role is to facilitate the discussion among members of the group in subjects relevant to the areas of study and informational needs. The flexibility of focus groups makes it a common approach for meeting many marketer and advertiser informational needs, particularly in the areas of new product idea generation; product positioning and product perceptions; creative product and package screening; and explorations of consumers' attitudes, beliefs, needs, and motivations.

Focus groups and minigroups are similar in orientation and structure. Each lasts about 1½ to 2 hours and uses a moderator who, relying on a discussion guide, moves the discussion through desired topic areas. The primary difference between focus groups and minigroups is in the number of participants. Focus groups generally consist of between 8 and 12 individuals. Minigroups are smaller, generally consisting of between three and six individuals.

ADVANTAGES OF FOCUS GROUPS.   The group nature of focus group discussion provides five potential advantages over personal interviews.

First, the interactive nature of the discussion helps focus group participants expand on and refine their own opinions. It is common for an individual's comments in a focus group to

- stimulate thoughts in other respondents,
- cause other respondents to view things differently,
- stimulate greater depth of discussion,
- remind individuals of things they may have forgotten, or
- help other respondents better verbalize their thoughts and opinions.

Second, focus groups are often more stimulating and exciting for participants versus depth interviews. The heightened interest that results from participating in a group discussion increases the likelihood that participants will pay attention, participate in the discussion, and provide more than superficial responses.

Third, focus groups can be more spontaneous than personal interviews. A well-moderated group encourages respondents to express their opinions and fosters active, positive interchanges between respondents. This spontaneity reduces defense mechanisms and self-editing and encourages respondents to share actual opinions. Furthermore, because there are always other participants in the group, the spontaneity of the group reduces the chances of participants "making-up" answers because they feel pressure to do so.

Fourth, focus groups are quicker to conduct and analyze versus personal interviews. Groups can be put together very quickly, often in a week or less, with reports of the findings following within a week or two of the final group.

Finally, the per respondent cost of focus group studies is generally less than the per respondent cost of personal interviews. A typical focus group, including moderator fees, typically costs about $2,500, much less than the cost of conducting a comparable number of personal interviews.

DISADVANTAGES OF FOCUS GROUPS.   In addition to the problems of generalizability shared by all qualitative research, focus groups have four significant disadvantages versus personal interviews.

First, there is always the possibility that one respondent will dominate the discussion or impose a particular point of view, setting a tone and direction counter to that of the group's or moderator's preference. For example, it may be difficult for participants to admit serving their children sugared cereal if one respondent begins the discussion by saying "Only mothers who don't care about their children's health serve their children cereal loaded with sugar."

Second, beyond the bias introduced by dominant respondents, there is the potential for moderator-introduced bias. A moderator can introduce significant bias into the group and the direction of the group's discussion by shifting or introducing topics too rapidly, by implicitly or explicitly encouraging certain points of view, or by failing to introduce or probe topics or responses.

Third, there is the possibility that group pressures can distort the expression of individual opinions. Some respondents may be reluctant to express opinions that they feel deviate from accepted or expressed group norms while others may not verbalize opinions that they feel run counter to the prevailing group consensus.

Fourth, and most important, the data and insights obtained from focus group discussions represent group, not individual, data. Focus group data reflects the collective ideas of the group, and, as a result, focus groups do not provide the depth of individual detail commonly obtained from personal interviews.[5]

APPROACHES TO COLLECTING QUALITATIVE INSIGHTS

There are three primary approaches to the collection of qualitative insights via personal interviews or focus groups. This section begins with a discussion of direct and projective question types and concludes with a discussion of process-oriented qualitative techniques.

Direct Question Types

Direct questions ask an individual to respond to a focused, generally narrow request for information. These question types include:

- Specification
- Structural
- Grand tour
- Idealization
- Hypothetical-interaction
- Third-person

SPECIFICATION QUESTIONS.   Specification questions are explicit requests for specific rational or emotional information. These questions are most useful in providing background information or for laying the foundation for more extensive discussion. Responses to these types of questions can be the starting point for delving deeper into respondent's attitudes, beliefs, and feelings. In spite of their direct and factual nature, however, these questions should always be asked in an open-ended manner, for example:

> What are the names of all the brands of soda that you have consumed within the past week?
>
> What are the most important reasons why you read the Daily Dirt Blog?
>
> How did you feel when you discovered the chips had no fat but 880 mg. of sodium per serving?

As can be seen, these questions typically ask "how" or "what." You should avoid wording these types of questions to allow for just a "yes" or "no" response.

You might think that specification questions should also allow you to ask "why," for example, "Why did you switch brands of toothpaste?" Qualitative interviewers have found, however, that "why" questions should probably be avoided. Dana notes, "Because 'why' questions ask informants to justify responses, thoughts or feelings, 'why' questions can potentially be interpreted by informants as threatening. If threatened, informants may become defensive in their responses, affecting the data obtained. If carried to an extreme, the researcher risks alienating the informant and thereby looses a valuable source for data collection [and] analysis."[6] "Why" questions are also difficult questions for respondents to answer because they require depth of self-analysis and introspection. For these reasons, it is recommended that you use alternate question forms to uncover "why" insights. Questions such as "Why did you switch brands of toothpaste?" for example, can be rephrased as "What are some reasons for your switch to your new brand of toothpaste?"

STRUCTURAL QUESTIONS.   Structural questions take a step beyond specification questions to help a researcher understand the *full range* of respondents' feelings and/or knowledge within a specific area. As a result, these questions are typically the starting point for the enumeration of a long list of thoughts or feelings. Here, for example, a respondent might be asked to explain "What are all the different ways that you and your friends talk about social networking sites?" or "What are all the different criteria you use to evaluate different search engines?"

GRAND TOUR QUESTIONS.   Grand tour questions[7] are less restrictive and more open-ended than the prior two types of questions. These questions ask a respondent to reconstruct a routine, procedure, activity, or event that took place at a particular time in his or her life. The respondent is the tour guide, describing for the "uninformed" interviewer the steps taken and the thoughts or feelings associated with each step. The respondent begins at the point in time specified in the question and continues on until the experience or event is fully described, for example:

> You mentioned that you purchased a new cell phone within the past month. Can you please describe for me the events that led up to the purchase and selection

of your particular phone? Start at the point when you first decided you needed a new phone and tell me your thoughts and actions at each step in the process.

You said that you just tried a no fat ice cream for the first time. Can you please describe for me your reactions and feelings the first time you ate this ice cream. What were you thinking prior to the first tasting? How did the tasting go? What were your thoughts after the tasting? I'd like to learn what you were thinking and feeling at each point.

Grand tour questions are an excellent way to move beyond specification and structural questions because they are nonthreatening, have no single correct answer, and establish rapport by showing that the interviewer is interested in the respondent's experiences. When using grand tour questions, keep in mind that this is a powerful technique that allows you to move beyond a discussion of content into one of process. You can use these types of questions to learn both what a person did (the content) and *why* he or she made certain decisions as well as the feelings associated with those decisions (the process). The following guidelines increase the success of grand tour questions:

- *Don't rush.* Pacing probes as a respondent talks allows him or her to better "engage in the complex task of remembering, reflecting, and, ultimately, articulating their thoughts. Conscious awareness of past memories is qualitatively different from current awareness . . . gathering and reconstructing these disparate traces of memory can take time . . . slowing down the interview pace and offering silence might give interviewees needed space to recognize, process, and verbalize the . . . internal experiences being requested."

- *Keep the focus on the past.* When answering grand tour questions, a respondent may slip into the present, commenting on current feelings compared to feelings encountered during the process being described. In these situations, prompts that employ words like *was*, *did*, and *then* work well to bring the respondent's focus back to his or her original memories.

- *Don't lose the focus on process.* Since it is easier to discuss content versus process, a respondent may focus his or her discussion of the former by describing "what I did." When this happens, it is important to acknowledge the importance of learning about the content, but then "gently redirect the participant back to inner processes." For example:

RESPONDENT: Well, I remember the first time I tried to set up my page on Facebook. The first thing I tried to do was add pictures to my page. What a mess that turned out to be.

INTERVIEWER: Were pictures important to you?

RESPONDENT: Yeah, that's the whole reason I set the page up.

INTERVIEWER: You said it was a mess, can you tell me what you mean?

RESPONDENT: I just couldn't get the page to look good, no matter what I tried. And the page never did look the way I wanted it to.

INTERVIEWER: And how did this make you feel? Can you describe for me what were you feeling at that point?

IDEALIZATION QUESTIONS.   Idealization questions ask a respondent to speculate about "the ideal," for example, the ideal product or ideal type of product category advertising. Once the ideal is described, specific, existing instances are then discussed within the context of the ideal. For example, a respondent might be asked to "describe the ideal dishwashing detergent" after which the characteristics of specific dishwashing products are compared to the ideal. The gap between existing and ideal product characteristics provides direction for identifying potential product gaps and new product opportunities. Alternatively, the interviewer can propose or describe the characteristics of the "ideal" and then ask the respondent to evaluate and respond to the description. Here, for example, the interviewer might say, "Here are some characteristics of what might be considered an ideal dishwashing detergent. It is extremely mild on the hands and is biodegradable. It works on all types of baked-on stains. How does this description match with your ideal dishwashing product? Are there any benefits missing? Are there any benefits that are not important to you?"

HYPOTHETICAL-INTERACTION QUESTIONS.   Hypothetical-interaction questions present a plausible situation and ask the respondent to verbalize how he or she would respond in that situation. The situation can describe a respondent's interaction with other individuals or products, for example:

> Imagine that the director and creator of Calvin Klein's jeans advertising were sitting across the table from you. Describe how you would feel and what you would be thinking. What types of questions might you ask these people? What would you anticipate their answers to your questions might be?

> Imagine that you were just invited to visit a new social networking site that describes itself as "the place where those in the know place their profiles." What would you expect the home page of this site to look like?

Hypothetical-interaction questions can also be used as the stimulus for more extended questioning designed to uncover brand beliefs and attitudes. Baumal[8] provides this example:

> First, I want you to close your eyes and think about the following. You have just won a radio contest—a free trip to a mystery vacation. You know that you have an all-expense-paid week's vacation, so you are excited. Now, I want you to picture yourself on the plane to the mystery destination, and you are very relaxed. You are in first-class and you are in a nice seat. You have a lot of legroom to stretch-out, so stretch out if you want to. You are enjoying a great movie on the in-flight entertainment system. As you continue this relaxing plane ride you are starting to envision your vacation. As the plane starts to descend, the pilot says "Ladies and gentlemen, we will soon be landing in Calgary." This is the first time you know where you are going.
>   Now, as you are sitting in the plane, what do you begin to feel towards the radio station for sending you to Calgary? What do you really want to tell them? What do you envision this vacation will be like for you?
>   Now, as you get off the plane, you look around the Calgary airport. What do you see? What do you smell? How does your luggage feel? How are you walking through the airport?

Next, you think about the kind of hotel the radio station will put you in. What kind of accommodations do you expect? Describe the room to me in detail.

Now, you are driving from the airport to your hotel and you are starting to get a good look at the city. As you look out the cab, you are going to see something that interests you. Look at it closely and describe it to me in detail. Now, you are going to look out the other side of the window and you are going to see something that repulses you. Look at it closely and describe it to me. Now, you get a call on your cell phone—it's a friend of yours that you share all your true feelings with—tell them what you see, think and feel about being in Calgary based on all your experiences so far.

Grand tour, idealization, and hypothetical-interaction questions draw upon a respondent's imagination and actual experiences. An interviewer using these types of questions works cooperatively with the respondent to make explicit underlying beliefs and attitudes and the reasons for these beliefs, attitudes, and behaviors. When used in a focus group setting, the moderator can use one person's grand tour or responses to an idealization question as the stimulus for further discussion. Grand tour, idealization, and hypothetical-interaction questions are often advantageously followed by third-person questions.

THIRD-PERSON QUESTIONS.   Third-person questions can be used to follow responses from the prior questions with nonthreatening challenges couched in the form of detached questions. A third-person question asks for elaboration within the context of an anonymous, absent person, for example,

You said that you think unlimited text messaging is the most important factor in the selection of a cell phone plan. Several others whom I've talked to have said the same thing. But, I've also heard quite a few individuals who have said that coverage and voice quality are the most important considerations. What do you think about this point of view? Do they have a point? What would you say to these people to convince them that your point of view is the most valid?

PROJECTIVE TECHNIQUES

The techniques discussed in the prior section are a relatively direct means of exploring individuals' attitudes and beliefs. There are times, however, when verbal, direct questions fail to get beneath the surface or when respondents are unable or unwilling to verbalize their thoughts and feelings. Donoghue provides a rationale for using projective techniques in these circumstances:

In certain circumstances it is impossible to obtain accurate information about what people think and feel by asking them to communicate their thoughts and feelings with direct questioning. In the typical interview, the subjects do not always share their innermost feelings with the researcher—who is after all a stranger. Moreover, the subjects are frequently unaware of their underlying motives, aspirations, values and attitudes in buying a product or choosing one brand instead of another. The may fear being irrational or "stupid" and may therefore be reluctant to admit certain types of purchasing behavior.[9]

In these cases, projective techniques are often a successful alternative to more direct and logical forms of questioning because they "are particularly useful at circumventing conscious resistance to direct questioning. They can be used to get participants' true opinion on a topic by getting them to comment about something indirectly, thus relieving inhibitions."[10]

Projective techniques have their roots in clinical psychology and are based on the *projective hypothesis,* which proposes that when people attempt to understand an ambiguous or vague stimulus, their interpretation and response to that stimulus reflects a projection of their needs, feelings, attitudes, and experiences. For example, when a young child hears a sound in another room late at night that he interprets as a "monster walking," he is projecting his fears onto the sound. The sound itself is an ambiguous, vague, but neutral stimulus. It is, in and of itself, neither good nor bad, fearsome nor friendly. What the child hears and verbalizes is a reflection of his underlying fears and attitudes. Projective techniques used in advertising and marketing research rely upon the same projective principle.

Keep in mind that in drawing meaning from projective techniques, "A subject's responses to projective techniques are not taken at face value . . . but are interpreted in terms of underlying meanings."[11] The challenge in using these techniques is to successfully discover these meanings.

The projective techniques used in advertising research can be divided into three groups:

- techniques that use verbal stimuli and responses (word association, sentence completion, and story completion),
- techniques that require the use of imagination or scenarios (personification, anthropomorphism, and role playing), and
- techniques that use pictures as stimuli.

Each of these techniques, which can be used in both group and personal interview settings, are discussed in the following sections.

Techniques Using Verbal Stimuli

WORD ASSOCIATION. Word association asks an individual to quickly respond to the presentation of words or phrases with the first thing or things that come to mind. This technique is commonly used to assess reactions to potential brand names, advertising campaign themes, and advertising slogans as well as to explore brand image. Word association works as follows: A respondent is first read (one at a time) a number of relatively neutral terms to help establish the demands of the technique. Then, words or phrases of interest to the advertiser are presented (again, one at a time), each of which is separated by several neutral terms (to reduce any bias due to anticipation or defense mechanisms).

For example, an airline might ask interviewees to respond to four potential taglines: "best in the sky," "on-time, every time," "your friend in the sky," and "the airline of pampered passengers." After all tag lines have been responded to, the interviewer can then return to and probe each response.[12]

SENTENCE AND STORY COMPLETION.   Sentence and story completion are considered by many researchers to be the most useful and reliable of all projective techniques. These approaches require a respondent to draw on his or her own attitudes and beliefs in order to complete an incomplete sentence or story.

Sentence completion requires a respondent to complete a sentence with the first phrase that comes to mind. For example, an individual might be asked to complete the sentence "The type of people who really like to spend lots of time on Facebook are. . . ." At first glance, it might appear that sentence completion is merely another way of asking an open-ended question (e.g., "What kind of people like to spend lots of time on Facebook?"). However, while open-ended and sentence completion formats are similar, each elicits different types of information. In direct questioning through open-ended questions, respondents typically give their answers after logical consideration and evaluation. However, because of the emphasis on speed of response in sentence completion tasks, internal defenses and self-editing tends to be greatly reduced.

Story completion is an expanded version of sentence completion. Story completion begins with an interviewer reading part of a story to the respondent. At some point, the narrative ends and the respondent is then asked to provide the end of the story. As with other projective techniques, it is hoped that the respondent will incorporate his or her own attitudes, beliefs, and experiences in the story ending. Imagine, for example, that First Savings Bank has aired an advertising campaign designed to increase favorable perceptions of the friendliness and responsiveness of their loan officers versus their major competitor, the First National Trust. A researcher could use direct questioning to examine differences in perceptions, or he or she could use story completion, as follows:

> Think about a man and woman who have been married for five years. They own their own home and have acquired enough equity in their home to take out a home equity loan. They wish to use the loan to finance a vacation.
>
> The husband, Tom, and wife, Mary, are discussing their own options after dinner one evening. They are tying to determine which banks to approach for the loan. They pick up the day's newspaper and see ads for First Savings Bank and First National Trust. They begin to discuss these banks.
>
> Tom says to Mary, "What about First Savings Bank?" Mary says
> _____
> (Probe for detail. Ask for dialogue from both Tom and Mary. After this segment is completed, continue)
>
> After they discuss the First Savings Bank, Mary says, "What about First National Trust?' Tom says _____.
> (Probe for detail. Ask for dialogue from both Tom and Mary. After this segment is completed, end)

Techniques Requiring Imagination or Scenarios

PERSONIFICATION AND ANTHROPOMORPHISM.   Personification and anthropomorphism[13] are techniques that ask individuals to take a leap in imagination in order to relate a brand or company to a well-known person, fictional character, or even an animal. In doing so, these approaches help researchers uncover subtle image characteristics that might otherwise require unusually high verbal facility to communicate.

There are two different approaches to personification and anthropomorphism. First, respondents can be asked a series of questions of the form:

> Think about a Jeep automobile. If a Jeep were to turn into a celebrity or other famous person, who would it be? Write down your first thought on the pad in front of you. Now, think about Chevrolet automobiles. If a Chevrolet were to turn into a celebrity or other famous person, who would it be? Write down your first thought on the pad in front of you.

> Think about a Jeep automobile. If a Jeep were to turn into an animal, what would it be? Write down your first thought on the pad in front of you. Now, think about Chevrolet automobiles. If a Chevrolet were to turn into an animal, what would it be? Write down your first thought on the pad in front of you.

Clearly, in this example, the brands would have different images (to be probed by the interviewer) if the response to Jeep was "Arnold Swartzeneger and a mountain lion" and the response to Chevrolet was "Paris Hilton and a mouse."

Second, a researcher can construct a list of personality characteristics and ask respondents to check all the characteristics that they feel apply to one brand or company versus another. The lists and checkmarks are not quantified, but instead are used as the basis for further discussion. Having individuals commit to their opinions in writing helps to both minimize group influences (in focus group settings) and to help respondents organize their thoughts prior to the start of discussion. An illustrative list of characteristics with directions to the respondent is shown in Figure 5.1.[14] Note how the list contains a mix of both positive and negative characteristics.

As with the prior approach, the value in this technique flows from the depth of discussion following characteristic selection.

ROLE-PLAYING.   One of the easiest projective techniques is role-playing. Here, rather than directly asking a person what he or she thinks, the question is couched in terms of "What would your neighbor think?" or "How do you think the average person would react?" This technique works well when the area under exploration is sensitive or responses may run counter to social or other norms. For example, a focus group might be composed of mothers, all of whom consistently serve their children sugared cereals for breakfast. They participate in this behavior even though they know there are better options and, as a consequence, they may be reluctant to admit they actually serve their children this type of cereal. In this case, a moderator using role-playing may ask, "Imagine that you are a mother who consistently serves her children sugared cereal. What do you think this mother is thinking? How does she feel about this?" Similarly, while an interviewer could ask respondents to describe how they feel they are treated by the

Below is a list of personality characteristics and two columns. In the first column, please check as many (or as few) of the characteristics that you think apply in any way to Facebook and its typical user. In the second column, please check up to three characteristics you think BEST describe Facebook and its typical user. Of course, there are no right or wrong answers.

This checklist is just to help you as we discuss Facebook and MySpace. I will not be collecting this form from you.

	Describes Facebook at all	Describes Facebook BEST
rebellious	[ ]	[ ]
ambitious	[ ]	[ ]
thoughtless	[ ]	[ ]
enthusiastic about life	[ ]	[ ]
lazy	[ ]	[ ]
arrogant	[ ]	[ ]
mature	[ ]	[ ]
optimistic	[ ]	[ ]
reliable	[ ]	[ ]
insecure	[ ]	[ ]
insensitive	[ ]	[ ]
serious	[ ]	[ ]
socially independent	[ ]	[ ]
adventurous	[ ]	[ ]
conventional	[ ]	[ ]
dull	[ ]	[ ]
creative	[ ]	[ ]
energetic	[ ]	[ ]
goal-oriented	[ ]	[ ]
unimaginative	[ ]	[ ]
results-oriented	[ ]	[ ]
risk-taker	[ ]	[ ]
relaxed	[ ]	[ ]

FIGURE 5.1 Personality Characteristics for use in Brand Personification

counter personnel of various department stores, it might be more insightful to ask each respondent to play the role and exhibit the behaviors of various stores' clerks.

Pictures as Stimuli

PICTURE PROJECTION.   Picture projection techniques use visual rather than verbal stimuli as the basis for respondent constructed stories or descriptions. A respondent is shown a picture and is then asked to provide the dialogue, thoughts, or feelings of other individuals in the drawing. The photographs shown in Photo 5.1 are examples of this type of projection technique and illustrate another way to assess perceptions, in this case the new car buying process and Ford dealerships. Respondents might be shown the pictures (in sequence) with the following introductions:

Picture A: This couple (picture shown on the top of Photo 5.1) is thinking about buying a new car, in particular, the Ford Focus. But first, they want to do their

PHOTO 5.1   Stimuli for Picture Projection

homework. What types of information do you think they are looking for? Can you name the specific Web sites that they might visit? Will they visit any blogs or other social networking sites? Why do you think this is the case? What, if anything, do you think they will print out and take to the dealership?

Picture B: The couple has arrived at the Ford dealership (picture shown in the middle of Photo 5.1). What's going through their minds as they are about to enter? Can you describe their thoughts and emotions? What are their expectations? Do they have any fears or anxiety? How do his thoughts and expectations differ from hers? How are both similar?

Picture C: As they approach the dealership, the couple sees two salespeople (pictures shown on the bottom of Photo 5.1). What are their first thoughts? Are they positive or negative? Do his thoughts differ from hers? How? Which salesperson do they approach? Why? What do they expect from the person they selected?

Picture projection can be used with both simple line drawings, finished drawings or photographs. In all cases the pictorial stimuli should allow the respondent to use his or her imagination to describe what is occurring.

PICTURE SORTS. Picture sorts, which are a useful way to obtain insight into how consumers distinguish between brands based on brand image, are appropriate for both individual interviews and focus group settings. This technique asks respondents to sort pictures of individuals based on the brands they think the pictured individuals are most likely to use. The technique requires a wide range of pictured individuals and that all brands of interest are identified in advance. The approach and goals of a picture sort are reflected in the following directions for a face-to-face interview:

1. Identify the target set of brands. These are the brands that your own brand currently competes with or aspires to compete with. Keep the number of brands relatively low, but nevertheless be certain that the set of brands includes the brands that are the category leaders or which may be important new category entrants. Prioritize the brands on the list, identifying no more than five brands (including your brand) to focus on in the next steps.

2. Place the logo or picture of each brand identified in the prior step on an index card plus add a card labeled "Other." Put all the cards out in a row (or two rows if space is short) in front of the respondent.

3. Explain to the respondent that you want to learn about how he or she thinks about the users of the different brands shown on the index cards. Give the respondent the deck of pictures. Ask the respondent to look through the pictures, one at a time, and to place the picture of each person on (or next to, below) an index card, indicating that the person pictured would be most likely to use that brand. Allow time to place all pictures, and let respondent know that he or she can move pictures from one brand to another, if desired. Continue until all pictures are placed.

4. For each brand, ask respondent to explain what individuals placed together have in common. When done, ask if there are any additional characteristics that distinguish individuals placed in different piles.

Focus groups use a similar process. Here, two or three groups can be formed and asked to perform the task cooperatively. Listening to each group as it works and then having each group provide a summary of the discussions that led to placement of pictures provides important insights into consumers' brand images. Alternatively, the entire focus group can work as one unit, discussing the placement of each picture and not accepting any placement until there is group consensus. As in the first approach, the discussion provides important insights.

Process Techniques

The prior sections described questions and techniques that can be used to provide insights into individuals' attitudes, beliefs, and behaviors. The three techniques presented in this section move beyond single questions or focused activities and require more extensive, active involvement on the part of the respondent.

REPERTORY GRID. The repertory grid is a simple yet powerful technique that helps marketers and advertisers identify the attributes and benefits consumers use to differentiate between competitive brands and products. Beyond this core application, the repertory grid can be used to determine the dimensions consumers use to evaluate any grouping of items, for example, advertising within a particular product category and package design for products within the same functional category. The repertory grid is best used in individual interviews.

The repertory grid is based on the psychological work of George Kelly[15] who proposed that each individual builds a system of bipolar constructs (also called dimensions) that help to reduce the complexity of attitudes and which subsequently guide behaviors. "Construct systems reflect our constant efforts to make sense of our world, just as scientists make sense of their subject-matter: we observe, we draw conclusions about patterns of cause and effect, and we behave according to those conclusions."[16] Constructs are typically simple, direct, easy to access and tend to divide a group of objects into two mutually exclusive groups. Constructs for a search engine might be, for example:

Cluttered results—uncluttered results

Provides useful search results—provides many wasted results

Quick—slow

The interview process described below illustrates how constructs are discovered, in this case for a set of competing brands.

1. Identify the target set of brands. These are the brands that your own brand currently competes with or aspires to compete with. Be certain that the set of brands includes the brands that are the category leaders or which may be important new category entries.

2. Place the logo or picture of each brand identified in the prior step on an index card.

3. Explain to the respondent that you want to learn his/her attitudes toward different brands and what he or she values and does not value with regard to these brands. The following instructions are a good model for explaining this task:

What to say . . .	*What to do . . .*
I'd like to know what you think about different brands, particularly how you distinguish between brands. I've put the logos of [number of brands] brands on these index cards, one logo on each card.	Show cards to respondent
I'm going to shuffle the cards and then give you three at a time to look at.	Shuffle cards
In looking at the brands on these three cards, which two would you say are the most similar?	Give first three cards to respondent. Wait for and record response. Put two selected cards close to each other in front of respondent, place the third, nonselected card apart but still in view.
What is the most important thing that these two brands have in common that distinguish them from the third brand?	Record response. Probe for "anything else?" When there are no additional responses, replace the cards in the deck, reshuffle, and repeat procedure with three new randomly selected cards. Continue until no additional insights are obtained.

As the interviews illustrate, the repertory grid method provides two important consumer insights. First, it identifies the constructs, dimensions, and benefits consumers use to distinguish between brands. Since these are consumer rather then advertiser-generated, the technique not only provides an understanding of the category from the consumers' perspective, it also has the additional potential to identify dimensions that were unknown to the advertiser prior to the research. Second, it provides insights into a brand's competitive position. The multiple shufflings of the deck results in random pairings of brands, allowing you to see how your and other brands are seen as similar or different to other brands.

The repertory grid approach is adaptable to different research and informational needs. You can, for example, present all of the index cards at one time to the respondent and then ask him or her to select the two brands from the deck that are most similar, explain why, and then select the one brand that is most dissimilar to the two selected, again explaining why. Or, you can present a pair of randomly selected brands to a respondent, asking for an explanation as to what the two brands have in common and how they differ.

Finally, as you think about exploring an individual's constructs, keep the following in mind:[17]

- *Construct systems are not static.* Individuals reassess constructs whenever they encounter new examples. Imagine that Mary uses the construct of "has exclusive information . . . just repeats same old information" to evaluate different music Web sites. Two of her favorite sites are *MaxMusic* and *MoreMusicNow*, both of which (in the past) she has evaluated quite positively on this dimension. However, after repeated recent visits to these two sites, she reassess her construct system: moving *MaxMusic* into the negative portion of the dimension and adding an entirely new construct "depth coverage of ska . . . lacking depth of ska information" to use in future evaluation of music sites.

- *Construct systems influence expectations and perceptions.* Construct systems are formed on the basis of past behaviors, and as a consequence, they set up expectations for how things will act in the future. If the *MaxMusic* site continues to exhibit a lack of exclusive information Mary may, after a while, stop using the site entirely, as she would expect this trend to continue.

- *Some constructs, and some aspects of construct systems, are more important than others.* "We feel, think, and behave according to our construct system . . . Some of our constructs—those which represent our core values and concern our key relationships—are complex, quite firmly fixed, wide-ranging, and difficult to change; others, about things which don't matter so much, or about which we haven't much experience, are simpler, narrower, and carry less personal commitment."

- *A person's construct system represents the truth as they understand it.* "Construct systems cannot be judged in terms of their objective truth—whatever 'objective' means in the world of personal feelings and choices. There is, therefore, no "right" or "wrong" outcome to repertory grid research."

LADDERING. Once you have identified the dimensions that consumers use to distinguish between brands (either through the repertory grid or through perceptual mapping, discussed in Chapter 18), laddering[18] works well to help you understand the meanings and values consumers associate with these dimensions. Laddering assumes that dimensions are only the starting point for consumers, and that that persuasive advertising strategy responds to the benefits and values that consumers assign to these dimensions. Means-end theory provides the rationale for wanting to understand the values assigned to dimensions, explained by MecAnalyst as follows:

> Product attributes are but means through which consumers achieve their ultimate values, ends, via the positive consequences or benefits accruing from the attributes. . . . In the means-end chain model, products are not chosen and purchased for themselves or their characteristics, but rather for the meaning they engender in the mind of prospects. In this way products, though selected for fairly concrete features, such as their characteristics and attributes (e.g., proportion of fat, color, origin, production method), and for the benefits which they are capable of providing—functional or psychosocial consequences (e.g., a healthy and tasty diet)—are in fact perceived subconsciously as aimed at and connected with the achievement of individual goals."[19]

A consumer may say, for example, that he bought an iPhone because of its G3 functionality (an attribute) but the real value attached to this function is that it impresses his friends, thereby increasing his own perceptions of status. The G3 functionality is only the means that helps achieve the more important end.

While there are several approaches to the collection of laddering data, the approach used by Johnson and Crudge to better understand search engine perceptions illustrates the most common approach:[20]

> Johnson and Crudge first used the repertory grid to identify the dimensions consumers use to distinguish one search engine from another. Laddering was then used to discover the values associated with each dimension, for example the dimension of "Interface Simple/Cluttered." Note that in laddering each dimension is written and presented as a continuum with two opposite poles. For this and the other dimensions, taken one at a time, each participant is asked to identify which end of the dimension is preferred, and then to explain why s/he prefers it. The question "Why is that important to you?" is the specific question asked. This question is then repeated after each subsequent answer until no further progress is made. At this point, focus is returned to the original dimension and the probe question is changed to "how is it different?" As before, this question is repeated until no additional insights are obtained. It is believed that the former question takes respondents higher up the ladder while the latter question takes respondents lower on the ladder.

An outlined example demonstrating laddering of the "Interface Simple/Cluttered" dimension described in the prior paragraph is provided in Figure 5.2a. Note that the rationale for the type of probe used at each stage is indicated in italics. A visual representation of the construct hierarchy is provided in Figure 5.2b.

MOOD BOARDS.   Mood boards are collages created by a respondent. The collage is intended to represent a respondent's thoughts and feelings with regard to a particular brand, company, product category, brand user group or other objects or individuals of interest. The creation of mood boards works well in both a personal and focus group setting.

The process of creating a mood board is straightforward. The interviewer provides each respondent (or group of respondents) with a large collection of magazines, preferably ones with a large number of photographs and illustrations. Sports, news, lifestyle, entertainment, and gossip magazines work well. A respondent is also given a large blank board, scissors, and glue. Imagine that you are responsible for the advertising for a travel site that is intended to cater to individuals aged 20 to 40 and that you want to use mood boards to understand these individuals goals, dreams, and attitudes with regard to international travel. The directions given to these individuals might be:

> I've provided a large pile of magazines, scissors, glue and a large blank board. Welcome back to kindergarten. I'd like you to think about your goals, aspirations and dreams with regard to international travel. Please go through the magazines and cut out those pictures that you think best represent these things for you personally, and then paste the pictures on the appropriate board. You can cut out any pictures you want . . . pictures of people, places, things and text . . . whatever you think provides a good representation. The choice is yours. When you are all done, I'd like you to explain your selections and your board to me.

Moving Up The Ladder

Interviewer: An interface can either be simple or cluttered. Which type of interface do you prefer?

Respondent: I prefer a simple interface.

Interviewer: Why is that important to you?

This question identifies the preferred pole on the continuum.

This question moves the discussion up the ladder.

Respondent: Because it is easier for me to find the SEARCH box on the page.

Interviewer: Why is that important to you?

This question continues to move the discussion upwards.

Respondent: Because it acknowledges that my time is valuable. It's much more efficient.

Interviewer: Why is that important to you (etc.)

Moving Down The Ladder

Interviewer: Keep thinking about simple versus cluttered interfaces. Can you think of a way in which they are different from each other?

This question moves the discussion down the ladder.

Respondent: A cluttered interface has lots and lots of banner ads and other types of annoying advertising.

Interviewer: Can you think of any other ways in which simple and cluttered interfaces differ?

This question seeks to determine additional differences, moving the discussion sideways.

Respondent: There's a lot of other visual distractions?

Interviewer: What do you mean by visual distraction?

This question seeks to clarify a vague answer.

Respondent: Links to places I don't care about.

Interviewer: Can you think of any other ways in which simple and cluttered interfaces differ (etc.)

FIGURE 5.2a   Example of Laddering Interview

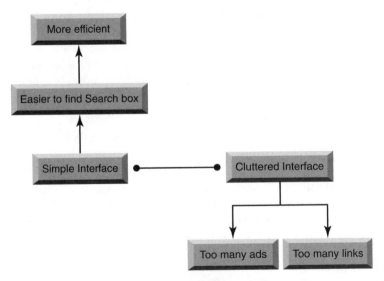

FIGURE 5.2b   Visual Representation of Laddering Interview

As with other process techniques, the value of this activity lies not only in the finished mood board but also in the discussion related to the process of how the board was constructed. Additionally, when used in focus groups, a "compare and contrast" discussion across the different boards often provides valuable insights.

AD CREATION.   Ad creation is a variation of mood boards. This technique helps an advertiser better understand consumers' attitudes toward category advertising and the relative importance of different product benefits. Ad creation works in both a personal and focus group setting, although the discussion in a focus group tends to be very illuminating when the following steps are followed.

1. Prior to the focus groups, obtain copies of your own and competitive brands' print advertising. Make a folder of the complete set of ads. Make enough copies of the folder to account for all focus groups (typically three times the number of focus groups). In a separate container, have scissors, blank paper, and glue sticks. You should have four containers prepared.

2. At the appropriate point in the focus groups, divide the group into smaller groups (typically three to four persons). Give each subgroup the folder with the ads and the container with the scissors, etc. and explain:

   The folder contains a wide range of advertising for [name or category of products]. Using these ads as your source, I'd like you to create an ad that represents your ideal ad for [name of product]. You can select, cut and then paste on the blank paper any images or text from any of the ads in the folder. I don't expect you to be artists, so please focus on what the ad says, either through word or copy, rather than worrying a lot about how the ad looks. You'll be working in a group, and so all decisions have to reflect the group's consensus, even though you might not agree on everything. I'll give you fifteen minutes or so to do this, after which I'll ask each group to show and explain its ad.

3. Allow each group to create its ad. Walk around the room to listen to conversations as each ad is created. These conversations provide very important insights.

4. When time is up, ask each group to present and explain the rationale for the elements in its ad.

THE QUALITATIVE INTERVIEW

The qualitative interview (whether in-person or in a focus group) begins well before an interviewer sits down with a respondent. The interviewer, agency research team, and client meet to discuss and identify key issues, required learning outcomes, goals, and desired techniques. Once there is consensus in these areas, the interviewer creates an interview guide. This guide, an excerpt from which is shown in Figure 5.3, provides an

Personal Interview Guide
(Online Advertising)

Introduction

- Explain purpose of interviews
- Introduce self
- Explain no right answers
- Explain taping, etc.
- Present, explain, and have respondent sign informed consent form

Context Questions

I'd like to begin by asking you about your Internet-related behaviors. This information will help us better focus on specific issues later in the interview. Let's begin by thinking about a typical day.

—How much time, overall, do you spend on the Internet in a typical day?
—What devices do you use to surf the Internet? [Probe for computers, cell phones, other mobile devices]
—What Web sites do you typically visit?
—How much time do you typically spend on each site?
—What are your reasons for visiting each site?

Advertising Awareness

Now, I'd like you to think about the three sites you indicated you spend the most time on. These were [insert names of sites]. Let's talk about them one at a time. [Repeat questions below for each site. Insert name of site where indicated.]

—Is there advertising on [name of site]?
—Does this advertising appear on the home page? on other pages? all pages?
—Think about the formats of advertising shown on [name of site]. Here is a sheet showing the various sizes of advertising that might be displayed on a Web site. Which, if any, of these formats appear on [name of site]?
—This advertising can either appear as a static ad (i.e., one without any movement), as an animated ad, or as a video ad. On [name of site] which forms of advertising do you remember seeing?

Reactions to Advertising

You mentioned that you've seen [insert types of advertising seen from prior set of questions]. I'd like to explore your reactions to this advertising?

—How often would you say that you pay attention to the advertising, that is, actually read one of the ads?
—What type of ad would you say that you pay the most attention to? The least amount of attention to? Can you describe how the ads either attract or don't attract your attention?
—How often would you say that you actually click on an ad to learn more?
—If any ads clicked on then ask: Can you explain the reasons for clicking on some ads and not others?
—If no ads clicked on then ask: It seems that you avoid clicking on all ads. Can you explain the reasons for this?
—Earlier you mentioned that three sites you visit very often are [insert names of sites]. Do you tend to pay more of less attention to ads on these sites versus other sites you visit? What do you think are the reasons for this?
—Still thinking about these sites, do you tend to click on ads on these sites more or less often versus other sites you visit? What do you think are the reasons for this?

FIGURE 5.3   Excerpt from Personal Interview Guide

ordered list of the questions to be asked as well as reminders for any required probes or follow-up questions. This document is a guide for the journey through the interview. The interviewer has complete control over the order in which the questions are asked as well as for the addition of any questions that might provide useful for clarification or additional insights.

While the questions on the interview guide do not need to be asked verbatim, it is nevertheless important that question wording be appropriate for qualitative research. In this regard, keep the following guidelines in mind:[21]

- Keep questions short and precise. Avoid questions that are overly long or that contain parenthetical phrases designed to "clarify," for example: "How do you view the relationship between the brand (by that I mean the brand name and image) and those who are loyal brand users (that is, individuals who buy the brand the majority of the time.)?"

- Ask only one question at a time. Avoid questions of the form: "How did you first become aware of changes to the brand's packaging, and how did this change make you feel?"

- Avoid questions in which the answer is either given or implied, for example, "Don't you think that brand quality is more important than absolute price?"

- Avoid "why" questions, as discussed on page 124.

Active Listening and Probes

Verbal questions are the stimuli that initiate the interview process. Probes and follow-up questions provide the opportunity for a deeper exploration of responses, for the clarification of issues, and for "pushing" respondent's to provide deeper, more meaningful responses.

A prerequisite to the meaningful probing of responses is active (as opposed to simple or passive) listening on the part of the interviewer or moderator. Simple listening shows the respondent that what he or she is saying is important. Verbal responses, such as "Yes, tell me more," "that's interesting, what else," and "I see" as well as non-verbal responses such as attentive body language, nods, smiles, and the maintenance of eye contact show a respondent that the interviewer is interested in what is being said and places value on the content being communicated. Active listening goes beyond simple listening. Active listening means hearing and responding to the significance of the respondent's remarks. Here, the interviewer attends to the "emotive aspects of what is said, the figures of speech, the inconsistencies, the buried connections, the obscure references, the startling insights, and the repetitions [in order to determine] what the person might have meant and what that person's remark might mean outside its immediate context."[22]

Active listening is important for several reasons. First, active listening shows that the interviewer is interested in and is paying close attention to what is being said. This communicates to a respondent that his or her responses are important. One way to indicate active listening is to use the respondent's own words in probes and follow-up questions, for example:

> Tell me more about your feeling that all gasolines are the same except for Shell.
>
> You mentioned that advertisers don't usually tell the whole truth about their products. Can you give me an example of when you saw this happen?

Drawing attention (in a nonthreatening and nonjudgmental way) to conflicting statements is another way to demonstrate this aspect of active listening, for example:

> Mary, at one point earlier in the group you said that you would never consider purchasing a luxury car. Just recently, however, you said that you might consider purchasing a Lexus or an Infiniti. Could you please help me understand your point of view? Can you please try and explain for me your attitudes toward purchasing luxury cars in general and purchasing an Infiniti or Lexus in particular.

Second, active listening tends to reinforce a respondents' perceptions that he or she and the interviewer are working on a common problem and that the interviewer is interested in truly understanding the respondent's unique points of view. Finally, the probes and follow-up questions that result from active listening increase the quality and depth of information communicated by the respondent.

Probes and follow-up questions accomplish these goals and provide the means for deeper information only if used appropriately. As a consequence, qualitative researchers recommend the following guidelines for the use of probes and follow-up questions:[23]

- Follow up on what the respondent says using the respondent's own words;
- Ask follow-up questions to resolve ambiguity and to increase clarity;
- Do not ask probes or follow-up questions for their own sake. Each must have a role in advancing the interview or discussion;
- Try not to interrupt or cause the respondent to lose his or her train of thought. Probe and follow up at logical stopping or transition points;
- Use probes to add depth by asking for concrete details;
- Use probes that are simple, direct, and easy for the respondent to understand;
- Use probes and follow-up questions to stimulate affective as well as cognitive responses.

Setting the Right Environment

The environment in which the interview or focus group takes place plays an important role in the quality of obtained insights. The potential for a successful qualitative research interview or focus group increases when the interviewer or moderator creates the proper environment.

Successful qualitative research is conducted in an environment in which respondents feel safe, comfortable, and free to express their opinions. This type of environment is most likely to occur when the interviewer or moderator

- personally does not act (and prevents others from acting) in a judgmental manner,
- establishes rapport, between himself or herself and the respondents and, in a group discussion, among the respondents themselves.

NONJUDGMENTAL MANNER. The interviewer or moderator must interact with respondents in a nonjudgmental manner; that is, he or she must ask questions, probe responses, and react to provided information without explicit or implicit indications of what is the "right," "better," or "expected" response. The best interviewers or moderators take a neutral stance. They do not let their own opinions be known, and they do not evaluate the responses of others. This does not mean, however, that the moderator must be distant or poker-faced. On the contrary, a relaxed, interested, and pleasant but neutral manner is very effective in encouraging respondents to feel comfortable expressing intimate or socially unacceptable sentiments as well as opinions that simply may run counter to prevailing group consensus.

The avoidance of explicit judgments (and the subsequent bias they cause) is relatively simple. The interviewer or moderator avoids leading or evaluative questions and probes, for example:

John, do you really mean to say that you actually believe what that advertiser said in his commercial?

How many others in the group participate in these sorts of unusual behaviors?

The avoidance of implicit judgments is also important, but is often more difficult to control. Here, for example, body language and note taking can introduce judgmental bias. Changes in the interviewer's body language, the tilting of an eyebrow, or the loss of eye contact can all signal evaluative judgments. Furthermore, if notes are taken sporadically, respondents may infer that comments that are written down are more important or more correct than comments not written down.

RAPPORT. The establishment of rapport between interviewer and respondent(s) is an important component of the interview or group setting. Lindlof[24] characterizes rapport as the "ability of both parties to empathize with each other's perspective" occurring when the "interviewer and interviewee are in basic accord on communication style and the subject matter that can and cannot be talked about." He goes on to point out that rapport is important because "it clears away the burden of having to translate what one wants to say into a formal or foreign style. It clears away the fear of being misunderstood. It means that, for this occasion, conditions are right for disclosing thoughts and feelings more readily."

Interview conditions and interviewer's actions affect the establishment of rapport. In terms of interview conditions, rapport is more likely to be established when the interview is conducted in comfortable surroundings and when initial contact between interviewer and respondent is positive (e.g., greetings are exchanged and hands are shaken). In terms of interviewer actions, rapport is more likely to be established when the interviewer

- pays attention to and follows up on what the respondent says,
- asks questions to clarify and expand on the respondent statements,
- probes for further information on respondent's cognitive and affective statements,
- follows up to learn more but does not interrupt to do so,
- displays appropriate emotions (e.g., laughs at respondent's jokes),
- tolerates silence and does not force responses,
- is attentive and appropriately responds to respondent's body language.

The creation of rapport between interviewer and respondent does not imply that interviewer neutrality needs to be abandoned. Patton explains the difference between these characteristics:

> Rapport is a stance vis-à-vis the person being interviewed. Neutrality is a stance vis-à-vis the content of what that person says. Rapport means that I respect people being interviewed, so that what they say is important because of who is saying it. . . . Yet, I will not judge them for the content of what they say to me. [25]

Focus groups and minigroups also require rapport among the group members. Respondents are more likely to express their true opinions if they believe that they have things in common with other members of the group and that other members of the group will not judge the "correctness" of their attitudes and beliefs.

SUMMARY

Qualitative advertising research entails the intensive observation and interviewing of a small number of individuals in order to acquire detailed, in-depth insights into their attitudes' beliefs, motivations, and lifestyles. The goal of qualitative research is to help develop a better understanding of why individuals act as they do, rather than developing numeric descriptions of what people do.

Qualitative research has several strengths and weaknesses versus quantitative research. Strengths include the depth of information provided, the opportunity to "get close to the data" by observing respondents themselves, and its cost and time efficiency. Weaknesses relate to problems of generalizability and projectability, the absence of numeric summaries, and greater potential for bias in findings interpretation.

Qualitative advertising research generally uses personal interviews or focus groups. Personal interviews, where individuals are interviewed one at a time, provide the greatest depth of detail and are most appropriate when

- the subject matter of the interview is confidential,
- group pressure is likely to distort responses,
- there are legal or confidentiality constraints on group discussion,
- a longer amount of time is required to establish rapport or an understanding of target attitudes and behaviors.

Focus groups, however, are appropriate when the spontaneity and interaction of the group discussion is desired.

The interviewer or focus group moderator is the key to obtaining valuable insights from a qualitative research study. The interviewer or moderator is more likely to conduct research that leads to valuable insights when he or she is well prepared, conducts the interviews appropriately, and uses appropriate questioning and projective techniques. Preparation for the interview entails obtaining an accurate and complete picture of the research study's background and informational needs, determining the most advantageous ways to obtain desired information, and preparing a well-tested and constructed discussion guide. Appropriate conduct of the interview or focus group entails using a nonjudgmental manner, establishing rapport, and being an active listener.

Qualitative questioning techniques can be classified in terms of the types of question or process used to elicit a response. Direct questions (specification, structural, grand tour, idealization, hypothetical-interaction, and third-person) ask an individual to respond to a focused and generally narrow request for information. Projective techniques ask individuals to use their imagination in response to a verbal or pictorial stimulus. The latter techniques include: word association, sentence and story completion, personification and anthropomorphism, role-playing, picture projection, and picture sorts. Additional techniques (repertory grid, laddering) rely on in-depth, sequential interviews or the interviewee's creation of a product such as an advertisement or mood board.

Review Questions

1. List three areas for which qualitative research is particularly well suited.
2. List three limitations of qualitative research.
3. What are the advantages and disadvantages of focus and minigroups?
4. What are the six types of direct questions asked in a qualitative interview? Briefly describe the use of each.
5. In what ways can you increase the success of grand tour questions?
6. Describe two approaches that may be used in formulating idealization questions.
7. Which types of questions focus on the imagination and actual experiences of a respondent? Provide an example of each.

8. What are the three main types of projective techniques?
9. What types of projective techniques use verbal stimuli? Provide an example of each.
10. What types of projective techniques use imagination or scenarios? Provide an example of each.
11. What types of projective techniques use pictures as stimuli? Provide an example of each.
12. How is a repertory grid prepared and administered?
13. What consumer insights are provided by the repertory grid approach?
14. Under what assumption does laddering operate? How does this approach help a researcher better understand the consumer?

15. What is a mood board? What is its primary use?
16. Briefly list and explain the steps of ad creation.
17. Define and provide an example of *active listening*.
18. What is the value of probes? How are probes best used during the qualitative interview?
19. Is rapport an important component of the qualitative interview? Why?
20. What are the indicators of good rapport?

Application Exercises

1. You are the supervisor of a qualitative research study. One of your assistants has conducted a qualitative interview. The objective of the interview was to determine people's reactions to the political advertising shown in a prior presidential campaign.

   You must provide a critique of the interview to your assistant, pointing out areas where your assistant performed well and areas in which there were problems, in other words, you want to help your assistant improve her qualitative interviewing skills. Read the following interview, and then prepare a written analysis of the interview. NOTE: Your job is to assess how well your assistant conducted the interview. You are not interested in the content of the interview per se. Also, the transcript begins after rapport has been established. Take each interviewer comment, question, or response, and discuss whether it was or was not appropriate. Justify your answer. If it was not appropriate, what advice would you give the interviewer to improve her performance. (In the interview transcript, "I" stands for the interviewer and "R" stands for the respondent. The transcript begins in mid-interview. The number after the "I" represents the number of the interviewer interaction and can be used as a reference in your answer. The respondent has been appropriately screened.)

   I (1): Let's turn our attention to the almost overwhelming number of political ads shown over the past three months. Specifically, I'd like to get your reactions of the advertisements for the presidential candidates. All right?

   R: Fine.

   I(2): Over the past three months, would you say that you saw more advertising for Obama or McCain?

   R: Obama.

   I(3): All right, let's focus on the advertising for Obama. In thinking back about this particular advertising, what thoughts or feelings come to mind?

   R: I think his advertising was the most straightforward.

   I(4): What do you possibly mean by straightforward?

   R: I think that it addressed the issues that needed to be addressed. His ad really didn't go into a lot of character attacks or go off on any tangential issues like McCain's ads did.

   I(5): You can't possibly believe that, do you?

   R: Yes.

   I(6): Any other thoughts or feelings?

   R: You know, I really don't like all that shrill stuff. The yelling and name calling. There was one McCain ad that really got me mad. I remember saying to myself: "Who would run such an ad?"

   I(7): OK . . . let's get back to Obama's ads. Many people liked the ad he aired the day before the election. The 30-minute infomercial. Did you happen to see this particular ad?

   R: Yup.

   I(8): How would you compare this ad to the commercial of the same length aired by McCain?

   R: I liked them both. They both really touched me.

   I(9): In what way?

   R: Different ways.

   I(10): You know, it would really be helpful if you could be more specific. Most people can explain these things. Give it a try. OK? Come on, you can do it?

   R: No, that's really all I can say.

I(11): One last question, how much did the ads influence who you wound up voting for?

R: I don't think I want to answer that.

I(12): OK, we're done.

2. Select an interview topic appropriate to one of your classmates, and then prepare a discussion guide. (Plan on conducting the interview for about 20 minutes). Record the interview. After the interview is complete, listen to the recording and prepare an assessment of how well you

   • were prepared for the interview and how this preparation affected the interview's success.

   • established rapport.

   • appropriately and successfully probed responses.

   • appropriately and successfully used projective and process techniques.

   Additionally, discuss what you believe to be the strengths and weaknesses of your performance as an interviewer. Provide examples.

3. Select four individuals with whom you can conduct personal interviews. All four individuals should be regular consumers of diet soft drinks. Your goal in each interview is to explore: (1) differences in perceptions of different brands of diet soft drinks, with particular attention to Diet Coke and Diet Pepsi, (2) how perceptions relate to levels of diet soft drink consumption, and (3) how perceptions relate to brand choice and brand image. Your interviews should use at least three of the techniques discussed in this chapter. Once the interviews are complete, write a short paper that describes what you learned.

4. You want to see how projective techniques that use verbal stimuli (see pages 128 to 129) help to identify and make explicit differences in individuals' perceptions of two streaming music sites: Pandora and Maestro.fm. Prepare a discussion guide that shows how each of these techniques could be used. In preparing your discussion guide, be certain to clearly present the wording and approach of each technique.

5. Select two brands that compete in the same category. Prepare a mood board to represent the users of each brand. Prepare a short paper that explains your rationale for the pictures selected for each board.

6. You wish to understand how your fellow students view their role on social networking sites. You will need to conduct two interviews. For the first interview, create an interview guide that probes why and how social networking sites are used, their advantages and disadvantages, and how the interviewee sees him or herself within his or her personal social network. Your guide can include any of the techniques discussed in this chapter except picture projection. For your second interview, extend the prior interview guide to include picture projection at the end of the interview. Show the interviewee the pictures displayed in Photo 5.2 and say "These pictures are representations of different social networking arrangements. Which picture best represents your social network and how do you see yourself within that social network? Why did you pick that picture?" Probe responses. After the completion of both interviews, write a short paper that describes what additional learning and insights were provided through picture projection. What were these approaches' strengths and weaknesses within the context of your interviews?

PHOTO 5.2

Endnotes

1. Interviewing, either one-on-one or in focus groups, is by far the most common form of qualitative research used by advertising researchers. There are, however, other approaches to qualitative research that while interesting and informative are less frequently used; for a review, see Research Methods Knowledge Base (2006). "Qualitative Methods" at http://www.socialresearchmethods.net/kb/qualapp.php, and for more extended discussion, see Thomas Lindlof and Bryan Taylor (2002). *Qualitative Communication Research Methods* (Thousand Oaks, CA: Sage Publications).

2. See, for example, D. K. Padgett (1998). *Qualitative Methods in Social Work Research: Challenges and Rewards* (Thousand Oaks, CA: Sage Publications).

3. Noell Rowan and Dan Wulff (2007). "Using Qualitative Methods to Inform Scale Development" *The Qualitative Report* 12 (3): 450–466.

4. Alfred Goldman and Susan McDonald (1987). *The Group Depth Interview: Principles and Practice* (Englewood Cliffs, NJ: Prentice-Hall).

5. The next chapter provides additional insight into the planning and conduct of focus groups.

6. Nancy F. Dana, et al. (undated). "Qualitative Interviewing and the Art of Questioning: Promises, Possibilities, Problems and Pitfalls" at http://www.coe.uga.edu/quig/dana92.html.

7. Grand tour questions are similar in approach to Interpersonal Process Recall. See Denise Larsen, Keri Flesaker, and Rachel Stege (2008). "Qualitative Interviewing Using Interpersonal Process Recall: Investigating Internal Experiences during Professional-Client Conversations" *International Journal of Qualitative Methods* at http://ejournals.library.ualberta.ca/index.php/IJQM/article/view/1617/1155. Several of Larsen et al.'s suggestions for this approach are drawn upon in this discussion and all quotes are from this source.

8. Brian Baumal (undated). "A New Definition Of Projective Techniques" at http://thinklounge.blogspot.com/2006/02/new-definition-of-projective.html.

9. Sune Donoghue (2000). "Projective Techniques in Consumer Research." *Journal of Family Ecology and Consumer Sciences,* 28: 47–53.

10. David Jacques (2005). "Projective Techniques: Eliciting Deeper Thoughts" at http://www.customerinput.com/journal/projective_techniques_eliciting_deeper_thoughts.asp.

11. Donoghue, op. cit.

12. The Word Association Thesaurus provides the most frequent associations with common words at http://www.eat.rl.ac.uk/.

13. For a more detailed discussion, see Anouk Hofstede et al. (2007). "Projective Techniques for Brand Image Research: Two Personification-Based Methods Explored." *Qualitative Market Research* 10 (3): 300–309. Personification occurs when people are used as a metaphor for the brand while anthropomorphism uses animals as a metaphor.

14. This list is adapted from Roy Posner (undated). "Traits of Human Consciousness" at http://www.gurusoftware.com/gurunet/Personal/Factors.htm.

15. George. A. Kelly (1955). *The Psychology of Personal Constructs* (New York, NY: Norton).

16. Enquire Within® (undated) "Kelly's Theory Summarised" at http://www.enquirewithin.co.nz/theoryof.htm.

17. Adapted and excerpted from Enquire Within®, op. cit. All quotes are from this source.

18. The seminal paper for laddering is Thomas J. Reynolds and Jonathan Gutman (1988). "Laddering Theory, Method, Analysis, and Interpretation." *Journal of Advertising Research* 28: 11–31. See also Tiana Veludo-de-Oliveira, Ana Ikeda, and Marcos Campomar (2006). "Laddering in the Practice of Marketing Research: Barriers and Solutions." *Qualitative Market Research* 9 (3): 297–306.

19. MecAnalyst (undated). "The Means-Ends Chain Model" at http://www.skymax-dg.com/mecanalyst/chain.html.

20. Frances Johnson and Sarah Crudge (2007). "Using the Repertory Grid and Laddering

Technique to Determine the User's Evaluative Model of Search Engines." *Journal of Documentation* 63 (2): 259–280.

21. Dana, op. cit.
22. Lidlof and Taylor, op. cit.
23. I. E. Seidman (1991). *Interviewing as Qualitative Research* (New York, NY: Teacher's College Press).
24. Lindlof and Taylor, op. cit.
25. Patton, op. cit.

CHAPTER 6

Focus Groups

Focus groups are one of the most common forms of qualitative research and are appropriate when interaction among respondents is believed to lead to significant insights into individuals' thoughts, attitudes, and behaviors. Focus groups are an inappropriate research technique when informational needs require numeric descriptions, when they are used as a substitute for more complex quantitative research, or when they are used simply because there is a feeling that we should do "something" (i.e., any) research before a decision is reached. The first part of this chapter provides an overview of appropriate focus group use. This is followed by a detailed discussion of the steps and procedures that underlie the planning and conduct of groups. The chapter concludes with guidelines for viewing focus groups as well as a discussion of online focus groups.

***

When you are done reading this chapter, you should have a better understanding of:

- when focus groups are most appropriately used
- the focus group planning process, including all materials that need to be developed in support of the groups
- how focus groups are conducted
- how to view groups to increase insights and usefulness
- the strengths and weaknesses of online focus groups.

Multiple definitions of "focus group" have been presented.[1] While there are variations in wording and emphasis across definitions, all ultimately define a focus group with a common set of criteria. A focus group can be defined as a group of 7 to 12 individuals who

- take part in a carefully planned series of discussions, which is
- held in a permissive, non-threatening environment, and is
- led by a trained moderator, where
- discussions are designed to uncover attitudes and perceptions in predefined areas of interest, to better
- enable decision makers to make more fully informed and more successful decisions.

Focus groups have been used to respond to a broad range of advertising-related needs, for example

- exploring issues related to advertising strategy, such as target audience selection, audience perceptions, and brand strengths and weaknesses;
- exploring reactions to alternative advertising messages and approaches;[2]
- understanding reactions to current approaches to brand and category advertising;[3]
- identifying perceived and desired category and brand benefits and exploring potential ways to express these benefits through advertising;
- developing and refining hypotheses regarding consumer motivations, especially with regard to how to "tap" these motivations in advertising;[4]
- developing and obtaining reactions to potential new products and new product ideas, as well as alternative product packaging ideas.[5]

The prior instances illustrate some of the areas in which focus groups can make an important contribution to the advertising planning process. However, while there is little debate that focus groups are useful when used appropriately, many caution against using focus groups in one specific situation: to make "go - no go" decisions on advertising creative. It is recommended that the evaluation of advertising creative in focus groups only be done to obtain an understanding of alternative approaches' potential strengths and weaknesses and *not* to select a "winning ad," which is better accomplished through quantitative research. The Business Research Lab notes that:

> It is better to test actual advertisements quantitatively, using a methodology which will, among other things, quantify the impact of a particular ad on purchase intent, product/service/corporate imagery, believability, recall of the actual ad and the message of the ad, and the extent to which people can identify the product/service/corporation being advertised.[6]

Those who argue for a quantitative approach to advertising selection claim that focus groups are an inappropriate place to select "winning ads" because, in this setting, consumers evaluate advertising from a high involvement analytical, logical "art- and copy-director" perspective, rather than the typical low involvement, feeling approach used to evaluate advertising in a naturalistic setting. After all, consumers watching Super

Bowl commercials at home rarely note that "the dialogue was a bit terse and there were a few distracting visual elements." Yet, this is how many react to advertising tests in a focus group setting. The focus group consumer mindset can be appropriate for obtaining *initial* reactions to advertising, but then these reactions need to be merged with professional judgment prior to determining the "winning" ad.

PLANNING FOR FOCUS GROUPS

Focus groups begin with the same planning and decisions as other types of research. The situation motivating the research is examined, a problem statement is formulated, informational needs are specified, and the selection of focus groups as a means of satisfying informational needs is made. Once these decisions are made, focus group planning begins. The steps involved in the planning and conduct of focus group research are shown in Figure 6.1. The discussion in this section explains each of these steps. The next section applies this discussion to actual focus group research.

Select a Moderator

Focus group planning begins with two simultaneous sets of activities. Figure 6.1 shows that one line of activity relates to moderator and moderator-related activities. The success of any focus group research is directly dependent on the skill and performance of the selected moderator. For this reason, this line of activity begins with the evaluation of potential moderators and the selection of the one moderator who will conduct the groups.

Many different aspects of moderator characteristics should be considered during the selection process. First, there are personality characteristics. Moderators who demonstrate excellence in focus group facilitation generally are

- genuinely interested in hearing other people's thoughts and feelings,
- able to verbalize and clearly express their own feelings,
- animated and spontaneous conversationalists,
- active listeners,
- able to understand how others feel and are able to see life from others' perspectives,
- cognizant of, and able to control, their own biases,
- inquisitive about "what makes people tick,"
- flexible and able to respond quickly to changing situations,
- innovative and able to see new ways to explore issues and facilitate the group discussion.

Second, it is important that group members be comfortable with the moderator's demographic characteristics. It would be a poor decision, for example, to have a male moderator conduct groups with women who will be asked to discuss their use of personal health and beauty aid products. Third, it is important that the moderator has good advertising and business sense. The moderator must be able to understand, from an advertising or business perspective, why the groups are being conducted, the types of information required, and how

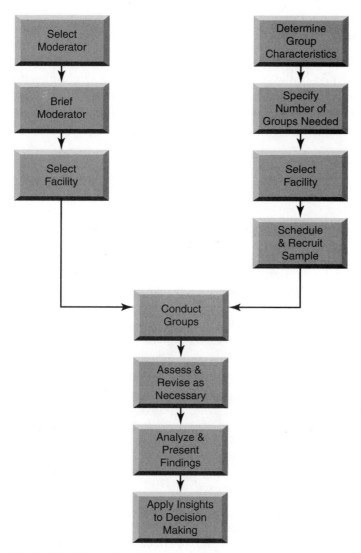

FIGURE 6.1 Steps in the Planning and Conduct of Focus Groups

this information will be used for advertising decision making. The moderator does not need, however, to have specific expertise in the business category under exploration.

Brief the Moderator

Once selected, the moderator is briefed on the research problem, research goals, informational needs, timing, and other study parameters and products, materials, or other tangible items (e.g., products to be tasted) to be used during the focus groups. This briefing typically takes several hours and helps the moderator understand what needs to be learned from the groups so that he or she is in the best position to keep the discussion focused on important areas and to circumvent or minimize irrelevant discussion. Remember that

> the objective of the moderator briefing should not be to try and make the moderator an expert in the area being researched, which could inhibit discussion by the respondents. Rather, the moderator should be sufficiently familiar with the material so that he or she can probe the important areas and become familiar with the language of the consumer with regard to the area being surveyed.[7]

Finally, moderator briefings are most productive when the moderator receives the documentation on the research study's background and informational needs in sufficient time to review before the formal briefing. The beginning of a moderator briefing is provided in Figure 6.2.[8]

Prepare, Evaluate, and Revise Discussion Guide

The discussion guide is typically drafted by the focus group moderator and is similar in format and approach to the personal interview guide discussed in Chapter 5 (pages 140 to 142). The focus group discussion guide presents the questions and topic areas to addressed in the group, noting the order of presentation and any required probes. Since the function of the guide to provide a roadmap for the group, it is not necessary to fully write out the questions to be asked. An example discussion guide is provided in Figure 6.3.

In 2000, the Centers for Disease Control and Prevention (CDC) was designated by Congress to take the lead in planning, implementing, and evaluating a national Youth Media Campaign to encourage tweens (boys and girls aged 9 to 13) to become more physically active. This campaign, *VERB: It's What You Do*, ran successfully from 2001 to 2006. Congress and the CDC are exploring the possibility of reactivating this campaign.

The initial campaign was developed through extensive formative research, including multiple focus groups and individual interviews with individuals in the target audience. These interviews, which explored tweens' attitudes and behaviors relevant to the campaign, provided the foundation for message strategy and advertising development.

Congress and the CDC are exploring the possibility of reactivating this campaign. However, given the large amount of time that has elapsed since the end of the original campaign, it is felt that focus groups would help to determine whether tweens' attitudes today are similar to or different from the tweens addressed in the original campaign. These focus groups would replicate those used in the original campaign's development. As a result, the current research is designed to provide information on psychographic audience segments that exist within the tween population and to determine the extent to which original and newly proposed messages resonate with different audience segments. Within this overall goal of the research, the proposed research will specifically

- identify specific youth segments within the tween population that may warrant tailored and unique message strategies;
- reveal the mindset of youth within these segments in order to facilitate message development;
- isolate the main message and message components that appear best able to generate appeal, relevance, and desired behavior among targeted segments.

A series of 16, geographically dispersed focus groups are planned. Participants will be assigned to specific focus groups according to their age, ethnicity, and current level of physical activity.

FIGURE 6.2 Sample Moderator Briefing

Moderator Guide for Formative Message Research
Tween Focus Groups

I. Introduction and Warm-Up

- **Welcome.** Explain purpose of the research (to learn more about participant's attitudes and behaviors, to talk about new advertising ideas, to get participant's reactions to ideas).
- **Approach.** No right or wrong answers. Everyone needs to talk—all opinions are important. Everything is confidential. No names used in report.
- **Logistics.** Group video taped. Observers on other side of the mirror.
- **Introductions.** Moderator. Respondents (first name, things like to do in spare time). Other icebreakers to get respondents comfortable with setting and other respondents.

II. Spare Time, Interests, and Physical Activity

- **Typical day.**
  - What is typical day like?
  - Most common activities?
  - Things would like to do but no time for.
  - Things would like to avoid

- **Spare time.**
  - How much? When?
  - Most common activities.

- **Passive versus active activities?**
  - Most common?
  - Any physical activities *(not mentioned in prior sections)*
  - Types of physical activities
  - Appeal of physical activity
  - *(PROBE: Barriers to engaging in more physical activity)*
  - *(PROBE: Views of type of individuals who have high participation in physical activity)*
  - *(PROBE: If high appeal but low participation, ask for reasons why)*

III. Reactions to Potential Messages

- **Explain process.** Going to show one idea at a time. Not finished yet, still may be changed. Your opinions help decide what changes might need to be made. Three different ads to look at.
- **Rotate presentation order across groups. Present each idea twice before starting discussion.**

  For each ad idea:

- **First impressions.** Have respondents write down the first two or three words (positive or negative) that come to mind. When all are done, have each respondent read their selection.
  - Why those particular words?
  - Agree or disagree with other's words? Why?

  (Cover all the following points. Cover the points, however, in the order that makes the most sense given prior responses.)

FIGURE 6.3 Sample Discussion Guide

- **Emotional reactions.**
  - What thoughts or feelings did you have as idea were presented?
  - Were reactions better or worse than other advertising typically seen?
  - Who was advertising talking to?
  - Was it talking to you?
  - What did you like? dislike?

- **Reactions to the message.**
  - What do you think is the main message or idea?
  - What in the ad gave you that idea?
  - What do you think of that message?
  - Is the message important?
  - Is the message believable?
  - Is the message appropriate/relevant to someone like you?

- **Motivation.**
  - What do you think you might do after seeing an ad with this idea?
  - Why do you feel that way?
  - *If motivation is low ask:* What, if anything, could be changed about the ad to make you more likely to do what is suggested?

  After all ads are viewed:
  - Have participants vote on most/least preferred. Explain why.

IV. Summary, Consensus, and Back-Room Questions

FIGURE 6.3   (Continued)

The draft discussion guide should be discussed with all individuals involved in the research prior to the initial focus group. During this discussion, the moderator should explain: (1) the rationale underlying the guide's organization, paying particular attention to question flow and sequence, (2) how question wording and sequencing will allow decision makers to obtain desired insights, (3) how the guide will be used as a road map, and (4) that question wording and sequence may be altered to reflect group direction and dynamics. This discussion may lead to revisions in the original draft.

Determine Group Characteristics

As illustrated in Figure 6.1, decisions related to group characteristics and the logistics of the research proceed at the same time the moderator is being briefed and the discussion guide is being developed. The first decision reached during this line of planning relates to group composition.

There is little doubt that group compatibility is a key contributor to group success. The more comfortable members of a group are with each other, the more likely they are to engage in conversation and provide deeper, more personal comments and insights. Kruger, in this regards, notes that relevant shared characteristics, compatibility, and interests "serve to enhance the permissive or nonthreatening environment in which [participants] can express controversial or private views."[9] As a result, it is important to plan each group in way that ensures high levels of compatibility. A researcher must think ahead and ask: "If all the people I invite to a group knew each other, would they all be friends?" Groups should be formed in a way that allows this question to be affirmatively answered.

Compatibility, it is important to note, does not mean that all members of a group are identical across all dimensions. Compatibility does mean that members of the group share enough characteristics in important, defining areas, to make each member comfortable with the others.

- *There are times when attitudes are the defining characteristic.* Focus groups exploring reactions to Tom Smith's political advertising would likely want to learn from those currently positive and negative toward candidate Smith. In this circumstance, it would likely be best to separate these two groups of individuals. Other respondents' characteristics such as age, gender, and income appear not to be related to Smith support, and thus are not a consideration in group composition. Thus, Smith will hold two types of groups: one focus group of "supporters" and one group of "nonsupporters." Similarly, focus groups probing perceptions of different types of wine might require separating those who consider themselves wine "connoisseurs" from those who consider themselves casual wine drinkers.

- *Demographics and product usage may be the defining characteristics in other circumstances.* Focus group exploration of hair coloring might entail seeking the reactions of men and women who do and do not color their hair. Because of gender differences in hair coloring, men and women would likely feel more comfortable in a same gender group. Moreover, the personal nature of hair coloring might make participants more comfortable if they were in a group with others of the same behavior. Thus, four types of groups would be required: (1) women who color their hair, (2) women who do not color their hair, (3) men who color their hair, and (4) men who do not color their hair. Other demographic criteria (such as age and income) are unlikely to be relevant to this set of group's composition.

Determine the Number and Location of Required Groups

The specification of group characteristics has implications for the total number of groups required. Once the number of distinct groups is determined, a researcher must then decide how many locations are needed and the number of groups to be conducted in each location.

It is generally unwise to conduct only one set of groups per location. Given small sample sizes and nonrandom sampling procedures, it is dangerous to rely on the perceptions, attitudes, and behaviors of one group of individuals. Thus, it is generally recommended to conduct at least two groups per location.

The number of locations selected for groups reflects the extent to which it is believed that geographic differences affect salient attitudes and behaviors. Where geographic differences are felt to exist, sets of groups should be held in geographically diverse locations. Geographic diversity provides greater insights and reduces the likelihood of respondents from a single geographic area skewing the results. However, geographic diversity becomes less important in the following circumstances:[10]

- The groups are designed to provide preliminary creative guidance;
- The groups are designed to confirm or extend actions based on more extensive prior research, for example, the revision of product positioning or a change in product labeling;
- The research is designed to support questionnaire development;

PHOTO 6.1a Traditional Focus Group Setting   **PHOTO 6.1b** Catalyst Ranch Focus Group Facility

- Sales data suggest that there are no regional variations in product purchase behaviors;
- Prior quantitative data suggest that there are no regional variations in relevant perceptions or attitudes.

Select the Facility

The focus group facility is the place where the groups will physically be held. While some advertising agencies have their own in-house facilities, most focus groups are held at facilities specially designed for the conduct and viewing of focus groups. Regardless of where the facility is located, it should have at minimum: a reception area in which to greet and organize respondents prior to the group, a conference room with a one-way mirror in which the group will be held, video and/or audio recording capabilities, and a viewing room. Most focus group facilities use the conference room approach, that is, a long table in the center of a larger room (see Photo 6.1a). Recently, however, researchers have found that respondents are more at ease and forthcoming with their opinions when the focus group takes place in a more natural and comfortable situation. The photograph shown in Photo 6.1b illustrates how Catalyst Ranch has designed its facility to maximize the friendliness of the group "room," thereby increasing respondents' willingness to talk and share.[11]

Beyond the physical layout of the facility, a facility should be also selected in a way that keeps participants' travel requirements in mind, ideally being located in a place that is conveniently located for all participants.

Schedule Groups, Specify Sample, and Recruit Participants

Focus groups in which the participants are not employed outside the home may be conducted in either the day or the evening. Groups conducted among those employed outside the home typically take place in the evening (common group times are 6 p.m. and 8 p.m.).

Most focus group facilities have the capability to recruit respondents. Here, the researcher specifies the characteristics of individuals required for each group, and the facility locates and recruits the respondents. A sample recruitment screener is shown in Figure 6.4. Note how the screener not only identifies desired participants and assigns each different type of participant to a different group, but also eliminates "undesirable"

Screener for Formative Message Research
Parent Focus Groups

DIRECTIONS TO RECRUITER: You are recruiting parents for four focus groups. Group meeting times are:

Tuesday, June 23	Group A	6 p.m.	(Women, child somewhat active)
	Group B	8 p.m.	(Women, child not active)
Wednesday, June 24	Group C	6 p.m.	(Men, child somewhat active)
	Group D	8 p.m.	(Men, child not active)

SCREENER:

Hello, my name is _____ from _____ a marketing research company. Can I please ask you just a few questions as part of a marketing research study? All of your answers are confidential, and I assure you that I am not selling anything.

1. First, can you please tell me if there are any children in your household between the ages of 9 and 13?

      Yes [ ] → CONTINUE WITH Q. 2
      No   [ ] → THANK AND DISCONTINUE

2. How would you describe your role in the raising of the 9- to 13-year-old children in your household?

      Primarily responsible for decision-making   [ ] → CONTINUE WITH Q. 3
      Share equally in decision-making   [ ] → CONTINUE WITH Q. 3
      Someone else is primarily responsible for decision-making [ ] → THANK AND DISCONTINUE

3. Do you or does any member of your household have a job that entails:

      Advertising or Marketing   [ ] → THANK AND DISCONTINUE
      Physical education or training [ ] → THANK AND DISCONTINUE

4. Have you participated in a focus group or other form of market research within the last 30 days?

      Yes [ ] → THANK AND DISCONTINUE
      No   [ ] → CONTINUE WITH Q. 5

5. *Confirm gender.*

      Female [ ] → CONTINUE WITH Q. 6
      Male   [ ] → SKIP TO Q. 7

6. Please think for a moment about your child who is aged 9 to 13. How would you describe this child's level of physical activity? On average, would you say that this child engages in some physical activity . . .

      frequently, at least once per day   [ ] → THANK AND DISCONTINUE
      often, less than once a day but several times a week [ ] → THANK AND DISCONTINUE
      sometimes, but less than once per week   [ ] → INVITE TO GROUP A
      rarely, almost no physical activity   [ ] → INVITE TO GROUP B

7. Please think for a moment about your child who is aged 9 to 13. How would you describe this child's level of physical activity? On average, would you say that this child engages in some physical activity . . .

      frequently, at least once per day   [ ] → THANK AND DISCONTINUE
      often, less than once a day but several times a week [ ] → THANK AND DISCONTINUE
      sometimes, but less than once per week   [ ] → INVITE TO GROUP C
      rarely, almost no physical activity   [ ] → INVITE TO GROUP D

FIGURE 6.4 Focus Group Screener

respondents who are: professional focus group participants (Question 4) or those involved in the advertising or marketing professions or are a "specialist" in the area (Question 3).

A well-written screener increases the probability that only those individuals of interest will be recruited for the groups. Nevertheless, even a well-written screener cannot compensate for a flawed recruitment process or problems with the database used to identify potential respondents. As a result, it is important that a researcher verify the appropriateness of the facility's recruitment process prior to the selection of that facility as the focus group recruiter. A verifiable statement of the facility's approach and procedures is a useful starting point, for example:

> At *Observation Baltimore*, recruiting is our priority. We exercise quality control at every stage of the recruiting process. Our quality extends from a professionally trained recruiting staff to call monitoring and daily maintenance of our extensive database. One key feature of our daily maintenance includes date of participation indexing to ensure fresh participants. We enter approximately 500 to 750 new participants into our database every month. Prior to a prospects entrance into our files, we conduct a thorough database search including name, address and phone number. This process assists us in discouraging professional respondents.[12]

An important part of respondent recruitment is the incentive. An incentive is a fee paid to respondents for participating in a focus group. The amount of an incentive generally reflects the difficulty in respondent recruiting. Easy to recruit respondents may be paid $30–$40, while harder to recruit respondents, such as those in specialized businesses, may be paid above $150.

The final part of the recruitment process actually takes place just before the groups begin. Recruited respondents are typically asked to arrive about 15 minutes prior to the planned group start time. Shortly after an individual arrives, he or she is given a written version of the screener (which was used for recruitment) to complete. This re-screening accomplishes several things. First, and most important, it confirms that participants do in fact possess the characteristics of interest. Second, "because the quality of the discussion depends heavily on the quality of the respondents, re-screening recruits prior to the start of the session helps provide quality assurance. Third, focus group facilities tend to recruit extra participants to help guarantee the desired show rate. Re-screening individuals will help you determine which ones you would like dismissed from the discussion,"[13] for example, those with characteristics that may hinder or disrupt the discussion, that is, a respondent who has a bad cough or appears unusually rowdy.

Conduct the Groups

Figure 6.1 shows that the successful conclusion of both planning paths is the conduct of the first set of groups. One common progression for focus group discussion is outlined next.

Prefatory remarks welcome the respondents, introduce the moderator, and explain the focus group setting and the rules that will govern the next two hours of discussion. Most prefatory statements contain the following elements:

- Introduction of the moderator by name;
- Explanation of the moderator's role ("to keep the discussion moving," "to help bring out thoughts and opinions," etc.);
- Specification of the topic under discussion ("tonight we will be discussing . . . ");
- Rules for participants: do not speak at the same time, address each other and not the moderator, be candid and truthful, and do not try for the right answer—there aren't any;
- Monitoring: one-way mirror, tape recording and/or audio recording, observers behind the one-way mirror;
- Rules for reporting: participants will not be quoted by name; all information is confidential and is only for internal agency for client use.

Introductions and personal information follow prefatory remarks. Here, each member of the group is invited to state his or her name and to tell something about him or herself that is related to the focus of the discussion. If appropriate, each respondent may also be invited to share basic demographic information, such as marital status, number of children, and occupation. There are three reasons for beginning the group in this way. First, it provides an opportunity for each respondent to talk, implicitly communicating that each person and his or her opinion is important. Second, it helps to establish group rapport by demonstrating similarities in important characteristics among the respondents. Third, shared information related to the group topic begins to focus respondents on the area of group discussion and inquiry.

Setting the context for discussion follows next. It is important for both the moderator and observers to understand the context of each individual's comments. Thus, groups often begin with a short series of questions that probe attitudes and behaviors specific to the group topic. Imagine a group designed to assess mothers' reactions to new children's cereals and positionings. At this stage in the group, to better understand the discussion that follows, the moderator might ask respondents to summarize their children's cereal-related behaviors, for example, the brands they typically buy, how often they purchase each brand, etc.

Discussion. The majority of group time is then devoted to the main discussion. The moderator uses open-ended questioning, probing and projective techniques discussed earlier to stimulate and lead the discussion.

Summary. A moderator, at the end of the main discussion, often develops and presents a summary to confirm his or her understanding of the group's primary comments and perspective. For example, at this point (near the end of the group) a moderator might say:

> We have covered a lot of ground tonight and I want to thank you for sharing your thoughts and opinions with me. We are close to finished, but

before we disband I would like to take just a few moments to make certain
that I correctly understand what you have said. OK. First, it seemed that
almost all of you felt that children's cereal advertisers place too much
emphasis on the premiums contained in the box. The group, fairly consensually, I think, believed that this was an unfair way to sell the cereal. Is this
right?

This type of recap serves three purposes. First, and perhaps most important, it makes certain that what the moderator thinks he or she heard is, in fact, correct. Second, group participants have one final opportunity to make their opinions known. Third, a clear and
concise prior summary is provided for individuals in the viewing room.

   Final questions. Moderators often excuse themselves from the discussion room after
the summary to take viewing room questions. At this time, the moderator might say:

You will recall that there were individuals in the viewing room watching the
group. Before I let you go, let me just check to see if they have any questions
that they would like me to ask you.

The moderator would then do a viewing room check to see if those in the viewing
room have any important, unresolved issues that need to be addressed. A viewer
might say, "The lady in the red dress said that she would never ever buy our product
again. But, others prevented her from saying why. Can you see what the main reasons
are?" The moderator takes questions from the viewing room and, if appropriate, communicates them to the group. The group then ends with a thank you and the payment
of incentives.

Assess Group Success and, If Necessary, Revise the Discussion Guide

Focus groups should be viewed as a dynamic rather than a static process, and consequently the discussion guide should be viewed as a fluid document subject to revision
and modification as necessary. At the end of the first set of groups, it is often advantageous to evaluate what transpired and to plan for the next set of groups. At this point, it
is important to prepare for the upcoming set of groups by noting

- information areas that should be probed in the same way in upcoming groups,
- information areas that should be explored differently in upcoming groups because
  the questioning or projective techniques were unsuccessful,
- new question areas that should be explored in upcoming groups,
- question areas that should be eliminated in upcoming groups.

Each of these modifications is reflected in a revised discussion guide.

Analyze and Present Findings; Apply Findings to Decision Making

Focus group research concludes similarly to other advertising research. The data, in this
case the group discussions, are analyzed, the major findings are presented, and the findings

are used to assist in the decision-making process. The analysis of focus group and other qualitative data is presented in Chapter 7.

VIEWING FOCUS GROUPS

As noted earlier, one of the great advantages of focus groups are their ability to allow for individuals at the agency and client to see and hear consumers firsthand. Mere viewing, however, is not enough to provide insights into the discussion's *meaning*. Focus group viewers must view the groups in a way that fosters an understanding of what is being said and that focuses on important aspects of the group's discussion. Viewer adherence to the following recommendations helps increase the likelihood of a positive, rewarding, and insightful viewing experience.

- *Come prepared.* Informed, prepared viewers are in the best position to participate in meaningful, productive group viewing and post-group discussions. At minimum, viewer preparation requires

  - familiarity with the research project's background, goals, and informational needs, and

  - that all required materials are handy and accessible (e.g., paper and pencil to take notes and a copy of the moderator's guide).

- *Start watching from the beginning.* The first brief sections of the focus group (introduction, personal information, setting the context) provide a great deal of meaningful background information and make explicit the context within which more detailed discussion will take place. It is important to pay attention to what is said in these early group discussions.

- *Focus on the big picture.* Focus group viewers often lose the forest by focusing on the trees. They may pay attention to the few unusual things that are said or they may become fixated on the comments from one or two individuals. Both viewing behaviors are dangerous and counterproductive. While detail is always important, it is most important to watch with an eye toward broad areas of group agreement and disagreement.

- *Listen to everyone.* Focus group viewers have a tendency to listen to and give more credence to individuals in the group who agree with their position and to discount the comments of those with whom they disagree. It is important that the opinions of all members of the group be given equal attention and consideration.

- *Listen to all comments.* A related viewer behavior is selective listening. Here, regardless of which participant expresses the thought, viewers tend to hear comments that agree with their position and to eliminate from consideration comments that run counter to their opinion. It is not unusual, for example, for a supporter of a particular point of view to quote all of the comments that agree with his or her point of view, even if there were an equal (or greater) number of counter comments. Selective listening has the potential to greatly distort the conclusions drawn from a group discussion and should be avoided.

- *Do not jump to premature conclusions.* Viewers should concentrate on listening to and interpreting the group discussion. Greenbaum notes that

  "the focus during the groups should be on intensive listening to the discussion, so that the observers can write down their interpretations of the discussion on the topics being discussed. After the groups, there is adequate time to review the notes and gather one's thoughts about the discussion in order to develop conclusions. This is an important point; many focus group observers jump to conclusions during the group discussion and therefore lose their objectivity. They then listen to the balance of the discussion (after their conclusion has been generated) with a biased mind, tending to hear only discussion points that support what they have already concluded."[14]

- *Do not let character judgments affect how the group members' comments are perceived.* Some viewers have a tendency to equate the value of the respondents' comments with the respondents' personal characteristics. In these cases, viewers believe that the comments of the more attractive, articulate, or entertaining respondents are more valid and insightful. This is a dangerous perspective and should be avoided.

- *Do not be biased by dominant personalities.* As discussed earlier, one risk of focus group research is the dominant personality, the person who speaks first (and often) and, in doing so, influences the direction and tone of the group's discussion. Viewers must be careful not to let this "louder voice" affect their interpretation of the overall group's perspective.

ONLINE FOCUS GROUPS

There is considerable debate over whether online focus groups should be considered "real" focus groups. Some argue that the absence of in-person interaction and the inability to utilize nonverbal cues prevent online approaches from being considered real focus groups.[15] Others argue that these groups satisfy the basic definition of focus groups: "a method of group interviewing in which the interaction between the moderator and the group, as well as the interaction between group members, serves to elicit information and insights in response to carefully designed questions."[16] We believe that debating the question "Are online focus groups 'real' focus groups?" to be both distracting and ultimately a waste of time. A more important question is: "Can online multi-person discussions (regardless of what you call them) provide valuable insights for advertising decision making?" The answer, we believe, is "yes" when (similar to all research techniques) this approach is used with a clear understanding of associated strengths and weaknesses. The remainder of this section describes approaches to online multi-person interviews.

There are three approaches to online multi-person interviews: synchronous, asynchronous, and hybrid. *Synchronous* approaches are the closest to traditional focus groups, as here all participants are online and interacting at the same time. Doyle Research provides a description of this approach:

> Using webcams and/or chat, discussions take place in real-time, in a password protected virtual focus group room, and provide the personal interaction of in-person research with the benefits of online. A shared screen feature allows a stimulus to be shown and marked up by both respondents and moderators, and a polling feature allows respondents to answer select questions privately before further discussion.[17]

Asynchronous approaches build the discussion over time as this approach makes it unnecessary for all group members to be online at the same time. Here an online chat room is created just for the group participants. The moderator asks questions, and group members post responses to the moderator's initial question as well as to other group member's comments. Throughout the discussion, the moderator interjects comments and additional questions, leading the discussion into new areas or asking respondents to clarify or elaborate on prior comments, or encouraging individuals to interact and respond to others' comments. *Hybrid* approaches combine asynchronous and synchronous approaches. Here, the research begins with asynchronous communication. This is followed by a synchronous focus group in which the major themes and areas of agreement/disagreement from the asynchronous communications are explored in greater detail.

All three approaches appear to have advantages over traditional focus groups in some circumstances. One set of advantages relates to logistics: online approaches work extremely when group members are dispersed geographically or when travel to a central location is otherwise difficult for either the group participants or for those who need to view the groups. This is a particular advantage of asynchronous approaches that permit individuals scattered across multiple time zones to participate in the same group. Beyond geography, the anonymity of online approaches makes it easier for researchers to contact and include hard-to-reach or stigmatized groups of individuals. A second set of advantages relates to the dynamics of the discussion.

> The Internet allows participants to overcome their inhibitions and social role constraints, thereby promoting freer and more spontaneous interaction . . . the anonymity of the setting appears to allow contributors to be more open and more willing to discuss private or emotionally involving experiences.[18]

In addition to these advantages, asynchronous and hybrid approaches appear to work quite well for topics and questions that require depth of thought prior to response. Both approaches allow individuals to think about, consider, and formulate a reply after reflection without the need for immediate response. The final set of advantages provides researcher benefits. Researchers who use asynchronous or synchronous approaches that require participation via written comments realize cost and time-savings due to the automatic and accurate capture of the discussion, significantly enhancing data analysis.

The advantages of online approaches only have value, however, if the quality of information is comparable or better than that obtained through traditional face-to-face focus groups. Research has shown that when used for appropriate topics, the quality of information and insights provided by online approaches are quite high. Tate et al. summarize the findings on data quality:

> Several studies . . . seem to suggest that the quantity and quality of data obtained online are broadly comparable to those obtained by traditional focus group discussions. Online data collection has the added advantage of providing an effective format to collect sensitive or personal health information. Self-disclosure, defined as "revealing personal information to others," is a key objective in focus groups, and lack of self-disclosure is often listed as a barrier to effective group discussions. The anonymity afforded by online communication is central in the explanation of increased levels of self-disclosure in online focus groups. The perceived privacy makes the online environment more conducive to eliciting honest and thoughtful responses. Furthermore, the visual anonymity provided by online focus groups may reduce the social desirability bias, allowing participants to feel more comfortable to voice their viewpoints. In traditional focus group discussions, participants may feel silenced or intimidated by more talkative participants. An important advantage of the online mode is the greater equality in participation than in traditional groups, providing a more balanced impression of all the viewpoints being expressed in the discussion. Finally, the absence of time-pressure in asynchronous forms of online discussion, allows considered responses that are lengthier and more detailed than those in synchronous or traditional forms. The aforementioned advantages attributed to conducting group discussions online enhance the accuracy and objectivity of the data obtained, and, consequently, the quality of the data.[19]

In sum, it appears that when justified by target characteristics or topic, online approaches are a viable, legitimate alternative to traditional focus groups.

APPLYING CHAPTER CONCEPTS

Individuals who drive while sleepy pose a significant threat to their own and others' safety. To better understand individuals with a high risk for drowsy driving, and to determine the best communication plan for persuading these individuals not to drive while sleepy, a series of focus groups were held. The groups were sponsored by the National Highway Traffic and Safety Administration. These focus groups provide excellent illustrations of the key principles discussed in the this chapter. Important materials from these groups are provided in the online supplemental readings.[20]

One of the first steps identified in Figure 6.1 is the moderator briefing. Note how the briefing for the sleepy driver groups (shown on page 3 of the supplemental readings) contains the key elements discussed earlier in the text (see pages 153 and 154) and serves a basis for a more detailed, in-person discussion with the group's moderator. In addition, note how the moderator briefing explicitly specifies the sequential nature of the planned groups and the specific goals for each group.

The focus group planners identified three types of individuals who are most likely to participate or play a role in driving while sleepy: young males, shift workers, and shift work supervisors. As with all focus groups, once individuals of interest were identified, the specific characteristics of each target group were defined so that a screener could be prepared. (The supplemental readings focus on shift workers.) Beyond demographics and job characteristics, individuals of interest were identified as follows:

- They had to be a licensed driver, although not licensed to drive commercial vehicles.

- They had to have a history of driving while sleepy as reflected in a "Yes" response to at least two of the following statements:

  - Have you ever fallen asleep or nodded off while driving?

  - Have you started to drive or continued driving an automobile when you felt very fatigued, drowsy, or sleepy three or more times during the past year?

  - Have you driven on a trip greater than one hour in length between midnight and 6:00 a.m. three or more times during the past year?

  - Have you driven an automobile after being awake for a period of 18 hours or longer three or more times during the past year?"

These target characteristics were then reflected in the screener used to recruit shift workers of interest. The screener is shown on page 4 of the supplemental readings.

Interactions with the moderator continued as the recruitment process proceeded. The moderator, the research team, and the client worked together to create the focus group discussion guide. As noted earlier in this chapter (see pages 154 to 156), the guide provides the road map for group discussion and makes explicit areas in which further probing is desirable. Two different discussion guides were needed for the shift worker sleepy driver groups. Each guide had to be customized to reflect the specific group's focus and goals.

- The first round of focus groups was designed to foster deeper insights into sleepy drivers' attitudes and behaviors. (This round consisted of initial groups with shift workers and a set of follow-up groups with shift workers and their supervisors.) The discussion guide beginning on page 6 of the supplemental readings is for the initial set of groups.

- The second set of focus groups was designed to obtain reactions to potential approaches to sleepy driving prevention messages. The discussion guide begins on page 10 of the supplemental readings, while the prevention messages explored in the group begin on page 13. Note how the concepts explored in these groups flow out of the insights gathered in earlier groups.

The results of the groups are provided in Sections A, B, and C of the supplemental readings. As mentioned, two rounds of exploratory groups were held with shift workers. The results of the first and follow-up groups are provided in Sections A and B. Section C presents reactions to the prevention message concepts shown in the second round of groups.

SUMMARY

Focus groups, the most common form of qualitative advertising research, can be defined as a group of 6 to 12 individuals who

- take part in a carefully planned series of discussions, which is
- held in a permissive, non-threatening environment, and is
- led by a trained moderator, where
- discussions are designed to uncover attitudes and perceptions in predefined areas of interest, to better
- enable decision makers to make more fully informed and more successful decisions.

Focus groups have been used to respond to a broad range of advertising-related needs:

- exploring issues related to advertising strategy, such as target audience selection, audience perceptions, and brand strengths and weaknesses;
- exploring reactions to alternative advertising messages and approaches;
- understanding reactions to current approaches to brand and category advertising;
- identifying perceived and desired category and brand benefits and exploring potential ways to express these benefits through advertising;
- developing and refining hypotheses regarding consumer motivations, especially with regard to how to "tap" these motivations in advertising; and
- developing and obtaining reactions to potential new products and new product ideas, as well as alternative product packaging ideas.

Focus group planning begins with two parallel activity paths. The first path relates to the moderator and consists of moderator selection and briefing and the creation of the focus group discussion guide. The second path relates to the logistics of the groups. Here, decisions are reached with regard to group characteristics, the number and location of the groups, facility selection, and participant recruitment. The successful completion of these two paths leads to the conduct of the groups themselves. A typical focus group passes through six stages: prefatory remarks, introductions and personal information, setting the context for discussion, main discussion, summary, final questions. The process concludes with an assessment of the success of the first set of groups, modifications and revisions (if necessary), analysis, presentation, and application to decision making.

The quality of information derived from focus groups is affected by observers' viewing behaviors. Observers should make certain that they come prepared, start watching from the beginning, focus on the big picture, listen to everyone, listen to all comments, do not jump to premature conclusions, do not let character judgments affect how the group members' comments are perceived, and are not biased by dominant personalities.

Advances in technology have resulted in viable alternatives to face-to-face focus groups. When justified by target characteristics or topic, online approaches are a viable, legitimate alternative to traditional focus groups.

Review Questions

1. How can focus groups be defined?
2. In what ways can focus groups contribute to advertising decision making?
3. Should focus groups be used to test and evaluate advertising creative? Why or why not?
4. What are important considerations in the selection of a focus group moderator?
5. What is the purpose of the moderator briefing? What topics are typically covered in the briefing?
6. What is a discussion guide? Describe how a discussion guide is developed.
7. What are important considerations in determining focus group composition? Why are different considerations appropriate for different types of groups?
8. How is the total number of required focus groups determined?

9. What are the key characteristics of a focus group facility?
10. What types of screener questions identify individuals who should be excluded from focus group participation?
11. What are the main stages in a focus group? What events occur at each stage?
12. Once written, should the focus group discussion guide ever be changed or modified? Why or why not?
13. What are the guidelines for focus group viewing? Why is each guideline important?
14. Are online focus groups "real" focus groups? Why or why not?
15. Under what circumstances do online focus groups have advantages over traditional face-to-face groups?

Application Exercises[21]

Application exercises 1 through 5 relate to concepts raised and discussed in this chapter.

1. You are the researcher working on the Dell Computer account. Dell is in the midst of evaluating its current advertising campaign and is particularly interested in exploring the attitudes and beliefs of 15- to 18-year olds with regard to (a) the process underlying computer purchase, (b) perceptions of Dell and competitive brands, and (c) the effects, if any, of advertising on brand perceptions and brand choice. You, as the researcher, have decided to hold focus groups to explore these issues and are just beginning the planning process. Your client, however, has never been to a focus group. Write the client a letter to explain what is about to happen. In your letter, be certain to address
   - What you have done so far to prepare for the groups. For example, how will you assure the client that the appropriate people will be attending and that the groups will be conducted in a beneficial and professional manner?
   - What the client can expect as he watches the groups. Discuss in detail, specific to these groups, the stages or progression the groups might proceed through, paying particular attention to the specific types and focus of

discussion that will occur at various points throughout the groups. Be specific. Explain what will happen when the groups first begin, what you expect to happen next, etc.
   - What is the best way to listen to, learn from, and draw conclusions from the group's discussion. Be concrete and avoid generalizations.

2. Your client is looking forward to the focus groups described in the prior exercise. You task now is to recommend the optimal number of groups. First, present a written recommendation for the groups: how many groups should be held, what city or cities should they take place in, and what are the characteristics of the individuals who will participate in each group? Second, based on this recommendation, prepare a screener to recruit the desired participants.

3. The focus groups described in the prior exercises are now just two weeks away. Prepare a discussion guide to be used in the groups.

4. You are the researcher working on the account team responsible for the advertising for K-Mart. K-Mart has decided to reposition itself. K-Mart's traditional appeal and customer base has been "middle-American" women aged 25 to 49, full-time homemakers, and "working-class" households with total annual incomes between

$15,000 and $35,000. K-Mart now wishes to appeal to a more contemporary, upscale clientele. Its new target includes both men and women aged 25 to 49, employed in white-collar jobs with annual household incomes of more than $40,000. K-Mart believes that it can appeal to this new target while at the same time keeping its traditional customer base.

K-Mart has authorized up to eight focus groups. How many groups do you recommend be conducted? Why? What are the specific characteristics of the people who would be attending each group? Why? Avoid generalities in your discussion. Be specific and provide a sound rationale for your decisions as to the number of groups you recommend and the characteristics of those attending.

5. Consider each of the following situations. Then, for each situation, decide whether you would recommend face-to-face or online focus groups. Explain and justify your recommendation.

   a. John Deere wishes to obtain farmers' reactions to its latest advertising campaign for tractors and to explore reactions to potential creative themes for a new campaign.

   b. Kraft General Foods wants to explore reactions to their trade advertising campaigns in focus groups with grocery store purchasing managers.

   c. Revlon wants to explore reactions to several new make-up formulations. This consists of women aged 25 to 44 who have purchased blush or eye shadow in the prior 60 days. Group participants will for each new product: be exposed to a description of the product, try the product, evaluate the product, and discuss the relationship between the new product description and actual product performance.

   d. Toys "R" Us wishes to probe what is "hot" in the video game market. Specifically, Toys "R" Us seeks to better understand perceptions of video games (both in general and in terms of specific titles) among boys aged 12 to 16.

Application exercises 6 through 11 relate to the drowsy driver focus groups discussed in the online supplemental readings.

6. Examine the screener used to identify shift workers of interest. What additions or modifications, if any, would you make to this screener? Are you satisfied with the wording and approach used to identify "sleepy drivers of interest?" Provide a rationale for your suggested changes or for leaving the screener "as is."

7. Examine and evaluate the discussion guides used for initial and follow-up groups. What additions, deletions, or other modifications would you make to each guide? Present your revised guides accompanied by a short paper that provides a rationale for your changes.

8. Read through the discussion guide. This guide uses logical/rational questions to probe respondents' attitudes toward sleep and drowsy driving. Revise the discussion guide to include at least three of the projective techniques discussed in Chapter 5. If you decide to use picture projection or other technique that requires a visual stimulus, make certain to attach copies of the stimuli you would use.

9. Read through the findings from the initial round of groups (Sections A and B) and the proposed prevention concepts (Section C). Keeping in mind what was learned in the initial round of groups, evaluate the concepts developed for the second round of groups. Does each concept reflect what was learned from initial groups? Would you modify, delete, or change any of the concepts? Are there additional concepts that should have been explored (and what would they be)? Prepare a short paper that provides your point of view in response to the prior questions.

10. Read through the reactions to the communication concepts provided in Section C. Which, if any, of the concepts would you recommend for use in a communication campaign? Provide support for your decision.

11. Assume that a third round of focus groups was desired. These focus groups would use what was learned from the second round of groups to obtain reactions to revised prevention concepts. You have been asked to create the messages/concepts that will be explored in these groups. Read the results of the reactions to the original concepts (Section C) and then present four concepts to be explored in these groups. Your concepts can be revisions of the initial concepts or entirely new concepts. Provide a rationale for the concepts you present.

Endnotes

1. See, for example, Iowa State University Extension (undated). "Can You Call It a Focus Group?" at http://www.extension.iastate.edu/Publications/PM1969A.pdf; Mary Marczak and Meg Sewell (undated). "Using Focus Groups for Evaluation" at http://ag.arizona.edu/fcs/cyfernet/cyfar/focus.htm; Richard A. Krueger and Mary Anne Casey (2009). *Focus Groups: A Practical Guide for Applied Research* (Thousand Oaks, CA: Sage Publications); David Gordon (1996). "Focus Groups." *Annual Review of Sociology* 22: 129–152.

2. See, for example, Ioni Lewis, Barry Watson, Katherine White, and Richard Tay (2007). "Promoting Public Health Messages: Should We Move Beyond Fear-Evoking Appeals in Road Safety?" *Qualitative Health Research* 17 (3): 61–74; Denise DeLorme, Scott Hagen, and I. Jack Stout (2003). "Consumer Perspectives on Water Issues: Directions for an Educational Campaign." *Journal of Environmental Education* 34 (2): 28–35. Beyond these readings, Lutz notes that: "The 1988 Republican focus group in Paramus, N.J., has reached legendary stature, and deservedly so, for that single gathering may have changed American history. George Bush was trailing Michael Dukakis by double digits, with the critical target group, so-called Reagan Democrats, trending toward the Massachusetts Governor. Assembled was just such a group, and they were fed a litany of Dukakis negatives, from Willie Horton to Boston Harbor. Individually, the negatives did not have a significant impact (although the prison furlough program evoked considerable unease). However, the cumulative effect of the information provided to the participants peeled them away from Dukakis one by one—and made it clear to the Bush camp exactly what had to be done to win." ("Focus Group Research in American Politics" at http://www.pollingreport.com/focus.htm).

3. See, for example, Elizabeth Waiters, Andrew Treno, and Joel Grube (2001). "Alcohol Advertising and Youth: A Focus-Group Analysis of What Young People Find Appealing in Alcohol Advertising." *Contemporary Drug Problems*, 28: 695–718; Gage Chapel, Kristen Peterson, and Roy Joseph (1999). "Exploring Anti-Gang Advertisements: Focus Group Discussions with Gang Members and at Risk Youth." *Journal of Applied Communication Research* 27: 237–257.

4. See, for example, Laura Bellows, Jennifer Anderson, Susan Martin Gould, and Garry Auld (2008). "Formative Research and Strategic Development of a Physical Activity Component to a Social Marketing Campaign for Obesity Prevention in Preschoolers." *Journal of Community Health* 33: 169–178.

5. Crest, for example, used focus groups to help it understand consumers reactions to a new line of toothpaste and to identify the three flavors that would comprise the line. Consumers picked rest introduced a new cinnamon, herbal, and citrus. See Louise Story (2005). "Consumers, Long the Targets, Become the Shapers of Campaigns," *New York Times* (July 1). To view a focus group discussion of alternative packaging ideas, see http://www.youtube.com/watch?v=_vII8dJsBZ0.

6. Business Research Lab (2007). "The Role of Focus Groups in Advertising" at http://www.busreslab.com/tips/tip9.htm.

7. Thomas L. Greenbaum (1983). *The Practical Handbook and Guide to Focus Group Research* (Lexington, MA: D. C. Heath and Company).

8. The content of the briefing as well as the discussion guide (shown in Figure 6.3) and screener (shown in Figure 6.4) are hypothetical and for illustrative purposes only. All three documents relate to the VERB campaign discussed in Chapter 1's online supplemental readings.

9. R. Krueger (1994). *Focus Groups: A Practical Guide for Applied Research (2nd ed.)* (Thousand Oaks, CA: Sage Publications).

10. Alfred E. Goldman and Susan McDonald (1987). *The Group Depth Interview: Principles and Practice* (Englewood Cliffs, NJ: Prentice-Hall).

11. The Catalyst Ranch Web site is http://www.catalystranch.com/.

12. Observation Baltimore at http://www.observationbaltimore.com/focus_group_facility_maryland_dc/qualiitative_research_analysis.html.

13. Research Inc. at http://www.researchincorporated.com/maximizing-results-at-a-focus-group-facility.

14. Thomas Greenbaum (2008). "Online Focus Groups are no Substitute for the Real Thing" at http://www.groupsplus.com/pages/qmr0601.htm.

15. Greenbaum, op. cit.

16. New York State Teachers College (2009). "Focus Groups," at http://www.programevaluation.org/focusgroups.htm.

17. Doyle Research located at http://www.doyleresearch.com/index.php/live-online. A video of this approach is found at http://www.youtube.com/watch?v=5Z6xYd7NZFk. For a listing of other companies engaged in this form of research, see the Green Book at http://www.greenbook.org/market-research-firms.cfm/online-focus-groups.

18. G. Graffigna and A. C. Bosio (2006). "The Influence of Setting on Findings Produced in Qualitative Health Research: A Comparison between Face-to-Face and Online Discussion Groups About HIV/AIDS." *International Journal of Qualitative Methods* 5 (3) at http://www.ualberta.ca/~ijqm/backissues/5_3/pdf/graffigna.pdf. For additional reviews of data quality from online approaches, see Katharine Hansen and Randall Hansen (2006). "Using an Asynchronous Discussion Board for Online Focus Groups: A Protocol and Lessons Learned" at http://www.quintcareers.com/KH_Teaching/ABR_2006.pdf and Kate Stewart and Matthew Williams (2005). "Researching Online Populations: The Use of Online Focus Groups for Social Research." *Qualitative Research* 5 (4): 395–416.

19. Kiek Tate et al. (2009). "Online Focus Groups as a Tool to Collect Data in Hard-to-Include Populations: Examples from Pediatric Oncology." *BMC Medical Research Methodology* at http://www.biomedcentral.com/1471-2288/9/15#IDALRX2E.

20. The supplemental readings are either adapted or taken directly from National Highway Traffic and Safety Administration (undated). "Development and Testing of Countermeasures for Fatigue Related Highway Crashes: Focus Group Discussions with Young Males, Shift Workers, and Shift Work Supervisors" at http://www.nhtsa.dot.gov/people/injury/drowsy_driving1/listening/toc.htm. The research was planned and reports were written by Toben F. Nelson, Nancy E. Isaac, and John D. Graham, Ph.D. of the Harvard School of Public Health.

21. All exercises are hypothetical.

CHAPTER 7

Analysis of Qualitative Data

A qualitative research study typically collects thousands of words that describe respondents' attitudes, express respondents' thoughts and opinions, and communicate respondents' feelings and emotions. Qualitative analysis attempts to make sense of this verbal data by going beyond the literal words themselves to discover underlying themes, commonalties, and differences among respondents. This chapter introduces you to the procedures underlying the analysis of qualitative data.

***

After reading this chapter, you should be able to:

- define the characteristics of qualitative data analysis
- identify the techniques by which insights are obtained and conclusions are drawn from qualitative data
- understand how to evaluate the quality of a quantitative analysis
- understand the strengths and weaknesses of qualitative data analysis software.

The goals of qualitative data analysis, as with any form of data analysis, are to produce findings that meaningfully relate to the problem motivating the research and to provide insights that help individuals make better decisions. These goals can be achieved only when the vast amount of verbal data collected during a qualitative research study is reduced to a set of well-defined and clearly explained patterns and themes. Unfortunately, there are few agreed-upon, externally objective techniques for accomplishing this. There are, for example, no mathematical formulae for determining statistical significance. There is no way to replicate perfectly the process by which an individual analyst infers themes from the data. In short, there are no absolute rules to guide a qualitative analysis except "to do the very best with your full intellect to fairly represent the data and communicate what the data reveal given the purpose of the study."[1] Thus, the extent to which qualitative research produces relevant, accurate findings is in great part dependent on the skills of the individual who conducts the analysis.

This is not meant to imply that qualitative data analysis is haphazard or subject to the whims of each individual analyst. Nothing, in fact, is farther from the truth. While there are no hard and fast rules governing the analysis of qualitative data, guidelines do exist. The greater the extent to which a researcher systematically applies these guidelines, the greater the likelihood that the analysis will accurately reflect real trends and patterns in consumer response. Patton, in this regard, points out the relationship between analytical procedures, analyst skills, and outcomes of the analysis:

> Guidelines and procedural suggestions are not rules. Applying guidelines requires judgment and creativity. Because each qualitative study is unique, the analytical approach used will be unique. Because qualitative inquiry depends, at every stage, on the skills, training, insights and capabilities of the researcher, qualitative analysis ultimately depends on the analytical intellect and style of the analyst. The human factor is the great strength and the fundamental weakness of qualitative inquiry and analysis.[2]

The remainder of this chapter presents strategies that guide the preparation, examination, and interpretation of qualitative data. The presentation and reporting of quantitative data is presented in Chapter 21.

ACTIVITIES CONDUCTED PRIOR TO DATA EXAMINATION

Two important activities take place during this initial stage: (1) a review of the research problem and informational needs, and (2) an evaluation of the study sample.

Review Problem Definition and Informational Needs

A useful qualitative analysis responds to the problem(s) motivating the research and the types of information required for relevant marketing or advertising-related decisions. Thus, this stage of analysis conducts an explicit review of the problem definition and informational needs. Notes and documents from agency and client meetings as well as the research proposal itself are reviewed. Since informational needs are also reflected in the discussion or interview guide, this is also reviewed. The outcome of the review is a list of specific areas that the analysis will address and the types of information that the analysis will provide.

Informational needs sometimes change during a qualitative research study. Some initial informational needs may become less important, and new informational needs may arise during the research. Additionally, it is possible that some important informational needs may not have been explicitly specified in initial discussions and research planning meetings. As a result, it is recommended that before the start of data analysis, all involved in the research meet to confirm that the focus of the proposed analysis will satisfy the current set of informational needs. The outcome of this meeting is either acceptance or revision of the list of analytical areas. The confirmation of informational needs and revision (if any) of the list of areas the analysis will address serves two important purposes. First, it provides an outline and focus for subsequent data analyses. As such, it lets the analyst focus on a well-defined set of topics. Given the vast amount of data collected by most qualitative research, the ability to focus the analysis is an important component of success. Kruger points out that:

> The challenge to the researcher is to place primary attention on questions that are at the foundation of the study. Focused analysis conserves resources, but more importantly it enables the analyst to concentrate attention on areas of critical concern.[3]

Second, an agreement of informational needs and analytical focus before data analysis verifies the types of information that will be addressed in the presentation of the study's findings and conclusions. This agreement greatly reduces the probability of a dissatisfied end user stating during a presentation: "This report is not complete. You should have looked at . . . ? I need to know about . . . ! Why is that information not here!"

Evaluate the Sample and Note Any Limitations

Next, the sample of respondents participating in the research is evaluated in terms of its "goodness" for providing reliable information relevant to the informational needs motivating the research.

Qualitative research rarely uses probability sampling, and therefore, it is typically acknowledged "up-front" that representativeness and generalizations to the broader population are limited. However, even when acknowledging these limitations, respondent characteristics must be still examined to confirm that (1) the sample possesses the desired set of demographic, brand-related and/or attitudinal characteristics, and (2) there is an absence of bias or confounding effects. The goal here is to make certain that the characteristics desired in the planned sample were actually present in the recruited sample. The following scenario illustrates the importance of this step.

> Imagine that Sony conducts a set of focus groups to probe college students' reactions to, perceptions of, and experiences with various brands of portable music players. Sony wishes to know the perceptions of those who currently own a Sony and those who own a competing brand. There are no problems with the respondents recruited for the Sony-owners group.

Respondents represent a good cross-section of the male and female college population and they possess specified brand and demographic characteristics. Moreover, these respondents did not know each other prior to attending the group. Recruitment for the group that owns other brands' products may be a problem, however. All of the participants in this group own the same competing brand, thus limiting the range of experiences with competing brands.

This limitation must be kept in mind during the analysis and must be acknowledged during the findings presentation.

DATA EXAMINATION

The next stage in qualitative data analysis entails a review of the raw data: audio or video-tapes, transcripts, any notes that might have been taken, and any respondent-generated materials.[4] At this stage, the goal is to immerse oneself in the data in order to experience the texture, tone, mood, range, and content of respondents' verbal (and if available non-verbal) communications. This immersion is not a results-oriented process, however. The goal is not to determine what the data means, but rather, the goal is to become more familiar with the data itself. Moustakas notes that this type of immersed data review lets an analyst "savor, appreciate, smell, touch, taste, feel [the information] without concrete goal or purpose."[5] The goal of data review, therefore, is an understanding of what respondents communicated. This understanding is facilitated when the following guidelines are kept in mind during the review process.[6]

Review the data with an open mind. The goal is to review and become refamiliar with what respondents did and said. Review comments and other materials without bias; do not selectively look for patterns of response that either confirm or disconfirm preconceived notions.

Try to understand the reasons underlying attitudes and behaviors. Statements of opinion or descriptions of a particular set of behaviors provide one level of information. An informed understanding of attitudes and behaviors, however, requires that the analysis be conducted on a second, deeper level. Here, it is necessary to get "beneath the surface" and understand *why* opinions are held or behaviors are exhibited. Thus, the initial review of the data should pay particular attention to the reasons individuals give for their attitudes and behaviors. Many respondents, for example, might state that they are offended by current approaches to perfume advertising. The widespread dislike of the advertising provides insights on one level. However, the implications of these stated attitudes for marketing and advertising would vary under the following conditions:

- Most respondents object because the advertising is felt to degrade women, portraying them as sexual objects;
- Most respondents objected because the advertising is felt to exclude them, being targeted to a younger audience;
- Most respondents object because they believe the advertising leads to increased promiscuity.

Respondents are often able to explain the reasons underlying their attitudes and behaviors. There are times, however, when respondents cannot verbally explain why they feel or act as they do. In these cases, underlying reasons can often be inferred from the words and analogies respondents use to describe the reasons for their opinions. Thus, an initial review of the data must be sensitive to both the direct and indirect methods that respondents use to express the reasons why they hold a particular belief or participate in certain behaviors.

Understand the Intensity of Respondents' Feelings and Points of View

Qualitative data analysis often seeks to uncover areas in which consensus of opinion does or does not exist among the sample of respondents. However, it is important to note both the *extent of consensus* and the *strength or conviction* with which expressed views are held. It is possible, for example, to use individual interviews to determine the initial appeal of two proposed advertising slogans. The pattern of responses to these slogans may indicate an overall consensus where most respondents liked both slogans, while a small portion of those interviewed did not like either slogan. This finding might suggest that either slogan can be selected. However, the intensity of respondents' reactions provides additional insights and can greatly influence the decision-making process. An examination of the intensity of responses might indicate the following:

Slogan 1: Most respondents liked (although in a quite lukewarm fashion) this slogan. A few respondents disliked this slogan very much. These respondents were quite outspoken in their distaste for the slogan.

Slogan 2: Most respondents liked this slogan very much. Respondents spent a long time describing the positive feelings evoked by the slogan. A few respondents disliked the slogan, but this dislike was not very strongly felt.

Thus, while the relative number of individuals liking and disliking each slogan was comparable, the intensity of opinions strongly suggests differences in the underlying reactions to each slogan. While the slogans appear equal on the surface (both appear to be liked by about the same proportion of respondents), the intensity of opinion clearly favors selection of Slogan 2 over Slogan 1.

Inferences of belief intensity can be drawn from the way in which a belief is expressed. Clear, unambiguous, forceful language is often an indicator of strong, intense feelings. A respondent who forcefully states "I hate that ad!" leaves little doubt that the opinion is genuine and intense. Repetition, where a respondent provides the same answer to several different (or differently worded) probes and questions, can also be a sign of belief intensity. Finally, respondents may signal a strongly held belief through irony, metaphor, or derisive humor. A respondent who looks at a new product concept and states (with a great deal of irony): "Oh, yeah sure, I'd buy this product. I've been waiting all my life for this product. Where, oh where, has it been?" is signaling a strongly held opinion.

Understand the Respondent, Not Individual Responses

Most respondents try to provide truthful responses to the questions they are asked. Sometimes opinions change during the interview or focus group, or initial statements do not present a complete view of an individual's beliefs. Thus, it is important to look at trends in the entire corpus of data rather than reviewing comments and statements on a response-by-response basis. The importance of this approach to data review becomes most apparent when self-contradictory statements are examined.

A self-contradiction occurs when statements made by a respondent at one point in the group or personal interview contradict statements made at other times. For example, a conversation early in a focus group could take this form:

Respondent 1: I never buy or use shampoos from the grocery store. They're really low in quality and they damage your hair.

Respondent 2: That's right. You really need to buy a salon shampoo. I know that's all I use. It's worth the price.

Respondent 1: There's just no comparison with how your hair looks. The shine and appeal is just so much greater after you shampoo with a salon shampoo. No grocery store brand can compare. So, I just don't buy them.

Later in the group, this conversation could take place:

Respondent 2: So what do you do?

Respondent 1: I buy it. There are times when I'm in the grocery store and I see a well-known brand. And it's on sale for a really good price. So I'll buy it. I really don't notice any short-term harm. And when I'm done with the bottle, I go back to my salon brand.

Respondent 1 provided contradictory statements. This respondent's initial comments were likely not attempts to mislead the moderator, but rather, they were honest expressions of her point of view. The respondent's initial comments were overstated and did not provide insights into her overall pattern of behavior. Only by examining the totality of this respondent's statements, especially her later statements in the context of earlier statements, can true insights into her attitudes and behaviors be understood.

Review with a Critical Eye and Ear

Most respondents try to tell the truth. They try to honestly express their attitudes and opinions and to accurately report their behaviors. However, some respondents, in some instances, will either intentionally or unintentionally not tell the truth. The challenge in qualitative analysis is to determine when to take respondents' comments at face value and when to discount or distrust their comments. It is important, for example, to distinguish between respondents who truly dislike a proposed television execution and those who may really like it but express negative reactions because all other group respondents express dislike.

Distinguishing between truth and falsity in respondents' comments is one of the great challenges of qualitative analysis. Contradictory statements provide some direction for distinguishing between truth and falsity. Here, one looks at the totality of response and infers the nature of true opinions. Other clues to false statements relate to social norms and social acquiescence. This occurs when respondents provide answers that they think the interviewer, moderator, or other group members want to hear. Responses that signal this type of false statement include the following:

- Simple responses (such as "Yes, that's true." and "No, I don't think so.") offered in response to probes but seldom volunteered.

- Responses that suggest either hostility or personal allegiance (such as "I've already said that twice!" and "You've convinced me.").

- Evasive responses that fail to explain a point of view (such as "It's like I said." and "You know what I mean.")[7]

During this portion of the analysis, it is also important to keep an eye and ear open for what is not said. Respondents can fail to mention a topic or provide a piece of information for one of four reasons. First, respondents may feel that the topic is not at all important and therefore, they may feel that there is little need to discuss and explore the topic. Second, respondents may assume that the topic is so important that it is unnecessary to mention, discuss, or explore it. (Respondents, for example, may not mention "avoidance of crashes" when asked to list the things they consider important in an airline. They assume that the importance of this characteristic is already known.) Third, the topic may be so personal or sensitive that the respondent does not feel like "opening up" in that particular area. The analyst, during the review process, must try to determine which of these causes is the reason why a particular topic has not been mentioned. The fourth reason is relatively easy to identify. Respondents will talk around the issue, talk in the third person, or otherwise avoid directly confronting the issue. Respondents may also explicitly state that they do not wish to pursue the topic. Distinguishing the first from the second situation is more difficult. Here, the analyst must look for cues in the discussion that point either toward or away from topic importance. When these cues are not present or are ambiguous, the analyst must be careful not to let his or her own biases influence inferences drawn from the interviews.

Reflection

Reflection is the final activity in this phase of data analysis. This is a time of "quiet contemplation . . . where the researcher deliberately withdraws" from the formal analytical process.[8] During this period (that typically lasts from one to several days), impressions and meanings from the prior review of the data "incubate" without structure or guidance as a prelude to the formal analysis, which takes place in the next set of activities.

THEME IDENTIFICATION, ANALYSIS, AND REVISION

Qualitative analysis typically centers around themes, where a theme is defined as the expression of a consistent and recurring idea found either explicitly or implicitly in the data. Themes help the end users of the research to understand the trends and patterns suggested by the data. This section describes the procedures by which themes are developed, evaluated, revised, and eventually accepted as a true representation of the research findings. Figure 7.1 illustrates the specific steps underlying this process, which do not follow a linear path. Rather, the development and evaluation of themes is a circular process entailing continuous data examination and theme revision.

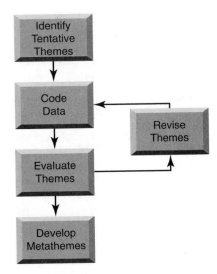

FIGURE 7.1 The Theme Development Process

The circular nature of this process is intentional and is a fundamental characteristic of the analysis process. The specific nature and value of this process has been described as:

> a loop-like pattern of multiple rounds of visiting the data as additional questions emerge, new connections are unearthed, and more complex formulations develop along with a deepening understanding of the material.[9]

It is important to note that the sequence of analysis proposed in this iterative process is one where, after data review and reflection, tentative themes are first proposed and then the data relevant to the evaluation of the theme is collected. Finally, based on data examination the theme is accepted, rejected, or modified. Bradley et al. note that "reviewing data (in this way) without coding helps identify emergent themes without losing the connections between concepts and their context."[10]

It can be argued that this approach is the reverse of the "proper" process where data is first organized, coded, and then the theme is allowed to "flow" out of the data. This reverse procedure will certainly, at the conclusion of the analysis, produce a set of findings. However, we recommend the theme → data → evaluation → revision procedure for several reasons. First, after data review and reflection, a researcher will certainly have themes in mind. It makes little sense (to us) to ignore these insights at the beginning of formal data analysis. Second, the uses of themes at the beginning of data analysis provide a tangible focus for the collection, coding, and evaluation of relevant data. Finally, the recommended process entails more extensive data analysis as one makes multiple passes through the data to confirm or disconfirm proposed themes.

Theme Development

Theme development begins with the list of areas to be addressed. Within each area, one or more themes relevant to that area are explicitly written. The theme represents the researcher's intuitive and informed judgment as to the content and pattern of findings in each topic area and, where appropriate, a specification of the underlying causes. The following illustrates a clear, concise, unambiguous theme that could be written at this stage of analysis.

> Overall, respondents reacted positively to the "Multi-music player" product concept. The product was seen as relevant, interesting and unique. Many expressed an interest in purchase when the product was priced under $90. Primary reasons for enthusiasm related to versatility and value. Neither gender nor income status appears related to level or type of response.

Coding Data According to Themes

Once all themes have been written, the researcher then examines and codes all available data. The coding of text, for example, interview or focus group transcripts, is relatively straightforward. The researcher reads through the transcript looking for statements that are related to each of the themes, where a particular statement can either be supportive of or contrary to the stated theme. Once a relevant statement is located, it is coded in the transcript with regard to its relevant theme and the direction of support (either positive or negative).

Examining Relevant Data

Each theme provides a concrete, tangible point of view that can be used to organize the findings and which can be confirmed or disconfirmed based on an examination of the trends in the coded data. Therefore, the next step in the process collects and examines the coded information relevant to each theme to determine the theme's correctness. A record sheet of the type shown in Figure 7.2 facilitates this process. The top of the form presents the theme—the analyst's view of a major pattern of response or finding. The theme shown on the top of the form in this example is the theme presented earlier in this section. The form following the theme is divided in half. Using the coding scheme developed in the prior step, evidence from the raw data that supports the theme is transcribed on the left side of the page, while evidence that disconfirms or contradicts the theme is transcribed on the right side of the page.

THEME: Overall, respondents reacted positively to the "Dual Player Zune" product concept. The product was seen as unique, and many expressed an interest in purchase when the product was priced under $50. Primary reasons for enthusiasm related to convenience and value. Neither gender nor income status appeared to be related to the response.

Evidence in support of theme   **Evidence in opposition to theme**

(Supportive evidence is placed in this column)   *(Counter evidence is placed in this column)*

FIGURE 7.2   Form for Recording Theme Support and Negation

When recording responses, it is important to record respondents' verbatim comments as well as any relevant demographic, attitudinal, or brand information. Verbatim comments, as opposed to paraphrased comments, are recorded for two reasons. First, the comments will be used later to provide the detail and substantiation for conclusions drawn in the written or oral presentation. Second, the verbatim comments shown on the record sheets provide a way for the analyst to justify and explain conclusions drawn from the data. (This aspect of the analysis is discussed in the next section.) Both uses of respondents' comments require the use of original, unaltered comments.

Theme Evaluation and Revision

Once all the comments relevant to a theme have been recorded, one re-examines the theme in light of the recorded data to determine the extent to which the theme should or should not be accepted given the pattern of the underlying data. An acceptable theme is one that accurately reflects the content of the recorded data. An unacceptable theme is one that does not accurately reflect the content of the recorded data and therefore must be rejected or revised. The process of theme evaluation proceeds as follows:

> The data is examined by the analyst. The theme is strengthened each time a piece of data is found that supports the theme. But, if some aspect of the data disconfirms the theme or relates to it ambiguously then the analyst redefines or restates the theme to accommodate the contrary data. The analyst keeps considering each piece of data and, as necessary, revising the theme until all the relevant data has been examined.[11]

This procedure of theme revision tends to produce themes that are highly accurate descriptors of the underlying data. Moreover, the process itself is an effective means of increasing and demonstrating the validity of conclusions reached, especially in light of the perceived subjective nature of qualitative data analysis.

As might be expected, few themes at this point are completely accepted in their original form or completely rejected. More typically, themes are modified or revised to improve clarity and increase accuracy. Theme revision generally takes one of two forms. First, a theme can be elaborated upon with additional levels of specificity and detail. Based on an examination of the relevant data, for example, the theme presented earlier in this section might be revised to read:

> Respondents' reactions to the "Multi-music player" were generally positive and the product shows some promise. The primary product appeal to both men and women was versatility. Respondents' favorable comments generally disappeared when the product was priced at $115. At this price level it was generally felt that the value (primarily provided by the versatility) was just "not there." Respondents felt that the appropriate price for the product was $90, a point at which there was a great deal of value. Beyond a lack of value related to price, primary reasons for negative response related to lack of a real need and perceptions that it is "just a gimmick."

Second, additional detail may be added to the theme to restrict its applicability to certain groups comprising the sample. The following might be a further revision of the prior theme:

> Respondents' reactions to the "Multi-music player" were generally positive and the product shows some promise. Women and men expressed positive reactions to the concept before the mention of price, although more women than men were favorable. The primary product appeal to both men and women was versatility. Women more so than men also displayed a positive response to two product features: the sound quality and size of the product. Respondents' favorable comments generally disappeared when the product was priced at $115. At this price level it was generally felt that the value (primarily provided by the versatility) was just "not there." Respondents felt that the appropriate price for the product was $90, a point at which there was a great deal of value. Beyond a lack of value related to price, primary reasons for negative response related to lack of a real need and perceptions that it is "just a gimmick."

Relating Individual Themes to Form Metathemes

Up to this point, individual themes describing trends and patterns in the data have been developed and evaluated. Moreover, individual themes have been modified to ensure that they are an accurate reflection of the data. One additional step is necessary to make the results of qualitative study maximally useful to those who use the information for decision making. The interrelationships of the individual themes must be made explicit to facilitate understanding of the overall trends and patterns in the data. Metatheme is the label given to themes that provide these interrelationships.[12] For example, the individual themes describing reactions to each of Sony's three new product concepts can be related to form a metatheme. This metatheme would summarize similarities and differences among each of the individual themes, as follows:

> *Metatheme: Overall, reactions to all three concepts were positive. Men and women, however, displayed different patterns of response.*
>
> Women tended to respond to each concept more favorably than men. They tended to react to the specific characteristics of each proposed concept and identified specific product attributes that led to product appeal. Additionally, women felt that all three concepts presented products that were "cutting edge" and that "would make their life better or more enjoyable."
>
> Men, on the other hand, were impressed by each product's convenience. Additionally, men were more price sensitive than women, often noting that the products were "just a gimmick" that in terms of the cost was just "not worth it."

Serendipitous Discoveries

The prior steps reflect a sequence of theme development, evaluation, modification, revision, and ultimate selection. The themes evaluated in this process are those that have been explicitly formulated in response to pre-identified areas of inquiry or informational need. However, one of the great advantages of qualitative analysis is the opportunity to gain insights in unanticipated areas. During each of the activities conducted in this stage of analysis, an analyst must be sensitive and open to unforseen or unanticipated insights. These insights should be recorded on forms similar to that shown in Figure 7.2 and evaluated similarly to other pre-identified themes.

EVALUATING THE ANALYSIS

Quantitative research relies on estimates of reliability and validity to help researchers determine how much confidence they can have in the data itself and the conclusions and insights drawn from data analysis. The outcomes of these estimates are numeric and typically open to only a narrow range of alternative interpretations. Since qualitative research is nonnumeric, many argue that the concepts of reliability and validity do not apply. Nevertheless, this does not mean that there is an absence of criteria for distinguishing between good/acceptable and bad/unacceptable qualitative analyses and reports. The quality of a qualitative analysis can be assessed by an examination of the way in which the study was planned and carried out, and the way in which the analysis was conducted and reported.

Crabtree and Miller[13] propose the following criteria for evaluating the design and analysis elements of qualitative research:

- *Was the appropriate method used to answer the questions motivating the research?* Is there an explanation, for example, for why focus groups were selected instead of individual in-depth interviews?

- *Was appropriate and adequate sampling used to answer the question?* Are there assurances that there is no inherent bias in sample selection and that enough people were studied to provide sufficient confidence in the strength of presented conclusions?

- *Was an iterative process of collecting and analyzing data used and data saturation achieved?* In qualitative research, the investigative team learns about the topic as the research progresses. The study design should consist of data collection and analysis, followed by more data collection and analysis, in an iterative fashion, until no new information is obtained. For example, were the learnings from initial focus groups or interviews used to inform and guide later interviews?

- *Was a thorough analysis presented?* A good qualitative study not only presents the findings but provides a thorough analysis of the data. Beware of studies that simply present superficial descriptions without interpretation.

- *Are the background, training, and preconceptions of the investigators described?* Because the investigators are being relied on for analysis of the data, we must know their training and biases. Once these characteristics are known, we can use them to evaluate their conclusions.

A researcher must also make certain that end users of the research understand how the themes were identified. This is called this *transparency.* Transparency does not mean that other researchers need to agree with the interpretation and conclusions. Rather, it means that other researchers must understand and agree with the steps taken to reach the conclusions. Transparency leads to greater credibility when several data-related questions are addressed and explained:

- Is there an absence of bias in data selection and examination. Was all data examined and considered? Was some data given more weight than others? Was some data eliminated from the analysis?
- Is there an absence of bias in the creation of themes?
- Is there sufficient evidence to support each presented theme?
- How were initial themes created and revised over the course of data analysis?
- Was the analysis carried out in a rigorous and systematic manner?

While transparency leads to greater credibility, greater credibility in turn leads to greater trust in the findings. The ultimate sign of an acceptable qualitative report is that the end users trust the conclusions, insights, and recommendations.

CAQDAS: COMPUTER-ASSISTED QUALITATIVE DATA ANALYSIS SOFTWARE

As the prior section indicates, the analysis of qualitative data can be time-consuming. In response, software programs have been developed to assist and guide the coding and analysis processes.

> Software which falls under the CAQDAS "umbrella" includes a wide range of packages but its general principles are concerned with taking a qualitative approach to qualitative data. A qualitative approach is one where there is a need to interpret data through the identification and linking or coding of themes, concepts, processes, contexts, etc. in order to build explanations or theories or to test or enlarge on a theory.[14]

The use of CAQDAS is not without debate. Drawbacks of CAQDAS are believed to include

- an analytical focus on small, isolated pieces of text, which may result in one missing real meaning available only through the analysis of larger segments.[15] The focus on the coding of small units of text may also result in over-coding, resulting in too many codes that prevent the researcher from seeing the overall picture.[16]
- an emphasis on literal content rather than process in the examination of interview and focus group transcripts.[17]
- the risk that the researcher may confuse the process of coding with the process of analysis, resulting in only superficial insights into the data and its meaning.

Others believe that potential problems with CAQDAS can be significantly reduced or eliminated when they are kept in mind during the use of this software. Retie et al. notes that "there is substantial literature on the advantages of CAQDAS. In particular it can facilitate data reduction, systematic coding, effective searching, the analysis of large data sets; the testing of hypotheses; and the identification of negative cases."[18] These advantages are most likely to occur when the CAQDAS program is used as a tool rather than as a replacement for analyst skill and judgment. In this regard, Silver and Lewis note that:

> While we would argue that some software packages may be more suited to certain types of approaches, their purpose is not to provide you with a methodological or analytic framework . . . As the researcher you should remain in control of the interpretation process and decide which of the available tools within a software [package] can facilitate *your* approach to analysis most effectively.[19]

A variety of CAQDAS programs are available to assist in the data analysis process. While there are some differences in approach across programs, all allow for the examination and analysis of text in multiple formats (such as Word documents and PDF files) and permit the analysis of photographs and rich media (such as sound and video files). Further information on two of the more popular CAQDAS programs can be found at their respective Web sites: NVIVO and XSIGHT (http://www.qsrinternational.com) and ATLAS.ti (http://www.atlasti.com/). Third-party evaluations of these and other CAQDAS programs can be found at the CAQDAS Networking Project Web site.[20]

SUMMARY

The analysis of qualitative data proceeds best when the analyst takes a systematic approach. The chapter presented one approach, consisting of three main stages.

- The first stage consists of *activities conducted prior to data examination.* Two important activities take place during this initial stage: (1) review of the research problem and informational needs, and (2) evaluation of the study sample.
- The second stage *entails a review of the raw data.* The goal is to immerse oneself in the data in order to experience and better understand the texture, tone, mood, range, and content of respondents' verbal and nonverbal communications. Immersion is followed by a period of reflection on what was read, viewed, and heard.
- The third stage is one of *theme identification, analysis, and revision.* Themes are generalizations that flow from the data and help decision makers better understand the trends and patterns suggested by the data. Theme development is a circular process of identification and revision. Once all themes have been identified, metathemes are created to reveal the interrelationships of individual themes.

Several criteria can be used to evaluate the reliability and validity of a qualitative analysis. These criteria appear in the following questions:

- Was the appropriate method used to answer the questions motivating the research?
- Was appropriate and adequate sampling used to answer the question?
- Was an iterative process of collecting and analyzing data used and data saturation achieved?
- Was a thorough analysis presented?
- Are the background, training, and preconceptions of the investigators described?

Computer Assisted Qualitative Data Analysis Software (CAQDAS), if used appropriately, can assist in the coding and analysis of qualitative data in many forms: written, pictorial, oral, or filmed.

Review Questions

1. Is there a single approach to the analysis of qualitative data? Explain.
2. What two activities are conducted in the first stage of qualitative data analysis?
3. Why is it necessary to review the problem definition and informational needs prior to the start of data analysis?
4. Why is it important to examine and evaluate the sample prior to the start of data analysis?
5. What guidelines help improve the quality and success of data examination?
6. Why is a time of reflection an important component of data analysis?
7. What is a *theme?*
8. What is the purpose of data coding?
9. Should the creation of themes precede or follow data coding? Why?
10. Should a theme ever be modified once it is created? Why or why not?
11. What is a *metatheme?* What is its function?
12. How can one tell if a qualitative analysis is reliable and valid?
13. What is *CAQDAS?* How does it assist in the analysis of qualitative data?
14. What are the strengths and weaknesses of CAQDAS?

Application Exercises[21]

1. The Sony Playstation advertising account has just been placed into review. Sony sends 20 agencies a questionnaire. Sony will examine responses to their questions and then select the four agencies that will participate in the "pitch." Your agency receives one of the questionnaires.

    Several of the questions on the questionnaire ask for your agency's analysis of Sony's and competitive brands' advertising. It is decided that to respond to these questions two types of research are required. First, several creatives and account executives will collect, examine, and review the advertising. This review will lead to the preparation of a point of view of the advertising's strengths and weaknesses from a professional advertiser's perspective. Second, the advertising will be shown to individuals in the advertising's target audience. Three focus groups will be held with these individuals, at which time they will be shown the advertising and their reactions will be explored. The reactions of the focus group participants will also be used to respond to Sony's questionnaire.

    Timing is tight. The groups will be held in two days. Three days later, the questionnaire must be submitted to Sony. Your supervisor says (not altogether jokingly) that you will have to begin writing the report of the findings from the focus groups while you are in the process of watching the groups. Describe each of the steps or actions that you will take from this point (two days prior to the groups) forward to ensure that the task of providing reliable, appropriate information is accomplished successfully.

2. A series of personal interviews have been held with individuals who are frequent car renters. Selected portions of the interviews are shown next. Review the set of interviews. Then analyze the data to discover underlying themes. Prepare a memo that presents each identified theme and your support for the validity of that theme.

    Sally, age 23: You know, after renting quite a number of cars I've realized a couple of things. You get what you pay for. And what I pay for, and what I expect to get, are attendants who are polite, bills that are right, and cars ready for me when I get to the rental counter. I've found I can get this from Avis or Hertz. Budget is just what it says it is.

    Jim, age 53: I hate traveling out of town, but lately I'm doing it more and more. So, I guess when I travel I try to make it as easy on myself as possible. I stay at the nicer hotels, and I try to keep things going smoothly. The last thing I need after getting off an airplane are rental car problems. I've had cars that were dirty, that needed gas, that smelled like cigarettes, that broke down. Usually from the cheap, that is, budget companies. Now I try to avoid these companies. I want, need, things to go smoothly. No hassles. Not with the car. Not with getting the car. A smile from behind the counter is so nice. Someone who knows what they are doing is even nicer. I get this with Hertz, usually Avis. Not very many of the other companies.

Adam, age 28: I like the smell of a clean car. Of a car that has the floors swept and the windows cleaned. I also hate standing in line. The men and women behind the counter need to be fast and efficient. I truly hate standing in line while some tourist takes three hours to fill out the rental papers. It's nice when there's a window or a club just for renters like me. Avis and Hertz have one. I don't think that Budget does.

Matthew, age 31: What's important to me. No hassle. No problems. A car that is prepared and ready for me. Attendants and counter people that know what they are doing. And that are helpful. And courteous. And have a smile. I rent from the big companies-except for Budget.

Kathy, age 54: After all these years it's still important that I make a good impression with my boss at work. One way I do this is by showing that I'm responsible in the way that I spend the company's money. Where do I rent? Budget.

Melanie, age 32: You know, I think that I've rented at least 75 cars. And things have clearly gotten worse. All the things that I used to look for and take for granted just a few years ago: nice people, smiling people, people who know what they are doing, just don't seem to exist anymore. Or at least there's not very many of them. I think that Hertz has hired the last of them.

Todd, age 53: I'll never forget the first time I rented a car. Now I'm an old pro, I guess. I've learned that there certainly are differences in what a rental company delivers. Their people, for example. Hertz and Avis must spend a lot of time training their people. They know what they're doing. And they do it well. I've come to expect and want this kind of treatment. Boo on Budget. Also, I like driving new cars. So it's important that the car I rent is ready for me. Not only there in the lot, but clean and gassed.

Diana, age 49: A car is a car. It gets you from here to there. It's just transportation. I don't need or expect anything special. I just don't want the price to take me "for a ride." All the companies are about the same, but I usually wind up renting from Budget.

3. Imagine that your assistant has prepared a draft report of Jeep focus groups. One section of this report addresses the use of anthropomorphism to investigate Jeep's image. The following appears in the report. What is your reaction to this analysis? Is this acceptable or not acceptable as written? What suggestions would you have for improvement? What themes do you see in the comments?.

At this point in the groups, the moderator asked the respondents who were participating in the group to imagine what the product would be if the product were an animal. (The product was a Jeep 4 × 4.) Each person in the group wrote down his or her answer and then provided his or her answer when asked by the moderator. There were 10 people in the group. Here are their responses:

MARY:	elephant
SUE:	rhinoceros
ELLEN:	elephant
THERESA:	hippopotamus
MARTHA:	ox
JOHN:	jaguar
MAX:	cougar
JOE:	lion
DAVID:	lion
GLEN:	tiger

As you can see, all of the women picked similar kinds of animals while all of the men picked similar animals, too. There were two pairs of agreement, one among the men and one among the women. The moderator then asked each person why he or she picked this animal. Here are the answers:

MARY:	because the car can go any-where, and so can an elephant
SUE:	a rhino is heavy and chunky, and so is a Jeep
ELLEN:	an elephant is big and boxy and can go along where ever he wants to go
THERESA:	hippos are big, boxy and ugly
MARTHA:	slow, lumbering, and good for doing a lot of heavy work

JOHN:	fast, manly, uncontrollable	DAVID:	uncontrollable, just like you feel when driving a Jeep
MAX:	sleek, in charge, fast		
JOE:	the king of the beasts, and a Jeep is king of cars	GLEN:	rough and tough

Endnotes

1. Michael Q. Patton (1990). *Qualitative Evaluation and Research Methods* (Newbury Park, CA: SAGE Publications). The discussion in the introduction of this chapter is also adapted from this source.
2. Patton, op. cit.
3. Richard A. Krueger (1994). *Focus Groups, Second Edition* (Thousand Oaks, CA: Sage Publications).
4. The basis of the review can be either audiotapes or transcripts. While both work well, we nevertheless recommend that tapes be utilized whenever possible. Tapes permit a greater understanding of the tone, conviction, and expression associated with individual consumers' responses. Imagine, for example, two respondents who answer a question "This one was good." The transcript merely reports their words. However, a tape recording provides a better understanding of the underlying meaning, for example, compare "This ONE was good" (meaning "This one in particular was good, the others were not") to "This one WAS good" (meaning "This one was at one time good, but it no longer is.").
5. Clark Moustakas (1981). *Rhythms, Rituals and Relationships* (Detroit, MI: Center for Humanistic Studies).
6. Several of these recommendations are adapted from Alfred Goldman and Susan McDonald (1987). *The Group Depth Interview: Principles and Practice* (Englewood Cliffs, NJ: Prentice-Hall) and Krueger, op. cit.
7. Goldman and McDonald, op. cit.
8. Patton, op. cit.
9. S. Berkowitz (1997). "Analyzing Qualitative Data." In J. Frechtling and L. Sharp (Eds.). *User-Friendly Handbook for Mixed Methods Evaluations.* at: http://www.nsf.gov/pubs/1997/nsf97153/start.htm
10. Elizabeth H. Bradley, Leslie A. Curry and Kelly J. Devers (2007). "Qualitative Data Analysis for Health Services Research." *HSR: Health Services Research* 42 (4): 1758–1772.
11. This process is an adaptation of a qualitative analytical procedure known as negative case analysis. See Thomas R. Lindloff (1995). *Qualitative Communication Research Methods* (Thousand Oaks, CA: Sage Publications) and Y. S. Lincoln and E. G. Guba (1985). *Naturalistic Inquiry* (Thousand Oaks, CA: Sage Publications).
12. "Meta" is a prefix that means "beyond," in either a literal or metaphorical sense. Thus, a metatheme is a theme that goes beyond individual themes to reveal their interconnections.
13. B. F. Crabtree and W. L. Miller (2006). "A Worksheet for Assessing Qualitative Articles" at http://www.qualres.org/HomeGuid-3934.html.
14. Christina Silver and Ann Lewis (2009). "Choosing a CAQDAS Package" at http://caqdas.soc.surrey.ac.uk/PDF/2009ChoosingaCAQDASPackage.pdf.
15. S. A. Bong (2002). "Debunking Myths in Qualitative Data Analysis" at http://www.qualitative-research.net/fqs/fqs-e/inhalt2-02-e.htm.
16. K. A. Roberts and R. W. Wilson (2002). "ICT and the Research Process: Issues Around the Compatibility of Technology with Qualitative Data Analysis" at http://www.qualitative-research.net/fqs-texte/fqs-e/inhalt2-02/2-02robertswilson-e.htm.
17. M. Catterall and P. Maclaran (1998). "Using Computer Software for the Analysis of Qualitative Market Research Data" *International Journal of Market Research* 40 (3): 207–222.
18. Ruth Rettie, Helen Robinson, Anja Radke and Xiajiao Ye (2008). "CAQDAS: A Supplementary Tool for Qualitative Market Research" *Qualitative Market Research: An International Journal* 11 (1): 76–88.
19. Silver and Lewis, op. cit.
20. See QUIC Working Papers at http://caqdas.soc.surrey.ac.uk/QUICworkingpapers.html.
21. All situations are hypothetical. Actual company names are used for illustrative purposes only.

CHAPTER 8

Observation Research: Human and Automated

Observation research collects information without asking verbal questions. A researcher identifies informational needs and then uses observation to collect data pertinent to those needs. This and the following chapter discuss the three primary types of observation research: human observation of others' behaviors, automated observation, and biometric (physiological) observation. This chapter focuses on the first two forms of observation, while the next chapter focuses on biometric observation.

***

When you are done reading this chapter, you should have a better understanding of:

- how human and automated observation is used
- the strengths, weaknesses, and limitations of each form of observation, and
- the range of insights provided by each form of observation and how these insights contribute to advertising decision making.

Observation is a natural behavior. When we stand in line at a grocery store, we observe other shoppers' behaviors. When we are walking by an outdoor restaurant, we observe the food that patrons are eating. When we walk into a class on the first day, we look around and think about the students awaiting the start of class. Observation research conducted to assist in advertising decision making uses observation in the same way except that here, the observations are systematically planned, conducted, and analyzed.

This chapter discusses two types of observation research commonly used to inform advertising decision making:

- *Human observation* uses a researcher to observe other people's behaviors. All of the data is collected by the human observer. Watching how shoppers read food labels prior to making their purchases is an example of this type of observation.

- *Automated observation* uses computers or mechanical tracking devices to observe behaviors. Once the observation procedures have been put into place, no human involvement is required for data collection. Cookies[1] placed on a computer to track the Web sites that individuals visit are an example of this form of observation.

The remainder of this chapter discusses each of these approaches to observation. For each form of observation, we discuss when the approach to observation is most appropriate, the type of data collected (qualitative or quantitative), and procedures used for data collection.

HUMAN OBSERVATION

Human observation research is most appropriate in four types of situations.

- *Where observations of behavior are more insightful than descriptions of behavior.* Imagine that Samsung wants to determine how well consumers are able to access and use their new cell phone's features. Observing how individuals actually interact with the phone is likely to provide more insightful, actionable information than asking survey questions after the individual interacted with the phone.

- *Where respondents may be unable to verbalize their attitudes.* Consider a case where television advertising has been developed for a new children's toy. You want to know the extent to which the commercial makes children interested in the toy. You show the commercial to children in the context of a children's television program. In this case, it would be better to allow the children the option of playing with the advertised and other toys and then observe their selections, rather than asking them survey questions to evaluate their interest.

- *When survey measures of attitudes may not accurately predict actual behaviors.* Many mothers, in response to survey questions, state that they are "in charge" and their children do not influence the purchase decision for snacks, soda, and cereal. Actual observations of how mothers and their children interact in the grocery store may provide more accurate insights into these interactions.

- *When behaviors themselves are the best source of insight.* Consider the music played in the background at a fast food restaurant. Does playing faster music make individuals eat faster and leave sooner? Observation research is best suited to answer this type of question.

Qualitative or Quantitative?

Human observation research can be either quantitative or qualitative depending upon the size of the sample, how the sample was selected and, most importantly, the type of data collected. Similar to focus groups, data collected from small convenience samples—especially data that consists of verbal descriptions—should generally be treated qualitatively. Information that can be represented numerically, from a relatively large number of randomly selected individuals, is generally treated quantitatively. The decision to collect either qualitative or quantitative data is reflected in the research design and responds to the advertiser's informational needs.

Consider a situation where you want to know if showing young children advertising which encourages physical activity actually motivates them to be more active.[2] You select a group of children and then randomly assign them to one of two conditions, as follows:

> Children in the treatment group watch an episode of The Simpsons® recorded from a television broadcast embedded with three 30-second advertisements promoting physical activity. Children in the control group watch the same episode embedded with child-appropriate advertisements, but without physical activity advertisements.

After viewing the program and advertisements, children are given time to play outdoors. During this play period, a trained observer who does not know to which group the children were assigned watches the children at play and collects the observational data. At this point, the data could either be qualitative or quantitative.

- Qualitative data would consist of the researcher taking notes about the children's play as well as recording his or her own thoughts about whether or not any specific instance of play could be considered "physical activity." The observer could take notes and create a narrative description of the types of activities the children engage in, their demeanor during play, whether or not they initiate physical activity alone or were encouraged by others, and what happens when one child encourages another to be physically active. These observations would then be examined and presented qualitatively.

- Quantitative data would consist of the researcher preparing a list of activities considered as "physical activity." This list would be prepared in advance of the observations. The observer would then observe each child and, when a listed activity occurs, record the amount of time spent on that activity. A stopwatch would be used to measure the amount of time.

Either approach is correct, although each provides different types of insights. Thus, the type of data collected in human observation research, similar to all research, is guided by the researcher's informational needs.

Types of Human Observation

Human observation research can be characterized in terms of four dimensions: the type of situation in which the observation takes place, observer presence, the level of observer participation, and the form of data recording.

SITUATION: NATURAL VERSUS ARTIFICIAL.   The *natural observation* of individuals, situations, objects, or events takes place as behaviors unfold at their own pace in their own environment. The prior example of observing children as they play was natural observation, as is

- observing sales clerks as they serve their customers,
- observing the label-reading behaviors of consumers purchasing certain types of canned foods,
- recording the time shoppers spend reading various point-of-purchase displays,
- noting the sequence and process individuals use in following a product's directions.

The natural observation of events, situations, and individuals is appropriate when the target behaviors are repetitive, frequent, and/or occur within a reasonably short time frame. The observation of store clerks or the behaviors of shoppers in busy supermarkets are situations appropriate for natural observation. When target occurrences or behaviors are not repetitive and frequent, the extended amount of time and associated cost required for data collection have great potential to outweigh the value of any collected information. As a consequence, artificial observation is typically used when these conditions are not met.

Artificial observation records target behaviors or events in the context of a fabricated situation. This situation may be a laboratory or a "real world" setting in which the researcher or other selected individual takes an active role in prompting the target behavior. Artificial observation permits a researcher to speed up the data gathering process by initiating the observational situation rather than waiting for it to occur naturally. Additionally, artificial situations permit a researcher to control extraneous variables that might have an impact on what is being observed. Mystery shopper research is an example of artificial observation. Here, rather than waiting for a customer to approach a sales clerk, the researcher plays the role of consumer and then observes how he or she is treated by the target employee.

OBSERVER OBTRUSIVENESS: OPEN VERSUS DISGUISED.   The second characteristic of observation research relates to the extent to which the presence of an observer is known to the individuals under observation. *Open observation* occurs when the presence of the observer is explicitly known, while *disguised observation* hides the presence of the observer from the person being observed.

Research has demonstrated that the known presence of an observer has great potential for altering the behaviors of the person being observed. Moreover, the potential for deviation from true or real behaviors increases with the obtrusiveness of the observer. Imagine a car manufacturer who wishes to observe the behaviors of individuals in its showrooms. The behaviors of these individuals would likely change if they knew that they were being watched. Thus, as a consequence of the potential bias introduced by the known presence of an observer, most field advertising and marketing research use disguised observation.

OBSERVER PARTICIPATION: ACTIVE VERSUS PASSIVE. An observer can be either an active or a passive participant in the behaviors being observed. An *active observer* typically takes part in the activities being observed. A "mystery shopper" who initiates conversations with sales personnel is an active participant in the research process. Similarly, a researcher who is also actively posting while observing the development of brand-related conversations on a blog is an active participant. A *passive observer* typically watches without interfering or interacting with the people or objects being observed. Thus, a "mystery shopper" who only watches how sales personnel interact with real shoppers is a passive observer.

Active and passive observation have complimentary strengths and weaknesses. An active participant is closer to the source of the data and has the opportunity to directly interact with those being observed in case questions arise or there is a need to clarify specific issues. These activities can be undertaken in both open and disguised observation. Active participation also allows the observer to subtly direct activities to allow the focus to be on the activities of highest interest, for example, when a discourteous mystery shopper would ask the sales clerk to "fix a problem." Passive observation requires that the researcher take events as they come. While this approach can be quite time-consuming, it nevertheless provides the cleanest data due to events and behaviors being allowed to unfold without any artificial influence. In doing so, passive observation eliminates the continual concern of active participation: "Would events and behaviors have been the same had the researcher not interfered?"

DATA RECORDING: STRUCTURED VERSUS UNSTRUCTURED. Observations can be recorded in either a structured or an unstructured manner. An observer recording data in a *structured manner* knows the types of information and behaviors in advance that are to be observed. Data pertinent to these areas are recorded on a checklist or observation form while all other information and behaviors are ignored. Data not initially collected numerically is typically coded after collection.[3] An observer recording data in an *unstructured manner* records his or her impressions of the observed behaviors in verbal form, typically as a narrative or field notes. There are no restrictions on the types of behaviors observed, although it is expected that pre-identified target behaviors will be specifically noted. Figures 8.1 and 8.2 (page 196) present hypothetical examples of structured and unstructured observations of children at play.

Structured and unstructured observations also have complementary strengths and weaknesses. Structured observations require greater time investment before the observation in order to create the observation form, but as a result, data collection and analysis are much more efficient than unstructured observations. Unstructured observations provide greater opportunity for discoveries in the field because the observer is not restricted to observing and recording a predetermined set of behaviors. However, when unstructured data is treated quantitatively, the time-consuming process of data coding must be completed prior to analysis.

Observational Checklist for Children's Play

Date: _____ Period Start: _____ Observer: _____

Period End: _____

Observation Number: _____

Physical Activity Time Start: _____
Physical Activity Time End: _____

Gender: Male ❑ Female ❑

Type of Activity: If on playground equipment check appropriate place(s) in picture below and/or check appropriate box(es).

Running/Tag ❑ Hide and Seek ❑ Catch/Kickball ❑ Other _____ ❑

Activities: Alone ❑
With Others ❑ —————> Initiated by child ❑
Initiated by other ❑ —————> Male ❑
Female ❑

FIGURE 8.1 Structured Observation (Children at Play)

Date: _____   **Observer:** _____

The play period began at 10:01 and ended at 10:13. Two girls came to the playground at the start of the play period. The first girl (Girl A) went immediately to the playground, while the second girl (Girl B) went to one of the benches and began to read a book.

Girl A began playing on the equipment at 10:02. She first took several turns on the slide, then moved on the climbing equipment, and then returned to the slide. She stopped playing at 10:04. She was clearly having a good time, smiling and laughing as she played. When Girl A stopped playing, she went over to Girl B, started a conversation, and pointed to the playground equipment. While I could not hear the conversation, it appeared that Girl A was encouraging Girl B to come play with her. After some reluctance, Girl B walked with Girl A over to the playground.

Girl A began to climb at 10:06. Girl B watched. As Girl A climbed, she would stop often to talk with Girl B as she hung from the bars. She reached the top of the bars at 10:08. From the top of the bars, Girl A motioned for Girl B to climb the bars and join her. Girl B shook her head and motioned "no" several times. After more encouragement from Girl A, Girl B began to climb the bars (very very slowly and carefully) at 10:10 and reached the top at 10:12. She smiled as Girl A gave her a hug. Both girls jumped down from the bars when the end of play period bell rang at 10:13, and both hopped and skipped back to their classroom.

(The teacher later returned to the playground to retrieve Girl B's book, which was left on the bench.)

FIGURE 8.2 Unstructured Observation (Children at Play)

Human Observation: Case Examples

The prior sections described four aspects of observation research. These aspects can be combined in a wide variety of ways to respond to an advertiser's informational needs. Moreover, when an advertiser's informational needs can only be partially answered by observation, these approaches can be combined with other research methodologies, such as surveys. The following three cases illustrate how these aspects of observation research are translated into practice.

CASE 1: DISCONNECT BETWEEN ATTITUDES AND BEHAVIORS.   This example uses observation that is natural, disguised, passive, and structured.

Advertisers generally assume that well-constructed attitude questions are a reliable means for predicting and understanding behaviors. There are times, however, when this linkage may not be fully understood or when a disconnect between expressed attitudes and actual behaviors is believed to exist. In these types of cases, observation research can provide the insights required to understand the relationship between attitudes and behaviors. This is what happened with Green Globe 21.

Green Globe 21 is an international certification program designed to promote sustainable travel and tourism.[4] The Green Globe 21 (GG21) ecolabel can be placed on products, places, or materials. Survey research found that tourists' attitudes toward the GG21 ecolabel were very positive and that they appeared to have a high awareness of sustainability issues. *There was some question, however, whether these positive, supportive attitudes translated into actual behaviors.* Observation research was used to determine whether these positive attitudes resulted in individuals actually seeking out GG21 eco-labeled products.[5] The research was conducted as follows:

> A tourist center was selected as the place of observation. The center contained numerous materials that were conspicuously labeled GG21 as well as other nonlabeled materials. The observation portion of the study was carried out in two phases. First, baseline data was collected. Here, visitor walking patterns around the center were observed and coded. The number and time spent looking at materials (both GG21 labeled and nonlabeled) was observed and recorded. Following the collection of this data, a large, attention-getting display and slideshow explaining Green Globe 21 was placed in the front of the center. The goal of this display was to passively prompt visitors to recall their expressed positive attitudes toward ecolabeling. Identical to the baseline phase, walking patterns and material interactions were observed and recorded. During this experimental stage, selected individuals were interviewed as they left the center.

The results of the observation analysis showed a significant disconnect between attitudes and behavior. Even though visitors' walking patterns showed that GG21 labeled materials had the opportunity to be viewed, barely any visitors took the time to stop and examine these materials. This was true of all visitors, but especially those who showed high levels of environmental concern and awareness of GG21 in post-visit interviews. In short, consumers' stated preference for green materials and ecolabeling did not translate into behaviors in which these materials were actively sought out.

CASE 2: SELF-REPORTED DATA REGARDING ATTITUDES AND BEHAVIORS MAY NOT BE ACCURATE.

This example uses observation that is natural, disguised, passive, and structured.

Sharp and Tustin[6] compared individuals' reported behaviors as communicated in focus groups with their actual behaviors with regard to alcohol purchase. After observing consumers shopping for alcohol, they concluded, "It seems that in an interview or group setting, where behavior is being discussed rather than observed, people claim to think about brand choice to a far greater degree than appears when behavior is observed and recorded. People also over-claim the influence of promotions and advertising." Specifically, they found that:

> Consumers claimed they regularly read product labeling and took over ten minutes in-store for a routine shop . . . this contrasted with the observational findings that showed that fewer than 10% of consumers read labels and, on average, shoppers took less than three minutes to enter, make a decision, pay and leave.
>
> In the interviews and focus groups, consumers consistently overstated both their brand loyalty, in terms of the number of brands they claimed to purchase, compared to the observational findings that revealed definite repertoire behavior and switching in the category. Recalled behavior gave an average usage of four brands while observational research findings showed the number to be somewhere closer to six brands.

In terms of the impact of point of sale promotional material, few respondents were observed to notice posters, gifts with purchase, or bonus stock offers, which are the typical promotional offers used in the category. In the interviews and focus groups respondents, in contrast, claimed these marketing offers were noticed and impacted on many purchase decisions.

About half the respondents thought they had bought a product on special. In fact the figure obtained through observation, was closer to 10%. In the focus groups and interviews, respondents spoke of their reliance on advertising for price comparisons, but few were observed to have this detailed material with them when they shopped, or were able to recall price specifics.

CASE 3: BEHAVIORAL RATHER THAN ATTITUDINAL CHANGE IS THE FOCUS.   This example uses observation that is artificial, open, passive, and structured.

The ultimate goal of some advertising is to change attitudes. Other advertising, while created to target specific attitudes, is nevertheless designed to change behaviors, and it is against this criterion that its success is determined. Observation is often a good means for assessing behavioral change, particularly for behaviors where people are being asked to learn and maintain new skills or there is a socially acceptable or desirable set of responses to survey questions. In these cases, researchers need to determine if actual behaviors, rather than just attitudes, have changed in response to message exposure, for example:

> A food safety issue of concern to health professionals is the handling of chicken. Raw poultry must be handled carefully to prevent bacterial cross-contamination with other food. This can occur if raw poultry or its juices contact cooked food or foods that will be eaten raw such as salad. An example of this is chopping tomatoes on an unwashed cutting board just after cutting raw chicken on it.
>
> Researchers wanted to know if they could improve chicken handling behaviors through a communication program that featured advertising as well as leaflets, newspaper articles, and other promotions.[7] A pre-post experimental design was used to assess the impact of the campaign where the behaviors of those exposed to the communication program were compared to individuals in a control (unexposed) group. The targeted behaviors were the use of separate or adequately washed and dried chopping boards and knives between the preparation of raw chicken and other foods, or the preparation of all other foods prior to preparing chicken.
>
> Observation was used for data collection. This allowed the researchers to determine what individuals actually do versus what they say they do with regard to the targeted behaviors. Observations and data coding occurred as follows: For each meal preparation session, participants were required to prepare a chicken salad from raw foods in a model domestic kitchen. Preparation of the chicken salad required handling raw chicken and ready-to-eat foods (salad ingredients and cooked ham) and thus involved opportunities for implementing cross-contamination behaviors targeted in this food safety initiative. Cumulative and targeted food safety practices were observed

using CCTV and recorded using detailed observational checklists. A risk-based scoring system was used to quantitatively assess food safety behaviors whereby demerit risk scores were awarded according to implementation of food-handling malpractices. A logarithmic scale was used to score food safety malpractices and was weighted towards high risk actions; therefore, the higher the total risk score attained, the more cumulative food safety malpractices were implemented.

The results found that this type of intervention can "result in a short-term improvement of consumer food safety behaviors. Interventions targeting specific food safety behaviors may produce a 'halo effect' upon other food safety behaviors that are known, yet not consistently implemented during domestic food preparation. Intervention effect was greater immediately after implementation of the strategy than four to six weeks later. Use of the risk-based scoring system and observation techniques were effective for assessing food hygiene behaviors and evaluating the effectiveness of interventions."

AUTOMATED OBSERVATION

A second form of observation is automated observation. Here human behaviors are observed, but the observational data is collected by machine rather than by people. This approach monitors and tracks consumers' behaviors, typically collecting quantitative data in a structured, disguised manner. There are two main forms of automated observation. First, automated observation *directly monitors consumer behaviors*. This occurs, for example, when cookies are used to track an individual's online behaviors or when loyalty cards are used at the supermarket. Second, automated observation monitors the *products of consumer behaviors*. This occurs, for example, when computers are used to measure online "buzz" or to monitor changes in brand perceptions in blogs or other forms of consumer-generated media (CGM). This section discusses each of these approaches to automated observation.

Observing Online Behaviors

Cookies are the most common way that advertisers observe online behaviors. Cookies and the observational data that they collect can be used, for example, to monitor online behaviors in order to evaluate Web site design or sales success. While cookies are used for a broad range of research, their most common use among advertisers relates to monitoring browsing and advertising response behaviors in order to increase advertising relevance and to evaluate the different components of a multi-media advertising campaign.

INCREASING ADVERTISING RELEVANCE.   A significant number of Web sites display advertising. These sites do not typically deliver advertising from their own servers but are instead fed advertisements from an advertising network's server. It is the network server that decides which ad will be seen in each individual viewing situation. Two individuals logging in to the same site at the same time may see very different advertisements. Cookies, which help to store and retrieve observations of past behavior, help the advertising network determine which ads should be served to each individual. This approach is typically summarized in a Web site's privacy policy, for example:

> [We] use third-party advertising companies including Google, among others, to serve ads when you visit our websites. These companies may use information (not including your name, address, email address, or telephone number) *about your visits to this and other websites in order to provide advertisements about goods and services of interest to you.*[8]

> When possible, we try to match the ads that we show you to your interests. We call this "ad matching," (sometimes also called ad customization) and we do this in order to make the ads you see more relevant and useful for you. *Ad matching uses data about your visits to both Yahoo! and our partner sites and about the ads you view and click.* . . . We (Yahoo!) look at a person's browsing activity, such as the types of content the person accessed, ads the person clicked, and searches the person conducted. Based on this, we infer certain interests the person has, and we show ads likely to meet the person's needs. For example, for people who like to check out the golf scores on Yahoo! Sports, we may show ads that focus on golf-related products and services.[9]

DoubleClick's DART is one of the largest ad serving networks. Advertisers use cookies and DART to maximize the probability that the advertising an individual sees is relevant, where relevance is based on that individual's prior responses to advertising. An individual who clicked on a gardening ad, for example, is more likely to be shown gardening ads in the future. This is because the prior gardening ad click-through has been associated with the unique cookie ID assigned to that individual. Doubleclick explains how the customized ad serving process works:

> Our clients store their ads on DoubleClick's ad servers. When you visit a Web page on which a client is using DoubleClick technology to deliver ads, coding that the website publisher placed in the Web page tells your computer's browser to send a request for an ad to the DoubleClick ad server. When the DoubleClick ad server receives a request, it will select an ad based on the criteria that the client has chosen together with *any information logged against the unique cookie id.*[10]

DART's goal is to use observation to increase advertising relevance and, by implication, increase advertising response. FetchBack approaches advertising targeting in a different way. FetchBack uses observation to match advertising exposure to prior Web behaviors, specifically by displaying advertising for a Web site to past visitors to that site. FetchBack explains this process as follows:

> Using our patent-pending technology we're able to deliver your message to visitors after they have left your site as they surf the Web. Your ads will appear to them as they surf their favorite internet sites—everything from popular news sites, social networking sites, to various blogs and informational sites. These are not pop-ups; these are advertisements that customers would normally see as they visit these webpages; only instead of a random ad being displayed, a targeted ad specifically for them will be shown.[11]

Several free programs can help you see how cookies and advertising serving software work together to monitor Web-related behaviors and then customize the advertising viewing experience. One such program is Ghostery, an add-on to the Firefox browser that makes explicit "the web bugs, ad networks and widgets that are monitoring your web surfing behaviors."[12]

MERGING ONLINE AND OFFLINE OBSERVATIONS.   DoubleClick and others use cookies to track prior response to advertising in order to maximize the relevance of future advertising when it is believed that consumers will respond more favorably as relevance increases. Other companies have expanded this level of observation to track a broad range of online and offline behaviors.

Coremetrics is one such company. Coremetrics believes that to be successful, "you must relentlessly follow your customers over time, both online and offline; anticipate their future buying decisions based on this history; and then tap that rich historical data to deliver the right message to each customer every time."[13] Coremetrics uses observation and tracking to provide the information required to accomplish this. Central to Coremetrics's approach is the Coremetrics Lifetime Individual Visitor Experience (LIVE) Profile. LIVE Profile tracks customers and prospects as they interact with businesses online, across multiple ad networks, or via e-mail, video, affiliate sites, social media, and more. It then integrates this data and offline information, providing a single comprehensive view of each visitor's behavior over time and across channels. LIVE Profiles are created by assigning

> each visitor a persistent cookie with a unique identifier. No other data is stored in the cookie. As that individual interacts with campaigns and content, Coremetrics builds a LIVE Profile for that unique visitor, and stores it in a massively scalable data warehouse. All individual actions are recorded in the warehouse and associated with the visitor's lifetime ID.

An example of the types of insights provided by LIVE Profiles is shown in Figure 8.3.[14]

EVALUATING COMPONENTS OF A MULTI-MEDIA ADVERTISING CAMPAIGN.   LIVE Profiles, and the example shown in Figure 8.3, illustrate how consumers are touched by multiple ads prior to the final purchase decision. As such, the traditional approach to measuring advertising success with regard to online advertising, attributing 100% of the influence for a "conversion" (i.e., a purchase or other desired behavior) to the last advertisement viewed, seems flawed. The Atlas Institute explains the problem with the approach:

> The problem with this approach is that it ignores the contributions of any previous ads that led the consumer down the road to that conversion. Additionally, a critical marketing concept, the *sales funnel*, is completely disregarded by the "last ad" model. The idea is simple, different marketing messages play different roles for consumers. Some marketing messages drive awareness, others close the deal. The "last ad" model is exceptional . . . if your only goal is to measure the bottommost touch point in the sales funnel.[15]

Coremetrics and the Atlas Institute, among others, are providing the means and motivation for advertisers to move away from the "last ad" mentality and begin to view

Mary Traversa Looks for a Vacation Get-Away:

Monday, July 23	Performs a Google search for "Vacations" Clicks on paid search result "Travelocity" Conducts Travelocity.com search Conducts search on TripAdvisor.com Prices two hotels
Tuesday, July 24	Clicks on Yahoo! banner ad for Sunrise Hotel Clicks on "Yahoo! paid ad for "NapaValley.com" Clicks on ad for Sunrise Hotel
Wednesday, July 25	Clicks on affiliate link for Sunrise Hotel Reserves a room at Sunrise Hotel in Sonoma valley for $355
Thursday, July 26	Directly accesses TripAdvisor.com Clicks on ad for EuroSpa Prices EuroSpa on Hotels.com Cancels Sunrise Hotel reservation Reserves room at EuroSpa for $325
Friday, July 27	Performs a Google search for "Napa Hotels" Clicks on paid ad for Serenity Hotel Directly accesses site for Serenity Hotel Cancels EuroSpa Reserves room at Serenity Hotel for $300
Saturday, July 28	Visits Expedia.com Prices Napa hotels Performs a Bing search for "Napa Hotels" Clicks on Bing banner ad for Sunrise Hotel Reserves room at Sunrise Hotel for $285 Cancels room at Serenity Hotel
Sunday July 29	Visits Orbitz.com Prices Napa Hotels Cancels room at Sunrise Hotel Reserves room at Serenity Hotel for $275

Insights:

* Mary first visited Sunrise Hotel via a Yahoo! banner ad, but returned to the hotel via an affiliate ad and a Bing banner ad. All three ads, not just the final Bing ad, played a role in the eventual reservation.

* Mary was favorable toward Sunrise Hotel, but concerned about the price (as noted in her bookings of decreasing amounts). Sunrise Hotel could have reached Mary with a special offer during the decision-making process and after the reservation was cancelled.

* Sunrise Hotel appears to directly compete with Serenity Hotel. Individuals who visit or search for Serenity Hotel can be shown special deals or packages for Sunrise Hotel.

* Sunrise Hotel needs to reinforce the purchase decision after the reservation is made to avoid continued shopping (especially price shopping) among those with current reservations.

FIGURE 8.3 LIVE Profile Insights Into Consumer Behavior

advertising within the context of multi-campaign attribution.[16] Here, the full range of a consumer's behaviors is observed, and different degrees of influence on the final conversion are attributed to multiple exposures prior to conversion.

Clearly, attributing levels of influence to different ads or other communications viewed prior to conversion is a data intensive activity. Automated observation allows for relevant data to be collected, and specialized computer software facilitates data analysis. The Atlas Institute, which calls its approach *Engagement Mapping*, explains how this is accomplished:

> Engagement Mapping is made possible by back-end technology that analyzes many factors behind the scenes, so marketers don't have to worry about the technological aspects managing the terabytes of data today's campaigns generate . . . Key influential factors can roll-up into a very straightforward site-by-site analysis to succinctly summarize Engagement ROI. Factors that can be taken into account include [ad] frequency, ad size, recency, ad format, interaction and order.[17]

Observing Offline Behaviors

While observing consumers' online behaviors is important for online advertisers and marketers, there is still a need to observe sales-related behaviors taking place offline. Store loyalty cards are one way that observation takes place offline. Loyalty cards are the credit card or keychain-sized cards with a barcode or magnetic stripe offered by most large retail chains, particularly supermarkets, pharmacies, and clothing stores. These cards work as follows:

- When scanned at the cash register, the card unlocks special discounts offered to "loyal" members.
- In return for the savings, cardholders agree to allow the grocery store to track their purchases each time they shop.
- Grocery stores use this information to decide which products to carry, what prices to charge, and in some cases, to target consumers with specific coupons and promotions on behalf of grocery manufacturers.[18]

The store, as might be expected, uses aggregate and masked data as part of its marketing research. These cards can be used to determine, for example, a given customer's favorite brand of laundry detergent or whether meat products are or are not purchased. Additionally, advertisers can match markets and, by placing different advertising in each market, can determine the differential effects of the advertising on brand sales. On an individual level, the observational data provided by these cards allows marketers to determine the success of promotional efforts or to customize offers to specific types of behaviors or purchase patterns.

Observing Consumer-Generated Media

As mentioned earlier, the second form of automated observation monitors the outcomes of individuals' behaviors. The most common form of this type of observation is the examination of consumer-generated media (CGM)

The term "consumer-generated media" was coined by Pete Blackshaw to describe the evolving consumer-created space on the Internet. CGM refers to a broad range of online word-of-mouth vehicles including, but not limited to, "consumer-to-consumer e-mail, postings on public Internet discussion boards/forums, Usenet groups and list-servs, consumer ratings Web sites or forums, blogs, moblogs (sites where users post digital images/photos/movies) vlongs (video blogs), social networking Web sites, and individual Web sites."[19] Given the widespread cumulative readership of these sites and the fact that consumers feel that this type of communication is seen as being more trustworthy than traditional media, advertisers and marketers have made significant commitments to monitoring CGM conversations/postings as they relate to their specific brands and brand image/reputation.[20] Nielsen-Online describes the importance of monitoring brand-related CGM:

> Consumer advocacy is the single-most important gauge of a brand's growth potential—and harnessing that advocacy is critical to the health and lifespan of any brand. Great brand and product experiences, amplified by advocates, power today's consumer-driven environment. Advocacy convinces consumers to visit your Web site, write positive things about you in the Web's public arena, try your products or services and tell others about your experience.[21]

The vast number of sources to be monitored necessitates automated observation, and there are a number of companies that provide this service. While each company approaches the task and reports the data slightly differently, all provide a core set of information based on their continuous observation of millions of CGM sources. The information typically provides by CGM observation includes:

- *Coverage.* The number of times a brand or issue is mentioned.
- *Depth.* The amount of brand detail. How deeply does the posting discuss a brand? Is it just a passing mention or does the CGM go into the subject in-depth with numerous comments and links?
- *Content.* The posting's objective. Was the posting designed to solve a problem, compare different brands, pass along information, advocate for a cause, criticize the organization, or simply allow the author to rant?
- *Sentiment.* The posting's sentiment. What was the tone and affect of the CGM? Was it generally positive, negative, or neutral?

The prior list describes two types of observations. The first two aspects are purely descriptive as the automated observation can use counts and similar measures to report the data.[22] The second two aspects describe the outcomes of analysis. Here, the computer software conducting the observation must analyze and evaluate the raw data in order to determine the nature and sentiment of the communication. Both types of data are important. Counts and similar measures provide the context for understanding the extent of brand discussion, but this data is of reduced value if an advertiser does not understand whether or not the discussion is positive, negative, or neutral. Clearly 1,000 positive communications have a very different implication for the brand in comparison to 1,000 negative postings. As a result, the validity of the procedures by which a company evaluates sentiment is of great importance. Figure 8.4 describes

Scout Labs' sentiment is "entity specific." What some products do when they produce "machine-generated sentiment" is that they count happy words vs. sad words in a news article. The "tone" of the article is shown by the happy word count. Consider "I love baseball. My happiest memories in life are from sitting in the bleachers at Fenway. It's the greatest game on earth. But guys like Bonds and A-Rod are bringing it down." Despite the high "happy" word count, this does not express a positive opinion about Barry Bonds or Alex Rodriguez.

In the Scout Labs application, we don't count happy words. We evaluate sentiment for each particular word or phrase you search for. We can tell that the sentiment for baseball is positive but negative for Bonds and Rodriguez. This is done via part of speech tagging: parsing the underlying semantic structure of a sentence and determining which emotion words apply to the key word. Emotion words come from dictionaries of standard English words and have been augmented with phrases and slang to better map to the world of social media. So Scout Labs' sentiment is entity-specific, which is very important.

Scout Labs' sentiment can be changed by users. We use confidence intervals to decide whether something is positive or negative, but if we get it wrong, you can change the score, immediately updating that item for yourself and the rest of your team. Charts and graphs update immediately as well. And the really cool part is that every time a user changes a sentiment value, that item becomes a labeled piece of data that we can use to abstract out additional rules and add words and phrases for our dictionary. So our ability to detect sentiment just gets better over time.

Does it work?

Yes. We have done extensive human vs. machine testing, and it's accurate in the 70%–80% range, meaning our algorithm agrees with humans' scores 70%–80% of the time. This is only slightly less than humans agree with each other. Some other insights and findings from our testing:

* *College educated people with business experience agree on the sentiment ratings for a blog post about 85% of the time.* Using less qualified people, such as you might find in a random Mechanical Turk experiment, produces lower rates of agreement. We were surprised that we couldn't get that rate higher. Some of the discrepancy stems from the human tendency to equate negative opinions and negative information: "I hate Coke" is a negative opinion; "Merrill Lynch just downgraded Coca-Cola" is negative information.

* *The Scout Labs sentiment feature agrees with college educated people about 75% of the time.* We try to pad that a little by being conservative about what we call positive or negative—we call things neutral if they're borderline.

* *The Scout Labs sentiment feature is terrible at detecting irony and sarcasm.* Posts that are heavy on the irony often end up classed as "neutral" because the machine can't even guess. Consider "Another winner from the almighty Microsoft." That's a tough one.

* *Machines don't understand business context.* Perhaps you work for Apple and every mention of an unlocked iPhone is negative because people shouldn't unlock their iPhones. An algorithm that uses grammar and vocabulary based rules cannot classify this post as negative about iPhone: "I love my iPhone. My boyfriend unlocked it for me last night."

So the Sentiment feature produces a pretty good guess. And our best guess plus your teams' efforts to quickly change the things we miss or get wrong means really high accuracy levels for you and your team with a minimum amount of work and expense.

FIGURE 8.4   How Sentiment is Evaluated at ScoutLabs

how sentiment is determined at ScoutLabs, while Figure 8.5 provides a visual example of sentiment reporting.[23]

APPLYING CGM OBSERVATIONS TO ADVERTISING DECISION MAKING. Advertisers use observations of CGM to inform planning and decision making in four primary ways.

Campaign Monitoring Advertisers can relate trends and shifts in CGM to their communication program, identifying those aspects of the program that seem to be working well and those that are problematic and need additional attention. Figure 8.6 illustrates this type of analysis. The figure shows the key events for the first 12 months of a new soft drink's communication campaign charted against the amount and direction of

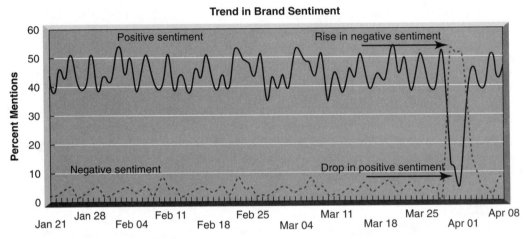

FIGURE 8.5 Sentiment Monitoring

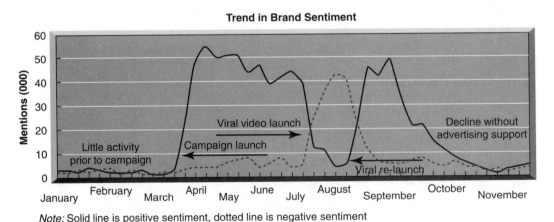

Note: Solid line is positive sentiment, dotted line is negative sentiment

FIGURE 8.6 Insights Provided by CGM Monitoring for Campaign Evaluation

consumer buzz. The trends indicate the following with regard to the impact of the communication program:

- Since this was a new soft drink, there was little CGM prior to the product introduction and the start of the advertising campaign. All of the CGM monitored during this period was pre-announcement speculation.

- The television campaign launched at the end of March. The campaign was extremely well received and generated increasing amounts of CGM. An examination of sentiment indicated that the additional CGM sentiment was overwhelmingly positive. As the campaign continued to run, some signs of "wear-out" occurred as the amount of positive sentiment began to slowly decline.

- A viral video campaign was launched in July to announce a summer promotion. It appears that this campaign was a disaster. Negative CGM mentions begin to spike very shortly after the launch of the viral campaign while positive CGM drops dramatically.

- The initial viral campaign is replaced by a second campaign several weeks later. This second viral campaign works well to reverse the prior trend, generating high levels of positive sentiment while significantly reducing the amount of negative sentiment.

- The second viral campaign ends in September, and no additional advertising communications are used for the rest of the year. From this point through the end of the year, CGM mentions fall off dramatically with both positive and negative sentiment bottoming-out at their pre-launch levels.

Image Monitoring Advertisers can monitor their own brand's image in CGM and track any changes in image versus key competitive brands. This information can then be used to determine if communication programs are needed to either reinforce or build brand image. Figure 8.7 displays data related to three competitive brands. The chart on the top of Figure 8.7 provides data for Brand A. Here, brand mentions are increasing and sentiment is increasingly positive. This brand, based on this data, would want to establish a communication program designed to capitalize on this momentum by reinforcing and extending these positive trends. The middle chart in Figure 8.7 shows the opposite situation. Here, there are always more negative versus positive mentions, but the gap between the two is becoming increasingly large. This brand is in trouble and the advertiser needs to develop a plan to reverse this trend. The bottom chart shown in Figure 8.7 shows a brand that may be fading from public awareness. While the overall ratio of positive to negative mentions is fairly constant, the overall number of mentions in CGM is declining. This appears to be a brand that is fading from public awareness and, as a result, a communication program designed to reverse this trend by fostering positive perceptions and increasing awareness may be warranted.

Each of the prior cases described a brand monitoring its image in isolation of other brands. CGM can be used, however, to place the CGM for one brand within the context

(Top)

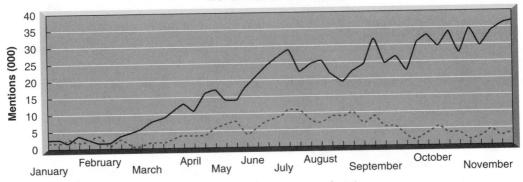

Note: Solid line is positive sentiment, dotted line is negative sentiment

(Middle)

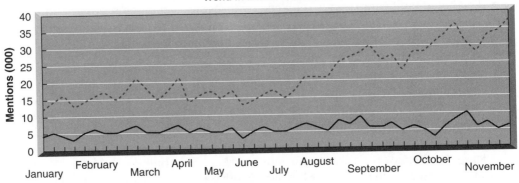

Note: Solid line is positive sentiment, dotted line is negative sentiment

(Bottom)

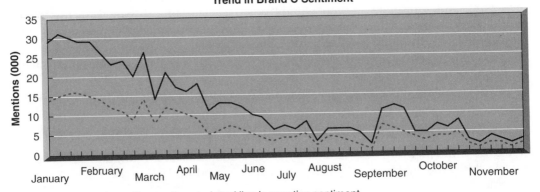

Note: Solid line is positive sentiment, dotted line is negative sentiment

FIGURE 8.7 CGM and Brand Image Monitoring

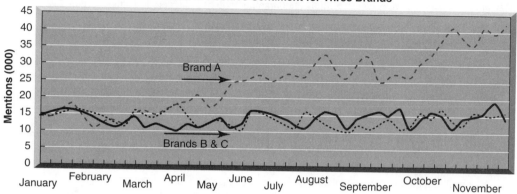

FIGURE 8.8 Comparative Brand Image Monitoring

of other brands' trends. The chart shown in Figure 8.8 illustrates this approach. The chart shows the number of positive CGM mentions for three brands. All three brands start at the same point, with about equal numbers of positive CGM brand mentions. Over time, however, Brand A differentiates itself from the other two brands with increasing levels of positive mentions.

Insights into Attitudes Observations of CGM can provide insights into consumers' mindsets, attitudes, and beliefs. This type of consumer understanding significantly increases an advertiser's ability to plan a successful communication program. The analysis provided in Figure 8.9 illustrates this approach.[24]

Crisis Management Observations of CGM can alert an advertiser to crisis situations requiring an immediate response. Spikes in CGM mentions coupled with negative sentiment indicate that immediate attention to brand maintenance is required. This was the case with Whole Foods, as discussed in Figure 8.10.[25]

Blu-Ray vs HD-DVD Case Study:
Online Mind Sharing Tell the Consumer Side of "The Stalemate" Story

It happens once in decades. A new digital storage format is introduced, taking consumer entertainment to a whole new level of audio-visual experience. A new format ends up changing how information and entertainment are produced, played and stored, and that is a big odds game with huge business implications.

When new generations of computer micro-processors are introduced, it would typically be two competing products launched almost simultaneously by Intel and AMD. In the micro-processor case consumer choice is relatively easy because both play all programs with little performance differences. By contrast, consumers have always needed to decide between alternative digital storage formats since developers typically secured exclusivity for their format with hardware (player) makers and content producers. In the early 80s, it was JVC's VHS vs Sony's Betamax. If you had a VHS player, you couldn't play videos that were available in Betamax format and vice versa. This meant that consumers "voted with their

---

FIGURE 8.9 CGM and Attitudes: The DVD Wars

wallet" in favor of one of the formats (thus encouraging content producers to channel product variety to that format). Investing in a new player meant risking choice of a player with inferior content variety. That is why new format generations trigger a "format war" as developing companies make every effort to drive decisive consumer patronage of their format.

This time, at the age of high-definition, it's Sony's Blu-Ray vs Toshiba's HD-DVD optical disk format. The "war of high-definition formats" has been waging for almost two years now. Both Sony and Toshiba invested heavily in marketing, sales promotions, and strategic alliances with content providers (such as with movie studios). But as the 2007 holiday season nears, the "war of formats" is at what has already been labeled as "the stalemate."

1st2c has looked into the consumer side of "the stalemate" and discovered that online mind-sharing provides surprisingly accurate diagnostics of the dynamics of the "war of formats." 1st2c Online Strategizing Research© discovered a much more cluttered consumer worldview and saw an underlying uncertainty about the future of digital storage as a whole. Emerging market dynamics suggests a need for new models for positioning and marketing of high definition players.

More than "another" war of formats

How do consumers react to the two formats? What drives their attention? Why do marketing initiatives deliver only short-term impact? These questions are being answered by hundreds of thousands of involved consumers engaged in online mind-sharing. 1st2c's deep Web monitor provides visceral understanding of the dynamics of the unfolding "war of formats" (see table below).

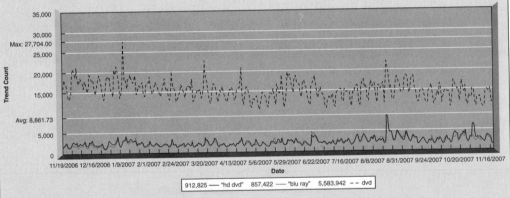

Trendline of Online Resonance on DVD vs "HD-DVD" and "Blu-Ray"

Perhaps the immediate striking insight is embedded in the evident continuous decline in attention to the DVD format as a whole, while at the same time attention to the new Blu-Ray and HD-DVD format is increasing only mildly and inconsistently. In other words, consumer engagement with the whole issue of optical disk format is eroding!

Deep diving into the networked market suggests that consumer choice mindset is not necessarily limited to Blu-Ray or HD-DVD. Active consumer mindset is far broader in encompassing additional types of solutions to the same core (content consumption and ownership) needs!

From our analysis, Blu-Ray and HD-DVD are actually in competition not only with each other (e.g., IP-based solutions are gaining popularity also among less techy consumers) and this increases consumers' perceived risk in choosing either.

FIGURE 8.9 (*continued*)

Focusing on the "war of formats" between Blu-Ray and HD-DVD, the state of shoulder-to-shoulder competition is evident. The striking similarity in trendlines of resonance between the two focal formats is typical to an undecided market. In such situations, consumers tend to discuss the respective merits of alternative offerings against any relevant market development.

Old marketing models may need rethinking

There is a deeper layer of insights embedded in online consumer resonance (see table below).

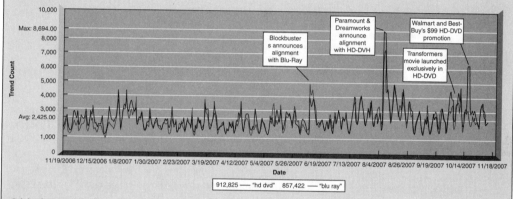

Critical events Influencing Online Resonance on "HD-DVD" and "Blu-Ray"

Throughout the last period, content-based initiatives drove surges in attention but didn't create decisive attention superiority to the respective format. This is visible for instance with Blockbuster's alignment with Blu-Ray (June 18), Paramount and DreamWorks alignment with HD-DVD (August 21), and the release of the Transformers movie on HD-DVD (October 16–24).

But something happened to the long standing "stalemate" in November. Online mind-sharing tells the story of a shake up in consumer mindset caused by big retailer competition. In late October Walmart, Circuit City, and Amazon lowered the price tag for Toshiba's HD-A2 HD-DVD player to $198 triggering surges in consumer talk, with notable advantage to HD-DVD. Immediately thereafter, on November 1, Walmart and Best Buy announced special sales promotion initiatives that dropped the price to $99. This time consumer resonance on HD-DVD rocketed leaving Blu-Ray far behind. For the first time in (at least) a year "the stalemate" was broken.

Is it the beginning of a momentum or just a short-term achievement for HD-DVD? A lot has to do with how marketers play their cards in the holiday season. But chattering consumers did provide a significant insight. So far, price-based leverages delivered better competitive differentiation than content-based leverages, at least in terms of consumer engagement.

The takeaways are clear and powerful.

Significant price cuts drive consumer action. There's no surprise about that. But when a net active audience is concerned, especially an intensively networking audience, online resonance is both a critical market undercurrents gauge and a powerful influence channel. What this deep dive into the networked marketplace suggests is examining the merits of "foot in the door" marketing strategies that motivate shift from "shopping" to "impulse" purchase behavior and leveraging them to drive a stalemate breaking mental shift.

FIGURE 8.9   *(continued)*

CGM Report: The Whole Foods Case Study

There's nothing wrong in a CEO doing his best to promote his brand. It is perfectly logical for a CEO to communicate with his networked market online. It is quite smart to do so in those places where your brand and business are discussed.

The unwritten rules of consumer-marketer interaction on Internet's social media have recently been fire-tested, and there's something to learn out of this experience for every marketer.

For eight years, John Mackey, the visionary entrepreneur who led the Austin, Texas-based natural foods chain Whole Foods chain to meteoric success, was active in Yahoo's stock community. Using the pseudonym "rahodeb" (his wife Deborah's name spelled backwards), Mr. Mackey has been posting messages on various issues regarding his business.

This phenomena known as "Sock Puppeting" exploded early June following an FTC anti-trust lawsuit alleging that Mr Mackey has been posting controversial company information, trashing competition, and touting management.

Social media fails to show "CGM autopilot" effect

Such a sensation-charged story, with an official "seal of seriousness," was sure material for a major online consumer backlash and potential consumer antagonism crisis for the Whole Foods brand. This was an exemplary case study for 1st2c, the forerunner of Online Strategizing Research©, to examine the DNA of an online consumer-driven crisis situation.

A day-by-day monitoring of online consumer resonance indicates that the stereotypical perception of social media as facilitating and encouraging consumers to mobilize against "misbehaving" marketers is too simplistic.

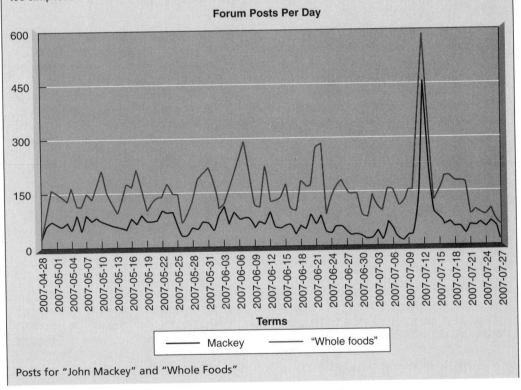

Posts for "John Mackey" and "Whole Foods"

FIGURE 8.10   CGM and Crisis Management: Whole Foods

The story breaking on July 12, 2007, did trigger a huge surge in consumer talk about both John Mackey and Whole Foods (see table above). However, as 1st2c tracking report shows, not only did consumer talk return to previous levels from the very next day but also talk on Mackey behaved differently than talk on Whole Foods. That following surge in talk correlated with media coverage to the issue and to Mackey's apology posted (this time) on Whole Food's corporate blog on July 17. Interestingly, blogs were more aggressive and attempting to mobilize mass action than social mind-sharing platforms (like forums and message boards).

Case study takeaways

Analyzing the nature of consumer response 1st2c analysts highlighted these insights:

1. CEO controversiality does not necessarily rub off on the brand if consumers do not perceive the CEO's "misbehavior" as compromising their health or interests in an immediate and critical way they are likely to judge his or her practices with limited collateral implications on the brand.

2. John Mackey "behaves" as a brand in terms of consumer attention. Many of the surges in talk about Mackey correlate with surges of talk about Whole Foods, sometimes in similar volumes. We have noticed such phenomena looking at consumer brands (mostly consumer goods) and see it as indicative of the significant impact these CEOs do or can have on brand equity, both on the negative and positive side.

3. Blogs represent a different audience and play a different role than social networks. Blogs are not the mirror of the market! In many cases, they are less so than social networks (forums, message boards, etc.). The active (vs. one shot) blogs tend to represent a more maven, activist and influence-oriented audience, while social networks tend to represent the "involved masses."

FIGURE 8.10 (*continued*)

APPLYING CHAPTER CONCEPTS

Two online supplemental readings illustrate the uses and power of observation research.

Video Consumer Mapping Study

The "Video Consumer Mapping Study" is the largest observational study of media use and consumption ever conducted.[26] The research, conducted on behalf of the Nielsen-funded Council for Research Excellence by Ball State University's Center for Media Design and Sequent Partners, observed and recorded the media usage of 476 adults in six geographically dispersed Designated Market Areas (DMAs). Media usage was recorded by extensively trained observers *every 10 seconds for an individual's full waking day period*. Observation rather than surveys was used to collect the data because prior research had demonstrated that media usage is complex, multifaceted, and not accurately reported in surveys or other self-reporting approaches. One of the principal researchers of this study notes that:

> Among the things that we learned [from prior research] is that people generally cannot report accurately how much time they spend with media. Some media tend to be over-reported whereas others tend to be under-reported—sometimes to an alarming extent. Clearly, that kind of variance puts into question one's ability to draw meaningful conclusions, and it convinced us that the observational method is the only real way to achieve accurate and reliable results.[27]

Beyond the belief that observation research provides more accurate data versus self-report data with regard to simultaneous multiple media usage, observation was also selected as the method of data collection due to the lack of availability of automatic data recording instruments. The researchers note that:

> There are no electronic monitoring systems which can capture media exposure (much less participant activities) across all media platforms and all locations. We therefore rely on a "shadowing" method in which human observers follow participants throughout the day. Shadowing overcomes the memory limitations and social desirability bias of recall data and the compliance problems of participant diary data.[28]

DATA COLLECTION.   The Alphasmart Dana™ smart keyboard was used to enter the observational data. The Dana keyboard is lightweight, has long battery life, and is extremely durable. Ball State University's Center for Media Design also developed the Media Collector™ software used by Dana for data input and coding. Dana, coupled with this software, allows quick and easy touch-screen and keyboard data entry while the on-screen menus remind observers of available coding categories.[29]

The use of a smart keyboard employing coding software resulted in the acquisition of quantitative data collected in a structured way. As discussed in the prior chapter, great care needs to be taken when developing the categories to be used for data coding. The following illustrates the considerations in this research:

> The location, activity and media exposure typologies are the heart of the method. They define what can be logged during observations and consequently what constitutes available data for analysis. While it is a truism that "the map is not the territory" (i.e., our descriptions of the world should not be confused with the world itself), all we have for analysis is the map—in this case, the parsing of the stream of lived behavior into discrete categories within coding typologies. Each category needs to be unambiguously defined and easily distinguished from other categories in a typology to allow for reliable application. Each typology should constitute a complete and valid inventory of the target domain, designed so only a small portion of entries end up in a catch-all "Other" category (without expanding beyond the cognitive limits of observers). Each typology must be able to generate data useful for answering the research questions.[30]

OBSERVER TRAINING.   Clearly, the quality of data in observation research rests upon the professionalism and expertise of the observers. As a consequence, observers for the Video Consumer Mapping Study underwent extensive training, typically over a four-day period. The goals of this training fell into three areas, as shown below:

Affective training goals
- Observers will recognize importance of the study
- Observers will recognize importance of their performance
- Observers will feel motivated for top performance

Cognitive training goals

- Observers will know relevant study policies and procedures
- Observers will master location, activity, and media coding systems
- Observers will know how to write clarification and correction comments

Behavioral training goals

- Observers will demonstrate basic operation of the Dana device
- Observers will demonstrate proper non-obtrusive behavior
- Observers will demonstrate acceptable inter-rater reliability

A detailed description of observer training follows.

Observer training prior to the first round of observation was completed at Ball State University; refresher training and training of replacement observers prior to Round II in Fall 2008 was completed in the DMAs selected for the study. All retained observers originally training for Round I in Spring 2008 completed refresher training.

Training materials and experiences incorporated into the four days of training included printed reference materials such as observer policies and procedures and category system definitions, interactive materials including extensive training PowerPoint™ slides and training videos for in-session practice (also made available on a CD-ROM for later reference), half-day practice observations with on-campus volunteer participants, paper-and-pencil tests of cognitive mastery of the material and a video-based real-time coding test of mastery of the observation device and category systems.

Training addressed a variety of topics beyond application of the coding systems. Observers were expected to be familiar with the observer responsibilities (including the rights of human research subjects), know and comply with guidelines for ensuring personal safety in the field, be aware of all grounds for termination of employment, be familiar with operation of the Dana™ device and Media Collector™ software, be able to operate the Observation Management System™ for scheduling of observations, and know how to reduce the obtrusiveness of their presence and minimize "observer effect."

Refresher training for the second round of observation was one day in length. PowerPoint™ materials for refresher training (and the decks for initial training of replacement observers) were modified to reflect learning from the experiences of round I, that is, category definitions further clarified with extra additional to challenging categories, procedural problems reviewed, additional examples added, minor changes to the software interface introduced and "rules of thumb" for dealing with unexpected situations encountered in the first round noted. Focus groups were held with observers after the first round of observation to identify areas for additional reinforcement or clarification in preparation for refresher training.[31]

A full presentation of the Video Consumer Mapping Study is provided in the online supplemental readings.

Campaigning with Social Media

The second report provided in the online supplemental readings is not a research study *per se*, but it does use observation to evaluate the success of a social media campaign. The campaign, designed by Amnesty UK, was designed to raise awareness of issues related to violence against women, in particular, the incidence of rape/other violence against women in the United Kingdom and the lack of support services for women who experience violence.[32] The success of the campaign was exclusively measured through the collection of observational data that reported the number of people who

- sent supporting e-mails,
- changed their Facebook or Twitter avatars,
- Tweeted the target message and/or became a Twitter follower,
- took a pledge,
- visited a target Web site.

The extent to which the campaign accomplished its goals, as reflected in the prior observational data, is provided in the report. As you read about the campaign and its results, be sure to notice how the observational measures used to evaluate the campaign are directly related to the campaign's approach and goals.

SUMMARY

Two common forms of observation research are human and automated.

Human observation research uses a researcher to observe other people's behaviors, and all of the data is collected by the human observer. This form of observation research, which can collect either qualitative or quantitative data, is appropriate in four types of situations:

- where observations of behavior are more insightful than descriptions of behavior.
- where respondents may be unable to verbalize their attitudes.
- when survey measures of behaviors may not accurately predict actual behaviors.
- when behaviors themselves are the best source of insight.

Human observation research can be characterized in terms of four dimensions: the type of situation in which the observation takes place (natural or artificial), observer presence (open versus disguised), the level of observer participation (active or passive), and the form of data recording (unstructured versus structured).

Automated observation uses computer or mechanical tracking devices to observe behaviors. No human involvement is required for this form of data collection. There are two main forms of automated observation where automation

- *directly monitors consumer behaviors.* This occurs, for example, when cookies are used to track an individual's online behaviors or when loyalty cards are used at the supermarket.
- *monitors the products of consumer behaviors.* This occurs, for example, when computers are used to measure online "buzz" or to monitor changes in brand perceptions in blogs or other forms of consumer-generated media.

Automated observation can help advertisers better target their advertising, evaluate components of a multimedia campaign, track brand awareness, evaluate brand sentiment, and monitor and respond to changes in brand sentiment or brand image.

Review Questions

1. Explain the difference between human and automated observation.
2. Name the four types of situations in which *human observation* is most appropriate.
3. In what situations should *qualitative* research be used when conducting human observations? When should *quantitative* techniques be chosen?
4. What four dimensions can be used to characterize *human observation research*?
5. Identify the differences between *natural* and *artificial observation*, and provide examples of each.
6. What is meant by *observer obtrusiveness*, and how can the degree of obtrusiveness affect participant behaviors?
7. How do the behaviors of an *active* versus a *passive* observer differ? What are the strengths and weaknesses of each approach to observation?
8. Briefly describe the differences between recording observations in a *structured* and *unstructured* manner. What are the strengths and weaknesses of each?
9. What are the two main forms of *automated observation*?
10. For what purpose are *cookies* used by advertisers? How do they function?
11. Provide an example of how to observe offline behaviors. Why are these behaviors important to advertisers?
12. What is meant by the term "*consumer-generated media*" (CGM)? Why has observing CGM become a priority for advertisers and marketers?
13. What type of information is generally provided by *CGM observation*?
14. In what ways is *CGM* used to inform planning and decision making? Briefly describe each of these uses.

Application Exercises [33]

Application exercises 1 through 5 relate to concepts raised and discussed in this chapter.

1. Tide is in the process of developing a series of point-of-purchase displays for its new cold water detergent. Prior to final approval, however, Tide wants to conduct observation research to determine the display's impact (if any) on shopper behavior. The displays are placed in 10 test grocery stores, and a trained observer is assigned to each store. Prepare a short paper that responds to the following issues related to this research:
   a. Think about the first three characteristics of observation research discussed in the text (the type of situation in which the observation takes place, observer presence, and the level of observer participation). For each characteristic, which do you recommend? Why?
   b. Your colleague recommends that one of the key measurements should be "time spent looking at the point of purchase display." You agree. What other measures do you feel should be included in the observation?
   c. Do you recommend the use of a structured or unstructured instrument for recording the observations? Why?
   d. Your client, while interested in your recommendation for the type of observation instrument, still wants to see a structured instrument. Please prepare one.
2. SmartRevenue is a marketing research company that conducts in-store observations. SmartRevenue notes that in grocery store research, it typically observes the following shopper behaviors:
   • How much time does the shopper spend browsing the category?
   • From which direction do shoppers enter the aisle?
   • How many pause and browse?

- What is the browsing pattern at the shelf? For example, do they start in the middle, from the left, or from the right side?
- Do they read product labels?
- Do they read shelf signage (i.e., price, promotion, etc.)
- Do they compare with other products? If so, what is the observed basis of comparison (e.g., price, size, brand, features)?
- How many pick up and put back products?
- How long does the shopper interact with the shelf?
- What is the shopper group configuration (e.g., with children, friends, parents, and spouse)?
- In which direction does the shopper exit (e.g., left, right, toward adjacent aisle, toward perimeter aisle)?
- What are behaviors of non-purchasers?[34]

Imagine that you want to conduct observation research on behalf of Macy's management to help them understand the clothing-related shopping patterns of young male shoppers. Prepare a short paper that modifies the prior list to accommodate the observation of clothing store behaviors. Be certain to add and provide a rationale for any additional measurements you think would be of value.

3. Visit three of your favorite Web sites that display advertising. Read the privacy policy of each site. Determine whether or not the sites use cookies to track visitors, and if so, how these are used.

4. Nielsen's BlogPulse (http://www.blogpulse.com/) allows you to search for brand names or other key terms and obtain the trend in blog mentions for up to the last 180 days. Pick three competitive brands and search for blog trends for the prior 180 days. Prepare a short paper that presents your analysis of the observed trends.

5. Your client wishes to hire a company to monitor consumer-generated media related to her brand. You have been asked to make a recommendation regarding the company to hire. You can obtain a list of potential companies through either a search engine search or Econsultancy's *Online Reputation and Buzz Monitoring Buyer's Guide 2008* at http://econsultancy.com/reports/online-reputation-and-buzz-monitoring-buyer-s-guide-2008.

Regardless of the approach you take, select three companies and then (a) provide an analysis of the companies strengths and weaknesses and (b) make a recommendation, with rationale, for the company you suggest your client hire.

Application exercises 6 through 10 relate to the Video Consumer Mapping Study provided in the online supplementatl readings.

6. The Video Consumer Mapping Study was not the first observational study of this type. An earlier study, sponsored by the Online Publishers Association, is located at http://www.online-publishers.org/pdf/opadayinthelife.pdf. Download a copy of the earlier research. Then, prepare a short paper that contrasts the two studies. What differences in approach did the Video Consumer Mapping Study take? Why were these differences important? What was learned in the first study that influenced the design of the Video Consumer Mapping Study?

7. Imagine that you have been asked to develop a one to two page briefing document that explains the Video Consumer Mapping Study and presents its most important findings. Prepare this briefing.

8. The researchers in the Video Consumer Mapping Study categorized all media in terms of four main "Screens": television, mobile, computer, and other. Prepare a short paper that presents your point of view on this approach to categorization. Please be explicit with regard to your acceptance of this approach. You are also encouraged to suggest any modification(s) you think would improve this approach.

9. Select one of the demographic groups discussed in the Video Consumer Mapping Study. Prepare a short paper that briefly summarizes the key findings for this group and which present implications for advertisers who wish to reach this group.

10. Identify (from your perspective) the most expected and unexpected findings of the Video Consumer Mapping Study. Prepare a short paper that presents these findings and explains your rationale for why they were expected and unexpected.

Application exercises 11 through 13 relate to Campaigning With Social Media provided in the online supplemental readings.

11. Campaigning With Social Media used a range of observations to evaluate the success of the campaign. Present a point of view regarding any additional types of observational data that could have been collected and why that data would be important.

12. Campaigning With Social Media evaluated the success of the campaign with "point-in-time" observational data. Prepare a short paper that discusses how this observational approach to campaign evaluation could have been expanded to also collect longitudinal data. Why do you think this more long-term approach to data collection would (or would not) have been valuable?

13. Campaigning With Social Media relied exclusively on observational data. Could additional data have been collected via surveys? If so, what specific survey questions would have provided additional insights into campaign success?

Endnotes

1. A cookie is "a small amount of information sent by a Web server to a Web browser with the expectation that, when the user visits the server (Web site) again, the browser will send the information back to the server. Web servers use cookies to store user-specific information on the user's computer. For example, a cookie may be used to store the user's Web site id on his/her computer so that the user does not have to supply the id every time when visiting the Web site. In successive visits to the Web site, the browser will send the cookie with the id to the server, thereby identifying the user." This definition is provided by David Kristol (undated). "Cookies and Advertising Networks" at http://www.silicon-press.com/briefs/brief.cookiead/index.html.

2. This example is based on Evan Atlantis, Jo Salmon, and Adrian Bauman (2008). "Acute Effects of Advertisements on Children's Choices, Preferences, and Ratings of Liking for Physical Activities and Sedentary Behaviours: A Randomised Controlled Pilot Study." *Journal of Science and Medicine in Sport* 11 (6): 553–558. The methodology has been altered, however, for the sake of the example. The actual advertisements used in their research can be seen at http://www.health.gov.au/internet/healthyactive/publishing.nsf/content/getmoving.

3. This is an important aspect of observational data. Numeric information can clearly be treated quantitatively. Narrative information, however, can be treated as *either* quantitative or qualitative depending upon the sample and how it was collected. Narrative material can always be numerically coded to permit quantitative analysis.

4. The Green Globe 21 homepage is at http://www.tianz.org.nz/Current-Projects/Environmental-Plan.asp.

5. This case reflects the work of Axel Reiser and David G. Simmons (2005). "A Quasi-Experimental Method for Testing the Effectiveness of Ecolabel Promotion." *Journal of Sustainable Tourism* 13(6): 590–616.

6. Anne Sharp and Michelle Tustin (2003). "Benefits of Observational Research." at http://smib.vuw.ac.nz:8081/WWW/ANZMAC2003/papers/RES02_sharpa.pdf.

7. Elizabeth C. Redmond and Christopher J. Griffith (2006). "A Pilot Study to Evaluate the Effectiveness of a Social Marketing-Based Consumer Food Safety Initiative Using Observation." *British Food Journal* 108 (9): 753–770. Quotes are from this source.

8. Anticlown Media Privacy Policy (2009) at http://www.anticlown.com/privacy_policy.php. Italics added.

9. Yahoo! privacy policy at http://info.yahoo.com/privacy/us/yahoo/opt_out/targeting/details.html Italics added.

10. DoubleClick (undated). "Privacy FAQ" at http://www.doubleclick.com/privacy/faq.aspx. Italics added.

11. FetchBack (2009). "Retargeting" at http://www.fetchback.com/retargeting.html.

12. The Ghostery web site is http://www.ghostery.com.

13. Coremetrics (2010). "Coremetrics Continuous Optimization Program" at http://www.coremetrics.com/solutions/continuous-optimization-platform.php.

14. The situation and explanation in Figure 8.3 is adapted from Coremetrics (2009). "Increasing Relevancy, Loyalty and Conversions Online" at http://www.coremetrics.com.

15. Atlas Institute (2008). "Engagement Mapping" at http://www.atlassolutions.com/.

16. Lovett defines multicampaign attribution as "the practice of attributing credit to all marketing exposures that led to a Web site and subsequently resulted in a conversion event, rather than attributing all credit to the exposure immediately preceding the conversion." See John Lovett (2009). "A Framework for Multicampaign Attribution Measurement" at http://www.coremetrics.com.

17. Atlas Institute, op. cit.

18. Boston University College of Communication (undated). "Grocery Store Loyalty Card Use Is Strong Despite Privacy Concerns" at http://couponing.about.com/od/groceryzone/a/loyalty_cards.htm.

19. Nielsen-Online (2006). "Consumer-Generated Media (CGM) 101: Word of Mouth in the Age of the Web-Fortified Consumer" at http://www.nielsen-online.com/downloads/us/buzz/nbzm_wp_CGM101.pdf. For a discussion of the full range of CGM, see Pete Blackshaw (2005). "The Pocket Guide to Consumer-Generated Media" at http://www.clickz.com/3515576.

20. For insights into an academic perspective on observations of CGM, see Mike Thelwall (2007). "Blog Searching: The First General-Purpose Source of Retrospective Public Opinion in the Social Sciences." *Online Information Review* 31 (3): 277–289.

21. Nielsen-Online (undated). "About Consumer Generated Media" at http://www.nielsen-online.com/resources.jsp?section=about_cgm&nav=7.

22. Nielsen-Online's Blog pulse provides this type of data without charge. See http://www.blogpulse.com/.

23. Figure 8.4 is quoted with permission from ScoutLabs at http://www.scoutlabs.com/2009/02/26/how-does-sentiment-work-and-how-accurate-is-it-anyway/. Figure 8.5 is adapted from ScoutLabs' Netflix case study at http://www.scoutlabs.com/cgi-bin/mt/mt-search.cgi?search=netflix.

24. The case was written by Ofer Friedman of 1st2C (http://www.1st2C.com) and is at http://cgmtrends.wordpress.com/2007/12/01/blu-ray-vs-hd-dvd-case-study-online-mind-sharing-tell-the-consumer-side-of-the-stalemate-story/. Reproduced with permission.

25. The case was written by Ofer Friedman of 1st2C (http://www.1st2C.com) and is at http://cgmtrends.wordpress.com/2008/01/06/1st2c-cgm-report-the-whole-foods-case-study/. The case study was conducted in September 2007. Reproduced with permission.

26. Findings from the study, provided in the online supplemental readings, are made available with the permission of the Council for Research Excellence at http://www.researchexcellence.com/ and The Nielsen Company.

27. Council for Research Excellence (2009). "Press Release" available at http://www.researchexcellence.com/vcm_pressrelease.pdf.

28. Council for Research Excellence (2009). "Video Consumer Mapping Study: Technical Appendix" at http://www.researchexcellence.com/vcm_technicalappendix.pdf.

29. Council for Research Excellence "Technical Appendix" op. cit.

30. Council for Research Excellence "Technical Appendix" op. cit.

31. Council for Research Excellence "Technical Appendix" op. cit.

32. The presentation of the campaign and its results is reproduced with permission of Amnesty UK (http://amnesty.org.uk).

33. Exercises 1 through 5 are hypothetical. Brand names and data are used for illustrative purposes only.

34. SmartRevenue (2009). "Ethnographic Observation" at http://smartrevenue.com/methods/observation.

CHAPTER 9

Observation Research: Biometrics

Chapter 8 discussed two common forms of observation research: human and automated. There is widespread agreement that these forms of research, when used appropriately, can provide important insights into individuals' attitudes and behaviors. A third form of observation research is biometric—the monitoring and analysis of physiological responses to advertising or other visual or verbal stimuli. This form of observation research is more controversial. This chapter explores biometric observation research and its application to advertising decision making.

***

When you are done reading this chapter, you should have a better understanding of:

- how each form of biometric observation is used
- the strengths, weaknesses, and limitations of each form of biometric observation
- how each form of biometric observation contributes to advertising decision making.

Biometric research measures an individual's voluntary and involuntary responses to stimuli such as advertisements, Web pages, or packages. The most commonly measured voluntary response is eye tracking, while the most commonly measured involuntary responses are brain waves or physiological responses such as galvanic skin response, heart rate, and blood pressure. Eye tracking, the least controversial and most widely accepted form of biometric observation, is discussed next. This is followed by a discussion of involuntary biometric observation, focusing on brain wave analysis and combined physiological measures.[1]

EYE TRACKING

The fusion of computer and video technology makes it possible to record the movements of an individual's eye as he or she watches a television commercial, reads an advertisement, looks at a product package, or interacts with a Web page. Current eye tracking techniques are unobtrusive and permit the respondent to act in a natural manner (see Figure 9.1). A respondent is seated in a chair, and an initial calibration of the eye tracking apparatus is conducted. A stimulus is presented next. While the respondent reads or views the stimulus, the eye tracking device transmits an undetectable beam of filtered light to his or her eyes. The reflection of this light from the eye to the tracking device identifies the visual focal point, indicating where the respondent is looking. Data recording is continuous and information on where, how long, and in what order the respondent looked is automatically recorded.[2]

FIGURE 9.1 Eye Tracking in Action

Eye tracking research can provide a wealth of information on an individual's visual behaviors as an advertisement or other stimulus is processed.[3] Advertising-related eye tracking research tends to focus on six key measures:

- *First fixation* identifies the visual element that attracts the greatest amount of initial attention. This element is the initial focal point in the ad.

- *Time to first fixation* is the amount of time that has elapsed from the start of visual processing until a specific element in the stimulus is viewed.

- *Most fiixation* identifies the visual element(s) that maintain attention. These are the element(s) that consistently attract attention across multiple viewers.

- *Individual gaze time* is the amount of time spent looking at individual element(s) in the ad. Longer gaze times reflect higher levels of interest or deeper levels of information/visual processing.

- *Total gaze time* is the sum of all individual gaze times and reflects how engaged a viewer is with the stimulus overall. Shorter total gaze times tend to reflect viewer confusion or disinterest while longer total gaze times are an indicator of increased engagement.

- *Movement between elements* indicates how the stimulus was processed. A systematic or structured approach, where one element leads the eye to the next logical element, is always preferable over the random viewing of elements.

These measures are important because they allow an advertiser not only to better understand how a stimulus is processed but also to better identify elements of an ad that are not being processed or which fail to attract attention.

Once eye tracking data is collected, it can be presented in any number of ways. The most common approaches are shown in Figure 9.2a through 9.2d and are described below.[4]

Consider the print advertisement shown in Figure 9.2a. This is the test advertisement. The image next to the advertisement (Figure 9.2b), presents *Gaze Paths*, individual search paths through the ad. Larger circles indicate greater amount of time spent in a particular area, while the numbers indicate the sequence of fixations. Note how low numbers tend to group together as do high numbers. This indicates that although there is variation across individuals, the visual pattern across individuals was fairly consistent.

The image shown in Figure 9.2c is a *heatmap*, one of the most common ways to present eye tracking data. A heatmap summarizes the viewing patterns of the entire sample by using colors (or shading when reproduced in black and white) to represent the amount of time spent viewing particular areas. The brighter the color, the longer the average individual spent looking at that area. Heatmaps thus provide insights into what individuals exposed to the stimulus are and are not likely to see. Heatmaps can be used several ways. First, heatmaps and Gaze Path charts can be used together: the latter informs the order of viewing, while the former informs the length or intensity of viewing on each step in the viewing path. Second, heatmaps can be used

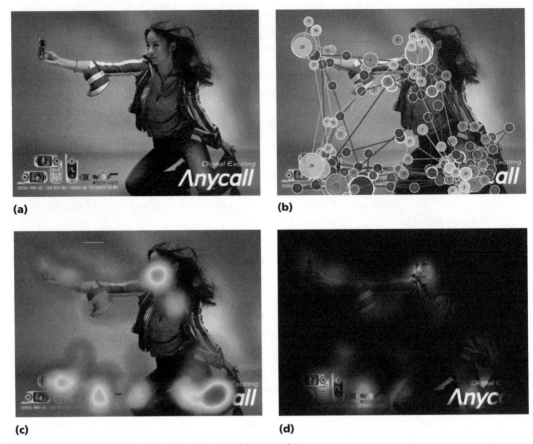

(a)   **(b)**

(c)   **(d)**

FIGURE 9.2 Methods for Reporting Eye Tracking Results

sequentially. Sequential changes in the primary viewing area (see Figure 9.3) illustrate how attention and engagement changes during each stage of stimulus processing.

Some find heatmaps cumbersome to use, especially if color reproduction is not available. (Distinctions between viewing areas are more difficult to see when a heatmap is reproduced in shades of grey.) An alternative to a heatmap is the *Opacity Chart* (Figure 9.2d). Here, viewership of the stimulus is represented by "openings" which correspond to colors in the heatmap. The more clearly a portion of the ad is seen the higher and more intense the level of viewing.

Application of Eye Tracking to Advertising Planning

Eye tracking data can contribute to improved advertising planning by helping advertisers make more informed decisions with regard to media selection and ad placement within a specific medium.

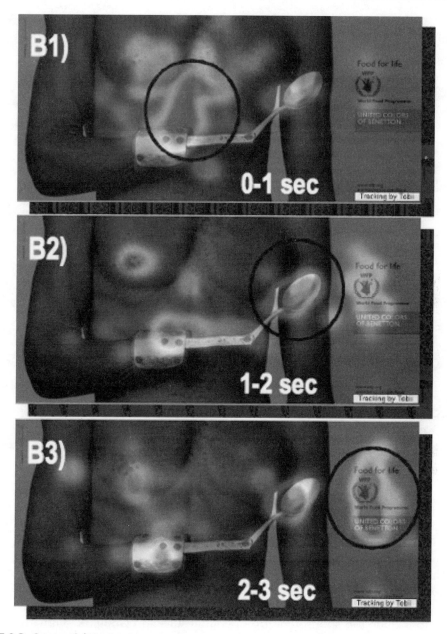

FIGURE 9.3 Sequential Heatmaps

One of the seminal studies conducted using eye tracking and the heatmap reporting method was Enquiro's eye tracking study conducted on Google's search results page. As the following discussion illustrates, this research played a critical role in helping advertisers better plan their search engine campaigns.

Enquiro used eye tracking data to discover Google's "Golden Triangle." The Golden Triangle is the distinct area of eye scan activity shown in Figure 9.4.[5] (As with

FIGURE 9.4 Google's Golden Triangle

all heatmaps reproduced in shades of grey, lighter areas indicate more intense viewing). The triangle extends from the top of the results over to the top of the first result, then down to a point on the left side at the bottom of the "above the fold" visible results. This key area was looked at by 100% of the participants. Generally, this area appears to include top sponsored, top organic results and Google's alternative results, including shopping, news, or local suggestions. Additionally, there seems to be a "F" shaped scan pattern, where the eye tends to travel vertically along the far left side of the results looking for visual cues (relevant words, brands, etc.) and then scanning to the right when something catches a reader's attention. Enquiro explains this importance of this triangle as follows:

> Think of the search results page as a shopping mall. Think of the eye activity
> as foot traffic. In a mall, you have anchor tenants who attract the majority of

traffic. Usually, malls try to have two or three anchor tenants distributed evenly around the perimeter of the mall so foot traffic is generated moving from anchor tenant to anchor tenant. All the other tenants take advantage of this by catching the attention of the foot traffic as they walk by.

The Google search results page has one anchor, and it's usually in the upper left corner. The anchor is the number one organic result. That's what we're all looking for. Everything else is a detour on the way. Yes, top sponsored results get high visibility and a reasonable number of click throughs, but more often than not, it's because they happened to catch our attention while we were looking for the top organic listing. With rare exceptions, we're not looking for a sponsored result.

Let's go back to our analogy. What would happen if a mall had only one anchor in a corner of the mall that every single shopper went to see? You would see a flurry of foot traffic in this corner of the mall and little everywhere else. The further you got from the anchor, the less traffic you would see. That's the Golden Triangle. And in this case, the anchor is very easy to see. It's firmly established in the upper left corner of the search results page. That's where our eyes first go to see the top organic listing. We may have to reorient ourselves from that orientation point, but that's where we'll start.[6]

The application of these results to advertising planning can be seen in the percentage of individuals viewing different ads.

> Visibility dropped quickly with organic rankings, starting at a high of 100% for the top listing, dropping to 85% at the bottom of the "above the fold" listings, and then dropping dramatically below the fold from 50% at the top to 20% at the bottom of the page. On side sponsored ads, the top ranked results received much more in the way of both eye activity and click through. About 50% of participants looked at the top ad, compared to only 10% who looked at ads in the sixth, seventh or eighth location on the page. In searches where top sponsored results are returned in addition to right sponsored ads, the top ads received much higher visibility, being seen by 80% to 100% of participants, as opposed to 10% to 50% of participants who looked at the side sponsored ads.[7]

The Google Golden Triangle eye tracking results led researchers to question whether this was a universal effect or if it was specific to Google. Current research indicates that while the general phenomenon is a constant, it does vary across search engines and cultures. The search process has nuanced but important differences across competitive search engines within the same country, with MSN having a much larger Golden Triangle versus Google.[8] Eye tracking research has also determined that individuals in the United States and China process Google's search page differently; where Google U.S.'s primary attention area is the Golden Triangle, Google China's primary perceptual area is a rectangle at the top of the search results page.[9] In all cases, understanding the differences in consumer processing allows for more successful advertising planning.

Application of Eye Tracking to Evaluation and Revision of Advertising Creative

As illustrated in Google's Golden Triangle, understanding how the context for advertising is processed provides important insights for advertising planning and media placement. Advertisers still need to make certain, however, that the strongest possible advertisement appears in that context. Eye tracking also makes a contribution here. Eye tracking is well suited to determining a stimulus' strengths and weaknesses and for providing direction for research-guided revision. The before and after ads along with the eye tracking results shown in Figures 9.5 and Figure 9.6 illustrate this application of eye tracking.[10]

The ad shown in Figure 9.5a is the test advertisement. The second visual (Figure 9.5b) is the Gaze Plot, which shows the order of fixations for seven participants. Each "bubble" is at least 250 milliseconds, and the size of the bubble reflects the length of the fixation. The bottom visual, Figure 9.5c, Hot Spots, translates the gaze data into an Opacity Chart. The visible areas in this chart reflect the areas (across all respondents) that were looked at the longest. Taken together, the Gaze Plot and Opacity Charts led to the advertisement being broken into four distinct segments: "Face and Body," "Headline," "Tagline," "Product Image." For this ad, the goal was to communicate the brand name "Magic Face," and as a result, the brand name was also considered a segment of the ad.

(a)   **(b)**

(c)

FIGURE 9.5 Tested Ad and Eye Tracking Results

(a)   **(b)**

FIGURE 9.6   Revised Ad and Eye Tracking Results

Two key measures were *time to first fixation* and *average gaze time*. Time to first fixation reflects the success or failure of each ad element to attract attention. Because most people spend only three or four seconds on a print ad before turning the page, it is critical to communicate the main message (in this case, the brand name) quickly. Therefore, the time it took people to look at the brand name is an important piece of data. The time to first fixation results are shown in the table below. Note how it takes a very long time for individuals to obtain product-related information via the brand name and product image.

Ad Component	Time to First Fixation (seconds)
Face and Body	0.33
Headline	1.38
Brand Name	3.36
Product Image	4.10
Tagline	4.14

While it takes a relatively long time to focus on product-related information, this would not necessarily be a significant weakness *if* individuals spent time in these areas of the ad once they arrived. This does not appear to be the case, however. As shown in the table below, very little time is spent on either the product image or the brand name.

Ad Component	Average Gaze Time (ms)
Face and Body	1,237
Headline	854
Tagline	790
Product Image	572
Brand Name	322

This data led to the following recommendation: move the ad's main message (in this case, communication of the brand name "Magic Face") closer to where people are naturally looking. The revised ad is shown in Figure 9.6a. Note how the brand name has been enlarged and how the copy has been moved to the other side of the ad, closer to the model's face and in an area at which the model is looking. The Opacity Plot for the revised ad is shown in Figure 9.6b. As with the original ad, all of the ad's primary elements are still clearly visible, indicating that the revision did not degrade the visual processing of the ad. The data related to time to first fixation and average gaze time indicate that the revisions significantly strengthened the ad. In particular, when comparing the pre- and post-revision data, note how time to first fixation has decreased for both the "Magic Face" brand name and tagline (see table below).

	Time to First Fixation (seconds)	
Ad Component	**Original Ad**	**Revised Ad**
Face and Body	0.33	0.47
Headline	1.38	1.71
Brand Name	**3.36**	**2.08**
Product Image	4.10	4.24
Tagline	**4.14**	**0.76**

Additionally, once individuals focused on these areas, they tended to stay longer. Note in following table how average gaze time has increased for the brand name without sacrificing time spent on the product image.

	Average Gaze Time (ms)	
Ad Component	**Original Ad**	**Revised Ad**
Face and Body	1,237	1,299
Headline	854	853
Tagline	790	509
Product Image	572	598
Brand Name	**322**	**604**

Combining Eye Tracking with Retrospective Interviews

Chapters 5 to 7 described qualitative techniques for obtaining insights into individuals' attitudes and beliefs. As discussed, these techniques are often used to obtain reactions to advertising or other consumer-focused communications. Here, a stimulus is shown, and the respondent is asked to verbalize his or her reactions either while processing the stimulus or after all processing has taken place. Bartels[11] believes that this process may be problematic regardless of when the verbalization occurs:

> Respondents can be asked to think aloud as they interact with the stimulus, verbalizing their thoughts and opinions as they occur. This approach, however,

may not provide accurate insights because the act of asking someone to voice his or her opinions as they occur may artificially influence the formations of those opinions.

Respondents can be allowed to interact with the stimulus and, when done, verbalize their thoughts and opinions. While this approach may be more realistic than the think-aloud approach, it does run the risk of information loss. In the time between the first impression and the beginning of the interview a lot can be lost. People forget. They change their minds. They make up stories without even knowing it. The gut reaction is a fleeting impulse, and once the moment has passed, the sensation is difficult to retrieve.

Bartels' suggested solution is the ActionReview Interview, a combination of eye tracking with post-tracking interviews. Here, a stimulus is presented and eye tracking data is collected. Next, the eye tracking data is played back to each respondent, while the respondents provide a narrative of their thoughts and feelings as the eye tracking data is viewed. This allows respondents to

> relive the gut reaction in vivid detail retrospectively . . . [Consider reactions to a Web page.] When asked to recall their impressions without the aid of eye tracking video, respondents tend to generalize (i.e., "I had trouble" or "It was easy to use"). Respondents often cannot recall moment-by-moment impressions; thus, information about useability, strengths and weaknesses is lost. However, when the respondent is provided with a visual cue that shows in great detail where he or she was looking, a wide array of specific information becomes available (i.e., "I was searching everywhere but couldn't find X," "I expected Y to be in the top navigation," "Z was the first thing I noticed," etc.) As each moment of the session is replayed, the respondent is able to relive that thought process and express it to the researcher to create a clear narrative of the interaction.

The ActionReview Interview is an excellent example of how the combination of different research techniques is able to provide insights beyond those provided by each technique individually.

Combining Eye Tracking with Facial Coding and Verbal Response

The prior example illustrates how the combination of two research techniques can provide important insights. Another research approach combines three data collection techniques: eye tracking, facial coding, and verbal response. (Facial Coding records the degree of emotional response generated by the stimulus, based on the Seven Core Emotions: surprise, fear, anger, sadness, disgust, contempt, or happiness.) Van Lun explains the rationale for this approach:

> Our brain processes information backwards. First a stimulus enters our old brain [where] it's processed intuitively and subconsciously. The old brain matches patterns, which means it automatically compares new experiences to previous ones. Then the stimulus is sent to our subconscious emotional brain where it assigns a value to the stimuli (e.g, an emotion). And eventually the stimulus is sent to our rational brain that fulfills a role more closely resembling

that of a lobbyist than having any real influence on the stimuli. It gives us an "intellectual alibi" that allows us to defend or justify purchases regarding family and friends and that way rule out cognitive dissonance . . . Because Facial Coding deals with these three processing levels, they also measure the three different levels:

- Eye Tracking in the old brain to figure out which stimuli are being observed, how long, with which intensity and in which order.
- Facial Coding to figure out what people feel during a witnessed stimulus (this is synchronized with Eye Tracking in "per second graphs").
- Rational response to the stimuli in which people have to give a vocal answer. This way, they measure if what people say matches what they feel (the facial expression).[12]

Sensory Logic[13] is a research company that offers both stand-alone facial coding and facial coding in conjunction with eye tracking. The Sensory Logic system offers an automated examination of facial expressions that entail a review and analysis of

43 muscles that correspond to 23 patterns of muscle activities known as action units. These correspond, in turn, to 10 emotional states. Data outcomes of the facial coding are: level of engagement, percentage of positive/negative/neutral emotions, and gauging of impact and appeal. In essence, this approach, prior to the use of verbal questions, allows the advertiser to determine the mood state associated with primary fixations on an advertisement or other communication.

A video presentation describing the application of facial coding to Obama and McCain ads from the 2008 election has been produced by Ad Age.[14]

Additional Examples of Eye Tracking Applications to Advertising

The online supplemental readings present additional examples of how eye tracking provides insights into a broad range of advertising-related issues and assists in advertising decision making.

NEUROMARKETING

Neuromarketing is the label given to the use of brain observation for marketing purposes. In its simplest form, brain wave observation examines changes in brain activity in the presence of advertising, packaging, or other communications. Neuromarketing uses state-of-the-art technologies such as functional magnetic resonance imaging (fMRI), magneto-encephalography, and more conventional electroencephalograms (EEGs) to observe which areas of the brain "light up" when test subjects are processing a stimulus. The activity of regions such as the nucleus accumbens, insula, and mesial prefrontal cortex give researchers insight into how consumers respond to specific stimuli.[15] The rationale for neuromarketing is straightforward:

The premise is that consumer buying decisions are made in split seconds in the subconscious, emotional part of the brain, and by understanding what we like, don't like, want, fear, are bored by, etc. as indicated by our brain's reactions to brand stimuli, marketers can design products and communications to better meet "unmet" market needs, connect and drive "the buy."[16]

The term "neuromarketing" is relatively new. The roots of neuromarketing, however, go back nearly 40 years.[17] While the general goals of this approach have not changed dramatically over time, two recent developments have significantly changed how these goals are achieved. One development is the availability of inexpensive, portable, extremely powerful computers. These computers allow for the collection, processing, and analysis of millions of pieces of data during one test session. The second development relates to the measurement equipment. Extremely sensitive equipment is now significantly less expensive, less intrusive, and more portable than in past years.

Brain wave analysis is no longer a "fringe" technique, as mainline advertisers are exploring neuromarketing applications, for example:

> Google is so confident that its InVideo Ads product—those semi-transparent/animated overlay ads it launched on YouTube last year—are game changers that the company is turning to brain wave researchers to prove their effectiveness. The search giant, in conjunction with MediaVest, has partnered with NeuroFocus, a researcher that specializes in biometrics, to gauge both how users respond to InVideo ads and how well those ads complement traditional banner ads.[18]
>
> The study discovered that viewers found the overlays "compelling and engaging" and that these ads generated a high amount of attention and emotional engagement for a variety of different brands and video types. In addition, including a companion banner alongside the overlay ad was found to improve brand response compared to banner ads alone.[19]

The two principal techniques for measuring brain wave patterns and activation are fMRI and EEG.[20]

- An fMRI uses magnetic resonance scanners to produce sets of cross-sections of the brain called tomograms. This ability allows fMRIs to identify the specific areas of the brain that are activated at a specific point in time. As opposed to an EEG that directly measures electrical activity, the fMRI observes and measures changes in blood flow and oxygenation in the brain and then relates the levels measured to brain activity. This linkage is possible because active nerve cells carry a great deal of oxygen while less active cells are far less oxygenated. The brain's response to the need for more oxygen in active areas is to increase blood flow to these areas.

- An *EEG* measures and records the brain's electrical activity and as a result provides insights into how much of the brain is engaged at a point in time but, unlike an fMRI, cannot pinpoint the specific areas being activated. An EEG requires that special sensors (electrodes) be attached to an individual's head, where these sensors are in turn attached to a computer that reads changes in brain activity. The EEG then reports which areas of the brain are activated and the strength of activity.

There is widespread consensus that both the fMRI and EEG provide highly reliable measures of brain activity. There are two distinct perspectives, however, on which type of measurement is of greater value.

fMRI: Activation of Specific Brain Areas

Some researchers are attempting to link changes in activity in specific brain areas to unobservable psychological outcomes such as emotional rewards, disgust, brand loyalty, and persuasion. A large body of research has identified the specific brain areas associated with these phenomena. As a result, when advertising exposure activates these or other known functional areas, neuromarketers assume that the associated psychological outcome has occurred. An increased activation in the brain's reward areas, for example, would be seen as a positive outcome of advertising exposure.

The case of Coke and Pepsi in the "Pepsi Taste Test" illustrates an early application of this type of research. McClure and his colleagues[21]

> gave 67 people a blind taste test of both Coke and Pepsi, then placed subjects in the scanner, whose magnetic field measures how active cells are by recording how much oxygen they consume for energy. After tasting each drink, all the volunteers showed strong activation of the reward areas of the brain—which are associated with pleasure and satisfaction—and they were almost evenly split in their preferences for the two brands. But when [McClure] repeated the test and told them what they were drinking, three out of four people said they preferred Coke, and their brains showed why: not only were the reward systems active, but memory regions in the medial prefrontal cortex and hippocampus also lit up. [According to the researchers] "This showed that the brand alone has value in the brain system above and beyond the desire for the content of the can." In other words, all those happy, energetic and glamorous people drinking Coke in commercials did exactly what they were supposed to do: they seeped into the brain and left associations so powerful they could even override a preference for the taste of Pepsi.[22]

More recently, Knutson and his colleagues at Stanford studied neural pathways in the brain related to reward and loss and were able to demonstrate the sequence of brain activity that precedes a decision to buy (or not to buy) a product. Once the sequence was established, the researchers could then forecast whether test subjects would buy other items by monitoring their brain patterns. Similarly, the area of the brain responsible for the assessment and development of "trust" has been identified. Neuromarketers are now testing advertising to see whether or not this specific area of the brain is activated by an ad, assuming that increased activation is an indication of increased trust in the advertising and brand. Lastly, Langleben and his colleagues at the University of Pennsylvania Annenberg School are using fMRIs to

> evaluate the feasibility of using functional Magnetic Resonance Imaging (fMRI) to study brain response to anti-smoking PSAs. In preliminary studies, researchers used perfusion fMRI to detect increased activity in the components of the brain limbic system in opiate-dependent patients in response to a ten-minute heroin-related video. The results indicated that: (1) brain response to media can be measured with fMRI, (2) brain response to media varies across target audiences, and (3) specific structures mediating strong interest could be activated in the target population but not the controls. Further, fMRI [has been

used] to detect differential response to the emotional image content. This pilot study takes an important first step toward exploring the feasibility of using magnetic resonance signal as a marker of cognitive (e.g., attention) and emotional (e.g., arousal) responses to different PSAs. Results from this would allow interpretation of the brain response to a PSA in terms of known brain localization of cognitive functions.[23]

Commercial companies such as MindSign are using fMRI testing in a more applied setting. MindSign explains its methodology as follows:

> We take your TV, Web video or radio ad, and show you what parts or scenes cause activation and what parts cause deactivation, which parts were the most engaging, and which parts were the least. We compare your ads to your competitor's ads to see which is more activating and at what parts. We then graph the brain responses to your ad versus our database and show you which parts of your ad are more activating than the average brain response to an advertisement, and which parts are less activating. We make a video graph, so you can watch your ad and see the brain reaction mapped over it in real-time—you can see what about your ad causes brain activation or deactivation moment by moment. Next, we do what we call TV Ad Re-Editing. We take brain reactions to several different versions of a TV or radio advertisement, keep the parts that cause activation and were greater than the database average, remove parts that cause deactivation and were below the database average, and edit together what's left into a coherent whole. We then rescan the new spot on the subject and show that the re-edited version has greater brain activation then the original sources.[24]

Figure 9.7 illustrates how fMRI data provides insights into consumer response. An ad for Virgin Mobile Phones is being tested. The scene being measured is shown in the upper

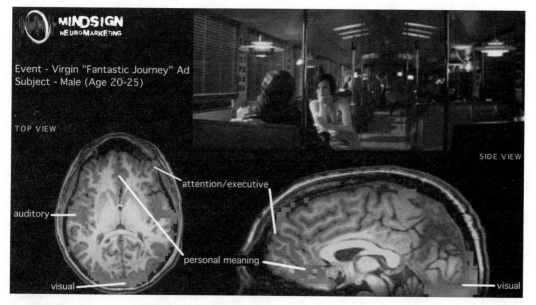

FIGURE 9.7 Example Results of MindSign fMRI Test

right-hand corner. Two views of the brain are provided and labeled where the darker areas of the brain are specific areas being activated. At this point, near the beginning of the ad, specific parts of the viewer's brain are being activated. Importantly (and positively) activation is in areas known to be related to personal meaning and attention. The viewer is engaged with the ad.

The online supplemental readings present more detailed insights into fMRI testing by showing changes in activation areas for the entire Virgin Mobile ad.

Overall Brain Activation (EEG) Plus Physiological Measures

The second approach to brain measurement for neuromarketing purposes is more holistic. Here, rather than trying to associate specific changes in brain activity with a specific psychological outcome, the goal is to determine the extent of overall brain engagement, operationalized, for example, as the degree to which an individual commits mental function to the processing of an advertising communication. Greater commitment (as reflected in greater overall brain activity which in turn is reflected in the EEG readings) is believed to lead to greater advertising success. Neuromarketers who take this approach often combine EEG data with physiological measures such as galvanic skin response and heart rate to compute an overall summary measure of an individual's reactions and level of engagement. Two representative companies that take this approach are Sands Research and One to One Insight.

SANDS RESEARCH.   Sands Research[25] uses proprietary algorithms to combine overall neural activity with other physiological measures to compute a stimulus' Neural Engagement Factor (NEF). The company argues that this measure of engagement better reflects advertising response and is therefore a better predictor of advertising success versus more traditional measures, such as focus groups or quantitative surveys.

Sands Research, similar to other neuromarketing firms, often uses external events to provide a measure of validity to its findings and conclusions. Dooley, for example, notes that:

> Earlier this year, Sands Research Inc., a leading provider of neuromarketing research studies, completed an extensive study into all 72 television commercials aired during NBC's 2009 Super Bowl XLIII broadcast. Each of the TV spots were ranked by the Company's Neuro-Engagement Factor (NEF) scoring system which is based upon measuring EEG (brain wave) activity from viewers and Sands Research's proprietary software and algorithms that measures the viewer's attention levels.
>
> Three out of the top five commercials identified from that Super Bowl study were nominated for the coveted Academy of Television Arts and Sciences' Creative Arts Emmy Award. This past weekend, top ranked Coca-Cola's "Heist" from Wieden + Kennedy, won the 2009 Emmy Award for outstanding commercial at the Creative Arts Emmy Awards. This commercial was the second highest rated Super Bowl commercial by Sands Research.[26]

ONE TO ONE INSIGHT.   One to One Insight[27] also combines physiological measures with EEG data to calculate a summary measure to represent an individual's engagement with a visual stimulus. This measure is supplemented with eye tracking information and a post-exposure interview to provide an additional perspective for interpretation and insights. One to One Insight calls this approach Quantemo™, which is described as follows:

> Quantemo™ allows for the simultaneous capture of multiple biophysical responses (breath rate, galvanic skin response, heart rate) in addition to eye tracking information. After recording the biophysical measures, Quantemo™ combines all of the measures into a single, representative measure of physiological engagement. The Quantemo™ Physiological Index or QPI serves as a single point of reference of the overall level of physical engagement (or disengagement) exhibited by a research participant. Positive QPI scores represent stronger physiological engagement while negative QPI scores represent weaker physiological engagement.[28]

The QPI is one component of an overall assessment of engagement. The final overall score (labeled the Quantemo Engagement Index or QEI) incorporates participant's reactions to PrEmo, a cross-cultural emotional tagging instrument developed by Technical University of Delft in the Netherlands. PrEmo asks respondents to report their emotions with the use of expressive cartoon animations.[29] The combined approach of biometric and self-report data allows researchers to correlate the objective physiological data of the QPI with the subjective, self-reported data. The QEI has been applied to a broad range of digital media. Recent research studies[30] include:

> *Implications of User Engagement with Search Result Pages* compares user engagement with Universal search results versus traditional text-only results by recording the users' eye tracking, physiological and emotional reactions, and click tracking behavior.
>
> *Emotion, Engagement, and Internet Video* uses the results from the various Quantemo™ data source and presents three insights concerning how users locate, respond to, and engage with Internet video.
>
> *Serious Games for Marketing* offers five insights for the design of future branding and marketing oriented activities in virtual worlds, such as Second Life.

Recent research conducted by One to One Insight illustrates the power of the QEI to discriminate responses to advertising. The company examined video game player's responses to advertising placed in video games using the full range of Quantemo tools: brain monitoring, physiological measures, eye tracking, and post-exposure surveys. All individuals were monitored as they played a video game with embedded advertising. With regard to the QEI, a direct relationship was found between level of QEI and brand recall/recognition. Higher levels of QEI were associated with higher levels of brand recall/recognition, as shown in the table below.[31]

QEI (Engagement)	% Brands Recalled
0.87	30.2
1.08	42.0
2.0+	>50.0

A full One to One Insight research report is provided in the online supplemental readings.

Exclusive Reliance on Physiological Measures

While some, such as Sands Research and One to One Insight, attempt to quantify advertising response through a combination of brain monitoring plus other physiological measures, others examine responses using *only* physiological measures such as heartbeat, galvanic skin response, and breathing patterns. One such company is Innerscope Research.[32]

Innerscope utilizes wearable sensor technology (a vest with monitoring sensors) to collect physiological information. Innerscope describes this vest as follows:

> The Innerscope Biometric Monitoring System contains a unique suite of biometric sensors imbedded in a comfortable, unobtrusive garment that detects and integrates key biometric measures that form the basis of human emotions: respiration, motion, heart rate and skin conductance. In conjunction, state-of-the-art eye tracking technology precisely identified where a person is looking during any time/response period. These biometric measures are time-locked to the media stimulus, allowing the direct relationship of collected data to stimulus processing.

Reference to external events is one way that Innerscope validates its procedure. Innerscope evaluated and then ranked Super Bowl ads using its Biometric Monitoring System. The company then looked at the number of comments and viewings the ads received on MySpace, assuming that more engaging ads would generate higher numbers as compared with lower engagement ads. When compared to rankings produced by EEGs, Innerscope's higher ranked ads did much better. Innerscope found that the top five ads as ranked by its methodology received 1½ more views and six times more comments as the top five ads as ranked by EEG testing.

Alternative Views

It is clear that neuromarketing is currently informing advertising decision making and has the potential to provide even greater insights in the future. Nevertheless, concerns have been raised regarding this approach. Some of these concerns relate to issues raised earlier in the chapter, that is, levels of external validity. Steinberg summarizes this point of view:

> Should the researchers be able to prove a commercial that provokes a rapid heartbeat, sweating, and movement in all the right facial muscles also leads to increased sales, they will likely have a hit on their hands. Until then, well, the testing goes on.[33]

A second issue relates to the ethics underlying the use of brain imaging techniques for advertising decision making.[34] Wilson and his colleagues summarize the ethical objections:

> Our contention is that neuroscience findings and methods hold the potential for marketing practices that threaten consumers' abilities to follow preferences and dictates according to free will and contradict Rawlsian justice. This context

suggests that external constraints on decision making imposed by applications of neural manipulation are possible violations. Transgressions are particularly troublesome when manipulation occurs without explicit awareness, consent, and understanding.[35]

Finally, some are concerned that the focus on neuromarketing distracts advertisers from what is believed to be their true goal: creating advertising that differentiates the brand and targets the consumers' heart. This point of view is addressed by Lowry:

> I find the whole practice of neuromarketing to be offensive and contrary to any principle of consumer experience. . . . Instead of messing with the customer's brain, focus on her heart: Develop an appealing and financially justifiable experience that she's willing to stand in line for. Customers are smarter and more empowered than ever before. It's time to stop insulting them. Treat them as honest partners in a reciprocal relationship. Treat them as individuals, not as machines, and appeal to their ability to make decisions. If you want them to make the right decisions, give them the right reasons—not a brain scan.[36]

APPLYING CHAPTER CONCEPTS

This chapter discussed a wide range of biometric approaches for exploring consumers' responses to visual stimuli, such as advertisements, product packaging, Web sites, and search engine results. The online supplemental readings provide actual biometric research studies and findings. As you read through each study, pay particular attention to the care taken regarding research design, data analysis, and data reporting.

Tobii Technology Eye Tracking Cases

The five case studies provided by Tobii Technology illustrate the diverse areas in which eye tracking can contribute to understanding consumer response and decision making. [37]

- The first two studies ("Print Advertisement" and "Media Research" cases) illustrate eye tracking application to the analysis of print advertising and demonstrate several things. First, the cases show how eye tracking data can help an advertiser understand how consumers are processing an ad and, as a result, identify areas of strength and weakness, particularly with regard to the ad's ability to focus attention on key elements such as the brand name. Beyond this shared finding of both cases, the first case illustrates how advertiser insights can be deepened when eye tracking data is supplemented by other research techniques. In this case, both quantitative and qualitative data were collected after the ad was viewed. Quantitative data focused on reactions to the ad, while qualitative measures focused on message communication.

- The "Online Marketing" case explored how the design and placement of large or moving banners on a Web page affected site visitors' behaviors as they viewed the page. Specifically, the research sought to answer two questions: "How does the design and placement of banners affect user behavior and Web site efficiency?" and

"How does the design and placement of banners affect users' total Web site experience?" Note that the approach taken in this research was different than that of the print eye tracking research. Here, rather than letting the user process the stimulus in the absence of direction, users were given specific tasks to accomplish. Eye tracking (supplemented with qualitative interviews) provided significant insights into how the design and placement of banners influenced how site visitors attempted to accomplish the assigned tasks.

- The prior study looked at how banner advertising affected Web page processing. The fourth study, "Online Banner Advertising," focuses on banner ads themselves. This research was designed to identify the relative strengths and weaknesses of two alternative banner ads. The specific questions addressed by the research were: "Which is the strongest banner creative?" "What is the most advantageous placement on the page for the banner ad?" and "What specific elements of the banner attracted the most attention?" The way in which eye tracking answered each of these questions led to significant improvement in visual processing and advertising response.

- The last study, "TV Sports Marketing and Eye Tracking," moves beyond advertising into an area of increasing interest to advertisers, sports marketing and promotion. This research was designed to help advertisers evaluate the extent to which brand exposure in a sporting event benefits the brand. Three key questions were addressed: "To what extent does a viewer focus on brands during a sporting event?" "How long is a brand viewed compared to the time it is visible?" and "What are the most efficient locations for brand placement?" Notice, as you read the results, how eye tracking is unique in its ability to answer all three questions.

Etre Web Site Analysis

Etre specializes in three aspects of Web design and evaluation: usability, accessibility, and findability (making content easy to find and simple to navigate).[38] The Etre cases provided in the online supplemental readings focus on the first area, usability and present Etre's analysis of four commercial Web sites. Each of the sites was tested among individuals aged 18 to 35, all of whom regularly used the Internet. Users were given nondirective instructions to just explore the Web site.

All four analyses illustrate a *very* important aspect of eye tracking research (and for that matter, research in general). While eye tracking instruments can provide a wealth of quantitative data regarding how a stimulus was processed, it still takes insightful, creative researchers to interpret the data and determine the data's implications for decision making. As you read through Etre's analysis of the four Web sites, notice how Etre applies its professional experience to go beyond what the data "says" to find crucial "meaning" in the data.

One to One Insight: Emotion, Engagement, and Internet Video

One to One Insight was introduced earlier in this chapter. The company measures individuals' emotional engagement with a visual stimulus through EEG monitoring combined with physiological measures. The online supplemental readings present one of the company's complete research reports, an exploration of the relationship between emotion, engagement, and reactions to Internet video.[39] This topic has significant importance as increasing numbers of advertisers turn to streaming and viral video for brand promotion. Several things are noteworthy about this report and the findings that it reports.

- The research report provides background and a context for understanding both the motivations for the research and the findings. These sections lay an important foundation for data interpretation.
- The methodology and key measures are well documented and explained.
- Similar to the Tobii "Print Advertising" case, multiple complimentary measures are used to acquire deep insights into consumer response.
- The results are organized around key insights rather than specific pieces of data. This focus on "meaning" and implications makes it much easier for readers to understand major findings. Additionally, all conclusions are supported with appropriate data.

MindSign fMRI Advertising Test of Virgin Mobile Phones "Fantastic Journey"

MindSign was also introduced earlier in this chapter as one of the few companies that conducts fMRI advertising testing. The online supplemental readings provide the results of the company's test of the Virgin Mobile Phones advertisement "Fantastic Journey."[40] As you watch the video or review the still pictures notice the sensitivity of the fMRI as specific, identifiable areas of the brain are activated or deactivated as the visual and verbal stimulus changes.

SUMMARY

Biometric research measures an individual's voluntary and involuntary responses to stimuli, such as advertisements, Web pages, or packages. The most commonly measured voluntary response is eye tracking, while the most commonly measured involuntary responses are brain waves or physiological responses such as galvanic skin response, heart rate, and blood pressure.

Eye tracking research monitors the manner in which a visual stimulus is processed. The six key measures obtained from eye tracking research are: first fixation, time to first fixation, most fixation, individual gaze time, total gaze time, and movement between elements. Eye tracking data can be presented as Gaze Path Charts, Heatmaps, and Opacity Charts. Many researchers note that insights from eye tracking research can be deepened if additional data is obtained through facial coding or retrospective interviews. Eye tracking research contributes to advertising planning, and creative development, evaluation, and revision.

Neuromarketing is the label given to the use of brain observation for marketing purposes. In its simplest form, brain wave observation examines the changes in brain activity in the presence of advertising, brands, or other communications. Neuromarketing uses state-of-the-art technologies, such as functional magnetic resonance imaging (fMRI), magneto-encephalography, and more conventional electroencephalograms (EEGs) to observe which areas of the brain "light up" when test subjects view or hear advertising or other communications. An FMRI allows researchers to identify specific areas of brain activation, while an EEG allows for an assessment of overall brain activity. EEG approaches to neuromarketing typically supplement brain data with physiological measures such as heart rate, blood pressure, and galvanic skin response.

Neuromarketing has been criticized on three grounds: the lack of external validity, ethics, and impact on advertising planning and creative development.

Review Questions

1. Define *biometric* research.
2. Explain how eye tracking data is collected.
3. What are the six key eye tracking measurements? Why is each important?
4. What is the relationship between a *Heatmap* and an *Opacity Chart?*
5. What is Google's Golden Triangle? What are the implications of this triangle for advertising planning?
6. Explain how eye tracking data contributes to the process of advertising development and revision.
7. What is a *retrospective interview?*
8. What are the advantages of combining a retrospective interview with eye tracking?
9. What is *facial coding?*
10. What are the advantages of combining facial coding with eye tracking?
11. Define *neuromarketing.*
12. What is the underlying premise of neuromarketing?
13. What is the difference between EEG and fMRI data?
14. Explain how fMRI data can contribute to advertising planning.
15. What types of physiological measures are commonly combined with EEG data?
16. Describe how neuromarketers are addressing the question of external validity.
17. Describe the relationship between brain activation, physiological measures, and engagement.
18. What are the three most common objections to neuromarketing?

Application Exercises[41]

Application exercises 1 through 5 relate to concepts raised and discussed in this chapter.

1. The ads shown in Figures 9.8a and 9.8b are alternative forms of the same ad. Both ads were tested by eye tracking as indicated in the heatmaps. While both ads have the same communication goal and copy elements, the orientation of the baby visual is different in the two ads. The data reporting *time to first fixation* and *average gaze time* for key segments of the ad are shown in the following tables. Based on this information, prepare a short paper that (a) discusses the impact of baby orientation on ad processing, and (b) makes

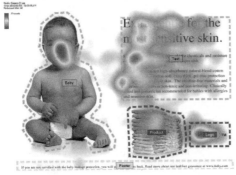

(a)

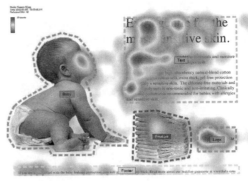

(b)

FIGURE 9.8 Eye Tracking Research Results for Application Exercise 1

recommendations for eliminating ad weaknesses and capitalizing on ad strengths.

Ad Component	Time to First Fixation (seconds)	
	Figure 9.8a	Figure 9.8b
Baby	1.10	1.75
Product	2.50	2.30
Text	.75	.10
Logo	2.75	2.65
Footer	3.75	3.65

Ad Component	Observation Length (seconds)	
	Figure 9.8a	Figure 9.8b
Baby	.75	.60
Product	.38	.30
Text	1.75	2.00
Logo	.42	.40
Footer	.62	.70

2. Your client, Pizza Hut, has asked you to provide a point of view regarding neuromarketing. Prepare a short paper that presents arguments for and against this approach to advertising testing.
3. Your client, McDonald's, has decided to test its newest ads using brain wave analysis. Do you recommend that it employ fMRI or EEG testing? Prepare a short paper that presents your recommendation with an explanation of why you consider your recommendation to be the preferred option.
4. Search for "neuromarketing" references in your preferred search engine. Prepare a short paper that summaries developments in this area that have taken place over the past six months.
5. Your client, Revlon, has decided to conduct advertising testing using brain wave analysis. Using your preferred search engine, identify three potential companies that might be used to conduct this research. Visit each site to

obtain an idea of each company's strengths and weaknesses. Then, prepare a short paper that (a) presents your analysis of the strengths and weaknesses of each identified company and (b) presents your recommendation, with justification, regarding the company you would recommend Revlon hire to conduct the research.

Application exercises 6 through 8 refer to the online supplemental readings.

6. The cases provided by Tobii Technology illustrate just some of the applications of eye tracking. Select a visual stimulus not addressed in the cases (e.g., Web sites with multiple ads for the same product/service, expanding online ads, advertising on social network sites) and then prepare a short paper that (a) specifies the types of research questions that would be of interest to an advertiser, (b) discusses how eye tracking can help answer identified questions, and (c) recommends additional types of data to be collected beyond that obtained through eye tracking. (For the last part, be specific as to the types of questions you would ask.)
7. Select a type of visual stimulus for which you think it is important to understand the effect of consumers' engagement on advertising response (e.g., video game advertising, product placement in television programs or movies). Using the One to One Insight report as a model, prepare a paper that (a) identifies the area of interest and research questions you think should be addressed, and (b) presents the Introduction and Study Design sections of the eventual full report.
8. The fMRI test of the movie trailer for Avatar is available at http://www.youtube.com/user/mindsignonline#play/all/uploads-all/1/KSKIkXvqruI. View the video and outcomes of its fMRI test, and then prepare a short paper that (a) discusses the strengths and weaknesses of the trailer and (b) provides recommendations for increasing the trailers' strengths and reducing its weaknesses.

Endnotes

1. Other physiological techniques such as facial analysis and voice pitch are also used. These techniques are typically employed to provide

additional detail to the primary involuntary physiological measures. For a detailed discussion of biometric measurement, see Yong J. Wang and

Michael S. Minor (2008). "Validity, Reliability, and Applicability of Psychophysiological Techniques in Marketing Research." *Psychology & Marketing* 25 (2): 197–232.

2. Eye tracking technology has advanced to the point that eye tracking data can now be collected in natural settings outside of the laboratory. See Tobii Technology (undated). "Tobii Glasses Eye Tracker Product Leaflet" at http://www.tobii.com/archive/files/20826/Tobii_Leaflet_ Glasses_ Eng_Web.pdf.aspx.

3. See Tobii Technology (undated). "Eye Tracking for Marketing Research Seminar" at http://www.slideshare.net/Tobii/eye-tracking-for-market-research-seminar.

4. Images reproduced with permission of Tobii Technology.

5. Images and quotations reproduced with permission of Enquiro (http://www.enquiro.com).

6. Enquiro (2005). "Enquiro Eye Tracking Resport I; Google. Sample" at http://www.enquiroresearch.com/images/Eyetracking2-Sample.pdf.

7. Eyetools (undated). "Google Search's Golden Triangle" at http://eyetools.com/research_google_eyetracking_heatmap.html.

8. The Yahoo!, Google, and MSN heatmaps can be seen at http://www.enquiroresearch.com/eyetracking-report.aspx.

9. See "Enquiro Presents: Chinese Eye Tracking Study" at http://www.slideshare.net/enquiro/enquiro-presents-chinese-eye-tracking-study-70751.

10. This case study provided by HCD Research (http://www.hdci.com) is reproduced with permission. The full presentation is available at http://www.slideshare.net/hedodiver/eyetracking-presentation-presentation.

11. Mike Bartels (2008). "The Objective Interview: Using Eye Movement to Capture Pre-Cognitive Reactions." *ORCA Views* Spring: 58-61. All quotes are from this source.

12. Erwin Van Lun (2008). "Facial Coding: What our Facial Expression Shows" at http://www.erwinvanlun.com/ww/full/facial_coding_facial_expression/

13. Sensory Logic's Web site is located at: http://www.sensorylogic.com.

14. The video is available at http://adage.com/brightcove/single.php?title=1825806615. See also Tobii Technology (2009). "Facial Coding Brochure" at http://www.tobii.com/ archive/files/19030/Facial+Coding+Brochure.pdf.aspx

15. Amber Haak (2007). "This is Your Brain on Advertising" at http://www.businessweek.com/globalbiz/content/oct2007/gb2007108_286282.htm.

16. Kevin Randall (2009). "Neuromarketing Hope and Hype: 5 Brands Conducting Brain Research." *Fast Company* at http://www.fastcompany.com/node/1357239/print.

17. See, for example, S. Weinstein, R. Drozdenko, and C. Weinstein (1984). "Brain Wave Analysis: An Electroencephalographic Technique Used For Evaluating the Communications-Effect of Advertising." *Psychology & Marketing* 1 (1): 17–42 and J. Cacioppo and R. Petty (1985). "Physiological Responses and Advertising Effects: Is the Cup Half Full or Half Empty?" *Psychology & Marketing* 2 (2): 115–126.

18. Mike Shields (2008). "Google, MediaVest Tap Biometrics for InVideo Ads Play" Mike Shields. *Mediaweek* p. 7. See also "Google Reading Brain Wave Patterns to Test Ads" at http://searchmarketingfornonprofits.wordpress.com/2008/12/02/google-reading-brain-wave-patterns-to-test-ads/.

19. Bob Heyman (2008). "Google's New Metric For YouTube Ads: Brain Waves" at http://searchengineland.com/google-explores-brain-waves-15256.

20. For additional detail on these and other techniques, see Peter Kenning, Hilke Plassman, and Dieter Ahlert (2007). "Applications of Functional Magnetic Resonance Imaging for Market Research." *Qualitative Market Research* 10 (2): 135-52 and Carl Senior, Hannah Smyth, Richard Cooke et al. (2007). "Mapping the Mind for the Modern Market Researcher." *Qualitative Market Research* 10 (2): 153–167.

21. S. M. McClure et al. (2004). "Neural Correlates of Behavioral Preference for Culturally Familiar Drinks." *Neuron* 44 (2): 379–87.

22. Alice Park (2007). "Marketing to Your Brain" available at http://www.time.com/time/magazine/article/0,9171,1580370,00.html. See also McClure et al. (2004). "Neural Correlates of Behavioral Preference for Culturally Familiar Drinks." *Neuron* 44: v379–387.

23. Neuroethics and Law Blog (2006) at http://kolber.typepad.com/ethics_law_blog/2006/08/neuromarketing_.html

24. MindSign (undated). "MindSign Services: Neuromarketing" at http://mindsignonline.com/services_madison.html.

25. Sands Research Web site is located at: http://www.sandsresearch.com.

26. See Roger Dooley (2009). "Emmy Awards Match Neuromarketing Study" at http://www.neurosciencemarketing.com/blog/articles/emmy-awards-neuromarketing.htm.

27. One to One Insight is a One to One Interactive company. Its Web site is http://www.onetooneinteractive.com/otoinsights. All quotes and descriptions are from this source. Quantemo is the registered trademark of One to One Insight, LLC.

28. Reprinted with permission from One to One Insight (2009). "Social Media for Marketing: An Analysis of Digg.com Engagement and User Behavior" at http://tr.im/otoinsights_digg.

29. One to One Insight (undated). "Quantemo" at http://www.onetooneglobal.com/insight/quantemo/what-is-quantemo/.

30. This research is available for downloading at http://www.onetooneinteractive.com/otoinsights/research-studies/.

31. One to One Insight (2009). "Player Engagement and In-Game Advertising" at http://www.slideshare. net/OnetoOneInteractive/otoinsights-player-engagement-and-ingame-advertising-1681643.

32. Innerscope Research is located at http://www.innerscope.com.

33. Brian Steinberg (2009). "Advertisers Aim to Measure Watchers' Responses" *Boston Sunday Globe* (September 3): G1.

34. For an extended discussion of the ethics of neuromarketing see Emily Murphy, Judy Illes, and Peter Reiner (2008). "Neuroethics of Neuromarketing." *Journal of Consumer Behavior* 7: 293–302.

35. R. Mark Wilson, Jeannie Gaines, and Ronald Hill (2008). "Neuromarketing and Consumer Free Will." *The Journal of Consumer Affairs* 42 (3): 389–410.

36. Lior Arussy (2009). "Neuromarketing Isn't Marketing." *Customer Relationship Management* (January): 12.

37. Cases are provided with permission of Tobii Technology. Tobii describes itself as follows: "Tobii Technology specializes in hardware and software solutions for eye tracking and eye control. This technology makes it possible for computers to know exactly where users are looking. Our products are widely used within scientific research and in commercial market research and usability studies, as well as by disabled people as a means to communicate. Tobii contributes with a wide range of Augmentative and Alternative Communication (AAC) products, as well as offers eye tracking technology to industrial partners within areas such as gaming, car safety and 3D displays. Using radical innovations in technology, Tobii's mission is to bring eye tracking into broader use in applications such as eye control interfaces for computers, design testing and medical diagnostics. Founded in 2001, Tobii has continuously shown very rapid year-to-year revenue growth, and has received numerous awards and recognitions for its accomplishments. The company is based in Stockholm, Sweden, with offices in the US, Germany, Norway, Japan and China. Our products are sold directly to customers and through resellers and partners worldwide." Additional information on Tobii Technology and eye tracking applications can be found at http://www.tobii.com.

38. Etre is located at http://www.etre.com. The case studies are provided by and used with permission of Etre.

39. The report is provided by and used with permission of One to One Insight (http://www.onetooneinsights.com) and is © One to One Insight, LLC., 2008. All rights reserved.

40. Visuals in the online supplemental reading are reproduced with the permission of MindSign. While this presentation uses selected still pictures from the test, a video of the entire test can be seen at http://www.youtube.com/user/mindsignonline#play/all/0/-05cOTWWQkg.

41. Application Exercises 2 through 5 are fictitious. The ads shown in Application Exercise 1 and accompanying data reflect actual eye tracking research and are provided courtesy of Tobii Technology.

CHAPTER 10

Data Collection Through Surveys

As seen in Chapters 8 and 9, observation research collects information from respondents without ever asking them a question. Survey research, on the other hand, uses questions to probe respondents' attitudes, beliefs, and behaviors. This chapter focuses on the methods used to collect survey information, considerations in the selection of survey research procedures, and the problems of error in the conduct of surveys.

✱✱✱

When you are done reading this chapter, you should have a better understanding of:

- the different options for collecting survey data, and the strengths and weaknesses of each option
- how to select the most appropriate data collection technique for different informational needs and research situations
- why response and nonresponse rates and nonresponse error are important considerations in evaluating the quality of survey data
- how to increase survey response rates.

Surveys provide a "point in time" snapshot of respondents' attitudes, beliefs, and behaviors. Surveys typically provide insights into these areas by using a questionnaire (also known as a survey) to ask respondents' questions of interest.

Advertising and marketing researchers typically utilize one of four survey data collection methods: personal (face-to-face) interviews, telephone interviews, mail or paper self-completed surveys, or online. (Hybrid methods, which combine one or more of the prior methods, are also increasing in usage.) Each approach has its own set of strengths and weaknesses, and as a consequence the appropriateness of each method for a particular research study must be evaluated in terms of which approach has the greatest likelihood of providing the most accurate information in the shortest period of time at the lowest cost. The following section begins with a description of the characteristics, strengths, and weaknesses of each individual data collection method. The section concludes with a discussion of hybrid data collection.

METHODS OF COLLECTING SURVEY INFORMATION
Personal Interviews

Personal interviews occur when an interviewer administers a survey to a respondent in a face-to-face setting. There are two main types of personal interviews: intercept and pre-recruited.[1]

An *intercept interview* recruits respondents "on the spot," for example, as an individual is walking through a shopping mall, grocery store, airport, or train station. All intercept interviews are generally conducted in the same way regardless of the location, as follows:

> A trained interviewer approaches an individual as he or she is walking through a high traffic public location. The interviewer is provided with a description of who should be approached; for example, he or she may be told to approach all women who appear to be between the ages of 18 to 49. The interviewer approaches individuals who meet the general target description, identifies himself or herself as a marketing researcher, and then asks a number of more detailed questions to make certain that the intercepted individual possesses the characteristics of the research study's sample. Respondents who qualify are invited to participate in the survey, which typically takes place in the research company's offices (if the intercept is in a mall) or in a private setting.

Mall intercept interviews are probably the most common setting for intercept interviews. Given the popularity of this setting, many marketing research companies have established permanent shopping mall research facilities.[2] The large number of facilities in shopping malls located in diverse geographic and socioeconomic areas permits researchers to reach a wide range of respondents with great efficiency.

Mall and other intercept approaches work well to obtain high-incidence individuals or those who are likely to have location-specific characteristics. (Car renters, for example, are likely to be found in airports.) Intercepts, however, are an inefficient way of locating individuals with less common characteristics. In these cases, personal prescreening and prerecruitment is necessary. Individuals in these cases are initially contacted first by mail, online, or telephone at which time arrangements for a personal interview are made.

Personal interviews, versus other forms of survey techniques, generally provide the highest level of data quality due to personal administration of the survey by a trained interviewer and the face-to-face contact between the interviewer and interviewee. In addition to data quality, personal interviews have several advantages over other data collection techniques:

- They work extremely well when the questionnaire is very long and/or complex.
- They permit the use of visual stimuli, such as the viewing of television commercials.
- They permit the interviewer to make very certain that the respondent understands individual survey questions or complicated instructions.

The primary disadvantage of personal interviews is their high cost and large amount of time required for completion. It is both expensive and time-consuming to train interviewers, conduct personalized interviews, prerecruit respondents (when necessary), and travel to the interview location. Moreover, in terms of sample characteristics, it is very difficult to obtain a true random sample. The selection of true random samples for survey research utilizing personal interviews are often time and cost prohibitive. As a result, generalizations to the broader population are often a problem (see Chapter 4).

Telephone Interviews

Telephone interviews are typically conducted by a team of trained interviewers telephoning from a central location.[3] Almost all telephone interviews use Computer Assisted Telephone Interviewing (CATI) where a telephone interviewer reads the survey questions off a computer and types in the responses as they are provided. CATI telephone interviewing offers many advantages over paper-and-pencil telephone interviews.

> One is the speed with which an interviewer can administer a survey since the computer automatically accounts for any branching questions, presenting the appropriate follow-up questions according to how previous questions were answered. The interviewer keys the answers in real time, which immediately creates a data file. This method decreases errors and helps note inconsistencies in respondent answers.[4]

Telephone interviews, similar to personal interviews, provide an opportunity for an interviewer to explain complicated instructions and questions, although explanations in these areas do tend to be more difficult over the telephone versus a personal setting. Beyond this similarity, telephone interviews present a different set of relative strengths and weaknesses versus personal interviews. On the positive side, telephone interviews

- especially those that are assisted by CATI, are able to administer interviews with very complex skip patterns. This is because the computer automatically calls up the next appropriate question based on the respondent's current answer;
- have lower marginal costs because individuals in the sample frame can be contacted several times if they are not available during the first contact;
- can more efficiently obtain a true random sample, increasing the generalizability and representativeness of the results.

On the other hand, telephone interviews have several limitations versus other forms of interviewing.

- Questionnaire length must be relatively short. It is very difficult to keep respondents on the telephone for an extended period of time.

- Question complexity must be relatively simple. Complex or detailed questions and scales are difficult for respondents to remember and answer accurately.

- It is difficult to collect sensitive data as individuals are often unwilling to give this information to strangers.

- Refusal rates are high.

- It is extremely difficult to use visual stimuli, for example, having a respondent view a television commercial.[5]

Care must be taken when selecting the sample for a telephone survey. A researcher providing or purchasing a list of names and telephone numbers must make very certain that the list is comprehensive and without bias. When lists are not available or are inappropriate, random digit dialing may be used.[6] Figure 10.1 presents The Pew Center for People & the Press approach to random digit dialing.[7]

The question of bias in telephone surveys is of rising concern as increasing numbers of individuals are eliminating landlines and moving toward exclusive reliance on cell phones. The Pew Research Center discusses its attempts to reduce this bias as follows:

> Unlike most other polling organizations, Pew's election surveys involved a "full dual frame design," (see Figure 10.1) in which people reached by cell phone who also have a landline are interviewed, as well as cell-only respondents. In contrast, most pollsters who included cell phones in their election surveys screened their cell samples for cell-only respondents.
>
> The difference between these two approaches can be seen as a tradeoff in methodological challenges. Supplementing a landline sample with cell-only respondents has the advantage of not "double covering" respondents who have both types of phones. This makes combining the samples more straightforward, but assumes that the landline sample is capable of accurately reaching all adults equally. If some adults have landline phones that they rarely or never answer because they favor their cell phones, they will be underrepresented in these surveys. Pew's approach of interviewing all adults in both the landline and cell phone samples ensures that every adult with a telephone is covered by the survey, but raises challenges in combining the data because some adults had a greater chance to participate if they have more than one telephone.
>
> Pew's methodology accounts for this double coverage by weighting respondents with both kinds of phones according to their probability of selection and the regularity with which they use each kind of telephone.

Mail Surveys

Mail surveys entail mailing each potential respondent a package containing a cover letter, the survey questionnaire, instructions for completion and return, and a stamped envelope

The typical Pew Research Center for the People & the Press national survey selects a random digit sample of both landline and cell phone numbers in the continental United States. As the proportion of Americans who rely solely or mostly on cell phones for their telephone service continues to grow, sampling both landline and cell phone numbers helps to ensure that our surveys represent all adults who have access to either. We sample landline and cell phone numbers to yield a ratio of approximately three landline interviews to each cell phone interview. This ratio is based on an analysis that attempts to balance cost and fieldwork considerations as well as to improve the overall demographic composition of the sample (in terms of age, race/ethnicity, and education). This ratio also ensures a minimum number of cell-only respondents in each survey.

Full Dual Frame Sample Design

Survey	Cell phone sample (25%)	Landline sample (75%)		
Population	Cell only (17.8%)	Dual users both landline and cell (66.6%)		Landline only (15.6%)

The design of the landline sample ensures representation of both listed and unlisted numbers (including those not yet listed) by using random digit dialing. This method uses random generation of the last two digits of telephone numbers selected on the basis of the area code, telephone exchange, and bank number. A bank is defined as 100 contiguous telephone numbers, for example 800-555-1200 to 800-555-1299. The telephone exchanges are selected to be proportionally stratified by county and by telephone exchange within the county. That is, the number of telephone numbers randomly sampled from within a given county is proportional to that county's share of telephone numbers in the United States. Only banks of telephone numbers containing three or more listed residential numbers are selected.

The cell phone sample is drawn through systematic sampling from dedicated wireless banks of 100 contiguous numbers and shared service banks with no directory-listed landline numbers (to ensure that the cell phone sample does not include banks that are also included in the landline sample). The sample is designed to be representative both geographically and by large and small wireless carriers.

Both the landline and cell samples are released for interviewing in replicates, which are small random samples of the larger sample. Using replicates to control the release of telephone numbers ensures that the complete call procedures are followed for the entire sample. The use of replicates also ensures that the regional distribution of numbers called is appropriate. This also works to increase the representativeness of the sample.

FIGURE 10.1 Pew Center for the People & the Press Approach to Telephone Sampling

addressed to the research company conducting the research. An incentive, such as a money or a small gift, may or may not be included in the package. Mail surveys thus differ from personal and telephone interviews because there is no personal interaction between the respondent and the interviewer. Respondents simply fill out and return the questionnaire at their convenience.

Mail surveys may be conducted in one of two ways. First, mailings to a selected sample of the population can be conducted. Similar to telephone surveys, the list of names and addresses can be generated internally or purchased. Second, a mail panel can be used. A mail panel is a continuing group of individuals who have agreed to participate in survey research studies. Panels are created and maintained by independent marketing research organizations such as Market Facts, National Family Opinion, and the National Panel Diary (NPD) Group. Panel sizes, which range from 100,000 individuals to over 1 million, provide several advantages over mailings to the general population:

- Response rates tend to be significantly higher. Panel members have agreed to answer questionnaires mailed to them.
- Cost efficiencies tend to be greater. Higher levels of response lower the per-interview cost.
- The selection of individuals with certain demographic or product usage characteristics can often be made without prescreening. This information has already been collected on all panel members by the marketing research company.
- Prescreening of low-incidence respondents can be efficiently conducted. A postcard with screening characteristics can be mailed to a large segment of the panel. Those with the appropriate characteristics are then mailed the main questionnaire.

Regardless of the form of the mail survey, this type of survey research has several strengths and weaknesses versus personal and telephone interviews. Strengths of mail surveys include:

- *Cost efficiency*. The cost per completed interview of properly designed mail surveys can be considerably lower than comparable personal or telephone interviews.
- *Respondent convenience*. Respondents may be more willing to participate because they can complete the questionnaire at their convenience.

Weaknesses of mail surveys include:

- *Low response rate*. Respondents may not complete or return the questionnaire, causing problems with the integrity of data.
- *Limited questionnaire length and complexity*. In theory, one can develop mail questionnaires of extreme length and complexity. However, response rate drops as questionnaire length and complexity increase.
- *Extended timing*. Response is mediated by mail delivery and thus data collection takes much longer than other methods.

Finally, the impersonal noninteractive nature of a mail survey is both a strength and a weakness. The impersonal nature often motivates respondents to provide more accurate data on personal feelings and sensitive subjects. However, respondents do not have the opportunity to clarify areas of confusion nor is there any external check that the questionnaire is being completed properly.

Closely related to mail surveys are self-administered surveys that are distributed in-person but are returned via the mail or at a central location. These surveys, which generally ask a limited number of questions, are most commonly used to measure customer satisfaction and the quality of a customer's brand-related experience. A sample of this type of survey is shown in Photo 10.1.

Customer Satisfaction Survey

Thank you for your visit to the Snakz Joint. We'd like to know what you may have liked or disliked about your experience. Please help us by completing this short survey.

Your date of visit _____ Time of visit _____
Number in your party _____

Was this your first visit:	Yes ☐	No ☐

How long (in minutes) did you wait to be seated? _____

Was your wait (check one box):
Longer than you expected ☐
Shorter than you expected ☐
About what you expected ☐

Did you have a reservation: Yes ☐ No ☐

Please tell us how you feel about the food, checking one box for each statement below.

	Very Pleased	Slightly Pleased	Slightly Displeased	Very Displeased
The temperature of the food when served	☐	☐	☐	☐
How the food tasted	☐	☐	☐	☐
Appearance of food on the plate	☐	☐	☐	☐
The food's value (in relation to cost)	☐	☐	☐	☐
Variety and selection	☐	☐	☐	☐

Please tell us how you feel about the staff, checking one box for each statement below.

	Very Pleased	Slightly Pleased	Slightly Displeased	Very Displeased
Courtesy	☐	☐	☐	☐
Appearance	☐	☐	☐	☐
Knowledge	☐	☐	☐	☐
Attentiveness	☐	☐	☐	☐
Warmth	☐	☐	☐	☐

Would you recommend Snakz Joint to your friends: Yes ☐ No ☐

IF "NO" can you please tell us why not?

PHOTO 10.1 Sample Self-administered Survey

Online Surveys

Online surveys are administered over the Internet or more recently, through one's mobile phone. These surveys are typically posted on a central Web site that allows individuals to respond on their computer or phone at a time of their choosing. This approach to surveys entails three components: the invitation, questionnaire design and posting, and data collection.

Invitations to the survey are most commonly made via an e-mail that invites members of the sample to participate in the survey. This e-mail typically contains a link that takes the respondent to the Web site hosting the questionnaire. The Web sites that host the questionnaire allow the researcher to design and post the questionnaire without the need for any additional software or hardware. As discussed in the next chapter, these sites allow for a wide range of questionnaire formatting options as well as branching and skip patterns. As a result, because the skip pattern is automatically followed by the computer, this form of interviewing is ideal for questionnaires that contain complex skip patterns.

Online surveys possess several strengths beyond the ability to execute complex skip patterns. First, many online survey sites allow for random assignment of individuals to different groups and for the random presentation of stimulus materials. This strength is of special importance when one uses these sites to collect experimental data. Second, question bias can be significantly reduced or eliminated through randomization of question response options. The options for a five-item ranking question, for example, can be placed in a different random order for each respondent. Third, data collection is typically very quick, as questionnaires from multiple members of the sample can be processed simultaneously. Fourth, costs are typically lower versus other forms of data collection. Lastly, "if you are interested in rare populations (e.g., people with a specific illness, opposite-gender twins, African-American Jewish women), online survey techniques allow you to draw responses from all over the world, resulting in a much larger sample size than you could gather via traditional methods."[8]

The primary caution regarding online surveys relates to sample composition. Since Internet access is not yet universal and comfort levels of Internet usage differ across age groups, there is always the question of sample representativeness. Some individuals in the sample frame may simply be unavailable through this data collection option.

Hybrid (Mixed-Mode) Surveys

Each of the prior approaches to data collection has a unique set of strengths and weaknesses. Given this situation, researchers are increasingly taking the position that in some circumstances, the "best" way to obtain data is one that is actually multi-modal, that is, the use of more than one approach to data collection. Survey Sampling describes this approach as follows:

> Multi-mode sampling is the process of accessing respondents using more than one mode for the same study. This could happen two ways: Different modes may be used only at the contact stage, while the sample itself remains on one mode-for example, contacting someone via e-mail to request that they do a study via phone or recruiting people via phone for an online or mail study.

Multi-mode may also apply to the questionnaire, where some portion of the sample answers online and another portion may answer via telephone.

Multi-mode is important because 30% of the US population does not have Internet access. Older, less affluent, rural populations are less likely to be online. But conducting an entire study via phone, mail, or face-to-face could be cost prohibitive. Here, a multi-mode solution could be employed to conduct as much as possible online, then supplementing with a phone or mail sample to fill in the population gaps.[9]

Hybrid designs have the potential to increase response rate and as a consequence increase data quality. Kroth et al. for example, found that participation rates increased 24% when those who did not respond to an invitation to participate in an online survey were offered the chance to participate via a mail survey.[10] In spite of this significant ability to increase response rates, these designs have two significant limitations. First, they are complex to put into practice, with different sample frames required for each mode of data collection. Second, hybrid designs assume that the same person (or a very similar one) would "give the same response to the same question irrespective of mode, sampling frame and sampling method."[11] Since this assumption has been called into question, the aggregation and analysis of hybrid design data is also complex.[12]

CRITERIA FOR SELECTING A DATA COLLECTION METHOD

Six factors should be considered when determining which survey method is the best for a particular research study. These factors are

- cost
- timing requirements
- sample, interview, and administrative control
- informational needs
- complexity of the topic and questionnaire
- interview length.

Cost

Cost is an extremely important consideration in the conduct of survey research. The cost of any particular research study reflects questionnaire length, required response rate, geographic coverage, and sample characteristics. However, when faced with comparable parameters in these areas, personal interviews (particularly those conducted in the respondent's home or place of business) tend to be considerably more expensive than other methods of data collection.

Study cost is the initial starting point in evaluating the suitability of alternative data collection methods. It is not the final or sole consideration. While it is clearly the researcher's duty to collect information in a cost-effective manner, the information must be reliable and valid. Selecting the absolute least expensive method of data collection is always inappropriate when, relative to other methods, there is a significant sacrifice in data quality. The inexpensive collection of unreliable data is no bargain.

Timing Requirements

Survey research methods differ in their speed of data collection.

Telephone and online surveys generally require the least amount of time to collect required data. Telephone surveys are relatively quick for two reasons: all training and coordination can be performed at a central facility, and teams of interviewers can work simultaneously. As a result, study timing can be shortened simply by adding more interviewers. Online surveys also collect data quickly because there is only a very small lag between time of respondent contact and survey administration. Also, because data is collected on a central server, multiple questionnaires can be completed simultaneously.

Mail surveys tend to take a great amount of time. Questionnaires must be put into the mail, processed and delivered by the post office, completed by respondents at their convenience, placed back into the mail, then processed and returned by the post office. Beyond the amount of time required for this initial mailing and return, additional time is often required for reminders, additional contacts, and follow-up mailings.

Personal interviews are almost always the slowest form of data collection, especially as sample sizes increase. This is primarily due to the need to schedule prerecruited interviews or identify qualified individuals via mall intercept.

Sample, Interview, and Administrative Control

Sample control refers to the extent to which a researcher can control who responds to the survey questionnaire. Obviously, it is important that the individual who meets the sample definition is the person who responds to the survey. The four methods of data collection differ in their ability to make certain that the target respondent is in fact the individual who participates in the research and provides the answers to the survey questions. Personal and telephone interviews provide the greatest degree of sample control. The personal contact and immediate nature of personal and telephone interviews help to ensure that the target respondent is the one providing responses. Mail and online interviews provide considerably less control. There is no assurance that the person to whom the questionnaire is directed is in fact the person who completes the questionnaire or, for that matter, that the person recruited to complete the questionnaire is being truthful with regard to personal or demographic characteristics.

Interview control refers to the extent to which a researcher has control over the circumstances in which a respondent provides his or her answers to the survey. Similar to sample control, personal and telephone interviews provide the greatest degree of interview control. An interviewer can make certain that the respondent participates in all required activities (i.e., listening to or reading a product description) and appropriately responds to the information requests of each survey question in the sequence dictated by the questionnaire. Additionally, the immediate nature of personal and telephone interviews permits an interviewer to address ambiguities or errors in response at the time they occur. Online data collection techniques provide a relatively lower degree of interviewer control. While the computer can be programmed to question inappropriate responses and to lead the respondent through the proper interview sequence, there is nevertheless no assurance when using this technique that the respondent has read all necessary material before proceeding to a set of questions. Mail surveys provide the least amount of interview control. There is no assurance that the respondent will read necessary materials, answer the questions in the proper sequence, or correct errors in response.

Administrative control refers to the degree to which a researcher is able to monitor interviewer quality, which can be done only in telephone or personal interviews. Supervisors at the telephone facility can monitor the quality of each telephone interviewer and immediately correct any problems with interviewer tone, style, or questionnaire administration. CATI programs assure that the survey will be conducted in an identical manner time after time and that skip questions are asked in the proper sequence. Personal interviews, particularly those conducted in the field, provide the least amount of administrative control. A researcher cannot possibly monitor each personal interview. Thus, while interviewer training is important in all survey methods, given the lack of administrative control it is most critically important in personal interviews.

Informational Needs

Some survey techniques work better than others when the survey topic is of a sensitive or personal nature.

Respondents tend to be more honest and candid in telephone and especially mail interviews versus personal interviews. First, telephone interviews tend to elicit fewer "socially acceptable" responses. Krysan, for example, conducted personal and mail surveys among comparable groups of African-American and white respondents. She found that mail survey respondents expressed more negative attitudes toward racial integration and affirmative actions than did those interviewed in a personal setting.[13] Along these same lines, Beebe et al. found that mail versus telephone surveys were the better way to collect sensitive, personal information, in this case reports of substance abuse.[14]

While telephone and mail surveys appear to be the better means for collecting sensitive information and for avoiding socially desirable responses, personal interviews appear to be a better means for collecting complete and considered responses. The personal nature of the interview situation, coupled with the physical presence of an interviewer, appears to better motivate consumers to consider each question and avoid quick and simple responses.

Complexity of the Topic and Questionnaire

Some research topics are inherently more complex than others. Research exploring consumers' attitudes toward government plans to revise health care or welfare addresses more complex issues than research designed to obtain reactions to a television advertisement. Additionally, regardless of the complexity of the topic, some questionnaires are more complex than others. Questionnaire complexity tends to increase as the number of skip patterns and verbally complex questions increases. A skip pattern instructs the respondent or interviewer to jump from one point to another on the questionnaire depending on an individual's response. Verbally complex questions are questions that require a respondent to expend a great deal of cognitive energy to process and remember elements or demands of the question, for example,

- multiple choice questions that have many possible choices,
- ranking questions that ask the respondent to remember a large set of objects and then place them in ranked order,

- constant sum questions that ask respondents to allocate points to a set of objects, and
- questions that have long lead-ins or provide information that must be remembered prior to answering.

Personal interviews are most appropriate when both the topic and questionnaire are complex. The personal nature of the interview provides the best setting for the discussion of complex issues, particularly because of the ease of presenting and probing responses to open-ended questions. Additionally, complex questions can be shown to the respondent reducing the demands on verbal memory.

Telephone interviews work well when the issue is complex and questionnaire complexity is entirely due to skip patterns. As with personal interviews, the interactive nature of the interview provides a good setting for the discussion of complex issues and for the use of open-ended questions. The use of computers to assist in the conduct of the interview (see the discussion of CATI presented earlier in this chapter) automates and minimizes errors in skip patterns and checks the appropriateness of responses. Telephone interviews are not appropriate when questionnaire complexity is due to verbal or question complexity. A respondent's inability to see a complex question may reduce his or her understanding of the question, thereby reducing the quality of the information provided.

Online interviews are appropriate for relatively simple topics with or without questionnaire complexity. The impersonal nature of the interview makes it difficult to use open-ended questions to probe attitudes in complex areas (especially since answers to these questions must be typed into the computer). However, a respondent's ability to see the questions and be guided by the computer permits relatively high levels of questionnaire complexity. Similar to computer assisted telephone interviewing, the computer program can make certain that responses to more complex questions are appropriate given the demands of the question.

Interview Length

Interview length refers to the amount of time required for a typical respondent to complete the survey. Interview length tends to increase as the absolute number of questions, question complexity, and the number of open-ended questions rises.

Personal contact is essential for longer surveys. The personal, face-to-face nature of the interview permits an interviewer to keep the respondent interested, attentive, involved, and a continuing participant in the research. Thus, longer interviews, especially those with many open-ended questions, generally use personal interviews as the data collection method. Mail, telephone, and interactive data collection techniques are generally appropriate only for shorter interviews.

- Lengthy mail interviews are visually overwhelming and require a considerable commitment of time and energy on the part of the respondent. Most respondents are unwilling to give such a commitment.
- Telephone interviews compete with other home or business activities, making it difficult to maintain respondent participation for more than 5 or 10 minutes.
- Lengthy interactive interviews share many of the same problems as mail interviews; that is, they require a commitment of time and energy that most respondents are unwilling to give.

RESPONSE RATE, NONRESPONSE RATE, AND NONRESPONSE ERROR

Response rate, a crucial element of a research study, refers to the percentage of the valid sample who participate in the research by completing an interview or survey. A low response rate can severely decrease the validity and generalizability of collected data, thereby reducing the ability of the data to positively and accurately contribute to the decision-making process. A response rate is calculated by dividing the number of respondents completing the survey by the number of respondents in the valid sample. A nonresponse rate is the complement of response rate and is computed by subtracting the response rate from 100%.

Figure 10.2 illustrates the calculation of response and nonresponse rates for a hypothetical telephone survey. In total, 1,200 homes were contacted through random digit dialing. Of these, 150 fell outside of the desired sample due to the telephone number being a disconnected number, a fax machine, or business. These numbers are subtracted from the total sample, leaving a working sample of 1,050 contacted homes. Of these remaining homes, 250 failed to meet at least one sample characteristic. These homes are also eliminated from the working sample, leaving a valid sample of 800 homes. Of these remaining 800 homes, 100 refused to participate in the interview, and 150 were not at home. Interviews were therefore conducted with individuals in the remaining 550 homes. The response rate was 68.8%, and the nonresponse rate was 31.2%.

Response and nonresponse rates are important indicators of data integrity. A high response rate, and thus a low nonresponse rate, generally indicates that there are no meaningful differences between those who responded to the survey and those who did not. A low response rate, and thus a high nonresponse rate, generally indicates a significant problem with the source of the data. It indicates that there is probably bias

Begin with original sample	**1,200**
Remove those not valid	(150)
Subtotal to obtain working sample	**1,050**
Remove those failing to meet sample definition	(250)
Subtotal to obtain valid sample	**800**
Subtract refusals	(100)
Subtract not at home	(150)
Subtract non-interviewed for other reasons	(0)
Subtotal to obtain number of participating respondents	**550**

To obtain *response rate* divide the number of participating respondents by the total valid sample:

$$550 \div 800 = 68.8\%$$

To obtain the *nonresponse rate* subtract the response rate from 100%:

$$100\% - 68.8\% = 31.2\%$$

FIGURE 10.2   Calculation of Response and Nonresponse Rates

in the data, reflecting the fact that the characteristics of those who participated in the research are different from those who did not participate.

The data shown in Figure 10.3 illustrate the danger of a nonresponse error. The data in the upper table presents the hypothetical results of an opinion survey taken before the

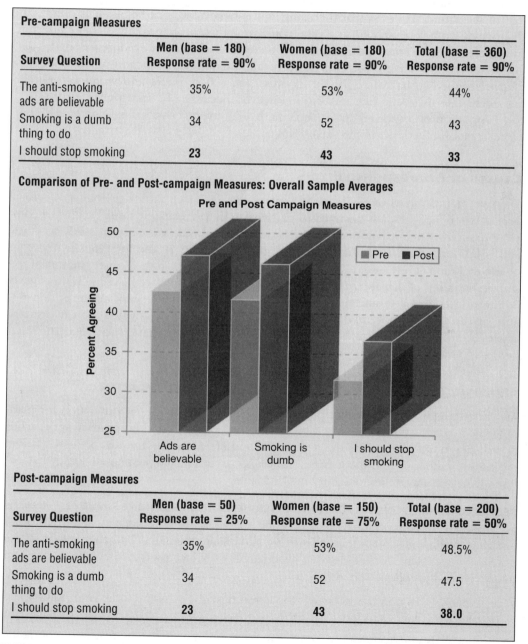

Pre-campaign Measures

Survey Question	Men (base = 180) Response rate = 90%	Women (base = 180) Response rate = 90%	Total (base = 360) Response rate = 90%
The anti-smoking ads are believable	35%	53%	44%
Smoking is a dumb thing to do	34	52	43
I should stop smoking	23	43	33

Comparison of Pre- and Post-campaign Measures: Overall Sample Averages

Post-campaign Measures

Survey Question	Men (base = 50) Response rate = 25%	Women (base = 150) Response rate = 75%	Total (base = 200) Response rate = 50%
The anti-smoking ads are believable	35%	53%	48.5%
Smoking is a dumb thing to do	34	52	47.5
I should stop smoking	23	43	38.0

FIGURE 10.3   Effect of Nonresponse Rate on Conclusions Drawn from Research

start of an antismoking advertising campaign. The response rates for men and women are high and equivalent, leading us to accept the findings, especially the overall averages, as representative of the population from which the sample was drawn. The middle chart compares precampaign with postcampaign averages on the three measures for the total sample. It appears that the campaign has exerted a positive impact on attitudes. All of the total sample's averages went up for all three measures, indicating that a greater percentage of the sample believes that the campaign is believable, that smoking is dumb, and that personal smoking should stop. The conclusion that the campaign has been effective, however, is incorrect and is directly due to the effects of the nonresponse error. The data shown in the lower table presents more detailed data regarding the opinions obtained after the campaign had aired for six months. Notice how men's and women's opinions are unchanged from the first measure. However, because of nonresponse error (i.e., a low proportion of responses from men) the overall averages increased due to the over-representation of women in the final sample.

Causes of Nonresponse Errors

The two main sources of nonresponse errors are refusals and not-at-homes. A refusal occurs when a participant declines to participate in the research study or fails to complete a survey once it has begun. The number of refusals varies from study to study and is influenced by a number of factors: the personality of the interviewer, the type of survey being conducted, a respondent's level of interest in the subject matter of the survey, the time of day the respondent is contacted, and the way in which the survey is introduced. Not-at-home nonresponse bias occurs when a respondent is unavailable at the time of potential contact. While, refusals have always been a primary cause of nonresponse bias, societal and lifestyle changes have increased the incidence of not-at-home bias.

Improving Response Rate to Reduce Nonresponse Error

An understanding of the sources of nonresponse errors provides a foundation for planning ways to reduce this type of problem in a particular survey. The primary approaches to reducing nonresponse bias due to refusals and not-at-homes are advance notification, incentives, callbacks, and recontacts. These approaches are implemented somewhat differently in personal, telephone, and mail surveys.[15]

REDUCING NONRESPONSE IN PERSONAL INTERVIEWS AND TELEPHONE SURVEYS.   Refusals are a problem in both personal interviews and telephone surveys. Since most refusals occur just after initial contact, it is important to try and ensure the immediate cooperation of the potential respondent. Techniques that have successfully increased cooperation in personal interviews and telephone surveys are to

- explicitly mention the interview topic and describe why the topic is important and relevant to the respondent.
- effectively and accurately describe the purpose and goal of the research, noting the importance of the individual's responses to achieving the goal.

- make certain that respondents do not feel threatened by participation in the research or by how their responses will be used.

- use incentives at levels appropriate to the demands of the survey. A $10 incentive increased the response rate in a research project that asked respondents to watch a particular television program,[16] while $2 or a small gift may be sufficient to effectively increased the response rate in a relatively short mall intercept study.

- use advance notification. Contact respondents in advance of the interview in order to gain cooperation. This is especially true of telephone surveys. Hembroff et al. for example, found that while some form of advance notification is better than nothing, letters are a more effective advance notifier versus postcards.[17]

Beyond these techniques that apply to both personal and telephone interviews, Feltser suggests some specific ways to positively increase the response rate in mall intercept interviews.[18] Feltser's suggestions include:

- *Keep the screener short, concise, and focused only on characteristics of primary importance.* "The border between screener and questionnaire proper gets pretty blurry now and then, particularly in two-stage studies where respondents do the indepth part back in the field office . . . consider the fancy footwork you'd need in order to keep a respondent happy and eager while you explain that the last six or seven minutes of questions was only the beginning and now there's lots more awaiting them back at the ranch ("More? I thought I just did your survey!"). A short, snappy screener always increases the odds that qualified contacts will hang in there to the end."

- *Minimize the skip patterns on the screener and make it easy for the recruiter to distinguish qualified from nonqualified respondents.* "The essence of successful mall interviewing is speed and efficiency. Experienced interviewers handle normal skip patterns easily, but they all have war stories. One outstanding example required interviewers to assign numerical values to responses, adding them here, subtracting them there, to determine whether the respondent qualified for the study. More common, but no less horrifying, are questionnaires with several instructions that say something like, "If respondent answered yes to Q. 4 and Q. 12b, ask Q. 23a; If respondent answered no to Q. 7, Q. 15, and Q. 16a or Q. 16b, ask Q. 23b." Skips that force an interviewer to move back and forth through the questionnaire pages not only make it easy to make mistakes, they also take time and let the respondent get bored and decide that going for a pizza would be more fun."

In addition to these respondent-centered techniques, careful training and monitoring of interviewers can reduce refusal rates. Here, it is important to make certain that interviewers are

- successfully trained to establish quick rapport with respondents. The tone of the interviewers voice has been shown to affect respondent cooperation and participation.

- carefully monitored with regard to their individual refusal rates. Interviewers who have exceptionally high refusal rates should be immediately retrained or replaced.

Nonresponse error due to respondent unavailability can be significantly reduced when multiple attempts to reach a specific respondent are used. Researchers have found that a second round of contact can double the response rate. The following guidelines have demonstrated effectiveness in increasing the success rate of repeated contact:

- Attempt recontact between three and six times.
- Vary the time of day during which calls are made. Use weekday evenings and weekend days to contact individuals who work full-time outside the home.

REDUCING NONRESPONSE IN MAIL SURVEYS.   The causes of nonresponse in mail surveys are different than that of personal interviews and telephone surveys. Researchers using mail surveys, assuming their list of names and addresses is accurate, have little problem in reaching respondents. The major problem in mail surveys relates to refusals; that is, many recipients of mail surveys simply do not take the time to complete and return the survey.

Advance notification is an effective means of inducing respondent cooperation and study participation. An advance notice briefly informs a respondent of the nature and importance of the study, the fact that they have been selected to participate, and the date around which they can expect to receive the survey questionnaire. In addition, the mailing itself can be constructed to increase the potential for study participation. Techniques that have been shown to increase response rate are to

- use a cover letter that clearly states the interview topic, describes why the topic is important and relevant to the respondent, effectively and accurately describes the purpose and goal of the research, and explains the importance of the individual's responses;
- include a postage-paid return envelope;
- prepare and print the questionnaire to maximize visual simplicity and professionalism;
- enclose monetary incentives with the questionnaire. Prepaid monetary incentives are the most powerful means of increasing response rates in both business and consumer mail surveys. Although larger incentives (those of $5.00 or more) tend to have a stronger effect than smaller ones ($1.00 or less), the actual difference is actually quite small.

Finally, after the surveys have been mailed, recontact is an effective means of increasing response rate. Nonparticipating respondents can be sent a postcard or letter requesting that he or she complete and return the questionnaire. However, given the fact that many respondents may no longer possess the originally mailed questionnaire, many researchers include a second questionnaire in the recontact mailing. Research has demonstrated that a significant increase in response rate is achieved with a single follow-up mailing.

REDUCING NONRESPONSE IN ONLINE SURVEYS.   Several techniques have proven effective in fostering participation in online surveys, thereby reducing nonresponse error. First, similar to mail surveys, a well-written, motivating invitation tends to encourage click-though and participation. Second, incentives tend to raise participation. Entering respondents into a drawing works well. Third, the use of personal salutations in the e-mail invitation also tends to increase participation. An e-mail addressed to "Dear Lisa" works better than one addressed to "Dear Student" or "Dear Panel Member."[19] In addition, Richard Gaunt suggests the following:

Make sure your survey link is clickable: survey software often generates very long links for individual surveys. You can often get around this by masking the link, like this "click to go to survey >>". However, some e-mail systems do not read masked links, so you may be better to copy the full link into the e-mail.

Reassure people about their privacy and confidentiality: people have to be reassured that their personal data and opinions will not be misused. A sentence covering these points should be found in the e-mail text and repeated on the first page of the Web survey.

Take care with the "From," "To," and "Subject": if possible, the e-mail address featured in the "From" field should be a real person. The "To" should only contain the e-mail address of the person receiving the e-mail. The "Subject" is also important and should be short and straight to the point.

Keep it short: you often can fall into the trap of over-explaining your survey and hiding the link somewhere in the e-mail text or right at the bottom. Try and keep your text brief—most people will decide in seconds if they want to participate or not—and they need to be able to understand why they should, for whom, and how long it will take.

An example of an e-mail invitation is shown in Figure 10.4.[20]

From: j.Mckenna@summit.net
To: g.daniels@gmail.com
Subject: SEO: NEW FRONTIERS 2010 CONFERENCE—Seeking your feedback

Dear Mr. Daniels,

On behalf of Summit, I'd like thank you for your participation in the 2010 SEO: New Frontiers conference.

The conference planners and speakers would very much appreciate your feedback on the conference. Your responses will help us better understand the strengths and weaknesses of this year's conference and will help guide the planning of next year's conference. This survey should take you less than five minutes to complete. All replies are anonymous and will be treated confidentially.

To complete the survey, please click here >>G.DANIELS SURVEY LINK

If this link does not work, please copy and paste the following link into your browser:

http://www.surveymonkey.com/SurveyPop.aspx?query=view&SurveyID=75&KiRb098765th

Thank you in advance; your feedback is very valuable to us. Please feel free to contact me by email or telephone (555-987-9087) should you have any questions or wish to discuss the conference in more detail.

Kind regards,
J. McKenna
Summit.net

FIGURE 10.4 Sample Email Survey Invitation

SUMMARY

Surveys provide a "point in time" snapshot look at respondents' attitudes, beliefs, and behaviors. Advertising and marketing researchers typically utilize one of four survey data collection methods: personal (face-to-face) interviews, telephone interviews, mail or paper self-completed surveys, or online. Each approach has its own set of strengths and weaknesses.

- *Personal interviews* generally provide the highest level of data quality. Other advantages include: appropriate for long and/or complex questionnaires, permit the use of visual stimuli, and permit the interviewer to make certain that the respondent understands questions asked. Disadvantages include high cost and amount of time required to conduct the interviews.

- *Telephone interview's* advantages include: ability to easily conduct interviews with complex skip patterns, lower marginal costs, and ability to obtain a true random sample. Limitations include: need for relatively short questionnaire length, need for relatively simple question structure, high refusal rates, and difficulty for using visual or other stimuli.

- *Mail surveys* allow respondents to answer at their own convenience and have generally good cost efficiencies. Limitations include: low response rates, limited questionnaire length and complexity, extended timing from mail-out to responses.

- *Online surveys* also allow respondents to answer at their own convenience and also have excellent cost efficiencies. Similar to CATI interviews, online interviews also handle complex skip patterns very well. The primary caution regarding online surveys relates to the concerns about sample representativeness.

Hybrid surveys, which combine one or more of the prior methods, are also increasing in usage.

Six criteria are commonly used for selecting a data collection method: cost, timing requirements, sample/administrative control, informational needs, the complexity of the topic and questionnaire, and interview length.

Response rate is an important way to evaluate the integrity of survey data. A high response rate, and thus a low nonresponse rate, generally indicates that there are no meaningful differences between those who responded to the survey and those who did not. A low response rate, on the other hand, generally indicates a significant problem with the source of the data and severely limits the extent to which a researcher can generalize the results to the larger population from which the sample was drawn. Response rates can be increased by taking actions designed toward reducing refusals to participate and not-at-homes.

Review Questions

1. What are the four primary ways for collecting data via surveys?
2. What is an *intercept* interview? How do intercept interviews differ from *pre-recruited* interviews? Which type of interview is most likely to take place in a mall?
3. What are the relative advantages and disadvantages of personal interviews?
4. What are the relative advantages and disadvantages of telephone interviews?
5. Describe possible sources of bias in telephone interviews.

6. What are the relative advantages and disadvantages of mail surveys?

7. What are the relative advantages and disadvantages of online surveys?

8. What is a mixed-mode survey? In what circumstances is this type of survey most appropriate?

9. What are the six considerations for selecting a data collection method? Why is each considera-

tion important? How does each consideration affect the evaluation of each data collection method's strengths and weaknesses?

10. Define *response rate* and *nonresponse error.*

11. How can nonresponse rate be reduced in personal and telephone interviews? In mail surveys? In online surveys?

Application Exercises

1. It has been decided that each of the following situations is best met through survey research. Consider each situation and then decide if you would recommend that the research be conducted through personal interviews, telephone interviews, mail surveys, or online. Your recommendation should reflect your decision as to the best means of data collection given each approach's relative strengths and weaknesses. Fully explain and justify your decision.

   a. Yolin Labs is a manufacturer of prescription drugs. Their latest product, which just received FDA approval, is a diet pill that curbs appetites for at least 16 hours. The pill is intended for individuals who are seriously overweight (defined as at least 75 pounds over the average weight for their age and height). Prior to the development of the advertising campaign, the agency and client wish to determine their target audience's current dieting practices and their reaction to this new medication.

   b. The editors of *Woman's Day* magazine have just completed a redesign of the magazine. The newly redesigned magazine will go on sale in about one week. The editors wish to determine their readers' reactions to the redesign three months after the introduction.

   c. Toyota is introducing three new minivans at the Detroit auto show. Toyota wishes to obtain reactions to these new models.

   d. Apple Computer is planning to specifically target primary and secondary school teachers in one part of their new advertising campaign. Prior to the development of the campaign, Apple needs to understand computer ownership among these individuals, computer brand perceptions, and the dimensions along which brands of computers are evaluated.

2. You are conducting a national survey among doctors and have expressed concern about a potentially high nonresponse rate. The survey asks about the influence of advertising on doctor's prescribing behaviors. First, select and defend a methodology to collect the data. Second, present a discussion of the nonresponse error and its likelihood to occur in the methodology you select. Third, explain why it is necessary to keep nonresponse errors to a minimum. Fourth, present specific recommendations for reducing nonresponse errors within the methodology you selected.

3. Consider the data shown below. Calculate the response and nonresponse rate.

Number in original sample	2,000
Number not valid	(300)
Subtotal	?
Failed to meet sample definition	(300)
Subtotal	?
Refusals	(150)
Not at home	(50)
Non-interviewed for other reasons	(0)
Subtotal	?

4. Imagine that Ford Motor Company initiated a new advertising campaign, which focused on the reliability of its cars. Prior to the start of the campaign, 750 interviews were attempted among three groups of consumers, and 750 interviews were attempted with the same three groups after the campaign had aired for two months. (250 interviews per group.) The key measures for three important subgroups of consumers are shown in the tables on the following page. Based on a comparison of the pre- and post-campaign total sample averages, Ford concluded that the campaign was a success. Do you agree with this conclusion? Why or why not?[21]

Pre-campaign Measures

Survey Question	Ford Owners (base = 200)	Former Ford (base = 210)	Never Owned Ford (base = 225)	Total (base = 635)
Ford cars are well made	55%	40%	20%	37.6%
Ford cars are reliable	65%	35%	15%	37.4

Post-campaign Measures

Survey Question	Ford Owners (base = 230)	Former Ford (base = 80)	Never Owned Ford (base = 75)	Total (base = 375)
Ford cars are well made	50%	40%	20%	42.1%
Ford cars are reliable	60%	35%	15%	46.0

5. Imagine that YouTube has redesigned its home page and wants to obtain visitors' reactions to the redesign. The survey will be conducted online. Write the e-mail invitation to the survey.

Endnotes

1. Personal interviews can also be conducted in-home through door-to-door interviews. However, due to the very high cost and time, as well as safety concerns, this technique is rarely used in advertising research.
2. A list of these companies can be found at the Green Book at http://www.greenbook.org/market-research-firms.cfm/mall-intercept.
3. A list of these companies can be found at the Green Book at http://www.greenbook.org/market-research-firms.cfm/interviewing-cati.
4. Smari.com (undated). "Computer Assisted Telephone Interviews (CATI)" at http://www.smari.com/cati.stm.
5. Stimuli can be mailed after the first contact, viewed by a respondent, and then discussed in a second telephone interview. There are, however, significant cost and methodological problems with this procedure.
6. The list procedure is often favored because it tends to create an unbiased sample. However, this technique also generates a sample that contains a relatively high number of disconnected numbers, business and government numbers, and nonexistent numbers. Thus, it is recommended that when this technique is used, the initial sample of telephone numbers be at least five times as large as the desired final sample size. The plus one technique tends to be more efficient in that there are typically fewer nonexistent numbers. This reflects the fact that numbers very close to currently existing numbers are also likely to have been assigned by the telephone company. Care must be taken to make certain that the telephone directory used represents the current state of the market.
7. See also Pew Research Center for the People & the Press (2009). "Sampling" at http://people-press.org/methodology/sampling.
8. Information Technology Services at the University of Texas Austin (2008). "Advantages of Online Surveys" at http://www.utexas.edu/learn/surveys/advantages.html.
9. Survey Sampling International (2008). "Multi-Mode Sampling" at http://www.surveysampling.com/en/methodologies/multi-mode-sampling.
10. Philip J. Kroth, Laurie McPherson, Robert Lawrence, William Pace et al. (2009). "Combining Web-Based and Mail Surveys Improves Response Rates: A PBRN Study From PRIMENet." *Annals of Family Medicine* 7 (3): 245–248.
11. George Terhanian (2006). "Multi-Modal Research and Data Linkage: Theoretical and Practical Advise" at http://www.slideshare.net.

See this source also for a discussion of data analysis in hybrid designs.

12. See, for example, Dirk Heerwegh and Geert Loosveldt (2008). "Face-to-Face Versus Web Surveying in a High Internet Coverage Population." *Public Opinion Quarterly,* 72 (5): 836–846.

13. Maria Krysan et. al. (1994). "Response Rates and Response Content in Mail Versus Face to Face Surveys." *Public Opinion Quarterly* 58: 381–99.

14. T. Beebe, J. A. McRae, P. A. Harrison et. al. (2005). "Mail Surveys Result in More Reports of Substance Abuse." *Journal of Clinical Epidemiology* 58 (4): 421–424.

15. From a methodological perspective, it is best to try and maximize response level and minimize the nonresponse error. The techniques described in this section present ways to accomplish this. When response rates remain low in spite of a researcher's efforts, statistical techniques can be used to compensate and adjust the data. These techniques, however, rely on many assumptions and may or may not in actuality increase the validity and representativeness of the data. For a discussion of these techniques, see G. Kalton (1983). *Compensating for Missing Survey Data* (Ann Arbor, MI: University of Michigan Institute for Social Research). For a current review of nonresponse errors and procedures for reducing nonresponse errors, see Nejdet Delener (1995). "An Integrative Review of Nonresponse Errors in Survey Research: Major Influences and Strategies." *Research in Marketing* 12: 49–80.

16. E. G. Goetz, T. R. Taylor, and F. L. Cook (1984). "Promised Incentives in Media Research." *Journal of Marketing Research* 21 (May): 148–154.

17. Larry A. Hembroff, Debra Rusz, Ann Rafferty et. al. (2005). "The Cost-Effectiveness of Alternative Advance Mailings in a Telephone Survey." *Public Opinion Quarterly,* 69 (2): 232–245.

18. E. B. Feltser (1996). "Pain-Free Mall Intercepts" at http://www.quirks.com/articles/a1996/19961102.aspx?searchID=28497451&sort=9.

19. See Dirk Heerwegh (2005). "Effects of Personal Salutations In E-Mail Invitations to Participate in a Web Survey." *Public Opinion Quarterly,* 69 (4): 588–598 and Steven R. Porter and Michael E. Whitcomb (2003). "The Impact of Content Type on Web Survey Response Rates." *Public Opinion Quarterly,* 67: 579–588.

20. The prior suggestions are from Richard Gaunt (2008). "Seven Tips for Better Email Invitations" at http://intelligentmeasurement.wordpress.com/2008/02/12/seven-tips-for-better-email-invitations-for-web-surveys/.

21. Data is hypothetical.

CHAPTER 11

Measurement

Quantitative advertising research is concerned with the collection, analysis, and interpretation of numeric data. The ability of numeric data to provide useful, reliable insights into an advertising-related problem is in great part dependent on the rigor underlying the measurement process. Not all measurements are appropriate for all situations. Not all measurements provide useful and reliable information. The quality of the measures you make directly determines the depth and quality of the insights you obtain. This chapter introduces you to the concept of measurement.

***

When you are done reading this chapter, you should have a better understanding of how to:

- describe the measurement process
- explain the four different levels of measurement
- determine a measure's reliability and validity.

Measurement is the way by which abstract, typically unobservable concepts are linked to observable events.[1] Researchers interested in "attitudes toward an advertiser" (the abstract, unobservable concept), for example, might use responses to questions on a survey (the observable event) to draw inferences about the extent to which an individual holds positive or negative attitudes toward the advertiser. The process by which a researcher moves from an unobserved concept to an observable event is an important one. A systematic approach of moving *from* a concept *to* an event increases the likelihood that conclusions drawn from the research are appropriate, reliable, and valid.

The remainder of this chapter describes a systematic approach to the measurement process. We begin by discussing the measurement process itself: the steps a researcher goes through when moving from the identification of "what I need to understand" to a determination of "what data will I collect?" This process applies to all types of data collection. Next, we discuss the role of levels of measurement in data collection. The chapter concludes with a discussion of reliability and validity, two evaluations of measurement "goodness" that apply to all measurements used in research.

THE MEASUREMENT PROCESS

The specific steps comprising the measurement process are shown in Figure 11.1 These steps, which are followed for each area explored and measured in a research study, can be grouped into three major tasks:

- Identify and define the concept of interest
- Specify an observable event
- Evaluate and revise the observable event

Task One: Identify and Define the Concept of Interest

The first task in the measurement process entails three sequential steps. As shown in Figure 11.1, this stage begins with a general notion of the area to be explored and ends with a detailed, explicit operational definition of what is to be measured.

IDENTIFY CONCEPT OF INTEREST.   All research is motivated by a need for information and insights. Well-designed research explicitly focuses its efforts in a specific area or direction. Thus, the measurement process begins by identifying the concept(s) of interest for study and exploration. A *concept* is an invented name for a property of an object, person, state, or event. Some concepts, such as age, gender, and income, present few measurement problems because they have well-defined meanings and can be easily reported and quantified. Other concepts explored in advertising research, such as advertising awareness, brand loyalty, communication recall, and Web site engagement cannot be explicitly observed and, as a result, are less concrete and present greater measurement challenges. In these types of cases, it is important to clearly define the concept and specific observable events that might be used to measure the

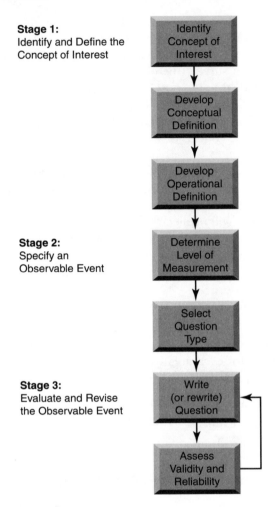

Stage 1:
Identify and Define the
Concept of Interest

Identify
Concept of
Interest

Develop
Conceptual
Definition

Develop
Operational
Definition

Stage 2:
Specify an
Observable Event

Determine
Level of
Measurement

Select
Question
Type

Stage 3:
Evaluate and Revise
the Observable Event

Write
(or rewrite)
Question

Assess
Validity and
Reliability

FIGURE 11.1 The Measurement Process

concept. This refinement of the concept of interest is accomplished through the creation of conceptual and operational definitions.

DEVELOP CONCEPTUAL DEFINITION.   A *conceptual* definition expresses a concept's central or core idea. It clearly states the major characteristics of the concept and distinguishes the target concept from similar, but different, concepts. Attitude toward an advertisement, for example, has been conceptually defined as "a predisposition to respond in a favorable or unfavorable manner to a particular advertising stimulus during a particular exposure situation."[2] This definition clarifies what researchers mean when they say that the research probes attitudes toward an advertisement. This conceptual definition also clearly distinguishes the research focus from similar research focused on related concepts such as "overall attitudes toward advertising."

Researchers need to be sensitive to the fact that for any particular concept there are multiple conceptual definitions. Consider, for example, the concept "brand loyalty," for which the following are all reasonable conceptual definitions:

- A consumer's commitment to repurchase the brand across repeated buying occasions.

- A consumer's predisposition to consistently speak positively about the brand to friends and others.

- A disposition toward a brand that is so favorable that it creates a "barrier to exit," making it difficult for other brands to compete.[3]

- Greater consumption of a particular brand versus consumers' average level of consumption.

In cases such as these, where there are multiple conceptual definitions, how is one selected? Typically through consensus. The process requires that all involved in the research agree on the selected conceptual definition. This is important because the conceptual definition directly leads to decisions regarding how the concept will actually be measured. Since different conceptual definitions can lead to different measures, the lack of agreement at the start of the research can lead to a client viewing the research presentation and saying" "Why did you measure brand loyalty like that? That's not at all what I mean when I speak about our brand loyal customers!"

DEVELOP OPERATIONAL DEFINITION.   Once a concept has been identified and conceptually defined, it is then operationally defined. An *operational definition* translates the concept into one or more observable events by explicitly describing the most important observable, defining characteristics of the concept. An operational definition serves as a bridge between the abstract, theoretical concept and real-world data collection.

While there can be some debate among researchers regarding a concept's conceptual definition, there can be great diversity of opinion as to a concept's operational definition. Consider, for example, the operational definitions of "affection" shown in Figure 11.2. While all four individuals are operating with the same conceptual definition (i.e., "a tender feeling or emotion for an other person"), each operationalizes that definition differently. That is, each person describes a different observable event to demonstrate or illustrate the concept.

- Mary feels that her boyfriend, Pete, has affection for her because his observable and measurable behaviors match her operational definition.

- John feels that Meg is not affectionate because her observable and measurable behaviors do not match his operational definition.

The differences in evaluating whether or not someone is "affectionate" differ across these individuals because of differences in operational definitions.

Similar to the different operational definitions of affection, differences in perspective among researchers often lead to differences in operational definitions. These differences are not a trivial matter. Different operational definitions lead to different measurements, which in turn can lead to different conclusions. Consider, for example, the operational definitions of brand loyalty presented earlier. The selection of the first operational definition (i.e., repeated purchases) might lead to a conclusion that brand

FIGURE 11.2 Differences in the Operational Definition of "Affection"

loyalty exists, while selection of the second operational definition (i.e., positive conversations about the brand) might lead the conclusion that brand loyalty is absent. The conclusions drawn are directly influenced by the operational definitions.

Figure 11.3 illustrates how advertising researchers starting with the same conceptual definition diverge as they operationally define the concept. As with conceptual definitions, there is no "right" operationalization of a concept, although there are ways to ensure that measure(s) once selected are both valid and reliable. These aspects of measurement are discussed later in this chapter.

Concept of Interest:	Attitude toward the advertisement	
Conceptual Definition:	A predisposition to respond in a favorable or unfavorable manner to a particular advertising stimulus during a specific advertising exposure	
Operational Definitions:	Ratings of the advertising using agree/disagree scales	
Researcher A	Four scales:	good/bad interesting/boring creative/uncreative relevant/not relevant
Researcher B	Two scales:	favorable/unfavorable pleasant/unpleasant
Researcher C	Six scales:	good/bad creative/not creative stimulating/not stimulating pleasant/unpleasant informative/not informative believable/not believable
Researcher D	Three scales:	boring/not boring excellent/poor exciting/not exciting

FIGURE 11.3   Differences in the Operational Definition of "Attitude Toward the Ad"

While the operational definitions for "attitude toward the advertisement" in Figure 11.3 are different from one another, together they illustrate the process of moving from the concept of interest to an operational definition. The following tasks underlie the process:

1. *Explicitly specify the concept of interest.* In this example, the area or concept of interest is "attitude toward the advertisement."

2. *Explore different aspects of the concept's meaning.* Think about the concept of interest from multiple perspectives. Ask yourself: "What do *I* mean by (concept of interest)? What do *others* mean when they say (concept of interest)?" In this example, the answers to these questions led to the conceptual definition: "a predisposition to respond in a favorable or unfavorable manner to a particular advertising stimulus during a particular exposure situation." The most important portion of this conceptual definition is the specification of response as "favorable" or "unfavorable."

3. *Explicitly specify what can be observed.* Ask yourself: "How will I observe (conceptual definition)? How have others observed (conceptual definition)?" In this example, the answers to these questions require the researcher to specify how favorable or unfavorable predispositions can be operationalized and made more concrete.

4. *Evaluate and select one or more of the alternatives identified in the prior step.* The selected alternative or alternatives become your operational definition. In this

example, the first operational definition shown in Figure 11.3 specifies that favorable and unfavorable predispositions toward an advertisement can be observed by asking a respondent to rate the ad in four different ways: good/bad. interesting/boring, creative/uncreative, and relevant/not relevant.

Finally, it is important to keep in mind that an operational definition implicitly defines the type of data that will need to be collected. Consider this common research problem:

> An advertiser wants to determine the extent to which his Web site engages site visitors. He conceptually defines engagement as the extent to which individuals respond favorably to site content.

This conceptual definition can lead to the following three different operational definitions:

1. Engagement is reflected in the amount of time and depth of interaction exhibited during a Web site visit. Higher levels of engagement are reflected in more overall time spent on the site, click-throughs to deeper site pages, and greater overall page views.

2. Engagement is reflected in consumer attitudes after site visit. Higher levels of engagement are reflected in more positive responses to survey questions that measure personal reactions to site content (i.e., interest, relevance, and appropriateness), feelings toward the site (i.e., enjoyment and likeability), and self-reporting of site behaviors (i.e., relative amount of time spent on site versus competitive sites).

3. Engagement is reflected in heightened physiological response to a Web site. This entails increased heart rate and increased amount of beta wave activity.

All three operational definitions of "engagement" are reasonable given the conceptual definition. Each, however, leads to a different form of data collection. The first operational definition requires the collection of actual respondent behaviors, while the second requires the collection of data via a survey or other type of questionnaire. The third operational definition requires the collection of physiological measures. None are inherently the "correct" operational definition. As stated earlier, what is important is that all involved in the research agree on the selected definition.

Stage Two: Specify an Observable Event

The second stage of the measurement process creates the observable events. Here, a researcher determines what *specific* types of questions or other data gathering sources that will be used to collect the information specified in the operational definition. The steps conducted in this phase (see Figure 11.1) are discussed in the following sections.

IDENTIFY THE APPROPRIATE LEVEL OF MEASUREMENT.   There are four levels of measurement: nominal, ordinal, interval, and ratio. Figure 11.4 shows the uses of each level. Note how each succeeding level of measurement provides different types of information and includes all the information provided by all lower levels. The following sections discuss the types of data collected at each level of measurement.

Level of Measurement	Classifying	Putting in Order	Determining Differences	Determining Ratios
Nominal	X			
Ordinal	X	X		
Interval	X	X	X	
Ratio	X	X	X	X

FIGURE 11.4 Levels of Measurement

Nominal Level of Measurement. Measurement on the nominal level is very common in advertising and marketing survey research. Nominal measurement occurs whenever the goal is the classification of the measured characteristic or attribute. A nominal level measure classifies by assigning each level of a characteristic or attribute to a distinct category, for example:

What is your gender?
Male ☞ (1)
Female ☞ (2)

This nominal level measure divides individuals into one of two categories based on the characteristic of gender: male or female. (The numbers after each nominal category are used for data analysis and are discussed later in this section.)

Nominal level measures are also common in observational or behavioral data collection. Click-throughs, for example, are a nominal level measurement used to evaluate the effectiveness of a banner ads. A cookie or other unobtrusive data collection instrument would record, for each individual, whether or not he or she clicked on a particular banner ad. In effect, the automated system monitoring banner response would answer the question:

Was the banner ad clicked on?
Yes ☞ (1)
No ☞ (2)

Similarly, a Web business can evaluate the appeal of an e-mail newsletter option by automatically recording, for each site visitor not previously subscribed, the answer to the question:

Did the site visitor register for the newsletter?
Yes ☞ (1)
No ☞ (2)

Nominal level measurement has three defining characteristics, each of which is illustrated in the prior examples. First, categories in nominal measurement are mutually exclusive and collectively exhaustive. This means that every level of the characteristic or attribute being measured fits into one and only one category and that every characteristic or attribute fits somewhere. In the gender example, the categories are mutually exclusive (no one can be both male and female) and exhaustive (everyone must be either male or female). Similarly all exposed to the banner ad had to either click or not. Second, for purposes of data analysis, numbers are assigned to each category of response. However, on this level of measurement, the numbers are merely labels for the categories that they represent. Thus, in terms of gender, a "1" represents the category of individuals classified as male while a "2" represents the category of individuals classified as female. The assignment of numbers is, however, totally arbitrary. We could have easily assigned a "1" to women and a "2" to men. The numbers only have value to the extent that they let us distinguish individuals in different classifications. Third, nominal measurement assumes internal category equivalence. All objects or people assigned the same category and represented by the same number are assumed to be the same. All individuals classified as "1," for example, are assumed have the same degree of "maleness."

Ordinal Level of Measurement. As indicated in Figure 11.4, ordinal level measurement arranges characteristics or attributes according to their magnitude in an ordered relationship along some explicit dimension, typically from greater to smaller or from more to less. An ordinal level survey question would be:

> Think about the taste of the five soft drinks that you just tasted. The name of each soft drink is shown below. Please rank the soft drinks to indicate your taste preference. Place a "1" next to the soft drink whose taste you most preferred, a "2" next to the second best preferred all the way through "5," which represents the drink whose taste you least preferred. Please use each number from "1" to "5" only once (there can be no ties).
>
> Coke   _____
>
> Dr. Pepper _____
>
> Pepsi   _____
>
> Seven-Up   _____
>
> Sunkist   _____

This question asks respondents to rank (i.e., place in order) five soft drinks according to taste preference from most to least preferred. An individual might provide the following responses to this ranking question:

> Coke   __5__
>
> Dr. Pepper __3__
>
> Pepsi   __4__
>
> Seven-Up   __1__
>
> Sunkist   __2__

As opposed to numbers that are used for classification on the nominal level, numbers on the ordinal level have some mathematical meaning. On this level of measurement, a number represents an object's position along the dimension of interest relative to all other objects. An analysis of the responses to the prior ranking question would indicate that this individual most prefers the taste of Seven-Up and least prefers the taste of Coke.

Ordinal measures thus provide insights into the *relative standing* of ordered characteristics. This is the total extent of an ordinal measure's interpretive value. Ordinal measures cannot provide any insights into the *relative distance* between ranked objects. It is tempting in this example to believe that the difference in taste preference between Seven-Up and Sunkist (ranked 1 and 2, respectively) is the same as the difference in taste preference between Sunkist and Dr. Pepper (ranked 2 and 3, respectively). After all, in the "real-world" the distance between number 1 and number 2 is the same as the distance between number 2 and number 3. But, this interpretation would be wrong. On the ordinal level of measurement numbers are only symbols that represent a place in an ordered array. As such, they are not subject to mathematical computations such as addition and subtraction. The reasons why ordinal measures only provide the order and not the distance between objects is illustrated in Figure 11.5. Consider the performance of the same three horses in three different races. The order is always the same where "Sam Fast" always wins by a considerable distance over "Becky Slow" and "Karl Wash," which always finish second and third very close to each other. The averages for the horses for the three races would be:

Sam Fast	1.0
Becky Slow	2.0
Karl Wash	3.0

These averages would indicate that there was the same distance between Sam and Becky as between Becky and Karl, but clearly this is not the case. Averaging the ordinal measures distorts our interpretation.

Ordinal measures can also appear outside of survey research. Eye-tracking data can, for example, indicate the order in which elements are noticed. We cannot, however, draw the conclusion that the item noticed second is noticed twice as fast as the item noticed fourth. Similarly, a Web site's detailed log can indicate the order of page views exhibited by each individual site visitor, but we cannot draw inferences that the order viewed is related to time viewed.

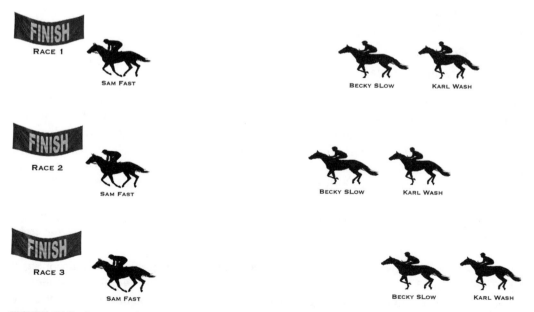

FIGURE 11.5   Inappropriate Averaging of Ordinal Measures

Interval Level of Measurement. Interval measurement contains all of the features of ordinal measurement with the additional characteristic that the distance or magnitude between any two adjacent numeric points on the scale is assumed to be equivalent. Consequently, interval measures provide deeper insights versus ordinal measures. Interval measures allow you to determine both the relative ranking of objects *and* the distance between the objects.

The Fahrenheit thermometer is an example of an interval scale. The difference in temperature between 34° and 35° is exactly the same as the difference between 64° and 65°. Similarly, time is measured on an interval scale. The same amount of time passed between the years 1901 and 1903 as passed between the years 1979 and 1981. Interval measures thus reflect the formal property of equal differences; that is, numbers on an interval scale can be compared to determine the relative distance between items. The distance between any two points is exactly the same. It is important to note, however, that interval scales do not have an absolute zero point and as a result it is not possible to make statements about how *many times higher* one score is than another. Equal differences on the time scale represent equal differences time, but the year 2000 is not twice as old as the year 1000.

Some interval scales, such as temperature and calendar years, are intuitively reasonable. Common sense dictates that no assumptions need be made as to the equivalence between points on the scale. Other scales, if constructed properly, have the assumption of equivalence between points even if this equivalence cannot be externally verified, for example:

Think about the commercial you just saw. Compared to other shampoo commercials how would you rate the believability of this specific commercial?

Very believable   ☞ (1)

Slightly believable   ☞ (2)

Slightly unbelievable   ☞ (3)

Very unbelievable   ☞ (4)

This type of scale assumes that response options represent a continuum on which the distance between points is equivalent. The scale shown assumes that the distance between "very believable" and "slightly believable" is the same as the distance between "slightly believable" and "slightly unbelievable." Therefore, the distance between a "1" that represents "very believable" and a "2" that represents "slightly believable" is considered to be the same as the distance between a rating of "2" and a rating of "3."

The power of interval scales versus nominal and ordinal scales is illustrated by the related questions and subsequent insights shown in Figure 11.6. While all the questions measure the same thing, note how interval scales provide much deeper insights into consumers' attitudes versus questions at the other levels of measurement. In sum, interval level measurement is very powerful. It permits you to draw all of the inferences allowed by ordinal and nominal scales while providing additional information on the distance between objects.

Situation: Respondents are given three formulations for a new diet soft drink. The goal is to select the formulation with the greatest appeal.

Nominal Level Measurement

Questions

Do you like the taste of Formulation A?   Yes ☐   No ☐
Do you like the taste of Formulation B?   Yes ☐   No ☐
Do you like the taste of Formulation C?   Yes ☐   No ☐

Results

Conclusion
All three formulations were well-liked.

Percent Liking Each Formulation

Ordinal Level Measurement

Question

Think about the taste of the diet soft drink formulations. Please rank the formulations to indicate your overall taste preference. Place a "1" next to the formulation whose taste you most preferred, a "2" next to the second best preferred, and a "3" next to the formulation whose taste you least preferred. Please use each number from "1" to "3" only once (there can be no ties).

Formulation A   _____
Formulation B   _____
Formulation C   _____

FIGURE 11.6   Power of Interval Scales

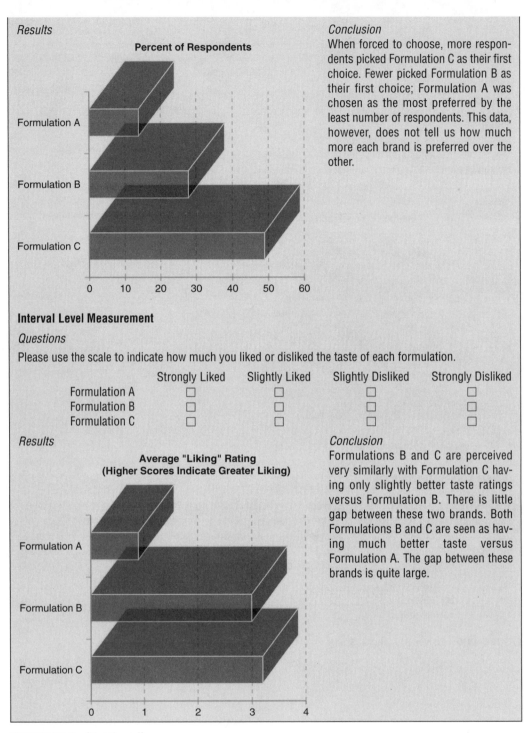

FIGURE 11.6 (Continued)

Ratio Level of Measurement. As shown in Figure 11.4, ratio measures have all the power of nominal, ordinal, and interval measures with the added, unique power that permits researchers to make comparisons among quantities; that is, we can interpret a "10" score on a ratio level measure to have twice as much of the measured characteristic as one with a "5." This is because ratio measures have equal distances between points *and* have a meaningful zero point. Exams that you take in class are a form of a ratio scale where you can receive any percentage between 0 and 100, and a score of 80 is considered to be twice as high as a score of 40.

A common form of ratio measure used in survey research is the constant sum scale. Here, a respondent is given a number of points and is told to distribute those points among a set of objects according to a specific criterion, for example:

Think about the reasons why you purchase a particular children's cereal. Several potential reasons are listed below. We are interested in knowing the relative importance of these reasons in your purchase decision. Assume that you have 100 points. Divide the points among the reasons below to indicate each reason's relative importance. The more points you give something, the more important it is. You can give as many or as few points as you wish to each reason. Please make certain that your total equals 100 points.

All natural	_____
Children like it	_____
Contains fruit	_____
Low price	_____
Low/no fat	_____
TOTAL	**100**

As this question illustrates, numbers on the ratio level of measurement indicate the actual amount of the property being measured. A measure of zero on a ratio measure truly indicates the total absence of the characteristic or attribute being measured. Thus, in the prior example, if "Children like it" averages 50 points and "Low Price" averages 25 points, then we can conclude that the former characteristic is twice as important as the latter.

Ratio level measures are very common in research that focuses on respondent behaviors. Research, for example, might ask a respondent to recall the number of ads viewed in a period of time, the number of ads viewed of a particular brand, the number of visits to particular types of Web sites, the number of Twitter messages sent in the last day, etc. Ratio level measures are also common in research that monitors respondent behaviors, especially Internet-related behaviors. Here, through the use of cookies or other passive means, research might determine, for example, the number of Web site pages viewed in the past day, the amount of time spent on specific Web sites, the number of videos forwarded to friends, or the number of banner ads clicked-on. Note that in all of the prior examples, "0" is a possible answer.

Summary: Selecting a Level of Measurement. Each of the four levels of measurement provides different types of information. On what basis, then, do you determine the appropriate level of measurement?

Level of measurement is determined by the characteristic or attribute being measured, the desired depth of detail required to answer the information needs of the research, and the level of detail required for planned or potential data analysis. While these issues vary across research studies, because higher levels of measurement contain all the descriptive power of lower measures *a general rule of thumb is try to collect information at the highest appropriate level of measurement.* For example, both nominal and ratio level measures can be used to determine an individual's age:

Nominal: Into which of the following groups does your age fall?

Under 18	☞ (1)
18 to 29	☞ (2)
30 to 49	☞ (3)
50 and older	☞ (4)

Ratio: What is your age? _____

A comparison of the data obtained by these two questions illustrates the advantages of collecting data at higher levels of measurement.

- First, data collected at higher levels is less limiting. Notice that the age groupings in the nominal level question are quite restrictive. One cannot determine, for example, the distribution of individuals within the 18- to 29-year-old age group, and the research cannot later examine and compare the responses of 18- to 24-year olds and 25- to 29-year olds. The ratio level measure, on the other hand, provides more detail since the age of every respondent is known, and as a result both of the prior limitations of the nominal level question are eliminated.

- Second, data collected at higher levels of measurement can always be turned into lower level data. The age data collected at the ratio level, for example, can always be grouped so that it is equivalent to that collected on the nominal level.

- Third, ratio versus nominal level measures can be examined with more powerful statistical techniques (see Chapter 16) leading to more confidence in the conclusions and insights drawn from the research.

IDENTIFY APPROPRIATE QUESTION TYPE.   Once concepts have been operationally defined and the appropriate level of measurement selected, specific questions are written to collect and record the desired information. Data collection in behavioral or observational research is almost always closed-ended. Here, as discussed in the prior two chapters, the "questions" in observational research are answered and appropriate data is collected through passive or other means of behavioral monitoring. Survey research has much greater latitude in data collection, and as a result either closed-ended or open-ended questions may be used.

Open-ended questions allow an individual or observer to reply in his or her own words without use of a fixed, predetermined set of answers. Typical open-ended questions are:

Tell me in your own words what did the commercial say or show about the advertised product?

What do you think are the primary benefits of a hair care product that combines shampoo and conditioner?

Why have you stopped using generic children's aspirin?

Open-ended questions have several advantages over closed-ended questions. First, open-ended questions permit respondents to answer a question in their own words. Respondents can state exactly what is on their mind without influence, as might occur when they must select an answer from a predetermined list of response options. Thus, open-ended questions are well-suited for exploring circumstances in which a researcher is either unable or unwilling to list all potential responses or the listing of responses might influence or bias the respondent. The two questions shown below illustrate the differences in the two approaches. Note how the open-ended question gathers the desired information without cueing the respondent as to possible answers.

Open-ended approach: Think about companies you've seen advertise themselves as "concerned about the environment." How do you feel about companies advertising and talking about themselves in this way?

Closed-ended approach: Think about companies you've seen advertise themselves as "concerned about the environment." Which, if any, of the words or phrases shown below reflect how you feel about companies advertising and talking about themselves in this way? You can check as many or as few (or even none) as apply.

> Honest
> Crass
> Only motivated by profit
> Sincere
> Helpful
> Deceptive

Second, open-ended questions can provide a context for interpreting an individual's answers to closed-ended questions. Here, open-ended questions can be written to allow a respondent to provide a rationale for his or her selection on a closed-ended question, for example:

1. Please use the following scale below to indicate the extent to which you liked or disliked the commercial you just saw.
   Strongly liked   (1)   CONTINUE WITH Q. 2
   Slightly liked   (2)   CONTINUE WITH Q. 2
   Slightly disliked (3)   SKIP TO Q. 3
   Strongly disliked (4)   SKIP TO Q. 3

2. What, in particular, did you like about the commercial?
   AFTER RESPONSE SKIP TO Q. 4

3. What, in particular, did you dislike about the commercial?

4. INTERVIEW CONTINUES

Third, open-ended questions are a good way to introduce a topic area. Once a subject is introduced, the questionnaire can then systematically reduce the breadth and increase the specificity of subsequent questions, Finally, because you don't need to know all possible answers in advance, open-ended questions tend to be easier to write versus many types of closed-ended questions.

Although the advantages of open-ended questions are significant, this type of question also has several disadvantages. First, responses can be incomplete, irrelevant and/or incomprehensible. Second, open-ended questions take more time to administer and place a greater demand on the verbal skills of the respondent. Third, and most important, the analysis of responses to open-ended questions is more time-consuming and difficult versus the analysis of closed-ended questions.

Closed-ended questions present a set of fixed alternative answers. Consequently, closed-ended questions versus open-ended questions tend to

- produce less variability in the range of response.
- be easier for a respondent to answer.
- be quicker to administer.
- be easier to examine and analyze.

The relative advantages of open-ended and closed-ended questions provide direction for determining which is most appropriate for a particular research situation.

Additional considerations relevant to the evaluation and selection of question type relate to researcher knowledge and respondent priming. Closed-ended questions should only be used when you are convinced that you have presented the full range of options. When presented with a list of items, respondents will generally use the list provided to answer the question; if the list is incomplete, the potential of the research to mislead judgment dramatically increases. Beyond list completeness, closed-ended questions have the potential to "prime" or "cue" the respondent. Open-ended questions are appropriate when the measurement goal is the attainment of unaided recall, opinions, or attitudes. Closed-ended questions are appropriate when the measurement goal is the attainment of aided recall, opinions, or attitudes. The difference between unaided and aided measurement, in this case advertising awareness, is illustrated in the following two questions:

UNAIDED ADVERTISING AWARENESS

Think about all the advertising that you have seen or heard in the past week. Please name any batteries that have advertised themselves as "environmentally-sensitive" or "better for the environment."

AIDED ADVERTISING AWARENESS

Think about all the advertising that you have seen or heard in the past week. Which, if any, of the batteries listed below have advertised themselves as "environmentally-sensitive" or "better for the environment?" Please check as many or as few as are appropriate.

> Energizer   ✐
> Eveready   ✐
> Ray-O-Vac   ✐

Stage Three: Evaluate and Revise the Observable Event

A survey question or observational instrument yields useful, accurate information only if it is reliable and valid. Thus, before initiating any research study, pilot research should be conducted to assess the reliability and validity of any untested measures. Reliability concerns the extent to which a survey question or other measurement procedure yields the same results over repeated trials. Validity concerns the extent to which the survey question or measurement procedure actually measures what it is intended to measure.

The determination of a measure's reliability and validity is a critical step in the measurement process. Figure 11.1 shows that only reliable and valid measures should be used in the actual conduct of research. Measures that are either unreliable, invalid, or both are rewritten and are then subjected to further assessment of reliability and validity before they are used in a research study. The next section discussed reliability and validity.

RELIABILITY AND VALIDITY: AN OVERVIEW

Reliability and validity are two independent yet related aspects of measurement. *Reliability* is an assessment of the extent to which a measure *consistently provides the same results*. A reliable measure is considered to be stable, that is, free from random error in yielding comparable results over multiple administrations. *Validity* is an assessment of the "goodness" of the measure. A valid measure is one that *accurately measures* what we think it is measuring. Any particular measure or set of measures can have one of four combinations of reliability and validity. Figure 11.7 provides illustrations of each of these combinations of outcomes. Imagine that arrows are shot at a target. A circle marks where each arrow lands. The arrows (representing measures) can be:

- *reliable but not valid:* all of the arrows are grouped together (indicating high reliability), but none of the arrows hit near the center of the target (indicating low validity).
- *valid but not reliable:* all of the arrows hit near the center of the target (indicating high validity), but the arrows are not grouped together (indicating low reliability).
- *neither valid nor reliable:* none of the arrows hit near the center of the target (indicating low validity), and none of the arrows are grouped together (indicating low reliability).
- *both reliable and valid:* all of the arrows are grouped together (indicating high reliability), and all of the arrows hit near the center of the target (indicating high validity).

Assessing Reliability

There are two main approaches to assessing the reliability of individual survey items: test-retest and alternative form.

Test-retest reliability is a common way of assessing a survey item's reliability. An estimate of test-retest reliability is obtained by repeating the administration of the test item under equivalent conditions to the same group of people. The results of the two administrations are then compared. The greater the similarity in response between the two administrations the greater the item's reliability. Imagine, for example, that a group of individuals is asked to (1) rank five brands of frozen dinners according to value (an ordinal measure) and (2) rate the taste of five brands of frozen dinners (an interval measure) as part of a survey administered on February 1 and February 14. The ordinal measure would have test-retest reliability if the relative order obtained in both administrations was consistent, while the interval measure would have test-retest reliability if the relative order and the relative distance between brands was consistent.

RELIABLE, BUT NOT VALID

All of the arrows (measurements) are consistent as evidenced in their clustering. This clustering makes them reliable.

The arrows are not on-target, severely reducing their validity.

VALID, BUT NOT RELIABLE

All of the arrows (measurements) are near the center of the target. This placement makes them valid.

The arrows are not clustered, severely reducing their reliability.

NOT RELIABLE AND NOT VALID

The arrows (measurements) are not clustered, severely reducing their reliability.

The arrows are also not on-target, severely reducing their validity.

RELIABLE AND VALID

All of the arrows (measurements) are consistent as evidenced in their clustering. This clustering makes them reliable.

All of the arrows (measurements) are also near the center of the target. This placement makes them valid.

FIGURE 11.7 Relationship of Validity and Reliability

The *alternative form* method of reliability estimation is similar to the test-retest method in so far as the same individuals participate in multiple administrations. However, this method differs from test-retest in one important regard: the same test is not given on the second testing. Rather, an alternative form of the first test is administered. Because it is assumed that the two forms of the test are designed to measure the same thing, reliability is estimated by comparing the responses to the two forms. The greater the correspondence in response between the two forms the greater the reliability.[4]

There are cases, however, in which a single measure cannot by itself carry out the operational definition of a concept or when sensitivity in measurement is desired beyond that which can be provided by a single question. As seen earlier in this chapter, measurement of attitude toward an advertisement may require asking several similar but not identical questions. *A set of questions is considered reliable if there is internal consistency in response.* Consider the following questions used to measure consumers' attitudes toward a celebrity product endorser:

Below are five scales. Use each scale to indicate how you feel about the celebrity you just saw in the advertisement. Place a check in the space in each scale that best represents your feeling.

The celebrity was . . .

Attractive	___ ___ ___ ___ ___ ___ ___	Unattractive
Not classy	___ ___ ___ ___ ___ ___ ___	Classy
Believable	___ ___ ___ ___ ___ ___ ___	Not believable
Not relevant	___ ___ ___ ___ ___ ___ ___	Relevant
Likeable	___ ___ ___ ___ ___ ___ ___	Not likeable

These scales would be internally consistent, and thus reliable, if individuals with positive attitudes tend to answer all questions positively while those with negative attitudes tend to answer all questions negatively.[5]

The definition of reliability is the same for passively obtained behavioral measures (such as recording the number of Web site visits through cookies) as it is for survey items. However, the approach used to assess reliability is different. In these circumstances, a measure's reliability is considered to be a reflection of recording accuracy *and* its subsequent ability to provide consistent information over time. If, for example, a cookie can be shown to accurately record the desired information then *on the recording level* the data is considered reliable. However, if a portion of site visitors is found to systematically delete these cookies, then even though data recording is accurate, the overall data collected would not be reliable as the information collected by the cookies is ultimately an incomplete and inconsistent measure of respondent behavior. When this occurs, just as in survey research, alternative means of data collection need to be identified.

Assessing Validity

A reliable measure consistently measures something. But, this something may or may not be what you want to measure. In other words, as shown in Figure 11.7, it is entirely possible that a set of survey items is reliable but not at all valid. Only valid measures actually measure what we want or, put in more formal terms, *validity only occurs when there is a high degree of correspondence between a concept's operational definition and the specific observable event used to record the concept.* With regard to advertising research, validity is commonly determined in one of three ways: face, concurrent, and predictive.[6]

Face validity is the most basic form of validity assessment. A measure has face validity when the subjective judgment of those with expertise agree that the measure accurately translates the operational definition into an observed event, in other words, when there is a consensus that the measure does in fact measure what it is supposed to measure. Face validity occurs, for example, whenever a questionnaire is reviewed, modified, and then approved by the client and agency personnel prior to use. Clear, unambiguous questions such as "Do you recall seeing any advertising for the Ford Taurus?" are generally felt to have face validity, in this case for the measurement of advertising recall. A question that attempts to measure brand loyalty by asking "Which brand is the best value for the money?" would lack face validity because individuals with expertise would notice that the attitude probed in the question (brand value) is different from the characteristic specified in the conceptual and operational definition (brand loyalty).

Problems with face validity often arise in behavioral or observational research. Consider, for example, monitoring changes in brain activity and other biometric responses during the viewing of a commercial, where changes in a specific direction are taken as indicators of commercial effectiveness.[7] The measure is reliable, in that the same results are obtained over repeated measurement. Assuming that the machines are calibrated correctly, the measurements are also valid *to the extent* the data does in fact accurately represent an individual's responses. But, are these measures valid measures of advertising effectiveness? There is considerable debate as to whether this is the case. The only individuals who are likely to rely on the data for decision making are those who believe that these measures have face validity.

Concurrent validity is assessed by comparing the results obtained from a new measurement with the results of an accepted measurement taken at the same point in time. For example, assume that an existing, well-accepted, 96 item survey provides excellent predictions of how specific individuals will react to different types of advertising. While the predictive ability of this survey is high, it nevertheless takes a long time to complete. In an attempt to fix this problem, a new, shorter survey consisting of only 15 items is developed. The new survey will have concurrent validity if its scores highly correlate with that of the existing test.

Predictive validity is estimated by determining the extent to which performance on one variable (measured today) accurately predicts performance on another variable (to be measured in the future). SAT scores, for example, are often used as predictors for first year college performance, as measured by a student's GPA. A high correlation between the two measures is considered evidence of predictive validity.

SUMMARY

Measurement is the process by which abstract, typically unobservable concepts are linked to observable events. The measurement process consists of seven steps representing three major stages (see Figure 11.1). The first stage, *identify and define the concept of interest*, begins with a general notion of the area to be explored (the concept of interest) and ends with an explicit operational definition of what is to be measured. The second stage, *specify an observable event*, creates the measurement instrument. This stage requires the researcher to determine the nature of the information needed and the most appropriate means for collecting this information. Here, decisions relate to the appropriate level of measurement and the appropriate question type (open- versus closed-ended). The four levels of measurement are:

- *Nominal:* Assigns responses to mutually exclusive and exhaustive categories.
- *Ordinal:* Places responses in sequential order according to a single explicit criterion.

- *Interval:* Places responses in sequential order with equal distances assumed between response options.
- *Ratio:* Contain all characteristics of prior levels of measurement with a true zero point.

The third stage, evaluate and revise the observable event, evaluates the measurement instrument. Acceptable measurement instruments are those that are both reliable and valid where

- reliability evaluates the extent to which a measure consistently provides the same results, and
- validity evaluates the extent to which a measure accurately measures what the researcher thinks it is measuring.

Measures that are not reliable and/or valid are revised or eliminated before they are used in a research study.

Review Questions

1. What does the term *measurement* mean?
2. What are the three main stages of the measurement process? What key events occur at each stage?
3. What is a *conceptual definition?*
4. What is an *operational definition?*
5. Why is an operational definition important?
6. Describe the process by which one moves from a concept of interest to an operational definition.
7. What is *nominal measurement?*
8. What are the characteristics of nominal measurement? Provide an example of a survey question written at the nominal level of measurement.
9. What is *ordinal measurement?* Provide an example of a survey question written at the ordinal level of measurement.

10. What is *interval measurement?* Provide an example of a survey question written at the interval level of measurement.
11. What is *ratio measurement?* Provide an example of a survey question written at the ratio level of measurement.
12. What are the relative advantages of open-ended versus closed-ended questions?
13. How is *reliability* defined?
14. What are the two ways by which reliability is estimated? Provide a brief description of each.
15. How is *validity* defined?
16. What are the three ways by which validity is estimated? Provide a brief description of each.

Application Exercises

1. Three researchers have proposed methods for measuring brand loyalty. They began with the same conceptual definition: brand loyalty is a consumer's preferential behavioral response to one or more products in a product category expressed over a period of time. Each researcher's question is shown below:

   TERRY: Think about all of the laundry detergents that you have purchased during the past two months. Fill in the space next to each brand to indicate the number of boxes/containers of that brand which you purchased.

   All   _____
   Cheer   _____
   Tide   _____
   Wisk   _____
   Other   _____

SUE: Think about your purchase of
            laundry detergent. Would you
            say that you ...

            Consistently purchase the
            same brand   _____(1)

            Do not consistently purchase
            the same brand   _____(2)

STACI: I am interested in learning
            how brand loyal you are to
            your laundry detergent. Would
            you say that you are...

            Extremely loyal   _____

            Slightly loyal   _____

            Slightly disloyal   _____

            Extremely disloyal _____

Prepare a short paper that describes the strengths
and weaknesses of each researcher's approach
to measuring the concept of "brand loyalty."

2. Advertising-related research is published in
   journals such as the *Journal of Advertising*,
   the *Journal of Advertising Research*, the
   Journal of Consumer Research, the *Journal of
   Marketing*, the *Journal of Marketing Research*,
   and *Journalism & Mass Communication
   Quarterly*. Concepts frequently explored in
   articles published in these journals include:
   attitudes toward the advertising, attitudes
   toward the brand, purchase intent, and attitudes
   toward the advertiser. Select one of these concepts, or another relevant to advertising research,
   and provide at least three different examples
   from the academic literature illustrating how the
   concept has been operationally defined. Present
   a point of view on the relative strengths and
   weaknesses of each approach.

3. Select one of the approaches identified in the
   prior question. How did the researcher address
   issues related to reliability and validity? Present
   a point of view on the adequacy of the procedures the researcher used.

4. Examine each of the following questions.
   Then, for each question: (a) identify the question's level of measurement and (b) present a
   point of view as to whether the question
   adheres to the principle of "collecting information at the highest appropriate level of measurement." If you feel that the question does not
   collect information at the appropriate level,
   present an alternative. Be certain to explain
   your recommendation.

a. Think about the following three
   products: Spiffo, Boffo, and Waxo.
   Select the one product you think
   cleans dirty floors the best?

   Spifo   _____   (1)

   Boffo   _____   (2)

   Waxo   _____   (3)

b. Into which of the following categories does your annual household
   income fall?

   Under $25,000   _____ (1)

   $25,000 to $34,999   _____ (2)

   $35,000 to $49,999   _____ (3)

   $50,000 to $69,999   _____ (4)

   $70,000 to $99,999   _____ (5)

   $100,000 and over   _____ (6)

c. How many children under the age of
   18 are currently living full-time
   in your household?

   Number of children _____

d. Please tell me whether you liked or
   disliked the advertising?

   Liked   _____   (1)

   Disliked   _____   (2)

e. Please use a scale of "0" to "10,"
   where "10" is the most favorable
   response, to indicate your estimation of the safety of each car
   brand shown below. Provide a rating for each brand

   Cadillac _____

   Ford   _____

   Toyota   _____

5. Imagine that you are hired as the consultant to
   your regional mass transit authority. The transit
   authority has allocated funds to develop and
   air an advertising campaign intended to
   increase mass transit ridership. In preparation
   for the campaign, they ask you to conduct
   research that will help them better understand
   (a) attitudes toward riding mass transit and (b)
   attitudes toward carpooling. Write a letter to
   the transit authority that explains how you will
   move from each general area of interest, to
   operational definition, to valid and reliable survey questions. Be specific in explaining the
   decisions and procedures that you will use at
   each stage of the measurement process.

Endnotes

1. This definition of measurement is taken from Edward G. Carmines and Richard A. Zeller (1980). *Measurement in the Social Sciences: The Link Between Theory and Data* (New York, NY: Cambridge University Press); M. W. Riley (1963). *Sociological Research: A Case Approach* (New York, NY: Harcourt Brace Jovanovich). It should be noted that this definition is different than the traditional definition of measurement presented in many texts, where measurement is defined as "the assignment of numbers to objects and events according to rules." Carmines and Zeller present a persuasive argument why this latter definition is inappropriate for social science research. See Edward G. Carmines and Richard A. Zeller (1979). *Reliability and Validity Assessment* (Beverly Hills, CA: Sage Publications). The discussion in this introductory section is based on that presented by Carmines and Zeller.

2. Scott B. Mackenzie, Richard J. Lutz, and George E. Belch (1986). "The Role of Attitude Toward the Ad as a Mediator of Advertising Effect: A Test of Competing Explanations." *Journal of Marketing Research* 23: 130–43.

3. Mohawk Fine Papers (undated) at http://www.mohawkpaper.com/resources/glossary/terms/.

4. Test-retest and alternative form reliability are typically assessed through the use of correlation, denoted as r_{xy}. Chapter 16 provides a detailed discussion of the correlation coefficient.

5. The statistical technique most commonly used for determining the reliability of multiple items is the coefficient alpha. For a discussion of this measure's characteristics, computation, and measurement, see L. J. Cronbach (1951). "Coefficient Alpha and the Internal Structure of Tests." *Psychometrika* 16: 297–334.

6. Construct validity is a fourth form of validity assessment. This form of validity is rarely used in applied advertising research due to its complexity. Construct validity is "concerned with the extent to which a particular measure relates to other measures consistent with theoretically derived hypotheses concerning the concepts (or constructs) being measured." To prove construct validity, the test measure(s) must: (a) correlate positively with other measures of the same concept, (b) show little or no correlation with theoretically unrelated concepts, and (c) correlate in a theoretically consistent way with measures of different but related concepts. See Donald S. Tull and Del I. Hawkins (1990). *Marketing Research: Measurement and Method* (New York, NY: Macmillan Publishing).

7. See, for example, Stewart Elliott (2008). "Is the Ad a Success? The Brain Waves Tell All" available at: http://www.nytimes.com/2008/03/31/business/media/31adcol.html.

CHAPTER 12

Writing Survey Questions

The quality of questions you ask in an interview or survey directly determines the accuracy and depth of the insights you obtain. In this chapter, you will learn how to write questions that successfully collect the information and insights required for sound advertising decision making. The next chapter provides direction for turning your well-written questions into a questionnaire.

***

After reading this chapter, you should be able to:

- understand the appropriate use of closed- and open-ended questions
- understand how to match question form and approach with information needs
- create well-written questions at all levels of measurement.

Quantitative survey research uses two types of questions: closed-ended and open-ended. A closed-ended question gives the respondent a predefined set of response options from which he or she can choose. An open-ended question permits the respondent to answer in his or her own words. Both types of questions provide valuable insights into a respondent's thoughts, beliefs, and attitudes. This chapter begins with a discussion of the types and characteristics of closed-ended questions, followed by a discussion of open-ended questions. The chapter concludes with the presentation of special considerations for open- and closed-ended question development.

WRITING CLOSED-ENDED SURVEY QUESTIONS

The prior chapter discussed the four levels of measurement (nominal, ordinal, interval, and ratio) and provided example questions written at each level. This section extends this discussion, providing specific guidance for creating the most commonly used types of questions at each level of measurement.

Nominal Level Questions

Nominal level questions categorize respondents and responses through the use of mutually exclusive response options. Three common types of nominal level questions are dichotomous questions, multiple-choice questions, and checklists.

DICHOTOMOUS QUESTIONS.   A *dichotomous question* is the simplest type of nominal measurement. It is used to classify individuals, objects, attitudes, or other responses into one of two exhaustive, mutually exclusive groups. The most common form of classification in dichotomous questions uses "yes" and "no" responses, for example:

Do you recall seeing any Bubble Yum advertising in the last 24 hours?

Yes _____

No _____

Dichotomous questions, however, are not limited to "yes" and "no" response options. They can be used whenever there is a need to divide respondents, attitudes, or behaviors into two groups, for example:

As a diet soda drinker, do you prefer diet soft drinks flavored with NutraSweet or Aspartame?

NutraSweet _____

Aspartame _____

What is your gender?

Male _____

Female _____

Dichotomous questions have several advantages over more complex questions: they are easy for a respondent to answer and they are simple to edit, code, tabulate, and analyze. Beyond these advantages, dichotomous questions also work well to move respondents though a questionnaire in a way that ensures that only relevant questions are asked of particular respondents. This is known as a "skip pattern" or "skip logic." Consider the four questions below:

1. Are you currently married or single?

   Married _____ ☛ CONTINUE WITH Q.2

   Single _____ ☛ SKIP TO Q.3

2. How long have you been married?

   _____ YEARS MARRIED ☛ CONTINUE WITH Q. 4

3. Have you ever been married?

   Yes   _____

   No   _____

4. INTERVIEW CONTINUES

The dichotomous Question 1 controls the skip pattern, selecting the appropriate next question based on an individual's response.

- Question 2 is only asked of those individuals who indicated they are married in Question 1.
- Question 3 is only asked of individuals who say they are not currently married in Question 1.
- After responding to the appropriate follow-up question, all respondents continue the interview with Question 4.

In spite of their advantages, dichotomous questions should not be used as a substitute for more detailed questions. It would be inappropriate, for example, to classify levels of brand usage through a dichotomous question that asks "Have you used three or more tubes of toothpaste in the past month?" A question of the form "How many tubes of toothpaste have you used in the past month?" would be more appropriate.

MULTIPLE-CHOICE QUESTIONS.   Multiple-choice questions are nominal measures that present three or more exclusive and exhaustive categories of response. These questions are used when the need is to categorize the characteristics or attributes of respondents or responses into smaller, more focused categories than are permitted by dichotomous questions. The collection of demographic information is a common use of this type of question. For example:

   Into which of the following groups does your total, annual household income fall?

Under $15,000	_____
$15,000–$24,999	_____
$25,000–$34,999	_____
$35,000–$44,999	_____
$45,000–$54,999	_____
$55,000 and over	_____

When writing multiple-choice questions, it is essential to make certain that the categories are exhaustive and exclusive. Categories are exhaustive when there is an appropriate response for every respondent, that is, every respondent fits someplace. Categories are exclusive when there is no overlap across response categories and each respondent fits into only one category. The following examples show the types of problems that arise when these conditions are not met. Consider this question:

How many children under the age of 18 are currently living full-time in your household?

1–2 _____

3–4 _____

5–6 _____

6 or more _____

This question's category options lack both exhaustiveness (what about respondents with no children?) and exclusivity (a respondent with six children fits into two categories). This question could be corrected as follows:

How many children under the age of 18 are currently living full-time in your household?

None _____

1–2 _____

3–4 _____

5–6 _____

7 or more _____

However, the more appropriate approach would be to collect this data at a higher level of measurement:

In the space below, please fill in the number of children under the age of 18 who are currently living full-time in your household.

_____ (Number of Children)

The example below also lacks exhaustiveness and exclusivity.

Which brand of laundry detergent did you buy last?

All _____

Cheer _____

Tide _____

Here, the absence of an "other" option prohibits the classification of respondents whose last purchase was not one of the listed brands (lack of exhaustiveness), while the question fails to account for a respondent who bought both Cheer and Tide the last time he or she was shopping (lack of exclusivity).

Multiple-choice questions are not restricted to the collection of demographic or behavioral information. This type of question can be used to probe attitudes and motivations as long as responses are constrained to one of the listed options, for example:

What is the one most important reason why you purchased a Toyota automobile?

Advertising	_____
Price	_____
Warranty	_____
Other	_____ SPECIFY: _____

Do you plan to purchase a home in the next 12 months?

Definitely yes	_____
Probably yes	_____
Probably no	_____
Definitely no	_____

Multiple-choice questions have several advantages: (1) the format is very flexible and appropriate to a wide range of situations; (2) they provide much of the same flexibility as open-ended questions, but without asking respondents to verbalize their thoughts and express themselves; and (3) versus open-ended questions, they are easier to code, edit, tabulate, and analyze.

There are several important considerations associated with the use of multiple-choice questions. First, as discussed earlier, it is necessary to make certain that the list of alternative answers is both exhaustive and exclusive. Second, it is important not to bias the respondent. Consider the question: "Which brand of automobile do you think has the best reliability?" While any of the response category orderings shown below are possible, only the first approach is acceptable.

Cadillac	Cadillac	Ford
Dodge	Ford	Saturn
Ford	Dodge	Cadillac
Saturn	Saturn	Dodge
Other (Specify)	Other (Specify)	Other (Specify)

Only the first approach places the response options in alphabetical order. Whenever a list of product names or similar options appear out of alphabetical order, respondents will assume that the choices appearing first are somehow "better." Third, when using multiple-choice questions to probe behaviors, make certain that: (1) you provide a "zero" option distinct from the other response options, (2) the response categories are relatively balanced, and (3) the "typical" behavior appears near the center of the list. Consider this question: "How many hours did you spend on YouTube in the past 24 hours. Please round to the nearest ½ hour?" The following response options would be unacceptable:

Less than 1 hour	_____
1 hour	_____
1½ to 5 hours	_____
5½ to 6 hours	_____
6½ or more hours	_____

While the categories are in fact exhaustive and exclusive, they nevertheless fail to allow us to distinguish between individuals who *never* participate in the behavior from those who participate *infrequently*. Additionally, the categories will not allow us to adequately differentiate among individuals with different *levels* of usage, as the vast majority of the sample is likely to fall into the 1½ to 5 hours group. A better set of response options would be:

0 - no time at all	_____
½ hour	_____
1 to 2 hours	_____
2½ to 4 hours	_____
4½ to 6 hours	_____
6½ or more hours	_____

This set of response options will allow us to distinguish between nonusers, light, medium, and heavy users of YouTube.

Dichotomous or Multiple Choice? Dichotomous and multiple-choice questions can be used to collect similar data, although each question does so with a different level of specificity. Dichotomous questions divide responses or respondents into two exclusive groups, while multiple-choice questions divide responses or respondents into three or more smaller, more narrowly defined groups. Given each question's level of specificity, it is recommended that dichotomous questions *only be used when the entire range of response consists of two categories.* The "gender" question, for example, where everyone is either male or female is an appropriate use of a dichotomous question. Now imagine that a commercial has been created for the Home Depot. This commercial is designed to appeal to individuals who have at least some college education. A test of the commercial is planned to confirm that the commercial does appeal to this group. The researcher includes the following question in order to identify these individuals:

What is your highest level of education?

High school diploma or less	_____
Some college or beyond	_____

While this question would accomplish the desired classification, it nevertheless violates the guideline of using dichotomous questions only when the entire range of response consists of two categories. As a result, the researcher is severely limited in the types of additional research questions that can be explored. The researcher would be unable to answer questions such as: "Do college graduates respond differently than those who have just some college?" and "Do those with a high school diploma respond similarly to those who have just some college?" In anticipation of these questions, a multiple-choice question would have been more appropriate, for example:

What is your highest level of education?

Less than high school	_____
High school diploma	_____
Some college	_____
College degree or higher	_____

CHECKLIST.   A checklist is a nominal measure that combines a series of related dichotomous questions into a single question. This approach results in a less time-consuming
and tedious method of data collection versus asking each question individually. Two
examples of checklist questions are:

> Think about all the music-related videos you've watched online in the past 24 hours.
> Which of the following types of music were featured in the videos? You can check as
> many or as few (or even no items) as apply.

Blues	_____
Classical	_____
Country	_____
Folk	_____
Jazz	_____
Techno	_____
Rap/Hip hop	_____
Rock/Pop	_____
Ska	_____

> Think about the commercial you just saw. Which of the following words or phrases
> describe how you feel about the commercial? You can check as many or as few (or
> even no items) as apply.

Entertaining	_____
Confusing	_____
Silly	_____
Believable	_____
Fun	_____
Annoying	_____
.	_____
.	_____
etc.	_____

These questions illustrate several important characteristics of checklist questions.
First, the question must *explicitly* define the criteria on which items in the checklist are to
be selected. Second, the question must not assume that the respondent will check any specific number of items. The instructions must make it clear that it is up to the respondent to
check as many or as few items (or even no items) as he or she feels is appropriate. Third,
the checklist itself must be constructed to reduce bias. Thus, lists of names or reasons for
purchase, as in the first prior example, should be in alphabetical order. Words and phrases,
as in the second prior example, should contain equal numbers of positive and negative
items placed in a random order.

Finally, the prior approach to checklist questions can be combined with a second
question to help identify those items on the checklist for which the respondent has the

strongest opinions. In this regard, the prior question on commercial liking could be changed as follows:

> Think about the commercial you just saw. In the first column below (labeled "Describes My Reactions"), please check the words or phrases that describe how you feel about the commercial. In this column, you can check as many or as few (or even no items) as apply. In the second column, labeled "Describes Best" please check the TWO words or phrases that **best** describe your reactions to the commercial.

	Describes My Reactions	Describes Best
Entertaining	_____	_____
Confusing	_____	_____
Silly	_____	_____
Believable	_____	_____
Fun	_____	_____
Annoying	_____	_____
.	_____	_____
.	_____	_____
etc.	_____	_____

Ordinal Level Questions

Ordinal level questions ask respondents to order a list of items in terms of a predefined characteristic. As discussed in the prior chapter, responses to these types of questions inform the researcher as to the *relative ordering* of items, although no inferences as to the *distances* between items can be drawn. The most common question at this level of measurement is rank order.

Rank order questions present a respondent with several characteristics, objects, or attributes and then requests the respondent to order or rank them with respect to a specific characteristic, which is made explicit in the lead-in to the list of items. The following rank order question might be asked of individuals who had just been exposed to the home pages of four social networking sites:

> You have just visited the home pages of four social networking sites: Bebo, Facebook, Myspace, and Twitter. Please rank the home pages with regard to their *overall appeal* to you. Place a "1" next to the site that has the greatest appeal, a "2" by the site with the next most appeal, through "4" which you would place next to the site whose home page you found least appealing. There can be no ties and please use each number only once.

> Bebo _____
>
> Facebook _____
>
> Myspace _____
>
> Twitter _____

Notice how the question is worded to explicitly state the respondent's task (rank the home pages), the characteristic to be used (overall appeal), and the method used to perform the ranking (a "1" for the most appealing, etc.). In addition, as discussed with regard to multiple-choice questions, the options have been placed in alphabetical order to avoid bias.

One thing you need be sensitive to in creating a rank order question is the number of listed items. Respondents are typically quite capable of ranking up to about six items; ranking lists with more items than this tend to be difficult for respondents and, as a result, have diminished ability to provide accurate insights into respondents' preferences.

Interval Level Questions

Questions at the interval level of measurement provide information on the rank order of items *and* provide an estimate of the relative distance between items.

Rating scales are one of the most common types of interval measures. These questions require a respondent to select one option from among the members of an explicit, well-defined continuum, for example:

How believable or unbelievable was the commercial you just saw?

Very believable	_____
Slightly believable	_____
Neither believable nor unbelievable	_____
Slightly unbelievable	_____
Very unbelievable	_____

This question illustrates the three characteristics of a well-written rating scale question:

- the lead-in is unbiased. Both ends of the rating scale are explicitly stated.
- the scale is constructed so that there are equal spaces or intervals between scale points. It is assumed that the distance between very and slightly believable is the same as that between slightly and very unbelievable.
- there is a direct correspondence between the information requested in the question itself and the scale used to gather the information. The question asks about believability and the scale options reflect this focus.

The rating scale questions shown in Figure 12.1 illustrate circumstances in which these criteria for well-written rating scales are violated.

As long as the prior three criteria are met, a researcher has a large amount of flexibility with regard to the scale options selected. The ultimate decision on the "best" option reflects the specific information need being addressed by the scale question. There are four important considerations.

First, because there is no set number of categories for rating scale questions, it is necessary to determine the number of categories to use. While any number of categories may be created depending on the nature of the attitude or behavior being investigated, a

(A) Problem with question lead-in. Only one end of the scale is mentioned. Scale options are acceptable.

Based on what you saw and heard in the commercial, how likely are you to purchase the advertised product?

Very likely _____

Likely _____

Unlikely _____

Very unlikely _____

(B) Problem with scale options. There are unequal spaces between scale options. Lead-in is acceptable.

Based on what you saw and heard in the commercial, how likely or unlikely are you to purchase the advertised product?

Very likely _____

Really likely _____

Somewhat likely _____

A little likely _____

Likely _____

Really unlikely _____

(C) Question lead-in is acceptable. Scale options are acceptable. There is a lack of agreement between lead-in and scale options.

Based on what you saw and heard in the commercial, how likely or unlikely are you to purchase the advertised product?

Strongly agree _____

Slightly agree _____

Slightly disagree _____

Strongly disagree _____

FIGURE 12.1 Example of Poorly Constructed Rating Scale Questions

general rule of thumb is that between four and seven response categories provide sufficient discrimination. However, if you do decide to use additional response options, you should be very certain that the finer distinctions represented in the scale options (such as the nine-item set below) are relevant and meaningful to the respondent. Consider the following two rating scales:

Very strongly agree	Very strongly agree
Slightly agree	Strongly agree
Neither agree nor disagree	Somewhat agree
Slightly disagree	Slightly agree
Strongly disagree	Neither agree nor disagree
	Slightly disagree
	Somewhat disagree
	Strongly disagree
	Very strongly disagree

The five-point scale assumes that respondents are able to evaluate the direction and general strength of their opinion. The nine-point scale assumes that respondents are able to make extremely fine distinctions.

Second, you must determine whether the scale should be balanced or unbalanced. A balanced scale provides an equal number of response categories on both ends of the continuum and the response options mirror each other. The prior believability question uses a balanced scale where there are an equal number of positive and negative choices and the adjectives used on the positive end are the same as those used on the negative end of the scale. An unbalanced scale violates either or both the characteristics of a balanced scale, for example:

To what extent are you pleased or displeased with the ability of Head & Shoulders shampoo to manage your dandruff?

Pleased	_____
Slightly displeased	_____
Somewhat displeased	_____
Strongly displeased	_____
Very strongly displeased	_____

It is recommended that unbalanced scales only be used in circumstances where the direction of response is generally known in advance of the research and finer distinctions on one end of the continuum are desired. Beyond this unique situation, we recommend against their use for two reasons:

- *Bias.* The question has the potential to bias the respondent. The appearance of four negative options and only one positive response option (as in the prior example) may lead respondents to believe that they should be displeased with the product.

- *Problems with data analysis and interpretation.* Data analysis is more complex versus balanced scales. An unbalanced scale is not a true interval measure because there are not equal distances between all scale options, and as a result the number of appropriate statistical procedures is limited and interpretation is often problematic.

Third, assuming that a balanced scale is used, you must decide whether the scale should contain an odd or even number of response options. Question A in Figure 12.2 uses an even number of categories, while Question B seeks to acquire the same information using an odd number of categories. Note that when an odd number of categories is used, the middle category is generally designated as "neutral," which is *not* the same as "no opinion." The decision to use odd numbers versus even numbers of response categories generally reflects your assumptions regarding the respondent's state of mind. Advocates of even-numbered categories avoid neutral points because they believe that attitudes cannot be neutral and that respondents should be forced to indicate some degree of attitude or opinion. Others argue that in many cases consumers may indeed be neutral and should be allowed to express that state of opinion.

Lastly, you must decide whether the question will use a frame of reference. *Noncomparative rating scales* ask a respondent to assign a rating without an explicit

(A) Even number of scale options.

To what extent do you agree or disagree with the statement: "Children under the age of 15 should have their parents approval before setting up an account on a social networking site such as Facebook."

Strongly agree   _____

Slightly agree   _____

Slightly disagree   _____

Strongly disagree   _____

(B) Odd number of scale options.

To what extent do you agree or disagree with the statement: "Children under the age of 15 should have their parents approval before setting up an account on a social networking site such as Facebook."

Strongly agree   _____

Slightly agree   _____

Neither agree nor disagree   _____

Slightly disagree   _____

Strongly disagree   _____

FIGURE 12.2   Odd and Even Number of Scale Options

frame of reference. For example, a scale designed to assess overall reactions to a specific commercial might ask:

> **Think about the commercial that you just saw. How believable or unbelievable would you say that the commercial was?**

Each respondent would answer this question using whatever frame of reference he or she prefers. Some respondents might compare the test commercial to other commercials in the same category, while others might compare it to "the last ads I saw," "the average ad," or "ads I like." The absence of an explicit frame of reference is appropriate whenever the research requires an absolute rating. *Comparative rating scales* provide a frame of reference, for example:

> **Think about the commercial that you just saw. How believable or unbelievable would you say that the commercial was compared to other beer advertising?**

As the name implies, comparative rating scales are appropriate whenever the research requires a relative rating.

ALTERNATIVE FORMATS FOR RATING SCALES.   The considerations for rating scales discussed in the prior section assume that all possible response options are labeled. This does not necessarily need to be the case, especially if greater differentiation among response options is likely to be of value. The four approaches shown in Figure 12.3 illustrate this flexibility in presenting a rating scale.

Question: Consider the commercial you just saw. How believable or unbelievable would you say the commercial was?

Possible Scale Options:

Please circle the number that best reflects your opinion.

Very believable   1   2   3   4   5   6   7   Very unbelievable

Please place an "X" in the space that best reflects your opinion.

_____ Very believable

_____

_____

_____ Neither believable nor unbelievable

_____

_____

_____ Very unbelievable

Please place an "X" in the space that best reflects your opinion.

Very Believable			Neither Believable nor Unbelievable			Very Unbelievable

In the space below, use any number between "1" and "10" to indicate your opinion. Higher numbers indicate higher levels of believability.

_____

FIGURE 12.3 Alternative Formats for Rating Scales

Beyond flexibility in the design of a single rating scale, it is also possible to combine individual but related scales into a single "super-question," for example:

> Think about Wal-Mart's recent attempts to promote its commitment to the environment. Read each phrase below and then indicate the extent to which you agree or disagree that the phrase describes Wal-Mart's environmental efforts. For each phrase, indicate your opinion by placing a check in the appropriate column.

	Strongly Agree	Slightly Agree	Slightly Disagree	Strongly Disagree
Is doing so only for profit	____	____	____	____
Is sincere	____	____	____	____
Is a good corporate citizen	____	____	____	____
Is a leader	____	____	____	____
Is exploitive	____	____	____	____

SEMANTIC DIFFERENTIAL. The semantic differential asks a respondent to rate an object on a number of related, seven-point scales bounded on each end by one of two bipolar adjectives. The following is an example of the semantic differential, in this case one used to evaluate reactions to a product spokesperson:

> Think about the spokesperson you just saw in the commercial. We'd like to know your reactions to this person. Each line below presents two opposite adjectives. On each line, please place a check to indicate your opinion of the spokesperson, where the closer your check is to one of the adjectives, the stronger you believe that adjective describes your reactions.

Trustworthy	____	____	____	____	____	____	____	Untrustworthy
Uninformative	____	____	____	____	____	____	____	Informative
Insincere	____	____	____	____	____	____	____	Sincere
Qualified	____	____	____	____	____	____	____	Unqualified

Two considerations are important in the use of semantic differential scales. First, the semantic differential may be unfamiliar to many respondents. Consequently, instructions must explicitly explain how to mark the scales. Second, care must be taken as to the placement of the bipolar adjectives. As seen in the prior example, adjectives appearing on the right side of the scale are both positive and negative. This increases the likelihood that the respondent will read each set of adjectives. Once the questionnaire has been administered, for purposes of data analysis and ease of presentation, all positive adjectives can be numbered similarly and placed on the same side of the continuum.

Ratio Level Questions

Questions at the ratio level measure objects, behaviors, and beliefs on a continuum with a fixed, zero origin. Placement on this continuum reflects the degree to which the measured object, behavior, or belief possesses more, less, or even none of the target characteristic. A common form of a ratio measure is the constant sum question.

A constant sum question is a ratio measure that requires a respondent to divide a preset quantity (the constant sum) among two or more objects or attributes in a way that reflects the respondent's relative preference for each object, the relative importance of each attribute or the degree to which the target object possesses each attribute. The general form of a constant sum question is as follows.

> Think about the reasons why you purchase a particular children's cereal. Some potential reasons are in the following list. We are interested in knowing the relative importance of these reasons in your purchase decision. Assume that you have 100 points. Divide the points among the following reasons to indicate the relative importance of each reason. The more points you give something, the more important it is. You can give as many or as few points as you wish to each reason. Please make certain that your total equals 100 points.

All natural	_____
Children like it	_____
Low fat	_____
Low price	_____
Low sugar	_____
TOTAL	_____100_____

The form of this question illustrates the characteristics of a well-written constant sum question: the focus for allocation is explicit (influence on purchase decision), the respondent's task is clearly described (allocate the points), and the criterion for point allocation is clear (more importance is reflected in more points).

There are two considerations in the writing of constant sum questions. First, the number of options needs to be manageable. Respondents generally have little trouble allocating points for up to about seven items. Beyond this, data quality tends to be lower. Second, the number of points to be allocated needs to be determined. While there is no rule for setting points, the total selected should be reasonable and easily divisible given the number of items (25 or 100 are the most common point totals used).

DEVELOPING OPEN-ENDED QUESTIONS

Quantitative research studies do not exclusively utilize closed-ended questions. Open-ended questions are also used to measure attitudes, beliefs, perceptions, and behaviors. In addition to the considerations relevant to all question types discussed in the next section, the writing of open-ended questions entails the following special considerations.

The question must be truly open-ended. Open-ended questions are used to minimize or eliminate potential bias when presenting a respondent with predetermined sets of responses. Thus, open-ended questions must be worded so that the respondent is permitted to respond in his or her own words without bias from the interviewer. Consider the question: "How satisfied are you with the product?" While this may appear to be an open-ended question, it is not. The interviewer has biased the respondent by assuming that he or she is in fact satisfied. A truly open-ended question does not presume which dimension of feelings, analysis or thought will be salient or meaningful for the respondent. Thus, a better open-ended question would ask: "What are your thoughts and feelings toward the product?"

The question must incorporate probes. Initial responses to an open-ended question generally lack depth. Respondents often give the easiest, most top-of-mind answer to an open-ended question. Additionally, respondents may not provide a response because they think it is obvious. For these reasons, probes must be used to determine whether there are additional attitudes, perceptions, etc. Common probes include: "Is there anything else?" "Do you have any additional thoughts or opinions?" and " Does anything else come to mind?" Following is an example of the use of probes in open-ended questions:

> What thoughts or feelings did you have as you watched the commercial? PROBE: Did you have any other thoughts or feelings? PROBE: "Anything else?" CONTINUE PROBING UNTIL NO FURTHER RESPONSE.

The question should be single-minded. Each open-ended request for information should be asked as a separate question. The independence of questions makes it easier for the respondent to focus on the specific request for information and facilitates question coding, analysis, and interpretation. For example, the question "Do any strengths and weaknesses of Suave shampoo come to mind?" should be divided into two separate questions: "Do any strengths of Suave shampoo come to mind?" and "Do any weaknesses of Suave shampoo come to mind?"

CONSIDERATIONS IN QUESTION DEVELOPMENT

Thus far we have seen that you have many options for the form of a particular measurement question. Different levels of measurement and types of measures within a level are often appropriate and available. However, regardless of the specific type of question or scale selected, all questions must satisfy a core set of requirements. This section describes these requirements.

Explicitly state the respondents' task in simple language. The question should clearly state what respondents must do to adequately answer the question. Respondents must be told whether they should state their opinion in their own words, how and where to place a mark to indicate their opinion, or order objects to represent relative rank. Do not assume that a respondent intuitively knows how to answer a specific type of survey question.

Use simple, active sentences and commonly used language. Questionnaires should communicate and facilitate response. They are not a device for impressing a respondent with the question-writer's literary skills. Additionally, avoid the use of industry or specialized jargon. If such jargon must be used, make certain that it is defined as part of the question. The following question illustrates what not to do.

> Think about the times that you were watching television and saw a commercial for which you had either a positive or negative reaction, that is, for which you felt good or bad during or after seeing the commercial. In these instances what in the commercial, that is, what visual or oral element, was the underlying stimulus for the causation of these feelings?

Avoid bias. Biased or leading questions implicitly communicate your point of view as part of the question, for example:

> Is it true that you still purchase white bread?
>
> Many people are engaged in activities to improve the environment. Which of the activities shown in the following list are you doing to improve the environment?

When respondents hear these questions, there is an increased probability that they will state what they think you want to hear as opposed to their own attitude or opinion. Questions can also be biased in a more subtle manner. For example, instructing a respondent to "Use the following scale to indicate how much you like the advertisement" implies that the respondent is expected to have liked versus disliked the commercial. To avoid this type of bias, a question should present both alternatives, for example, "Use the following scale to indicate how much you liked or disliked the commercial." Finally, leading a respondent also biases the question and response. Questions should not begin with phrases such as "Don't you think . . ." or "Wouldn't you agree that . . ."

Avoid multiple informational requests in a single question. Similar to considerations for writing an open-ended question, each question should have a single-minded focus. Instead of asking "What is your favorite brand of shampoo and how often do you use it?" ask two questions. First ask "What is your favorite brand of shampoo?" and then ask "How often do you use it?" The separation of questions makes it easier for a respondent to answer and facilitates data coding and analysis. Moreover, the elimination of multiple informational requests greatly reduces problems in data interpretation. For example, a "yes" response to the question "Are you aware of cigarette advertising and do you approve?" may be in response to either the first part (awareness), the second part (approval), or both parts. You have no means of determining to which part of the question the "yes" refers.

Avoid ambiguity. Ambiguous words are words that are open to multiple interpretations. All words used in a question should be unambiguous in their interpretation, even when the questions appear on their face to be extremely simple, for example, "What kind of shampoo do you use?" Some respondents may interpret "kind" to refer to the brand name, while others may interpret "kind" to mean form (gel or liquid) or type (dandruff, conditioning, or regular).

The problem of ambiguity is especially pronounced when one attempts to measure quantities and time. Consider the following response options:

Very long ago	Infrequently
Long ago	Sometimes
Recently	Often
Very recently	

Both scales of options are ambiguous because respondents can provide multiple, idiosyncratic interpretations to the descriptors. One respondent might interpret "recently" to mean "yesterday," while another might interpret the same term to mean "within the past week." Similarly, respondents can provide multiple interpretations to words such as "often" and "sometimes." Ambiguity in the measurement of time and quantities can be eliminated through the use of specific numeric descriptions.

Avoid assumptions. Well-written questions do not presume or assume a particular respondent's state of mind. For example, asking "What did you like about the commercial?" presumes that the respondent did, in fact, like something. A better form of the question is: "What, if anything, did you like about the commercial?" Questions should also avoid assuming knowledge on the part of a respondent. For example, asking "What was the price of the last brand of toothpaste you purchased?" assumes that the respondent remembers the price. It would be better to first ask, "Do you recall the price of the last brand of toothpaste you purchased?" If the answer is "yes" then ask, "What was the price?"

Justify requests for personal information. Respondents are typically quite cooperative when asked for information on behaviors and attitudes as long as these requests are seen as legitimate and impersonal. However, respondents are often reluctant to provide personal information such as age, education, income, or information on sensitive topics, for example, finances or the use of personal hygiene products. In these latter instances, the probability of obtaining information is increased when you justify and explain the need for the requested information. A request for demographic and related types of information can be prefaced by a statement such as "The following questions will be used only to help us classify your responses." A request for sensitive information may be prefaced by a statement such as, "Now I'd like to ask you a few questions related to. . . . I know that these questions probe personal and perhaps sensitive areas, but I would really appreciate your cooperation. All of your answers, of course, are strictly confidential."

Provide a reasonable time frame for behavioral questions. All questions that measure behaviors need to provide a time period in which the target behavior took place and that time period needs to be reasonable given individuals' memory. While respondents will try to answer any question asked, the quality of the data provided declines significantly as time periods and memory demands increase. The first question below fails to provide any time period while the second question provides an inappropriately large time period for the behavior being measured:

> How many times do you visit YouTube?

> How many times did you visit YouTube in the past month?

A more appropriate approach to this question area would be:

> How many times did you visit YouTube in the past 24 hours?

QUESTION WRITING: AN EVALUATION

The target audience for the questionnaire shown in Figure 12.4 is college students. There is a problem with how every question is written. Read through the questionnaire and determine the problem with each question and then propose a solution. Once you've examined and rewritten each question, continue reading to assess your answers.

Question 1: The response categories are inappropriate. Almost all students will fall into the first category. The response categories are also not exhaustive (what about someone under age 18?) or exclusive (a 28-year old fits into two categories). The range of the categories is odd and without any apparent underlying rationale. Finally, the question does not collect data at the highest level of measurement. A better question would be:

> What is your age? _____

Question 2: The question asks for two pieces of information and yet only one set of response options is provided. It is possible for an individual to answer these questions "yes/yes," "yes/no," "no/yes" or "no/no" but none of these responses are possible given the way the question is written. At minimum, it is necessary to break the question into two:

> Do you find your classes interesting?
>
> Yes _____   No _____

> Do you find your classes useful?
>
> Yes _____   No _____

This approach, however, only allows us to assign responses to one of two categories, and does not allow us to distinguish the *degree* that classes are felt to be interesting or useful. A better approach to

---

CAMPUS SURVEY

1. What is your age?

[ ] 18–24   [ ] 24–28   [ ] 28–29   [ ] 30   [ ] 31 and older

2. Do you find your classes interesting and useful?

Yes   [ ]

No   [ ]

3. Do you plan on purchasing a new car?_____

4. What kind of computer do you plan on purchasing next?_____

5. Everyone we talk to has to tell us his or her income in order for us to classify his or her answers. It is important that you not lie to us. How much do you really make in an average year?

[ ] Under $5,000

[ ] $5,001 to $10,000

[ ] $10,001 to $20,000

[ ] $20,000 or more

6. How often do you read your college newspaper in a typical month?

Regularly [ ]   Often [ ]   Infrequently [ ]   Never [ ]

7. How much do you agree or disagree with the statement: "My campus newspaper is an objective source of information about campus activities."

[ ] Strongly disagree

[ ] Disagree

[ ] Slightly agree

[ ] Strongly disagree

[ ] Extremely unimportant

8. How much do you agree or disagree that a handheld calculator should have a lifetime warranty?

[ ] Extremely important

[ ] Important

[ ] Neither important nor unimportant

[ ] Unimportant

[ ] Extremely unimportant

9. Read each of the items shown below. Check all that apply to Apple.

___ Fun

___ Easy

___ Stylish

___ Contemporary

___ Cutting-edge

FIGURE 12.4 Sample College Student Survey Questions

10. Imagine that you are going to buy a personal computer. Thinking about approximate prices, durability, speed, functionality, warranty, chip manufacturer, availability of software, and technical support, please allocate points to indicate how important the following characteristics of a computer are. Put the characteristics shown below in order.

_____ Color

_____ Style

_____ Size

11. Here are five points. Show me what is important about pizza below.

Taste	_____	Online ordering	_____
Delivery time	_____	Friend's recommendations	_____
Price	_____	Accepts charge cards	_____
Location	_____	Runs daily specials	_____
Advertising	_____		

FIGURE 12.4   (Continued)

improving this question would be to increase the level of measurement and assess these attitudes through rating scales:

How interesting or uninteresting do you find your classes?

Very interesting   _____

Slightly interesting   _____

Slightly uninteresting   _____

Very uninteresting   _____

How useful or not useful do you find your classes?

Very useful   _____

Slightly useful   _____

Slightly useless   _____

Very useless   _____

Question 3: This is not a true open-ended question as only a "yes" or "no" is a sufficient response. "New" is ambiguous; does "new" refer to a brand new car (i.e., never had another owner) or does it refer to any car (regardless of the number of prior owners) that would be new for the respondent? Finally, there is no time frame. The following question resolves these problems:

How likely or unlikely are you to purchase a new (never before owned) car within the next three months?

Extremely likely   _____

Likely   _____

Unlikely   _____

Extremely unlikely   _____

Question 4: The question assumes that the respondent is in fact planning to purchase a computer. There is no time frame. "Kind" is ambiguous;

does "kind" refer to type (laptop, tower), make (Mac, PC), or function (best for games, best for graphics)? The following series of questions resolves these problems:

1. Are you planning on buying a computer within the next three months?

   Yes   [ ] → CONTINUE WITH QUESTION 2

   No   [ ] → SKIP TO QUESTION 3

2. What brand of computers are you considering purchasing? Check as many or as few (or even no) brands shown in the list below.

   Apple   _____
   Dell   _____
   HP   _____
   Sony   _____
   Toshiba   _____
   Other   _____

3. SURVEY CONTINUES

Question 5:   The lead-in question wording is inappropriate. The multiple-choice categories are exhaustive but not exclusive (a person earning $20,000 fits into two options). While the category ranges are generally appropriate for college students, there should be a "zero" category to allow the researcher to distinguish those with no income from those with a low income. Finally, since this question is asking for sensitive information, a "decline to answer" option is appropriate. A better alternative is:

In order to classify your answers, we'd like to know your annual income. As I indicated earlier, this answer as well as all your other answers are strictly confidential. Into which of the following ranges does your income fall?

Zero - no income   _____
$1 to $5,000   _____
$5,001 to $10,000   _____
$10,001 to $15,000   _____
$15,001 to $20,000   _____
$20,001 and over   _____
Refuse to answer   _____

Note that this question does violate the rule of asking for data at the highest level of measurement. However, individuals are more willing to indicate where within a range of income theirs falls rather than answering the question "What is your annual income?"

Question 6:   The time frame is much too long for anyone to recall accurately. "How often" is vague; does this refer to the number of times per day that a respondent might read the same issue or the number of different issues? The scale is inappropriate as the terms are vague and subject to multiple interpretations. Finally, data can be collected at a higher level of measurement. A better version of the question is:

Your college newspaper is issued Monday to Friday. How many issues did you read last week? _____ (Please fill in a number between 0 and 5.)

Question 7: The response options are incorrect as the positive choices are not mirror images of the negative choices. While the scale items can appear in either order of agreement (agree . . . disagree, disagree . . . agree), the order should be the same at that which appears in the question lead-in, in this case the order should be agree . . . disagree. The following question fixes these problems:

How much do you agree or disagree with the statement: "My school newspaper is an objective source of information about campus activities."

Strongly agree _____

Slightly agree _____

Slightly disagree _____

Strongly disagree _____

Question 8: The lead-in to the question is acceptable. The scale is also acceptable. The scale, however, does not match the lead-in. The question below has a consistent lead-in and scale:

How important or unimportant is it to you that a computer have a lifetime warranty?

Very important _____

Slightly important _____

Neither important nor unimportant _____

Slightly unimportant _____

Very unimportant _____

Question 9: The instruction "check all that apply" is biased in that it assumes the respondent will check at least one. The list should contain a mix of positive and negative words/phrases placed in random order, but only positive words/phrases are present. Finally, "Apple" is vague and ambiguous. Is the respondent to rate Apple the company, the iPhone, iPod, or other Apple product? Better instructions and list of options would be:

Think about Apple, not any one particular product but rather the brand overall and what you think the brand represents. Which of the following words or phrases describe how you feel about Apple, the brand? You can check as many or as few (or even no items) as apply.

Fun _____

Boring _____

Classy _____

Stylish _____

Outdated _____

Overpriced _____

Cutting-edge _____

Trend-setter _____

Question 10:   The lead-in is written very poorly: there is no specific indication for the criteria to be used to evaluate the listed items; there is no direction for how the respondent is to indicate the rank order; it is overly complex. There are also problems with the list of items: the list of items is different than that discussed in the lead-in, and items should be in alphabetical order. A better question would be:

> Imagine that you are going to buy a personal laptop computer. I'd like to find out what is most important to you in this decision. Below are five characteristics of a personal computer. Place a "1" next to the characteristic that would exert the greatest influence, a "2" by the next most important characteristic, through "5" which you would place next to the characteristic you feel exerts the least amount of influence on your purchase decision. There can be no ties and please use each number only once.

> Color   _____
> Price   _____
> Processor speed _____
> Screen size   _____
> Weight   _____

Question 11:   The lead-in provides no guidance for what is being rated, how the point allocation should take place, or what criteria should be used for the allocation. The list is too long and should be in alphabetical order. Finally, and the number of points is too small. An improved question would be:

> Think about the reasons why you purchase pizza from a particular business. Some potential reasons are in the following list. We are interested in knowing the relative importance of these reasons in your purchase decision; that is, why you purchase from one company versus another. Assume that you have 100 points. Divide the points among the following reasons to indicate the relative importance of each reason. The more points you give something, the more important it is. You can give as many or as few points as you wish to each reason. Please make certain that your total equals 100 points.

> Accepts credit cards   _____
> Delivery time   _____
> Friend's recommendation   _____
> Location   _____
> Online ordering   _____
> **TOTAL**   __**100**__

APPLYING CHAPTER CONCEPTS

This chapter's online supplemental readings provides two examples of superior research. Both studies are creative in their approach and insightful in their findings and implications. Relevant to the discussion in this chapter, both studies use well-written survey questions to collect the data. Beyond these attributes, data analysis is clear and informative, and the presentations themselves are visually interesting, well organized, and easy to follow.

Razorfish Digital Brand Experience Report/2009

Razorfish[1] is one of the world's largest interactive marketing and technology companies. Razorfish's success is in great part dependent upon how well it understands consumer behaviors and attitudes as well as media developments. This understanding is often acquired through original research such as the Digital Brand Experience Report/2009. The Digital Brand Experience Report/2009 is designed to provide an in-depth understanding of how the evolving digital environment is changing the way that consumers interact with brands. Razorfish summarizes the key findings of the 1,000 interviews comprising the research as follows:

> Experience matters. A lot. So much so that experiences are becoming the new advertising or marketing. And these experiences are having an inordinate amount of impact on how consumers perceive a brand and ultimately purchase products. Moreover, we also found that consumers are actively engaged with brands across the entire digital spectrum. Consumers may be in control but so are brands which are so deeply embedded in the culture that consumers can't imagine not making them a part of their world—on Facebook, Twitter or even their own blogs.[2]

The full Digital Brand Experience Report/2009, including the actual survey questions and data set, is provided as one of this chapter's online supplemental readings. As you read through the report, note

- the overall flow of the presentation; that is, how the authors move from topic to topic in a way that builds a cohesive, coherent picture of the findings and implications.
- the successful integration of data tables with the text.
- how the authors go beyond data tables to visually present and summarize key insights and implications.
- how the data and findings themselves are seamlessly integrated into the narrative without breaking the narrative flow.
- the Executive Summary (pages 7 to 12) which both clearly summarizes the key findings and encourages the reader to read the more detailed findings.
- how secondary research is cited and integrated with the findings to provide a context for interpreting the current research findings.

Finally, keep in mind that the findings are of value *only* because the survey questions themselves were well-written and relevant to the research focus. Be certain to review the survey questions and detailed findings beginning on page 41 of the report.

People From Cossette

Cossette[3] is an international, full-service communications company with offices in Canada, the United States, and the United Kingdom. It is one of the top communications companies in the world, servicing clients locally, nationally, and globally. The Cossette 2009 Social Media Study was designed to gather insights on consumers who use social media, specifically, to provide an in-depth understanding of social media penetration as well a social media users' motivations, behaviors, and attitudes. More than 3,000 individuals participated in the online survey.

The full report is provided as an online supplemental reading. As you read through the report, note that this report, although different than the Digital Brand Experience Report/2009 in visual approach and organization, nevertheless shares many of that report's strengths with regard to

- the overall flow of the presentation. Note how the authors have logically organized and sequenced the topics of discussion, moving within a topic from more general to more detailed findings.
- the successful integration of data tables with the textual explanations, making certain that the text provides a summary of the findings rather than simply repeating all of the numeric information from the data tables.
- how the authors creatively use data tables to visually present and summarize key insights and implications. Large amounts of complex data are presented in a way that makes the findings readily accessible.
- how the implications of the findings are made explicit and justified by the underlying data.

Finally, as with the Digital Brand Experience Report/2009, the strength and value of this research is a direct reflection of the quality of the survey questions used to collect the data. As you read through the presentation, be certain to notice the actual survey questions that are shown on the bottom of the presentation slides.

SUMMARY

Researchers ask questions to obtain the information needed for advertising decision making. Better-written questions obtain better, more reliable, and insightful information.

Questions may be written at one of four levels of measurement: nominal, ordinal, interval, and ratio where questions written at different levels have different uses and characteristics:

- Nominal level questions are primarily used to classify responses and respondents. Common forms of nominal level questions are dichotomous, multiple-choice, and checklist. Nominal level questions are defined by response options that are exhaustive and mutually exclusive.
- Ordinal level questions, such as rank order questions, ask respondents to order a set of objects according to an explicit criterion or dimension.
- Interval level questions, such as rating scales and the semantic differential, allow researchers to determine both order and distance between responses.

- Ratio level questions, such as constant sum, have a true zero point and thus allow for magnitude comparisons (i.e., a conclusion that Brand A is twice as preferred as Brand B).

The quality of open- and closed-ended questions can be improved by adhering to several "rules of thumb" for question development: use simple language and simple, active sentences; avoid bias, ambiguity, assumptions, and multiple requests for information; justify requests for personal information; and provide a reasonable time frame for behavioral questions.

Review Questions

1. What are the functions of *dichotomous* question? At what level of measurement is this question type written?

2. What is a *multiple-choice* question? At what level of measurement is this question type written?

3. What are the defining characteristics of multiple-choice questions?

4. Why is having a "zero" or "none" response important in classification questions?

5. What are the defining characteristics of *checklist* questions? At what level of measurement is this question type written?

6. What are the defining characteristics of *rank order* questions? At what level of measurement is this question type written?

7. What are the defining characteristics of *interval level* questions?

8. How does one determine the number of response options for a *rating scale* question?

9. Why is *frame of reference* an important consideration in rating scale questions?

10. What are the defining characteristics of *semantic differential* questions? At what level of measurement is this question type written?

11. Provide an example of a *ratio level* question. What are its defining characteristics?

12. What are important considerations in the creation of *open-ended* questions?

13. In what circumstances are open-ended questions more appropriate versus closed-ended questions?

14. What eight considerations help improve the quality of survey questions?

Application Exercises

Application exercises 1 through 3 reflect chapter content and discussion.

1. Each of the following questions has at least one problem with style or form. Identify the problem(s) associated with each question, and then rewrite the question so that it is a well-written survey question.

    a. How many pets do you currently own and what are their ages?

    b. What kind of car do you currently own?

    c. Everyone whom we talk to needs to tell us their income so that we can classify their answers. Into which of the following categories does your total after tax annual household income fall?

    under $10,000   _____
    $10,000 to $25,000   _____
    $25,000 to $28,000   _____
    $29,000 to $31,500   _____
    over $31,500   _____

    d. Which of the following best reflects the extent to which you agree or disagree with this statement: "Most corporations in America are concerned about the environment."

    Strongly agree   _____
    Agree   _____
    Neither   _____
    Slightly disagree   _____
    Strongly disagree   _____

e. To what extent do you plan on purchasing a new car in the next 12 months?

Yes   _____

No   _____

Not sure   _____

f. Most parents are very concerned about how they will pay for their child's college education. I'm sure you are one of those parents. These parents all try to save as much as they can for their child's education. I'm sure you are, too. How much money, on average, would you say you save per year for your child's education?

None   _____

Under $1,000   _____

Under $5,000   _____

Under $10,000   _____

More than $10,000 _____

g. How often do you shampoo your hair?

Very frequently   _____

Frequently   _____

Occasionally   _____

Infrequently   _____

Never   _____

h. Please put the brands below in order to indicate your preference.

Coke   _____

Dr. Pepper   _____

Sprite   _____

Mountain Dew   _____

Red Bull   _____

2. The Quicko Baking Company has used past research to identify four important attributes in a cake mix: ease of preparation, consistency, color, and aroma. Quicko must now decide which of these four attributes is the most important to the target consumer when he or she decides on the purchase of a cake mix. Use a rank order, rating scale, and constant sum question to identify the most important cake mix attribute. Which question type do you feel works the best? Why?

3. Millie Laboratories has just introduced a new dog flea collar called Prescription Flea Control. Now, it wishes to measure consumers' reactions to and perceptions of this flea collar before developing its new advertising campaign.

Millie developed a sampling plan and screened potential respondents for desired target audience characteristics and awareness of the Prescription Flea Control Collar as well as the flea collars marketed by Hartz and Pet-Pro. Questions 1 to 10 shown in Figure 12.5 are some of the questions asked of respondents. Review these questions and then address the following:

- Evaluate the form and style of each question. Is each acceptable as written? If not, how would you rewrite or revise the question?

- What types of questions are represented on the questionnaire? What level of measurement does each represent? Are the level of measurement and type of question appropriate for the type of information desired?

- There is a great deal of redundancy in this questionnaire. What other types of questions or scales could have been used to collect the desired information in a more efficient manner? Would there have been any sacrifice in the depth of information acquired by using these alternative approaches?

- Rewrite the questionnaire to reflect your views as to the best means for obtaining the desired information.

Application exercises 4 through 9 refer to the Razorfish Digital Brand Experience Report/2009 provided in the online supplemental readings.

4. Question 7 (presentation page 45) is a checklist question. Prepare a short paper that addresses the following with regard to using this question in future research: First, if the question is kept in this form, are there any additional options you would add to the original checklist? If so, what would the additional options be? Second, discuss the relative advantages and disadvantages of collecting this information through

1. We are interested in your overall opinion of the effectiveness of three flea collars. These collars are manufactured by Hartz, Millie Labs, and Pet-Pro. Please rank the flea collars marketed by these three companies by placing a "1" by the company with the most effective flea collar, a "2" by the next most effective, and a "3" by the least effective.

    Hartz   _____

    Millie Labs   _____

    Pet Pro   _____

2. Now I would like to have your opinion on a few statements that could be used to describe the flea collars manufactured by Hartz. If you agree completely with the statement, then give it a "10." If you disagree completely, then give it a "0." You can use any number between "0" and "10" to indicate the extent to which you agree or disagree.

    Are safe for my pet   _____

    Are made without pesticides   _____

    Are FDA approved   _____

    Work for at least 90 days   _____

    Are a good value for the money   _____

3. Now I would like to have your opinion on a few statements that could be used to describe the flea collars manufactured by Millie Labs. As before, if you agree completely with the statement, then give it a "10." If you disagree completely, then give it a "0." You can use any number between "0" and "10" to indicate the extent to which you agree or disagree.

    Are safe for my pet   _____

    Are made without pesticides   _____

    Are FDA approved   _____

    Work for at least 90 days   _____

    Are a good value for the money   _____

4. Lastly, I would like to have your opinion on a few statements that could be used to describe the flea collars manufactured by Pet-Pro. Again, if you agree completely with the statement, then give it a "10." If you disagree completely, then give it a "0." You can use any number between "0" and "10" to indicate the extent to which you agree or disagree.

    Are safe for my pet   _____

    Are made without pesticides   _____

    Are FDA approved   _____

    Work for at least 90 days   _____

    Are a good value for the money   _____

FIGURE 12.5 Survey Questions for Application Exercise 3

5. Think about your last five purchases of dog flea protection collars. How many were of each of the following brands?

Hartz   _____

Millie Labs   _____

Pet-Pro   _____

Store brand/generic   _____

Other   _____

6. Think about your next five purchases of dog flea protection collars. How many will be of each of the following brands?

Hartz   _____

Millie Labs   _____

Pet-Pro   _____

Store brand/generic   _____

Other   _____

7. When deciding on a dog flea collar, how important or unimportant is it to you that the collar has FDA approval?

Extremely important   _____

Important   _____

Unimportant   _____

Extremely unimportant   _____

8. When deciding on a dog flea collar, how important or unimportant is it to you that the collar is pesticide free?

Extremely important   _____

Important   _____

Unimportant   _____

Extremely unimportant   _____

9. Finally, I would like to ask you a few questions to help us classify your answers. Into which of the following age groups does your age fall?

Under 25   _____

25 to 34   _____

35 to 44   _____

45 to 54   _____

55 and older   _____

10. Which of the following describes your highest level of education?

Not a high school graduate   _____

High school graduate   _____

Some college   _____

College graduate   _____

Advanced degree   _____

FIGURE 12.5   (Continued)

an open-ended question versus the checklist approach.

5. Question 10 (presentation page 46) is a classification question. Prepare a point of view that addresses the following: First, leaving the question as is, what are the advantages and disadvantages of following up this question with an open-ended question that probes *why* a home page has or has not been customized? Second, discuss the advantages and disadvantages of following up this question (to be asked only of those who answered "yes") with a question designed to identify the specific *way(s)* in which the home page had been customized.

6. Question 14 (presentation page 49) asks for all sources of online news. What is your point of view regarding asking a companion question that requests the respondent to identify his/her *primary* source of online news?

7. Question 16 (presentation page 50) asks respondents to indicate how often they participate in various brand-related activities. Prepare a short paper that presents your point of view regarding the response options available to the respondents. Be certain to answer these two questions: First, what are the strengths and weaknesses of the current options? Second, what are the relative advantages and disadvantages of using a specific time frame (e.g., once a day or more, once every two to three days, etc.) versus the current options?

8. Questions 17 and 18 (presentation page 51) are classification questions that probe the effects of brand-related experiences on brand attitudes and purchase behaviors. Prepare a point of view that discusses the advantages and disadvantages of asking one or more open-ended questions after each question (to be asked only of those who answered "yes") designed to identify the specific experiences that affected attitudes and behaviors. Write out this sequence of questions.

9. Imagine that you want to expand the list of outcomes measured in questions 20, 22, 24, 26, and 29 (presentation pages 52, 53, 54, 55, 57). Propose three additions to the list and provide a rationale in support of the value of these additions.

Application exercises 10 through 14 refer to the Cossette 2009 Social Media Study provided in the online supplemental readings.

10. Questions 10 and 11 (presentation pages 9 and 10) ask about "ever" consulting different information sources. Imagine that these questions will be used in future research. Prepare a short paper that contrasts the relative strengths and weaknesses of the current approach with two alternative approaches: (1) consultation *within different time periods* (i.e., "yesterday," "within last week," etc.) and (2) the *amount* of consultation (i.e., the number of times consulted within a given time period.) Conclude your paper with your recommended approach. Be certain to support your recommendation.

11. Questions 6 through 9 (presentation pages 12 and 13) use open-ended questions to collect information on respondents' behaviors. Prepare a short paper that contrasts this approach to the use of a checklist question to collect similar information. What are the relative strengths and weaknesses of each approach? Conclude your paper with your recommended approach. Be certain to support your recommendation.

12. Question 12 (presentation page 33) asks respondents to rate the relative value of "information produced by other citizens" to traditional sources of advertising such as television and radio. Prepare a short paper that proposes two other ways to measure the relative value of citizen-produced information. Write the actual survey questions. Then, evaluate the strengths and weaknesses of the approach used in the Cossette research and your two proposed approaches. Conclude your paper with your recommended approach. Be certain to support your recommendation.

13. Question 29 (presentation page 44) probes social media users' self-image using a 10-point rating scale. Imagine that you have been asked to expand this list of self-image items. Propose six more statements that could be added to the existing list. Include these items in a short paper that provides a rationale for the proposed statements.

14. Question 29 (presentation page 45) also probes social media users' perceptions of the social networking environment. Imagine that you have been asked to expand this list of items. Propose six more statements that could be added to the existing list. Include these items in a short paper that provides a rationale for the proposed statements.

Endnotes

1. The web site for Razorfish is http://www.razorfish.com.
2. Razorfish (2009). "Feed: The PDF" at http://feed.razorfish.com.
3. Cossette is located at http://www.cossette.com.

CHAPTER 13

Questionnaire Design

The creation of well-written survey questions is a critical step in the research process. But, your set of questions cannot be asked haphazardly. They must be organized in a way that elicits the appropriate responses from each participant in the research study. The most commonly used method for organizing questions is, not surprisingly, the questionnaire, which can be thought of as the conduit between researcher and respondent. In this chapter, you'll learn a systematic approach to questionnaire construction.

***

When you are done reading this chapter, you should have a better understanding of how to:

- determine the type of questionnaire to use in different research situations
- describe and prepare the parts of a questionnaire
- prepare and lay out the questionnaire
- explain how pretesting can dramatically improve the quality of the questionnaire and the information that it collects.

The quality of the information gathered by a questionnaire is dependent on how carefully the questionnaire is constructed. Not all questionnaires successfully collect the desired information. Some questionnaires are organized in a confusing manner and, consequently, respondents are unable to devote full attention to answering the survey questions, instead devoting considerable energy to trying to figure out what is being asked. Some questionnaires bias responses to questions asked toward the end of the interview with earlier questions. Some questionnaires are incomplete and, as a result, the researcher is left without the data to answer many of the questions that motivated the research in the first place. Careful and precise preparation of the questionnaire is needed to overcome these and other difficulties.

The best way to avoid errors when preparing the questionnaire is to take a systematic approach to design and construction. The key issues that should be addressed in preparing the questionnaire are shown in Figure 13.1. The remainder of this chapter discusses each of these issues.

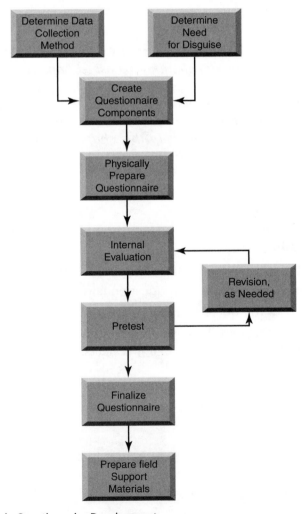

FIGURE 13.1 Steps in Questionnaire Development

DETERMINE THE DATA COLLECTION METHOD

Chapter 10 discussed the four primary approaches to data collection: personal interviews, mail, telephone, and online. Not only does each approach have a unique set of strengths and weaknesses, but each approach also requires different types of questionnaires. Questionnaires written for face-to-face interviews look and read differently than questionnaires written for telephone or self-administered online studies. In these latter circumstances, an absence of face-to-face contact generally requires a less complex questionnaire. Additionally, self-administered questionnaires and questionnaires administered by an interviewer are written for the "eye" and can use pictures or a variety of manipulatives. Telephone questionnaires are typically written more conversationally for the "ear" and, obviously, cannot use pictures or other visual aids. Thus, as shown in Figure 13.1, the first step in questionnaire design requires the selection of the data collection method.

DETERMINE THE NEED FOR DISGUISE

The next step in the questionnaire design process determines the need for disguise.

Disguise refers to the extent to which the purpose and/or sponsor of the research is hidden from the respondent. *Undisguised questionnaires* make the purpose and sponsor of the research explicit to the respondent, often through the questionnaire's introduction or the wording and focus of specific questions. *Disguised questionnaires* provide a general overview of the research but hide more detailed information on research goals and sponsor from the respondent. The decision whether to disguise a questionnaire depends on the extent to which it is felt that a respondent's knowledge of the purpose and/or sponsor of the research will influence his or her responses. The greater the likelihood of influence or bias, the more appropriate it becomes to disguise the questionnaire.

When you decide to disguise your questionnaire, you must make certain that there are no clues as to the specific purpose and/or sponsor of the research. Consider Shell Oil Corporation, which may want to obtain consumers' perceptions of it and its products compared to other oil companies. An undisguised questionnaire might use the following introduction:

> Thank you for agreeing to participate in this study of consumer opinions, sponsored by a major oil company. In this study we will ask you about your opinions toward a number of oil and gasoline companies and their products and services. Remember, there are no right or wrong answers to any questions. Just tell me your honest opinion.

This introduction leaves little doubt as to the focus of the interview. However, consumers' responses might be biased by knowing that the research is sponsored by an oil company. Consequently, it might be wise to disguise the questionnaire as follows:

> Thank you for agreeing to participate in this study of consumer opinions. In this study we will ask you about your opinions toward a number of different companies and their products and services. Remember, there are no right or wrong answers to any questions. Just tell me your honest opinion.

Finally, there are times that you might decide that a mixed approach is best. In these cases, you begin the survey in the disguised mode and then move to a series of undisguised questions.

When thinking about the use of disguise, keep in mind that disguised and undisguised questionnaires provide different perspectives on the same set of information. This is because each type of questionnaire provides a different frame of reference for the respondent. In the prior example, a disguised questionnaire implicitly compares Shell to a number of consumer product companies, some of which are oil companies and some of which are not. The undisguised questionnaire only compares Shell to other oil companies. It is entirely possible that the ratings of Shell obtained in these two formats will be different. Neither is correct nor incorrect. It is just important that you keep the frame of reference in mind when evaluating the strengths and weaknesses of a disguised versus undisguised format for a particular research problem.

CREATE QUESTIONNAIRE COMPONENTS

After you choose the type of questionnaire, you next create each of the four main components of the questionnaire: introduction, screener, main body of information questions, and classification questions (see Figure 13.1).

Introduction

The introduction is a statement that explains the purpose and goals of the research and asks for the respondent's cooperation and participation in the research study. The introduction's specific wording is dependent on the need for disguise, the complexity of the study, and the sensitive nature (if any) of the type of data collected. The goal of the introduction is to motivate the respondent to participate, thereby reducing nonresponse error (see Chapter 12). While the specific wording of questionnaire introductions will vary among research studies, there are some common elements that most introductions contain. These are:

- *an explicit or implicit reference to importance.* The introduction should communicate that the study itself is important (and is therefore worthy of the respondent's investment of time to complete the questionnaire) and that the respondent's own opinions are important (thereby increasing the likelihood of participation).

- *general information on the rationale and goals of the research.* The amount of detail will depend on the extent of disguise.

- *an explicit request for participation.* The introduction might say, "We would greatly appreciate you sharing your thoughts and opinions."

- *reassurance that the task of participating is not too burdensome or time-consuming.* You might say that "Most of the questions are easy and quick to answer. We anticipate that you can complete the survey in no more than 10 minutes."

- *the need for truthful answers,* for example: "We are interested in your opinions. There are no right or wrong answers."

- *the promise of confidentiality*, for example: "Your responses will be kept completely confidential. No one will see your individual answers."
- *the reassurance that this is real, legitimate research,* for example: "We are conducting this research to find out the opinions of people like you. This is not a sales pitch. We are not trying to sell you anything and no salesperson will call."

The level of detail provided in a questionnaire introduction varies among data collection methods. Introductions in face-to-face and telephone research tend to be relatively short. These introductions quickly explain the reason for the research, assure confidentiality and the absence of a "sales pitch," and invite the potential respondent to participate, for example:

Good morning. My name is Elyse McKenna and I am calling from Elyse McKenna Marketing Research, an independent marketing research company. I am not a salesperson and this is not a sales call. Instead, we are talking to a number of individuals like yourself to better understand their attitudes toward San Diego radio stations. The executives at these stations are very interested in the opinions of people like you. They will consider your opinions when deciding on their musical selections, radio personalities, promotions, and advertising. I have just a few questions to ask you and the entire survey will take 10 minutes or less. Most of the questions are easy and quick to answer and, of course, there are no right or wrong answers. We just need your truthful opinions. Naturally, all of your answers will be strictly confidential.

The introduction to mail or other self-administered questionnaires tends to be longer and more detailed, because in these situations there is no interviewer present to answer any of the respondent's questions, especially with regard to the study's purpose and use of the data. Additionally, the introduction to self-administered questionnaires must contain directions for returning the completed questionnaire. Photo 13.1 presents the introduction to a self-administered questionnaire for a radio station study.

Screener

A screener works like a gate: it admits into the study all individuals who possess all of the target characteristics and eliminates all the individuals who lack at least one of the identified characteristics. The use and characteristics of a screener, therefore, depends on the specifics of the research study's sample population.

Some studies are conducted among a random sample of the adult population. In these cases, a very brief or even no screener is typically necessary. More often, however, advertising research is conducted among the subsets of the total population that possess a specific combination of demographics and category- or product-related characteristics. In these cases, the introduction is followed by a screener, a short series of questions that identifies those respondents who should be included in the study. Screener complexity is dependent on the detail in the sample definition (see Chapter 4). Figure 13.2 presents a screener that can be used in a mall-intercept study. Note the importance of explicit instructions for following the screener flow and for determining whether the individual meets the research target audience characteristics. In this screener, the initial set of questions (Questions 1 to 3) screen for desired demographic and behavioral characteristics.

Elyse McKenna Marketing Research
48474 Tribortona Road
Randallville, Illinois 60021

June 23, 2010

Mr. Johan Harding
23837 High Crest Blvd.
Tolono, California 92009

Dear Mr. Harding:

Elyse McKenna Marketing Research is an independent marketing research company. We have been chosen by a number of Southern Illinois radio stations to find out what people like you think about your local radio programming and a number of different radio stations.

Your opinions, as a radio listener, are important to us. The executives and programmers at your local stations will consider your opinions when deciding on their musical selections, radio personalities, promotions, and advertising.

You can use the enclosed survey to let us know what you think. Just read each question carefully and then answer it honestly. There are no right or wrong answers and the entire survey can be completed in less than 10 minutes.

When you have completed the survey, please return it in the enclosed postage paid envelope.

I look forward to receiving your questionnaire. And, of course, all of your answers are strictly confidential. You do not have to put your name on the survey.

If you have any questions please do not hesitate to contact me at 555-765-9878.

Won't you take a few minutes to let us know what you think?

Best regards,

Elyse McKenna

Elyse McKenna

PHOTO 13.1 Introduction to a Self-Administered Questionnaire

Target Audience Definition: All respondents must be women between the ages of 25 and 49 who are employed full-time outside the home. All must have dieted at least once within the past 12 months. Those who are currently on a diet must have purchased (for personal consumption) a reduced calorie frozen dinner within the past week. Those who are not currently dieting may not have purchased (for personal consumption) a reduced calorie frozen dinner within the past month.

APPROACH WOMEN WHO APPEAR TO BE BETWEEN THE AGES OF 25 AND 49.

Hello, my name is _____ of Mall-Vue Research Services. Today, we are talking with a number of women to help us better understand their opinions and attitudes. We are trying to talk to different types of women so, before we begin, I'd like to ask you just a few short questions.

1. Into which of the following categories does your age fall?

under 25	❏	.... THANK AND DISCONTINUE
25 to 34	❏	.... CONTINUE WITH Q. 2
35 to 49	❏	.... CONTINUE WITH Q. 2
50 and older	❏	.... THANK AND DISCONTINUE

2. Are you currently employed full-time outside the home?

yes	❏	.... CONTINUE WITH Q. 3
no	❏	.... THANK AND DISCONTINUE

3. Have you dieted, that is, regulated the type and amount of your food consumption in order to maintain a desired weight or reduce your weight, in the last twelve months?

yes	❏	.... CONTINUE WITH Q. 4
no	❏	.... THANK AND DISCONTINUE

4. Are you currently on a diet?

yes	❏	.... CONTINUE WITH Q. 5
no	❏	.... SKIP TO Q. 6

5. Which of the following products have you purchased for your own personal consumption within the past week? READ LIST.

reduced calorie salad dressing	❏
reduced calorie soft drink	❏
reduced calorie frozen dinner	❏ ... IF YES, INVITE TO INTERVIEW
	IF NO, THANK AND DISCONTINUE

6. Which of the following products have you purchased for your own personal consumption within the past month? READ LIST.

reduced calorie salad dressing	❏
reduced calorie soft drink	❏
reduced calorie frozen dinner	❏ ... IF NO, INVITE TO INTERVIEW
	IF YES, THANK AND DISCONTINUE

FIGURE 13.2   Sample Screener

Question 4 continues screening for behavioral characteristics and permits a jump to the appropriate set of diet-related questions. Question 5 screens current dieters' purchase of reduced calorie frozen dinners, while Question 6 screens past dieters' purchase of reduced calorie frozen dinners. Note that the screener is structured in a way that the only members of the target sample "pass" through the entire screener.

It is important that the screener *only* contain the questions necessary to distinguish target from nontarget individuals. The inclusion of any nonessential questions only lengthens the screener, increasing the likelihood that the person being screened will either discontinue or drop out. Since, the sole purpose of a screener is to screen respondents, important but nonessential screener questions should be incorporated into the main body of the questionnaire.

Main Body

The main body of the questionnaire contains the questions that address the research study's information needs. The prior chapter provided detailed instruction for writing these questions.

Once the questions have been written, they must be placed into a logical order on the questionnaire. When performing this task, keep the following guidelines in mind:

- *Begin with simple, nonthreatening, interesting, easy-to-answer questions.* Simple questions ease the respondent into the interview. They show that the task of participation is not difficult. The more comfortable the respondents are, the more likely they are to participate in and complete the survey.

- *Group questions on the same topic together; complete one topic before moving on to another.* Interviews typically ask respondents to answer questions that they had not given much thought to before the survey. As a result, respondents must give some thought to each question before answering it. Once they are thinking about a particular area, it is important to stay focused on this area as this increases the potential for obtaining meaningful answers. Moving from topic to topic without a logical flow increases the potential for shallow, top-of-mind responses.

- *Within a topic, move from the most general questions to the most specific.* More general questions provide a means of introducing the topic and focusing the respondent's thoughts on the topic. Once the respondent is focused, it is much easier for him or her to answer questions of greater detail or specificity.

- *Place difficult or sensitive questions at the end of the questionnaire.* Hopefully, by the end of the questionnaire the interviewer will have established some rapport with the respondent increasing the respondent's comfort level in answering these types of questions. While no rapport is established in mail surveys, it is hoped that the investment in time to complete the questionnaire up to this point will motivate the respondent to invest a little additional time to answer these questions.

- *Avoid biasing questions appearing later in the questionnaire with questions asked earlier in the questionnaire.* You must be very careful that questions asked early in the interview do not provide the information required for the answering of later questions. For example, asking the question a "How would you rate the cleaning ability of each of these detergents?" will bias answers to this question when asked later in the interview: "What aspect of your detergent would you like to see improved?"

- *Address the most important topics first.* There is some evidence to suggest that the quality of responses declines as the respondent becomes fatigued. Thus, questions probing the most critical information areas should appear earlier in the questionnaire.

Classification

Questionnaires typically conclude with a series of questions that collect relevant demographic, brand usage, or behavioral information not collected as part of the screener or in the main body of the questionnaire. Demographic questions may address age, gender, education, income, ethnicity, and family/marital status. Brand usage and behavioral questions may also be included in the classification questions if the information collected by these questions is important for the analysis of different subgroups within the total sample. Remember, the purpose of all classification questions is to provide a means for examining important subgroups within the larger sample.

PHYSICALLY PREPARE THE QUESTIONNAIRE

The next step (as shown in Figure 13.1) is to take all of the written, sequenced survey questions and construct the questionnaire that will be used for data collection. Three areas must be addressed as you begin to layout and prepare the questionnaire: (1) visual appearance, (2) transitions between major topic areas and between individual questions, and (3) interviewer/respondent instructions. Each of these areas is implemented differently in self-administered versus questionnaires administered by an interviewer.

Self-Administered Questionnaires

Good organization is important in all questionnaires. Good visual appearance is most important in self-administered questionnaires as questionnaires administered by an interviewer (e.g., in personal or telephone interviews) are unlikely to be seen by the respondent.

An individual who is asked to complete a self-administered questionnaire will take a quick look at the questionnaire and then decide whether to invest his or her time to complete it. Any indication that the questionnaire will be too difficult or time-consuming to complete will generally cause a respondent to refuse and drop out of the study. As a result, it is very important that a self-administered questionnaire be uncluttered, easy to follow, and typed in an easy-to-read typeface. Visual appearance and layout are also important in questionnaires administered by an interviewer. Here, good visual appearance and layout help to ensure that the interviewer will conduct the interview in the proper manner.

The self-administered questionnaire shown in Photo 13.2 has good visual layout and appeal. The questionnaire is uncluttered, easy to read, and demonstrates several other aspects of good preparation and layout.

- *Questions are distinguished from responses.* Questions are shown in bold type, responses in normal type. This arrangement helps reduce the likelihood that a question will inadvertently be skipped.

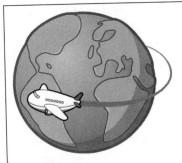

Aztec International Airlines

Dear Passenger:

Aztec International is very pleased that you've chosen to fly with our airline. In order to keep improving our service, we'd like to hear about your experience.

Could you please take just a moment to complete this short survey? Your flight attendant will pick up your survey shortly before landing.

Thank you for your help.

Max Light,
Director, Operations

1. **Please tell us your . . . .**

   Flight number   _____

   Today's date   _____

2. **How would you rate your overall satisfaction with this flight? Please check one of the boxes below.**

   Very satisfied   ❑ 1
   Slightly satisfied   ❑ 2
   Slightly dissatisfied   ❑ 3
   Very satisfied   ❑ 4

3. **Please rate each of the following with regard to *your service* on this specific flight. Please check one box for each item.**

	Excellent	Good	Fair	Poor
Courtesy	❑ 1	❑ 2	❑ 3	❑ 4
Attentiveness	❑ 1	❑ 2	❑ 3	❑ 4
Friendliness	❑ 1	❑ 2	❑ 3	❑ 4
Professionalism	❑ 1	❑ 2	❑ 3	❑ 4

PHOTO 13.2   Sample Paper and Pancil Questionnaire

4. Please rate each of the following with regard to *your meal* on this specific flight. Please check one box for each item.

	Excellent	Good	Fair	Poor
Appearance	❑ 1	❑ 2	❑ 3	❑ 4
Taste	❑ 1	❑ 2	❑ 3	❑ 4
Variety	❑ 1	❑ 2	❑ 3	❑ 4

5. Did you check any luggage for this flight?

Yes	❑ 1	☞	PLEASE CONTINUE WITH Q. 6
No	❑ 2	☞	PLEASE SKIP TO Q. 7

6. Was your luggage checked . . .

Efficiently?
Yes	❑ 1
No	❑ 2

Courteously?
Yes	❑ 1
No	❑ 2

7. How did you purchase your ticket?

Online from a travel site	❑ 1
Online, direct from Aztec Intl.	❑ 2
Travel agent	❑ 3
Phone, direct from Aztec Intl.	❑ 4
Other _____	❑ 5

8. Would you recommend Aztec International to a friend?

Yes	❑ 1
No	❑ 2

PHOTO 13.2 (Continued)

- *Response coding is unobtrusive.* The numeric codes used to represent specific responses are small and are placed so that they do not interfere with the text of either the question or response options.

- *Questions do not continue across columns or pages.* Questions that continue across pages have a tendency to confuse respondents and interviewers.

- *Columns are used to help maintain the respondent's focus, save space, and simplify response.*

Online Questionnaires

Questionnaires administered online have their own unique set of considerations that relate to (1) form and visual appearance of the questionnaire itself, (2) the range of question types available across survey companies, and (3) the way in which specific questions are presented across survey companies.

QUESTIONNAIRE FORM AND VISUAL APPEARANCE.   Several considerations regarding online questionnaire form and visual appearance need to be kept in mind. These include the following.

The use of pictures is not a trivial decision. When pictures are used, they should have an explicit research-specific function and should have a real and meaningful link to the research question. This is because pictures have the potential to influence and bias responses, for example:

- Witte et al. conducted research to determine respondents' views toward four endangered species. Some respondents were asked their opinion with a picture of the species present, while others responded to a text-only version. Those exposed to the picture were significantly more likely to express support for endangered species protection.[1]

- Couper et al. examined the influence of pictures on reports of different behaviors, such as shopping, travel, and eating out. Some respondents saw low frequency pictures of the behavior (e.g., people eating at a fine restaurant), while others saw high frequency pictures (e.g., people eating at a fast food restaurant). Regardless of the specific behavior being measured, those who saw the high frequency picture consistently reported more frequent behaviors.[2]

Carefully consider how may questions to present on a single Web page. The administration of an online survey provides a continuum of options. At one end of the continuum, the entire questionnaire is placed on a single Web page, through which the respondent scrolls until the end is reached. At the other end of the continuum, each question is placed on a separate page. In the center are approaches that use multiple pages, but group related questions together on a single page.[3] In general, the single page approach works best for shorter questionnaires; cuing respondents into the length of a long questionnaire (all placed on a single page) can raise drop out and discontinuation rates. The middle approach, grouping related questions together on a single page, tends to work best for longer questionnaires, especially if the respondent is explicitly told the percentage of the total questionnaire completed as each page is completed. This is particularly true of longer, multi-page questionnaires, where the drop out rate tends to increase dramatically after the second page.

Understand the relationship between space provided and depth of response in open-ended questions. It appears that respondents use the space provided to answer an open-ended question as a visual cue for the amount of response desired by the researcher. Answer length tends to increase when more space is provided. As a result, it is necessary to carefully match the amount of space provided with the anticipated response. Too little space will restrict responses, while too much space might motivate the respondent to "fill the space up" with information of little value.

How input boxes are labeled affects the quality of data provided. Similar to the use of pictures, the labeling of input boxes is not a trivial consideration, but rather has a significant effect on data quality. Christian et al., for example, varied the way in which dates and months were requested. She found that there were important differences across input options, as noted by the percentage of individuals providing accurate information. More than twice as many students provided accurate information when the input boxes were labeled "MM/YYYY" versus "Month/Year."[4]

Not all response formats for closed-ended questions are equivalent. Consider the question "Which of the following is most important to you in selecting a breakfast cereal?" where the respondent can choose from 11 potential answers.[5] The 11 options can be presented to respondents as either an ordered list, a drop box that requires scrolling, or a drop box that requires no scrolling. After comparing the responses to these three alternatives, Couper concluded that

> the choice of response format used in Web surveys leads to different response distributions. Radio buttons and drop boxes may not be equivalent measurement tools. It seems clear that scrolling drop boxes (where some but not all of the response options are visible) should be avoided. Drop boxes may be useful when the respondent must search along a list of response options (e.g., state or country of residence) for a well-known target answer. But for questions . . . in which respondents are formulating answers rather than matching options to an existing answer, the choice of a particular response format should carefully balance design considerations with the response process.

RANGE AND APPEARANCE OF QUESTION TYPES.   Almost all online survey companies[6] permit the use of the most common question types: single selection multiple-choice questions, checklists, single and multiple rating scales, and open-ended responses.[7] The format of these questions, however, varies widely across companies. Beyond these basic question types, there are significant differences across companies with regard to their ability to present more complex question types. Only Zoomerang and Psychdata, for example, allow ranking questions, and only PsychData allows for constant sum questions. As a result of these differences, we encourage you to take advantage of free trial offers to familiarize yourself with each company's approach.

Transitions

Transitions are the conversational, connective material that provide a sense of flow and continuity to the questionnaire. Transitions help respondents maintain their focus during a long series of questions, give warning that a change in topic or focus is imminent, and provide justification for sensitive information. While the wording of transitions among questionnaires will vary, there are some general rules for transitions. These are presented and discussed in Figure 13.3

Interviewer and Respondent Instructions

Two types of instructions are provided in a questionnaire: (1) instructions for completing an individual question and (2) instructions for moving from one question to another.

Questions written for self-administered questionnaires generally provide all the information a respondent needs to answer the question. Consequently, question-specific instructions are rare in self-administered surveys. However, there are times in surveys

Poorly Written Transitions

Potential to bias response

Now I'd like to talk to you about advertising. There's so much of it I know that you must have seen some.

Too long; too detailed. Increases difficulty level of the questionnaire

Now I would like to ask you some questions about how you feel toward various advertisers, in particular, those advertisers who have made some environmentally related claim for their product. In this context, for this discussion, an environmental claim is an explicit or implicit communication that promises that the use of a particular product will be beneficial to the environment. An environmental claim, for example, may make reference to biodegradability, ozone, the elimination of CFCs and HCFCs, recylability, or compostability.

Too demanding; damages rapport

Now, and I can't stress this enough, you really need to tell us how you feel about beer advertisers.

Well-Written Transitions

Lends conversational tone; helps to maintain rapport

There is certainly a range of opinions with regard to this issue. I'd like to find out what your opinions are.

Alerts respondent to the introduction of a new topic

Thank you for sharing your opinions with regard to _____. Now, I'd like to move to another topic. Can we please discuss _____?

A second goal of this survey is to better understand people's opinions about _____. Can we please discuss this topic for a moment?

Alerts respondent to more detailed questions within a topic.

I'd like to learn more with regard to what you think about _____. There are a few specific areas I'd like to explore.

Provides a reason for collection of sensitive or personal information.

Finally, there are just a few more questions that I'd like to ask you. These questions are important because they let us combine your answers with those similar to you.

This last set of questions is very important to us. These questions help us understand who we talked to and the similarities and differences in opinions held by different individuals.

FIGURE 13.3 Guidelines for Transitions

conducted by an interviewer when you want to communicate instructions to the interviewer. In these cases, instructions for the interviewer are generally distinguished from the questions themselves by using all capital letters, for example:

> For you personally, what is the most important consideration in deciding which cell phone service to use? DO NOT READ LIST. CHECK FIRST MENTION.

SKIP PATTERNS. Beyond question-specific instructions, instructions are also needed to help respondents or interviewers move between questions. This is because questionnaires often use skip patterns. As discussed in earlier chapters, a skip pattern is a series of questions asked of some respondents but not others where the answers to earlier questions determine which later questions are asked. In paper-and-pencil self-administered surveys, skip patterns are incorporated into the questionnaire, as shown in the following series of questions.

1. Now, I would like to focus on advertising for children's toy stores. Think about any advertising that you might have seen over the past week for a children's toy store. Do you recall seeing any advertising for this type of store?

    Yes [ ](1)   ->   GO TO Q.2
    No   [ ](2)   ->   GO TO Q.4

2. Do you recall seeing or hearing any advertising for Toys-R-Us?

    Yes [ ](1)   ->   GO TO Q.3
    No   [ ](2)   ->   GO TO Q.4

3. Would you say that this advertising was primarily directed toward parents, primarily directed toward children, or directed equally toward parents and children?

    Parents   [   ](1)
    Children   [   ](2)
    Both   [   ](3)

4. Questionnaire continues ......

Question 1 probes overall advertising awareness for children's toy stores. Respondents not aware of any advertising are skipped forward to the next section of the questionnaire (beginning with Question 4). Question 2 probes advertising awareness for Toys-R-Us, the focus of the research. As with the prior question, respondents not aware of Toy-R-Us advertising are sent to the next section of the questionnaire. Question 3 is, as a result, only asked of those familiar with Toys-R-Us advertising. No skip instructions are required for this question, because those asked this question move on to Question 4 when done.

Skip patterns in telephone and online surveys are programmed into the survey. The computer examines the responses to one question and then decides, based on that answer, what the next question should be. This is all done automatically in a way that is hidden from the respondent. As a way of confirming the accuracy of the skip pattern, some online survey companies will print a visual confirmation of a questionnaire's skip pattern. Figure 13.4, prepared by PsychData, shows the skip pattern for the prior four Toys-R-Us questions. It is always recommended that skips patterns be closely examined prior to the actual launch of a survey.

Skip patterns thus make certain that appropriate questions are asked of the correct individuals. The complexity of skip patterns, however, makes them a common source of error in questionnaire construction. When developing and preparing your skip patterns, make certain that

- *all responses are accounted for.* Examine Questions 1 and 2 in the prior series of questions. All responses are assigned a destination. This greatly reduces the potential for incorrect or inappropriate movement between questions.

Saturday, November 28, 2009

Toys-R-Us

*1) [Multiple Choice: Single Select (vertical)]
Now, I would like to focus on advertising for children's toy stores. Think about any advertising that you might have seen over the past week for a children's toy store. Do you recall seeing any advertising for this type of store?
   Yes

   Logic
   If [Yes] is selected, then skip to question [#2]

   No

   Logic
   If [No] is selected, then skip to question [#4]

*2) [Multiple Choice: Single Select (vertical)]
Do you recall seeing or hearing any advertising for Toys-R-Us?
   Yes

   Logic
   If [Yes] is selected, then skip to question [#3]

   No

   Logic
   If [No] is selected, then skip to question [#4]

3) [Multiple Choice: Single Select (vertical)]
Would you say that this advertising was primarily directed toward parents, primarily directed toward children, or directed equally toward parents and children?
   Parents
   Children
   Both

4) [Free Response: One Line Answer (2 character limit)]
This question continues the questionnaire . . . .

FIGURE 13.4 PsychData Confirmation of Skip Patterns

- *all skip directions send the respondent somewhere appropriate.* Make certain that when you send a respondent to a particular question (e.g., "GO TO QUESTION 6"), that a question with that number appears on the questionnaire and is the appropriate question to ask next.

Skip patterns are common within a single questionnaire, and the prior guidelines help to ensure that they work as intended. There are times, however, when the information needs require that skips also take place across different questionnaires. Consider an online research study in which you are trying to learn more about individuals' behaviors on and commitment to Facebook. In order to best understand these issues, you have developed multiple sets of questions: a common set of questions that will be asked of all respondents, and additional sets that are customized to light, moderate, and heavy users of Facebook. While you could place all these questions in a single questionnaire, this would unfortunately result in a questionnaire with many, many questions, increasing the chances of a problematic skip pattern. Instead of combining all these questions into a single questionnaire, you could skip across questionnaires, where:

> Questionnaire I contains the screener questions, the common set of questions to be asked of all respondents and the skip questions that will determine levels of Facebook usage.

> Questionnaires II to IV contain the questions customized for individuals at each of three levels of Facebook usage.

To our knowledge, only PsychData permits this type of cross-questionnaire skipping.

INTERNAL EVALUATION

Prior to pretesting the questionnaire, you and others associated with the project should review the questionnaire. Prior to review by nonresearchers, you should make very certain that

- *the questionnaire is complete and concise.* Research objectives and information needs should be cross-referenced to the numbers of all questions contained in the questionnaire. A questionnaire is complete when questions contained in the questionnaire all correspond to identified information needs and there are no questions that do not correspond.

- *questions themselves are clear, unambiguous, and appropriate for the type of information needed.*

- *the layout is clear and easy to follow.* You must make certain that there are no vague or ambiguous instructions and that all skip patterns do, in fact, lead the respondent to the proper place on the questionnaire.

Once you and your research team have decided that the questionnaire satisfies each of these requirements, you then submit the questionnaire for internal agency and client review. It is important that those who will ultimately use the data as a basis for decision making "buy-into" the instrument used to collect the information. This helps to ensure that the discussion of the research results focuses on what is learned rather than how the information was collected.

PRETEST THE QUESTIONNAIRE

Pretesting is a crucial step in the questionnaire development process. A pretest is important because it offers the insights needed for improving the questionnaire's wording, structure, format, and organization. No questionnaire is ever perfect after the initial draft and review. Remember, if the questionnaire used in the actual research is faulty, then the quality of the information collected will be significantly diminished. Problem areas typically of interest during a pretest include:

- *problems with administration.* Did the questionnaire take as long as expected to administer? Did it take longer? If it is too long, what can be done to shorten the questionnaire without sacrificing important questions?

- *problems related to question comprehension.* Were there any questions that were hard for the respondent to understand? Was this difficulty due to the amount of information contained in the question? Was this difficulty due to the question's length? Were any questions ambiguous? How can problem questions be rewritten to make the information needed explicit and unambiguous?

- *problems related to question demands.* Were technical terms used without definition? How might these be explained to reduce confusion? Were common words used in unusual ways or contexts? How can the use of these terms be clarified? Were there any questions that asked for difficult pieces of information (e.g., "What percent of the time would you say that price is an important factor in the brands of chips you purchase?")? Were there any questions that asked for information that is not likely to be known (e.g., "How many miles did you drive last year?" and "How much beer advertising have you seen in the past three months?")? How can these questions be rewritten to better collect the desired information?

- *problems related to response options.* Are there any questions for which "Don't Know" or "No Answer" is the most common response? Are there any questions that "Other" gathers a significant percentage of responses? Are there some scales that do not provide enough levels of distinction (e.g., an agree-neutral-disagree scale)? Are there some scales that provide too great a level of distinction?

- *problems related to organization and question sequencing.* Did the questionnaire flow as well as expected? How well did transitions and interviewer/respondent instructions work? Do any transitions or instructions need to be rewritten? Do any transitions need to be added or deleted? Did all skip patterns work as expected? Do any skip patterns need to be revised? Were any questions asked later in the questionnaire biased by earlier questions?

Cognitive interviews are the best way to pretest a questionnaire because they help researchers understand how respondents interpret and construct answers to questions. Specifically, cognitive interviewing entails "administering draft survey questions (to a small number of target audience individuals) while collecting additional verbal information *about* the survey responses, which is used to evaluate the quality of the response to help determine whether the question is generating the information that the author intends."[8] There are two approaches to cognitive interviewing: think-aloud and active probing.[9]

The *think-aloud method* asks respondents to verbalize their thoughts as they are answering a survey question. Here, the interviewer reads each question to the respondent (one at a time) and then records and/or notes the process each respondent used to comprehend and answer the question. The interviewer is therefore a passive participant in the process, typically only asking a variation of the question "Tell me what you are thinking about this question." Consider the apparently straightforward question "How many times have you talked to a doctor in the last 12 months?" The think-aloud method might obtain the following response:

> I guess that depends on what you mean when you say "talked." I talk to my neighbor, who is a doctor, but you probably don't mean that. I go to my doctor about once a year, for a general checkup, so I would count that one. I've also probably been to some type of specialist a couple of more times in the past year—once to get a bad knee diagnosed, and I also saw an ENT about a chronic coughing thing, which I'm pretty sure was in the past year, although I wouldn't swear to it. I've also talked to doctors several times when I brought my kids in to the pediatrician—I might assume that you don't want that included, although I really can't be sure. Also, I saw a chiropractor, but I don't know if you'd consider that to be a doctor in the sense you mean. So, what I'm saying, overall, is that I guess I'm not sure what number to give you, mostly because I don't know what you want.

Willis observes that:

> from this "think-aloud protocol," the interviewer may observe that the individual attempts to answer this question by attempting to recall each visit individually, rather than by estimating. It might be concluded that the individual has trouble determining whether a visit was really in the last 12 months. If, after interviewing several subjects, it becomes clear that none could really "think through" with confidence the number of times they had been to a doctor, one might decide that the reference period is simply too long to provide adequate answers. More significantly, the larger problem here seems to be that the subject is clearly unsure about what is to be included and excluded from the question, as far as both (a) whether this refers only to doctor contacts that pertain to his/her health, and (b) the type of physician or other provider that is to be counted.

The second approach to cognitive interviews is *active probing*. Here, after the interviewer asks each survey question (again one at a time); and after an answer or response is obtained, the interviewer probes further in order to understand the basis of the response. The interviewer is an active participant in the process, asking specific questions to develop a better understanding of the relationship between the desired information and the answer provided by the respondent. The most common types of probes include:

Comprehension/Interpretation Probe	What does the term "social media" mean to you?
Paraphrasing:	Can you repeat the question I just asked in your own words?
Confidence judgment:	How sure are you that you visited a social networking site five times in the past week?

Recall probe:	How do you remember that you saw advertising for Twitter on television?
General probes:	How did you arrive at that answer? Was that easy or hard to answer? I noticed that you hesitated—tell me what you were thinking.

Once pretesting is concluded, a debriefing with the agency and client should take place. The debriefing should systematically discuss potential problems with the questionnaire and provide suggestions for improvement/revision given the pretesting results.

PREPARE FIELD SUPPORT MATERIALS

Once the questionnaire has been pretested and revised, it is ready for use as a data collection instrument. As discussed in Chapter 1, field services are often used to collect the data. In these cases, the questionnaire and appropriate supporting materials are sent to the field service, interviews are conducted, and the questionnaires are returned for data coding and analysis. Potential problems with field service data collection are minimized when the questionnaire is accompanied by two types of support materials:

- A cover letter that (a) identifies the study, (b) itemizes materials sent to the field service, (c) discusses data collection techniques, (d) presents a detailed description of the sample and any special quotas, (e) identifies any special material or equipment requirements, and (f) confirms study cost, timing, and procedures for return of the questionnaires and any other test-related materials,

- A memo describing the questionnaire and any particular administrative details of which interviewers should be aware.

APPLYING CHAPTER CONTENT

The online supplemental readings provide three examples of extremely well-written questionnaires.

VERB Campaign Evaluation

Chapter 1 introduced the Centers for Disease Control and Prevention's VERB campaign, which had the broad goal of increasing physical activity of youth aged 9 to 13 ("tweens"). As with most major communication campaigns, periodic evaluations were conducted to determine campaign effects. This chapter's supplemental readings provide the questionnaires used to collect the evaluative data. Since there were two targets for the campaign, two questionnaires were necessary: one for parents and one for children.[10]

PARENT QUESTIONNAIRE.   Chapter 1 discussed how questionnaire content is selected to respond to decision makers' information needs. In the case of campaign evaluation research, the questionnaire must help decision makers answer the question "How well did the communication campaign accomplish explicit campaign goals?" Given this perspective, it is not surprising that the questions asked on the VERB parent questionnaire reflect the specific parental goals of the VERB campaign as they relate to parents' attitudes, behaviors, and awareness of the VERB campaign itself. This questionnaire is organized as follows:

Questionnaire Page	Specific Questions	Purpose
A-7:		Introduction to the research and informed consent
A-8	P1 to P2a	Confirmation that the interview is being conducted with the correct respondent
A-8	PINTRO	Transition and focus on upcoming set of questions
A-9	P3, P4	Attitudes and influences regarding child's physical activities
A-9	P_D1, P_D2	Special questions for parents of child with a disability
A-10	P5, P6	Attitudes and influences regarding child's physical activities
A-10	P8	Parent reporting of child's involvement in school activities; attitudes and influences regarding activities
A-11, 12	P10 to P11c	Parent participation in physical activities
A-12	P11d	Child's video game and media habits
A-13	P12 to P13d	Parental involvement in child's activities
A-13	P13d	Parent self-participation in physical activities
A-14	P7, P14	Parental attitudes toward physical activity
A-14	P_14a	Parent reporting of child's media habits
A-15	P_14b, P_14c	Parental knowledge of physical activity recommendations
A-15, 16	P_14e to P15	VERB campaign awareness
A-16 to 19	P16 to P23	Classification questions

CHILD QUESTIONNAIRE.   The questions asked on the child questionnaire also reflect the specific goals of the VERB campaign with regard to childrens' attitudes, behaviors, and awareness of the VERB campaign. Note how the introduction and questions have been appropriately written for the age and language skills of younger respondents. The questionnaire is organized as follows:

Questionnaire Page	Specific Questions	Purpose
A-20	C1	Classification question, used to skip to appropriate question set
A-20	C2	Classification question, used to skip to appropriate question set
A-21	C3	Child's physical activities (types in last seven days)
A-22	C4 to C5c	Amount of time child spent in physical activities (last seven days)
A-22	C6	Classification question, used to skip to appropriate question set
A-23	C7	Child's physical activities (types yesterday)
A-24	C_7x	Amount of time spent in physical activities (yesterday)
A-24	C_7a to C_7c	School-related activities
A-25, 26	C8	Child's attitudes toward physical and leisure activities
A-27	C_8a, C_8b	Child's self-image
A-27	C_8c	Child's view of others
A-27	C9	Child's trial of new activities
A-28, 29	C10 to C14	Child's leisure activities
A-29 to 34	C15 to C_23ov	VERB campaign awareness and understanding

Generation Next

The Pew Research Center for the People & the Press notes that "A new generation has come of age, shaped by an unprecedented revolution in technology and dramatic events both at home and abroad. They are Generation Next, the cohort of young adults who have grown up with personal computers, cell phones and the Internet and are now taking their place in a world where the only constant is rapid change."[11] Pew conducted research to better understand the attitudes and behaviors of members of this generation (which consists of individuals born between 1981 and 1988.)

The telephone questionnaire used for data collection in the Generation Next research study is provided as an online supplemental reading.[12] As you read through the questionnaire, note the following:

- the use of open-ended questions whenever there was a need for unprimed or top-of-mind responses.

- the use of bold typeface and capital letters to distinguish interviewer instructions from the survey questions.

- the use of randomization in questions 8, 10, 12, 46, 47, 48, 49, 59, and 60. Whenever there is a long list of items, there is always the potential for items asked early in the list to influence or bias responses to later items by creating an implicit frame of reference. Randomizing the order of list item presentation across respondents significantly reduces this potential form of bias.

- the use of rotation in questions 4, 5, 6, 9, and 54. Whenever a respondent is asked to choose one item in a pair, the potential exists for the first item to exert more influence simply because it was asked first. Pew attempted to significantly reduce this form of bias by rotating across respondents the item that was read first.

SUMMARY

The best way to avoid errors when preparing a questionnaire is to take a systematic approach to design and construction (as illustrated in Figure 13.1). The first steps in the questionnaire development process typically address the questions: "What method will I use for data collection?" and "Is questionnaire disguise necessary?"

A questionnaire typically consists of four components. The *introduction* explains the purpose and goals of the research and asks for the respondent's cooperation and participation in the research. The *screener* makes certain that the information is collected only from appropriate individuals. The *main body* of the questionnaire contains the questions that explore areas of interest. *Classification questions* collect any relevant demographic, brand usage, or behavioral information not collected as part of the screener or main body of the questionnaire.

The questions appearing in the questionnaire must be sequenced so that they facilitate data collection. Additionally, the sequenced questions must be presented with appropriate transitions and directions for the respondent and interviewer. The final result must be a clean, visually appealing questionnaire.

Before using a questionnaire in the field, it must be evaluated by others at the agency and client. Once these individuals have approved the questionnaire, and any required revisions based on their comments are made, it must be pilot tested. The final questionnaire reflects what was learned during pilot testing.

Review Questions

1. Why does the questionnaire development process start with the need to determine the data collection method?

2. What is meant by questionnaire disguise? In what circumstances is disguise warranted?

3. What are the four main components of a questionnaire?

4. What are the characteristics of a questionnaire *introduction*?

5. What is the function of the questionnaire *screener*?

6. List six considerations for the sequencing of questions in the main body of the questionnaire. Why is each consideration important?

7. Why is the visual appearance of a questionnaire important?

8. What are important considerations in the use of pictures within questionnaires?

9. What types of considerations are unique to online questionnaires?
10. What are *transitions?* What is their primary purpose?
11. What is a *skip pattern?*
12. When does the internal evaluation of a questionnaire take place?
13. What criteria should one use to internally evaluate a questionnaire?
14. What problems should one look for during a questionnaire pretest?
15. What is *cognitive interviewing?* What are its main forms?

Application Exercises

Application exercises 1 through 5 reflect chapter content and discussion.

1. The William Pace Advertising Company wishes to determine consumers' awareness of and reactions to its current advertising campaign for the NorthWest Consolidated Banking Corporation (NWCBC). Quantitative research will be conducted. The campaign target, and therefore the research sample, consists of adults aged 50 and older who live in Detroit and currently carry an ATM card. The campaign is designed to communicate the benefits of NWCBC's redesigned ATM machine.

   Your client at NWCBC asks you whether you intend to disguise the research. What questions would you ask NWCBC and/or what types of information would you like to see to make this determination? What factors might lead you to disguise the NWCBC questionnaire? What are the relative advantages and disadvantages of disguise for this specific research project?

2. The Bottled Beer Company has developed a program to help parents discuss drinking with their younger children. This program is advertised in a number of women's and family-oriented magazines. One ad in this campaign is specifically directed toward mothers who have younger female daughters (i.e., those between the ages of 8 and 14). Assume that the company wishes to determine its target mothers' awareness of and (among those who remember seeing the ad) reactions to the ads.

   You are unsure, however, whether the research will be conducted over the telephone or through the mail. As a result, (a) write the introduction and screener for a telephone study and (b) write the introduction and screener for a mail study. What special considerations do you need to keep in mind as you prepare each introduction and screener? When you are done, examine the telephone and mail versions. What are their common elements? How were these elements expressed in both versions? What information does one version have that is missing in the other version? Why do these differences occur? How are the screeners handled in both versions? How does each version provide instructions and direction for qualifying or disqualifying a respondent from participating in the study?

3. The San Ystero Regional Blood Center is conducting research to determine donor and nondonor awareness and perceptions of the Regional Blood Center, past donor behaviors, influences on donor and nondonor behavior, and attitudes toward blood donation. The questionnaire drafted by its pro bono agency's research department is shown in Figure 13.5. The survey is designed to be used for telephone interviews and is targeted to take from five to seven minutes to complete.

   As an initial step in the evaluation process, you make certain that all key areas relevant to research goals are addressed in the questionnaire. You construct the following chart:

Area of Research Focus	Questionnaire Items
Donor behavior classification	1, 2, 3, 5, 19
Awareness and perceptions	4, 6, 7, 8, 18
Donor behaviors in San Ystero County	9, 10, 15, 16
Influences on donors and nondonors	11, 12, 13, 14, 20, 21, 22, 23
Attitudes toward donating	17
General classification	24, 25, 26, 27, 28, 29

San Ystero Regional Blood Center Survey

ID_ _ _ _   (1–4)

Hello, my name is _____. I am a student at San Ystero State University. The university is helping the San Ystero Regional Blood Center with an important piece of research. Would you be willing to answer a few questions about donating blood? The survey will only take a few minutes and your participation would be a great help. We need to understand the attitudes and opinions of people like you. This is not a call to donate blood. Of course, all your answers will be strictly confidential.

1. First of all, what is your age? FILL IN BELOW.

_____ IF BETWEEN 17 AND 59 CONTINUE WITH Q. 2
         IF OVER AGE 60 TERMINATE INTERVIEW   (5–6)

2. Have you ever donated blood before?

Yes   ❐ (1)   ⇨   SKIP TO O. 5
No   ❐ (2)   ⇨   SKIP TO Q. 4   (7–8)

3. At what age did you first donate blood? RECORD AGE BELOW.

_____   (8–9)

4. If you wanted to donate blood would you know where to go?

Yes   ❐ (1)
No   ❐ (2)   (10)

5. How many times have you donated blood? RECORD NUMBER BELOW.

_____   (14–12)

6. Have you ever heard of the San Ystero Blood Center?

Yes   ❐ (1)   ⇨   CONTINUE WITH Q. 7
No   ❐ (2)   ⇨   SKIP TO Q. 9   (13)

7. Do you know where the nearest branch of the San Ystero Blood Center is located?

Yes   ❐ (1)   ⇨   CONTINUE WITH Q. 8
No   ❐ (2)   ⇨   SKIP TO Q. 9   (14–15)

8. How did you find out about this location? READ LIST. CHECK ONE RESPONSE.

Driven by the center	[ ]	(1)
Asked center for directions	[ ]	(2)
Friend or relative	[ ]	(3)
Someone took me to the center	[ ]	(4)
Yellow Pages	[ ]	(5)
Other	[ ]	(6)
Don't know or can't remember	[ ]	(7) (16)

9. Have you ever given blood through the San Ystero Regional Blood Center?

Yes   ❐ (1)
No   ❐ (2)

10. At which center did you donate? READ LIST. CHECK ONE RESPONSE.

The East City location	[ ]	(1)
The North City location	[ ]	(2)
The North Suburban location	[ ]	(3)
Don't know or can't remember	[ ]	(4) (19)

11. Have you ever been asked through the media to donate blood?

Yes   ❐ (1)
No   ❐ (2)   (20–22)

12. How did you feel about these appeals? READ CHOICES BELOW. CHECK RESPONSE. Did you feel . . .

Very pressured	[ ]	(1)
Somewhat pressured	[ ]	(2)
Not at all pressured	[ ]	(3) (19)

(continued)

FIGURE 13.5 San Ystero Regional Blood Center Questionnaire

13. Have you ever been personally asked to donate blood?

Yes ☐ (1) ⇨ CONTINUE WITH Q. 14

No ☐ (2) ⇨ SKIP TO Q. 15   (20)

14. How did you feel about these appeals? READ CHOICES BELOW. CHECK RESPONSE.

Did you feel . . .

Very pressured	[ ] (1)	
Somewhat pressured	[ ] (2)	
Not at all pressured	[ ] (3)	(21)

15. Have you donated blood in San Ystero County within the last five years?

Yes ☐ (1) ⇨ CONTINUE WITH Q. 16

No ☐ (2) ⇨ SKIP TO Q. 17   (22)

16. Where did you donate? RECORD LOCATION BELOW.

_____ (24–25)

17. Here are some reasons others have given for donating blood. For each reason that I read to you, please tell me, using a scale 0 to 100, how much you agree or disagree that the statement that I've just read is true of your own personal feelings, thoughts, or opinions. A '0' means that you absolutely agree that the statement is not true of you and a 100 means that you absolutely agree that the statement is true of you. You can pick any number between 0 and 100 but the number that you pick must fall within the range of 0 to 100. Remember, pick a number to indicate how much you agree or disagree that the statement is true of you. Record number in appropriate space.

I give because I enjoy participating in community service

_____ (26–29)

I give because it is the right thing to do

_____ (30–31)

I gave because I was asked to

_____ (32–34)

I gave because there was a community shortage

_____ (35–37)

18. Now I'd like to get your impressions of the San Ystero Regional Blood Center. For each statement that I read to you, please tell me if you agree or disagree. Specifically, tell me if you strongly agree, slightly agree, slightly disagree, or strongly disagree. READ EACH STATEMENT AND CHECK RESPONSE IN APPROPRIATE COLUMN.

	Strongly agree (1)	Slightly agree (2)	Slightly disagree (3)	Strongly disagree (4)
The centers are clean and neat	____	____	____	____
The centers are convenient	____	____	____	____
My experience was positive	____	____	____	____
The staff was friendly	____	____	____	____

19. Have you ever donated blood?

Yes ☐ (1) ⇨ SKIP TO Q. 23

No ☐ (2) ⇨ SKIP TO Q. 23   (38)

20. Has a friend or relative ever asked you to donate blood?

Yes ☐ (1) ⇨ SKIP TO Q. 23

No ☐ (2) ⇨ SKIP TO Q. 23   (39)

21. Please listen to each statement that I read and tell me whether or not that statement describes you.

I am afraid of needles		
Describes	[ ] (1)	
Does not describe	[ ] (2)	

How afraid of needles are you?   (40)

Very afraid	[ ] (1)	
Somewhat afraid	[ ] (2)	
Just a little afraid	[ ] (3) (41)	

I am certain that if I gave blood I would faint

Describes	[ ] (1)	
Does not describe	[ ] (2) (42)	

How certain are you?

Very certain	[ ] (1)	
Somewhat certain	[ ] (2)	
A little certain	[ ] (3) (43)	

(continued)

FIGURE 13.5 (Continued)

22. Have you ever heard an appeal on the radio or television to give blood?

Yes   ☐ (1)

No   ☐ (2)   (44)

23. Have you ever received any phone calls from San Ystero Regional Blood Center asking you to donate blood?

Yes   ☐ (1)

No   ☐ (2)   (45)

How long ago was this call? _____ (46)

Did you fulfill your civic duty and give blood? (47)

24. Now, I'd like to end with just a few more very important questions. (49)

25. What is your current marital status?

Married   ☐ (1)   ⇨   SKIP TO Q. 26

Single   ☐ (2)   ⇨   SKIP TO Q. 27   (38)

26. How many children do you have?

_____ (50)

27. What is your approximate household annual income, before taxes, in thousands?

_____ (50–52)

28. What is your highest level of education completed?

Less than high school diploma	[	] (1)
College graduate	[	] (4)
High school	[	] (2)
Master's degree	[	] (5)
Some college	[	] (3)
Advanced degree	[	] (6) (53)

Thank you for your time. AFTER INTERVIEW RECORD GENDER.

Male	[	] (1)
Female	[	] (2) (54)

FIGURE 13.5 (Continued)

On the basis of this table and your examination of the questionnaire, are all areas adequately addressed? If not, what specific questions would you add?

Once you are certain that the questionnaire addresses all appropriate areas, examine the questionnaire itself. With your knowledge gained from the prior chapter on question writing and from this chapter on the design of the questionnaire, what suggestions do you have for improving the questionnaire? Revise the questionnaire as needed. Then, pilot test the questionnaire. What additional insights into questionnaire form and structure did the pilot test provide? How would you revise the questionnaire based on the results of the pilot test?

4. Set up a free account at one of the online survey companies. Take your final questionnaire from the prior exercise and create an online version. Print out a copy of your online questionnaire.

5. Each of the questionnaires shown in Figures 13.6 through 13.10[13] are based on "real-world" questionnaires that have been used for data collection.[14] While all of the questionnaires are good starts, each can be improved through the use of skip patterns, improved question wording, additional questions, proper spelling, and better question flow. For each questionnaire, prepare a short analysis that describes the questionnaire's strengths and weaknesses, and then (in light of your analysis) revise the questionnaire accordingly.

Ad Blocking Survey

1) On a scale of 1 to 10, where 1 is the least knowledgeable and 10 is advanced knowledge, how would you rate your knowledge of computing and the Internet?

--Select--
-1
-2
-3
-4
-5
-6
-7
-8
-9
-10

2) Have you heard of the term "ad-blocker" before, or are you aware of what ad-blocking software and techniques do?
○ Yes   ○ No

3) Do you use any form of ad-blocking method and if so, what?

(1000 characters remaining)

4) Please identify your major reasons for using an ad-blocker (choose all options that apply).
❏ Ads are a waste of your bandwidth
❏ Ads cause slow-down problems for your computer
❏ Ad-blocker was installed for you by someone else
❏ Find that ads are a irritant and detract from website content
❏ Other (please specify)

5) Please identify the major sorts of ads you wanted to block (choose all options that apply).
❏ All ads in general
❏ Flash ads
❏ Text ads
❏ Banners
❏ Pop-ups/Pop-unders
❏ Floating ads
❏ Ads from a specific provider
❏ Ads on a specific website
❏ Other (please specify)

6) If a site was able to get around your ad-blocker and show you ads as you surfed, would this adversely affect how you felt about the site? Would you stop using the site if this was the case?
○ Yes
○ No

7) Can you explain your response to the prior question?

(1000 characters remaining)

8) Would you pay to use a site without ads, for example, paying a subscription fee for a given time period for example a day or a year?

9) Do you have any final comments on ad-blocking that you feel are important for us to know?

FIGURE 13.6 Ad Blocking Survey

Attitudes Toward Internet Advertising

We are really interested in your opinion. The questions below deal with the topic of Internet advertising. Please take a moment to read the instructions and complete the survey. There are no right or wrong answers and your identity is anonymous. This survey will take about five minutes to complete. You must complete all the questions in order to submit your answers. Thank you for your time.

1) How often do you use the Internet?
   - ○ Less than once per week
   - ○ About once per week
   - ○ 2 to 4 times per week
   - ○ 5 to 6 times per week
   - ○ Daily

2) When using the Internet, about how long do you stay logged on (consider the whole day)?
   - ○ Less than one hour
   - ○ At least one but less than two hours
   - ○ At least two but less than five hours
   - ○ Five or more hours

The next few questions deal with Internet advertising. For the purposes of this survey, Internet advertising refers to any type of advertising on the Internet designed to get you to buy or request more information about a product of service. Internet advertising examples include banner ads, text links, e-mail ads, and pop-up window ads.

3) Please select the item below which best describes your feelings in general toward Internet advertising.
   - ○ I'm very bothered by it
   - ○ I'm somewhat bothered by it
   - ○ It doesn't bother me
   - ○ I enjoy it somewhat
   - ○ I enjoy it

For each advertising characteristic listed below, select the statement that best indicates how your opinion is affected about an ad based on its characteristics.

		Doesn't affect my opinion	Could affect my opinion	Affects my opinion somewhat	Affects my opinion
4)	Download speed	○	○	○	○
5)	Graphics quality	○	○	○	○
6)	Text content	○	○	○	○
7)	Annoyance	○	○	○	○
8)	Offensiveness	○	○	○	○

Please rate your feelings toward the Internet advertising methods listed below. Use a scale of 1 to 5 to indicate your feelings where 1 is negative and 5 is positive. You can use the same number more than once.

		1	2	3	4	5
9)	Banner ads	○	○	○	○	○
10)	Text links	○	○	○	○	○
11)	E-mail ads	○	○	○	○	○
12)	Pop-up window ads	○	○	○	○	○

The next few questions seek your opinion about the characteristics of Internet advertising. Please select an option below to indicate how often you have noticed the advertising characteristic used, such as "download speed" or "text content," for each advertising method.

The **"download speed"** of the web sites I visit are slow because of:

		Never	Rarely	Sometimes	Often	Always
13)	Banner ads	○	○	○	○	○
14)	Text links	○	○	○	○	○
15)	Pop-up window ads	○	○	○	○	○

FIGURE 13.7   Attitudes Toward Internet Advertising

Poor quality **"graphics"** are used in:

		Never	Rarely	Sometimes	Often	Always
16)	Banner ads	O	O	O	O	O
17)	E-mail ads	O	O	O	O	O
18)	Pop-up window ads	O	O	O	O	O

Unappealing **"text content"** is used in:

		Never	Rarely	Sometimes	Often	Always
19)	Banner ads	O	O	O	O	O
20)	Text links	O	O	O	O	O
21)	E-mail ads	O	O	O	O	O
22)	Pop-up window ads	O	O	O	O	O

The advertising methods below can be classified as **"annoying"**:

		Never	Rarely	Sometimes	Often	Always
23)	Banner ads	O	O	O	O	O
24)	Text links	O	O	O	O	O
25)	E-mail ads	O	O	O	O	O
26)	Pop-up window ads	O	O	O	O	O

The advertising methods below can be classified as **"offensive"**:

		Never	Rarely	Sometimes	Often	Always
27)	Banner ads	O	O	O	O	O
28)	Text links	O	O	O	O	O
29)	E-mail ads	O	O	O	O	O
30)	Pop-up window ads	O	O	O	O	O

31) Consider all your prior responses. Which type of Internet advertising method is most preferred by you?
    O Banner ads
    O Text links
    O E-mail ads
    O Pop-up window ads

32) Based on your response to the last question, which advertising characteristic was the most important in determining your response?
    O Download speed
    O Graphics quality
    O Text content
    O Ad affect (annoying or offensive)

Please indicate how much you agree or disagree with each of the statements shown below.

"I would be more likely to purchase or seek information about the advertised product or service if the ads advertising them were...

		Strongly disagree	Disagree	Indifferent	Agree	Strongly agree
33)	faster downloading	O	O	O	O	O
34)	more interesting	O	O	O	O	O
35)	less annoying or offensive	O	O	O	O	O

FIGURE 13.7 (Continued)

Brand Awareness and Attitudes

This survey is about informal family restaurants.

1) When thinking about informal family restaurants, what restaurant comes to mind first?

   [_____]

2) What other informal family restaurants come to mind? (Please list up to five)

   [_____]
   [_____]
   [_____]
   [_____]
   [_____]

3) Have you heard of any of the following informal family restaurants? (Please select all you are aware of, including those you mentioned in the previous questions.)
   ❏ Olive Garden
   ❏ Denny's
   ❏ Sizzler
   ❏ Coco's
   ❏ TGI Friday's
   ❏ Chili's
   ❏ Applebee's
   ❏ None of these

How often do you typically visit each of the following informal family restaurants?

		Never visit	Once every 4 months or less often	Once every 2 to 3 months	Once a month	2 to 3 times a month	4 to 11 times a month	12 or more times a month
4)	Olive Garden	O	O	O	O	O	O	O
5)	Denny's	O	O	O	O	O	O	O
6)	TGI Friday's	O	O	O	O	O	O	O
7)	Applebee's	O	O	O	O	O	O	O

Which of the following informal family restaurants have a location near your home, school or place of work.

Please select all that apply in each column.

		Near home	Near work	Near school
8)	Olive Garden	O	O	O
9)	Denny's	O	O	O
10)	TGI Fridays	O	O	O
11)	Applebee's	O	O	O
12)	None of the above/Not applicable	O	O	O

How would you describe your overall opinion of the following informal family restaurants?

		Very Unfavorable	Unfavorable	Slightly Unfavorable	Neutral	Slightly favorable	Favorable	Very favorable
13)	Olive Garden	O	O	O	O	O	O	O
14)	Denny's	O	O	O	O	O	O	O
15)	TGI Friday's	O	O	O	O	O	O	O
16)	Applebee's	O	O	O	O	O	O	O

FIGURE 13.8 Brand Awareness and Attitudes

How likely are you to recommend each of the following informal family restaurants?

		Very unlikely	Unlikely	Slightly unlikely	Neutral	Slightly likely	Likely	Very likely
17)	Olive Garden	O	O	O	O	O	O	O
18)	Denny's	O	O	O	O	O	O	O
19)	TGI Friday's	O	O	O	O	O	O	O
20)	Applebee's	O	O	O	O	O	O	O

Think about advertising for specific menu items.

In the past 30 days, where have you seen or heard menu item specific advertising for the following informal family restaurants? (Please check all that apply for each restaurant.)

		Outdoor	At the restaurant	Online	TV	Print	In a movie theater	Radio	Other	Did not see advertised in past 30 days
21)	Olive Garden	☐	☐	☐	☐	☐	☐	☐	☐	☐
22)	Denny's	☐	☐	☐	☐	☐	☐	☐	☐	☐
23)	TGI Friday's	☐	☐	☐	☐	☐	☐	☐	☐	☐
24)	Applebee's	☐	☐	☐	☐	☐	☐	☐	☐	☐

How would you rate your overall reactions to each restaurant's advertising?

		Very favorable	Favorable	Neutral	Unfavorable	Very unfavorable
25)	Olive Garden	O	O	O	O	O
26)	Denny's	O	O	O	O	O
27)	TGI Fridays	O	O	O	O	O
28)	Applebee's	O	O	O	O	O

29)   Can you please explain your rating of Olive Garden advertising?

(1000 characters remaining)

30)   Can you please explain your rating of TGI Friday's advertising?

(1000 characters remaining)

31)   Please rank the following restaurants in terms of your preference for each restaurant's advertising where 1 is the most preferred and 4 is the least preferred.

☐ Olive Garden
☐ Denny's
☐ TGI Friday's
☐ Applebee's

FIGURE 13.8   (Continued)

Brand Image and Advertising Awareness

Thank you for taking the time to participate in our survey. We value your privacy, your identity and responses are anonymous, strictly confidential, and wil be used for research and informational purposes only. Thank you in advance for your thoughtful input.

1) When thinking of companies that are making a commitment to help the environment, what ONE company comes first to mind?

How familiar would you say you are with each company listed below? (Select one answer for each)

		I know a lot about the company	I know a fair amount about the company	I know a few things about the company	I have only heard of the name before	Never heard of
2)	Apple	○	○	○	○	○
3)	Sony	○	○	○	○	○
4)	Dell	○	○	○	○	○
5)	Toshiba	○	○	○	○	○
6)	HP	○	○	○	○	○

Have you seen any ONLINE ADVERTISING for the following companies within the past 30 days? (Select one answer for each)

		Yes	No	Not sure
7)	Apple	○	○	○
8)	Sony	○	○	○
9)	Dell	○	○	○
10)	Toshiba	○	○	○
11)	HP	○	○	○

Where else might you have seen advertising for any of these companies within the past 30 days? (Check all that apply)

		Television	Radio	Newspaper	Magazines	Mobile Phone	Other
12)	Apple	○	○	○	○	○	○
13)	Sony	○	○	○	○	○	○
14)	Dell	○	○	○	○	○	○
15)	Toshiba	○	○	○	○	○	○
16)	HP	○	○	○	○	○	○

What is your overall impression of the following companies? (Select one answer for each)

		Very favorable	Somewhat favorable	Somewhat unfavorable	Very unfavorable	I have no opinion
17)	Apple	○	○	○	○	○
18)	Sony	○	○	○	○	○
19)	Dell	○	○	○	○	○
20)	Toshiba	○	○	○	○	○
21)	HP	○	○	○	○	○

What is your overall impression of the companies' advertising?

		Very favorable	Somewhat favorable	Somewhat unfavorable	Very unfavorable	I have no opinion
22)	Apple	○	○	○	○	○
23)	Sony	○	○	○	○	○
24)	Dell	○	○	○	○	○
25)	Toshiba	○	○	○	○	○
26)	HP	○	○	○	○	○

FIGURE 13.9 Brand Image and Advertising Awareness

27) Which of the following companies, if any, uses the message "Always Green" in its advertising? (Select one)
- O Apple
- O Sony
- O Dell
- O Toshiba
- O HP
- O Samsung
- O Lenvino
- O Acer
- O None of these
- O I am not sure

28) Based on anything you've seen or heard or any impressions you may have, which of these companies do you think are environmentally friendly? (Please check all that apply)
- O Apple
- O Sony
- O Dell
- O Toshiba
- O HP
- O None of these
- O I am not sure

29) Have you ever heard of the phrase "Computing Without Limits"?
- O Yes   O No

30) Which of the following companies do you associate "Computing Without Limits" with? (Please check all that apply)
- O Apple
- O Sony
- O Dell
- O Toshiba
- O HP
- O None of these
- O I am not sure

Based on anything that you've seen or heard or any impressions you may have, which of these companies do you think are providing innovations that enable...? (Please select all these apply)

		More powerful computing	Expanding computing to poorer countries	Making computing more affordable	Making computing "greener"
31)	Apple	O	O	O	O
32)	Sony	O	O	O	O
33)	Dell	O	O	O	O
34)	Toshiba	O	O	O	O
35)	HP	O	O	O	O

Please indicate how strongly you agree or disagree with each statement regarding **Sony**. (Select one answer for each)

Sony is...

		Strongly agree	Agree	Neither agree or disagree	Disagree	Strongly disagree	I have no opinion
36)	Global	O	O	O	O	O	O
37)	Trusted	O	O	O	O	O	O
38)	Reliable	O	O	O	O	O	O
39)	Modern	O	O	O	O	O	O
40)	Dynamic	O	O	O	O	O	O
41)	Innovative	O	O	O	O	O	O
42)	An industry leader	O	O	O	O	O	O
43)	A company that cares	O	O	O	O	O	O

FIGURE 13.9 (Continued)

Parents' Attitudes Toward Child-Directed Food Advertising

1) I'd like to begin by asking about all types of food and drink advertising on television and online. Let's focus first on television. To what extent, if at all, are you concerned about the advertising of food products at times when children are likely to see it?
   O Not at all concerned
   O A little concerned
   O Somewhat concerned
   O Very concerned

2) Now, to what extent, if at all, are you concerned about the advertising of food products on web sites where children are likely to visit?
   O Not at all concerned
   O A little concerned
   O Somewhat concerned
   O Very concerned

3) Focusing now on unhealthy food products, to what extent, if at all, are you concerned about the advertising of UNHEALTHY food products at times when children are likely to be watching television?
   O Not at all concerned
   O A little concerned
   O Somewhat concerned
   O Very concerned

4) Still focusing on unhealthy food products, to what extent, if at all, are you concerned about the advertising of UNHEALTHY food products on web sites where children are likely to visit?
   O Not at all concerned
   O A little concerned
   O Somewhat concerned
   O Very concerned

5) To what extent do you think television or online food advertising provides accurate information about the nutritional quality of the product being advertised?
   O Not at all
   O A little
   O Somewhat
   O A great deal

6) Do you think that there is a difference in the information accuracy of television and online food advertising?
   O Yes
   O No

7) What do you think is the difference?

   (1000 characters remaining)

I'd like you to tell me to what extent, if at all, you are concerned about the following aspects of food advertising at times children watch television. Please check one answer for each item.

		Not at all concerned	A little concerned	Somewhat concerned	Very concerned
8)	The use of popular personalities or characters to promote unhealthy foods to children.	O	O	O	O
9)	Food advertising that promotes free toys or gifts with products.	O	O	O	O
10)	The amount of television advertising of unhealthy food at times when children watch television.	O	O	O	O
11)	Television food advertising that promotes only the healthy aspects of the product	O	O	O	O

FIGURE 13.10 **Parents' Attitudes Toward Child-Directed Food Advertising**

12) Are you aware that food and drink products are advertised to children in the following ways ... (Please check all that apply)
- ❑ Online games
- ❑ Email or SMS messages
- ❑ Children's magazines
- ❑ Through competitions
- ❑ In school materials
- ❑ Through school fundraisers
- ❑ Sponsorship of childrens' sporting events

13) Thinking back to television advertising, regulations are currently in place that monitor and control television advertising to children. Did you know that these sorts of regulations existed?
- ○ Yes
- ○ No
- ○ Don't know

14) Based on the food advertising you've seen at times your children watch television, do you agree or disagree that the current regulations are effective?
- ○ Strongly agree
- ○ Agree
- ○ Neither agree nor disagree
- ○ Disagree
- ○ Strongly disagree

15) Do you agree or disagree that the government should introduce stronger restrictions on food advertising when children watch television?
- ○ Strongly agree
- ○ Agree
- ○ Neither agree nor disagree
- ○ Disagree
- ○ Strongly disagree

16) Below are some suggestions that people have made about the advertising of food on television. Please check the ONE suggestion you most strongly support.
- ○ A total ban on ALL food advertising
- ○ A ban on ALL food advertising at times when children watch television
- ○ A total ban on advertising of unhealthy foods
- ○ A ban on advertising of unhealthy foods at times children watch television
- ○ None of the above

Please take another look at the list of possible options. Please tell me, in general terms, whether you support or oppose each suggestion. Check one answer for each option.

	Strongly support	Support	Neither support not oppose	Oppose	Strongly oppose
17) A total ban on ALL food advertising	○	○	○	○	○
18) A ban on ALL food advertising at times when children watch television	○	○	○	○	○
19) A total ban on advertising of unhealthy foods	○	○	○	○	○
20) A ban on advertising of unhealthy foods at times children watch television	○	○	○	○	○

PFIGURE 13.10 (Continued)

Application exercises 6 through 9 refer to the VERB questionnaires provided in the online supplemental readings.

6. Prepare a short paper that discusses the strengths and weaknesses of the parents' and child's questionnaire?[15] What specific suggestions would you make to improve each questionnaire? Prepare revised questionnaires to reflect your recommendations.

7. Each questionnaire was last used in 2006. Imagine that the VERB campaign was restarted this year with the same goals and objectives. How would you update each questionnaire to account for social changes, and changes in the potential range of parent's and children's experiences since the questionnaires were last used? Prepare a short paper describing areas of modification to each questionnaire, and then revise each questionnaire accordingly.

8. Take your revised parent questionnaire from the last exercise, and translate it from a telephone to a self-administered online survey.

9. Do you think that the children's questionnaire should remain a telephone questionnaire or would it work better as a self-administered online questionnaire? Prepare a short paper that presents your point of view. Provide specific examples from the questionnaire to support your decision.

Application exercises 10 through 12 refer to the Pew Generation Next questionnaire in the online supplemental readings.

10. The Pew questionnaire covers a great many topics, each of which provides insights into the attitudes and behaviors of Generation Next. Review the questionnaire, and make a list of the broad areas explored in the questionnaire. Then, select one area, and recommend additional questions that will allow the area to be surveyed in greater depth. Write and submit your questions, numbering the questions to indicate where they would appear in the questionnaire.

11. Review the list of areas covered by the Pew survey. (This list was created for the prior application exercise.) Identify an area of attitude or behavior that is not on the list. Write a series of at least six questions that collect information in this area. Number the questions to indicate where you would place them in the questionnaire.

12. The Pew Generation Next interview was conducted over the telephone. Prepare a paper that presents your point of view regarding whether this interview could be conducted as a self-administered online survey? What are the advantages, if any, of an online approach? What, if any, are the limitations or disadvantages? Be certain to support your point of view with specific examples.

Endnotes

1. James C. Witte, Roy P. Pargas, Catherine Mobley, and James Hawdon (2004). "Instrument Effects of Images in Web Surveys: A Research Note." *Social Science Computer Review* 22 (3): 363–369.

2. Mick P. Couper, Roger Tourangeau, and Kristin Kenyon (2004). "Picture This! An Analysis of Visual Effects in Web Surveys." *Public Opinion Quarterly* 68 (2): 255–266.

3. For more detailed discussion, see Andy Peytchev, Mick P. Couper, Sean E. McCabe, and Scott D. Crawford (2006). "Web Survey Design: Paging Versus Scrolling." *Public Opinion Quarterly* 70 (4): 596–607.

4. Leah M. Christian, Don A. Dillman, and Jolene D. Smyth (2007). "Helping Respondents Get It Right the First Time: The Influence of Words,

Symbols, and Graphics in Web Surveys." *Public Opinion Quarterly* 71 (1): 113–125.

5. This example and the results discussed are from Mick P. Couper, Roger Tourangeau, Frederick G. Conrad, and Scott D. Crawford (2004). "What They See Is What We Get: Response Options for Web Surveys." *Social Science Computer Review* 22 (1): 111–127.

6. Three commonly used online research companies are PsychData (http://www.psychdata. com), SurveyMonkey (http://wwwsurvey monkey.com), and Zoomerang (http://www. zoomerang.com).

7. Almost all companies also allow for pictures to be integrated into the questionnaire.

8. Paul C. Beatty and Gordon B. Willis (2007). "Research Synthesis: The Practice of Cognitive Interviewing." *Public Opinion Quarterly* 71 (2): 287–311.

9. The discussion of cognitive interviewing techniques draws primarily from Gordon B. Willis (1999). *Cognitive Interviewing: A "How To" Guide"* available at http://appliedresearch. cancer. gov/areas/cognitive/interview.pdf. All quotes are from this source.

10. Sources for the questionnaires are as follows: The parent questionnaire is located at http:// www.cdc.gov/youthcampaign/research/PDF/ ymcls_parent.pdf, while the child questionnaire is located at http://www.cdc.gov/youth campaign/research/PDF/ymcls_child.pdf,

11. Pew Research Center for the People and the Press (2007). "A Portrait of "Generation Next." How Young People View Their Lives, Futures and Politics (Overview)" at http://people-press. org/report/300/a-portrait-of-generation-next. The full report is located at http://people-press. org/reports/pdf/300.pdf.

12. The original questionnaire with topline data is located at http://people-press.org/reports/ questionnaires/300.pdf. Note that the introduction and informed consent are not shown.

13. All questionnaires were developed at PsychData (http://www.psychdata.com). Questionnaires have been reformmated for use in the text.

14. Brand names on the questionnaires have been changed from the original to maintain confidentiality. The questionnaire shown in Figure 13.10 uses some questions from Coalition on Food Advertising to Children (2007). "National Community Survey of TV Food Advertising to Children" at http://www.health.qld.gov.au/ph/ documents/hpu/Survey_TVFoodAdChild.pdf. This questionnaire, however, is different than that used by the Coalition. Note also that screener and classification questions are not shown.

15. This chapter presented both VERB questionnaires as examples of well-written and well-organized questionnaires. Nevertheless, it is still possible that each might still be improved.

CHAPTER 14

Experimentation

Descriptive research such as consumer surveys lets advertisers take a "snapshot" of consumers in order to better understand their current attitudes and behaviors. There are times, however, when advertising decision makers require more than a description and instead require an understanding of cause and effect. This understanding is obtained using experimental research in which a researcher changes or alters something in the consumers' or product's environment in order to see what happens. This chapter discusses the role of experiments in advertising research.

***

When you are done reading this chapter, you should have a better understanding of how to:

- identify characteristics of experiments and distinguish experimental versus nonexperimental approaches to data collection
- explain the factors that influence an experiment's ability to provide a sound basis for decision making
- describe the options a researcher has in designing experiments
- describe how advertisers address the issues of internal and external experimental validity

Advertisers and marketers have two ways of understanding the consumer, the product, and the marketplace. Descriptive research provides a look at consumers' attitudes, beliefs, lifestyles, and behaviors at a particular point in time. A descriptive study, for example, might survey individuals in the advertiser's target audience to determine the extent to which they are aware of the advertising and can recall key ideas communicated by the advertising. An experimental study moves beyond description. *The goal of an experiment is to determine* **causality**—*the effect of changes in one area on one or more other areas.* An experiment might vary the amount of advertising placed in particular markets to determine how advertising weight affects target audience advertising awareness and message recall. Here, some individuals would be exposed to a great deal of advertising, while other individuals would be exposed to very little advertising. This experiment would try to answer the question: "To what extent does the amount of advertising exposure affect advertising awareness and message recall?"

This chapter discusses experimentation. We begin with an example that illustrates the differences in insights provided by survey and experimental research. Next, we discuss the characteristics and components of experiments, paying particular attention to the requirements that must be satisfied for one to accept the causality inferred from an experiment. This is followed by a focus on the concepts of internal and external validity. Internal validity determines the extent to which we have confidence that observed results are due to the experimental manipulations. External validity influences the extent to which the experimental results are generalizable to the "real world."

SURVEYS VERSUS EXPERIMENTS

Surveys and other forms of personal interviews are an excellent (and sometimes only) way to collect information on individuals' attitudes and beliefs. There are times, however, when advertisers need to move beyond attitudes and beliefs in order to understand individuals' behaviors. When behaviors are the focus, advertisers have two options: surveys can be used, where respondents are asked to recall and report on their behaviors, or experiments can be used to bypass recall and actually observe behaviors. The following situation illustrates the differences in the two approaches.

Imagine that you are an advertiser who uses banner ads to promote your products.[1] You want to conduct research to determine which aspects of banner ads are most likely to motivate individuals in your target audience to "click." You conduct a survey among a random sample of your target audience, asking them to indicate which aspects of banner ads are most likely to influence a click-through. You find, as shown in the following table, that these individuals say that they are most influenced by ads that they consider relevant and which provide a discount code. While these findings are not unexpected, you are surprised at the low level of influence attributed to ad size which you always believed to be very influential.

Banner Ad Characteristic	Percentage of Respondents Saying "Very Influential" for Click
Relevant to my interests	75%
Provides discount code	72
Entertaining	53
Provides useful information	33
Ad size	19

Given your surprise at the survey results and the importance of the conclusions for future and media planning, you decide to further explore the relationship between banner ad characteristics and click-through in an experiment. Here, you randomly select members of your target audience and manipulate the characteristics of the banner ads to which they are exposed. This manipulation allows you to isolate the effects of relevance, discount codes, and ad size. You then track and measure how these manipulations affect click-through. When this is done, you discover that relevance, discount code, and ad size are all equally important overall. The table below summarizes this finding, where the percentage of the sample with a click-through is higher for relevant versus nonrelevant ads, higher for ads with discount codes versus those without, and higher for larger versus smaller ads.

Banner Ad Characteristic	Percentage of Sample Clicking-Through
Relevance	
High relevance	5.6%
Low relevance	3.4
Discount Code	
Present	5.7%
Absent	3.3
Ad Size	
Larger	5.9%
Smaller	3.1

This outcome is important because the survey results would have led you to conclude that ad size is not important, which it clearly is. But the experiment can provide even greater insight into the relationship between banner characteristics and click-though. The experiment found that:

- There is a relationship between discount codes and relevance: discount codes are an important influence *but only* when the level of relevance is low. When an ad is seen as relevant, it is equally likely to be clicked upon whether a discount code is present or not. When an ad is seen as not relevant, click-through increases when the ad contains a discount code.

- There is a relationship between ad size and relevance: ad size is important *but only* when ads do not contain a discount code. Larger ads are equally likely to be clicked upon whether a discount code is present or not. When an ad is smaller, click-through increases when the ad contains a discount code.

These results, which indicate that influences on click-though are much more complex than indicated in the survey, provide excellent guidance for future ad development and media planning.

The difference between the survey and experimental results illustrates the limitations of survey research as a means for exploring individuals' behaviors and influences on these behaviors. Survey results become less reliable for explaining behaviors when:

- survey questions require recall, especially over longer time periods.
- individuals are asked for introspection in areas of behavior they do not normally think about.
- individuals are asked to use memory to attribute cause and effect.
- there may be complex, multiple, or interrelated influences on behavior.

In these situations, experimentation or the actual monitoring of behaviors is the preferred alternative to surveys.

THE CHARACTERISTICS OF EXPERIMENTS

Experiments are appropriate whenever one needs to understand causation, the effect of changes in one area on other areas. Every experiment consists of four basic steps, regardless of who is conducting the experiment or the subject matter that the experiment addresses. When you conduct an experiment, you:

- identify what you need to learn,
- take the relevant actions (conduct the experiment by manipulating one or more variables),
- observe the effects and consequences of those actions on other variables, and then
- determine the extent to which the observed effects can be attributed to actions taken.

Each of these parts of an experiment is illustrated in the following example:

Peter wants to develop a pizza crust with better texture than the crusts he has made in the past. So, he conducts an experiment to see how the amount of water added to the batter affects crust texture. Peter mixes three different batches of crust making certain that he uses the same ingredients in the same quantity in each crust except for the amount of water. Crust A is made with one cup of water, Crust B contains 1½ cups of water, while Crust C contains two cups of water. All ingredients are added and mixed in the same order. Peter's oven is large enough to hold one crust at a time. He bakes each crust for the same amount of time at the same temperature in the same pan. He mixes each crust batter immediately before baking and lets the oven cool down between each baking. Peter then observes and evaluates each crust when it comes out of the oven. He decides that Crust C has a better texture: it is firmer, crisper (without burning), and has a better color. Peter decides that the recipe for Crust C is the better of the three recipes.

Peter's pizza crust experiment illustrates the four steps underlying the conduct of an experiment. Peter decided that he wanted to understand the effect of water content on crust texture, took the relevant action by varying the amount of water in the recipes, observed the effect of water variation on crust texture, and decided (because of the care he took in the design and conduct of the experiment) that he could have confidence in the conclusion that the amount of water in Crust C results in the best crust. Because Peter took care in the design and conduct of this experiment, the nature of cause and effect is clear.

Independent and Dependent Variables

Every experiment has at least one independent variable, one dependent variable and a manipulation. A variable is an object, event, idea, feeling, time period, or any other type of thing you wish to measure. There are two types of variables: independent and dependent. The *independent variable* is what the experiment manipulates. The amount of water in Peter's crust experiment was the independent variable. The *dependent variable* is what the researcher is interested in explaining, and as a result, is the measure used to evaluate the influence of the independent variable. The dependent variables in Peter's crust experiment were his ratings of crust firmness, crispness, and color.[2] Finally, independent variables are *manipulated* in some systematic way. Variations in the amount of water in each crust reflected manipulation of the independent variable.

When thinking about experimental design, many people have trouble identifying the dependent and independent variables. An easy way to remember is to insert the names of the two variables you are using in this sentence in the way that makes the most sense. Then, you can figure out which is the independent variable and which is the dependent variable:

> Independent variable causes a change in Dependent Variable, and it isn't possible that Dependent Variable could cause a change in Independent Variable."[3]

For example:

> The amount of water causes a change in pizza crust characteristics, and it isn't possible that pizza crust characteristics could cause a change in the amount of water.

Requirements for Causality

All experiments try to claim causality, that is, to claim that the manipulations of the independent variable(s) caused a change in the dependent variable(s). While it is easy to make a claim for causality, for example, "smoking causes cancer," it is quite another thing to prove this claim in a convincing, problem-free experiment.

Well-designed experiments permit one to attribute causality with a high degree of certainty, that is, to presume that the cause of changes in the dependent variable(s) is due to manipulations of the independent variables(s). However, before this causal relationship can be accepted, several critical criteria must be satisfied.[4]

1. *Events must take place in the proper order.* For one event to cause another, it must precede it. Peter's experiment satisfies this criterion because his manipulation of water content preceded crust evaluation.[5]

2. *Events must take place at the same time and show an explicit relationship.* This attribute of causation, labeled concomitant variation, requires that causes and effects must occur or vary together. In other words, "concomitant variation says that if across a range of situations that lead to a certain effect, we find a certain property of the effect varying with variation in a factor common to those situations, then we can infer that factor as the cause. For example, imagine that you felt somewhat sick having eaten one oyster, whereas your sister felt rather not well having eaten a few, and your father became critically ill having eaten 10 in a row. Since the variation in the number of oysters corresponds to variation in the severity of the illness, it would be rational to infer that the illnesses were caused by the oysters."[6] Peter's experiment satisfies this criterion because crust quality varied in a predictable way as the result of water manipulation.

3. *Alternative explanations must be reduced and eliminated whenever possible.* While it is impossible to eliminate all alternative explanations for experimental results, better experiments eliminate as many alternative causal factors as possible. When all reasonable alternative explanations for the results are eliminated, then you can have confidence that the manipulations of the independent variable caused the observed changes in the dependent variable. Consider what happens when Sally conducts her own pizza experiment in this way:

> Sally begins her experiment in exactly the same way as Peter. She carefully prepares each recipe manipulating only the water content. However, because she is pressed for time and has a shortage of pizza pans, she bakes Crust A in her oven and pan, she bakes Crust B in a neighbor's oven in a different brand of pizza pan, and she bakes Crust C in a second neighbor's oven using a third brand of pan.

This experiment fails to eliminate two reasonable alternative explanations of the results. The differences in crust quality could be due to differences in the ovens or due to differences in the pans.

4. *Strength of association.* The cause and effect relationship must be supported and verified by significant outcomes from appropriate statistical tests.

While all four criteria for the acceptance of causation are essential, the third criterion is perhaps the most crucial because it affects an experiment's internal validity. *Internal validity* refers to the extent that one can eliminate alternative explanations for the observed experimental results. The greater a researcher's ability to show that the manipulation of the independent variable caused the observed changes in the dependent variable, the higher the level of experimental internal validity and the resulting greater confidence one has in inferring causation. Peter's pizza experiment had high internal validity because of the care he took in the preparation and baking of each crust. Consistency in these areas helped to eliminate alternative explanations. Sally's pizza experiment lacked internal validity because there were several reasonable alternative explanations of the results. Crust differences in Sally's experiment could be attributed to differences in ovens or pans.

The next section discusses the factors that can affect the internal validity of an experiment.

PROBLEMS AFFECTING INTERNAL VALIDITY

Internal validity is reduced whenever alternative explanations of the results can be found. Researchers have identified many different types of problems (typically referred to as "threats") that can negatively impact an experiment by raising alternative explanations of the relationship between independent and dependent variables, thereby decreasing a researcher's confidence in any conclusions drawn from the research.[7] These threats to internal validity fall into the following areas, with the specific threats in each area noted in parentheses:

- problems associated with an initial, pretest survey (premeasurement, interaction, and testing)
- problems due to data collection (instrumentation)
- problems associated with the sample (maturation, selection, and mortality)
- problems caused by the study context (history)
- problems attributable to researcher behavior (bias)

Premeasurement and Interaction

Premeasurement and interaction threats to internal validity are closely related. Either or both may occur whenever individuals are interviewed at the start of an experiment, before they are exposed to the independent variable. *Premeasurement* threats occur whenever an interview administered before the start of an experiment has a direct effect on a respondent's attitudes, actions, or behaviors *during* the experiment. *Interaction* threats occur whenever an interview administered before the start of the experiment affects a respondent's sensitivity or responsiveness to the independent variable.

The following situations illustrate how problems with premeasurement and interaction can reduce internal validity:[8]

PREMEASUREMENT   Tom resides in a test market selected by Wisk, a manufacturer of laundry detergent. Wisk is about to conduct a test of a new advertising campaign in the test market. Tom is selected to participate in the research study that will track changes in product perceptions and purchase behaviors. Before the start of the study, Tom completes a questionnaire that asks him to rate five brands of laundry detergent and to describe his purchase behaviors of the past four months. After he completes the questionnaire, he says to himself: "I've recently tried all the brands the questionnaire asked me about except Wisk. I haven't bought Wisk in a long time. I wonder why? Next time I think I'll get some." Tom's next purchase of laundry detergent is Wisk. Four weeks later, Tom fills out another questionnaire that shows he has purchased Wisk.

Wisk attributes this positive shift in Tom's behavior to the effects of the advertising. However, Tom's purchase had nothing to do with the advertising test. In fact, he did not even see any Wisk advertising. Tom's purchase was directly affected by the questionnaire he filled out before the start of the test.

INTERACTION   Tom's neighbor, Mary, is selected to participate in another research study. This study is designed to probe the influence of heath care advocacy advertising on consumer attitudes. Before the start of the study and the advertising campaign, Mary completes a questionnaire that explores her attitudes toward health care reform and health care advocacy advertising. At the end of three months, during which time the advertising appears, Mary completes another survey that again explores her attitudes toward health care reform and health care advocacy advertising. Mary shows a large shift in attitude between the first and second questionnaires.

The study sponsor attributes the changes in Mary's attitudes to the impact of the advertising and generalizes these changes to the broader population. But, Mary is not representative of the broader population because her behaviors changed after filling out the initial questionnaire. After Mary completed the first questionnaire, she said to herself: "That's an interesting topic. I haven't seen any advertising about health care reform, yet. I'd better watch out for it." The first questionnaire sensitized Mary. She was much more likely than the average consumer to watch for this advertising, and as a result, her change in attitude may be larger than the typical consumer who was not sensitized.

In the cases of Tom and Mary, decision makers have attributed changes in the dependent variable (purchase behavior and attitudes) to the advertising exposure (the independent variable). But this linkage may not be true (and in these cases are not true) given the presence of the two uncontrolled threats to internal validity. The presence of these threats to internal validity obscures the interpretation of the findings and reduces our confidence in attributing changes in the dependent measures to the independent variable.

Finally, while premeasurement and interaction threats to internal validity are related, it is important to understand their differences. Premeasurement threats to validity occur *without* exposure to the independent variable. All observed attitudinal or behavioral changes are the result of exposure to the initial measurement instrument. Interaction threats to validity occur whenever the independent variable is more likely to be noticed and reacted to then it would be without exposure to the initial measurement instrument. This distinction is important for the design of experiments. As you will see in the next section, some experimental designs eliminate premeasurement threats without eliminating interaction threats.

Testing

Testing threats to internal validity can result from repeated administrations of the same questionnaire or survey, when it is administered once before the treatment (the pretest) and once again after the treatment (the post-test). It is possible that changes in scores between these two administrations happen not because of the independent variable's effect but rather because of repeated testing. For example, a consumer might show better understanding of product benefits after exposure to a test ad when this understanding is compared to responses given on a pretest. This improvement, however, might not necessarily reflect any change in knowledge or understanding, instead it might simply reflect the respondent's better ability to answer the test questions "correctly" on the second try.

Instrumentation

Instrumentation refers to changes made to the measurement instrument (e.g., the questionnaire) or data recording techniques during the experiment. Such changes

Changes in the Measurement Instrument

Harris Toys is interested in determining the effects of two advertising campaigns on product perceptions and purchase behaviors. They select four comparable markets. The new campaign will be shown in two markets; the remaining markets will not receive any advertising. Prior to the start of the campaign, participants in all markets are questioned about their current product perceptions. One of the key scale questions, which probes the value of Harris' toys, is found to be confusing and difficult for respondents to answer. This question is changed, and the new, revised version appears on the questionnaire used to measure attitudes and behaviors at the conclusion of the experiment. The change in the question makes it impossible to accurately compare attitudes on the pretest with attitudes expressed on the post-test.

Changes or Noncomparability in Recording Techniques

Harris Toys has also developed two new versions of a preexisting toy. First, they take the old version of the toy, give it to children, and note their reactions by recording their play behavior on an observation protocol. Three days later, they give each of the new toy versions to the same children and again record their reactions. However, different individuals record the children's reactions. Because the recording requires judgment, a subjective analysis of the behaviors being displayed, there is no assurance that the judgment used to obtain ratings of the old toy is comparable to the judgment used to rate reactions to the revised toy.

Changes in Data Collection Methods

In January 2009, Talpin Bank conducts a study of consumers' attitudes toward Chicago banking and financial institutions. The study uses face-to-face personal interviews conducted among a representative sample of the target audience. While the study collected a great deal of valuable information, the use of face-to-face interviews was very costly and time-consuming. One year later, in January 2010, the bank uses the same questionnaire but conducts the study by mail among a second representative sample. The differences in data collection methods prevent the bank from confidently comparing attitudes in 2009 and 2010.

Inconsistent Interviewing

The Remmie Corporation has hired a field service to conduct 300 mall intercept interviews. The interviews need to be completed within two weeks. After one week, 100 interviews had been completed. A discussion with the interviewers reveals that a great deal of time is devoted to clarifying questions and to probing answers. In the interest of meeting the time deadline, interviewers are told to minimize these activities. The change in interviewing can have a dramatic effect on information content and quality and thus affects the internal validity of the research.

FIGURE 14.1 Instrumentation Threats to Internal Validity

affect the internal validity of the experiment because one does not know whether to attribute differences in attitudes or behaviors observed before and after the experimental manipulation to the manipulation itself, or to changes in the measurement instrument, recording techniques, data collection methods, or inconsistent interviewing. An example of each of these sources of instrumentation threats is presented in Figure 14.1.

Maturation

Respondents' attitudes, behaviors, and physiology change during an experiment. They can become tired, hungry, thirsty, bored, and disinterested as the experiment progresses. Maturation threats to internal validity refer to these types of changes, all of which have the potential to affect and distort the levels of the dependent variable. Respondents at the end of an experiment may be less interested in the experiment and the experimental topic than when they began. This may cause them to provide superficial answers on the questionnaire administered at the end of the experiment.

Selection and Mortality

Selection and mortality threats to internal validity are related to the composition and characteristics of the groups comprising the experimental study.

True experimental designs require at least two groups of individuals, a test group and a control group formed through random assignment. The control group is not exposed to the experimental manipulation and serves as a basis of comparison for the test group, which is exposed to the experimental manipulation. Selection threats to internal validity occur whenever the characteristics of these two groups are not equivalent before the start of the experiment.

Selection threats occur whenever, at the start of the experiment, the test and control groups differ in terms of relevant demographics, attitudes, or behaviors. Selection threats pose significant problems with data interpretation because the researcher does not know whether to attribute differences in response between groups to initial group differences or to the experimental manipulation. As will be seen later in this chapter, random assignment can typically eliminate this threat.

Mortality threats arise when respondents drop out of a study between the pretest and the post-test and, as a result, it cannot be determined whether differences between the two tests are the result of the experimental treatment or are the result of different group characteristics at the two stages of measurement. Mortality threats can occur whether or not there is a control group, as illustrated in the following examples:

- Imagine that an advertiser wishes to see if changes to an advertising campaign's essential message result in more favorable attitudes toward the product. A group of 500 individuals are recruited and are given a survey to complete prior to advertising exposure (this is the pretest). After advertising exposure, they answer the same questions as in the pretest. The researcher then compares the before and after exposure ratings. The favorable ratings rise from an average of 2 to an average of 6 on a 10-point scale where "10" is the best score. The advertiser concludes that the advertising was a success. This conclusion is incorrect, however. Due to mortality, many of those who were initially unfavorable toward the product dropped out of the experiment. As a result, the majority of those who completed the post-test were already favorable toward the product *even before seeing the advertising*. The advertising appeared to have a positive effect, but actually didn't.

- Assume that a test and a control group are well matched before the start of the study and that each group consists of a representative sample of the U.S. adult population. During of the study, 10% of the individuals in both groups drop out of the study. However, in the control group, the dropouts are individuals aged 18 to 24 (thus increasing the mean age of this group), while in the test group the dropouts are individuals aged 45 and older (thus decreasing the mean age of this group). Consequently, differences in attitudes or behaviors at the conclusion of the experiment cannot unambiguously be attributed to the influence of the independent variable. The difference in mean age between the two groups at the end of the experiment may have affected responses to the dependent measures.

History

History refers to any events or influences beyond those intentionally manipulated by the researcher that occur during the experiment and that have the potential to affect the experimental outcome as measured by the dependent variable(s). Historical threats to an experiment's internal validity come from several sources.

- *Some historical threats are the result of circumstances beyond any person's control.* For example, an experiment designed to measure the effect of various promotions on soft drink consumption might be distorted by several weeks of unexpected unseasonably hot or cold weather. Similarly, an advertising test designed to promote fish as a healthy choice could be influenced by news reports of high mercury levels in fish. Finally, the test of a new campaign featuring a well-known celebrity can be influenced if the celebrity is the focus of either very good or very bad publicity.

- *Some historical threats are the result of deliberate actions taken by others.* Wondra hand lotion, for example, was test marketed in Milwaukee. During the test, large and atypical discounts were offered by Wondra's competitor significantly distorting sales figures. Sales figures dropped, indicating (on the surface) the advertising campaign was not motivating sales. The drop in sales, however, was due to the deep discounting of Wondra's competitor.

Researcher Bias

Unlike some of the prior threats to internal validity, researcher bias is under the direct control of the person planning and conducting the experiment. Researcher bias can be eliminated through raised self-awareness and proper planning.

Researcher bias occurs whenever the actions of the experimenter affects the outcome of an experiment. Bias can occur during any part of an experiment, for example[9].

- A researcher can bias the results at the very start of the research because of the way individuals are assigned to different groups. When random sampling is not used, a researcher can assign "better" people to the test conditions, where "better" is defined "as most likely respond in the desired way to the independent variable."

- A researcher can bias the results during the experiment by subtly treating individuals in different groups differently, where the difference in treatment reflects the researcher's expectations about the outcome of the experiment, which is subtly communicated to the participants.

- A researcher can bias the results during data analysis through inconsistent data processing. When interpreting open-ended responses, for example, a researcher's analysis and classification of ambiguous responses can be influenced by what the researcher wants the outcome of the experiment to be.

Since all forms of researcher bias have the potential to lead to incorrect conclusions, it is incumbent on the researcher to have nonbiased interactions with both study participants and study data.

EXPERIMENTAL DESIGN

The threats to internal validity discussed in the prior section can, to a greater or lesser extent, be controlled through experimental design. Some experimental designs attempt to control all threats to internal validity, while other designs are able to control only a few.

Usually, information accuracy and cost increase as more controls are built into the experimental design. Given this relationship between cost and control, it is not necessarily the case that a researcher always wants to select the design that controls all threats to internal validity. Good research design requires a balance between the accuracy of the information collected and the cost required to collect that information. A researcher must identify the experimental design that, given the magnitude of the decision and information needs, provides the best balance between accuracy and cost.

This section discusses both quasi-experimental and true experimental design, noting the strengths and weaknesses of each design. Each design will be discussed in the context of the following situation:

> **The American Savings Association (ASA) wants to improve consumers' attitudes towards Savings & Loans, particularly in the areas of stability, friendliness, and community involvement. An e-mail campaign has been developed to address these issues. It is hoped that consumers' attitudes in these areas will have improved as a result of exposure to the campaign. The e-mail campaign consists of four mailings taking place one week apart. The initial mailing, which addresses safety issues, is shown in Photo 14.1.**

Quasi-Experimental Designs

The effectiveness of the e-mail campaign conducted by the ASA could be evaluated by one of three common quasi-experimental designs. These designs are called quasi-experimental because they are not true experiments. These approaches attempt to uncover a causal relationship, but do so relatively poorly because they fail to eliminate a large number of threats to internal validity. As a result, the outcomes of quasi-experimental designs are difficult to interpret and are only slight improvements over descriptive studies as a basis for decision making. Marketers and advertisers who use these designs when a true experiment is needed do so at their own risk. The three common types of quasi-experimental designs that could be used by the ASA are:

- one group post-test only
- one group pretest to post-test
- two group post-test with control

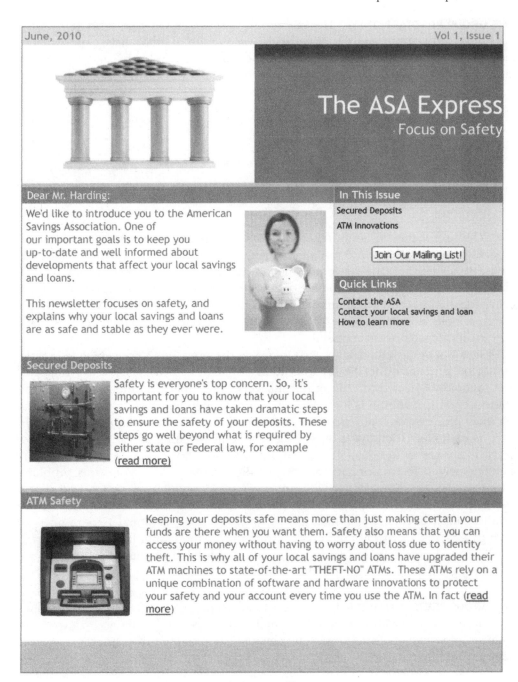

PHOTO 14.1 • Initial American Savings Association E-mailing

ONE GROUP POST-TEST ONLY.   The one group post-test-only design (also known as the "let's at least do something" design) takes a single group of individuals, exposes them to the treatment or experimental manipulation (the independent variable), and then measures the dependent variable(s) as part of the post-test, as shown below.

The use of this design in the ASA e-mail campaign would result in the following quasi-experiment: The ASA e-mails individuals who have provided their e-mail address on the ASA Web site. One week after the last mailing, each individual is contacted by e-mail and asked to complete an online questionnaire that measures perceptions of the stability, friendliness, and community involvement of their community's Savings & Loans. The ASA looks at the opinions expressed on the questionnaire and then decides whether the e-mail campaign was successful.

This is a very weak design. First, because the sample is a convenience sample, it cannot be generalized to the broader adult population. However, even if the sample was randomly selected, the design is still very weak. Because there is no control or reference group, the ASA is forced to rely entirely on judgment to interpret the results. For example, assume that "friendliness" is measured using a five-point scale in which a "5" is extremely friendly. Is an average friendliness rating of 3.0 good or bad? The ASA has no way of knowing because it did not know how "friendly" Savings & Loans were perceived to be prior to the start of the campaign.[10] Beyond this problem in interpretation, the ASA cannot with any degree of confidence attribute the post-test ratings to the e-mail campaign. These ratings (reflecting historical threats to internal validity) may have been influenced by news stories, personal experiences with Savings & Loans, or word of mouth occurring during the month-long e-mail campaign. Finally, the design fails to control for several additional threats to internal validity, specifically maturation, selection, and mortality.

ONE GROUP PRETEST TO POST-TEST.   The one group pretest–post-test design (also known as "before and after without control") is similar to the design just discussed *except* that a premeasure is taken before experimental manipulation of the independent variable. This design would be represented as:

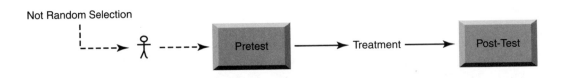

This design is frequently used for tests of product pricing, packaging, and advertising response, as follows:

Pretest	**Treatment**	**Post-test**
Measure product brand share	Alter pricing	Measure product brand share
Measure customer satisfaction	Alter product formulation	Measure customer satisfaction
Measure product perceptions	Run new advertising	Measure product perceptions

In each case, the impact of the experimental treatment is assessed by comparing levels of the dependent measure in the post-treatment measure to levels observed in the pretreatment measure. For example, if product perceptions improve after the airing of the new ads, it is assumed that the rise in perceptions was caused by the new ads.

The ASA would use this design as follows: The ASA selects a sample of adults for study participation. Each individual is contacted by e-mail and interviewed before the first e-mailing (via an online questionnaire) regarding his or her perceptions of Savings & Loan stability, friendliness, and community involvement. The ASA begins its test e-mailing one week after the conclusion of these pretest interviews. One week after the last e-mailing, each individual is contacted by e-mail and asked to complete an online questionnaire that similarly measures perceptions of Savings & Loan stability, friendliness, and community involvement. The ASA compares the opinions expressed on the post-exposure questionnaire to precampaign levels and then decides whether any changes between the pretest and post-test levels are indicative of a successful campaign. For example, if "safety" ratings on the pretest averaged "2" and on the post-test averaged "4," the ASA would conclude that the campaign successfully improved "safety" perceptions.

The weakness of this approach becomes evident when we try to assign cause and effect by claiming that the e-mail campaign was responsible for the rise in positive attitudes. First, there is no control for any historical threats to internal validity. Similar to the prior design, the post-test ratings may have been influenced by news stories, personal experiences with Savings & Loans, or word of mouth occurring during the month-long e-mail campaign. Second, the design fails to eliminate any problems associated with the initial pretest survey: taking the pretest could have sensitized individuals to the forthcoming e-mails, thereby altering their inclination to immediately delete unknown commercial e-mails, or it could have affected their attitudes or perspective when they received the test e-mails. Third, the design fails to eliminate any problems associated with the sample itself, for example, maturation. Over the course of the research, individuals could have dropped out, resulting in only a subset of the total pretest sample providing post-test data. Because the ASA doesn't know what types of people dropped out, conclusions drawn from the pretest to post-test comparison are quite weak. Imagine, for example, that many individuals initially negative toward Savings & Loans dropped out of the study. As a result, the positive ratings at the end of the study would be attributable to initially favorable attitudes among those who remain in the study, rather than the positive effects of the e-mail campaign.

TWO GROUP POST-TEST WITH CONTROL.   The two group post-test with control is an attempt to address the problems with the prior designs. Symbolically, this design is represented as:

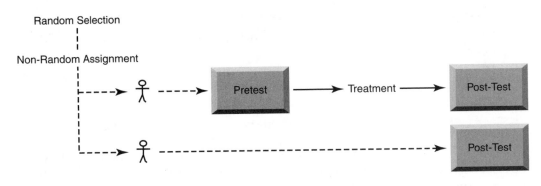

The ASA would use this design as follows: The ASA selects a random sample of adults for study participation. Next, it uses a nonrandom technique to assign individuals to the two groups: in this case, it assigns the first 100 people to the pretest/post-test group, the next 100 people to the post-test only group, etc. The ASA sends members of Group 1 one e-mail per week. The members of Group 2 do not receive any ASA e-mails. One week after the last e-mailing, individuals in both groups are contacted by e-mail, and asked to complete an online questionnaire that asks for perceptions of Savings & Loan stability, friendliness, and community involvement. The ASA compares the two groups' opinions as expressed on the post-test surveys. More positive attitudes in the treatment group versus the post-test only group are attributed to the success of the e-mail campaign.

This approach and conclusion might appear reasonable. Unfortunately, even in the presence of significant post-test differences in attitudes between the two groups, any conclusions drawn as to cause and effect may not be correct. The main problem with this approach lies in the characteristics of the two groups. *Because true random assignment was not used to form the groups, there is no way to tell (or to even assume) any equivalence in pretest scores.* If the pretest attitudes are not similar, then conclusions drawn from differences in post-test measures can be quite misleading. The data presented in Figure 14.2

Group	Pretest	Post-test
Treatment	3.2	4.5
No Treatment	(3.3)	3.1

Note: "Safety" measures are a five-point scale where higher numbers are more positive

Group	Pretest	Post-test
Treatment	4.3	4.3
No Treatment	(3.3)	3.3

Note: "Safety" measures are a five-point scale where higher numbers are more positive

FIGURE 14.2   The Effects of Non-random Assignment on Data Interpretation

illustrates this design problem, where the scores in parentheses are unknown to the researcher. The top table presents a situation in which the initial attitudes of the two groups on the measure of "safety" were in fact similar at the start of the experiment. Given similar initial ratings, differences in the post-test scores can, in the absence of other threats to internal validity, be attributed to the treatment, in this case receipt of the e-mailing. But a researcher never knows from this design whether or not this is actually the case. The bottom table in Figure 14.2 shows a situation in which initial attitudes in the two groups were not equivalent at the start of the survey. Neither group's attitudes changed, but because the treatment group was higher than the control group at the start of the experiment, the treatment was assumed to have a positive impact when in fact it did not.

True Experimental Designs

True experimental designs differ from quasi-experimental designs in two important ways. True experimental designs (1) have a control group and (2) use random assignment to form test and control groups. Random assignment in this context means that each study participant has a known and equal chance of being assigned to *either* the control or treatment group. The use of random assignment is particularly important because randomization helps to control many threats to internal validity. Thus, in spite of the fact that true experimental designs are more costly and time-consuming versus quasi-experimental designs, they tend to collect information that provides a sounder basis for decision making. The five most common types of true experimental designs are:

- simulated pretest to post-test
- post-test only with control
- pretest to post-test with control
- Solomon four-group design
- Factorial designs

Each of these designs controls for different threats to internal validity, and all provide greater confidence in conclusions versus quasi-experimental designs.

TWO GROUPS—TWO MEASURE DESIGNS.   The two most common forms of experimental advertising research require two groups of respondents and measurement at two different points in time. These designs, the *simulated pretest to post-test* and *post-test only with control,* are popular because of their ability to control most threats to internal validity while minimizing the number of required groups of respondents and measurements. Both designs accomplish this because they assume that the random assignment of individuals to the two groups results in equivalency across groups in terms of levels of pretreatment attitudes or behaviors.

Simulated Pretest—Post-test. The *simulated pretest to post-test* experimental design controls for premeasurement and interaction threats to internal validity, particularly in experiments dealing with consumer attitudes and knowledge. The experimental design controls these threats to validity by using one group of randomly assigned respondents for the pretest measurement and a second group of randomly assigned respondents for the treatment and post-test measurements, as follows:

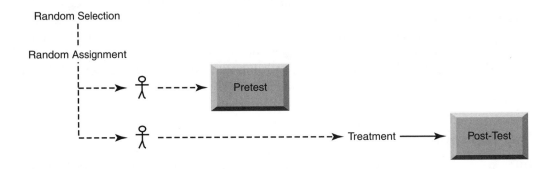

Because different individuals are administered the pretest and the post-test, premeasurement or interaction threats to validity cannot arise. However, other threats such as history, maturation, instrumentation, and selection can still occur. Data analysis in this design compares post-test measures in the treatment (test) group to pretest measures in the control group. In the absence of other explanations, differences in these measures are attributed to the experimental treatment because the design using random assignment assumes that attitudes in the control and test group were equivalent at the start of the research.

The ASA would use this design as follows: Members of the target audience for the e-mail campaign would be identified through appropriate random sampling techniques. Once identified, half would be randomly assigned to the control group and half would be randomly assigned to the treatment group. Those in the control group would be administered a questionnaire that measures attitudes toward Savings & Loans. When the administration of this questionnaire is complete, individuals in the treatment group would begin to receive the e-mail campaign. One week after the last campaign e-mailing, members of the treatment group would be administered the same questionnaire as was used in the control group's pretest. The post-treatment scores for the treatment group are then compared with the pretest scores of the control group. If the groups are of sufficient size and random assignment and selection of respondents were performed properly, then any differences in the two groups' attitudes can be attributed to the effects of the e-mail campaign in addition to any effects produced by either history, maturation, instrumentation, or selection.

Post-test Only with Control. The *post-test only with control* experimental design also utilizes two groups of respondents and two measures. This design, however, differs from the simulated pretest–post-test design in the way that it measures treatment effects. The simulated pretest to post-test design estimates treatment effects by comparing one group's pretest to a different group's post-test. This design estimates treatment effects by exclusively comparing post-test measures, one measure obtained from the treatment group and one obtained from the control group, as follows:

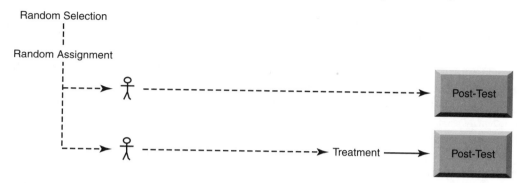

In the absence of other explanations, differences in the two groups' post-test measures are attributed to the experimental treatment because, due to random sampling and random assignment, the groups are assumed to be equivalent at the start of the experiment.

The post-test only with control design is a more powerful design than the simulated pretest–post-test design because it controls for a greater number of threats to internal validity. Because both post-test measures are taken at the same point in time, this design is able to control for history, maturation, and instrumentation, as well as premeasurement, and interaction threats to internal validity.

The ASA would use this design as follows: Members of the target audience for the e-mail campaign would be identified through appropriate random sampling techniques. Once identified, half would be randomly assigned to the control group and half would be randomly assigned to the treatment group. After the groups are formed, individuals in the treatment group would begin to receive the e-mail campaign. One week after the last e-mailing, members of both groups would be administered the same questionnaire. The post-test scores for the treatment group are then compared to the post-test scores of the control group. As with the prior design, if the groups are of sufficient size and the random assignment and selection of respondents were performed properly, then any differences in the two groups' attitudes on the post-test can be attributed to the effects of the e-mail campaign.

TWO GROUPS WITH FOUR MEASURES: THE PRETEST TO POST-TEST WITH CONTROL.   The prior design assumed, but never verified, that random assignment resulted in equivalent pretreatment attitudes in the treatment and control groups. This design, the *pretest to post-test with control,* makes certain that there is equivalency between the treatment and control groups before the start of the research. This certainty is obtained by testing both groups before the start of the research, as follows:

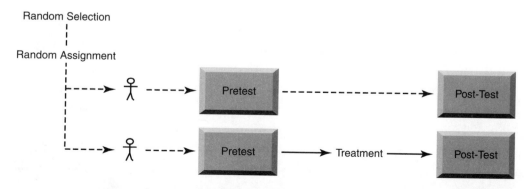

This common and very strong design is appropriate whenever a researcher needs explicit evidence of group equivalency before the start of the treatment or whenever there is some doubt as to the extent of group equivalence.

The ASA would use this design as follows: Members of the target audience for the e-mail campaign would be identified though appropriate random sampling techniques. Once identified, half would be randomly assigned to the control group and half would be randomly assigned to the treatment group. After the groups are formed, individuals in both groups would be asked to complete the pretest questionnaire. Next, individuals in the treatment group would begin to receive the e-mail campaign. One week after the last e-mailing, members of both groups would be administered the same questionnaire designed to collect post-test data. This powerful design allows a researcher to make certain that there is no meaningful difference in the pretest scores for the two groups prior to comparing the differences in the group's post-test scores.

The pretest to post-test with control design is an alternative to the post-test only with control design. Both experimental designs control for premeasurement, history, maturation, and instrumentation threats to internal validity. However, the post-test only with control eliminates interaction threats, while the pretest to post-test with control eliminates selection threats. Neither design eliminates challenges to internal validity due to mortality. Consequently, design selection reflects a researcher's information needs, anticipated threats to validity, and budget.

FOUR GROUPS—SIX MEASURES: THE SOLOMON FOUR-GROUP DESIGN.   The *Solomon Four-Group design* is both the most powerful and the most resource-intensive experimental design. The design is powerful because it controls for all major threats to an experiment's internal validity. As shown in the following diagram, it accomplishes this by combining a pretest to post-test with control design (the top two rows of the diagram) with the post-test only with control design (the bottom two rows):

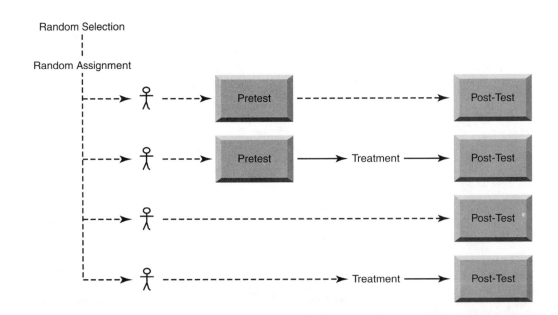

The ASA would use this design as follows: Members of the target audience for the e-mail campaign would be identified though appropriate random sampling techniques. Once identified, respondents would be randomly assigned to one of four groups. Once the groups are formed, before the start of the e-mail campaign individuals in Groups 1 and 2 would be administered the pretest. After the pretest results are obtained, individuals in Groups 2 and 4 would begin to receive the e-mail campaign. One week after the last e-mailing to these groups, members of all groups would be administered the same questionnaire designed to collect post-test data.

The number of measurements taken as part of this design allows for a variety of comparisons during data analysis. Each set of comparisons eliminates different threats to internal validity and allows a researcher different insights into data trends, treatment effects, and overall experimental results. It should be noted that in spite of its experimental power, the Solomon four-group design is rarely applied advertising and marketing research, primarily due to its complexity, cost, and timing.

More Complex Experimental Designs

The prior examples presented the most basic forms of experimentation. There was only one independent variable, and this variable had only one level (present or absent). Advertising research often requires more complex experimental designs. These designs might entail manipulating different levels or aspects of a single independent variable or they might require the simultaneous manipulation of two or more independent variables.

MORE THAN ONE LEVEL OR ASPECT OF A VARIABLE.   A true experimental design can be expanded for circumstances in which different levels or aspects of a single independent variable need to be studied. A variable has *different levels* when you experimentally vary the *quantity* of that variable, giving more or less of it to different groups of individuals. For example:

- The ASA might want to determine how the number of e-mails an individual receives affects subsequent attitudes toward Savings & Loans. As a result, they can form four experimental groups, in which members of Group 1 receive one e-mail (in total), members of Group 2 receive four e-mails, and members of Group 3 receive seven e-mails.

- An advertiser might want to see how the length of a viral video affects individuals' attitudes toward the advertiser. Three videos of different lengths (:15, :60 and :90) can be created, with individuals in different experimental groups being exposed to one of the videos.[11]

A variable has *different aspects* when you experimentally vary the *characteristics* of that variable. For example:

- An advertiser wants to determine whether a male or female spokesperson is most appropriate for the product. Two commercials, using the same script, are filmed where one commercial uses a female spokesperson and second uses a male. Reactions to the two ads are measured experimentally, where individuals randomly assigned to Group 1 view the female spokesperson ad and individuals randomly assigned to Group 2 view the male spokesperson ad.

- A blogger wishes to determine where to place ads on his blog so that click-throughs can be maximized. Three versions of the blog are developed, where ads are either placed on the top of page (version one), the right-hand side of the page (version two), or integrated into the blog itself (version three). Each visitor to the blog is randomly assigned to view one of the three versions.

Any true experimental design can be expanded to accommodate multiple levels or aspects of an independent variable. The design selected is determined by the information needs motivating the experiment and the specific threats to internal validity that need to be controlled. The simulated pretest–post-test design, for example, could be an appropriate way to determine whether the length of video differentially affects attitudes toward the advertiser. In this case, the experimental design would be:

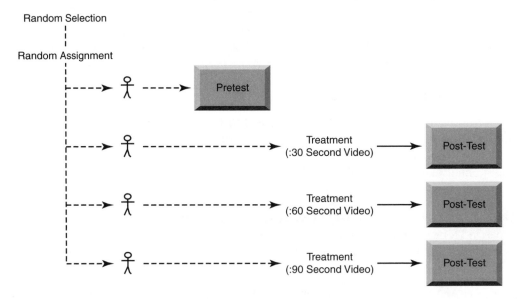

As in the prior case of just one treatment group, each group in this design consists of a randomly selected sample of adults who, once identified, are randomly assigned to one of the four groups. Individuals in Group 1 are only administered a pretest. Individuals in Group 2 are shown the :30 video, while individuals in Groups 3 and 4 are shown the :60 and :90 videos, respectively. After exposure to the video, all respondents in the treatment groups are given a post-test questionnaire to complete. Questions on the post-test questionnaire are identical to those used on the pretest questionnaire given to Group 1.

Imagine that a summary measure, the "Average Advertiser Rating," is calculated based on the post-test measures. This measure reflects that average score of all measures of attitudes toward the advertiser and is scaled so that larger numbers indicate more positive attitudes. The "Average Advertiser Rating" for the Control Group (Group 1) was 3.2 (out of a possible 7) while the scores for the three treatment groups are shown in the following table:

Length of Video	Average Advertiser Rating
:30 seconds	6.7
:60 seconds	5.3
:90 seconds	4.9

Had the advertisers tested any one of the videos, the test would have been considered a success as the "Average Advertiser Rating" for any of the videos was much higher than that of the control group. However, only by testing different lengths of the video was the advertiser able to conclude that the :30 video was by far the strongest of the three.

FACTORIAL DESIGNS: MORE THAN ONE MANIPULATION. There are times when an advertising researcher needs to manipulate and observe the effects of two or more independent variables at the same time where each of these variables has two or more levels or aspects. Imagine, for example, a creative team in the following situation:

> We have debated for days our creative options for the new advertising campaign. Two problems remain. First, we cannot decide if we should use a celebrity or an ordinary person as the spokesperson in the commercial. Second, we cannot decide if the tone and manner should be humorous or serious. We need research to answer three questions for us. In terms of the persuasiveness of the commercial:
>
> 1. What is the effect of varying the commercial's spokesperson?
> 2. What is the effect of varying the commercial's tone?
> 3. What is the effect of varying the spokesperson and tone at the same time; for example, does response to the celebrity spokesperson remain constant or change when the tone of the commercial changes?[12]

A factorial design could be used to answer these questions. A factorial design is an experimental procedure that simultaneously measures the effect of two or more independent variables, each with different levels, on one or more dependent variables. Factorial designs are typically diagramed as squares (for two factors) or cubes (for three factors), where each column and row represents one of the factors.[13] The factorial design that would be used to address the issues of spokesperson and commercial tone is graphically represented below. The columns represent the levels of one main effect (type of spokesperson), while the rows represent the levels of the second main effect (commercial tone). Respondents are randomly recruited and then randomly assigned to one of the four cells. Each respondent sees one ad. Respondents assigned to the upper left cell, for example, will see a serious ad with a celebrity spokesperson, while respondents assigned

Type of Spokesperson

	Celebrity	Regular
Serious Approach	Celebrity in Serious Commercial	Regular Person in Serious Commercial
Humorous Approach	Celebrity in Humorous Commercial	Regular Person in Humorous Commercial

to the lower right cell will see a humorous ad with an ordinary spokesperson. After an ad is seen, a post-test questionnaire is given.[14]

Factorial designs consist of main effects and interactions. A main effect is the separate influence of each independent variable on the dependent variable(s). In this example, the main effects are the spokesperson and tone. The effect of *combinations* of main effects on the dependent variables(s) is the interaction. Interaction occurs when the simultaneous effect of two or more independent variables is different from the sum of their independent effects. In this example, an interaction would occur if responses to a particular spokesperson-tone combination were different from independent responses to spokesperson alone or tone alone. Chapter 16 provides a detailed discussion of the analysis and interpretation of factorial designs.

CONDUCTING EXPERIMENTS ONLINE

A critical decision that must be made with regard to experiments relates to how individuals will be exposed to the stimulus. The ASA experiment e-mailed the stimulus to individuals in the experimental group(s). Other experiments, especially those exploring the results of advertising exposure, typically use a laboratory setting to show different experimental groups the appropriate stimulus. The high use of the laboratory setting was due, in great part, to the inability of online research companies to handle true random assignment. Fortunately, this is changing.

PsychData[15] is one of the few companies with the capability to conduct online experiments with random assignment. The company accomplishes this by allowing a researcher to randomly assign sampled individuals to different experimental conditions. Imagine, for example, that a researcher wanted to conduct the factorial experiment described in the prior section. Creating this experiment on PsychData would be straightforward. The researcher would:

- Create and then upload the stimuli, in this case the four commercials. Each stimulus would represent one of the four experimental conditions.

- Create a link to each stimulus.

- Tell PsychData that there are four stimuli and that exposure to each stimulus should be randomized.

- Provide PsychData with the links to each stimulus. PsychData confirms the links and random assignment with feedback such as that shown in Figure 14.3. (Note that in this example respondents are not shown the URL of the link, but rather the coded link name.)

The online survey software at PsychData will then randomly assign each individual participating in the research to one of the four experimental conditions.

INTERNAL VALIDITY: A BROADER VIEW

The prior section shows how experimental design affects internal validity by allowing or eliminating alternative explanations of the experimental results. Internal validity improves as more threats to internal validity are eliminated. Beyond these specific

Random Assignment

[Random Stimulus Assignment 1]

Prior to beginning the research, we'd like you to watch a television commercial. You can view the commercial by clicking on the link below. The commercial will open and play in a new browser window. Please close the browser window when the commercial is done and then continue with the survey.

View Commercial A/NBV/127

[Random Stimulus Assignment 2]

Prior to beginning the research, we'd like you to watch a television commercial. You can view the commercial by clicking on the link below. The commercial will open and play in a new browser window. Please close the browser window when the commercial is done and then continue with the survey.

View Commercial A/POL/654

[Random Stimulus Assignment 3]

Prior to beginning the research, we'd like you to watch a television commercial. You can view the commercial by clicking on the link below. The commercial will open and play in a new browser window. Please close the browser window when the commercial is done and then continue with the survey.

View Commercial A/KJU/749

[Random Stimulus Assignment 4]

Prior to beginning the research, we'd like you to watch a television commercial. You can view the commercial by clicking on the link below. The commercial will open and play in a new browser window. Please close the browser window when the commercial is done and then continue with the survey.

View Commercial A/KMB/588

FIGURE 14.3 • Random Assignment in Online Experiments

aspects of internal validity, Krathwohl[16] argues that an experiment's internal validity is also affected by the nature of the experiment's predictions and results. This broader view of internal validity suggests that an experiment's internal validity improves under the following circumstances:

- *Internal validity increases with stronger predictions.* Strong predictions state the direction and size of changes that will occur in response to the experimental manipulations. "Indicating simply when the effect will occur is the weakest prediction. A stronger prediction adds the direction of effect, a still stronger one the size and nature of the change." A researcher, for example, might wish to explore the relationship between advertising exposure and brand attitudes. A statement that "exposure will affect attitudes" is the weakest prediction because it does not specifically identify the nature of the relationship between exposure and attitudes. A stronger prediction would add directionality (i.e., "increased advertising exposure will positively improve brand attitudes"), while an even stronger prediction would address the nature of the change (i.e., "increased advertising exposure will improve brand attitudes in the areas of product performance and quality").

- *Internal validity is greater when a change in the cause is followed by large changes in effect.* The results of experiments are typically evaluated by the use of inferential statistics that determine if there are statistically meaningful differences among experimental conditions. However, not all statistical significant differences are meaningful and not all meaningful differences are statistically significant. As a consequence, studies that exhibit large changes in the dependent variable(s) tend to produce results that are both meaningful and statistically significant, thereby improving the experiment's internal validity.

- *Internal validity is greater when the effect reverses a prevailing tendency or condition than when the change simply produces more of the same.* An experiment that improves brand attitudes among those negative toward the product tends to have more internal validity than an experiment that improves brand attitudes among those who are already positive.

We agree with Krathwohl and recommend that these factors be considered during the planning stages of any experiment.[17]

EXTERNAL VALIDITY

Internal validity affects the extent to which you can have confidence in the integrity of the data collected in an experiment. Once internal validity is achieved, it is important to determine the extent to which the experiment has external validity. External validity is concerned with the extent to which the results of the experiment can legitimately be generalized beyond the narrow confines of the experiment itself. External validity addresses the question: For what other populations, measurements, and settings can similar results be expected?

Population-related external validity is heightened when systematic, appropriate, and random sampling procedures are used to select individuals from the population of interest and, when experimentation is used, to assign selected individuals to specific treatment and control groups. The external validity of research that utilizes convenience or haphazard samples, for example, is always quite low.

Measurement-related external validity is heightened when steps are taken to ensure that the measures used to collect the data are actually collecting the right data. The following situation provides an illustration:

> Peter is conducting research to measure restaurant customers' satisfaction with the serving staff. He experimentally varies the amount of trips made to a table and the extent of interaction between customer and staff. He decides to use the amount of the "tip" as the measure of satisfaction, assuming that larger tips reflect greater satisfaction. The external validity of Peter's research is dependent upon the extent to which his measure is a valid measure of satisfaction and the extent to which this measure is agreed to be appropriate versus other measures, such as the number of return visits, recommendations to friends, length of time dining, etc.[18]

Setting-related external validity is always a concern of advertising researchers who have to decide whether to conduct an experiment in a laboratory or in a natural setting. There is always a trade-off with regard to internal and external validity between the two approaches.

- A laboratory study is by its very nature an artificial situation. A well-constructed laboratory study will have very high internal validity (since the researcher can control appropriate threats) but very low external validity since there is no assurance that the way individuals act in such an artificial and well-controlled environment is the same as they would act in the real world.

- A field experiment is a much more natural setting. Experiments conducted in this setting tend to have very high external validity because of the natural setting but quite low internal validity, since it difficult to control many threats to internal validity outside of the lab.

There is no "right' approach. Most research situations can be explored in either a laboratory or a field setting. The better decision is the one that provides the desired trade-off between internal and external validity.

APPLYING CHAPTER CONCEPTS

This chapter discussed how well-designed experiments increase advertisers' insights and improve advertising decision making. Two extremely well-designed and analyzed experiments are provided in the online supplemental readings.

IAB Advertising Effectiveness Study

The Internet Advertising Bureau's (IAB) Advertising Effectiveness Study fundamentally altered how advertisers viewed banner advertising and, as a result, repositioned online advertising as a legitimate and important advertising medium. Keep in mind that while no one doubts the importance of online advertising today, attitudes were very different in 1997. Few advertisers had a good understanding of how advertising in this new medium worked and even fewer were confident that it even worked at all. Within this context, banner advertising was not viewed as a critical component of an advertising plan. Some felt that banner advertising occupied the same niche as direct mail, as both forms of advertising could be measured by response rate (click-throughs in the case of banner advertising). Others felt that banner advertising was equivalent to outdoor advertising asking "what can those little billboards accomplish?" The IAB Advertising Effectiveness Study resulted in a paradigm shift. The research repositioned online advertising by demonstrating that advertising in this medium works much more like television advertising than direct mail or outdoor. The research found that after only a single exposure online advertising can increase brand awareness, enhance product perceptions, and improve product purchase intent. Perhaps most important, these positive outcomes were achieved *in the absence of click-throughs.*

Key summary sections from the 1997 Advertising Effectiveness Study are provided.[19] Report page 6 provides background on the study and insights into methodological considerations. Report pages 12 to 15 provide an overview of the experimental design. Note how key issues of experimental research (sampling, random assignment, experimental design, and the use of control groups) are all addressed. Finally, report pages 7 to 11 summarize the findings. Note, how the presentations of the results of a complex experimental design do not have to be complex themselves. The results of this research are presented in a way that highlights the key findings and builds a persuasive, easy-to-understand explanation of how banner advertising worked.

Massive Video Game Advertising Test

Jumper (the movie), released in 2008, starred Hayden Christensen, Jamie Bell, and Rachel Bilson. The overlap between the movie's assumed target audience and video game players motivated research to determine whether advertising *Jumper's* DVD release in video games was appropriate and effective.

Massive Incorporated[20] designed an executed an exemplary "real-world" experiment to determine whether the placement of in-game advertising for the *Jumper* DVD release improved attitudes toward the movie and fostered increased interest (including purchase intent) in the DVD. Massive executed a multi-title, multiple creative, time-sensitive in-game advertising campaign and then surveyed gamers playing *Skate* and *Rainbow 6: Vegas 2* to determine the advertising campaign's impact on preidentified key measures. (Examples of advertising placement in these games are shown in Photos 14.2 and 14.3.) Massive worked with Interpret Research to recruit 603 console gamers aged 13 to 34 into a control group (which did not see the in-game ads) and a test group (which did see the ads). Both groups answered an online questionnaire that measured their awareness and

PHOTO 14.2   Advertising Placed Inside a Video Game (courtesy Massive, Inc.)

PHOTO 14.3 Advertising Placed Inside a Video Game (courtesy Massive, Inc.)

opinions of the film and purchase intent for the DVD.[21] The results were impressive. Among gamers who saw the ads there was:

- a 39% increase in awareness for the Jumper DVD release.
- over 100% increase in film ratings and purchase consideration.
- up to 80% increases in positive ratings of the film's attributes.

Importantly, gamers who saw the ads were very positive. The presence of the ads was felt to improve the game experience by adding realism and "looking cool."

The full report of this experimental research is provided in the online supplemental readings.[22] As with the IAB Study, note how great care is taken to make certain that the experiment is well-designed and executed. Also, note how data is presented in way that makes it easy for users of the research to see and understand key findings and implications.

SUMMARY

Advertisers conduct experiments to determine how different actions affect consumer attitudes, beliefs, or behaviors. Experiments help answer questions related to advertising strategy, creative development, new product introductions, product packaging, advertising content, media mix, and advertising spending.

A true experiment has at least one independent variable, one dependent variable, and a manipulation. All experiments try to claim causality, that is, to claim that the manipulations of the independent variable(s) caused a change in the dependent variables. In order for one to attribute causality, four criteria must be met:

- events must take place in the proper order,
- events must take place at the same time and show an explicit relationship,
- alternative explanations must be reduced or eliminated, and
- strength of association must be statistically verified.

The extent to which a researcher can confidently conclude that actions affect outcomes (i.e., that there is cause and effect) is dependent on how well the experiment is planned and conducted. Experimental designs that reflect better planning and control, and thus increase confidence in the results, are simulated pretest–post-test, post-test-only with control, pretest–post-test with control, and Solomon four-group. These designs, versus quasi-experimental designs, increase confidence because they eliminate many of the threats to internal validity.

External validity is concerned with the extent to which the results of an experiment can legitimately be generalized beyond the narrow confines of the experiment itself. External validity addresses the question: For what other populations, measurements, and settings can similar results be expected? Population-related external validity is heightened when systematic, appropriate, and random sampling procedures are used to select individuals from the population of interest and, when experimentation is used, to assign selected individuals to specific treatment and control groups. Measurement-related external validity is heightened when steps are taken to ensure that the measures used to collect the data are actually collecting the right data. Setting-related external validity is a concern of advertising researchers who have to decide whether to conduct an experiment in a laboratory or in a natural setting, acknowledging the generalization problems associated with each option.

Review Questions

1. What is the goal of an experiment? Why is this goal important?
2. What is the difference between a survey and an experiment?
3. Define the characteristics of an experiment.
4. What is an *independent* variable?
5. What is a *dependent* variable?
6. How does the concept of *manipulation* relate to independent and dependent variables?
7. What are the necessary criteria for claiming causality?
8. What threats to internal validity are associated with an initial, pretest survey? Briefly describe each.
9. What threat to internal validity is associated data collection? Briefly describe this threat.
10. What threats to internal validity are associated with the sample? Briefly describe each.
11. What threat to internal validity may be caused by the study context? Briefly describe this threat.
12. What threat to internal validity is related to the researcher? Briefly describe this threat.
13. How does a true experimental design differ from a quasi-experimental design?
14. Name and describe the characteristics of two quasi-experimental designs? What are the strengths and weaknesses of each design?
15. Name and describe the characteristics of four true experimental designs? What are the strengths and weaknesses of each design?
16. What are the characteristics of a factorial design, and in what circumstances is this design most appropriate?
17. What is the difference between main effects and interactions effect in a factorial design?
18. What are considerations related to evaluating an experiment's external validity?

Application Exercises[23]

Application exercises 1 through 5 reflect chapter content and discussion.

1. Spritzz is a wine cooler that has been distributed in three states: Delaware, New Hampshire, and Maine. It has been successful in these states, although it has never been advertised. Its average share of the wine cooler market in these states is about 15%. A new management team at Spritzz has identified two goals for the upcoming year.
   • First, they want to increase Spritzz's market share in Delaware, New Hampshire, and Maine. Management believes that one way to increase market share is to begin advertising in these states.
   • Second, management wants to expand Spritzz's area of distribution. They believe that they can successfully market the brand in denser, more urban states such as New York and New Jersey. Management believes that consumers in these areas would respond well to Spritzz's natural taste.

   As the Research Director at Spritzz, you realize that you have no way of knowing whether management's assumptions are correct. You convince management to explore the truth of these assumptions using experimentation. Prepare a memo to Spritzz management that proposes two experimental designs. The first design should help answer the question: "To what extent will increased advertising in existing markets affect market share?" The second design should address the question: "How successfully can Spritzz be marketed in urban areas?" Be certain to clearly explain and justify your recommendations. Remember, individuals in management are not researchers, so be certain to provide sufficient detail (explained in clear language) to help them understand both the methodology you recommend and what they will learn from the experiment.

2. You are an advertising researcher who wishes to explore the effect of television commercial exposure on children's play behavior. You think that there is a relationship between exposure to children's toy commercials and possessiveness during play. Specifically, you hypothesize that the more toy commercials a child sees the more possessive he or she will become.

   You have access to a day care center with 200 children. In addition to a large, common area play room, the center has eight individual rooms. Each individual room has a video tape player, a television set, many toys and games, and a one-way mirror, through which you can unobtrusively watch the children in the room. Present and defend a research design, including key measures, that you would use to experimentally determine whether there is a relationship between exposure to children's toy commercials and possessiveness during play.

3. Pizza Pie, a local pizza chain, wants to determine consumers' reactions to three different coupon offers. Pizza Pie creates two groups of individuals from a list of past customers. Each group of 400 receives one of the coupons. A third coupon is placed in the Sunday paper. A count of redeemed coupons is conducted for two weeks after mailing or publication. Evaluate this methodology. Is it a proper experiment? Can the results confidently be used for future planning? What experimental problems exist? What threats to internal validity are uncontrolled? Evaluate Pizza Pie's approach and then propose an improved experimental design to answer its information need.

4. The Norris Agency has prepared two new advertising campaigns for its client, the Old World Rice Company. Old World likes the current campaign, but has said, "We'll run either of the new campaigns if you can prove to us that it is better than the current one. But, you pay for the test." The agency has allocated enough money to conduct and analyze a total of 1,500 interviews. With this budget constraint in mind, propose and defend an experimental design to determine the campaign that is the strongest in terms of changing consumer attitudes toward the brand and in motivating consumers to purchase the product.

5. Select an advertising-related experiment from one of the following academic journals: *Journal of Advertising, Journal of Advertising Research, Journal of Marketing, Journal of Marketing Research, Journal of Consumer Behavior,* and

Journal of Consumer Marketing. Evaluate the strengths and weaknesses of the design used in the study. What threats to internal validity were controlled for? Which threats were not? Was the design appropriate for the type of information needed and research question explored? Why or why not? Explain and justify your point of view. How does the laboratory field setting of the experiment affect the interpretation and generalizability of the results? If the research was conducted in the field, present a plan for exploring the research question in a laboratory setting. If the research was conducted in the laboratory, present a plan for exploring the research question in a field setting.

Application exercises 6 through 9 refer to the IAB Advertising Effectiveness Study provided in the online supplemental readings.

6. The IAB Study used a post-test only with control research design. The methodology states that:

> Because test and control respondents were randomly assigned and identically matched, the hypothesis is that responses from test and control cells should be statistically identical unless the single additional exposure to the Web ad banner caused an effect. A methodology of this type sets a high standard for advertising effectiveness because it precisely measures the effect of one additional exposure to a Web ad banner, as opposed to measuring the cumulative impact of advertising. As a result, the findings may conservatively state the effectiveness of Web advertising.

Comment on this statement and the use of the post-test only design. Is this statement justified by the design? Did the research control for all potentially confounding variables? If not, which variables do you feel were not controlled or accounted for?

7. Imagine that you have been asked to propose the use of a pretest–post-test design instead of the post-test only design used in the IAB Study. Prepare a short paper that (a) presents a detailed description of how this design could be accomplished and (b) provides a point of view on the relative merits of the pretest–post-test design versus a post-test only design.

8. The IAB Study's Executive Summary details the key measures used in the research. Prepare a short paper that recommends (with justification) additional measures that might have been valuable to include in the research. Would the measures you recommend require a change in the research methodology? Why or why not?

9. The range of online advertising has expanded since the initial IAB Study. Internet advertising now comes:
   - in multiple sizes, with or without movement and sound,
   - with or without the ability to expand with a click or mouseover,
   - with or without the ability to overlay the Web page,
   - with the ability to appear multiple times on the same page.

   Assume that, in light of these developments, you have been asked to plan an experiment that will allow advertisers to better understand consumer response to these new advertising forms. Focus on one of the prior developments or one of your own choices and then prepare a short paper that (a) formulates a research question, (b) explains why the question is important, (c) presents a detailed description of the experimental methodology recommended to answer the question, and (d) identifies key measures. Make certain to fully explain and support all recommendations.

Application exercises 10 through 13 refer to the Massive in-game advertising test provided in the online supplemental readings.

10. The Massive Study, similar to the IAB study, uses a post-test only design. Prepare a short paper that discusses the use of this design versus a pretest–post-test design. What are the relative advantages and disadvantages of each experimental design for the questions motivating the research?

11. Two related but independent studies are reported by Massive (i.e., the effect of Jumper advertising in *Rainbow 6: Vegas 2* and *Skate)*. Each study utilized its own control group. Prepare a short paper that provides a point of view on this approach. Was it necessary for each study to have its own control group, or could the same control group have been used for both

studies? What are the relative advantages and disadvantages of each approach?

12. The Massive research report details the key measures used in the research. Prepare a short paper that recommends (with justification) additional measures that might have been valuable to include in the research. Would the measures you recommend require a change in the research methodology? Why or why not?

13. Imagine that your client, Oreo, wants to determine whether in-game advertising can be beneficial to the brand. First, visit the Massive site (http://www.massiveincorporated.com/ demosandvideos.html) and learn about in-game advertising and the type of advertising available. Next, review the types of games in which advertising can be placed (http://www. massiveincorporated.com/networkcontent.html). Once you have completed this, prepare a short paper that presents your point of view regarding how an in-game test of Oreo should be conducted. Make certain that you address issues related to sampling, experimental design (including game selection and types of ads to be tested), and identification of key measures.

Endnotes

1. The content for this example is adapted from Lightspeed Research and the Internet Advertising Bureau (2009). "Relevant Advertising With Bucks Off Captures Online Consumers" at http://www.mediapost.com/publications/?fa= Articles.showArticle&art_aid=102593. The situation and all data are fictitious.

2. An experiment can have more than one independent and dependent variable. Peter, for example, could have added "taste" as an additional dependent variable.

3. Graphing Tutorial (undated) at http://nces.ed. gov/nceskids/help/user_guide/graph/variables. asp.

4. These criteria for causality are adopted from those proposed by Bradford Hill. See "Hills Criteria for Causation" at http://www. drabruzzi.com/hills_criteria_of_causation.htm for a more detailed discussion.

5. While this criterion appears to reflect common sense intuition, it is nevertheless important because cause and effect can, at times, become quite confused. Consider an experiment in which one varies the amount of advertising exposure and then measures consumers' awareness of the advertising and product purchase. Assume that both measures rise. One could conclude that increases in advertising awareness (and thus more exposure and attention to the advertising) caused more people to try the product. However, it is also possible that as people increasingly purchased the product, they became more aware of the product's advertising. Which event, advertising awareness or product purchase, preceded the other?

6. Joe Lau and Jonathan Chan (2009). "TUTORIAL S05: Mill's Methods for Identifying Causes" at http://philosophy.hku.hk/think/sci/mill.php

7. For the original thinking on these potential threats internal validity, see D. T. Campbell and J. C. Stanley (1963). *Experimental and Quasi-Experimental Designs for Research* (Chicago, IL: Rand McNally).

8. Unless otherwise noted, all situations presented in this chapter are hypothetical and for illustrative purposes only.

9. The examples listed are common forms of researcher bias. See D. L. Sackett (1979). "Bias in Analytic Research." *Journal of Chronic Diseases* 32 (2): 51-63 for a comprehensive list of experimenter biases.

10. Note that this problem is not solved even if the Association sets a target for "friendly" ratings, for example, saying that the campaign would be considered successful if the "friendly" rating averages a 4 out of 5. As with the prior example, without a frame of reference there is no way of knowing if a "4" is good (i.e., a rise from the past average of "3") or bad (i.e., a decline from the past average of "5").

11. When conducting experiments that manipulate the quantity of a variable, it is important that there be relatively large differences across the different levels. It would not be wise, for example, to test the effect of one versus two e-mails (as in the first example) or the difference in

effect of a :15 versus :30 video (as in the second example).

12. This type of question addresses the interaction between factors. An interaction occurs when the effect of one variable depends on one or more other variables. Consider the independent variables "adding sugar to coffee" and "stirring." Neither of the two individual variables has much effect on sweetness (the dependent variable) but a combination of the two does. In this example, an interaction might indicate that a celebrity spokesperson is *only* effective when humor is used.

13. A factorial design can have any number of factors, but designs with more than three are very difficult to present visually, as they require one to draw in four or more dimensional space.

14. This is a post-test-only experimental design, as it is assumed that through random assignment to the cells, pretest attitudes will be equivalent across the four cells.

15. PsychData is located at http://www/psychdata. com.

16. The points presented in this section are from David R. Krathwohl (1985). *Social and Behavioral Science Research: A New Framework for Conceptualizing, Implementing and Evaluating Research Studies* (San Francisco, CA: Jossey-Bass).

17. Krathwohl (op. cit.) presents five additional criteria for the evaluation of internal validity. Internal validity is believed to increase: "With controlled application of the cause, treatment or instigating condition"; "The more a complexly patterned cause is predictably mirrored by the effect"; "If an instigating condition or cause can be controlled at will, producing a pattern of cause on demand"; "The greater the range of instigating conditions over which the predictions can be shown to hold"; "The more time elapses between the instigating condition and the effect, assuming one can accurately predict the time of appearance of the effect." The reader is encouraged to use this source for an extended discussion of these issues.

18. This example is adapted from Bellarmie (undated) at http://cas.bellarmine.edu/Osborn/hypertut_piv/external_validity_is_concerned_w.htm.

19. Reproduced with permission of the Interactive Advertising Bureau at http://www.iab.net. We encourage you to review the wide range of excellent research conducted by the IAB at http://www.iab.net/insights_research.

20. Massive Incorporated at http://www.massiveincorporated.com/.

21. The use of in-game advertising such as that reported in the research is growing at an astounding rate, and is now estimated to exceed $1 billion. For an overview of in-game advertising, see Adweek (2008). "Video Game Advertising" at http://www.adweek.com/aw/photos/stylus/43082-1020VideoGames-lo-res.pdf.

22. Reproduced with permission of Massive Incorporated.

23. Exercises 1 through 5 are hypothetical.

CHAPTER 15

Descriptive Statistics

Chapters 12 and 13 showed you how to write well-written survey questions and how to turn these questions into a well-constructed questionnaire. Quantitative data analysis begins once all the responses to the questionnaire have been collected. Data analysis has two components: the mathematical summarization of the data (telling you what the data "is") and data exploration (helping to tell you what the data "means"). Because advertising management is much more interested in how the data helps them make better decisions, this chapter focuses on the latter aspect of data analysis, using math only as a tool to help you improve your skills in drawing meaning from the data.

***

This chapter is organized as follows:

■ the first section, *Basic Math and Key Measures,* explains the five primary measures needed to analyze quantitative data. Most of these measures will already be familiar, making the math less intimidating and more approachable.

■ the second section, *Making Certain You Have Good Data,* describes the start of the data analysis process, focusing on how to ensure that your data is reliable enough to serve as the basis for subsequent decisions.

■ the third section, *Data Analysis by Question Type,* shows how each of the specific types of questions introduced in Chapter 13 are examined and analyzed.

- The fourth section, *Looking at Subgroups,* shows how to take the last step toward data meaning, moving away from an analysis of the total sample into analyses of smaller groups of respondents.

- The last section, *Data Analysis in Action,* brings all of the prior information together through a step-by-step demonstration of the entire data analysis process.

BASIC MATH AND KEY MEASURES

Five basic and easy-to-compute measures provide all the math needed to derive meaning in most data analysis situations. These measures are: percentage, average, median, mode, and standard deviation.

Percentage

You already know about a percentage, it's a number that you calculate after every exam. When you calculate your percentage score, you divide the number of correct answers by the total number of questions and then multiply by 100. Sixteen correct answers out of 20, for example, would give you a score of 80%.

The use of percentages for the analysis of survey data works exactly the same way: we divide the number of people giving a particular response by the total number of people answering the question. The table below shows how this is done, where the first column shows the possible answers to the survey question, the second column shows the number of people selecting each option, and the last column shows the percentage of people selecting each option. The 82.5% male percentage, for example, is obtained by dividing 33 by 40 and then multiplying by 100.

Gender	Number of Respondents	Percent of Respondents
Male	33	82.5
Female	7	17.5
Total	**40**	**100.0**

Note how we can check to make certain that the percentages have been calculated correctly: the total of the percentage column should always add up to 100%.

You can always calculate percentages manually. However, if you conduct your survey using one of the online survey sites such as Zoomerang or SurveyMonkey, the site will automatically provide percentages for you. Figure 15.1 provides an example for a survey with 10 respondents. Zoomerang's presentation of results shows the percentage of respondents selecting each option for each question.

Average

The second basic measure is an average, which is also a number frequently used to calculate class performance.[1] Your class average summarizes your performance on all graded tests and assignments and is computed as follows:

1.	How believable or unbelievable was the message in the commercial you just viewed?				
Extremely believable				2	20%
Somewhat believable				0	0%
Somewhat unbelievable				6	60%
Extremely unbelievable				2	20%
			Total	10	100%

2.	What is your highest level of education?				
Some high school or less				0	0%
High school graduate				1	10%
Some college				4	40%
College graduate				4	40%
Advanced degree				1	10%
			Total	10	100%

FIGURE 15.1 Zoomerang Data Reporting

You add up the total number of points you've received and then divide this number by the total number of possible points. This final number is then multiplied by 100. If, for example, you receive 70 out of 90 possible points on the first exam and 88 out of 110 possible points on your second exam, then your overall average would be 79 (calculated as the sum of the two scores, 158, divided the total possible, 200, multiplied by 100).

Similar to helping you understand your standing with regard to class performance, averages are a useful way to summarize responses to *certain types* of survey questions. (We discuss when to use averages later in this chapter.) We calculate an average for a survey question in much the same way as you calculate a class average, except in the case of survey questions we divide the total number of points for the question by the *total number of people answering the question.* Imagine, for example, that you want to discover if consumers find the message in a commercial relevant, so you ask the following question:

Thinking back to the commercial you just saw, how relevant or not relevant would you say the commercial's message was? Would you say that it was . . .

Extremely relevant   _____ (1)

Somewhat relevant   _____ (2)

Somewhat irrelevant   _____ (3)

Extremely irrelevant   _____ (4)

Note how each response option has been assigned a value. Ten consumers rate the commercial as follows: 1, 2, 3, 2, 3, 4, 4, 2, 1, 2. The average relevance rating would be 2.4, calculated by dividing the sum of all of the individual scores, 24, by the number of people answering the question, 10.

The prior procedure is the easiest way to calculate the average response to a question. You can, however, also calculate the average by using a question's percentage distribution, such as the one shown in Figure 15.1. In this case, you

- multiply the number of people giving each response by the value of the response, and then
- total across all responses, and then
- divide by the number of people who answered the question.

This process is illustrated in the table below, which uses the data from Question 1 in Figure 15.1. The overall average for this question would be 2.8 (28 ÷ 10).

Response Options	Value	Number of Respondents			Total
Extremely believable	1	X	2	=	2
Somewhat believable	2	X	0	=	0
Somewhat unbelievable	3	X	6	=	18
Extremely unbelievable	4	X	2	=	8
Total			**10**		**28**

Median and Mode

The median and mode are two additional ways to summarize responses to a survey question, although they are typically only used in special circumstances.

The *median* is the number that appears in the middle of an ordered set of data. You can think about a median score like this: when you drive along a divided highway, you'll often see signs that say "Keep Off Median" meaning that you can't drive on the grassy area in the middle of the highway. The median is in the middle. A median score is the same thing, and while it is not a grassy area, it does refer to the number in the middle of a data set *when the scores are ordered from lowest to highest.*[2] Imagine that you ask five people their age in a survey and you get the following responses: 21, 23, 26, 25, 99. The average age would be 38.8 (calculated by dividing the sum of all the ages, 194, by the number of people, 5, and then multiplying by 100). But this average seems not to fit the data, as no respondent has an age around 39 and in fact four out of the five respondents are aged 26 or younger. The average is high because of the one individual who is aged 99.

When you have an average that is distorted by a few either very high or very low scores, then the median often becomes a better way to summarize the set of scores.[3] The first step in calculating the median is to put all the scores in order; lowest to highest typically works best. Next, you need to find the middle score. The procedure for doing this depends upon whether there are an odd or even number of scores.

- When you have an odd number of scores, the median is the score exactly in the middle of the ordered set of data. You can count to the middle, or you can use the formula below to find the middle score:

  Position of the median = (Total number of measurements + 1) ÷ 2

- When you have an even number of scores, the median is the average of the two middle scores.

Looking back to the age data presented earlier, the median age would be 25, obtained by first putting the scores in order (21, 23, 25, 26, 99) and then finding the score that is in the middle (21, 23, **25**, 26, 99). Note how this number is much more representative of the ages in the data set versus the average.

The *mode* is the number in a set of responses that appears most often. This measure is infrequently used in the reporting of survey results, but under some circumstances is nevertheless a useful number when the aim is to obtain additional insights into the responses to a particular survey question. The mode is useful when we want to know the most frequent response. To find the mode, simply look at the distribution of responses to find the most commonly given response. The mode for Question 1 in Figure 15.1, for example, would be "Somewhat unbelievable" as this would be the most frequently given response, with 6 out of 10 individuals (60%) choosing this option.[4]

RELATIONSHIP OF THE MEAN, MEDIAN, AND MODE. The mean, median, and mode each provides a different insight into a set of scores' distribution. Imagine that 100 students take an exam. The distribution of exam scores is symmetrical when the mean, median, and mode are nearly identical (see Figure 15.2a). In these cases: (a) the distribution to the right of the mean, median, and mode is a near mirror image of the distribution to the left of these measures and (b) the majority of scores fall into the center of the distribution. This distribution is the typical "bell curve" that you are likely familiar with from class grade assignment. When the distribution is (or is near) symmetrical, then the mean is an accurate and preferred descriptor of the distribution.

Distributions do not have to be symmetrical, however.

- A distribution in which the value of the mode falls below the median that in turn falls below the mean is said to skew left. This distribution has a large number of values at the lower end of the distribution and few values at the high end of the distribution. The distribution of exam scores shown in Figure 15.2b is skewed left as many students scored low on the exam.

- A distribution in which the value of the mode falls above the median that subsequently falls above the mean is said to skew right. This distribution has a large number of values at the high end of the distribution and few values at the low end of the distribution. The distribution of exam scores shown in Figure 15.2c is skewed right as many students scored high on the exam.

The more skewed the distribution the less well the average provides an acceptable summary of that distribution. As a result, for heavily skewed distributions, either the median or the mode is often the preferred descriptor versus the average. Your selection of one or the other should always be guided by the goal of accurately summarizing the scores in the distribution.

Standard Deviation

The fifth measure that is useful for helping find meaning in data is the standard deviation, which is a measure of a set of scores' dispersion. Dispersion refers to how spread out or clustered a set of scores is around the mean. It is an important measure because it helps

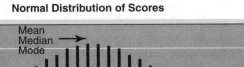

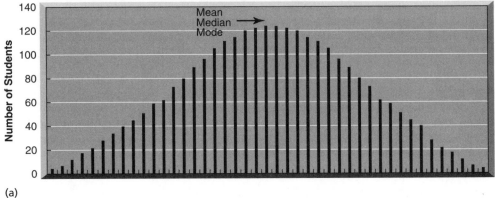

(a)

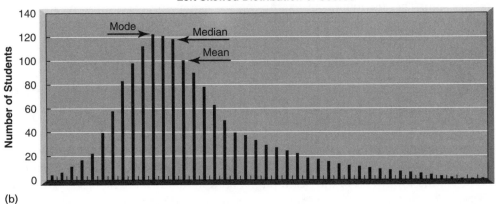

(b)

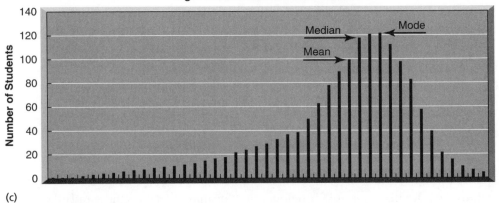

(c)

FIGURE 15.2   Types of Distributions

you understand the distribution of scores, which as discussed in the prior section affects the extent to which you can use the average score as an appropriate summary measure.

Consider the data shown in the following table. The data represents 50 consumers' purchase intent after seeing one of three commercials. The data in each column represents the percentage of people selecting each response (for each commercial) and the data on the bottom of the table reports the average purchase intent for each commercial.

Response Options	Ad 1	Ad 2	Ad 3
Strong positive (1)	20%	50%	5%
Slight positive (2)	20	0	15
Neutral (3)	20	0	60
Slight negative (4)	20	0	15
Strong negative (5)	20	50	5
Mean	**3.0**	**3.0**	**3.0**

The mean purchase intent for each commercial is identical, although the underlying distributions are quite different. Responses to Ad 1 are evenly spread out among the five response options, while responses to Ad 2 fall exclusively at the ends of the purchase intent scale. Responses to Ad 3 more closely resemble a normal distribution where most responses are in the center of the distribution and the percentage of responses declines as you move to the extremes of the scale.

The standard deviation is a way to understand and compare distributions of scores without having to actually plot and examine each and every score. For any particular scale, the greater the standard deviation the greater the dispersion of scores and, as a result, the less accurate the mean for summarizing the set of scores. The table below adds the standard deviation to the prior table.

Response Options	Ad 1	Ad 2	Ad 3
Strong positive (1)	20%	50%	5%
Slight positive (2)	20	0	15
Neutral (3)	20	0	60
Slight negative (4)	20	0	15
Strong negative (5)	20	50	5
Mean	**3.0**	**3.0**	**3.0**
Standard Deviation	**1.4**	**2.0**	**.8**

The standard deviation is the smallest for Ad 3, larger for Ad 1, and much larger for Ad 2. A researcher seeing these differences in standard deviations should conclude that underlying patterns of response to the three commercials are very different and, as a result, there is a need to look deeper into the trends in the responses to this question. When this is done, the researcher would conclude that only in the case of Ad 3 is the mean a good summary measure of the distribution.[5]

It is important to remember that when comparing standard deviations, any particular standard deviation is a reflection of the underlying scale. Thus, for example, the standard deviations for scales that all have five options can be compared even though the scales measure different things. This is illustrated by the data shown in the following table, which shows responses to three five-point scales. Even though the scales measure different things, because the scales have the same number of options, their means and standard deviations can be compared. In this case, the dispersion of the "Believability" scale is much greater than that of the "Liking" and "Relevance" scales; in other words, respondents had a greater range of attitude with regard to commercial believability versus liking and relevance, for which lower and comparable standard deviations indicate less dispersion and greater agreement.

Response Options	Believability	Liking	Relevance
Strong positive (1)	40%	15%	5%
Slight positive (2)	5	10	20
Neutral (3)	0	55	40
Slight negative (4)	10	10	25
Strong negative (5)	45	10	10
Mean	**3.2**	**2.9**	**3.2**
Standard Deviation	**1.9**	**1.1**	**1.0**

Standard deviations cannot be compared, however, when scales have different numbers of options. The tables below show the distribution of responses to two questions: "Message Importance" and "Message Uniqueness." Here, the importance scale has five options, while the uniqueness scale provides seven options. In spite of the distributions being exactly the same (with all responses evenly split between the two most extreme options), the means and standard deviations are indeed different.

Response Options	Importance
Strong positive (1)	50%
Slight positive (2)	0
Neutral (3)	0
Slight negative (4)	0
Strong negative (5)	50
Mean	**3.0**
Standard Deviation	**2.0**

Response Options	Uniqueness
Very strong positive (1)	50%
Strong positive (2)	0
Slight positive (3)	0
Neutral (4)	0
Slight positive (5)	0
Strong negative (6)	0
Very strong negative (7)	50
Mean	**4.0**
Standard Deviation	**3.0**

A standard deviation indicates the dispersion of scores because it is calculated by a formula that includes the subtraction of the overall mean from each individual score. The formula is

$$sd = \sqrt{\frac{\sum\limits_{i=1}^{m}(X_i - \overline{X})^2}{N-1}}$$

where:

sd is the standard deviation,

$\sum\limits_{i=1}^{m}(X_i - \overline{X})^2$ is the sum of the difference between every individual score and the mean, squared, and

$N - 1$ is the number of scores in the sample minus one.

This process is illustrated for a set of 10 respondents in Figure 15.3.

Step 1: Calculate the Mean

Mean = (2 + 1 + 4 + 5 + 5 + 4 + 4 + 5 + 5 + 5) ÷ 10
      = 40 ÷ 10
      = 4.0

Respondent	Response	Step 2: Compute Difference From Mean	Step 3: Square Differences
1	2	−2	4
2	1	−3	9
3	4	0	0
4	5	+1	1
5	5	+1	1
6	4	0	0
7	4	0	0
8	5	+1	1
9	5	+1	1
10	5	+1	1
		Step 4: Find Total	**Total = 18**

Step 5: Divide summed "squared differences" by sample size minus one

Step 5 = 18 ÷ (10 − 1)
       = 18 ÷ 9
       = 2

Step 6: Take square root of prior number to find standard deviation

Standard deviation = √2
                   = 1.41

FIGURE 15.3 Manual Calculation of Standard Deviation

Fortunately, standard deviations almost never need to be calculated by hand. Computer data analysis programs such as SPSS can easily calculate this statistic. Additionally, spreadsheet programs such as Excel have the calculation of standard deviations as a built-in function.

MAKING CERTAIN YOU HAVE GOOD DATA

It is unavoidable in survey research that even though considerable time and effort was spent designing the questionnaire, some respondents will answer the questions incorrectly. Here, "incorrectly" does not mean providing information that disconfirms your initial beliefs, but rather incorrect in the sense that no answer to a question was given or the answer provided was inappropriate or nonsensical, for example, saying that one's age was "999." Since successful advertising and related decisions are based on good (i.e., correct and appropriate) responses, you must "clean" your data set prior to conducting any analyses of the data.

Data Review, Decisions, and Editing

The first step in preparing data for analysis is to check the responses to each question, looking both for questions that have a large number of missing responses or questions that have odd, inappropriate, or unexpected responses or patterns of response. You can perform this initial review either by using the percentage distributions provided by the survey company or by examining the actual raw data file and generating your own percentage distributions. Once you've reviewed each question on your survey, you'll have to decide which questions are problematic and what to do with each: accept as is, eliminate, or edit. The following scenario illustrates this process.

Consider the information provided by Zoomerang for the four questions shown in Figure 15.4.[6] Examine each question to see whether there is anything odd in the pattern of responses.

Each question should have raised some concerns as you conducted your initial review of the data.

- Question 1 focuses on a beer advertiser's most direct competition. Almost all those who answered this question (90%) chose Heinekin. While this high percentage of respondents choosing a single response might not be expected, the data appears to be "good" as there does not appear to be any problem with question wording or response options. An appropriate decision at this point would be to accept and use the data as is.

- Question 2 shows the same pattern of response as Question 1, with all respondents choosing just one response. However, a close review of this question's response options shows that there were typographical errors—the final two options should have read "unimportant" instead of "important." As a result, the scale is incorrect and the data from this question is not useable.

- Question 3 is a problem, but for a different reason. You'll note that 10 individuals responded to each of the prior questions. These 10 individuals comprise the total sample, but only two individuals answered this question, probably because it was

1. Which brand of beer do you most prefer to drink when you are out with friends?

Budweiser		0	0%
Coors		1	10%
Heinekin		9	90%
Miller's		0	0%
Samuel Adams		0	0%
Other, please specify		0	0%
	Total	10	100%

2. When you are out with friends, how important or unimportant is price when choosing a beer for your own consumption?

Very important		10	100%
Important		0	0%
Important		0	0%
Very important		0	0%
	Total	10	100%

3. Beer advertisers often use special promotions to entice individuals to try their brand. These special promotions can include things such as price off, special purchases, coupons or similar. We would like to know what you think about these special promotions and how they might have affected you personally with regard to the brand of beer that you are likely to drink when you are out with friends. How important or unimportant to you are these promotions as they relate to the brand of beer you order when out with friends, where the phrase "out with friends" means someplace other than where you live.

Very important		0	0%
Important		1	50%
Unimportant		1	50%
Very unimportant		0	0%
	Total	2	100%

4. How many hours per week do you spend on social networking sites?

View 10 Responses

4. How many hours per week do you spend on social networking sites?

#	Response
1	12
2	16
3	20
4	11
5	19
6	112
7	23
8	14
9	1
10	18

FIGURE 15.4   Responses to Four Survey Questions

too long and confusing. This question, like any question that has a high number of "no responses," should be eliminated from the analysis.

• Question 4 illustrates an additional type of problem. All respondents provided a response, which is a good sign. Two respondents, however, provided answers that seem unreasonable. Respondent number 6 says that 112 hours was spent on social networking sites in the past seven days, an average of 16 hours a day. Respondent 9 says that only one hour was spent. Cases like these require that you use your judgment with regard to next steps. You can examine the total pattern of response for these two individuals: if the pattern seems reasonable, you can accept the data as it is; if the pattern seems reasonable but this one measure seems odd or inconsistent, you can recode the response as "missing" (thus assuming that it was an error on the part of the respondent); or if the pattern of response is problematic across a number of questions, you can eliminate the respondent from the sample. Regardless of the action you take, you should be prepared to report any changes to the data and to provide a rationale for your decisions.

The examination of your data on the question level should be followed by a review of each respondent's individual pattern of response. Here, you are looking for any respondents who have a large number of missing or odd responses across all survey questions. The information shown in Figures 15.5 and 15.6 illustrate why this is important and how to conduct this review.

Figure 15.5 shows a fictitious sample's response to four questions that probe attitudes toward YouTube advertising. Ten individuals in total participated in the survey. The responses appear quite reasonable on the question level (see Figure 15.5): each question shows a range of response, and it appears that the answers from only two respondents are missing from each question. The pattern of percentages is deceptive, however.

Figure 15.6 shows the responses of each respondent on the four survey questions (where the numbers represent the code used for the response and a blank indicates that no response was provided). This data indicates that the first 6 respondents answered all of the questions while respondents 7 through 10 only answered half of the questions. Partial or incomplete surveys are a problem; including the responses of those who skip a significant number of questions in the final data analysis has the potential to skew or distort the findings. For this reason, researchers typically delete from the sample those respondents who have failed to answer a large number of questions.[7] Additionally, the responses of respondents 4, 5 and 6 shown in Figure 15.6 also appear to be a problem, as each individual gave the exact same answer to *all* questions. When every answer is the same, then it is quite likely that the respondent did not give the survey his or her full attention and the responses are probably not valid.[8] These respondents should also be eliminated prior to data analysis.

Once you are confident that you have "good" data, the next step is to analyze the data, turning it into useful, actionable information. The following section will show how to do this.

DATA ANALYSIS FOR SPECIFIC QUESTION TYPES

Imagine that Bebo (http://www.bebo.com) wants to obtain reactions to its social networking site, paying particular attention to determining how individuals react to advertising on its home page. Some of the questions Bebo might ask are shown in Figure 15.7 (pages 409–410). These questions are the basis for this and the next section's discussion.

Question 1: How helpful or not helpful do you find the advertising on YouTube?

Response Options	Percent of All Respondents	Percent of Respondents Answering
Very helpful	60%	75.0%
Slightly helpful	10	12.5
Slightly unhelpful	0	0.0
Very unhelpful	10	12.5
	80%	
Missing	*20*	
Total	**100%**	**100.0%**

Question 2: On your last visit to YouTube, did you click on any advertising?

Response Options	Percent of All Respondents	Percent of Respondents Answering
Yes	40%	50%
No	40	50
	80%	
Missing	*20*	
Total	**100%**	**100%**

Question 3: How annoying or not annoying would you say that YouTube advertising is?

Response Options	Percent of All Respondents	Percent of Respondents Answering
Extremely annoying	30%	37.5%
Slightly annoying	40	50.0
Not at all annoying	10	12.5
	80%	
Missing	*20*	
Total	**100%**	**100.0%**

Question 4: How much do you agree or disagree with the statement: "YouTube advertising is for people like me"?

Response Options	Percent of All Respondents	Percent of Respondents Answering
Strongly agree	20%	25.0%
Slightly agree	30	37.5
Slightly disagree	30	37.5
Strongly disagree	0	0.0
	80%	
Missing	*20*	
Total	**100%**	**100.0%**

FIGURE 15.5 Summary of Responses to Four Survey Questions

Respondent #	Question 1	Question 2	Question 3	Question 4
1	1	1	3	2
2	1	2	1	3
3	4	2	2	2
4	1	1	1	1
5	1	1	1	1
6	2	2	2	2
7	1		2	
8	1		2	
9		2		3
10		1		3

FIGURE 15.6   Individual Responses to Four Survey Questions

Classification, Checklist, and Other Nominal Level Questions

Questions 1 through 3 on the survey shown in Figure 15.7 are nominal level questions, questions designed to classify respondents or to assign responses to discrete categories. Because the numbers used to code responses to nominal level questions have no intrinsic meaning, averages are inappropriate.[9] Instead, percentages are the most common way to report and summarize the data collected by these types of questions.[10] As discussed earlier, the percentage of respondents providing each response is calculated by dividing the number of respondents who select a particular response by the total number of respondents who answered the question, as illustrated in the following table:

Demographic Characteristic	Number of Respondents	Percent of Respondents
Current educational status		
Not enrolled in any school	55	11%
Enrolled in high school	125	25
Enrolled as college undergraduate	275	55
Enrolled for advanced degree	45	9
		100%
Social Site Used Most Often		
Facebook	265	53%
Myspace	175	35
MyAOL	50	10
Other	10	2
		100%
Ever visited Bebo		
Yes	145	29%
No	355	71
		100%
Total respondents	**500**	

Social Networking Survey

1 What is your current educational status?

- Not enrolled in any school
- Enrolled in high school
- Enrolled as college undergraduate
- Enrolled for advanced degree

2 Which social netowrking site do you use most often?

- Facebook
- Myspace
- MyAOL
- Other, please specify

3 Have you ever visited Bebo?

YES   NO

4 Which, if any, of the words below descibe how you feel about advertising on Bebo? You can check as many or as few (or even no) responses, as appropriate.

- Valuable
- Informative
- Distracting
- Annoying
- Interesting
- Intrusive

5 Which, if any, of the words below descibe how you feel about advertising on MyAOL? You can check as many or as few (or even no) responses, as appropriate.

- Valuable
- Informative
- Distracting
- Annoying
- Interesting
- Intrusive

6 Below are listed three social networking sites. Please rank these sites in terms of your perceptions of each site's ease of use. Place a "1" next to the site that you think is the easiest to use, a "2" next to the site that is next most useable and a "3" next to the site that is the least useable. Use each number only once and there can be no ties.

Bebo	
Facebook	
MyAOL	

FIGURE 15.7 Bebo Survey Questions

7   Please indicate the extent to which you agree or disagree with the statement: "Bebo's homepage is visually appealing."

Strongly agree	Slightly agree	Neither agree nor disagree	Slightly disagree	Strongly disagree
1	2	3	4	5

8   Please indicate the extent to which you agree or disagree with the statement: "Bebo's homepage makes me want to join."

Strongly agree	Slightly agree	Neither agree nor disagree	Slightly disagree	Strongly disagree
1	2	3	4	5

9   Please indicate the extent to which you agree or disagree with the statement: "Bebo's homepage is for people like me."

Strongly agree	Slightly agree	Neither agree nor disagree	Slightly disagree	Strongly disagree
1	2	3	4	5

10   Below are some benefits of social networking sites. Assume that you have 100 points to distribute across these benefits, where more points indicate greater importance of that benefit to you. Please allocate your points ... you can give as many or as few (or even no) points to any one benefit. When you are done, make certain that your total adds to 100.

Blog	
Instant message	
Post pictures	
Post videos	

SUBMIT

FIGURE 15.7   (Continued)

As the prior table (page 408) illustrates, the initial reporting of percentages should always present the data in the form collected by the survey question; that is, there should be a one-to-one match between the response categories used in the survey question and the response categories shown in the table. Once this is done, you can then summarize the data in ways that do not directly correspond to the original response categories. In these cases, the original response categories are combined in some logical fashion, and the total percentages for the new categories are presented. The responses to the educational status question can, for example, be recomputed to allow for an easier to see comparison of those who are in *any* type of school versus *no* school:

Demographic Characteristic	Number of Respondents	Percent of Respondents
Current educational status		
Not enrolled in any school	55	11%
Currently enrolled in any school	445	89
Total respondents	**500**	**100%**

or to compare the size of the groups who are currently not enrolled, enrolled in high school, and enrolled in any type of college. In this case, the table would be:

Demographic Characteristic	Number of Respondents	Percent of Respondents
Current educational status		
Not enrolled in school	55	11%
Currently enrolled in high school	125	25
Currently enrolled in any college	320	64
Total respondents	**500**	**100%**

Keep in mind that while the number of supplemental tables that can be constructed is near limitless, management information needs will dictate which supplemental tables will have the most value.

Checklist Questions

Question 4 on the survey shown in Figure 15.7 is an attempt to gauge individuals' reactions to advertising on the Bebo social network site. A checklist was used, and respondents were allowed to check as many or as few options as reflect their opinions. Six checklist items in total, three positive and three negative, were used.

The first step in the analysis of checklist questions is to calculate the percentage of respondents who checked each item. The table below provides this data, presenting the data in the same order as the items appeared on the questionnaire.

Statement	Number of Respondents	Percent of Respondents
Valuable	145	29.0%
Informative	33	6.6
Distracting	227	45.4
Annoying	359	71.8
Interesting	57	11.4
Intrusive	26	5.2
Total respondents	**500**	**

** *Does not add to 100% due to multiple responses*

The prior table accurately presents the data. However, because there is no logical organization to the ordering, it is difficult to see the overall pattern of response. Both the following two tables fix this problem, but in different ways. The first table orders items by absolute level of selection, making it easier to see which items have relatively more or less agreement. The second table groups positive and negative items together (and then orders items within each category) to make it easier to see which positive and negative items have relatively more agreement.

Statement	Number of Respondents	Percent of Respondents
Annoying	359	71.8%
Distracting	227	45.4
Valuable	145	29.0
Interesting	57	11.4
Informative	33	6.6
Intrusive	26	5.2
Total respondents	**500**	**

** Does not add to 100% due to multiple responses

Statement	Number of Respondents	Percent of Respondents
Negative Attitudes		
Annoying	359	71.8%
Distracting	227	45.4
Intrusive	26	5.2
Positive Attitudes		
Valuable	145	29.0
Interesting	57	11.4
Informative	33	6.6
Total respondents	**500**	

Note: Percentages do not add to 100% due to multiple responses

The presentation of percentages for checklist items is often sufficient for discovering overall patterns of response. There is, however, an additional computation that can provide deeper insight into respondents' thoughts and attitudes. This computation, which requires that you manipulate the raw data file, entails examining and then classifying each respondent's pattern of response according to a predetermined set of criteria. Given both positive and negative items on a checklist, for any individual respondent one of three patterns of response is possible:

- a respondent checks *only* positive attributes
- a respondent checks *only* negative attributes
- a respondent checks *both* positive and negative attributes

Distinguishing between these three types of individuals is important, because it allows you to identify the relative percent of respondents who are entirely positive, entirely negative, or have mixed feelings. Classifying individuals in this way provides you with the ability to distinguish between patterns of response that appear identical on the surface. We will apply this approach to the analysis of the next survey question.

Question 5 on the survey shown in Figure 15.7 (similar to Question 4) asks respondents to check their feelings toward advertising that appears on MyAOL's homepage. At first glance, the responses to Bebo (from the prior question) and MyAOL appear to be similar, as shown in the table below:

Statement	% of Respondents Bebo	% of Respondents MyAOL
Negative Attitudes		
Annoying	71.8%	73.1%
Distracting	45.4	42.4
Intrusive	5.2	6.3
Positive Attitudes		
Valuable	29.0	30.1
Interesting	11.4	10.4
Informative	6.6	6.3

Note: Percentages do not add to 100% due to multiple responses

Without further analysis, a researcher might conclude that reactions to advertising on the two sites' homepages are identical. However, this conclusion proves false when we look at the percentage of people who are entirely positive, entirely negative, or have mixed reactions to the two sites' homepage advertising. This analysis is shown below.

Response Pattern	% of Respondents Bebo	% of Respondents MyAOL
All items checked are positive	27.3%	27.3%
Checked both positive & negative	61.8	5.5
All items checked are negative	10.9	67.2

This analysis shows that reactions to the advertising on the two sites are very different. The same proportion of the sample had entirely positive attitudes toward the advertising on each site. However, most of the remaining reactions to Bebo were mixed, with few individuals having entirely negative attitudes. Reactions to MyAOL were very different, with few individuals having mixed feelings and most individuals having entirely negative reactions. This data indicates that MyAOL's homepage advertising is perceived as being much more of a problem than Bebo's homepage advertising. Importantly, this insight into consumers' attitudes was masked by the initial analysis of the individual item percentages.

Insights from supplemental analyses such as this often prove very valuable in helping management see and understand the important meaning and implications of the data.

Ranking and Other Ordinal Level Questions

Question 6 on the survey shown in Figure 15.7 is a rank order question, a question that collects data on the ordinal level of measurement. Similar to the nominal level questions discussed earlier, only percentages (and medians and modes) are appropriate for summarizing responses to ranking or other ordinal level questions.[11]

The first step in the analysis of ranking data is the creation of a frequency distribution that reports the number of each ranking assigned to each ranked item; in this case, we want to count how many "1," "2," and "3" ranks were given to each of the three social networking sites. A frequency distribution for the 500 respondents who ranked the three sites might be:

Ranking Level	Bebo	Facebook	MyAOL
1	380	100	20
2	80	240	180
3	40	160	300
Total Rankings	**500**	**500**	**500**

The table shows, for example, that 380 people gave Bebo a ranking of "1," 80 people gave it a ranking of "2," and 40 people gave it a ranking of "3." Since all 500 people in the sample provided rankings, the total rankings for each site add up to a total of 500.

The next step in the analysis and presentation of ranking data is the translation of each frequency distribution into a percentage distribution for each ranked item. This is done by dividing each number of responses in a column by the total responses for the column. For each networking site in this example, this would be as follows:[12]

Ranking Level	Bebo	Facebook	MyAOL
1	76%	20%	4%
2	16	48	36
3	8	32	60
Total Percentages	**100%**	**100%**	**100%**

The data in this table is read both down (by column) and across (by row).

- Reading from top to bottom of each column helps you understand the pattern of response for each site independent of the other sites. You can see that individuals responded very favorably to Bebo and very negatively to MyAOL, where the majority of rankings for Bebo were "1" (76%) while the majority of rankings for MyAOL were "3" (60%).

- Reading across within a row allows you to compare across sites. You can see that Bebo received the greatest number of "1" rankings (76%), far exceeding the number of "1" rankings given to Facebook (20%) and MyAOL (4%).

Both readings of the data indicate that Bebo's homepage is the most preferred of the three sites.

Once the summary chart for ranking data is created, additional summary measures can be calculated to simplify the data and to assist in communicating key findings. In this case, for example, we can present a computation that subtracts the percentage of worst rankings (in this case "3" rankings) from the percentage of best ("1") rankings in order to obtain an overall assessment of positive preference. The results of this computation are shown in the table below, where the new measure is called "Net Best Rankings." The 68% reported for Bebo, for example, is computed by subtracting the percentage of "3" rankings from the percentage of "1" rankings, in this case 76 − 8.

Ranking Level	Bebo	Facebook	MyAOL
1	76%	20%	4%
2	16	38	36
3	8	32	60
Net Best Rankings	**68%**	**−12%**	**−56%**

This summary measure clearly reinforces the prior conclusion that Bebo has the most preferred homepage: only Bebo had more individuals giving it a "best" versus a "worst" ranking.

Rating Scales and Other Interval Level Questions

Questions 7 to 9 in Figure 15.7 are rating scales that ask respondents to indicate the extent to which they agree or disagree with a particular statement. These measures provide more detailed information on reactions to the Bebo homepage. The most common way to report interval level data is through percents and averages, although medians and modes can also be used if they are felt to be useful.

The first step in the analysis of interval level data (for each question individually) is the calculation of the percentage of respondents who select each response option and the calculation of an overall average and standard deviation. The table that reports this information for Question 7 is shown below. The majority of respondents were positive toward

Bebo's Homepage is Visually Appealing	Number of Respondents	Percent of Respondents
Strongly agree (1)	239	47.8%
Slightly agree	107	21.4
Neither agree nor disagree	74	14.8
Slightly disagree	37	7.4
Strongly disagree (5)	43	8.6
Total	**500**	**100.0%**
Overall Average	*2.1 (sd = 1.3)*	

Bebo's homepage, and as a result the average is near the value of the "Slightly Agree" response option.[13]

Once detailed data has been reported for each response option, the data can then be simplified to make the underlying trends easier to see. One approach is to combine choices that are directionally related, in this case by combining both positive "agree" choices (i.e., "strongly agree" and "slightly agree") in a single summary measure and both negative "disagree" choices (i.e., "strongly disagree" and "slightly disagree") in a separate summary measure. The table that presents this data for Question 7 is shown below.

Bebo's Homepage is Visually Appealing	Number of Respondents	Percent of Respondents
Agree	346	69.2%
Neither agree nor disagree	74	14.8
Disagree	80	16.0
Total	**500**	**100.0%**

Finally, similar to the approach taken for ranking data, we can subtract the percentage of negatives from positives in order to obtain a measure of overall positive responses. This data has been added to the prior table below:

Bebo's Homepage is Visually Appealing	Number of Respondents	Percent of Respondents
Agree	346	69.2%
Neither agree nor disagree	74	14.8
Disagree	80	16.0
Total	**500**	**100.0%**
Overall Positive Ratings	*266*	*53.2%*

The 53.2% overall positive percentage shown in the "Overall Positive Ratings" line is computed by subtracting 16.0 from 69.2. This indicates that there were many more respondents positive versus negative with regard to this question.

Each of the prior approaches provides a slightly different look at the responses to each individual question. When you have a set of multiple, related questions, however, it is often useful to prepare a summary table that presents the key findings from multiple questions. The specific form of the table and data it presents will vary depending upon the specific points that you want to communicate. When you want to focus on just one area, then multiple measures for that area can be presented in a single table. The table below, for example, presents summary measures only for Bebo when reporting the responses to Questions 7 to 9.

Reactions to Bebo's Homepage	Average Response	Overall Positive Responses
Visually appealing	2.1	63.2%
Makes me want to join	2.8	53.2
Is for people like me	2.4	58.7

Now imagine that the survey also asked individuals to rate Facebook and MyAOL on these same scales. In this case, you might want to construct a table that focuses on just one summary measure, reporting that measure for all three rated sites, as shown below.

Average Reactions to Site Homepage	Bebo	Facebook	MyAOL
Visually appealing	2.1	3.1	4.2
Makes me want to join	2.8	2.8	4.4
Is for people like me	2.4	2.5	3.9

This type of chart makes it very easy to see relative strengths and weaknesses. Here, Bebo's average ratings are generally equivalent to (or slightly better than) those for Facebook, and the ratings for both Bebo and Facebook are much more positive than MyAOL.

Constant Sum and Other Ratio Level Questions

Question 10 on the survey shown in Figure 15.7 is a constant sum question, a question that collects data on the ratio level of measurement. Similar to the interval level questions discussed in the prior section, percentages and averages, as well as medians and modes, are appropriate for summarizing responses to this type of question.

The first step in the analysis of constant sum data is the creation of a distribution that reports the average number of points given to each listed item. A distribution for the 500 respondents who ranked the importance of each site attribute is shown below. Note that in the preparation of this table: (a) the sum adds to the number of points (100), not the number of respondents, and (b) the items evaluated have been placed in descending order rather than the order in which the items appeared on the questionnaire.

Activity Characteristic	Average Number of Points Given to Each Site
Post pictures	42
Blog	38
Post videos	12
Instant message	8
Total	**100**

The table shows that the ability to post pictures and blog were perceived as the most important benefits, receiving nearly the same high number of points. The ability to post videos and instant message were seen as the least important benefits as indicated in their low number of points. At this point, given this data, you might conclude that a focus on either posting pictures or blogging could safely be selected as the site attribute that should be promoted and featured on Bebo's homepage. But, without additional analyses, it would be premature to do so. The calculation of averages for constant sum data is an important first step that provides an overview of respondents' attitudes. Additional analyses are required, however, to make certain that the averages do not lead to erroneous conclusions. These additional analyses require an examination of each of the distributions underlying the constant sum averages. One approach to examining the underlying distribution is to group the point allocations into larger groups, noting the *percentage of the sample* that falls into each group. When performing this analysis, the focus shifts from the averaging of points (as shown in the prior chart) to an examination of the sample's allocation behavior. We can, for example, create two categories of response, as follows:

- Extremely important: Percent of sample who allocated more than 75 points to an attribute
- Extremely unimportant: Percent of sample who allocated less than 25 points to an attribute

The results of this analysis are shown in the table below, where the percentages reflect the percentage of respondents falling into each category.[14]

	Post Pictures	Blog	Post Video	IM
Extremely Important	74%	48%	17%	16%
Extremely Unimportant	15	37	59	24%

The table indicates that in spite of the roughly equivalent *average* number of points given to posting pictures and blogging (from the prior table), the underlying pattern of response presents a quite different picture. Respondents were overwhelmingly in favor of posting pictures, with 74% of the sample giving it 75 or more points and only 15% of the sample giving it 25 or fewer points. The pattern for blogging is quite different, with relatively equal numbers of people feeling that it was important and unimportant. This analysis is valuable because it shows that the conclusion drawn just from the averages, that either posting pictures or blogging could be selected as the primary homepage feature, is incorrect. Posting pictures is clearly the more powerful benefit.

THE IMPORTANCE OF SUBGROUP ANALYSIS

All of the prior approaches entailed examining, summarizing, and reporting the results for the total sample. It is often very useful, however, to examine and compare the responses of two or more smaller groups that comprise the sample. An analysis of smaller subgroups often provides deeper insights into data trends and provides a basis for drawing important meaning from the data. We illustrate the logic of subgroup analysis by working through a portion of the data collected by the questions shown in Figure 15.7.

As discussed previously, the overall average rating for Bebo's homepage as being "for people like me" was 2.4 (which is positive and slightly above average). But we might want to know whether this average rating reflects the opinions of the entire sample or whether it differs across groups of consumers. We might want, for example, to compare the opinions of younger versus relatively older individuals. This analysis is shown in the following table.[15]

Bebo's Homepage is for People Like Me	Respondents Aged 18 to 24	Respondents Aged 25 to 34
Strongly agree (1)	5%	35%
Slightly agree	18	21
Neither agree nor disagree	18	19
Slightly disagree	30	20
Strongly disagree (5)	29	5
Total	**100.0%**	**100.0%**
Average	**3.6**	**2.4**

The subgroup analysis provides important insights. The total sample's slightly positive average masked the fact that younger individuals are negative while older individuals are positive.

You can take subgroup analyses to any level of detail. The prior analysis compared two age groups and found that older individuals were more positive than younger individuals. But, we can zoom in even further to determine if the positive reactions of 30 to 39 years old vary as a function of education. In this more detailed analysis, we can compare the opinions of individuals aged 30 to 39 *with* a college education to those aged 30 to 39 *without* a college education. The following table shows the results of this comparison, where it appears that within this age group less well-educated individuals are more positive than those with a college education.

Bebo's Homepage is for People Like Me	Respondents Aged 30 to 39 Without a College Education	Respondents Aged 30 to 39 with a College Education
Strongly agree (1)	35%	11%
Slightly agree	23	28
Neither agree nor disagree	23	20
Slightly disagree	11	38
Strongly disagree (5)	8	3
Total	**100.0%**	**100.0%**
Overall Average	***2.3***	***2.9***

There are no rules for determining which subgroup analyses are likely to provide important insights. You should be guided by your senses of creativity and inquiry.[16] Nevertheless, there are some guidelines to assist you in the process:[17]

- *Think about the data from the research end user's perspective.* What questions are they likely to ask? What areas of the findings will they find most intriguing? What findings are they least likely to accept? What depth of detail is required for management to make fully informed decisions? Once you have answered these questions, conduct the appropriate subgroup analyses to provide the details.

- *Look for the unexpected.* Be creative in the questions you ask; don't just focus on the obvious or anticipated findings. You find valuable meaning in the data by discovering unexpected trends and relationships in subgroup analyses.

- *Be open-minded.* When you see the unexpected, take a step back and ask yourself why the results might be as they are. Ask new questions and reformulate old questions. Answer these questions with the appropriate subgroup analyses.

- *Be sensitive to sample size.* The size of individual subgroups typically declines as the groups are more narrowly defined. If you focus on very narrowly defined groups, be wary of analyzing groups that contain a small number of individuals. If there are few respondents in one or more individual groups, you should be cautious in accepting the findings.

DATA ANALYSIS IN ACTION

Up to this point, you have seen how descriptive statistics can be used to summarize research findings. The discussion in this section will take you through the process of discovering meaning in data and will show you how subgroup analyses contribute to this discovery.

The Situation

Imagine that the agency creative department develops a new commercial and asks that you conduct research prior to production to identify the commercial's strengths and weaknesses. You plan a research study where all 20 respondents are members of the product's target audience and the survey uses five measures to test reactions to the commercial.[18] The data collected by these measures, including demographic information, are

- Respondent's age
- Respondent's gender
- Rating of purchase intent after seeing the commercial
- Rating of commercial message believability
- Rating of commercial message uniqueness
- Reactions to the commercial (two checklist items)

All data were collected after an individual viewed the test commercial.

The Analysis

The data collected from the 20 respondents are shown in the following table, where:

- *Age* is coded "1" or "2," where a "1" represents an individual who is 25 to 34 years old and a "2" represents an individual who is 35 to 49 years old.

- *Gender* is coded "1" or "2," where a "1" represents a woman and a "2" represents a man.

- Ratings of *purchase intent, message believability and message uniqueness* are all on a five-point scale where higher numbers indicate more positive responses.

- *Checklist reactions* use an "x" to indicate an item was checked. A blank space indicates that an item was not checked.

Respondent Number	Gender	Age	Purchase Intent	Believability	Uniqueness	Checklist "Interesting"	Checklist "Confusing"
1	1	1	1	3	3	X	X
2	1	1	2	4	2	X	X
3	1	1	2	4	1	X	
4	1	1	5	4	4	X	
5	1	1	1	5	2	X	
6	2	1	1	3	2	X	X
7	2	1	5	5	5	X	
8	2	1	5	4	4	X	
9	2	2	5	4	5	X	
10	1	2	2	4	2	X	X
11	2	2	5	4	4	X	
12	2	2	4	4	5	X	
13	1	2	2	4	1	X	X
14	2	2	4	4	5	X	
15	2	2	1	4	1	X	X
16	1	2	2	4	1	X	
17	1	2	2	5	2		
18	2	1	5	5	3		
19	2	1	4	5	5		
20	1	2	4	5	5		

As mentioned earlier, one way to approach data analysis is to imagine the types of questions the end users of the research will ask and then carry out the necessary computations to answer these questions. Since this is a commercial test, the most fundamental question likely to be asked by those who designed the commercial is: *How did the commercial do?*

An answer to this question requires an examination of all of the measures for the total sample, using descriptive statistics to summarize the results. This will provide our first look at how all respondents reacted to the commercial. To conduct this analysis, we need to first identify the appropriate descriptive statistics for each measure, as follows:

Measure	*Level of Measurement*	*Appropriate Descriptive Statistic(s)*
Purchase intent	Interval	Mean, percentage, median, mode
Believability	Interval	Mean, percentage, median, mode
Uniqueness	Interval	Mean, percentage, median, mode
Checklist items	Nominal	Percentage

With this in mind, the bottom two rows of the following below present the appropriate descriptive statistics for all 20 individuals in the sample. Note that averages have been calculated only for interval level measures, not for gender and age, which will be used as classification variables.

Respondent Number	Gender	Age	Purchase Intent	Believability	Uniqueness	Checklist "Interesting"	Checklist "Confusing"
1	1	1	1	3	3	X	X
2	1	1	2	4	2	X	X
3	1	1	2	4	1	X	
4	1	1	5	4	4	X	
5	1	1	1	5	2	X	
6	2	1	1	3	2	X	X
7	2	1	5	5	5	X	
8	2	1	5	4	4	X	
9	2	2	5	4	5	X	
10	1	2	2	4	2	X	X
11	2	2	5	4	4	X	
12	2	2	4	4	5	X	
13	1	2	2	4	1	X	X
14	2	2	4	4	5	X	
15	2	2	1	4	1	X	X
16	1	2	2	4	1	X	
17	1	2	2	5	2		
18	2	1	5	5	3		
19	2	1	4	5	5		
20	1	2	4	5	5		
Average			**3.1**	**4.2**	**3.1**	–	–
Percentage			–	–	–	**80%**	**30%**

The averages and percentages shown in the prior table indicate that overall the commercial performed fairly well. Purchase intent was at the midpoint of the scale, message believability was high, and message uniqueness was at the midpoint of the scale. Most respondents found the commercial interesting and less than one-third found it confusing.

At this point, it would be easy to think that your job is done. You might look at the data and conclude that the commercial's performance isn't too bad—certainly some room for improvement, but overall acceptable to take forward to production. However, if this was your conclusion, you would be terribly wrong; you would be recommending a course of action that could doom the brand to failure.

You would have reached the wrong conclusion not because your calculations were incorrect, but because you stopped your analysis too soon, failing to anticipate additional questions the members of the creative team might ask about the research results. The commercial audience, for example, is composed of both younger and older men and women. As a result, a logical next question to ask would be: *Did the commercial work equally well among all members of the target audience?*

This is a critical question, one that a researcher looking to find meaning in the data should anticipate. To answer this question, we will perform subgroup analyses, calculating the appropriate descriptive statistics for each subgroup. Two divisions will be necessary, one by age and one by gender. The next table looks at subgroups determined by respondent age.

Respondent Number	Gender	Age	Purchase Intent	Believability	Uniqueness	Checklist "Interesting"	Checklist "Confusing"
1	1	1	1	3	3	X	X
2	1	1	2	4	2	X	X
3	1	1	2	4	1	X	
4	1	1	5	4	4	X	
5	1	1	1	5	2	X	
6	2	1	1	3	2	X	X
7	2	1	5	5	5	X	
8	2	1	5	4	4	X	
18	2	1	5	5	3		
19	2	1	4	5	5		
Average			**3.1**	**4.2**	**3.1**	–	–
Percentage			–	–	–	**80%**	**30%**
9	2	2	5	4	5	X	
10	1	2	2	4	2	X	X
11	2	2	5	4	4	X	
12	2	2	4	4	5	X	
13	1	2	2	4	1	X	X
14	2	2	4	4	5	X	
15	2	2	1	4	1	X	X
16	1	2	2	4	1	X	
17	1	2	2	5	2		
20	1	2	4	5	5		
Average			**3.1**	**4.2**	**3.1**	-	-
Percentage			-	-	-	**80%**	**30%**

This table shows the original data set divided into two age groups. All of those in the younger group (those coded with a "1" for age) have been placed together in one group, while all those in the older group (those coded with a "2" for age) have also been grouped together. Once this is done, the appropriate descriptive statistics are calculated for *each* group, also shown in the table.

There appears to be no difference in commercial performance by age group:

• The averages for the rating scales are identical (purchase intent for both age groups equals 3.1; message believability for both age groups equals 4.2; message uniqueness for both age groups equals 3.1)

• The percentages of respondents in each group who say the commercial is interesting (80%) and confusing (30%) are the same.

It therefore appears that the commercial is working equally well for all individuals in the target audience *regardless of age*.

Next, we can see whether a respondent's gender makes a difference in commercial response. The next table looks at subgroups determined by gender.

Respondent Number	Gender	Age	Purchase Intent	Believability	Uniqueness	Checklist "Interesting"	Checklist "Confusing"
1	1	1	1	3	3	X	X
2	1	1	2	4	2	X	X
3	1	1	2	4	1	X	
4	1	1	5	4	4	X	
5	1	1	1	5	2	X	
10	1	2	2	4	2	X	X
13	1	2	2	4	1	X	X
16	1	2	2	4	1	X	
17	1	2	2	5	2		
20	1	2	4	5	5		
Average			2.3	4.2	2.3	–	–
Percentage			–	–	–	80%	40%
6	2	1	1	3	2	X	X
7	2	1	5	5	5	X	
8	2	1	5	4	4	X	
9	2	2	5	4	5	X	
11	2	2	5	4	4	X	
12	2	2	4	4	5	X	
14	2	2	4	4	5	X	
15	2	2	1	4	1	X	X
18	2	1	5	5	3		
19	2	1	4	5	5		
Average			3.9	4.2	3.9	–	–
Percentage			–	–	–	80%	20%

This table shows the original data set divided into the two gender groups. All women (those coded with a "1" for gender) have been placed together in one group, while all men (those coded with a "2" for gender) have also been grouped together. Once this is done, the appropriate summary measures are calculated for *each* group.

There appears to be important, meaningful differences in commercial performance when women's responses are compared to men's responses:

- Men are much more positive toward the commercial versus women. Men's purchase intent is much higher (3.9 versus 2.3), and they are much more positive toward commercial message uniqueness (3.9 versus 2.3). Both groups find the commercial believable.

- While both men and women find the commercial interesting, women more than men (40% versus 20%) find the commercial confusing.

It therefore appears that it would have been a mistake to recommend taking this commercial into production, as women have a very negative reaction to the commercial.

These data trends would likely lead to one additional question: *What can we do to fix the commercial?*

A look at the data in the prior table shows that most (but not all) women had a low purchase intent while most (but not all) men had a high purchase intent. Thus, because the low purchase intent group consists of both men and women, one more sort of the data is necessary in order to answer this final question. We need to compare all those who had low purchase intent to those who had high purchase intent.

The next table shows the original data set divided into the two purchase intent groups. All individuals with a low purchase intent (those coded with a "1" or "2") have been placed together in one group, while all those with a high purchase intent (those coded with a "4" or "5") have also been placed together.[19] Once this is done, the appropriate descriptive statistics are calculated for *each* group, as shown in the following table.

Respondent Number	Gender	Age	Purchase Intent	Believability	Uniqueness	Checklist "Interesting"	Checklist "Confusing"
1	1	1	1	3	3	X	X
2	1	1	2	4	2	X	X
3	1	1	2	4	1	X	X
5	1	1	1	5	2	X	
6	2	1	1	3	2	X	
10	1	2	2	4	2	X	X
13	1	2	2	4	1	X	X
15	2	2	1	4	1	X	X
16	1	2	2	4	1	X	
17	1	2	2	5	2		
Average			1.6	4.0	1.7	—	—
Percentage			—	—	—	90%	60%
4	1	1	5	4	4	X	
7	2	1	5	5	5	X	
8	2	1	5	4	4	X	
9	2	2	5	4	5	X	
11	2	2	5	4	4	X	
12	2	2	4	4	5	X	
14	2	2	4	4	5	X	
18	2	1	5	5	3		
19	2	1	4	5	5		
20	1	2	4	5	5		
Average			4.6	4.4	4.5	—	—
Percentage			—	—	—	70%	0%

This final analysis provides you with the final piece of the puzzle and clear direction for how to improve the commercial:

Those with low purchase intent were much less likely to feel that the commercial's message was unique (average rating of 1.7), while those with high purchase intent were very likely to feel the message was unique (average rating of 4.5). Clearly, the creative team will have to figure out a way to improve the communication of message uniqueness.

How can they do this? The commercial needs to be made less confusing. Most of those with a low purchase intent (60%) found the commercial confusing, while no one in the high purchase intent group felt this way.

Conclusion

The prior analysis illustrates two key points, both meriting explicit mention.

First, the statistics used to describe a set of data do not have to be complex or sophisticated in order to be useful. The prior analysis relied exclusively on averages and percentages.

Second, the value of data analysis lies not in the number or sophistication of statistics used, but rather in the *types* of analyses conducted. The prior analysis was meaningful and had value for the creative team because the researcher anticipated the types of questions members of the creative team would have had and then conducted the specific analyses required to answer these questions. This approach led to an actionable piece of research that helped the research's end users make sounder decisions.

SUMMARY

The goal of descriptive data analysis is to find meaning in the data. Five mathematical computations help researchers uncover meaning: percentage, average (or mean), median, mode, and standard deviation. The type of computation applied to a specific measure is dependent upon that measure's level of measurement:

- Percentage, median, and mode are appropriate for data collected at all levels of measurement.
- Averages and standard deviations are only appropriate for data collected at the interval and ratio levels of measurement.

It is necessary, prior to data analysis and reporting, to make certain that the data is "good" (i.e., there are no problems with the underlying pattern of response). The analysis of data "goodness" examines the data on two levels: overall sample and individual respondent. Problems on either level can result in data being eliminated from subsequent analyses.

Data analysis always begins with an examination of total sample responses. These analyses should always be supplemented with analyses of key subgroups within the larger sample.

Review Questions

1. List and briefly explain the five main measures used to analyze quantitative data.

2. How is a percentage calculated? What percentage would 34 correct answers out of 49 be?

3. What are the different ways to calculate an average?

4. How is a median determined when there are an odd number of scores? When there are an even number of scores?

5. For what situations is the mode a useful analytical tool? For what situations is the mean a useful analytical tool?

6. What are three possible data distribution patterns? Which distribution is best described by referring to the mean?

7. In preparing data for analysis, what are the first things to check for in a set of responses?

8. What is the most appropriate way to report nominal level questions? Why?

9. How should the initial reporting of percentages be presented? What are alternative presentation styles that may also be used?

10. How can checklist items be analyzed?

11. What are ranking questions, and how should they be analyzed?

12. Describe the advantages of using multiple tables to present interval level questions.

13. Explain the steps used for analyzing constant sum data.

14. Why are more analyses then just averages necessary for constant sum data?

15. What is the value of conducting subgroup analyses?

16. Why are wrong conclusions often reached despite correct calculations? How can this scenario be avoided?

Application Exercises

1. Your client is Veree-Tastee Doggee Treats. A quantitative research study was conducted to: (1) determine which benefit to feature in a commercial for a new Veree-Tastee Doggee treat and (2) identify the executional (creative) approach in which to feature this benefit. Research was conducted among 70 consumers, all of whom own at least one dog and who purchased at least one box of dog treats (any brand) within the past 30 days. After screening and the collection of demographic information, respondents were asked the questions shown in Figure 15.8.

    The data representing respondents' ratings and rankings are shown in Figure 15.9. Prepare an analysis (with detailed write-up) that identifies the strongest benefit and executional approach. Be very certain to provide numeric support to support your recommendations and point of view. In addition to the incorporation of key findings into your written discussion, be certain to provide appropriate data tables. In examining the data, keep the following in mind when trying to determine whether or not the difference between two numbers is significant and important: With regard to benefits, differences in averages (means) of four points or more are important

and meaningful. Scores that are closer than the prior differences should be considered as "not different." (Remember, averages should not be calculated for the ranking data.

2. Two researchers design a project to determine the individual and combined effects of exposure to advertising on the Web and on television. They pick Gap sweaters as the test product. Consumers are recruited through random-digit telephone dialing and are randomly assigned to one of four groups:

    Group 1:   NO exposure to test advertising

    Group 2:   Exposure to test advertising ONLY on the Web

    Group 3:   Exposure to test advertising ONLY on television

    Group 4:   Exposure to test advertising on BOTH Web and television

    At the conclusion of the study, respondents are asked two questions:

    1. Do you recall seeing any advertising for Gap sweaters?

        Yes   _____ (1)

        No   _____ (2)

    2. How interested are you in purchasing a sweater from the Gap? Rate your interest on

Q2. (asked prior to exposure to any concepts or executions)
In the past 60 days, how many boxes of Veree-Tastee Doggee Treats did you purchase?

4 or more boxes   [   ] 1

1 to 3 boxes   [   ] 2

0 boxes   [   ] 3

Q3. I've placed four cards in front of you. Each card is labeled. Each card discusses one potential benefit of Veree-Tastee Doggee Treats. Please read the description on each card. When you are done reading the cards, I'd like you to use the grid below to indicate how important you feel each benefit is to you personally as you think about buying dog treats.

Each benefit is listed below. Assume that you have 100 points. Divide the points among the benefits to indicate what you feel is the relative importance of each benefit. The more points you award a benefit the more important you feel it is. You can give as many or as few points as you wish to any benefit, and you do not have to give any points to a benefit if you don't want to. Please just make certain that when you are done, you've used all 100 points.

Avoidance of tooth browning   _____

Decay in teeth is slowed   _____

Fun for dog to eat   _____

Nutrition for a full day's needs   _____

TOTAL   100

Q4. (asked after respondent is shown storyboards for four executions)
You've just seen four ideas for Veree-Tastee Doggee Treats. I'd like to know your preferences. The names of each execution are shown below. Please number them in your order of preference, placing a "1" in front of the one you most prefer, a "2" in front of the next preferred, a "3" in front of the next preferred, and a "4" in front of the one least preferred. There can be no ties.

Couch   _____

Day Out   _____

Nine Yards   _____

Teeth   _____

FIGURE 15.8 Survey Questions for Application Exercise 1

a scale from 1 (extremely low) to 7 (extremely high).

The data is shown in Figure 15.10. Your analysis of the data must lead to an explicit answer to each of the following three questions:

- Which medium or media would you recommend if the strategic goal was *just* an increase in ad recall? Why?

- Which medium or media would you recommend if the strategic goal was **just** an increase in intent to purchase? Why?

- Which medium or media would you recommend if the strategic goal was to obtain the

best combination of recall and intent to purchase?

Be very certain to provide numeric support to support your recommendations and point of view. In addition to the incorporation of key findings into your written discussion, be certain to provide relevant data. Finally, in examining the data, keep the following in mind when trying to determine whether or not the difference between two numbers is important. With regard to average (mean) purchase intent, differences of .4 or more are meaningful. Differences less than .4 indicate that the two scores are not meaningfully different.

		Q3: Benefits				Q4: Liking			
Respondent #	Usage Class	Avoidance	Decay	Fun	Nutrition	Couch	Day Out	Nine Yards	Teeth
1	2	35	30	30	5	3	2	1	4
2	2	34	33	27	6	3	2	1	4
3	3	75	15	0	10	2	4	3	1
4	3	15	70	0	15	1	3	4	2
5	1	5	5	85	5	2	3	1	4
6	1	25	0	75	0	1	2	3	4
7	2	30	30	30	10	2	1	3	4
8	2	29	0	70	1	3	2	1	4
9	1	24	1	74	1	1	2	3	4
10	2	39	45	15	1	3	1	2	4
11	1	0	1	98	1	1	3	2	4
12	3	25	50	0	25	1	3	4	2
13	3	15	50	0	35	2	4	3	1
14	2	33	20	46	1	3	2	1	4
15	3	25	65	5	5	4	3	2	1
16	1	1	2	92	5	3	2	1	4
17	2	40	25	30	5	2	3	1	4
18	1	20	1	79	0	3	1	2	4
19	2	10	35	35	20	2	1	3	4
20	2	12	40	30	18	3	2	1	4
21	2	31	31	31	7	3	2	1	4
22	2	35	30	30	5	4	2	1	3
23	3	37	25	3	35	1	3	4	2
24	3	50	0	5	45	2	3	4	1
25	1	2	2	94	2	3	2	1	4
26	2	30	30	30	10	1	3	2	4
27	1	0	5	94	1	3	2	1	4
28	2	30	40	25	5	3	2	1	4
29	3	95	0	0	5	2	1	4	3
30	3	57	32	3	8	2	4	3	1
31	2	25	25	35	15	3	2	1	4
32	1	20	5	75	0	1	2	3	4
33	3	45	0	1	54	3	2	4	1
34	1	22	2	74	2	2	3	2	4
35	2	10	30	30	30	3	2	1	4
36	1	15	35	50	0	1	2	3	4
37	2	30	30	30	10	3	4	2	1
38	1	0	4	95	1	3	1	2	4
39	3	25	50	0	25	1	4	3	2
40	3	50	35	0	15	3	1	4	2
41	2	30	40	10	20	3	4	1	2
42	1	6	1	90	3	3	2	1	4
43	2	15	40	30	15	3	2	1	4
44	3	45	15	5	35	2	4	3	1
45	3	80	0	0	20	2	3	4	1
46	1	23	2	75	0	2	1	3	4

FIGURE 15.9 Data for Application Exercise 1

Respondent #	Usage Class	Q3: Benefits				Q.4: Liking			
		Avoidance	Decay	Fun	Nutrition	Couch	Day Out	Nine Yards	Teeth
47	2	10	35	35	20	3	2	1	4
48	2	10	35	30	25	3	2	1	4
49	1	1	0	99	0	1	3	4	2
50	2	20	38	38	4	3	1	2	4
51	3	30	25	0	45	2	3	4	1
52	3	69	25	5	1	4	3	2	1
53	3	78	20	1	1	2	3	4	1
54	3	64	35	0	1	2	3	4	1
55	3	64	35	0	1	1	4	3	2
56	3	15	70	0	15	2	3	4	1
57	3	20	54	1	25	2	4	3	1
58	3	25	50	0	25	2	3	4	1
59	3	49	49	1	1	2	3	4	1
60	3	25	49	1	25	1	4	3	2
61	3	25	65	5	5	2	3	4	1
62	3	70	25	0	5	2	4	3	1
63	3	79	20	1	0	2	3	4	1
64	3	49	50	0	1	2	3	4	1
65	3	50	35	0	15	2	4	3	1
66	3	15	70	0	15	2	4	3	1
67	3	30	54	1	25	2	4	3	1
68	3	100	0	0	0	1	2	4	3
69	3	25	50	0	25	1	2	4	3
70	3	100	0	0	0	1	2	4	3

FIGURE 15.9 (Continued)

Group Number	Recall Ad	Intent to Purchase	Group Number	Recall Ad	Intent to Purchase
4	1	7	2	1	4
4	1	7	2	1	4
4	1	7	2	1	4
4	1	7	2	1	4
4	1	7	3	1	4
4	1	7	3	1	4
4	1	7	3	1	4
4	1	7	3	1	4
3	1	6	2	1	3
1	1	5	3	1	3
2	1	5	2	1	2
2	1	5	4	1	2
3	1	5	4	1	2
3	1	5	4	1	2
3	1	5	4	1	2
3	1	5	4	1	2
2	1	4	4	1	2

FIGURE 15.10 Data for Application Exercise 2

Group Number	Recall Ad	Intent to Purchase	Group Number	Recall Ad	Intent to Purchase
4	1	1	2	2	4
4	1	1	2	2	4
4	1	1	3	2	4
4	1	1	3	2	4
1	2	7	1	2	3
4	2	7	1	2	3
4	2	7	1	2	3
1	2	6	1	2	3
2	2	6	1	2	3
3	2	6	1	2	3
1	2	5	1	2	3
2	2	5	1	2	3
2	2	5	2	2	3
2	2	5	3	2	3
2	2	5	3	2	3
3	2	5	1	2	2
3	2	5	1	2	2
3	2	5	1	2	2
3	2	5	1	2	2
3	2	5	2	2	2
1	2	4	2	2	2
1	2	4	2	2	1
1	2	4			

FIGURE 15.10 (Continued)

Endnotes

1. When used for data analysis purposes averages are often referred to as the "mean." The two terms can be used interchangeably.

2. This example is from AlgebraLab, "Finding the mean, median, and mode" at http://www.algebralab.org/lessons/lesson.aspx?file=Algebra_StatMeanMedianMode.xml.

3. Think about the distortion of an average by a small number of high or low scores in a situation such as this: Your scores on five exams (all worth 100 points each) were 98, 99, 96, 92, 12. Your overall average would be 79.4. But, it is unlikely that you would agree that this average (likely a C+) is a good indicator of your class performance; after all, four out of five exams were nearly perfect. Your median score, 96, much better represents your overall level of performance. Similar logic is used when evaluating the "goodness" of an average versus a median to summarize a data set.

4. Technically, modes are reported in terms of the number underlying the response, rather than the words expressing the response. So, in this example if the numbers assigned to the response options went from "1" that represents "Extremely believable" to "4" that represents "Extremely unbelievable," then the mode would be "3," the number that represents "Somewhat unbelievable."

5. It should be evident that for any particular scale, the greater the dispersion in the underlying responses the greater the standard deviation. If there is no dispersion, that is if every observation equals the mean score, then all deviations from the mean will be zero and the resulting standard deviation will be zero. Standard deviations will be greatest when all scores are equally split between the two extreme scale values.

6. All data and research findings shown in this example and throughout the remainder of the

chapter are fictitious and provided for illustrative purposes only.

7. The ultimate definition of "large" is a judgment call on the part of the researcher. The Agency for Healthcare Research and Quality (AHRQ), for example, recommends eliminating any respondent who answered less than one entire section of the survey or who answered fewer than half of the items throughout the entire survey. See http://www.ahrq.gov/qual/hospculture/hospcult7.htm.

8. AHRQ (undated). "Chapter 6. Preparing and Analyzing Data and Producing Reports" at http://www.ahrq.gov/qual/mosurvey08/medofficetab2.htm

9. Here is why averages are not appropriate for nominal level data: Consider a survey question that asks for the respondent's gender, where a "1" stands for "male" and a "2" stands for female. The assignment of numbers to each gender category is entirely arbitrary and could easily be reversed. They have no intrinsic meaning. If you were to calculate an average of the responses to this question, you'd find that the average gender on the survey was 1.4. This number has no meaning and cannot be interpreted. Just who (what?) is a person who has an average gender of 1.4?

10. Medians and modes may also be used to report data collected by questions at this level of measurement, but they are used much less frequently.

11. Some statisticians argue that ordinal data, such as rankings, can be added and averaged, for example, finding that a particular response option has an average ranking of 1.3 while another has an average of 2.6. But, because ordinal data only reports rank order and not distance between ranks, it would be incorrect to conclude that a ranking of 1.3 (with "1" being the best) is twice as good as a ranking of 2.6. Woolf, in this regard, points out that "as a rule, ordinal data is considered nonparametric and can not be added . . . it does not make sense to add together first and second place in a race - one does not get third place" (see http://www.webster.edu/~woolflm/statwhatis.html).

12. The 76% reported for "1" rankings for Bebo is computed by dividing the number of rankings at that level by the total number of rankings, in this case 380 ÷ 500. Also note that since this table is reporting percentages, the sum of each row and column equals 100%.

13. The average is actually 2.076, but has been rounded to 2.1.

14. Note that the percentages in each column do not add to 100% since not all respondents will fall into one of these categories.

15. The tables generated by subgroup analyses are often called "cross tabulations" or "cross tabs." Wisco Survey Power describes the process as follows: "Cross-Tabulation is used to show relationships between answers made for two survey questions. The responses (variable) from two questions are displayed in a table. The choices for the first question are displayed to the left (the row labels) of the table data. The second question choices are displayed across the top of the table (the column headings). The counts (or percentages) indicate the number (or percentage) of survey responses that match both the column heading choice and the row label choice." See http://www.custominsight.com/articles/crosstab-sample.asp.

16. Given the data collected by the questions shown in Figure 15.7, you might want to compare, for example, Bebo, Facebook, and MyAOL users; high schoolers to undergraduates; those who think blogging is most important to those who think posting pictures is most important; or those who have visited Bebo to those who have not.

17. Adapted from CustomInsight at http://www.custominsight.com/articles/crosstab-sample.asp.

18. A real research study would use more respondents and measures. However, for purposes of this discussion, we will keep it simple so that we can focus on the analysis rather than the calculations.

19. There were no individuals who had a "3" on this scale, making the assignment straightforward. If there were such individual, however, they would be eliminated from this particular analysis.

CHAPTER 16

Inferential Statistics

Descriptive statistics help you better understand the data you've collected so that you can draw appropriate conclusions from the research. In some cases, data analysis stops at this point. Percent distributions and averages may provide all the information required for decision making. In many cases, however, additional analyses are needed so that decision making can be even better informed. Here, there is a need to determine the relationship between observed measures and the statistical differences between measures. These more advanced techniques are the focus of this chapter.

***

When you are done reading this chapter, you should have a better understanding of:

- what statistical significance is and why it is important
- how to evaluate different levels of response from a single group of individuals
- how to evaluate the meaningfulness of differences in levels of response among two or more groups of individuals
- how to determine the simultaneous and independent influence of two or more experimental factors
- how to determine the relationship between two or more measures.

Imagine that you are presenting the findings of a research study with top management. You spend an hour presenting the descriptive statistics for research that explored target audience attitudes and preferences toward three proposed advertising campaigns. At the end of the meeting, you say: "You've seen the average scores for all of the key measures. Based on these averages, I'd recommend that the second campaign be selected." This recommendation has important implications, for $30 million will be spent in support of the campaign. Given the importance of the decision, the agency Creative Director asks "How confident are you in your recommendation?" Without inferential statistics, you can't objectively answer this question. And without this objective level of confidence, you increase your chances of making the wrong recommendation.

Inferential statistics provide a range of support for decision making and provide the basis for objectively determining the amount of confidence you can have in drawing conclusions from a set of data. Advertising researchers typically use these statistics to answer two simple, but tremendously important questions:

- How much confidence can I have that the *difference* between two or more measures is real and meaningful, and not just the result of random fluxuation in the data?

- How much confidence can I have that the *relationship* I am seeing between two or more measures is real and meaningful?

This chapter will show you how inferential statistics helps to answer these questions. First, however, it is important to understand the basis of statistical decision making, *statistical significance.*

STATISTICAL SIGNIFICANCE

While the calculations used to determine statistical significance can be quite complex, the concept of statistical significance is actually quite simple and straightforward.[1] Statistical significance helps you to decide whether the *differences* you see in the averages (or percentages) between two or more groups are "real" or whether they are due to chance. Similarly, statistical significance tells you whether the *relationship* you see between two variables is real or due to chance. "Real" is important; the more "real" the results are, the more confidence we have in our decisions based on the results.

Statistical significance is expressed as a number between 0 and 1, and unlike the scores you receive on an exam, lower numbers are better. The level of significance (expressed by the Greek letter alpha, α) represents the probability that the difference you see is due to chance. The lower the number the less chance plays in the results, and as a consequence the more the confidence you can have that the difference is a real one. Once calculated, for ease of interpretation, an α is turned in a percentage. When $\alpha = .1$, for example, the level of chance is 10%, so that we can be 90% confident that the results are real.[2]

What is a "good" alpha? When α is .05 or less, indicating that there is only a 5% probability or less that the results are due to chance, researchers typically claim that the findings are *statistically significant* and as a result that the observed differences are real. Keep in mind, however, that

> while this level is generally agreed to . . . there is nothing magical about a 5% chance, it's simply a convenient convention and could just as easily be 10% or

1%. The arbitrariness of the 5% threshold is most obvious when alpha values are near the cut-off. To call one finding significant when the alpha value is 5% and another not significant when it is 6% vastly overstates the difference between the two findings.[3]

As a result, you need to bring sensible judgment to the interpretation of levels of significance. But in most research, an alpha of .05 or less is a good cut-off for determining statistical significance.

Consider this example: *Indy 2010* is an online interactive car racing game. You want to find out whether explicitly incorporating the Ford Mustang into the game has any effect on players' attitudes and preferences toward the car.[4] You arrange to have the Mustang appear in half of the players' game while the other half of players are not exposed. All participants are randomly selected and randomly assigned to one of the conditions. After an hour of playing, a pop-up window appears and asks the players whether they would answer a few short questions about the game. The questions related to Mustang are shown below where the "awareness" measure is the percentage of the sample mentioning Mustang when asked "What car names and types come to mind?" and the remaining three measures are each group's average rating on a 1- to 5-point scale where higher numbers are more positive. Positive scores in the difference column indicate higher scores for the exposed versus unexposed group.

Measure	Not Exposed to Mustang	Exposed to Mustang	Difference
Top of mind awareness of Mustang	73%	81%	+8%
Overall positive opinion of Mustang	3.0	3.5	+0.5
Consider Mustang for next purchase	2.9	3.6	+0.7
Consider Mustang a real "power car"	3.1	4.1	+1.0

Those exposed to the Mustang in the video game always have higher (more positive) scores. A researcher looking just at these numbers might conclude that Mustang's presence in the game achieved success in all four of the areas measured, and as a result, game placement is a viable option if Ford wants to change a broad range of attitudes toward Mustang. But would this conclusion be correct? The table below adds the alpha value to each measure.

Measure	Not Exposed to Mustang	Exposed to Mustang	Difference	α
Top of mind awareness of Mustang	73%	81%	+8%	.09
Overall positive opinion of Mustang	3.0	3.5	+0.5	.11
Consider Mustang for next purchase	2.9	3.6	+0.7	.09
Consider Mustang a real "power car"	3.1	4.1	1.0	.04

The levels of statistical significance show that we can only have confidence that the game helped to change perceptions of Mustang as a power car. Only this measure has an α level at .05 or less. The changes in the other areas were positive but did not reach the level of statistical significance. Thus, based on the results, a more correct conclusion might have been that:

Placement in the game works well to foster power car perceptions of Mustang and shows some success in changing attitudes toward Mustang in other areas. If Ford wants to focus on improving power car perceptions, then game placement is an excellent option. If Ford wants to use game play to generate awareness and to improve attitudes in the remaining two attitudinal areas, then ways should be explored to determine how the current Mustang presentation can be strengthened with specific focus on the areas that showed near statistical significance.

Most data analysis programs automatically calculate an α for you, and in fact, in this chapter there are only three instances in which an easy manual calculation is necessary to find the level of statistical significance. With this in mind, we can now explore ways in which inferential statistics can help you better understand the nature of the results obtained in specific research situations. Figure 16.1 serves as a guide to the various types of analyses discussed in this chapter.

MAKING JUDGMENTS ABOUT A SINGLE MEASURE FROM ONE SAMPLE

Two types of analyses may be conducted when a single sample is available.

- The first type of analysis compares a sample mean or percentage to the corresponding mean or percentage in a larger population. Here, for example, an advertiser

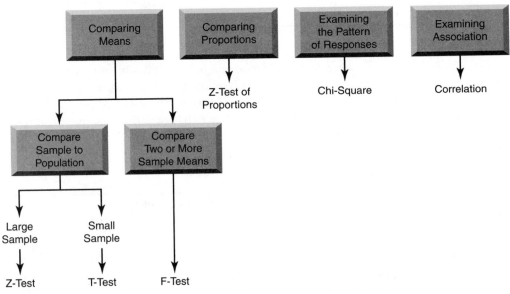

FIGURE 16.1 Statistical Analyses Discussed in Chapter 16

may have a database of scores from past commercial research and might want to compare the tested performance of each proposed new commercial to the average score of past commercials. This would allow the advertiser to see whether or not a new commercial meets or exceeds the average performance of past efforts.

- The second type of analysis examines the internal characteristics of a single sample. Here, for example, an advertiser may show a group of consumers four commercials and ask them to select the one that they felt best communicated a particular message. Each commercial is selected by a certain percentage of the sample as the "best." The advertiser would then determine whether the pattern of preferences within this sample reflects a significant preference of one commercial over the others.

The next two sections explain the procedures that can be used to analyze data and determine statistical significance in each of these types of circumstances.

Comparing a Sample Average to a Population Average

One of two tests can be used to compare a sample mean to a population mean.[5] The test selected is determined by the sample size. The math underlying both tests is quite simple and requires only minimal manual computation.[6]

LARGE SAMPLE SIZE.   A large sample size is generally considered to be 30 or more individuals.

Imagine that McDonald's tests every proposed commercial before it is produced. Over time, several hundred of these tests are conducted. McDonald's can use the population of prior tests to evaluate the performance of new, proposed commercials where it has decided only those commercials that are statistically better than the average of prior commercials on the key measure of "purchase intent" will be produced.

McDonald's tests a new commercial. The data needed to calculate whether or not the commercial is significantly better than the average of past commercials is shown below (where higher numbers represent higher purchase intent):

	Test Commercial	Population of Commercials
Average purchase intent	3.9	3.1
Standard deviation	not required	1.6
Sample size	100	not required

A comparison of the test commercial to the population of commercials is carried out through the following three steps:[7]

1. Subtract the population average from the sample average, in this case, the test commercial. The result is .8 (3.9 − 3.1 = .8).

2. Divide the population standard deviation by the square root of the sample size. The result is .16. (The square root of 100 is 10, so the computation is 1.6 ÷ 10 = .16).

3. Divide the number obtained in Step 1 by the number obtained in Step 2. The result is 5.0 (calculated as .8 ÷ .16).

The value obtained in the last step is a Z-score, which can be interpreted using one of three approaches, all of which reach the same conclusion. First, a statistical table can be used.[8] These tables, however, tend to be cumbersome and tricky to use and, as a result, can lead to interpretive error. Second, you can compare the Z-score obtained to the Z-score required for α at 95% and 99% levels of confidence (i.e., when α equals .05 and .01, respectively). These levels are shown below:

- A Z-score of 1.96 or greater exceeds the 95% level of confidence. There is less than a 5% probability that the difference is due to chance.
- A Z-score of 2.58 or greater exceeds the 99% level of confidence. There is less than a 1% probability that the difference is due to chance.

In this case, the Z-score of 5.0 exceeds 2.58 indicating that we can be more than 99% confident that the difference between the test commercial and the average of all prior commercials is real and not due to chance. McDonald's can confidently conclude that the test commercial is better than the average of prior commercials. Finally, to find the exact level of significance, you can use an online calculator, such as that provided by SISA.[9] Using this calculator, we find that a Z-score of 5.0 results in an α of less than .001, indicating that there is actually less than 1 chance in 1,000 that the observed differences are due to chance.

SMALL SAMPLE SIZE.   When the sample size is less than 30, an alternative test, the t-test, is used to compare a test mean to the population mean. The t-test is very similar to the Z test in approach. However, while the Z test uses the *population* standard deviation in Step 2, the t-test utilizes the *sample* standard deviation, otherwise the steps are the same. Consider the data shown below:

	Test Commercial	Population of Commercials
Average purchase intent (5 highest)	3.2	3.6
Standard deviation	1.5	not required
Sample size	25	not required

A comparison of the test commercial to the population of commercials is carried out through the following three steps:[10]

1. Subtract the population average from the sample average, in this case, the test commercial. The result is −0.4 (3.2 − 3.6 = −0.4).
2. Divide the test sample standard deviation by the square root of the sample size. The result is .3 (The square root of 25 is 5, so the computation is 1.5 ÷ 5 = .3).
3. Divide the number is obtained in Step 1 by the number obtained in Step 2. The result is −1.33 (calculated as −0.4 ÷ .3).

An interpretation of the t-value uses two of the same options as the interpretation of the Z-score except that here you also need to know your *degrees of freedom,* which is the number in your sample minus one (or in this example 24). First, a statistical table can be used.[11] As with the Z-score table, this table can also be cumbersome and tricky to use and, as a result, can lead to interpretive error. Second, you can use an online calculator, such as that provided by SISA. When the t-score of −1.33 and 24 degrees of freedom are input into the calculator, we obtain a significance value of .196. This level of significance is greater than the traditional cut-off values of .01 or .05, and thus indicates that we cannot be confident that the difference between the test commercial and the average of all prior commercials is "real" and not due to chance. McDonald's cannot confidently conclude that the test commercial is different than the average of prior commercials.[12]

Comparing a Sample Proportion to a Population Proportion

The prior Z and t-tests used interval data to compare sample and population means. A similar approach can be used to compare the responses on a nominal or ordinal measure to the scores in the larger population. This is a test of proportions.

Think about McDonald's trying to assess the impact of proposed commercials on consumers' intention to eat at McDonald's. However, rather than using a purchase intent rating scale, after seeing a test commercial respondents are asked: "The next time you go to a fast food restaurant, where will you go?" The percentage of respondents answering "McDonald's" is tallied. McDonald's can compare the proportion of respondents saying "McDonald's" after seeing a test commercial to the average percentage saying "McDonald's" within their population of prior tests. The data they would use is:

	Test Commercial	Population of Commercials
Percent choosing McDonalds	75%	57%
Percent choosing "all others"	not required	43%
Sample size	50	not required

A comparison of the test commercial to the population of commercials is carried out through the following five steps:[13]

1. Turn the population and sample proportions into decimals. Then, subtract the population proportion from the sample proportion, in this case, the test commercial. The result is .18 (.75 − .57 = .18).

2. Multiply the two population proportions. The result is .25 (.57 × .43 = .25).

3. Divide the number from Step 2 by the sample size. The result is .005 (.25 ÷ 50).

4. Take the square root of the number obtained in Step 3. The square root of .005 is .071.

5. Divide the number from Step 1 by the number in Step 4. The result is 2.53 (.18 ÷ .071 = 2.53).

The value obtained is a Z-score, which is interpreted similarly to the Z-score discussed earlier. You can find the level of statistical significance by using a statistical table, you can compare this score to the critical cut-off points, or you can use an online calculator. In this case, the online calculator indicates that a Z-score of 2.53 translates to an α of .011. This indicates that McDonald's can be nearly 99% confident that the differences are real and not due to chance.[14] Given that α is less than the .05 level of significance,

McDonald's concludes that the proportion of respondents who say they intend to try McDonald's after seeing the test commercial is higher than the average proportion of individuals saying "McDonald's" in the population of test commercials.

Examining the Internal Characteristics of a Single Sample

The prior tests took a single measure, a mean or proportion, from a single sample of respondents and compared this measure to the same measure in the relevant population. There are times, however, when an advertiser needs to examine the overall pattern of response to a single measure. The most common approach to examining the internal characteristics of responses to a single measure is chi-square. The *chi-square test* (represented by the symbol χ^2) allows you to examine the frequency distribution within a single sample and then determine whether the pattern is significantly different than the one you would get purely by chance.

Imagine that McDonald's has four commercials and wishes to determine which commercial best communicates the target message. All four commercials are shown to a sample of consumers and, after all are seen, each respondent selects the commercial he or she thinks was the best communicator. Chi-square lets the advertiser examine the pattern of response to determine whether or not, from a statistical perspective, the pattern obtained is real and not due to chance. The commercial preference data for this example is as follows:

Commercial	Number of Respondents Selecting Each Commercial
1	152
2	114
3	91
4	79

Fortunately, because of the extensive math required to calculate the chi-square statistic, online calculators are available to perform the calculations.[15] To make the underlying data trend more visible, the following table expands the prior table as follows:

- the count of individuals selecting each commercial is turned into a percentage distribution.
- the expected number of individuals selecting each commercial has been added. This percentage and actual number assumes that if chance selection was occurring, an equal percentage of individuals would select each commercial. The use of percentages and actual estimates in the third and fourth columns makes it easier to compare the actual to estimated pattern of response. The data in the second and fifth columns are what is used in the actual chi-square analysis.

Using the data from this expanded table and the online chi-square calculator, the results of the chi-square calculation and its level of significance have also been added to the bottom of the table.

Commercial	# of Respondents Selecting Each Commercial	% of Respondents Selecting Each Commercial	Expected % Selecting Each Commercial	Expected # Selecting Each Commercial
1	152	35%	25%	109
2	114	26	25	109
3	91	21	25	109
4	79	18	25	109
Chi-Square = 28.42	$\alpha < .001$			

The level of significance indicates that the results are not random or due to chance. The probability of this pattern not being "real" is less than 1 in 1,000. Thus, McDonald's can conclude that consumers' reactions to the commercials are indeed different and that, based on the preference data, Commercial 1 was the preferred commercial.

MAKING JUDGMENTS ABOUT A SINGLE MEASURE FROM TWO OR MORE INDEPENDENT SAMPLES

A great deal of advertising research entails comparing measures from two different samples, for example, conducting an experiment where you want to compare the results of the control to the test group or where you want to find out if the differences between two subgroups (such as men versus women) on the same survey are statistically different. In these cases an F-test is used.[16] Fortunately, since statistical programs such as SPSS, online calculators, and spreadsheet programs such as Excel are available to perform the mathematical computations, we'll focus on interpretation rather than the computations themselves.

Comparing Two Means

Advertisers are often interested in comparing two groups of individuals who vary in some important way; for example, the groups may differ in terms of an advertising-related variable such as advertising awareness, advertising exposure, or exposure to different forms of advertising. Additionally, advertisers may want to compare groups that differ on specific characteristics; for example, they may want to compare the attitudes of brand users versus nonusers or younger versus older consumers. This section provides two examples of situations where two means are compared.

TWO CONDITIONS, ONE GROUP PER CONDITION.   Imagine that you have developed two ads that are to be placed into rotation in Google Adwords. While both ads will be shown in response to the same search terms, the ads differ in the benefit they offer to the consumer: the first ad stresses customer service, while the second ad stresses low prices. Adwords lets you monitor the purchase amount resulting from the click-through for each of the ads. Note that this is ratio level data, as an individual can have a purchase of $0 indicating that no purchase was made. Data is collected for a month, and is shown in the following table.

Key Measure	Ad Focus: Customer Service	Ad Focus: Price Low
Average purchase	$23.87	$16.29

The F-test is the appropriate statistical test to use in circumstances such as this. The following table adds the results of the F-test:

Key Measure	Ad Focus: Customer Service	Ad Focus: Low Price	F-value	α
Average purchase	$23.87	$16.29	54.9	<.001

The F-value, which takes into account sample size, the differences between the averages and standard deviation, is used to determine the level of significance. This statistic is reported in the last column. The appropriate α for a specific F-value can be obtained through the use of a statistical program such as SPSS or a spreadsheet program such as Excel. In this case, the α level indicates that the difference between the two ads is significant in favor of the customer service ad. The chances of these differences being seen due to chance are less than 1 in 1,000.

ONE SURVEY, TWO SUBGROUPS.   Chapter 15 discussed the value in examining the responses of subgroups of individuals to survey questions. When the data being examined is at the interval or ratio level of measurement, an F-test can be used to determine whether the responses of different subgroups are statistically significant. When the data is at a lower level of measurement, then different tests must be used. The most common of these tests, chi-square, is discussed later in this chapter.

Imagine that you have conducted a survey on which you ask the five-point rating question: "How likely or unlikely are you purchase an iPhone in the next month?" Higher numbers indicate a greater likelihood to purchase. The average for the total sample was 3.0, indicating a neutral response. However, when the ratings of the 100 men versus 100 women participating in the survey are separated the following data appears:

Key Measure	Men	Women
Average purchase intent	4.1	1.9

The following table adds the results of the F-test:

Key Measure	Men	Women	F-value	α
Average purchase intent	4.1	1.9	75.9	<.001

As in the prior example, the F-value determines the level of significance, which is reported in the last column. The α level indicates that there is a significant difference between men and women with intent to purchase an iPhone. Men express a significantly higher intent to purchase versus women. The chances of this difference being due to chance is less than 1 in 1,000.

Comparing Three or More Means

While the prior examples compared two means, the exact same processes can be used to compare three or more means. These means can represent the levels of response in different experimental conditions or can reflect the responses of different subgroups within the same survey.

THREE OR MORE CONDITIONS.   Imagine that after the test described in the beginning of the prior section, the advertiser decides to keep the customer service ad but now wants to test two additional ads: the first ad stresses quick delivery, while the second ad is a revised version of the low price ad. Again, data is collected for a month and is shown below:

Key Measure	Ad Focus Customer Service	Ad Focus: Quick Delivery	Ad Focus: Low Price (Revised)
Average purchase	$23.87	$21.23	$32.59

The following table adds the results of the F-test.

Key Measure	Ad Focus: Customer Service	Ad Focus: Quick Delivery	Ad Focus: Low Price (Revised)	F-value	α
Average purchase	$23.87	$21.23	$32.59	47.43	<.001

When testing three or more means, an F-test tells you whether all of the means should be considered the same (when α is greater than .05) or if one or more means are significantly different than the others (when α is less than .05). Thus, in reading the α level of significance column in the prior table, we see a significant difference in the average purchase amount generated by each ad. But, we don't know which one is the "best."

A determination of statistical significance is the first step in exploring the differences between three or more means. When significance is found, the second step compares all pairs of means in order to determine which are significantly different from each other.[17] When this is done for the three ads' average purchase amount, the following data is obtained:

Key Measure: Average Purchase	F-value	α
Comparing means of "Customer Service" and "Quick Delivery"	3.35	.46
Comparing means of "Customer Service" and "Low Price (Revised)"	23.22	<.001
Comparing means of "Quick Delivery" and "Low Price Revised)"	28.76	<.001

The pattern in the levels of significance indicates that the "Customer Service" and "Quick Delivery" ads generated, on average, equivalent purchase amounts. The amounts generated by these two ads were not statistically significant. The "Low Price Ad (Revised)" is statistically different than other two ads, as the level of significance for both comparisons is less than .001. An examination of each ad's average purchase amount shows that "Low Price Ad (Revised)" generated a significantly *higher* purchase amount versus the other two ads.

ONE SURVEY, THREE OR MORE SUBGROUPS.   The prior procedure can also be used to compare three or more subgroups responding to the same survey. Imagine, for example, that now you wanted to examine iPhone purchase intent among different age groups. The relevant data from the five-point purchase intent question is shown below, where higher scores indicate greater purchase intent:

Key Measure	Age 18 to 24	Age 25 to 49	Age 50+
Average purchase intent	4.7	3.0	1.3

The following table adds the results of the F-test.

Key Measure	Age 18 to 24	Age 25 to 49	Age 50+	F-value	α
Average purchase intent	4.7	3.0	1.3	81.23	<.001

As in the prior example, the F-test tells you whether all of the means should be considered the same (when α is greater than .05) or if one or more means are significantly different than the others (when α is less than .05). Thus, in reading the α level of significance column in the prior table, we see that there is a significant difference in average purchase intent. But, we don't know which groups are significantly different from each other. This is accomplished by comparing each pair of means, as follows:

Key Measure: Purchase Intent	F-value	α
Comparing means of 18 to 24 year olds versus 25 to 49 year olds	16.24	.01
Comparing means of 18 to 24 year olds versus 50+ year olds	70.23	<.001
Comparing means of 25 to 49 year olds versus 50+ year olds	18.56	.01

The pattern in the levels of significance indicates that all three groups differ from each other. An examination of each group's average purchase intent indicates that the purchase intent of those aged 18 to 24 is significantly higher than the purchase intent of the other two age groups and that the purchase intent of those aged 25 to 49 is, in turn, greater than the purchase intent of those aged 50+.

FACTORIAL DESIGNS: MAKING JUDGMENTS ABOUT THE SIMULTANEOUS INFLUENCE OF TWO OR MORE VARIABLES

The examples discussed in the prior section manipulated only one variable at a time. Individuals, for example, saw one ad or another. There are times, however, that you want to find the influence of two or more variables at the same time. The advantage of simultaneously manipulating two or more variables is that you are able to see if there is an interaction between the variables; that is, you can determine the extent to which variables work together or act independently to affect the dependent variable(s). A nonsignificant interaction means that the variables work independently while a significant interaction indicates that the combined impact of one or more variables is greater (or less) than the influence of each variable individually. A factorial design allows you to manipulate two or more variables at the same time.

A factorial design is described in terms of its main factors and the levels within each factor. While there is no mathematical limit to the number of factors and levels in any particular research situation, practical considerations tend to keep both factors and levels low. Imagine, for example, that you develop four viral ads for a new campaign. The ads, while all designed to communicate the same message, vary along two factors: the use of humor and the gender of the spokesperson. "Humor" and "Gender" are the factors. Each factor has two levels: the two levels of humor are "Absent" and "Present," while the two levels of "Gender" are "Male" and "Female."[18] The four ads and their characteristics are as follows:

Name of Viral Ad	Humor	Gender
Logo	Yes	Male
Trial	Yes	Female
Guitars	No	Male
Text	No	Female

Thus, for example, the ad named "Logo" uses humor with a male spokesperson, while the ad named "Text" uses a female spokesperson with no humor. Figure 16.2 visually

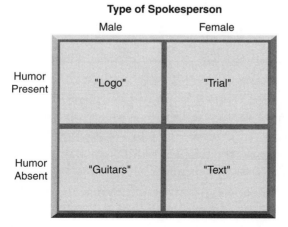

FIGURE 16.2 Factorial Design

shows this research study's design. Note that every cell is filled by one of the test ads. The goal of all four ads is to improve attitudes toward the brand, using the measure "How much do you agree or disagree with the statement: This is a brand for me." as the key measure. A five point-scale was used where higher scores indicate more agreement.

The most common potential outcomes of this type of 2 × 2 factorial design are examined in the next sections, as follows:

- neither factor is significant, no interaction between factors
- one factor is significant, no interaction between factors
- one factor is significant, with interaction between factors
- two factors are significant, no interaction between factors
- neither factor is significant, with interaction between factors

Neither Factor Is Significant, No Interaction Between Factors

This example presents an instance in which neither of the factors (the independent variables) have any significant effect on ratings of personal relevance (the dependent variable) and there is no interaction between the factors.

The first step in the analysis calculates the average for each factor independently and for each combination of factors. The outcome of these calculations is shown in the table below.

Measure: Ratings of Personal Relevance	Average Rating
Spokesperson	
Male ("Logo" and "Guitars" combined)	3.7
Female ("Trial" and "Text" combined)	3.9
Humor	
Present ("Logo" and "Trial" combined)	3.7
Absent ("Guitars" and "Text" combined)	3.9
Individual Ads	
"Logo"	3.6
"Trial"	3.8
"Guitars"	3.8
"Text"	4.0

The data indicates that

- the overall average for the two ads with a male spokesperson was 3.7, while the overall average for the two ads with a female spokesperson was 3.9;
- the overall average for the two ads with humor was 3.7, while the overall average for the two ads without humor was 3.9;
- the average for "Logo" was 3.6, while the average for "Text" was 4.0.

A statistical analysis program such as SPSS or a spreadsheet program such as Excel would then examine the pattern of response across the four groups and the main effects. Based on this examination, an F-value is computed for each factor (i.e., "Gender" and "Humor") and for the interaction between the two factors. The F-value is then translated into an α. This information is shown in the following table

Factors Evaluated	F	Level of Significance (α)
Gender (Alone)	2.34	.15
Humor (Alone)	2.48	.17
Spokesperson × Humor Interaction	1.83	.25

The prior two charts taken together are interpreted as follows:

- Gender as a main effect had little influence on ratings of commercial relevance. There was no significant difference (α is greater than .05) when the gender of the spokesperson was varied. This can be seen in the closeness of the mean scores for male and female spokespeople.

- Humor as a main effect had little influence on ratings of commercial relevance. There was no significant difference (α is greater than .05) when humor was either present or absent. This can be seen in the closeness of the mean scores for the commercials with and without humor.

- There was no significant interaction between the two main effects as the α for the interaction is greater than .05.

These findings are illustrated in the graph shown in Figure 16.3. Note how the lines for both main effects are parallel to each other (indicating no interaction) and very close together (indicating that neither main effect is significant).

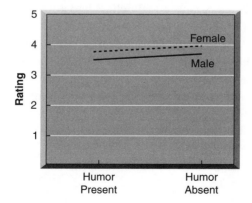

FIGURE 16.3   Factorial Results: Nonsignificant Main Effects, Nonsignificant Interaction

One Factor Is Significant, No Interaction Between Factors

This example presents an instance in which the only one of the factors has a significant effect on ratings of personal relevance and there is no interaction between the factors.

As in the prior example, the first step in the analysis calculates the average for each factor independently and for each combination of factors, as shown below.

Measure: Ratings of Personal Relevance	Average Rating
Spokesperson	
Male ("Logo" and "Guitars" combined)	3.7
Female ("Trial" and "Text" combined)	2.5
Humor	
Present ("Logo" and "Trial" combined)	3.0
Absent ("Guitars" and "Text" combined)	3.2
Individual Ads	
"Logo"	3.6
"Trial"	2.4
"Guitars"	3.8
"Text"	2.6

The F-values and levels of significance computed for each factor and for the interaction between the two factors are shown in the following table.

Factors Evaluated	F	Level of Significance (α)
Gender (Alone)	42.45	.001
Humor (Alone)	.97	.92
Spokesperson × Humor Interaction	1.02	.85

The prior two charts taken together are interpreted as follows:

- Gender of the spokesperson as a main effect had a profound influence on ratings of commercial relevance. There was a significant difference (α is less than .05) when the gender of the spokesperson was varied. As reflected in the mean scores, relevance was rated higher (more positively) when the spokesperson was male versus female.

- Humor as a main effect had little influence on ratings of commercial relevance. There was no significant difference (α is greater than .05) when humor was either present or absent. This can be seen in the closeness of the mean scores for the commercials with and without humor.

- There was no significant interaction between the two factors as the α for the interaction is greater than .05.

These findings are illustrated in the graph shown in Figure 16.4. Note how the lines for both factors are parallel to each other (indicating no interaction) with the space between them quite large (indicating a significant main effect). The graph indicates that the male spokesperson was always responded to in a more positive way versus the female spokesperson; that is, regardless of whether or not humor was present, the male spokesperson received higher ratings versus the female spokesperson.

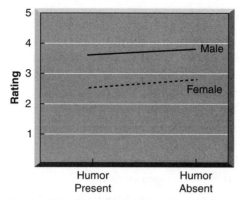

FIGURE 16.4   Factorial Results: One Significant Main Effect, Nonsignificant Interaction

One Factor Is Significant, There Is an Interaction Between Factors

This example presents an instance in which only one of the factors has a significant effect on ratings of personal relevance *but* there is an interaction between the factors.

As in the prior examples, the first step in the analysis calculates the average for each factor independently and for each combination of factors, as shown below.

Measure: Ratings of Personal Relevance	Average Rating
Spokesperson	
Male ("Logo" and "Guitars" combined)	3.3
Female ("Trial" and "Text" combined)	2.2
Humor	
Present ("Logo" and "Trial" combined)	2.7
Absent ("Guitars" and "Text" combined)	2.8
Individual Ads	
"Logo"	2.8
"Trial"	2.6
"Guitars"	3.8
"Text"	1.8

The F-values and levels of significance computed for each factor and for the interaction between the two factors are shown in the following table.

Factors Evaluated	F	Level of Significance (α)
Gender (Alone)	32.45	.001
Humor (Alone)	2.97	.15
Spokesperson × Humor Interaction	17.92	.01

The prior two charts taken together are interpreted as follows:

- Gender as a main effect had a significant, independent influence on ratings of commercial relevance. There was a significant difference (α is less than .05) when the gender of the spokesperson was varied. Overall, the male spokesperson generated higher levels of personal relevance versus the female spokesperson.

- Humor as a main effect had no independent influence on ratings of commercial relevance. There was no significant difference (α is greater than .05) when humor was either present or absent. This can be seen in the closeness of the mean scores for the two ads with and two ads without humor.

- There was a significant interaction between the two factors as the α for the interaction is less than .05. This indicates that we need to be cautious in interpreting the data relevant to the main effects. When the individual commercial means are examined, we see a much higher score for the "Guitars" ad and a much lower score for the "Text" ad versus the other two ads. These means, coupled with the significant interaction term, indicate that when humor is present the gender of the spokesperson does not affect reactions to the commercial, but when humor is absent reactions are much more positive when the commercial uses a male versus female spokesperson.

These findings are illustrated in the graph shown in Figure 16.5. Note how the lines now run at an angle to each other, rather then running parallel. This pattern, when lines run at an angle or cross, is the visual indication of an interaction. The lines' closeness when humor is present and greater distance when humor is absent indicate that humor *only* exerts an influence on relevance ratings when it is absent and *only* results in higher ratings when a male spokesperson is used.

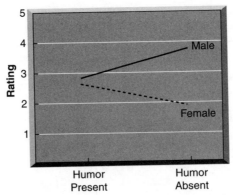

FIGURE 16.5   Factorial Results: One Significant Main Effect, Significant Interaction

Two Factors Are Significant, No Interaction Between Factors

This example presents an instance in which both of the factors have a significant effect on ratings of personal relevance and there is no interaction between the factors.

As in the prior examples, the first step in the analysis calculates the averages for each factor independently and for each combination of factors, as shown below.

Measure: Ratings of Personal Relevance	Average Rating
Spokesperson	
Male ("Logo" and "Guitars" combined)	2.3
Female ("Trial" and "Text" combined)	3.7
Humor	
Present ("Logo" and "Trial" combined)	3.7
Absent ("Guitars" and "Text" combined)	2.3
Individual Ads	
"Logo"	3.0
"Trial"	4.4
"Guitars"	1.6
"Text"	3.0

The F-values and levels of significance computed for each factor and for the interaction between the two factors are shown in the following table.

Factors Evaluated	F	Level of Significance (α)
Gender (Alone)	18.23	.001
Humor (Alone)	17.81	.001
Spokesperson × Humor Interaction	6.02	.43

The prior two charts taken together are interpreted as follows:

- Gender exerted an independent influence on ratings of commercial relevance. There was a significant difference (α is less than .05) when the gender of the spokesperson was varied. As reflected in the mean scores, relevance was rated higher (more positively) when the spokesperson was female versus male.

- Humor exerted an independent influence on ratings of commercial relevance. There was a significant difference (α is less than .05) when humor was present versus absent. As reflected in the mean scores, relevance was rated higher when humor was present.

- There was no significant interaction between the two factors as the α for the interaction is greater than .05.

These findings are illustrated in the graph shown in Figure 16.6. Note how the lines for both factors are parallel to each other (indicating no interaction) with the space between them quite large. The slope or angle of the parallel lines coupled with the large space between them visually indicates the significance of both main effects without any interaction.

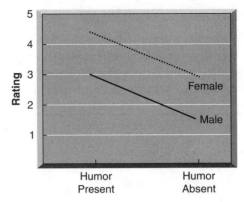

FIGURE 16.6   Factorial Results: Two Significant Main Effects, Nonsignificant Interaction

Neither Factor Is Significant, There Is an Interaction Between Factors

This example presents an instance in which neither of the factors has a significant effect on ratings of personal relevance *but* there is an interaction between the factors.

As in the prior examples, the first step in the analysis calculates the averages for each factor independently and for each combination of factors, as shown below.

Measure: Purchase Intent	Average Rating
Spokesperson	
Male ("Logo" and "Guitars" combined)	3.1
Female ("Trial" and "Text" combined)	3.1
Humor	
Present ("Logo" and "Trial" combined)	3.2
Absent ("Guitars" and "Text" combined)	3.0
Individual Ads	
"Logo"	2.0
"Trial"	4.4
"Guitars"	4.2
"Text"	1.8

The F-values and levels of significance computed for each factor and for the interaction between the two factors are shown in the following table.

Factors Evaluated	F	Level of Significance (α)
Gender (Alone)	1.45	.91
Humor (Alone)	1.87	.88
Spokesperson × Humor Interaction	17.92	.001

The prior two charts taken together are interpreted as follows:

- Gender as a main effect had no significant influence on ratings of commercial relevance. There was no significant difference (α is greater than .05) when the gender of the spokesperson was varied. This can be seen in the closeness of the mean scores for the two commercials with a male spokesperson and two commercials with a female spokesperson.

- Humor as a main effect had no significant influence on ratings of commercial relevance. There was no significant difference (α is greater than .05) when humor was present or absent. This can be seen in the closeness of the mean scores for the two commercials with humor and two commercials without humor.

- There was a significant interaction between the two factors as the α for the interaction is greater than .05. The significant interaction requires that we move beyond the main effect averages and examine each of the individual commercial averages. When this is done, it can be seen that a female spokesperson has the most positive effect when humor is present while a male spokesperson has the most positive effect when humor is absent.

These findings are illustrated in the graph shown in Figure 16.7. Note how the lines run at an angle to each other, rather then running parallel. As in the prior example of an interaction, this pattern is the visual indication of an interaction. The graph visually shows that a female spokesperson is most effective when humor is present while a male spokesperson is most effective in the absence of humor.

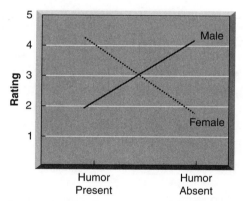

FIGURE 16.7 Factorial Results: Nonsignificant Main Effects, Significant Interaction

MAKING JUDGMENTS ABOUT THE RELATIONSHIP BETWEEN TWO OR MORE MEASURES

Correlation

The most common technique for determining the relationship between two variables is *correlation*, a statistical measure of the covariation or association between two variables.[19] For example,

> height and weight are related; taller people tend to be heavier than shorter people. The relationship isn't perfect. People of the same height vary in weight, and you can easily think of two people you know where the shorter one is heavier than the taller one. Nonetheless, the average weight of people

5′5″ is less than the average weight of people 5′6″, and their average weight is less than that of people 5′7″, etc. Correlation can tell you just how much of the variation in peoples' weights is related to their heights.[20]

A correlation coefficient (noted by the symbol *r*) consists of two parts:

- The *sign* of the correlation coefficient, either + or −, indicates the *direction* of the association.
- The *numeric component*, which ranges from −1 to +1, indicates the *magnitude* of the association.

If the value of *r* equals +1.0 then there is a perfect positive correlation between the two variables. All of the observations fall on a straight line and as one variable increases so does the other (see top left-hand graph in Figure 16.8). If the value of *r* equals −1.0, then there is a perfect negative correlation. Here, all of the observations fall on a straight line but as one variable increases the other decreases (see top right-hand graph in Figure 16.8). The total absence of a relationship between two variables occurs when *r* = 0 (see bottom graph in Figure 16.8).

Correlation thus tells you about the simultaneous movement of two measures. Imagine, for example, that after viewing a commercial, respondents used a five-point

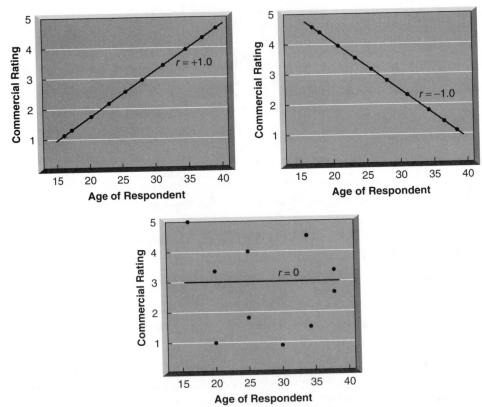

FIGURE 16.8 Positive, Negative and Absence of Correlation

scale to rate commercial liking and a different five-point scale to rate commercial believ-ability. In both cases, a "5" was the most favorable response. The correlation between the two variables is +.89. The + would be interpreted to mean that the two ratings move in the same direction; that is, respondents who provided a high liking score also tended to provide a high believability score, while respondents who provided a low liking score also tended to provide a low believability score. The .89 correlation indicates that there is a strong relationship between the two ratings.

The absolute value of a correlation coefficient provides a great deal of insight regarding the relationship between two measures. However, similar to the analyses dis-cussed earlier in this chapter, it is also possible to determine the statistical significance of the correlation coefficient. Fortunately, there are online calculators that can accomplish this when the r value and the number of individuals in the sample are known.[21] Keep in mind that when determining statistical significance, sample size plays a key role in deter-mining significance; that is, the same r value will have different levels of significance for different sample sizes. This is illustrated in Figure 16.9.

Correlations can also be calculated for multiple pairs of measures. When this occurs, the set of correlations is reported in the form of a correlation matrix, as shown in Figure 16.10. The correlation between any two variables is found by locating the value at the inter-section of the column specifying the first variable and the row specifying the second variable. For example, in Figure 16.10 the correlation between commercial believability and commercial liking is .87, while the correlation between age and believability is −.88. Each "*" in the correlation matrix was provided by the statistical program that calculated the correlations, where an "*" indicates a statistically significant correlation.

Be careful in interpreting correlation as *correlation does not imply causation.* Correlation indicates the relationship between two variables. A strong positive correlation only indicates that the two variables move together in the same direction. Correlation,

Number in Sample	Correlation	Level of Significance
25	.15	.47
50	.15	.30
100	.15	.14
200	.15	.03
25	.25	.23
50	.25	.03
100	.25	.01
200	.25	<.001
25	.30	.15
50	.30	.03
100	.30	.002
200	.30	<.001

FIGURE 16.9 Impact of Sample Size on Statistical Significance of Correlation

	Age	Income	Rating of Ad Believability	Rating of Ad Liking	Purchase Intent
Age	1.0				
Income	.67*	1.0			
Rating of ad believability	−0.88*	.02	1.0		
Rating of ad liking	.09	−0.05	.87*	1.0	
Purchase intent	−0.15	.04	.83*	.89*	1.0

*indicates a correlation significant at .05 or less

FIGURE 16.10 Correlation Matrix

however, does indicate causation; it does not indicate that one variable *causes* the movement in the other or that a change in one will result in a change in the other. For example, it would be erroneous to conclude from a +.89 correlation between commercial liking and purchase intent that causing people to like the commercial more will cause people to have higher levels of purchase intent.

Chi-Square

The type of analysis conducted among subgroups of individuals is determined by the data's level of measurement. As discussed earlier, and F-test can be used when the data being examined is at the interval or ratio level of measurement. When the level of measurement is at a lower level (nominal or ordinal), then the chi-square test must be used. Similar to the chi-square test discussed earlier (see pages 440 to 441), this test also can be used to see if the pattern of response among different subgroups is significantly different than chance.

Imagine the same scenario as that discussed for the single group chi-square: An advertiser has four commercials and wishes to determine which commercial best communicates the target message. All four commercials are shown to a sample of consumers and, after all are seen, each respondent selects the commercial he or she thinks was the best communicator. Now, however, the advertiser wants to see if there are differences between subgroups in the pattern of response. The following approach might be taken.

Since the advertiser already knows that Commercial 1 is preferred overall (see pages xxx to xxx), he can compare the preference for just this commercial among men and women. The table that provides the relevant data is shown below:

Preference of Commercial 1	Men	Women
Preferred	92	60
Did Not Prefer	21	87

The table indicates that 92 men preferred Commercial 1 (versus 21 men who preferred another commercial) and that 60 women preferred Commercial 1 (versus 87 who preferred another commercial). The chi-square computation, which can be accomplished via an online calculator[22], compares mens' and womens' patterns of response to see if there are any differences. This computation results in a chi-square value of 41.71 and an α of $<.001$, indicating that the two patterns of response are statistically different from each other. Commercial 1 appears to be the preferred commercial for men but not for women. Given this result, follow-up analyses can be conducted to identify the preferred ad for women.[23]

A chi-square analysis is not limited to only two subgroups. A similar analysis, for example, can be performed for three different age groups: those aged 18 to 24, 25 to 34, and 35 to 49. As with the comparison of men versus women, the relevant data for preference of just Commercial 1 for each age group is shown below.

Preference of Commercial 1	Aged 18–24	Aged 25–34	Aged 35–49
Preferred	63	57	61
Did Not Prefer	32	38	27

The chi-square computation compares the pattern of preference for the three age groups. In this case, the chi-square value of 1.84 and an α of .39 indicates that the patterns of response are not statistically different from each other (as the α is greater than .05). All three age groups are similar in their preference for Commercial 1.

A CAUTION REGARDING STATISTICAL TESTS

Statistical tests are powerful tools that help researchers determine how confident they can be in the conclusions that they draw from survey data. However, the power of these tools means that they must be used with care. Be certain that when using these techniques, you *let statistical tests inform your judgment, not replace it.* Don't confuse statistical significance with practical significance. Don't confuse the lack of significance with the lack of importance.

SUMMARY

Inferential statistics provide the basis for objectively determining the amount of confidence a researcher can have in drawing conclusions from a set of responses. Advertising researchers typically use inferential statistics to answer two important questions:

- How much confidence can I have that the *difference* between two or more measures is real and meaningful, and not just the result of random fluxuation in the data?
- How much confidence can I have that the *relationship* I am seeing between two or more measures is real and meaningful?

The specific type of statistical test used to address these questions and to evaluate group differences and relationships between measures is determined by the nature and size of the sample and the data's level of measurement. The appropriate test to use in various circumstances is summarized below:

Comparison	Sample Size	Statistical Test
Means		
Sample mean to population mean	Large	Z-test
Sample mean to population mean	Small	t-test
Two or more sample means	N/A	F-test
Factorial design	N/A	F-test
Proportions		
Sample proportion to population proportion	N/A	Z-test of proportions
Two sample proportions	N/A	Z test of proportions
Pattern of Observations		
Percentage distributions	N/A	Chi-square
Association		
Association of two or more variables	N/A	Correlation

Statistical tests must be conducted and interpreted with care and with an understanding of their limitations. The results of statistical tests should inform a researcher's judgment, not replace it.

Review Questions

1. Define and explain *statistical significance.* What is the value of this statistic?

2. What is an *alpha* level? Why is it important and how is it interpreted?

3. What types of analyses can be used to make judgments about a single measure from one sample?

4. What types of analyses can be used to compare a sample average to a population average?

5. How does sample size affect the type of analysis used to compare a sample average to a population average?

6. What types of analyses can be used to compare a sample proportion to a population proportion?

7. Explain the value of the *chi-square* analysis. In what circumstances is this analysis appropriate?

8. What types of analyses can be used to make judgments about a single measure from two or more independent sample?

9. How does the F-test allow you to compare three or more means?

10. What is a *factorial* design?

11. Why is understanding *interaction* in a factorial design important?

12. Define and explain *correlation.*

13. What are some cautions in interpreting and applying statistical significance?

14. What is the normal curve? How is the normal curve used in the calculation of statistical significance?

15. How is probability related to the normal curve?

16. What is meant by *hypothesis testing?*

17. What is the *null hypothesis?* What is its role in hypothesis testing?

Application Exercises

1. Each of the situations described below represents a circumstance in which an advertiser needs to rely on research data to aid in decision making. For each hypothetical situation, do the following: (a) read the question or questions posed, (b) conduct the statistical test or tests that will provide you with the insights to answer the question(s), and (c) use the data and the results of your statistical test to answer the question(s).

- *Based on ratings of believability and purchase intent, which of the two tested commercials should be recommended for production?* The research was conducted among a sample of the commercials' target audience. 100 respondents saw Commercial A and 100 different respondents saw commercial B. Believability and purchase intent were both measured through the use of 5-point scales where "1" was the least positive (i.e., extremely unbelievable; would definitely not buy) and "5" was the most positive (i.e., extremely believable; would definitely buy) response option.

Measure	Commercial A	Commercial B
Believability:		
Mean	4.2	3.7
Stand. Dev.	1.3	1.1
Purchase Intent:		
Mean	4.3	3.3
Stand. Dev.	1.1	1.2

- Over the years, the AAbCo Corporation has used a number of celebrities as its corporate spokespeople. This year, AAbCO is considering a new individual who, for security reasons, has been identified as Person X. The appeal of the potential spokesperson was assessed by showing a group of 45 target audience individuals the person's picture and then asking for a rating of appeal. Appeal was measured through the use of 7-point scale where "1" was the least positive (i.e., extremely unappealing) and "7" was the most positive (i.e., extremely appealing) response option. The ratings of Person X as well as the data for all past spokespeople

were shown in the table below *Would you recommend Person X?*

	Person X	Past Spokespeople
Appeal (mean)	4.5	5.5
Standard Deviation	1.5	not required
Number in sample	45	not required

- San Diego University has initiated a communication program designed to enhance the University's image among graduating high school seniors in cities greater than 100 miles from the University. This was done in an effort to recruit seniors from beyond the immediate San Diego area. The University interviewed 100 individuals prior to the start of the program. After the communication program has run for a year, the University surveys the attitudes of 200 target individuals: 100 men and 100 women. The key measure used to evaluate the program is "consideration of San Diego University" measured on a 7-point scale of "1" (would not at all consider) to "7" (would definitely consider). *Overall has the campaign been successful when compared to attitudes prior to the start of the program (as indicated in pre-survey measure)? Is the campaign more successful among women or men, or does it affect the attitudes of each gender group equally?*

	Men	Women	Pre-Survey
Consideration (mean)	4.1	4.5	3.2
Did Not Prefer	1.1	1.1	1.3

- The Becker Brewing Company has reformulated its no-alcohol beer. It is hoped that no-alcohol beer drinkers, especially those aged 25 to 39, will prefer the reformulated product to both the old Becker product and its major competitor. Taste tests are conducted. Target audience individuals are given a sample of the Old Becker formulation, the New Becker formulation, and O'Dools (Becker's major competitor). After tasting all three brands, each respondent is asked to name the one brand that he or she prefers. The actual number of respondents and their preferences are shown in the table below. *Overall, is the new Becker formulation preferred over the old formulation and O'Dools? Has Becker accomplished its goal by fostering preference among the target audience of individuals 25 to 39?*

Brand Preferred	Total Sample	Age 25–32	Age 33–39
Becker old formulation	72	36	36
Becker new formulation	97	32	75
O'Dools	86	37	49

• The North Coast Environmental Action Committee is planning a communications program designed to increase the public's recycling behaviors. Specifically, the program is designed to increase individuals' stated inclination to recycle aluminum cans. Two versions of the campaign are developed. One version uses fear of negative consequences to motivate recycling (i.e., more garbage, more landfills, etc.), while another version uses positive appeals (i.e., a better world for all of us). Each campaign is shown to 100 individuals. After viewing each campaign, a respondent is asked: "After viewing this advertisement, would you say that you are now more or less likely to recycle aluminum cans?" *Which campaign, if any, would you recommend?*

	Fear Appeal	Positive Appeal
% Saying "More Likely"	73	92
% Saying "Les Likely"	27	8

2. Identify an advertising-related problem that can be explored in a 2 × 2 factorial design. Prepare a short paper that (a) explains the problem and what you hope to learn, (b) identifies and explains each factor and level within each factor, and (c) provides and discusses your expected results.

3. Explain the implications of the correlation matrix shown in Figure 16.10 for creative planning.

4. Each of the situations described below represents a researchable circumstance that an advertiser and his or her agency might encounter. Read each hypothetical situation and then (a) translate each situation into a null and alternative hypotheses or hypotheses, (b) explain why you decided to make the comparison one-tailed or two-tailed, (c) state whether the preferred outcome is acceptance or rejection of the null hypothesis, and (d) set an appropriate probability level for acceptance or rejection of the null hypothesis.

• KXXC is a local radio station. In March it measured awareness of its new morning format. Between March and August, it spent $100,000 advertising its new format. In August it again measured awareness. KXXC wants to compare awareness at these two points in time in order to determine the extent to which awareness has increased.

• David Palmer is running for a seat on the city council. His friends, who are helping with his advertising, have suggested two slogans: "Put Palmer on the Council" and "Palmer: The Citizen's Choice." David's staff conducts research to determine which slogan should be selected.

• The San Diego Union-Tribune has just redesigned its business section. The paper wants to determine readers' reaction to the new design versus the prior design. It is hoped that the redesigned business section is more appealing than the prior format.

Theory Underlying Statistical Significance

Researchers need to be confident in conclusions that they draw from research studies. When, for example, researchers compare two average scores and then decide that one is in fact higher or better than the other, they want to be certain that the differences between the mean scores reflect *real* differences as opposed to random error in the data. They want to have confidence that the marketing and advertising decisions based on inferences and conclusions drawn from the data are the right decisions. Because few data-based decisions can be made with absolute certainty, confidence in decision making is typically expressed in terms of a probability. A researcher might say, for example, "I've just tested two commercials. In examining the scores that represent responses to these commercials I want to be confident that any observed differences are meaningful and that decisions I reach based on the data reflect the proper interpretation of the data. The data primarily involves mean level of response. I want to be 95% certain that the difference between the means of the two commercials is real and not due to error."

In order to understand how levels of confidence are determined, it is necessary to understand the relationship between the normal curve, standard deviation, and probability.

THE NORMAL CURVE

The frequency and percentage distribution of responses to a particular research question can take a variety of shapes. Some distributions are symmetrical where the mean, median, and mode are identical; some distributions are skewed to the left or right where the mean, median, and mode assume different values; some are bimodal or multimodal where the distribution begins to resemble a range of mountains and valleys. While distributions can assume any of these or other forms, the first type of distribution is of the most interest and importance to researchers. This distribution, called the bell shaped curve, has three defining characteristics. A bell shaped curve is

- *symmetrical*—if we divide the curve at its exact center the left hand half would be an exact mirror image of the right hand half.
- *unimodal*—there is only one mode, which appears in the exact center of the curve.
- *unskewed*—the mean, median, and mode have identical values.

There are an infinite number of bell-shaped curves, differing in the extent to how sharply the curve rises toward the central peak. Statisticians are interested, however, in one unique member of the set of bell-shaped curves: the standard normal distribution or normal curve. The standard normal distribution is important because it provides a basis for: (1) describing distributions of responses to a particular survey question, (2) interpreting the magnitude of a standard deviation and (3) determining the probability of observing any particular level of response. Each of these factors is an important component of statistical tests and analyses.

The Standard Normal Curve, Standard Deviation and Area Under the Curve

The characteristics of the standard normal curve let you determine the area under any particular segment of the curve. The boundaries of a segment under the curve are defined in terms of standard deviations from the mean, expressed as a Z-score. The normal curve shown in Figure 16.11 illustrates the relationship between area and standard deviation.

The majority of the area of a standard normal distribution lies within one standard deviation on either side of the mean. The fact that the majority of the area under the curve lies close to the mean is reasonable considering that the mean is located at the highest peak of the curve. As shown in Figure 16.11, about 34% of the total area of the normal curve lies within one standard deviation to the positive side of the mean while about 34% lies within one standard deviation to the negative side of the mean. Thus, about 68% of the total area under the normal curve lies within ± one standard deviation of the mean. (In reference to Figure 16.11, this would mean that about 68% of all students scores lie within ±1 standard deviation from the overall test average.) Two standard deviations from the mean contains almost all the area under the curve, 95.44%, while very little additional area lies outside of three standard deviations.

Area under the curve is therefore related to standard deviation. If you know the standard deviation from the mean of any point on the normal curve, you can determine the area beneath the curve from the mean to that point or the percent of the total area of the

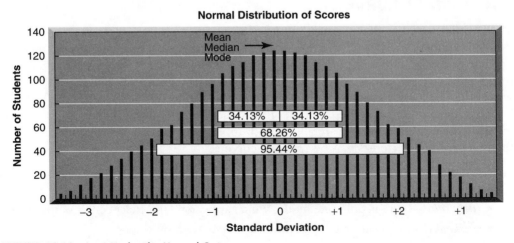

FIGURE 16.11 Area Under the Normal Curve

curve up to and beyond that point. Furthermore, if you know the placement of any two points in terms of their standard deviation from the mean, you can calculate the percent of area falling between and outside of the range bounded by those points. Fortunately, you need not manually calculate area under the curve, the results of the calculations can be found through the use of statistical tables or through the use of online calculators.[24]

Area Under the Curve and Probability

A *probability* can be thought of as the likelihood of a particular event occurring. A probability of 50% means that the event should occur, on average, 50 times out of every 100 or one out of every two. A probability of 1% indicates that the event should occur, on average, one time out of every 100. The area under the normal curve plays an important role in statistical analysis and subsequent decision making because area under the curve can be translated into a probability. This probability reflects the likelihood of obtaining any particular value given its distance from the mean.

The relationship between area under the curve and probability can be seen by re-examining Figure 16.11. Imagine, for example, that we want to estimate the probability of two scores: one being *within* one standard deviation of the mean with the other being *more than* one standard deviation from the mean. Figure 16.11 shows that the area between negative one and positive one standard deviation from the mean is 68.26%. This percentage represents the probability of obtaining a score within this range. The probability of obtaining a score outside of this range is 31.74% (100% − 68.26%).

The next section discusses how probabilities are used to determine the importance and significance of observed differences between two means.

Hypothesis Testing

Advertising research that ends with the presentation of measures such as percentages and means is descriptive. A researcher performs the appropriate calculations and then presents the characteristics of the sample in terms of the descriptive measures. Judgment is used to assess whether levels of response are high or low. Other more powerful research analyses use inferential statistics. Inferential statistics let you mathematically evaluate levels of response and the importance of differences in levels of response across different groups. In doing so, inferential statistics lets you determine the *level of confidence* that you can have in the conclusions you draw from, and subsequent decisions based on the data. Consider the following scenario:

> Pace Manufacturing Company has developed a new line of children's play action figures. It is particularly interested in one figure, Shamantweto, because it feels that it will appeal equally to both boys and girls. The Shamantweto brand manager, Roberta Harris, has asked her advertising agency to help her evaluate the toy's appeal prior to development of the advertising campaign.
>
> Kelly Gifford is the research associate at Pace's agency. Kelly designed the research and created a questionnaire that collected a broad range of information and reactions from the sample of 100 target audience boys and 100 girls who participated in the study. One of the key questions Kelly asked was:
>
> > "Which of the following faces shows how much you like this toy. Put a check next to the one that best shows how much you liked or disliked Shamantweto."

After all the data was collected, Kelly used the appropriate descriptive statistics to provide insights into the distribution of boys' and girls' response to Shamantweto. She summarized her analysis with the following chart:

Measure	Boys	Girls
Strongly like (5)	20%	10%
Slightly like (4)	40	20
Neutral (3)	25	35
Slightly dislike (2)	10	30
Strongly dislike (1)	5	5
Average (mean)	3.6	3.0

Kelly then presented her conclusion to Roberta: "As you can see the mean or average appeal of the product was higher among boys versus girls. The mean response among boys was slightly positive at 3.6 while the average response among girls was neutral at 3.0. The distribution of responses in both cases was quite similar. There were few scores at the extreme ends of either distribution and most scores fell near the center. Given similar distributions and a higher mean appeal among boys versus girls, I'd have to say that our initial assessment was wrong. Shamantweto should be marketed only to boys."

Roberta looked at Kelly and said: "How confident are you in this decision?"

Kelly replied: "I think the decision is right, after all, the mean rating among boys is more than a half rating point higher than the mean rating among girls. And, there are no odd skews in the distributions of responses that would lead us to question the validity of these means for describing the set of boys' and girls' responses."

Kelly used descriptive statistics and judgment to decide that toy appeal was higher among boys versus girls. However, given the importance and consequences of many research-based decisions, such as target audience selection in Kelly's case, Kelly should have used inferential statistics to inform her judgment after the descriptive analysis was concluded.

Implicit in inferential statistics are hypotheses. An *hypothesis* is an unproven belief about the nature of the world. For example, an advertising manager for a laundry detergent might hypothesize that if the new advertising campaign changes consumers' attitudes toward the product's cleaning ability, then the brand's share will increase. A media planner might hypothesize that a proposed media plan will generate higher levels of awareness among older versus younger brand users. A creative might hypothesize that the new campaign will be better liked and be better believed among current users of the product versus those who use competitive products. Kelly and Roberta's initial hypothesis was that Shamantweto would appeal equally to both boys and girls.

Researchers translate verbal hypothesis such as these into formal mathematical statements. In fact, every verbal hypothesis is expressed as two or more formal hypotheses: one null hypothesis and one or more alternative hypothesis. A null hypothesis (represented by the symbol H_0) is a statement about the status quo. A null hypothesis expresses the belief that there are no real, meaningful differences between groups and that any observed differences are insignificant and can be attributed to random error. Researchers typically develop null hypotheses so that they can (hopefully) disprove them in favor of the alternative

Example A: A One-tailed test in which the alternative hypothesis is the preferred outcome.

The Quincy Agency has developed a media plan specifically targeted toward men and women who are aged 55 and older. It is therefore hoped that advertising awareness among those who are aged 55 and older (A_{55+}) exceeds the awareness of those aged under 55 (A_{55-}).

$$H_0 : A_{55+} = A_{55-}$$
$$H_1 : A_{55+} > A_{55-}$$

Example B: A two-tailed test in which the direction of difference is not specified and the preferred outcome is one of the alternative hypotheses.

A new children's cereal has been created. It is expected (and hoped) that the cereal will appeal (A) more to one gender than another, although the specific gender to which the cereal will have the greatest appeal is unknown. The differential appeal will lead to media and creative efforts that specifically target the needs of the gender among which the cereal has the most appeal.

$$H_0 : A_{boys} = A_{girls}$$
$$H_1 : A_{boys} > A_{girls}$$
$$H_2 : A_{boys} < A_{girls}$$

Example C: A two-tailed test in which the direction of difference is not specified and the preferred outcome is acceptance of the null hypothesis.

The advertising campaign for Dandy Detergent has just begun to air. The campaign is designed to equally increase positive attitudes toward the brand (PA) among both frequent and infrequent users of the brand.

$$H_0 : PA_{frequent\ users} = PA_{infrequent\ users}$$
$$H_1 : PA_{frequent\ users} > PA_{infrequent\ users}$$
$$H_2 : PA_{frequent\ users} < PA_{infrequent\ users}$$

FIGURE 16.12   Hypothesis Testing

hypothesis or hypotheses. An alternative hypothesis or hypotheses (represented by the symbol H_1, H_2, etc.) express the belief that any observed differences between groups are in fact real and attributable to some difference in the characteristics of the groups. The process of translating verbal hypotheses into null and alternative hypotheses is illustrated in Figure 16.12. Note that while Examples A and B show how the preferred outcome is often rejection of the null hypothesis, Example C illustrates how the acceptance of the null hypothesis can in certain circumstances be the preferred outcome.

Figure 16.12 also illustrates the concept of "tails." A tail refers to the directionality of the anticipated differences as expressed in the alternative hypotheses. A one-tailed test specifies the direction of difference between the two groups and thus utilizes only one alternative hypothesis. Example A is a one-tailed test. A two-tailed test merely specifies that there will be differences between the groups without specifying the direction of difference. As a consequence, a two-tailed test requires two alternative hypotheses. Example B is a two-tailed test.

Once you have expressed your beliefs regarding research outcomes as null and alternative hypotheses, you must then decide how stringent you will in determining the circumstances in which the null hypothesis is rejected in favor of an alternative hypothesis. This is your confidence in the decision reached and requires you to set a level of significance.

In its most formal sense, a level of significance (represented by the symbol alpha, α) represents the probability of rejecting the null hypothesis as false when it is in fact true, in other words, in concluding that meaningful differences exist when in fact they do not. You may adopt whatever level of significance appears to be appropriate to the purposes and potential consequences of decisions based on the research. Generally, the greater the consequences of the decision, the higher you would set the level of significance, thereby reducing the chances of rejecting the null hypothesis when it is in fact true. Common levels of significance are .05 and .01, meaning that there is a 5% or 1% chance, respectively, of rejecting the null hypothesis when it is in fact true.

Levels of significance (and thus levels of confidence) are evaluated in light of the probabilities derived from areas under the normal curve. With a one-tailed test at the .05 level of significance, the null hypothesis is rejected when probability of the observation is equal to or below 5%. This is the point approximately 1.6 standard deviations from the mean. With a two-tailed test at the .05 level of significance, the .05 is divided by two and the null hypothesis is rejected when the probability of the observation is equal to or below 2.5%. This is the point approximately ±2 standard deviations from the mean.

Endnotes

1. This discussion focuses on the interpretation of levels of statistical significance. The Addendum to this chapter provides a discussion of the theory underlying this measure.
2. The 90% is calculated by subtracting the α level (in this case 10%) from 100%.
3. American College of Physicians, "Primer on Statistical Significance and P Values" at http://www.acponline.org/clinical_information/journals_publications/ecp/julaug01/primer.htm.
4. This scenario and data is hypothetical and for illustrative purposes only.
5. Remember from Chapter 15 that averages or means can only be calculated for interval and ratio level data.
6. All of the examples in this chapter are fictitious. Brand names are used for illustrative purposes only.
7. If you are hesitant to perform these calculations by hand, they are easily performed in Excel or similar spreadsheet program. The actual formula used for this calculation is:

$$Z = \frac{\overline{X} - \mu}{\dfrac{\sigma}{\sqrt{N}}}$$

where,

Z represents the Z-score, the score used to determine the level of significance.

X represents the mean of the sample (in this case, the test commercial).

μ represents the population mean (in this case, the mean of all past commercials contained in the population database of commercials).

σ represents the population standard deviation.

N represents the number of observations in the sample.

8. One such table is located at http://www.epatric.com/documentation/statistics/z-score_table.html.
9. The calculator is located at http://www.quantitativeskills.com/sisa/calculations/signif.htm.
10. The actual equation used for these calculations is:

$$t = \frac{\overline{X} - \mu}{\dfrac{s}{\sqrt{N}}}$$

The symbols used in this equation are the same as in the Z test except that s represents the sample standard deviation and the outcome of the calculations is the t-statistic.

11. One such table is located at http://www.math. unb.ca/~knight/utility/t-table.htm.

12. Note that the direction (sign) of the Z and t-values tell you the direction of the difference. When then sign is positive (as in the Z-test example), then one concludes that the score of the test sample is higher (better) than that of the population. When the sign is negative (as in the t-test example), then one concludes that the score of the test sample is lower (worse) than that of the population.

13. The actual formula used for these calculations is:

$$Z = \frac{p - P_u}{\sqrt{\dfrac{P_u Q_u}{N}}}$$

where,

Z represents the Z-score, the score used to determine the level of significance.

p represents the sample proportion selecting the target response option.

P_u represents the population proportion selecting the target response option.

Q_u represents the population proportion selecting the alternative response option.

N represents the number of observations in the sample.

14. The Z-score of 2.53 is just a bit short of the 2.58 level needed for the .01 level of statistical significance.

15. A chi-squared calculator that is formatted for a single group analysis is located at http://www. graphpad.com/quickcalcs/chisquared1.cfm.

16. Some researchers recommend using a t-test when comparing only two means. However, for sample sizes greater than 30, as is the typical research case, the results are identical.

17. This approach works well when the number of comparisons is relatively low. However, when the number of comparisons increases, it is possible that some comparisons will be statistically different simply due to chance. In these circumstances, tests other than an F-test are more appropriate for making multiple comparisons. See the discussion at Hyperstat beginning at http://davidmlane.com/hyperstat/B99961.html.

18. Factorial designs are often described numerically. The viral ad example would be described as a 2 × 2 design, indicating that there are two levels of the first factor and two levels of the second factor. Additionally, since factorial designs are not limited in the number of factors or levels, this example could be modified to add a third factor with three levels, for example, three types of music. This latter approach would be described as a 2 × 2 × 3 design. Also note that factors are also referred to as "main effects."

19. The manual calculation of a correlation coefficient is tedious. Statistical programs such as SPSS or spreadsheet programs such as Excel can quickly calculate the correlation among one or more pairs of variables.

20. Creative Research Systems (2009). "Correlation" at http://www.surveysystem.com/correlation. htm.

21. A calculator to determine the statistical significance of the correlation coefficient can be found at http://faculty.vassar.edu/lowry/tabs. html#r.

22. One such calculator is available at http:// people.ku.edu/~preacher/chisq/chisq.htm.

23. Note that the underlying assumption of multiple group chi-square is different than that of a single group. In a single group analysis, the chi-statistic compares the actual distribution to the distribution that would have occurred by chance, that is, equal numbers of respondents per cell. In multiple group analyses, chi-square does not assume equal distributions per cell but rather compares the actual distribution to the number that would be expected in a cell given the row and column averages.

24. An online calculator can be found at http:// davidmlane.com/hyperstat/z_table.html.

CHAPTER 17

Segmentation

Very few products are marketed or advertised to a target audience defined as "all adults" or "all consumers." Advertisers have learned that "universal" products or "universal" advertising campaigns produced to meet the needs of the "average consumer" are rarely successful, in great part because in today's marketplace there is no such thing as an "average consumer." Today's marketplace is fragmented, consisting of small, distinct groups of consumers that have different attitudes, personal characteristics, product needs, and media habits. To successfully advertise a product or service to one of these groups, marketers and advertisers must first identify and understand the unique characteristics of that group. Advertising target audience selection, product positioning, creative strategy, advertising essential message, and media selection are all influenced by group characteristics.

Marketers and advertisers use consumer segmentation to identify and understand the groups of consumers that comprise the marketplace for a particular product or service. This chapter introduces you to consumer segmentation.

***

When you are done reading this chapter, you should have a better understanding of how to:

- explain the reasons marketers and advertisers segment markets
- describe how segmentation research influences advertising planning
- evaluate and select segments for communications targeting
- identify the criteria that can be used to define consumer segments
- plan and conduct original segmentation research
- identify and understand commonly used syndicated segmentation research.

A great deal of advertising research aggregates the data collected by the research study. In these cases, the findings summarize and describe relevant aspects of the total sample of individuals who participated in the research. Consumer segmentation research is just the opposite. A consumer segmentation study seeks to break down a population of individuals into smaller subgroups where individuals in a specific subgroup are similar to each other in terms of important characteristics and possess characteristics different from individuals in other groups.

The general approach to and characteristics of segmentation are illustrated in a study conducted by the Pew Internet & American Life Project.[1] First, Pew formulated the research question: "Does age affect online behaviors?" Next, the research asked a sample of individuals questions related to Internet usage, making certain that there was a large range of ages within the sample. This dispersion of age within the sample was important, since age was the focus of the research question. Once the data was obtained, individuals in the sample were classified (segmented) by age, in this case, into one of six age groups (see Figure 17.1). Finally, the differences and similarities in patterns of Internet usage by age group were examined. A table summarizing the key findings is provided in Figure 17.2.[2] This approach illustrates three important aspects of a well-conceived segmentation study:

- *Successful segmentation research starts with a well-formulated research question.* Prior to data collection, a researcher needs to explicitly identify the criteria that will be used to segment and describe the sample.

- *Each group is unique* with respect to the segmentation focus, in this case, age. Individuals within a group are homogeneous (i.e., very similar to each other with respect to the criteria used to segment the sample), and there is heterogeneity across groups (i.e., each segment is distinct and has its own profile and identity, different than the other groups).

- *There is a relationship between segments and outcomes.* In this case, individuals in different age groups showed distinctly different patterns of behavior.

A second more visual example of segmentation is shown in Figure 17.3.[3]

Generation Name	Birth Years	Ages in 2009	Percent of Population	Percent of Internet-Using Population
Gen Y (Millennials)	1977–1990	18–32	26%	30%
Gen X	1965–1976	35–44	20	23
Younger Boomers	1955–1964	45–54	20	22
Older Boomers	1946–1954	55–63	13	13
Silent Generation	1937–1945	64–72	9	7
G.I. Generation	1936 and earlier	73+	9	4

FIGURE 17.1 Pew Generational Segmentation: Age Segments

Generational Differences in Online Activities

	Online Teens^ (12–17)	Gen Y (18–32)	Gen X (33–44)	Younger Boomers (45–54)	Older Boomers (55–63)	Silent Generation (64–72)	G.I. Generation (73+)	All Online Adults^^
Go online	93%	87%	82%	79%	70%	56%	31%	74%
Teens and Gen Y are more likely to engage in the following activities compared with older users:								
Play games online	78	50	38	26	28	25	18	**35**
Watch videos online	57	72	57	49	30	24	14	**52**
Get info about a job	30~	64	55	43	36	11	10	**47**
Send instant messages	68	59	38	28	23	25	18	**38**
Use social networking sites	65	67	36	20	9	11	4	**35**
Download music	59	58	46	22	21	16	5	**37**
Create an SNS profile	55	60	29	16	9	5	4	**29**
Read blogs	49	43	34	27	25	23	15	**32**
Create a blog	28	20	10	6	7	6	6	**11**
Visit a virtual world	10	2	3	1	1	1	0	**2**
Activities where Gen X users or older generations dominate:								
Get health info	28	68	82	74	81	70	67	**75**
Buy something online	38	71	80	68	72	56	47	**71**
Bank online	*	57	65	53	49	45	24	**55**
Visit govt sites	*	55	64	62	63	60	31	**59**
Get religious info	26~	31	38	42	30	30	26	**35**
And for some activities, the youngest and oldest cohorts may differ, but there is less variation overall:								
Use email	73	94	93	90	90	91	79	**91**
Use search engines	*	90	93	90	89	85	70	**89**
Research products	*	84	84	82	79	73	60	**81**
Get news	63	74	76	70	69	56	37	**70**
Make travel reservations	*	65	70	69	66	69	65	**68**
Research for job	*	51	59	57	48	33	9	**51**
Rate a person or product	*	37	35	29	30	25	16	**32**
Download videos	31~	38	31	21	16	13	13	**27**
Participate in an online auction	*	26	31	27	26	16	6	**26**
Download podcasts	19	25	21	19	12	10	10	**19**

^Source for Online Teens data: Pew Internet & American Life Project Surveys conducted Oct.–Nov. 2006 and Nov. 2007–Feb. 2008. Margin of error for online teens is ±4% for Oct.–Nov. 2006 and ±3% for Nov. 2007–Feb. 2008.

^^Source for Online Adult data: Pew Internet & American Life Project Surveys conducted August 2006, Feb.–March 2007, Aug.–Sept. 2007, Oct.–Dec. 2007, May 2008, August 2008, November 2008, and December 2008. Margin of error for all online adults is ±3% for these surveys. The average margin of error for each age group can be considerably higher than ±3%, particularly for the Matures and After Work age groups. See Methodology for average margins of error for each generational group.

~Most recent teen data for these activities comes from the Pew Internet & American Life Project Teens and Parents Survey conducted Oct.–Nov. 2004. Margin of error is ±4%.

*No teen data for these activities.

FIGURE 17.2 Pew Generational Segmentation: Patterns of Internet Usage

FIGURE 17.3 Obama Segmentation (reproduced with permission of SocialMedia8)

HOW ADVERTISERS USE SEGMENTATION

The primary assumptions of segmentation are straightforward.

- Because each segment is homogeneous with respect to the basis for the segmentation, advertisers expect individuals in a segment to respond in a similar way to the same communication plan and messages.

- Because segments are formed to accentuate differences across segments, advertisers do not expect the same communication plan or message to work for multiple segments.

These assumptions provide advertisers with several reasons for using segmentation.

First, and perhaps most important, segmentation permits advertisers to increase the relevance (and thus potential impact) of their messages. Segmentation provides the information required for the planning and presentation of advertising communications that exactly fit and respond to the characteristics, needs, attitudes, and lifestyles of a unique segment of a broader target audience. Thus, while an advertiser may want individuals in all segments to engage in the same end-behavior, the messages used to move individuals toward this goal will vary across segments. This approach to message customization can be seen in the two ads for ExecTrade shown in Figure 17.4. Both ads seek the same end behavior: opening an account at ExecTrade. The ads differ, however, in that they target two different segments of consumers where individuals in different segments are looking for different benefits. Individuals targeted by the right ad are most interested in maximizing returns, while the left ad targets individuals who are most interested in service personalization.

FIGURE 17.4   Segmented Advertisements for ExecTrade

The use of segmentation to increase message relevance is true of messages communicated in all media, but can be particularly true of messages communicated via e-mail. Marketers can segment their database of current, prior, and potential customers to make certain that individuals in each segment receive the most relevant and appropriate message. This level of customization can be accomplished with relatively little effort or cost. SubscriberMail notes that: "Dynamic content can make sending targeted content to recipients easy. Dynamic content allows you to create a single e-mail message that delivers multiple versions based on recipients' demographic profile or other data."[4] As a result, messages to different groups of individuals can be customized to reflect a segment's past purchase history, past e-mail activity, Web site activity, personal interests, or other relevant data.

Second, segmentation permits an advertiser to respond to the current structure and realities of the marketplace. It is usually easier to take advantage of market segments that already exist than to try to create new segments. Segmentation, therefore, improves the communication planning process by helping an advertiser understand the consumer segments that comprise the marketplace and how brands are positioned against each other within and across these segments. This understanding makes explicit the range of available positioning, target audience, and message options.

Third, segmentation helps refine and increase the efficiency of communication plans. Different segments often have different media habits and receptivity to different types of communication efforts. The identification of a specific segment's media preferences helps a media planner better match media selection with target audience media habits.

Finally, segmentation helps an advertiser uncover new opportunities in secondary, but typically smaller, segments. Jello, for example, used segmentation to discover and target a group of mothers who were concerned about the fat and cholesterol in their children's snacks. This group, traditionally not Jello users, was targeted in a special print advertising campaign that communicated the fat-free, cholesterol-free character of Jello.

In sum, marketers and advertisers conduct and use consumer segmentation research because it makes them more efficient and increases their chances for success.

Criteria for Selecting Segments

Once an advertiser acknowledges that segmentation can help improve advertising planning and communication effectiveness, it then becomes necessary to select one of the segments as the target for the communication campaign. Advertisers use several criteria to evaluate the relative appeal and value of different segments.[5] Two sets of criteria can be used to evaluate segments. First, there is a set of six criteria and accompanying questions that can be applied to all situations, regardless of whether the ultimate goal is product-related (i.e., purchase of a particular product) or strictly behavioral (i.e., begin participating in a target behavior such as "start eating healthier" or stop a target behavior such a "stop using drugs"). Second, there are four additional criteria that apply only to product-related segmentation.

The criteria and accompanying questions that apply to all segmentation situations are:

- *Size.* Is the segment of sufficient size to justify the expenditures of time and energy required to develop a customized communication program?
- *Media Accessibility.* Can members of the segment be efficiently reached though traditional and new media vehicles?
- *Message Availability.* Can a communication message or appeal be created that responds to the unique attitudes, needs, and behaviors of segment members?
- *Responsiveness.* If a communication message can be developed, to what extent are members of the segment likely to pay attention and respond to this message in the desired way? Are members of the segment "open-minded" or "set in their ways?"
- *Sustainability.* Is the segment stable or likely to grow for the long term, or is the segment likely to disappear or merge with other segments?
- *Evaluation.* Can efforts toward the segment be measured in order to determine the strengths, weaknesses, and outcomes of the communication campaign?

Beyond these criteria that apply to the evaluation of all segments, product-related segment evaluation applies the following additional criteria:

- *Profitability.* If the communication campaign is successful, will this result in sufficient increases in sales to justify the campaign?
- *Competition.* To what extent do competitive brands have an interest in the segment? Will communication efforts have to combat heavily entrenched brands?
- *Defendability.* If the communication campaign is successful, is there likely to be a significant competitive response? Can such a response be defended against?

- *Compatibility*. Are members of the segment, and the types of products they desire, compatible with existing or desired company goals, perspectives, and objectives?

VARIABLES USED IN SEGMENTATION

The Pew generational segmentation divided the adult U.S. adult population into six segments based on age. Age, however, is only one of many variables that can be used in segmentation research. Variables used in segmentation research typically fall into four broad categories:

- demographics
- geography
- psychographics (personal attitudes, values, motivations, and lifestyle)
- relevant attitudes and behaviors[6]

It is important to note that any of the variables within these broad categories can be used in one of two ways. They can be used as either *classification* or *descriptive* variables.

Classification variables are the basis for segment formation and can be selected from any of the prior categories. The Pew generational study discussed earlier used a demographic variable, age, as the basis for group formation. Age, therefore, was the sole classification variable. Classification variables are not limited, however, to just a single variable from a category. Multiple variables from a category can be used; for example, a segmentation could be conducted using multiple demographic variables (e.g., age, gender, and income) or multiple behaviors. Additionally, the formation of segments is not limited to variables from a single category. A study of video game players could use both demographics and attitudes toward gaming as the classification criteria, resulting in four groups: Young Dedicated Gamers, Young Casual Gamers, Older Dedicated Gamers, and Older Casual Gamers. Once classification variables have been used to form segments, *descriptive variables are used to describe the members of each segment*. The descriptive variables in the Pew generational study are all related to online behaviors. The descriptive variables in a segmentation of video game players could include behaviors such as the types and amount of games played, situations in which games are played, and purchase behaviors.[7]

The remainder of this section discusses the most commonly used variables within each of the four broad categories mentioned earlier. Note that while all variables can be used as either classification or descriptive variables, we will discuss each when used for purposes of segment creation.

Demographic Segmentation

Demographic variables include characteristics such as age, gender, race, ethnicity, household characteristics, occupation, level of education, and social class.

AGE.   Age is an important demographic variable since individuals of different ages are likely to have different attitudes, behaviors, product needs, and product perceptions. The Pew generational segmentation discussed earlier is an example of using age as a classification variable. While age has the potential to form meaningful segments, this potential is only realized when appropriate age ranges are used to define the segments. Defining age segments too broadly tends to blur the differences between age segments. Defining age segments too narrowly results in too many small segments. The presence of either condition significantly reduces a segmentation's usefulness. Thus, age segments must be defined with care.

Shifts in the size of various age groups are also an important consideration in age-based segmentation. The shrinking teenage market, coupled with the large and growing size of the "aging boomer" market, for example, has prompted jeans marketers and advertisers to shift their target audience focus from the former to the latter group and alter the focus of the product's key benefit from "tight fit style" to "relaxed comfort." Similarly, Maybelline has developed and advertised a line of beauty products for "aging boomers" who wish to look younger.

GENDER.   Social and cultural forces, as well as physiological and psychological factors, contribute to differences between men and women in attitudes, behaviors, product perceptions, and product usage. As with age, an understanding of the differences between men and women in a product category provides advertisers with a basis for customizing product positionings and advertising messages.

HOUSEHOLD.   A household can consist of a single individual, two individuals (friends, partners or married), a nuclear family (with or without two parents, with or without the two biological parents), an extended family, or another combination of adults with or without children. Additionally, when present, children in a household can be of any age. Marketers and advertisers often segment the population based on household characteristics to identify product needs and advertising opportunities. The marketing and advertising of single serving size food products, for example, responded to the rise in single-person households.

LIFE STAGE.   Age, gender, household size, and other demographic variables are often combined to form multidimensional life stage or family life-cycle segments. Figure 17.5 illustrates one approach to life stage segmentation.[8] The segments in Figure 17.5 represent the Travel Industry of America's segmentation of traveling households into life stage segments. Three core life stage groups—Singles, Couples, and Parents—are defined by combining household composition, marital status, and the presence/absence of children. These groups are then further segmented according to age and for some segments, employment. This results in the 11 life stage segments shown in Figure 17.5. Importantly, these groups not only reflect life stage, but also relate to three well-accepted generational cohorts: Generation X/Generation Y (Young), Baby Boomers (Middle), Empty Nesters and Seniors (Older).[9]

Life stage segmentation need not rely on age or household characteristics as the primary classification variables. Morton, for example, has created five life stage segments based on career and work, as follows:[10]

- *Provisional Adulthood:* Choosing a career and entering the workforce.
- *Early Adulthood:* Progressing in careers and settling into work.
- *Middlescense:* Reexamining work.

- *Age of Mastery:* Adjusting to realities of work and approaching retirement.
- *Age of Integrity:* Disengaging from paid work and searching for new achievement outlets.

Geographic Variables

Geographic location provides clues about how individuals live, think, and relate to various brands and product benefits. It is a common belief that different geographic areas, formed by different patterns of population dispersion, reflect different types of cultural

Young Singles:	Household head age 18 to 34 and Male living alone or with non-spouse relative or roommate of the same gender; or Female living alone or with non-spouse relative or roommate of the same gender
Middle Singles:	Household head age 35 to 54 and Male living alone or with non-spouse relative or roommate of the same gender; or Female living alone or with non-spouse relative or roommate of the same gender
Older Working Singles:	Household head age 55 or older who is employed and Male living alone or with non-spouse relative or roommate of the same gender; or Female living alone or with non-spouse relative or roommate of the same gender
Older Retired Singles:	Household head age 55 or older who is retired or not employed and Male living alone or with non-spouse relative or roommate of the same gender; or Female living alone or with non-spouse relative or roommate of the same gender
Young Couples:	Household head age 18 to 34 and Husband and wife; or Male living w/female that is not a roommate/relative; or Female living w/male that is not a roommate/relative
Middle Couples:	Household head age 35 to 54 and Husband and wife; or Male living w/female that is not a roommate/relative; or Female living w/male that is not a roommate/relative
Older Working Couples:	Household head age 55 or older, at least one employed and Husband and wife; or Male living w/female that is not a roommate/relative; or Female living w/male that is not a roommate/relative
Older Retired Couples:	Household head age 55 or older, both retired or both not employed and Husband and wife; or Male living w/female that is not a roommate/relative; or Female living w/male that is not a roommate/relative
Young Parents:	Household head age 18 to 34 and Children in household under age 18
Middle Parents:	Household head age 35 to 54 and Children in household under age 18
Older Parents:	Household head age 55 or older and Children in household under age 18

FIGURE 17.5   TIA Segmentation of Traveling Households

development, behavioral patterns, attitudes, and perceptions. Consequently, marketers and advertisers often use geographic variables to identify consumer segments based on geographic boundaries and population characteristics. The most common criteria used in geographic segmentation research are: region, population size, population density, city size, and climate.

Geographic segmentation can contribute to several types of marketing and advertising planning. Marketers who understand regional differences in product preferences can make certain that the characteristics of their products respond to the needs and desires of a particular region. Campbell's, for example, has introduced spicier versions of its soups to better satisfy consumers' preference for spicier food in the West and South. Advertisers who understand regional variance in product usage can also create better, more efficient media plans.

- Different purchase patterns in different geographic areas suggest the need for different media schedules. Barbeque sauce is purchased all year in warmer climates, and thus may require a different advertising schedule than cooler markets where product purchase is concentrated in the summer months.

- Different levels of product purchase in different geographic areas often suggest the need for different levels of media allocation, since many advertisers wish to concentrate their advertising spending in those geographic areas that show higher levels of consumption. Sparkling water, for example, shows higher consumption in urban areas in the Northeast and West, while powdered soft drinks show higher consumption in the Midwest.

While geographic segmentation has significant application to product development and message strategy, it also has application to non-product categories where geography plays an important role, for example, in tourism and tourism planning. Nyaupane and Graefe, for example, found that those who traveled a long distance to visit a specific place (in this case a National Forest) had demographics, attitudes, and motivations different than those who traveled a short distance to visit the same place.[11] This would imply that message strategies would be more effective if customized to each group; that is, the communication plan designed to reach distance travelers would be different than that designed to reach those more local.

Psychographic Variables

The term "psychographic" describes an individual's general attitudes, values, motivations, and lifestyle. A psychographic segmentation, therefore, divides the population into groups based on characteristics in one or more of these areas. Psychographic segmentation assumes that what people think, how they are motivated, and how they lead their lives are often strong determinants or predictors of their use of specific types of goods and services as well as their choice to participate (or not participate) in certain behaviors. The Center for Generational Studies, for example, notes the distinct differences in the psychographics of those classified as "Generation X" and "Millennial" (see Figure 17.6).[12]

ATTITUDES AND VALUES. Individuals who are in the same demographic category often have different attitudes and values. Consequently, consumers' attitudes and val-

> **Generation X Consumer Themes**
>
> They feel life is too short not to have fun.
> They like choice. If they are not offered the right options, they will attempt to create them.
> Xers seek extensive peer input.
> Money comes in the forms of credit cards and clicks.
> They're willing to wait to purchase quality.
> Xers are passionate about controlling their time.
> Xers want to interact with media rather than watch.
> They prefer non-textual information.
> To Xers, simplicity means practicality.
> They look for straightforward information.
> They like sales and service that anticipates their needs.
> They are innately suspicious of advertising.
> They research thoroughly before shopping.
> They consider it acceptable to lead a salesperson on with no intention of buying.
> They are comfortable challenging salespeople.
> They pride themselves on working smarter and purchasing smarter.
>
> **Millennial Consumer Themes**
>
> They expect computers to assist decision making.
> Money comes in the forms of credit cards and clicks.
> They are inherently skeptical of all media.
> Immediate outcome/gratification is critical.
> Debt is an acceptable form of being.
> Many have come of age with a regular infusion of discretionary income.
> They are conditioned to receive free "stuff."
> They are highly influenced by friends and congregate in groups.
> They want media they can call their own.
> They are highly brand conscious, especially with apparel and wear "badged" items.
> Attracted to immediate opportunities for affluence.
> They have become experienced consumers at an early age.

FIGURE 17.6 Center for Generational Studies Segmentation: Gen Y and Millennial Insights

ues often provide a useful basis for market segmentation. Attitudes and values can include attitudes toward life, career, self-image, and the importance of status and recognition.

An exploration of attitudes and values helps advertisers better understand important differences within individuals of the same age group and among individuals of different age groups. Attitudes toward oneself and the future are, for example, an effective way of distinguishing different psychographic segments within the demographic segment of "mature individuals" (defined as those who are aged 50 and older). Morgan and Levy,[13] for example, identified four attitudinal segments within this market:

- *Upbeat Enjoyer.* Individuals who are most likely to feel that their best years are now and in the future. High priorities are looking good and staying active. They feel financially secure.

- *Insecure.* Individuals who feel that they have not been successful in life and that the best years of their lives lie in the past. They are afraid they will not have enough money for the future; they invest conservatively, shop for value, and are generally uncomfortable with their appearance.

- *Threatened Active.* Individuals who have a positive outlook on life, although the outlook is tempered by worries about crime. Very resistant to change, they want to keep living in their own homes and working at their current job. These individuals do not worry about "looking young."

- *Financial Positives.* Individuals who are more open to change and more concerned about looking good. They feel financially secure, successful, and optimistic.

Thus, while the age composition of all four groups is similar, the attitudes within each group are very different, indicating that one single advertising message is unlikely to be effective in reaching the entire "mature market."

MOTIVATIONS.   Perceptions and behaviors are often influenced by underlying motivations. Consequently, the motivations that underlie consumer behavior often provide an insightful basis for segmenting a product category and advertising audience. Motivational segmentation assumes that if you understand an individual's motivations for buying or not buying a product (or, more broadly, for participating or not participating in a particular type of behavior), then you can tailor your advertising message to capitalize on (or counter) those motivations.

Quidel Corporation provides an excellent example of motivational segmentation and the tailoring of communications (in this case, package design) for different motivationally defined consumer segments. Quidel is a manufacturer of home pregnancy tests, ovulation tests, and other home-based medical products. The company markets two different home pregnancy tests: Conceive and RapidVue. The package of Conceive brand pregnancy test features an adorable baby smiling at the potential purchaser from a pink box. The package exudes warmth and friendliness. The package of RapidVue brand pregnancy test is much starker. There are no warm, happy colors. There is no smiling baby. The product name is printed in brick-red lettering against a mauve background. However, while the packaging of the two brands is very different, the product inside each package is identical. Each package is nevertheless designed to appeal to a different motivational segment. Conceive is marketed to those who desire to conceive, RapidVue is marketed to those who do not.[14]

LIFESTYLE.   Lifestyle segmentation divides the population based on interests, activities, hobbies, participation in various forms of social events, sports, and other activities. Segmentation based on these and related measures helps advertisers understand the relationship between how consumers lead their lives and the types and brands of products that they use. Lifestyle segmentation has proven to be a useful way of segmenting the market for "badge" products (i.e., products that are conspicuously consumed or displayed) such as liquor, automobiles, cigarettes, and clothing.

Category and/or Brand-Related Attitudes and Behaviors

Segmentation based on category and brand-related attitudes and behaviors is a very common form of consumer segmentation. Desired benefits is a common classification variable for this type of segmentation. When specifically used for product-related segmentation, classification variables typically relate to aspects of product usage or brand loyalty.

PRODUCT USAGE SEGMENTATION.   Product usage segmentation is straightforward. The population is divided to reflect patterns in brand and product usage, quantity of consumption, or the situation in which the product is used. These characteristics may be used independently or in combination with other brand or product-related characteristics for example:

- Segmentation based on brand usage divides the population into groups that differ with respect to patterns of brand usage, typically the brand used most often. Beer drinkers, for example, could be segmented to reflect the beer brand that had the greatest consumption within the prior month.
- Segmentation based on product usage divides the population into groups based on the types of products consumed. Beer drinkers could be segmented to reflect the type of beer (import, domestic, premium, super-premium) that had the greatest consumption within the prior month.
- Segmentation based on quantity of consumption divides the population on the basis of amount of product consumed. Beer drinkers could be segmented to reflect the total amount of beer consumed within the prior month.
- Segmentation based on situation of consumption divides the population to reflect the circumstances in which the product is used. Beer drinkers could be segmented to reflect where the product is primarily consumed, for example, at restaurants, at home, and at a bar.

BRAND LOYALTY.   Brand loyalty is a measure of consumer attachment to a particular brand. Loyalty can range from absolute commitment to a total lack of preference. Segmentation based on brand loyalty divides the population to reflect loyalty to a particular brand. An understanding of the attitudes, demographics, and motivations of different loyalty groups helps an advertiser to identify the creative approach and essential message that is most likely to reinforce loyalty among its own users and reduce loyalty among its competitors' users.

BEHAVIORS IN NON-PRODUCT CATEGORIES.   Individuals' behaviors can also be used as classification variables in non-product categories; in fact, they are appropriate in any instance where differences in behaviors across individuals are believed to exert an important influence on the target audience's attitudes or behaviors. For example:

- Ruiz and his colleagues segmented consumers based on the behaviors exhibited during a visit to the mall.[15] Four segments were identified: *Recreational Shoppers, Full Experience Shoppers, Browsers, and Mission Shoppers.*

- The Ontario Ministry of Tourism has conducted multiple segmentation studies using behaviors as the classification variable. These studies include: a segmentation of outdoor activities participated in while on vacation, types of cultural and entertainment pursuits while on vacation, and types of shopping conducted while on vacation.[16]

- Behaviors combined with attitudes were an important classification variable in segmentation designed to better understand groups of consumers with regard to health and eating habits. The Centers for Disease Control and Prevention created five segments to describe attitudes and behaviors regarding nutrition, physical activity, and weight control.[17]

NEEDS OR BENEFITS.   Needs or benefits segmentation can be used for either product- or non-product categories. A product-related benefit segmentation related to mobile phones could, for example, use benefits sought from mobile phones as the classification variables. Similarly, a non-product category segmentation related to vacation travel could use destination-related benefits as the classification variables. In both cases, segments would be formed where members of the same segment would have the same needs or seek the same benefits. Importantly, a needs or benefits segmentation does not have to exclusively focus on needs that are currently being met or benefits that are being received. Some segments may represent individuals with needs that are currently unmet by available options.

Belles points out the direct linkage between understanding a segment's desired benefits, product positioning, and communication focus. He uses the beverage marketplace as the context:

> Beverage marketers may be best served . . . by classifying their products according to the new evolving needs states that define our customers. "We're in the carbonated soft drink business" or "We sell bottled water" or "I'm a beer marketer" or "I sell spirits" will be replaced by "We're in the beverage energy marketplace" or "We sell dehydration beverages" or "I'm a mood-enhancement beverage marketer" or "I'm into beverage status beverages. . . ." This redefinition of the marketplace is much like the business school case study that redefined the buggy whip manufacturer's playing field. Those who continued to say that they sold buggy whips slowly went out of business; those who redefined their market as 'transportation' prospered.[18]

Haley provides an example of a product-related benefit segmentation, in this case, of benefits sought from toothpaste.[19] Four benefit segments exist within the toothpaste category where each segment most values a different benefit. The benefit segments are

- *worriers,* who are most concerned about decay prevention. They tend to have large families, are heavy users of toothpaste, and tend to prefer Crest.

- *sociables,* who are most concerned about their appearance and teeth brightness. They tend to be younger, value sociability, lead an active lifestyle, and tend to prefer Ultra Brita.

- *sensory,* who are most concerned about the product itself, especially a toothpaste's favor and appearance. Sensory individuals tend to be children and prefer flavored toothpastes. The preferred brand is Stripe.

- *independents,* who are price-driven. They tend to be men who are value-oriented and, as a consequence, tend not to be brand loyal instead buying whatever brand is on sale.

A toothpaste advertiser who uses this segmentation would be able to customize a message to meet the specific benefits sought by a particular segment. Additionally, advertisers could use this segmentation to determine how well their brands are performing in segments in which they currently compete and to determine opportunities for product expansion.

CONDUCTING ORIGINAL SEGMENTATION RESEARCH

The planning and conduct of original segmentation research begins similarly to other research (see Chapter 1). The need for the research is identified, segmentation is selected as an appropriate response to information needs, and sample and sampling issues are addressed (see Chapter 4). Segmentation research then follows the steps shown in Figure 17.7. This section discusses the major events and decisions that take place at each step. A benefit segmentation study designed to help Brazil in tourism planning for individuals residing in the United States is used to illustrate the process "in action." The research was conducted by Firefly Research.[20]

Explicitly State the Research Question(s)

The chapter noted earlier that successful segmentation research starts with one or more well-formulated research questions. These questions make explicit the information that needs to be collected for both classification and descriptive variables. The specifics of these variables are determined in the next step. At this point, the research questions need to note only the categories of variables that will be explored in the research. Firefly Research proposed two core questions:

> Do visitors to Brazil differ with regard to the benefits they seek during their visit? If so, do these differences result in different benefit-driven segments?

> If different segments do exist, are there significant differences in group characteristics? Specifically, are there differences with regard to group: demographics, travel behavior, personality characteristics, interests, expectations, and attitudes?

Identify the Range of Classification and Descriptive Variables

As discussed earlier, classification variables are the characteristics that individuals within a segment share and that differ among individuals in different segments, while descriptive variables provide the basis for understanding the characteristics of each segment once they have been formed. The potential for successful group formation and description increases in direct proportion to the appropriateness and relevance of the specific classification and description variables selected for inclusion in the research. In both cases, the extent of insights provided by these variables is directly related to the care with which they are selected, their relevance to the segmen-

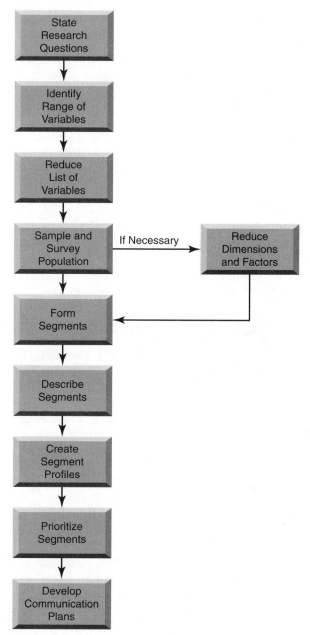

FIGURE 17.7 Steps in Original Segmentation Research

tation, and their ability to provide an understanding of the characteristics of each segment.

The importance of these variables requires that the researcher make certain that all potential variables have been identified and considered. This can be accomplished through a review of prior related research or through the conduct of qualitative research such as in-depth personal interviews or focus groups. Firefly Research used both approaches. First, the company conducted an extensive review of prior research on destination tourism. Their review uncovered several important insights:

- benefits sought by travelers can be explored in two ways, either directly through survey questions or indirectly though an analysis of the types of activities in which visitors participated;
- travelers have a wide and diverse set of reasons for destination travel. Firefly identified over 200 types of direct benefits sought; and
- the most useful segments are those that are described through a combination of demographics, behaviors, personality characteristics, motivations, and attitudes.

These insights led to a second step: a series of four focus groups with individuals who traveled to Brazil for personal reasons within the past 12 months. Two of the groups consisted of first-time visitors to Brazil, while the remaining two groups consisted of repeat visitors. All participants were the decision maker for the trip. The groups were used to obtain deeper insights into Brazil travelers' attitudes, behaviors, and motivations. Information gathered from both the literature review and focus groups was used to create a list of nearly 400 classification and descriptive variables.

Reduce the List of Segmentation and Descriptive Measures

The prior step resulted in a large number of variables. This step reduces the number of variables to a manageable number. This can be accomplished through judgment or through the use of statistical techniques such as factor analysis. The variables that "pass through" this step are those that will be translated into specific questions on the questionnaire. Firefly Research used its own judgment, in consultation with its client, to identify its final list of variables, making certain that the final list addressed all important areas of inquiry.

Sample and Survey the Population

The questionnaire is developed after classification and descriptive variables are specified. As with all survey research, it is recommended that the questionnaire be pilot-tested and revised prior to its final use.

Once the questionnaire is finalized, it is then time to sample and survey the population of interest. (See Chapter 4 for a review of sampling-related issues.) The sample design for every segmentation study is different, as each plan must reflect the specific characteristics of the population of interest. As a result, some sample plans may seek to maximize generalizability through random sampling, while other plans may need to sacrifice some generalizability in order to focus on harder to locate individuals. Firefly Research's sampling plan, designed to efficiently locate and interview travelers to Brazil, attempted to balance these two considerations, as follows:

The five United States airports with the largest number of direct flights to Brazil were identified. For a one week period, all flights to Brazil from each airport were identified. Random sampling was used in the waiting area of each

Brazil-bound flight to identify individuals to be interviewed. Respondents were screened to eliminate those under the age of 18 and to select only those traveling to Brazil for personal reasons. When an individual was traveling with a family, the decision maker (or shared decision maker) for the trip was identified and interviewed. Interviewing began one hour prior to flight boarding and continued until the boarding process was completed.

If Necessary, Reduce the Data to a Manageable Number of Factors or Dimensions

When a questionnaire contains multiple related items, it is likely that individuals will respond to many of the items in a similar way. When this is felt to be the case, it is beneficial to group similar items together as the first step in data analysis. Factor analysis is the statistical technique that can accomplish this.[21] Factor analysis groups related questions together so that the researcher can identify broader trends and relationships among the individual measures.

A factor analysis of responses to Firefly Research's questionnaire resulted in five benefit factors (as shown in Figure 17.8). Each of these factors represents a specific type of benefit individuals seek when they go on a Brazilian vacation. Note how similar activities are grouped together within the same factor and how Firefly Research gave each factor a name that summarizes and describes the benefits comprising that factor.

Use the Classification Variables to Form Segments

Segments are formed using a statistical technique called cluster analysis that places respondents with similar patterns of response to the classification variables in the same segment.[22] As discussed earlier, the criteria governing segment formation are

- responses to the classification variables must be similar within segments and different across segments,
- segments must be of sufficient size, and
- the internal characteristics of each segment must be reasonable with regard to interpretation and should be able to serve as the foundation for future communications planning.

Firefly Research formed four segments. The data shown in Figure 17.9 provides the size of each segment and illustrates the differences across the four segments with regard to benefits sought in a Brazilian vacation. Larger positive numbers reflect greater benefit importance, while larger negative numbers reflect greater lack of importance. The column labeled "Segment 1," for example, shows that individuals in this segment (who represent about 10% of the total sample) most value outdoor adventure and least value cultural and fun around the clock activities. Note how the profiles of the four segments are quite different, indicating a successful segmentation.

Benefit Factor 1—Fun Around the Clock:	Dancing, drinking Gambling Party boat tours Sunbathing Swimming Other relatively passive sports Other forms of indoor/outdoor entertainment
Benefit Factor 2—Ecotourism:	Visit natural wonders Visit botanic, zoological gardens Nature-oriented excursions Visit historical, archeological sites Visit small towns and villages
Benefit Factor 3—Culture:	Attend musical concerts, plays Attend local cultural events Visit museums, galleries, etc.
Benefit Factor 4—Outdoor Adventure:	Hiking, camping Fishing Sailing, boating Snorkeling, scuba diving Surfing
Benefit Factor 5—Shopping:	Visit urban shopping centers Shop in rural villages

FIGURE 17.8 Benefit Segmentation: Benefit Factors

	Segment 1: Thrill Seekers	Segment 2: Do It Alls	Segment 3: Hedonists	Segment 4: Culturals
Size of Segment	10%	35%	25%	30%
Benefit Factors				
Fun Around the Clock	−1.61	1.12	1.46	−.53
Ecotourism	−.79	1.84	−.08	−.60
Culture	−1.45	1.38	−1.81	1.70
Outdoor Adventure	1.60	1.37	−1.80	−.80
Shopping	.02	−1.82	−.44	1.62

FIGURE 17.9 Benefit Segmentation: Benefit Segments

Once the segments are formed, classification variables are used to make group characteristics explicit. In this research, data from both Figures 17.8 and 17.9 would be used
to create an initial description of each group. Additionally, this data would be used to

determine a descriptive name for each segment. Descriptions and names of the four benefit segments follows.

Segment 1: Thrill Seekers seek active outdoor adventures. They are the smallest segment, representing 10% of the total sample. This segment's interest in outdoor activities coupled with a lack of interest in each of the remaining types of activities differentiates it from the other segments.

Segment 2: Do It Alls are the largest segment, representing 35% of the sample. Individuals in this segment like to explore the destination fully, and as a result, seek diverse benefits falling into a broad range of activities, where they are most interested in activities associated with ecotourism. These individuals are not at all interested in shopping.

Segment 3: Hedonists represent 25% of the sample. Individuals in this segment are most interested in activities that are not strenuous and which provide instant gratification. These are the activities that are classified as "Fun Around the Clock." They are uninterested in other types of activities.

Segment 4: Culturals represent 30% of the sample. They are interested in the performing arts and other cultural activities as well as shopping-related activities.

Describe Segments Using Descriptive Variables

This step determines the extent to which segments differ with regard to demographics, attitudes, values, and other descriptive areas included in the research. This is typically done by cross-tabulating the descriptive variables with each of the segments. The key cross-tabulations for the four segments are shown in Figures 17.10 to 17.13. (Note that higher numbers in Figure 17.12 indicate greater importance while higher numbers in Figure 17.13 indicate stronger agreement.)

Create a Summary Sheet, Narrative or Persona for Each Segment

Data tables are the starting point for the presentation of segmentation insights. Insights are typically best communicated when the underlying data is used to describe each segment in one of three ways:

- A summary sheet can be created for each individual segment. This sheet (see Figure 17.14 on page 490) typically names the segment; provides a picture of the typical segment member; and then lists the key characteristics, values, behaviors, and beliefs of the segment.

- A narrative can be written. This narrative (see Figure 17.15 on page 491) provides a more "literary" description of the segment and its defining characteristics, values, behaviors, and beliefs.

- A persona can be written. A persona (see Figure 17.16 on page 492) names and describes the typical individual in a segment, communicating all segment characteristics as a reflection of a single individual.[23]

	Segment 1: Thrill Seekers	Segment 2: Do It Alls	Segment 3: Hedonists	Segment 4: Culturals
Gender				
Female	39%	52%	53%	67%
Male	61	48	47	33
Age				
18 to 34	69	43	66	50
35 to 54	27	41	31	40
55 and older	4	16	3	10
Education				
High School or less	22	14	19	12
University	60	52	71	52
Postgraduate	18	34	10	36
Occupation				
Employed full-time	79	77	71	71
Median Household Income	$37,000	$43,000	$47,000	$56,000

FIGURE 17.10 Benefit Segmentation: Segment Demographics

	Segment 1: Thrill Seekers	Segment 2: Do It Alls	Segment 3: Hedonists	Segment 4: Culturals
Travel Frequency				
More than 1 trip/year	55%	20%	42%	73%
Trip Organization				
Strong interest in self- organized vacation	80	86	82	61
Strong interest in all- inclusive vacation	10	25	66	60
Travel Party				
Spouse/partner	35	33	4	55
Family with child	2	19	1	12
Family without child	3	21	1	2
Friends	25	20	20	27
Alone	35	7	74	4
Information Source				
Internet	69	36	48	52
Travel agent	22	43	69	74
Travel books	51	24	44	32
Friends and family	65	66	69	57
Newspaper travel section	33	30	28	29
Travel brochure	30	33	44	42
TV Travel show	11	17	11	11

FIGURE 17.11 Benefit Segmentation: Travel Behaviors and Interests

	Segment 1: Thrill Seekers	Segment 2: Do It Alls	Segment 3: Hedonists	Segment 4: Culturals
Relative Appeal				
Health service	2.3	4.1	3.6	3.3
Child day care	1.2	2.6	1.3	2.1
Telecom service	2.2	3.9	3.4	3.6
Local tourist office	1.9	3.9	3.3	2.9
Banking service	2.7	4.1	3.6	3.6
Local transportation	2.3	3.9	3.4	3.9
Low local crime rate	3.4	4.4	4.4	4.2
Clean food and water	3.3	4.7	4.8	4.4
Friendly locals	4.3	3.5	3.5	4.4
Affordable accommodations	4.1	4.5	4.5	4.4
Affordable flights	4.6	3.8	3.6	3.3
Good local prices	4.2	4.4	4.6	4.1

FIGURE 17.12 Benefit Segmentation: Decision Drivers

	Segment 1: Thrill Seekers	Segment 2: Do It Alls	Segment 3: Hedonists	Segment 4: Culturals
Attitude Statement				
My interests are pretty narrow	1.7	2.0	2.5	2.3
I like traveling where lots of tourists go	1.7	3.0	2.9	2.6
I try to mingle with the locals whenever possible	3.8	2.9	2.7	2.8
I stay away from tourist areas—local hangouts are the best places to go	3.7	2.5	2.3	2.6
I like to learn about new things	3.3	2.9	3.3	2.8
I consider myself an intellectual	2.1	3.1	2.8	2.7
I like to learn about art, culture and history	1.9	3.6	3.3	3.1

FIGURE 17.13 Benefit Segmentation: Attitudes

The Thrill Seeker

At a Glance	• Always up for a novel adventure • Is a doer versus an armchair participant • Self-reliant and self-confident • Traveling is a priority despite relatively lower income
Demographics	• Predominantly male (61%) • Relatively younger (most are 18 to 34) • Well educated (60% university; 18% postgraduate) • Employed full-time (79%) • Modest median income (about $37,000)
Travel Priorities	• Require affordable transportation, accommodations and local expenses • Want to avoid tourist traps and instead hangout with the locals, doing what the locals do • Want to try new and different things, from food to adventure, taking full advantage of the outdoor opportunities, local sports, immersion in unique local culture
Travel Planning Sources	• Internet (69%) • Recommendations of friends and family (65%) • Travel books (51%) • Very unlikely to use pre-planned packaged vacation
Physical Activities	• Camping • Hiking • Extreme sports • Participating in local sports • Doing what the natives do
Travel Companions	• Doesn't necessarily need company • About equally likely to travel with spouse/partner, friends, or alone
Media Opportunities	• Internet travel ads in conjunction with hiking/camping/sports web pages • Internet travel ads on web sites with more adventure-oriented (less traditional) focus for Brazil • Extreme sports advertising exposure

FIGURE 17.14 Benefit Segmentation: Summary Sheet for Thrill Seekers Segment

Travel Priorities

- to learn about art, culture & history
  - I like traveling where lots of tourists go
  - try to mingle w/the locals whenever possible
  - Like to learn new things

Travel Planning Sources
- family and friends   - Clean food & water
  - Travel agent   - Affordable accommodations
  - Internet   - Good local prices
  - Travel brochure   - Low local crime rate

Physical Activities
- Visit small towns
- Nature oriented excursions
- Visit Natural wonders

Travel Companions
- Travel w/a spouse/partner

Media Opportunities
- Brochure - family & friends

Com 509

Do it All

Female: 52%
Male: 48%

18-34 - 43
35-54 41
55+ - 16

Highschool - 14
University - 52
Post grad - 34

AT A GLANCE: Doesn't travel alot.
• Associated with ecotourism. Doesn't
really like shopping

Demographics:
• Mainly Women 52%
• between ages 18-34
• Attend University
• 77 full time
• 43,000$

- Travel
- Internet
- Travel agent

Michael O'Connell is thinking about where to go on his next vacation. He is 28 years old, loves to travel, and tries to get away at least twice a year. For Michael, traveling is a priority, even though his income is modest. He can do this because he's an adventurous traveler. He seeks out affordable transportation both to his destination and when he arrives, he has modest needs with regards to accommodations (unique, off-the-beaten-track places to stay are a positive part of the adventure). Michael has no interest in typical tourist traps or organized tours.

Michael's idea of a great vacation is one that takes advantage of the unique characteristics of the country he is visiting. Sometimes he like to travel alone while at other times he likes to travel with another person. In either case, Michael is confident and self-reliant. Michael likes to hike, camp, and participate in local and extreme sports. When he is not experiencing the great outdoors and enjoying the scenery, he likes to immerse himself in the local culture, meeting the people, eating the native cuisine and enjoying the local hangouts.

Given this kind of itinerary, Michael enjoys planning his own vacations. He is happy to listen to recommendations from friends or family, but Michael is likely to investigate his vacation options online and in travel books. In this way, he can avoid the tourist routes and instead find the unique activities which he will enjoy while he is soaking up the local culture. Michael avoids travel agents.

On the last trip Michael took, he and his girlfriend went to Brazil. He loved it and decided that he would return again in an instant. The people were welcoming and he managed to take full advantage of the rich landscapes and rugged terrain. The food was great and by staying off the tourist paths, his trip was both affordable and unique.

FIGURE 17.15 Benefit Segmentation: Narrative Description for Thrill Seekers Segment

Evaluate Segments for Communication Priority

One of the final steps in segmentation research is the selection of one or more segments for marketing and advertising focus. Because not all segments within a population have equal appeal from a marketing or advertising perspective, marketers and advertisers must examine the internal characteristics of the segments to evaluate each segment's appeal as a potential target audience.

SYNDICATED APPROACHES TO SEGMENTATION

The prior sections discussed how marketers and advertisers conduct and use segmentation research as well as the procedures that underlie the conduct of an original segmentation. There are times, however, when original segmentation research is too costly or time-consuming, or when existing data sources do not provide the required information. In these cases, marketers and advertisers might use a syndicated approach to segmentation. Syndicated approaches generally fall into one of three categories:

- psychographic segmentation
- product usage segmentation
- geodemographic segmentation

The remainder of this chapter discusses each of these syndicated approaches to segmentation.

Michael: The Thrill Seeker

"I can't wait to get to Brazil. What a great time I'll have there, exploring the amazing terrain, sports, and hanging out with the locals!"

Personal Profile

Michael O'Connell loves to travel and usually does so more than once a year. Although his income is modest, the adventure of travel and the promise of new experiences beckons him. Michael is now looking forward to heading to Brazil on his next vacation in search of more adventure and a chance to get to know the locals and hangouts in a new locale.

Michael is self-confident and self-reliant. While he is happy to listen to places his family and friends recommend for travel destinations, Michael loves to hop on the Internet and read travel books seeking out new experiences where he can enjoy camping, hiking and/or local outdoor activities. He is looking for novel places as opposed to tourist traps and he is happy to design his own trip itinerary so he can avoid the tourist hangouts and instead incorporate camping, hiking and a taste of the people and sports of the place he is visiting. The cost of flights and accommodations is a significant consideration as Michael wants to be able to travel often and his income is somewhat modest. His funds go farther, however, because he is looking for an authentic local experience and not top-of-the-line tourism services.

Personal Information

Age: 28

Education:
BA and above

Employment:
Full time; income $37,000

Key Words:
Adventure, experience, sports, local hangouts, off-the-beaten-path

Goals	Information Sources	Questions
• Affordable travel costs (flights and accommodations) • Adventurous activities: local sports, camping, hiking, sea activities if on coast (not beach-bathing) • Immersion in the country visited	• Internet • Travel books • Family and friends	• What do the locals do and where? (sports, outdoor activities, hangouts) • What can I do there that I cannot do elsewhere? • Where can I go to avoid tourists and fully experience the local culture?

FIGURE 17.16   Benefit Segmentation: Persona for Thrill Seekers Segment

Psychographic Segmentation: VALS™

VALS™ segments adults on the basis of the psychological traits that motivate and drive consumer behavior.[24] Strategic Business Insights explains the relationship between traits and behaviors as follows:

> VALS uses psychology to describe the dynamics underlying consumer preferences and choices. VALS identifies the psychological motivations that predict consumer differences. VALS uses proprietary psychometric technology to measure concepts that researchers have proved empirically correlate with consumer behavior.[25]

VALS divides the U.S. adult population into eight groups based on their responses to the "VALS questionnaire" (see Figure 17.17). Classification variables, discussed earlier in the chapter, were used to identify the eight segments during the initial VALS development. Using classification variables, the VALS research ream developed the VALS questionnaire to enable marketers and adverisers to identify each individual's specific VALS type. The VALS questionnaire is also integrated into larger custom or syndicated research questionnaires which allows marketers and advertisers to see the product, service, and media preferences, as well as additional descriptive variables, of each VALS segment. An

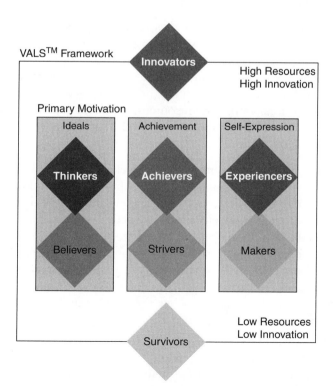

FIGURE 17.17 VALS Types (reproduced with permission of Strategic Business Insights, SBI. Source at http://www.strategicbusinessinsights.com/VALS)

example of this latter integration is Mediamark Research & Intelligences' (MRI) *Survey of American Consumers*, which is discussed later in this chapter.

Figure 17.17 illustrates the two primary dimensions of the VALS framework: primary motivation (the horizontal dimension) and resources (the vertical dimension). VALS describes each of these dimensions as follows:

- *Motivation.* The concept of primary motivation explains consumer attitudes and anticipates behavior. VALS includes three primary motivations that matter for understanding consumer behavior: ideals, achievement, and self-expression. Consumers who are primarily motivated by ideals are guided by knowledge and principles. Consumers who are primarily motivated by achievement look for products and services that demonstrate success to their peers. Consumers who are primarily motivated by self-expression desire social or physical activity, variety, and risk. These motivations provide the necessary basis for communication with the VALS types and for a variety of strategic applications.

- *Resources.* A person's tendency to consume goods and services extends beyond age, income, and education. Energy, self-confidence, intellectualism, novelty seeking, innovativeness, impulsiveness, leadership, and vanity play a critical role. These psychological traits in conjunction with key demographics determine an individual's resources. Various levels of resources enhance or constrain a person's expression of his or her primary motivation.[26]

The combination of motivation and resources results in three broad motivational categories: Ideals, Achievement, and Self-Expression (see Figure 17.17). Six VALS segments fall into these categories. The other two VALS segments, Innovators and Survivors, don't easily fit into them. Survivors, with many resource constraints, (e.g., little money, poorer health, low tolerance for risk) consume little and are motivated mostly by low cost and brand familiarity. Innovators, with many resources, are exceptionally active in the marketplace, making it hard to put them into any one motivation category. The eight VALS segments are described below.[27]

- *Innovators* are successful, sophisticated, take-charge people with high self-esteem. Because they have such abundant resources, they exhibit all three primary motivations in varying degrees. They are change leaders and are the most receptive to new ideas and technologies. Innovators are very active consumers, and their purchases reflect cultivated tastes for upscale, niche products and services. Image is important to Innovators, not as evidence of status or power but as an expression of their taste, independence, and personality. Innovators are among the established and emerging leaders in business and government, yet they continue to seek challenges. Their lives are characterized by variety. Their possessions and recreation reflect a cultivated taste for the finer things in life.

- *Survivors* live narrowly focused lives. With few resources with which to cope, they often believe that the world is changing too quickly. They are comfortable with the familiar and are primarily concerned with safety and security. Because they must focus on meeting needs rather than fulfilling desires, Survivors do not show a strong primary motivation. Survivors are cautious consumers. They represent a very modest market for most products and services. They are loyal to favorite brands, especially if they can purchase them at a discount.

The Ideals group consists of the Thinker and Believers segments.

- *Thinkers* are motivated by ideals. They are mature, satisfied, comfortable, and reflective people who value order, knowledge, and responsibility. They tend to be well-educated and actively seek out information in the decision-making process. They are well-informed about world and national events and are alert to opportunities to broaden their knowledge. Thinkers have a moderate respect for the status quo institutions of authority and social decorum, but are open to consider new ideas. Although their incomes allow them many choices, Thinkers are conservative, practical consumers; they look for durability, functionality, and value in the products they buy.

- *Believers,* like Thinkers, are motivated by ideals. They are conservative, conventional people with concrete beliefs based on traditional, established codes: family, religion, community, and the nation. Many Believers express moral codes that are deeply rooted and literally interpreted. They follow established routines, organized in large part around home, family, community, and social or religious organizations to which they belong. As consumers, Believers are predictable; they choose familiar products and established brands. They favor American products and are generally loyal customers.

The Achievement-oriented group consists of Achievers and Strivers.

- *Achievers,* motivated by the desire for achievement, have goal-oriented lifestyles and a deep commitment to career and family. Their social lives reflect this focus and are structured around family, their place of worship, and work. Achievers live conventional lives, are politically conservative, and respect authority and the status quo. They value consensus, predictability, and stability over risk, intimacy, and self-discovery. With many wants and needs, Achievers are active in the consumer marketplace. Image is important to Achievers; they favor established, prestige products and services that demonstrate success to their peers. Because of their busy lives, they are often interested in a variety of time-saving devices.

- *Strivers* are trendy and fun loving. Because they are motivated by achievement, Strivers are concerned about the opinions and approval of others. Money defines success for Strivers, who don't have enough of it to meet their desires. They favor stylish products that emulate the purchases of people with greater material wealth. Many see themselves as having a job rather than a career, and a lack of skills and focus often prevents them from moving ahead. Strivers are active consumers because shopping is both a social activity and an opportunity to demonstrate to peers their ability to buy. As consumers, they are as impulsive as their financial circumstance will allow.

The Self-Expression group consists of Experiencers and Makers.

- *Experiencers* are motivated by self-expression. As young, enthusiastic, and impulsive consumers, Experiencers quickly become enthusiastic about new possibilities but are equally quick to cool. They seek variety and excitement, savoring the new, the offbeat, and the risky. Their energy finds an outlet in exercise, sports, outdoor recreation, and social activities. Experiencers are avid consumers and spend a comparatively high proportion of their income on fashion, entertainment, and socializing. Their purchases reflect the emphasis they place on looking good and having "cool" stuff.

- *Makers,* similar to Experiencers, are motivated by self-expression. They express themselves and experience the world by working on it—building a house, raising children, fixing a car, or canning vegetables—and have enough skill and energy to carry out their projects successfully. Makers are practical people who have constructive skills and value self-sufficiency. They live within a traditional context of family, practical work, and physical recreation and have little interest in what lies outside that context. Makers are suspicious of new ideas and large institutions such as big business. They are respectful of government authority and organized labor, but resentful of government intrusion on individual rights. They are unimpressed by material possessions other than those with a practical or functional purpose. Because they prefer value to luxury, they buy basic products.

Marketers and advertisers use the VALS typology in several ways. First, VALS can contribute to target audience selection and message planning. The specific types of products used by individuals in each segment can be identified using surveys, and those segments with the highest usage can be targeted. Luxury items, for example, sell best to Innovators, Experiencers, and Achievers; snowboards and skateboards sell best to Experiencers; and basic hunting equipment sells best to Makers. Additional applications of VALS to target audience selection and communication planning include

- a large pension plan provider to the United States which conducted a custom research survey of its participants, incorporating VALS to identify which of its participants it could service electronically. By understanding the motivations of these consumers, the provider was able to revise its Web site and communications to serve its participants' needs better.

- an electric utility which used VALS to increase participation in its energy conservation program by developing a targeted direct mail campaign. Using VALS/MRI data, the utility identified two distinctly different VALS segments as key targets. By developing unique strategies for each audience and identifying zip codes with high proportions of each target using GeoVALS™, the utility reported a 25% increase in participation.[28]

Second, VALS data can help marketers and advertisers better understand how to position their products, for example:

- A leading U.S. bank used VALS/MacroMonitor data from Consumer Financial Decisions to reposition several ubiquitous products in commodity categories. By understanding the emotional benefits sought by target consumers, the advertising agency was able to define unique selling propositions for each product that linked to the corporate branding strategy. The bank achieved about one-third of its customer-acquisition goal 12 weeks into the first campaign.

- One of the premier U.S. community real estate developers included VALS in a custom research survey of homeowners to increase the developer's understanding of which amenities would be most attractive to add to its communities. VALS enabled the developer to link its own research to nationally syndicated MRI data to identify a broad diversity of leisure preferences.[29]

Third, VALS can make a contribution to product design and development, for example:

- An international consumer electronics firm used VALS to anticipate consumer demand for a new consumer media product for delivery over the Internet. By using VALS/MRI data, the company was able to customize the product feature set and delivery style to meet the needs of two key VALS consumer targets.

- A major telecommunications product company used VALS to select an early adopter target for a new telecommunications concept. VALS enabled the company to develop the product prototype and prioritize features and benefits, with a focus on the early adopter target. The company used VALS to select the best name and logo, choose an overall positioning strategy, and set an initial price point.[30]

Category and Brand Usage Behaviors

Experian Simmons and Mediamark Research & Intelligence (MRI) are two marketing research companies that provide an extensive database on the demographic, self-concept, attitudes, media habits, and product usage of a nationally representative sample of adults. Simmons and MRI make this information available by subscription to advertisers, marketers, and media companies that use the data to segment the population into groups that reflect differences in product- or media-related behaviors.

The core of the Simmons or MRI database is an extensive questionnaire that collects information on a respondent's demographics, attitudes, media habits, and usage of more than 6,000 brands and products.[31] An excerpt from the MRI questionnaire, for toothpaste and related products, is shown in Figure 17.18. Notice how the questionnaire goes beyond brands to collect information on toothpaste types, kinds, and forms.

Exploration of the Simmons and MRI databases is typically done interactively using specialized software created by each respective company. The data shown below illustrates the type of information provided by each company.[32]

		U.S. Adults	Fident	Islands	TresBon
GENDER: FEMALE	Sample	14,165	926	218	1,545
	(000)	114,462	6,960	1,789	14,176
	Horizontal %	100%	6.1%	1.6%	12.4%
	Vertical %	52.1%	63.2%	74.4%	46.7%
	Index	100	121	143	90

HEALTH AND BEAUTY AIDS

Page 3

TOOTHPASTE
001

You Personally: Used in last 6 months / Times/ last 7 days

TOTAL:		00
TYPES:		
Baking Soda		01
Baking Soda and Peroxide		02
Non Baking Soda		03
KINDS:		
Tartar Control		04
Regular		05
FORMS:		
Gel		06
Paste		07
BRANDS:		
Aim		08
Aquafresh		09
Aquafresh Extra Fresh		10
Aquafresh Extreme Clean		11
Aquafresh Whitening		12
Arm & Hammer Advance White		13
Arm & Hammer Dental Care		14
Arm & Hammer Complete Care		15
Other Arm & Hammer		16
Close-Up		17
Colgate 2 in 1		18
Colgate Luminous		19
Colgate Max Fresh		20
Colgate Regular		21
Colgate Sparkling White		22
Colgate Tartar Protection		23
Colgate Total		24
Colgate with Baking Soda and Peroxide		25
Other Colgate		26
Crest Dual Action Whitening		27
Crest Pro-Health		28
Crest Regular Gel		29
Crest Regular Mint Paste		30
Crest Tartar Protection Gel		31
Crest Tartar Protection Paste		32
Crest Vivid White		33
Crest Whitening Expressions		34
Crest Whitening Plus Scope		35
Other Crest		36
Mentadent		37
Pepsodent		38
Rembrandt		39
Sensodyne		40
Tom's of Maine		41
Ultra Brite		42
		999
OTHER (Write In)		
PROPERTIES:	116-0	
Whitening		1
Sensitive		2

DENTAL FLOSS
002

You Personally: Used in last 6 months / Times/ last 7 days

TOTAL:		00
TYPES:		
Waxed		01
Unwaxed		02
KINDS:		
Flavored		03
Unflavored		04
BRANDS:		
Butler		05
Glide		06
Johnson & Johnson Reach		07
Oral-B		08
Reach Access Flosser		09
Generic (No Label)		10
Store's Own Brand		11
		999
OTHER (Write In)		

TOOTHBRUSHES
003

You Personally: Bought in last 6 months / Number in last 6 months

TOTAL:		00
TYPES:		
Battery-Operated		01
Electric		02
Manual		03
KINDS:		
Firm Bristle		04
Medium Bristle		05
Soft Bristle		06
FORMS:		
Angled Handle		07
Straight Handle		08
BRANDS:		
Aquafresh		09
Butler G-U-M		10
Colgate 360˚		11
Colgate Motion		12
Colgate Navigator		13
Colgate Plus		14
Colgate Wave		15
Colgate Total Professional		16
Other Colgate		17
Crest SpinBrush		18
Crest SpinBrush Pro		19
Mentadent		20
Oral-B AdvancePower		21
Oral-B Advantage		22
Oral-B CrossAction		23
Oral-B Indicator		24
Oral-B ProfessionalCare		25
Oral-B Pulsar		26
Oral-B Triumph		27
Other Oral-B		28
Reach Advanced Design		29
Reach Max		30
Other Reach		31
Sonicare Elite		32
Sonicare IntelliClean		33
Other Sonicare		34
Generic (No Label)		35
Store's Own Brand		36
		999
OTHER (Write In)		

MOUTHWASH
005

You Personally: Used in last 6 months / Times/ last 7 days

TOTAL:		00
BRANDS:		
Biotène		01
Cepacol		02
Chloraseptic		03
Crest Pro-Health Rinse		04
Green Mint		05
Lavoris		06
Listerine (Yellow)		07
Listerine Cool Mint (Blue)		08
Listerine FreshBurst (Green)		09
Other Listerine		10
Listermint		11
Oasis		12
Scope Original (Green)		13
Scope Peppermint (Blue)		14
Tom's of Maine		15
		999
OTHER (Write In)		

DENTAL RINSE
006

You Personally: Used in last 6 months / Times/ last 7 days

TOTAL:		00
BRANDS:		
ACT Fluoride Rinse		01
Colgate Fluorigard		02
Crest Pro-Health Rinse		03
Crest Whitening		04
Listerine Whitening		05
Oral-B		06
Plax		07
Rembrandt		08
		999
OTHER (Write In)		

BREATH FRESHENERS
007

You Personally: Used in last 6 months / Times/ last 7 days

TOTAL:		00
TYPES:		
Spray/Drops		01
Mints		02
Gum		03
Liquid		04
Thin Film		05
BRANDS:		
Binaca		06
Cool Mint Listerine PocketPaks Strips		07
Other Listerine PocketPaks Strips		08
Listerine Pocketmist		09
Eclipse Flash Strips		10
MintAsure		11
Sweet Breath		12
		999
OTHER (Write In)		

LIP CARE
008

You Personally: Used in last 6 months / Times/ last 7 days

TOTAL:		00
BRANDS:		
Blistex		01
Burt's Bees		02
Carmex		03
ChapStick Lip Balm		04
ChapStick Lip Moisturizer		05
ChapStick Ultra SPF 30		06
Other ChapStick		07
Herpecin-L		08
Natural Ice		09
Neosporin LT Lip Treatment		10
Neutrogena		11
Softlips		12
Vaseline Lip Therapy		13
Other Vaseline		14
		999
OTHER (Write In)		

TOOTH WHITENERS (not toothpaste)
004

You Personally: Used in last 6 months / Times/ last 7 days

TOTAL:		00
FORMS:		
Strips		01
Gel		02
BRANDS:		
Aquafresh White Trays		03
Crest Night Effects		04
Crest Whitestrips		05
Listerine Whitening Strips		06
Rembrandt		07
Plus White		08
		999
OTHER (Write In)		

FIGURE 17.18 MRI Questionnaire: Toothpaste (reproduced with permission of Mediamark Research & Intelligence)

Data is reported in rows and columns. Columns are formed by classification variables, and rows reflect descriptive variables. In this case, consumers have been segmented with regard to the *brand of toothpaste used most within the past seven days* (the classification variable). Three brands are of interest: Fident, Islands, and TresBon. The row is labeled "GENDER: FEMALE" indicating that the data all of these rows refers to female users of each brand. Beyond the brand information, the first column of data, labeled "U.S. Adults," provides data on the total U.S. adult population, which provides a frame of reference for data interpretation.

A full data report provides five types of information for each descriptive variable, as follows:

- The row labeled "Sample" reports the number of people in the Simmons or MRI database falling into a particular category, in this case "Females." Reading across the "Sample" row, there are 14,165 women in the sample, of which 926 used Fident the most in the prior seven days, 218 used Islands, and 1,545 used TresBon. The number reported in the sample column is always important to check in order to make certain that the sample is of sufficient size to warrant confidence in the data.

- The next row, labeled "(000)," projects the sample to the total adult population. The three zeros indicate that numbers reported in this row should have three zeros added when read. Thus, reading across the "(000)" row, there are an estimated 114,462,000 women in the United States, of which it is estimated that 6,960,000 used Fident the most in the prior seven days, 1,789,000 used Islands, and 14,176,000 used TresBon. While these numbers do not directly translate into brand share, they do provide some guide as to relative brand strength. Clearly, the number of women using TresBon is much larger than the other two brands.

- Absolute numbers are often hard to interpret, so group size with regard to a particular descriptive variable is typically translated into a percentage. This percentage is reported in the row labeled "Horizontal %." Reading across this row, it can be seen that the 6,960,000 female users of Fident represent 6.1% of all women. Similarly, 1.6% of women report using Islands and 12.4% report using TresBon. The percentages shown in the "Horizontal" column simplify the determination of relative strength as it allows a researcher to move from raw numbers to more easily interpretable percentages.

- The next row, labeled "Vertical %" looks at the distribution *within* each brand-user segment. Reading across this row, it is estimated that 52.1% of all adults are women. Furthermore, it is estimated that 63.2% of Fident users are women, 74.4% of Islands users are women, and 46.7% of TresBon users are women.

- The final row, labeled "Index," places the vertical percentages in context. The index indicates the extent to which the percentage of a segment's users who fall into a specific descriptive category is larger or smaller than the percentage of all adults falling into that category. Higher indices (typically those over 115) indicate that a group is significantly more likely to display a specific characteristic while lower indices (typically under 85) indicate that a group is significantly less likely to display a specific characteristic. Indices between 86 and 114 are generally considered average. The basis for estimating likelihood is the total U.S. population.

Consider Fident users, of which 63.2% are women. The index first compares the percentage of Fident users who are women (63.2%) to the percentage of women in the total population (52.1%). Next, it divides the first number by the second and multiplies the result by 100. In this case, the index of female Fident users is 121, calculated as $(63.2 \div 52.1) \times 100$. This Index is over 115, which indicates that Fident users tend to skew female; that is, there are more female Fident users than would be expected by the size of the overall female adult population. Islands also skews female (even more so than Fident) with its index of 143. TresBon, in contrast to these two brands, does not skew toward female users. The index for female users of TresBon falls in the average range, indicating that there is just the expected number of female users, not significantly more or less. In sum, both Fident and Islands can be thought of as "women's brands," while TresBon is a brand that has appeal to both men and women.

Once sample sizes and relative brand strength have been examined, advertisers typically use the information reported in the "Vertical %" and "Index" columns to better understand different brand-user segments. The data shown in Figure 17.19 shows an excerpt from a report of two toothpaste brand-user segments.[33] The two segments of toothpaste brand users are quite different, although both brands have a predominantly female user base. (This, as discussed previously, is reflected in the over 115 indices for women and the under 85 indices for men.) An analysis and interpretation of this data would be as follows:

- Fident skews younger as 61% of its users are under 35 and both the 18 to 24 and 25 to 34 years old groups index over 115. All age groups over 35 have indices below 85. Furthermore, while the percentage is relatively low, Fident's user base has a higher than expected percentage of Asians and of those who are not married (as evidenced in the below 85 index for "Married").

- Islands has a quite different user profile. Islands' users tend to be between 35 and 64 (as reflected in the high indices for these age groups and the low indices for the remaining groups). 69% of Islands' users fall into this age range. In addition, Islands' user base has a higher than expected percentage of Black/African-Americans and those who are married. Islands' user base also contains fewer than expected Asians (as indicated in the lower than 85 index).

The ability to segment by brand usage or related variables helps advertisers understand the types of users attracted by their own and competitive products, which in turn allows them to begin to identify the most appropriate communication messages. Beyond demographics, however, both Simmons and MRI allow brand-defined segments to be analyzed in terms of attitudes and psychographics. This data extends demographic profiles and helps advertisers refine and focus the communication message. The data shown in the following table presents each brand user segments' level of agreement with five key attitudinal statements. A high index indicates greater than average agreement with the statement, while a low index indicates lower than average agreement. Clearly, women users of the two brands are quite different with respect to this set of attitudes.

		US Adults	Fident	Islands
Gender				
Male	Vertical	48%	37%	26%
	Index		77	53
Female	Vertical	52%	63%	74%
	Index		122	144
Age:				
18–24	Vertical	19%	25%	12%
	Index		132	55
25–34	Vertical	17%	36%	11%
	Index		212	65
35–49	Vertical	28%	18%	38%
	Index		64	136
50–64	Vertical	22%	13%	31%
	Index		59	141
65+	Vertical	14%	8%	8%
	Index		57	57
White	Vertical	78%	75%	59%
	Index		96	76
Black/African-American	Vertical	11%	11%	26%
	Index		100	236
Asian	Vertical	4%	8%	3%
	Index		200	75
Married	Vertical	54%	33%	68%
	Index		61	126

FIGURE 17.19 Fictitious Data for Two Toothpaste Brand-User Segments

Attitudes	Fident (women only)	Islands (women only)
I spend what I have to in order to look younger	180	60
I like to stand out in a crowd	152	72
It is important to keep young looking	138	61
I like to enjoy life now, not worry about future	135	74
It is important to be attractive to opposite sex	137	77

Finally, beyond demographics and attitudes, Simmons and MRI data provide insights into brand-related behaviors. Imagine, for example, that you are the brand manager for Crest toothpaste. The data collected by MRI (refer to the questionnaire shown in Figure 17.18) could help answer the following questions when Crest toothpaste usage is selected as the classification variable and other brands, both within and related to the toothpaste category, are used as the descriptive variables:

- What is the brand switching behavior of Crest toothpaste users? When there is switching, what toothpaste brands do they switch to? Do they switch to other Crest brands of toothpaste or to competitive brands?

- How loyal are Crest toothpaste users?

- What brands does Crest toothpaste most directly compete with? Do different Crest toothpaste formulations compete with other Crest toothpaste products or with competitive toothpaste brands?

- Do Crest toothpaste users also use Crest toothbrushes? If not, what brand of toothbrush are they most likely to use?

- Do Crest toothpaste users also use Crest dental rinse? If so, which specific type? If not, what brand of dental rinse are they most likely to use?

- Do Crest toothpaste users also use Crest tooth whiteners? If so, which specific type? If not, what brand of tooth whitener are they most likely to use?

Geodemographic Segmentation

Geodemographic segmentation is an analysis of people in terms of where they live. Geographic segmentation accomplishes this analysis by dividing the United States into very small geographic areas and then describing the individuals who live in that area in terms of demographics, media usage, lifestyle choices, possessions, and purchase behaviors. The core premise of geodemographic segmentation is that similar people live in similar places, partake in similar activities, share common beliefs, and live similar lifestyles, in other words, that "birds of a feather flock together." Geodemographic segmentation performs its clustering analysis as follows:

- Information is obtained from the latest United States census, automobile registration records, magazine subscriber lists, buying clubs, consumer product usage surveys, syndicated and proprietary research studies, self-report surveys, and other sources of consumer information.

- The information from these sources is aggregated on the census block level. A census block (about 340 households) is selected as the basic unit of geography because it typically represents an actual neighborhood.

- The characteristics of each census block in the United States are identified and examined. Then, based on this analysis, each census block is assigned to a segment (also known as a cluster) so that census blocks within a cluster are similar to each other and dissimilar to census blocks in other clusters.[34]

There are similarities and differences in the outcomes of these procedures among geodemographic research companies. Companies are similar in that the final segmentation reflects a continuum of economic, life stage, and lifestyle characteristics. Geodemographic clusters range from very wealthy individuals living in exclusive areas leading "the good life" to very poor, inner-city individuals living at the barest level. Geodemographic research companies differ, however, in the specific types of information used to form their clusters, the total number of clusters formed, and how the clusters are labeled and described. Three of the leading geodemographic systems—Claritas' PRIZM, ClusterPLUS, and MOSAIC— have, for example, segmented U.S. neighborhoods into 67, 38, and 60 clusters, respectively. Each system provides a descriptive name for each individual cluster and groupings of individual clusters into larger segments. Two illustrative PRIZM descriptions are:[35]

> *Segment 7. Money and Brains.* The residents of Money & Brains seem to have it all: high incomes, advanced degrees, and sophisticated tastes to match their credentials. Many of these city dwellers–predominantly white with a high concentration of Asian Americans–are married couples with few children who live in fashionable homes on small, manicured lots.

> *Segment 47. City Startups.* In City Startups, young, multiethnic singles have settled in neighborhoods filled with cheap apartments and a commercial base of cafés, bars, laundromats, and clubs that cater to twentysomethings. One of the youngest segments in America–with 10 times as many college students as the national average–these neighborhoods feature low incomes and high concentrations of Hispanics and African-Americans.[36]

Marketers and advertisers use geodemographic segmentation to locate new customers, evaluate alternative retail store sites, select print and broadcast media vehicles, target direct mail, and develop new products, for example:

- Imagine a direct mail campaign that receives a positive response from a particular zip code or geodemographic cluster. A geodemographic cluster system can then be used to identify other zip codes or clusters that display similar characteristics and would therefore be thought to be more likely to also display a positive response.

- Consider a retail Web site that knows the addresses of those who have made a purchase. The retailer can geodemographically code each purchaser. Once the geodemographic code is known, e-mail correspondence and future offers can be customized for the characteristics of that unique individual in a way that reflects the characteristics of the individual's geodemographic cluster.

APPLYING CHAPTER CONCEPTS

As this chapter has discussed, segmentation has the potential to be a powerful tool. This potential is only realized, however, when the research is well-planned, segments are well-formed, and insights into each group are relevant and detailed. The online supplemental readings provide two examples of research with these characteristics.

A Typology of Information and Communication Technology Users[37]

A 2007 Pew Internet & American Life project sought to explain how different groups of individuals use information and communication technology to express themselves online and participate in online activities. With this goal in mind—the segmentation of information and communication technology users—research was conducted to classify Americans into different groups of technology users in relation to three dimensions: assets, actions, and attitudes.

> *Assets:* Pew asked about individuals' use of the Internet, cell phones, and other devices that connect to the Internet (e.g., video or digital cameras), and services that facilitate digital consumption, participation, and electronic communication (e.g., broadband and non-voice applications on cell phones).

> *Actions:* Pew asked about online activities and behaviors, such as downloading audio and video, generating original online content, and the wide range of things people do with their cell phones and computers.

> *Attitudes:* Pew asked people about the extent to which they believe information and communication technologies help them be more productive at work, to pursue hobbies, and to keep up with family and friends. Pew also asked about information overload and technology's capacity to offer more control over individuals' lives.

The research identified 10 segments of individuals, which in turn comprise three larger groups.

- At one of the continuum are the *Elite Users* of information and communication technologies. (This group consists of 31% of all U.S. adults and four segments, see Figure 17.20.) Elite Users have the most information technology, are heavy and frequent users of the Internet and cell phones, and, to varying degrees, are engaged with user-generated content. Members of all four Elite Users segments typically have high levels of satisfaction about the role of information and communication technology in their lives. The four segments comprising this broad group differ, however, on whether they believe the wide range of information, technology, and communication options is positive or negative.

- *Middle-of-the-Road Users* (20% of all U.S. adults) consists of two segments whose outlook toward information technology is task-oriented (see Figure 17.20). Middle-of-the-Road Users tend to use information and communication technologies for specific tasks more than for self-expression. While the two segments in this group share similar behaviors and orientation, they differ with regard to their views of communication technologies: one segment finds their pattern of information technology use satisfying and beneficial, while the other finds it burdensome.

- Individuals with *Few Technology Assets* (49%) lie at the other end of the continuum. Four segments comprise this group, united in the belief that modern and widely accepted technology resides on the periphery of their daily lives. Some find it useful, others don't, and others simply stick to the "plain old" telephone and television.

An excerpt from the Pew Internet & American Life report is provided in the online supplemental readings. The following excerpts are provided:

- The *Executive Summary* (report pages i to vi) provides an overview of the findings, paying particular attention to the defining and distinguishing characteristics of each

	Group Name	% of Adult Population	Key Insights
Elite Tech Users (31% of U.S. adults)	Omnivores	8%	They have the most information gadgets and services, which they use voraciously to participate in cyberspace and express themselves online and do a range of Web 2.0 activities such as blogging or managing their own Web pages.
	Connectors	7%	Between featured-packed cell phones and frequent online use, they connect to people and manage digital content using information communication technologies (ICTs)—all with high levels of satisfaction about how ICTs let them work with community groups and pursue hobbies.
	Lackluster Veterans	8%	They are frequent users of the Internet and less avid about cell phones. They are not thrilled with ICT-enabled connectivity.
	Productivity Enhancers	8%	They have strongly positive views about how technology lets them keep up with others, do their jobs, and learn new things.
Middle-of-the-Road Users (20% of U.S. adults)	Mobile Centrics	10%	They fully embrace the functionality of their cell phones. They use the Internet, but not often, and like how ICTs connect them to others.
	Connected But Hassled	10%	They have invested in a lot of technology, but they find the connectivity intrusive and information something of a burden.
Few Tech Assets (49% of U.S. adults)	Inexperienced Experimenters	8%	They occasionally take advantage of interactivity, but if they had more experience, they might do more with ICTs.
	Light But Satisfied	15%	They have some technology, but it does not play a central role in their daily lives. They are satisfied with what ICTs do for them.
	Indifferents	11%	Despite having either cell phones or online access, these users use ICTs only intermittently and find connectivity annoying.
	Off The Network	15%	Those with neither cell phones nor Internet connectivity tend to be older adults who are content with old media.

FIGURE 17.20 Pew Information and Communication Technology Segments

of the 10 information and communication technology groups. Note how these groups meet the criteria discussed earlier in this chapter: with regard to classification and descriptive measures, individuals within a group are very similar to each other and very different from individuals in other groups.[38]

- A detailed description of one segment within each of the three broad groups follows the Executive Summary. *Omnivores* (who are part of the Elite Users) are described on report pages 8 to 11, *Mobile Centric* (who are part of the Middle-of-the-Road Users) are described on report pages 21 to 23, and *Inexperienced Experimenters* (one of the four Few Technology Assets groups) are described on report pages 27 to 29. Notice how the in-depth discussion of each group provides comparable, detailed information that relates back to the initial informational focus of the study: assets, actions, and attitudes.

- An overview of the study methodology concludes the excerpts (report pages 54 to 55).

Generation C

This chapter discussed the four main types of classification and descriptive variables: demographics, psychographics, geography, and brand and category attitudes and behaviors. The Pew information and technology segments were formed through a combination of measures. There are times, however, when the basis for segmentation relies exclusively on one type of measure. This is the case of Generation C, which is defined by a set of category attitudes and (especially) behaviors.

The label "Generation C' was coined by Trendspotting[39] and refers not to a demographic group but rather to individuals of all ages who produce and share content. These individuals mix their own music, edit their own videos, post their photography to the Internet, or write books and blogs. They are active social networkers and represent a large group of individuals, estimated to now exceed 53 million U.S. adults. Generation C's motivation for participating in these activities is personal and expressive; they write a blog for the fun of it, or they put together a slideshow of photos to e-mail to friends and family.

The identification of segments such as Generation C is only the first step in the development of successful advertising strategy. Successful strategy requires one to completely understand the characteristics of a segment and to identify the implications of these characteristics for future decision making. The online supplemental readings present an excellent example of this type of in-depth understanding and analysis: Dan Pankraz's presentation *Generation C - A Look Into Their World*. This presentation demonstrates the type of in-depth analysis required for successful strategy development and illustrates that this analysis can be as creative and compelling as the topic (or in this case, segment) that is being described.[40]

SUMMARY

Consumer segmentation is the process of dividing a population into distinct smaller subgroups where individuals in a specific group are similar to each other in terms of important characteristics and possess characteristics different from individuals in other groups. Marketers and advertisers segment populations because it makes them more efficient and increases their chances for marketplace success. Segmentation accomplishes this by helping marketers and advertisers take into account and respond to differences within the consumer's audience.

Consumer segmentation research defines segments using characteristics that fall into one or more of the following areas:

- demographics (age, gender, household, life stage, race, ethnicity, social class, lifestyle),
- geographics (region, population size, population density, climate),
- psychographics (attitudes, values, motivations, and lifestyle), and
- category and brand-related attitudes and behaviors (product usage, brand loyalty, and benefits).

The segmentation research used by a marketer or advertiser can either be customized to meet a unique information need or it can be an adaptation of consumer segmentation research developed and syndicated by others. Regardless of the approach taken, similar criteria are used to select segments for communication emphasis. The most commonly used criteria applicable to all segmentation research are segment size, media accessibility, message availability, responsiveness, sustainability, and evaluation. Four additional criteria are applicable to product-related segmentation: profitability, competition defendability, and compatibility.

Customized (original) segmentation research begins similarly to other quantitative research. The need for the research is identified, segmentation is selected as an appropriate response to the information need, and sample and sampling issues are addressed. The actual segmentation research then proceeds through the following steps:

- Explicitly state the research question(s)
- Identify the range of classification and descriptive variables
- Reduce the list of segmentation and descriptive variables
- Sample and survey the population
- If necessary, reduce the data to a manageable number of factors or dimensions
- Use the classification variables to form segments
- Describe segments using descriptive variables
- Create a narrative or persona for each segment
- Evaluate segments for communication priority
- Develop segment-specific communication strategy

There are three major syndicated approaches to segmentation: psychographic, brand and product usage, and geodemographics.

- VALS is one of the most commonly used psychographic segmentations. VALS divides the adult population into eight groups based on their responses to the VALS questionnaire. The main dimensions of the VALS segmentation are primary motivation and resources. VALS consists of the following groups: Innovators, Survivors, Thinkers, Believers, Achievers, Strivers, Experiencers, and Makers.

- The data provided by Experian Simmons and Mediamark Research & Intelligence permits consumer goods segmentation. Marketers and advertisers use to data to better understand the demographic, attitudinal, and brand usage characteristics of segments defined in terms of category and brand-specific behaviors.

- Geodemographic segmentation segments the population on dimensions related to demographics, media usage, lifestyle choices, possessions, and purchase behaviors. These characteristics are used to classify each census block or household in the United States into a cluster so that blocks and households within a cluster are similar to each other and dissimilar to those in other clusters. While there is a variance among geodemographic research companies in terms of the number of clusters formed, the final segmentation of each company typically reflects a continuum of economic, life stage, and lifestyle characteristics.

Review Questions

1. What is the goal of a consumer segmentation study?
2. What are the defining characteristics of segments?
3. What are the two underlying assumptions of segmentation research?
4. Identify and briefly describe the reasons why advertisers use segmentation research.
5. List and briefly describe the criteria used to select segments in all types of segmentation research.
6. List and briefly describe the criteria used to select segments in product-related segmentation research.
7. What are the four main categories of variables used in segmentation research?
8. Define classification and descriptive variables? What is the function of each?
9. Describe how demographic characteristics can be used as classification variables.
10. Explain life stage segmentation.
11. Describe how geographic characteristics can be used as classification variables.
12. Define psychographics.
13. What are the primary types of psychographic measures?
14. Describe how psychographic characteristics can be used as classification variables.
15. Describe how category and brand-related behaviors can be used as classification variables.
16. Can behavioral segmentation only be conducted for consumer products? Explain.
17. What are the steps through which an original segmentation study passes?

18. Why is it important to start a segmentation study by explicitly stating the research question(s)?
19. How does a researcher identify and select classification and descriptive variables?
20. How are classification variables used to form segments?
21. What is a persona? How is it used to communicate segment characteristics?
22. What are the three main approaches to syndicated segmentation?
23. What type of segmentation is VALS?
24. What is VALS' basic assumption? On what two dimensions does VALS base its classification?
25. What are the defining characteristics of VALS Innovators and Survivors?
26. What two groups comprise VALS Ideals segments? What are their defining characteristics?
27. What two groups comprise VALS Achievement segments? What are their defining characteristics?
28. What two groups comprise VALS Self-Expression segments? What are their defining characteristics?
29. Describe how VALS contributes to advertising planning and decision making.
30. Describe how Experian Simmons and MRI data contribute to advertising planning and decision making.
31. Define geodemographic segmentation. How do advertisers and marketers use geodemographic segmentation?

Application Exercises

Application exercises 1 through 8 reflect chapter content and discussion.

1. Your agency has just acquired the Health Nation account. Health Nation is a holding company that owns Health Maintenance Organizations (HMOs) in 11 cities (Atlanta, Boise, Boston, Chicago, Denver, Los Angeles, New Orleans, New York, Phoenix, Spokane, and Tulsa). Health Nation has requested the agency to develop one advertising campaign that can be used in all cities in which they do business. They suggest a 30-second commercial targeted to all adults. They suggest further that the commercial should have a five-second donut in the center where the names of their specific hospitals in each city can be inserted.

As the agency researcher, you suggest that the development of a single commercial targeted to all adults may not be the best approach. You feel that this target definition may be too broad and that there may be important differences among (1) the 11 cities in which the advertising is scheduled to appear and (2) different groups of individuals within each city. As a result, you believe that segmentation research may be a necessary prerequisite to the advertising planning process. Others at the agency are not convinced of the importance of segmentation in this instance after you informally propose the idea.

Write a memo to others on the agency brand team (consisting of account management, creative, and media) that attempts to convince them that segmentation research is necessary in this instance. Your memo should, at minimum, address the following issues:

- The reasons why segmentation is necessary.
- The manner in which the segmentation will contribute to better, more successful advertising.
- The characteristics that you propose using to segment and describe the population (with a justification for their selection).
- The potential outcomes and application to advertising planning process.

When writing your memo, remember that your audience is not interested in a theoretical discussion. Be certain to present your argument, examples, and recommendations within the context of your client, Health Nation. Feel free to incorporate relevant information from secondary sources that supports your argument.

2. Congratulations. Your memo was successful. The agency and Health Nation have agreed to conduct segmentation research before the development of the advertising campaign. Health Nation, however, is still unclear on the details. Write a letter to Mary Ford, Health Nation's Director of Advertising, that describes the specific steps you will ttake to conduct the research and the outcomes that she can expect from each step. Be certain to

- focus the discussion on Health Nation;
- provide detailed, relevant examples of actions, decisions, and potential outcomes; and
- inform Mary of your expectations of her (i.e., at what stages will she need to be involved and what types of decisions will she have to make?).

3. Figures 17.14 through 17.16 present three different ways to describe Firefly Research's *Adventurers* segment. Select one of the remaining three segments from this research, and then review the data presented in Figures 17.8 through 17.13. Create a summary sheet, narrative, and persona to describe the segment of your choice.

4. Figure 17.12 presents the decision drivers identified by Firefly Research. Create a list of 10 additional decision drivers that you believe can help to differentiate the four segments. Prepare a short paper that provides that rationale for your recommendation.

5. Figure 17.13 presents the attitude statements used by Firefly Research. Create a list of 15 additional attitude statements that you believe can help to differentiate the four segments. Prepare a short paper that provides that rationale for your recommendation.

6. The VALS Web site allows you read about the eight VALS groups and then take a survey to determine your VALS group. In order to prepare for this activity, first review the discussion of VALS types on pages 494 to 496. Next complete each of the following steps, putting your response together in exactly the manner described.

Page 1:   Before taking the survey, predict your VALS group. Write one to two paragraphs that explain your rationale for group selection. Be certain to relate your discussion to the descriptions provided on the VALS Web site.

Page 2:   Read about the VALS survey at http://www.strategicbusinessinsights.com/vals/presurvey.shtml. Then, using the link on the bottom of the page, take the survey. Print out the "Results" page that notes your VALS classification.

Pages 3–4: Compare your prediction with the actual classification. If the classification was not as expected, speculate as to why not. Regardless of whether or not your prediction was correct, review the questionnaire and select the four to seven questions you think carried the most weight in determining your assignment. Provide and then, explain why you selected these items. (Note: There is not a one-to-one relationship between individual VALS questions and a VALS group; the scoring algorithm is complex.)

Page 5:   Select one of the remaining VALS groups (you cannot select the group predicted in the prior exercise or, if different, the group in which you were classified). Answer the survey in a way that reflects how you believe a member of the selected group would answer. Did VALS predict membership in your selected group? Explain the results.

7. Select a brand. Identify the VALS segment to which you think the advertising for that brand should be targeted. Discuss and provide a rationale for your selected segment.

8. You are the researcher on the Lean Cuisine account. The types of information collected on Lean Cuisine and competitive products are shown in Figure 17.21, an excerpt from the MRI questionnaire. Use the discussion on page 502 as a model to identify at least seven questions that the data can help answer regarding the users of Lean Cuisine and competitive brands. Present your questions.

Application exercises 9 through 10 refer to the Pew research study provided in the online supplemental readings.

9. Examine the characteristics that distinguish the 10 segments in the Pew study. Prepare a short (less than 20 questions) survey that could be used to assign individuals to one of the ten segments. Then, compare your questionnaire to that used by Pew to label individuals with regard to segments.[41] Prepare a short paper that compares your questionnaire to that used by Pew, paying particular attention to areas of overlap and divergence.

10. The Pew Web site allows you to take a survey and determine, based on the survey responses, the technology segment to which you most likely belong (see Endnote 41). Review the characteristics of the 10 technology segments shown in Figure 17.20, and then using this survey do the following:

   • Before taking the survey, predict your technology segment. Write two to three short paragraphs that explain your rationale for group selection. Then, take the Pew survey. Was your prediction correct? If your prediction was not correct, why (based on your answers to the Pew survey) do you think you were assigned to that group?

   • Select one of the remaining nine technology segments (you cannot select the segment predicted in the prior exercise). Answer the survey in a way that reflects how you believe a member of the selected segment would answer. Did the Pew survey predict membership in your selected segment? Explain the results.

Application exercises 11 through 12 refer to the Generation C report in the online supplemental readings.

11. The Generation C presentation notes that this segment of individuals is older than might be expected (average age 24) and contains a broad age range of individuals (generally those aged 10 to 35). This might imply that there are "mini-segments" within this larger segment. Prepare a short paper that compares 14- to 17-year-old Generation C members to those aged 30 to 35.

Page 93

FOOD

CANNED TOMATOES

	Your Household: Used in last 6 months	Cans/last 30 days
	802	
TOTAL:	☐	____ 00
TYPES:		
Crushed	☐	____ 01
Diced/Chunky/Wedge	☐	____ 02
Paste	☐	____ 03
Sauce	☐	____ 04
Stewed	☐	____ 05
Whole	☐	____ 06
Other	☐	____ 07
BRANDS:		
Contadina	☐	____ 08
Del Monte	☐	____ 09
Hunt's	☐	____ 10
Muir Glen	☐	____ 11
Progresso	☐	____ 12
Red Gold	☐	____ 13
Ro*Tel	☐	____ 14
S & W	☐	____ 15
Store's Own Brand	☐	____ 16
OTHER (Write In)	☐	____ 999

CANNED OR JARRED VEGETABLES

	Your Household: Used in last 6 months	Cans or jars/last 30 days
	803	
TOTAL:	☐	____ 00
TYPES:		
No Salt	☐	____ 01
Salt-Packed	☐	____ 02
KINDS:		
Beans	☐	____ 03
Carrots	☐	____ 04
Corn	☐	____ 05
Mixed	☐	____ 06
Peas	☐	____ 07
Spinach	☐	____ 08
FORMS:		
Canned	☐	____ 09
Jarred	☐	____ 10
BRANDS:		
Allens	☐	____ 11
Bush's	☐	____ 12
Del Monte	☐	____ 13
Food Club	☐	____ 14
Freshlike	☐	____ 15
Goya	☐	____ 16
Green Giant	☐	____ 17
Hanover	☐	____ 18
Le Sueur	☐	____ 19
Libby's	☐	____ 20
Stokely's	☐	____ 21
S & W	☐	____ 22
Veg-All	☐	____ 23
Store's Own Brand	☐	____ 24
OTHER (Write In)	☐	____ 999

CANNED STEWS

	Your Household: Used in last 6 months	Cans/last 30 days
	804	
TOTAL:	☐	____ 00
BRANDS:		
Castleberry's	☐	____ 01
Dinty Moore	☐	____ 02
Store's Own Brand	☐	____ 03
OTHER (Write In)	☐	____ 999

CANNED OR JARRED SPAGHETTI & MACARONI

	Your Household: Used in last 6 months	Cans/jars last 30 days
	805	
TOTAL:	☐	____ 00
BRANDS:		
Chef Boyardee	☐	____ 01
SpaghettiOs	☐	____ 02
Store's Own Brand	☐	____ 03
OTHER (Write In)	☐	____ 999

SPAGHETTI/PASTA SAUCE

	Your Household: Used in last 6 months	Containers/last 30 days
	806	
TOTAL:	☐	____ 00
TYPES:		
Canned	☐	____ 01
Jarred	☐	____ 02
KINDS:		
Low Fat/Low Sugar	☐	____ 03
Regular	☐	____ 04
FORMS:		
Refrigerated	☐	____ 05
Non-Refrigerated	☐	____ 06
BRANDS:		
Barilla	☐	____ 07
Bertolli	☐	____ 08
Classico	☐	____ 09
Del Monte	☐	____ 10
Francesco Rinaldi	☐	____ 11
Healthy Choice	☐	____ 12
Hunt's	☐	____ 13
Muir Glen	☐	____ 14
Newman's Own	☐	____ 15
Prego Chunky Garden	☐	____ 16
Prego Meat Sauce	☐	____ 17
Prego Organic	☐	____ 18
Prego Regular	☐	____ 19
Other Prego	☐	____ 20
Progresso	☐	____ 21
Ragú Cheese Creations	☐	____ 22
Ragú Chunky Gardenstyle	☐	____ 23
Ragú Light	☐	____ 24
Ragú Old World Style	☐	____ 25
Ragú Organic	☐	____ 26
Ragú Rich & Meaty	☐	____ 27
Ragú Robusto!	☐	____ 28
Other Ragú	☐	____ 29
Store's Own Brand	☐	____ 30
OTHER (Write In)	☐	____ 999

CANNED TUNA

	Your Household: Used in last 6 months	Cans/last 30 days
	797	
TOTAL:	☐	____ 00
TYPES:		
Low Sodium	☐	____ 01
Regular	☐	____ 02
FORMS:		
Packed in water	☐	____ 03
Packed in oil	☐	____ 04
KINDS:		
Solid white	☐	____ 05
Chunk light	☐	____ 06
Chunk white	☐	____ 07
BRANDS:		
Bumble Bee	☐	____ 08
Chicken of the Sea	☐	____ 09
Geisha	☐	____ 10
StarKist	☐	____ 11
3 Diamonds	☐	____ 12
Store's Own Brand	☐	____ 13
OTHER (Write In)	☐	____ 999

PACKAGED, FROZEN, REFRIGERATED PASTA

	Your Household: Used in last 6 months	Packages/last 30 days
	808	
TOTAL:	☐	____ 00
TYPES:		
Dry	☐	____ 01
Frozen	☐	____ 02
Refrigerated (Fresh)	☐	____ 03
FORMS:		
Long	☐	____ 04
Stuffed	☐	____ 05
Other	☐	____ 06
BRANDS:		
American Beauty	☐	____ 07
Barilla	☐	____ 08
Barilla Plus	☐	____ 09
Buitoni	☐	____ 10
Celentano	☐	____ 11
Contadina	☐	____ 12
Creamette	☐	____ 13
De Cecco	☐	____ 14
Di Giorno	☐	____ 15
Dreamfields	☐	____ 16
Golden Grain/Mission	☐	____ 17
Light 'n Fluffy	☐	____ 18
Mueller's	☐	____ 19
No Yolks	☐	____ 20
Pennsylvania Dutch	☐	____ 21
Prince Pasta	☐	____ 22
Ronzoni	☐	____ 23
Rosetto	☐	____ 24
San Giorgio	☐	____ 25
Skinner	☐	____ 26
Stouffer's	☐	____ 27
Uncle Ben's	☐	____ 28
Store's Own Brand	☐	____ 29
OTHER (Write In)	☐	____ 999

LUNCH COMBINATIONS/ KITS

	Your Household: Used in last 6 months	Packages/last 30 days
	810	
TOTAL:	☐	____ 00
BRANDS:		
Armour LunchMakers	☐	____ 01
Bumble Bee Lunch on the Run	☐	____ 02
Lunchables (Oscar Mayer)	☐	____ 03
Lunchables Maxed Out	☐	____ 04
Lunchables Pizza (Oscar Mayer)	☐	____ 05
Starkist Lunch To-Go	☐	____ 06
Store's Own Brand	☐	____ 07
OTHER (Write In)	☐	____ 999

FIGURE 17.21 MRI Questionnaire: Prepared Dinners (reproduced with permission of Mediamark Research & Intelligence)

Beyond differences in age, income, and other demographics, how do you think the two groups differ in terms of key attitudes, behaviors, and motivations? Beyond the content of the paper itself, write and include a persona for each mini-segment.

12. The Generation C presentation ends with a list of 10 things to keep in mind with regard to reaching these individuals. Prepare a short paper that adds five additional items to this list. Be certain to fully explain and provide a rationale for your additions, using secondary research where appropriate.

Endnotes

1. The Pew segmentation study is entitled "Generations Online 2009" and is at http://www.pewinternet.org/Reports/2009/Generations-Online-in-2009.aspx?r=1. The generational classification is from this source.

2. The data presented in Figure 17.2 is from Pew Internet & American Life Project "Generations Online 2007" at http://www.pewinternet.org/Infographics/Generational-differences-in-online-activities.aspx.

3. Figure 17.3 is reprinted with permission of SocialMedia8 (http://www.socialmedia8.com/) and is taken from *Barak Obama Strategy Case Study* at http://www.slideshare.net/socialmedia8/case-study-the-barack-obama-strategy. This case is an excellent introduction to the use and power of segmentation in the development of message strategies.

4. SubscriberMail (2008). "Email Segmentation Strategies" at http://www.subscribermail.com.

5. For an extended discussion of the criteria used to evaluate segments, see Sally Dibb (1999). "Criteria Guiding Segmentation Implementation." *Journal of Strategic Marketing* 7 (2): 107–129.

6. These four categories are the most common categories of segmentation variables. A fifth approach to segmentation, cognitive segmentation, has been proposed but is not yet widely accepted. For insights into cognitive segmentation, see Francois Carrillat et al. (2009). "Cognitive Segmentation: Modeling the Structure and Content of Customers' Thoughts." *Psychology & Marketing* 26 (6): 479–506.

7. Another example of classification and descriptive variables can be found in Howard B. Moss, Susan D. Kirby, and Fred Donodeo (2009). "Characterizing and Reaching High-Risk Drinkers Using Audience Segmentation." *Alcoholism: Clinical and Experimental Research* 33 (8): 1336–1345. This study used drinking behaviors as the classification variables and then used demographics, geographic information, lifestyles, health-related behaviors, interests, and cultural values as the descriptive variables.

8. For additional insights into life stage segmentation, see Interactive Advertising Bureau (2008). "The IAB Lifestages Segmentation Study" at http://www.iab.net/insights_research/530422/1672/223276 and Bryan Brenner (2009). "Life-Event Segmenting Offers Optimaization of Benefit Effectiveness." *Journal of Financial Service Professionals* (May): 26–29.

9. Travel Industry of America (2002). "Travel Through the Life Stages, 2002 Edition" at http://www.tia.org/uploads/research/pdf/lifestage02_es.pdf

10. Linda Morton (2008). "Market Segmentation by Life Stage" at http://www.strategicmarketsegmentation.com/blog/market-segmentation-by-life-stage-market-segments/

11. Gyan P. Nyaupane and Alan R. Graefe (2008). "Travel Distance: A Tool for Nature-Based Tourism Market Segmentation." *Journal of Travel & Tourism Marketing* 25 (3): 355–366.

12. The Center for Generational Studies (2008). "The Psychographics of the Emerging Consumer" at http://www.gentrends.com/ClientResources/IAAM%20Psychographics%20web.pdf.

13. Carol M. Morgan and Doran J. Levy (1993). *Segmenting the Mature Market* (Chicago, IL: Probus Publishing Company).

14. Rita Koselka (1994). "Hope and Fear as Marketing Tools." *Forbes*: 78–79.

15. Jean-Paul Ruiz, Jean-Charles Chebat, and Pierre Hansen (2003). "Another Trip to the Mall: A

Segmentation Study of Consumers Based on Their Activities." *Journal of Retailing and Consumer Services* 11: 333–350.

16. See Ontario Ministry of Tourism at http://www.tourism.gov.on.ca/english/research/travel_activities/ index.html.

17. Centers for Disease Control and Prevention (undated). "Segmenting Audiences to Promote Energy Balance" at http://www.cdc.gov/nccdphp/dnpa/socialmarketing/pdf/audience_segmentation.pdf.

18. Michael C. Bellas (2006). "Motivational Need States and How We Need to Think." *Beverage World* (June 15): 67.

19. Russell I. Haley (1995). "Benefit Segmentation: A Decision-Oriented Research Tool." *Marketing Management* 4 (1): 59–63.

20. This discussion is modeled after Emine Sarigollu and Rong Huang (2009). "Benefit Segmentation of Visitors to Latin America." *Journal of Travel Research* 43(February): 277–293. The methodology, data, conclusions, and implications, however, are fictitious in order to better illustrate discussion points. Figures 17.14 through 17.16 are original to this text. Firefly Research is a fictitious company.

21. Factor analysis is discussed in the next chapter.

22. The most common form of cluster analysis is the "nearest neighbor approach." Here, each respondent's pattern of response is examined. The first two cases combined into a cluster are those that have the smallest distance (or largest similarity) between them. The distance between a new cluster and each succeeding new case is then computed as the minimum distance between an individual case and a case in the cluster. At every step, the distance between two clusters is the distance between their two closest points. This process forms segments such that cases within a segment are very similar to each other and very different from cases in other clusters.

23. For additional information on personas, see Tina Calabria (2004). "An Introduction to Personas and How to Create Them" at http://www.steptwo.com.au/papers/kmc_personas; George Olson (2004). "Making Personas More Powerful: Details to Drive Strategic and Tactical Design" at http://www.boxesandarrows.com/view/making_personas_more_powerful_details_to_drive_strategic_and_tactical_design; Steve Mulder (undated). "The User Is Always Right: Making Personas Work for Your Site" at http://www.slideshare.net/MulderMedia/the-user-is-always-right-making-personas-work-for-your-site.

24. Entry to the VALS Web site is at http://www.strategicbusinessinsights.com/vals. VALS is the registered trademark of Strategic Business Insights.

25. Strategic Business Insights (2009). "About VALS" at http://www.strategicbusinessinsights.com/vals/about.shtml

26. Strategic Business Insights (2009). "US Framework and VALS Types" at http://www.strategicbusinessinsights.com/vals/ustypes.shtml.

27. All VALS segment descriptions are provided by Strategic Business Insights, op. cit.

28. Strategic Business Insights (2009). "Applications of VALS: Communications" at http://www.strategicbusinessinsights.com/vals/applications/apps-com.shtml.

29. Strategic Business Insights (2009). "Applications of VALS: Positioning" at http:// www.strategicbusinessinsights.com/vals/applications/apps-pos.shtml.

30. Strategic Business Insights (2009). "Applications of VALS: New Product Development" at http:// www.strategicbusinessinsights.com/vals/applications/apps-npd.shtml.

31. Both Experian Simmons (http://www.smrb.com/web/guest/home) and MRI (http://www.mediamark.com/showcontent.aspx?content=~/The_Survey_of_the_American_Consumer/000_The_Survey_Of_the_American_Consumer.xhtml) use complex sampling procedures to ensure that their samples of about 20,000 adults is representative of and generalizable to the overall U.S. population. For additional information on data collection procedures, see the each company's Web site.

32. All data is fictitious and used for illustrative purposes only.

33. This excerpt shows just some of the demographic information provided by Simmons and MRI. Additional information, for example, includes more detailed information on household characteristics, marital status, income, employment, and education.

34. The creation of geodemographic clusters based on information aggregated on the census block

level is a common and accepted procedure. However, one drawback of the use of aggregated data is the assumption that individuals within a census block are homogeneous. A new generation of geodemographic clustering makes this assumption unnecessary. Geodemographic research companies have refined their coding and analytical procedures to bring classification down to the household level. As a result, two houses side by side on the same street can be assigned to different clusters.

35. PRIZM allows you to see its system in action through the identification of clusters most associated with a zip code of the users' choice. This interactive tool can be found at http://www. claritas.com/MyBestSegments/Default.jsp?ID= 20&SubID=&pageName=ZIP%2BCode%2BLook-up.

36. Segment descriptions can be found at http:// www.claritas.com/MyBestSegments/Default. jsp?ID=30&SubID=&pageName=Segment% 2BLook-up.

37. Study descriptions and outcomes are adapted from John B. Horrigan (2007). "A Typology of Information and Communication Technology Users" at http://pewresearch.org/pubs/471/ a-typology-of-information-and-communication-technology-users and the study itself: "A Typology of Information and Communication Technology Users" at http://www.pewinternet. org/Reports/2007/A-Typology-of-Information-and-Communication-Technology-Users.aspx. The excerpt from the full research report as well as Figure 17.21 is from this latter source.

38. Note that the report uses "ICT" as a acronym for "information and communication technologies."

39. Trendspotting's Web site is http://www. trendspotting.com/.

40. The presentation is reproduced with permission and is available at http://www.slideshare. net/guest7e5b6a/generation-c-a-look-into-their-world-by-dan-pankraz-presentation. Additional insights on Generation C can be found at Pankraz's blog at http://danpankraz.wordpress. com.

41. The Pew questionnaire is located at http:// www.pewinternet.org/Participate/What-Kind-of-Tech-User-Are-You.aspx.

CHAPTER 18

Brand Mapping

Successful advertising strategy requires that an advertiser understand consumers' brand perceptions, in particular, the importance of various product attributes, the criteria consumers use to differentiate brands, and the perceived strengths and weaknesses of competitive brands. Brand mapping is the label for a set of techniques advertisers use to obtain insights in each of these areas. This chapter introduces you to three types of brand maps.

***

When you are done reading this chapter, you should have a better understanding of:

- the principal approaches to brand mapping
- the procedures used to construct each type of brand map
- how each approach to brand mapping makes a contribution to brand understanding, brand positioning, and advertising strategic decision making.

Advertisers rely on research to help them understand how consumers perceive the strengths and weaknesses of their brand and competitive brands. Brand maps facilitate this understanding by translating numeric data into visual representations. But brand maps can do more even more. Brand maps can help advertisers better understand the benefits valued by different groups of consumers or they can make explicit consumer perceptions across a broad range of attitudes. This chapter discusses three types of brand maps: perceptual maps, correspondence maps, and concept maps.

PERCEPTUAL MAPS

Perceptual maps, the most common form of brand map, provide a visual representation of consumers' attitudes, typically in terms of the perceived strengths and weaknesses of brands that compete in the same category. When used in this way, a perceptual map tells us: (1) the dimensions consumers use to evaluate brands, (2) the strengths and weaknesses of brands with regard to these dimensions, (3) a brand's competitive set, and (4) the brand's strengths and weaknesses with regard to consumers' perceptions of the ideal brand.

This section focuses on perceptual maps, as follows: The initial discussion focuses on why perceptual maps are important and how they provide insights into consumers' brand attitudes. This discussion is followed by a description of the research steps used to create a perceptual map. The section ends with a discussion of how perceptual maps contribute to advertising strategy.

What Perceptual Maps Tell Us

THE DIMENSIONS CONSUMERS USE TO EVALUATE BRANDS.   Research indicates that consumers try to evaluate brands using the least amount of time and energy. They accomplish this by identifying and then using a few broad dimensions[1] to compare brands or products rather than by remembering and using all of the multiple, narrower individual product attributes. It is much easier, for example, to remember that a particular laundry detergent "cleans extremely well" rather than having to remember that it "gets colored clothes clean," "gets out stains well," "brightens whites," etc. Here, "cleans extremely well" is a dimension, a broad descriptor that encompasses all of the more specific attributes. Perceptual mapping makes explicit the dimensions consumers use to evaluate brands and products. Consumers in highly complex or high involvement categories typically use more dimensions to evaluate brands and products; less complex and lower involvement categories are typically those where fewer dimensions are used.

The perceptual map shown in Figure 18.1a is the beginning of a map of social networking sites.[2] The map indicates that consumers use two dimensions to evaluate social networking sites: how easy or difficult it is to use the site and how passé (old and dated) or cutting-edge the site is thought to be. Note that each dimension is a continuum and that both ends of each continuum are labeled, with the positive ends of each continuum pointing up and to the right. The use of two dimensions results in four quadrants, labeled in Figure 18.1b from I to IV. Quadrant II is generally the best place for a brand

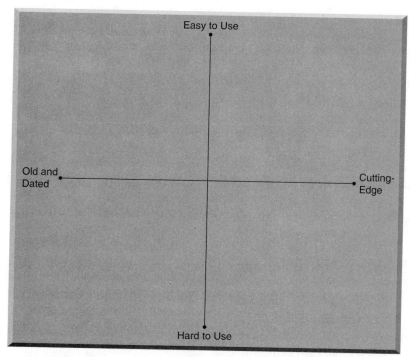

FIGURE 18.1a   Dimensions Used to Form Perceptual Map

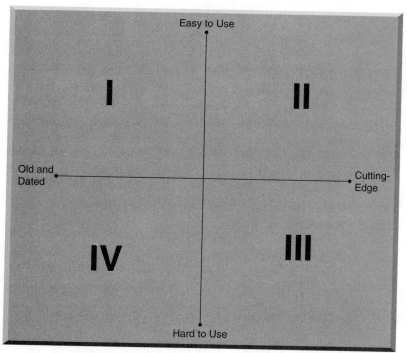

FIGURE 18.1b   Perceptual Map Quadrants

to be as it is the place where positive aspects of both dimensions fall. Quadrant IV is generally the worst place for a brand to be as it is the place where negative aspects of both dimensions fall.

STRENGTHS AND WEAKNESSES OF INDIVIDUAL BRANDS. Once dimensions are identified, individual brands are plotted on the map. As discussed earlier, brands that fall into Quadrant II are typically in the strongest competitive position, while the brands that fall into Quadrant IV are in the weakest position. Brands in the remaining two quadrants may have a mix of strengths and weaknesses or may be successful niche brands.

Figure 18.2a plots eight social networking sites on the perceptual map. Note that of all the brands plotted, only two fall into Quadrant II. These two brands are poised for success, being seen as both easy to use and cutting-edge. Four brands fall into Quadrant IV and are likely in serious trouble, offering nothing positive to the user as they are seen as both hard to use and passé.

IDENTIFYING THE COMPETITION. The closer two brands are on a perceptual map, the closer they compete in the consumers' mind. The further apart brands are, the less similar consumers' perceive them to be. The map shown in Figure 18.2a indicates that:

- Facebook and Bebo are in direct competition with each other, and are set apart from other social networking sites.
- Classmates, Friendster, Zorpia, and Yahoo! 360 are seen as similar, competitive sites.
- Myspace does not directly compete with other sites.
- Zanga does not directly compete with other sites.

THE IDEAL BRAND. Brands located in Quadrant II typically have a competitive advantage, as they are positively perceived on both dimensions. In order to determine which of the brands in Quadrant II is the relatively stronger, a perceptual map may also plot the "Ideal" brand, the brand that in the consumer's mind has all strengths and no weaknesses. Figure 18.2b adds the ideal brand to the perceptual map. Note that while the Ideal brand in this example is expected to be both easy to use and cutting edge (because it falls in Quadrant II), it is much more important that it be easy to use. As a result, although both Bebo and Facebook lie in Quadrant II, Bebo versus Facebook is the relatively stronger brand because it is closer to the Ideal.

Constructing a Perceptual Map

The prior section provided direction for interpreting a perceptual map. This section provides a step-by-step explanation for constructing a perceptual map. Fortunately, much of the computational "heavy lifting" is done by computer, leaving a researcher free to focus on the interpretation of the findings. The discussion focuses on constructing a perceptual map for Internet retail bookstores.[3]

ATTRIBUTE IDENTIFICATION. Perceptual maps begin with the creation of a list of specific category attributes. Because dimensions are built up from individual attributes, it is very

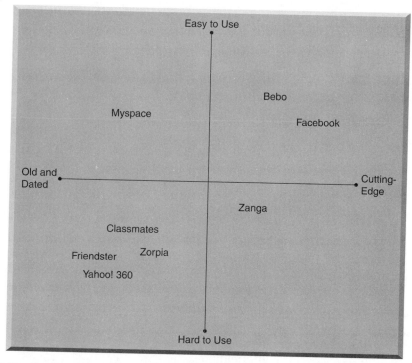

FIGURE 18.2a   Perceptual Map of Social Networking Sites

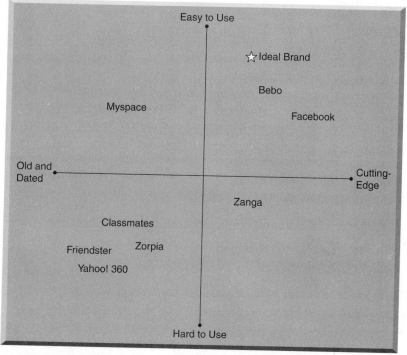

FIGURE 18.2b   Perceptual Map of Social Networking Sites: Ideal Brand Added

important that the list of brand and product attributes contain *all* attributes that are known to be (or that judgment or research indicates could potentially be) important in consumers' evaluation of target brands or products. Important dimensions cannot be discovered in the absence of their component attributes.

Next, rating scales are developed. These scales ask respondents to rate each brand or product (plus the Ideal brand) on each attribute. A consumer might, for example, be asked the following question:

> Below are listed the names of six Internet retail bookstores. Please indicate the extent to which you feel the phrase "the site always has what I'm looking for" applies to each bookstore. You can use any number between "1" (to represent "applies perfectly") and "10" (to represent "does not apply at all").

The rating of all brands on all attributes, and the subsequent mathematical combination of attributes into broader dimensions, reflects the underlying assumption of perceptual maps, that is, that a respondent's ratings of specific attributes reflect the underlying dimensions used to distinguish between brands. The 10 attributes used to evaluate the online bookstores are:

> The site always has what I'm looking for
> The site is a fun place to shop
> The site makes shopping easy
> The site's design makes shopping safe
> The site protects my personal information
> Shopping on the site is really boring
> I'm always surprised at what I find
> I'm not afraid to register on the site
> I look forward to shopping here
> The site will never misuse my personal data

DETERMINING THE NUMBER OF DIMENSIONS.   Chapter 16 explained correlation and the correlation coefficient, a computed number (such as +.76) that indicates the relationship between two measures. The sign indicates the direction of the relationship, while the strength of the relationship is reflected in the size of the coefficient. The larger the coefficient the stronger the relationship.

Examining and interpreting the correlation of one pair of measures is straightforward: you just need to note the direction and size of the correlation coefficient. Calculating and then examining correlation coefficients for multiple measures is more difficult because of the large number of correlation coefficients that need to be examined. The intercorrelation of 15 measures, for example, results in 105 pairs of correlations. *Factor analysis* solves this problem by identifying the relatively small number of factors or dimensions that represent the relationships among a large number of variables.

The process of factor analysis begins after consumers rate each of the target brands or products on each individual attribute. A statistical analysis program examines the set of ratings data and calculates the correlation coefficient for each pair of variables. After all pairs of correlation coefficients have been calculated, the program manipulates the pairs of correlation coefficients in order to create enough factors (typically equivalent to the number of attributes) to account for 100% of sample variance.[4] This can be seen in the following table. In the first column, the rows are numbered from 1 to 10, reflecting the fact that 10 attributes were evaluated. The total for the last column is 100%, noting that 100% of the variance has been accounted for.

Factor	Eigenvalue	Percent of Variance
1	5.71	57.1%
2	2.11	21.1
3	.67	6.7
4	.52	5.2
5	.38	3.8
6	.21	2.1
7	.18	1.8
8	.09	.9
9	.07	.7
10	.06	.6
TOTAL	**10.00**	**100.0%**

The remaining data provide more specific information.

- The second column reports eigenvalue, the amount of variance explained by each factor. This column is only important to the extent that it allows us to calculate the percentage in the next column.

- The third column translates eigenvalues into percentages. The total of the eigenvalue column is always equal to the number of attributes used in the research. Thus, factor one, with an eigenvalue of 5.71, accounts for 57.1% of total sample variance (calculated as 5.71 ÷ 10, the factor eigenvalue divided by the total number of attributes). The percent of variance is a very important calculation. It indicates a factor's importance to consumers. The greater the percent of variance accounted for by a factor, the more important that factor is to consumers when evaluating the brands and products explored in the research.

A researcher examines the percent of variance explained by each factor and then selects the number of factors to be used in subsequent analyses. Typically, *a researcher tries to select the least number of factors that explain the highest amount of sample variance.* It is understood that this is, in part, a subjective judgment. "High" is a relative term that will vary from study to study, but a total of 70% or more is generally acceptable. In this example, two factors would likely be selected as together they account for 78.2% of the variance. This number seems reasonable, as not much is gained by adding a third additional factor.[5] Once the number of factors is determined, the factor analysis computer program reanalyzes the data restricting the number of factors to the number selected by the researcher.

Next, the factor loading for each attribute is computed and examined. A factor loading indicates the degree of association between an individual measure and a factor,

Table A: Original Factor Loadings

Attribute	Factor 1	Factor 2
The site always has what I'm looking for	.987	.231
The site is a fun place to shop	.675	.033
The Web site makes shopping easy	.656	−.123
The site's design is makes shopping safe	.034	.567
The site protects my personal information	−.231	.655
Shopping is really boring	−.756	.343
I'm always surprised at what I find	.790	−.321
I'm not afraid to register on the site	.321	.791
I look forward to shopping here	.887	.321
The site will never misuse my personal data	−.188	.765

Table B: Ordered Factor Loadings

Attribute	Factor 1	Factor 2
The site always has what I'm looking for	**.987**	.231
I look forward to shopping here	**.887**	.321
I'm always surprised at what I find	**.790**	−.321
Shopping is really exiting	**.756**	−.343
The site is a fun place to shop	**.675**	.033
The Web site makes shopping easy	**.656**	−.123
I'm not afraid to register on the site	.321	**.791**
The site will never misuse my personal data	−.188	**.765**
The site protects my personal information	−.231	**.655**
The site's design is makes shopping safe	.034	**.567**

FIGURE 18.3 Association Between Attributes and Factors

and is interpreted similar to a correlation coefficient: a positive factor loading indicates a positive association between a measure and a factor, while a negative loading indicates a negative association. The strength of association is reflected in the numeric portion of the factor loading. Factor loadings, showing the relationship of each attribute with each factor, are typically presented in a format similar to that shown in Table A in Figure 18.3.

Once this table is generated, it then becomes necessary to find the one factor with which each attribute has the strongest association. This is easily found: it is the largest number in each row regardless of the sign. The first attribute, "the site always has what I'm looking for," for example, is most associated with Factor 1. The fifth attribute, "the site protects my personal information," is most associated with Factor 2. Once the association of each attribute with each factor has been determined, it is often useful to reorder and highlight the associations to make the pattern easier to see, as demonstrated in Table B in Figure 18.3. In addition, interpretation is easier when each attribute has a positive association with its factor. Negative signs can be eliminated by reversing the attribute description and then reversing the signs of the associated factor loading. For example, the negative sign for "really boring" was eliminated when the description was changed to "really exciting." Compare this statement and factor associations in Tables A and B in Figure 18.3.

Next, the researcher names each factor where the name chosen reflects the common or shared characteristics of the attributes most associated with that factor. Names are based on researcher judgment, and dimension names can reflect either logical or emotional sets of underlying attitudes. As illustrated earlier, dimension names should be a continuum and should accurately reflect the common characteristics of the underlying attributes. In this example, the two factors might be named:

- Factor 1: Shopping experience (excellent to poor)
- Factor 2: Shopping safety (very safe to not at all safe)

The prior steps allow a researcher to determine the number and characteristics of the dimensions consumers use to evaluate brands in a category. The final step is to place the brands on each map. In order to do this, a researcher needs to know each brand's average score for each factor. This computation is performed by the statistical analysis program. The score calculated for each brand represents the average rating of each brand for all of the measures comprising an individual factor. The average factor scores for seven Internet bookstores are shown in the following table. These numbers are used to place the brands on the map, resulting in the perceptual map shown in Figure 18.4. Note that the ends of the dimensions are labeled with the appropriate end of the factor continuum.

Brand Safety	Factor 1 Shopping Experience	Factor 2 Shopping
Amazon	3.5	3.5
Alibris	1.3	4.7
Bestsellers	4.0	−3.2
Bookdepot	3.5	−4.2
Bookspot	2.2	−3.8
Booktopia	−4.0	−4.2
Bookworld	−2.2	4.5
IDEAL	4.5	4.5

Note: Range of scores is −5 (lowest) to +5 (highest)

The key insights provided by the perceptual map shown in Figure 18.4 are:

- The Ideal brand is in the upper right-hand corner of Quadrant II. This means that consumers want both an excellent shopping experience and high shopping safety.
- Amazon and Alibris are in the best competitive position in Quadrant II. These brands are seen as most similar by consumers, although Amazon in the stronger competitive position being placed closer to the Ideal brand.
- Booktopia is in the worst position in Quadrant IV. The brand is alone in being seen as possessing neither of the benefits valued by consumers.

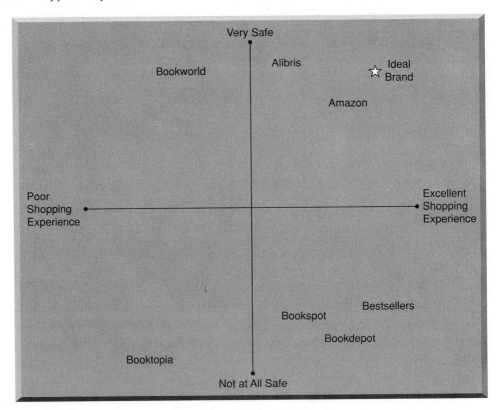

FIGURE 18.4   Brand Placement: Internet Bookstores

- Bookworld has no direct competition, as it is alone in Quadrant I. It possesses one out of the two benefits valued by consumers.
- Bookspot, Bestsellers, and Bookdepot directly compete with each other in Quadrant III. All three brands possess just one of the two benefits valued by consumers.

The last and most important step in perceptual mapping is to answer the question: "What do we do now?" Approaches to using perceptual maps for strategic planning are discussed in the next section.

Perceptual Maps and Advertising Strategy

Perceptual maps make a valuable contribution to the advertising planning process by identifying the dimensions consumers use to evaluate brands and their perceptions of brands on these dimensions. Advertisers using this information can decide on any number of actions that take into consideration their brand's placement. The following discussion illustrates some of the more common decisions, using the perceptual map shown in Figure 18.4.

BRANDS IN A STRONG COMPETITIVE POSITION.   Amazon and Alibris are in a strong competitive position relative to the other brands by virtue of their placement in Quadrant II. Consumers believe that these two sites possess both important benefits: shopping safety and an excellent shopping experience. Amazon, however, relative to Alibris, is in the stronger position due to its closer placement to the Ideal brand. Brands in this quadrant typically select one of three strategic approaches, depending upon their position, the position of competitors, and the position of the Ideal brand.

- Amazon would likely attempt to *defend* its strategic place. It is the strongest brand of all seven and closest to the Ideal brand. Amazon needs to continue to reinforce current perceptions with regard to both its specific characteristics and the characteristics desired of the Ideal brand.

- Alibris is faced with a different situation. While its own brand perceptions are very positive, it is in a relatively weaker position versus Amazon. Given this situation, three options are available if Alibris desires to change its competitive position. The result of each of these options, if successful, is shown in Figure 18.5. First, Alibris can reinforce current positions of its brand while attempting to degrade perceptions of Amazon. If successful, this strategy would move Amazon away from the Ideal, leaving Alibris the closer brand (Figure 18.5a). Second, it can attempt to improve its own image, by passing Amazon and moving itself closer to the Ideal (Figure 18.5b). In this case, since it is seen as being close to the Ideal on "Safety," it would have to focus entirely on improving perceptions of its shopping experience. Finally, Alibris can leave its own and Amazon's placements alone, attempting to move the Ideal brand closer to its brand, in effect trying to convince consumers that safety is more important than a superior shopping experience. If successful, Alibris will be the brand closest to the Ideal brand (Figure 18.5c).

BRANDS WITH A MODERATELY STRONG COMPETITIVE POSITION. Again referring to Figure 18.4, Bookworld, Bestsellers, Bookspot, and Bookdepot are in moderately strong competition positions, being placed in quadrants where they are perceived as having strength on one dimension and weakness on the other. Strategies available to these brands take into account their distance from the Ideal brand and the placement and number of competitive brands sharing their quadrant.

- Bookworld is in a unique position, as it is the only brand in its quadrant. Consumers' perceptions of Bookworld "Safety" are as high as both Alibris and the Ideal Brand. Two options are available to this brand. First, it can choose to remain where it is, becoming a niche brand catering to individuals who value just the single dimension of shopping safety. Second, it can attempt to improve consumers' perceptions of its shopping experience. If this latter strategy is successful, the brand would move from Quadrant I to Quadrant II, greatly improving its competitive position and actually moving the closest to the ideal brand (see Figure 18.5d).

- Bestsellers, Bookspot, and Bookdepot are in a very different position, as there are three closely placed brands in this quadrant. It is a highly competitive quadrant where all three brands are seen as being comparable, and as a result, where it would be difficult for one brand to distinguish itself from another if it remains in its current place. The most common option for brands in this position is to break away from the pack, in this situation by improving perceptions of shopping safety. Successful brands would move from Quadrant III to Quadrant II.

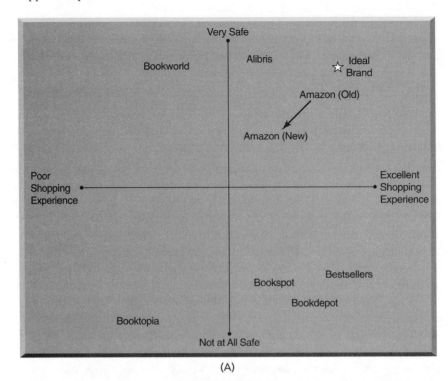

(A)

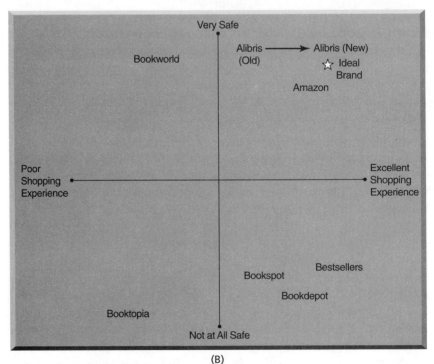

(B)

FIGURE 18.5 Potential Strategic Options

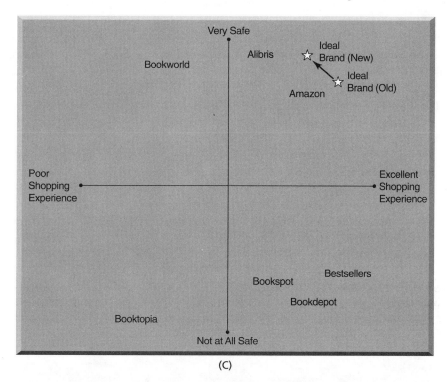

(C)

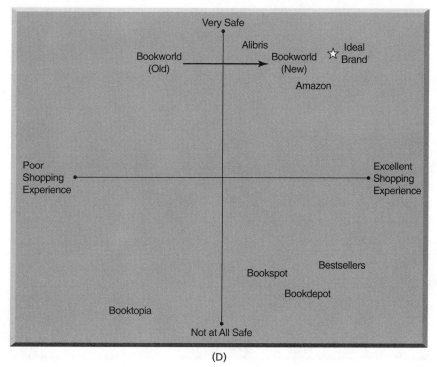

(D)

FIGURE 18.5 Potential Strategic Options (Continued)

Finally, there is a high risk but high reward option for brands in Quadrants I and III. Rather than attempt to move the brand into Quadrant II, a brand might decide to try and convince consumers to evaluate brands based on an entirely new dimension. If successful, and assuming this new dimension is a unique strength of the brand, the brand would find itself in the strongest competitive position, being the only brand close to the Ideal due to its strength in the original and new dimension. Imagine that Bestsellers is, of all the brands, the best "corporate citizen," donating 25% of all corporate revenue to charity, employing state-of-the-art environmental controls, purchasing energy from sustainable sources, etc. If Bestsellers can convince the target that this is much more important than having an excellent shopping experience, then the resulting map would resemble the one shown in Figure 18.6. Bestsellers moves closest to the new Ideal brand and becomes the only brand in this quadrant because it is the only brand with positive perceptions on the new dimension. Note that in this map brand placement reflects each brand's original perceptions of "Safety" and its new perceptions of "Corporate Citizen."

BRANDS IN A WEAK COMPETITIVE POSITION.   Brands in Quadrant IV face almost insurmountable hurdles to marketplace success because they are perceived as possessing *none* of the attributes of value to consumers. Since it is extremely difficult to reposition a

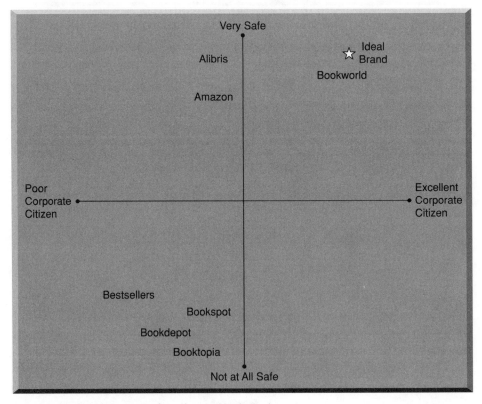

FIGURE 18.6 Brand Placement After Change in Dimension

brand through diagonal movement (i.e., moving directly from Quadrant IV to Quadrant II), these brands face a long and costly road to success. (Note that moving on the diagonal is very difficult and typically not recommended as this entails changing perceptions in multiple areas at the same time). Brands in this quadrant must first invest in their brands so that they deliver what is important to consumers and then must change consumers' perceptions to match these brand changes.

CORRESPONDENCE MAPS

Correspondence maps are similar to perceptual maps in that they provide a visual representation of consumers' brand perceptions and brand competitive sets. However, as illustrated by the correspondence map shown in Figure 18.7, these maps differ from perceptual maps in an important way. Correspondence maps do not provide insights into dimensions. Instead, they identify the set of specific attributes with which a brand is most associated. The closer brands and attributes are to each other, the more strongly associated they are in the consumer's mind.

Given correspondence maps similarity to perceptual maps, it is not surprising that similar procedures are used for its creation. We can use the online bookstore example to illustrate the steps.

ATTRIBUTE IDENTIFICATION. Similar to perceptual maps, correspondence maps begin with a list of specific category attributes. Since brands and individual attributes will be

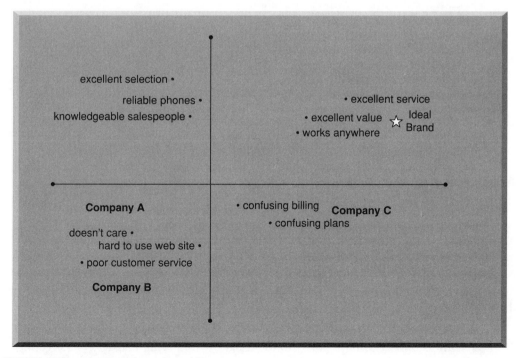

FIGURE 18.7 Correspondence Brand Map

mapped together (see Figure 18.7), it is very important that the list of brand and product attributes contain *all* attributes that are known to be (or that judgment or research indicates could potentially be) important in consumers' evaluation of target brands or products. Beyond these attributes, it is also possible to include attributes that are not currently available but may be introduced in the future. This allows an advertiser to see whether any brands are already associated with the attributes.

Next, measures at the nominal level are created. These measures are designed to determine whether or not specific attributes are associated with specific brands and, if desired, the Ideal brand. Thus, unlike the use of rating scales in perceptual maps, these measures elicit yes/no responses, as follows:

> **Different online bookstores have different characteristics. I'd like to read you a list of characteristics, one at a time. After each characteristic, I'll read a list of online bookstores. For each bookstore, please tell me whether that bookstore does or does not possess that characteristic. You can say "yes" if it does possess the characteristics and "no" if it does not.**

Once all attributes have been associated with all brands, a statistical analysis program performs both factor and correspondence analysis. Correspondence analysis then plots the data in a two-dimensional visual, where distances between brands and attributes reflect degree of association. Closer placement on the map indicates a stronger relationship. The correspondent map shown in Figure 18.7 presents consumers' views of four different cell phone companies. The map indicates that

- no brands are viewed as being close to the Ideal, where the Ideal brand is most associated with the attributes "excellent service," "excellent value," and "works anywhere";
- brand C is closest to the Ideal of all competitors. This brand, however, is strongly associated with the attributes "confusing billing" and "confusing plans";
- no brand is associated with the grouping of positive attributes in the upper left-hand corner. These attributes are of secondary importance, however, since they are far from the Ideal brand; and
- brands A and B are viewed as similar to each other and far from the Ideal. Both brands are associated with multiple negative attributes.

Application to Advertising Strategy

Correspondence maps, similar to perceptual maps, allow advertisers to determine, *from the consumers' perspective,* the strengths and weaknesses of their current positioning and the brands with which they most directly compete. This information can then be used to identify, *from the advertisers' perspective,* the extent to which the brand should defend its current positioning or alter its positioning in an attempt to move to a different place on the map, perhaps filling a currently open niche. Each of these two options can be seen in the map shown in Figure 18.7.

- Brand C is in the strongest competitive position. Its place in the marketplace can be strengthened by moving it closer to the Ideal by improving consumers' perceptions of its service, value, and reliability, while at the same time moving away from its association with the negative attributes of confusing billing and plans.

- Brands A and B are in very weak competitive positions. These brands need to differentiate themselves from each other, move away from the set of perceived negative associations, and improve their association with positive attributes (either those close to the Ideal or those in the upper left-hand corner that are currently unassociated with any brand).

BRAND CONCEPT MAPS

Both perceptual and correspondence maps allow you to visualize the relationship between multiple brands and either dimensions or attributes. Brand concept maps provide greater detail on how consumers perceive one individual brand. A simplified brand concept map for Volkswagen is provided in Figure 18.8.[6] The map represents the most important attributes consumers associate with Volkswagen where Volkswagen is most associated with the attributes "fun to drive," "neat colors" and "not expensive." Note that in a brand concept map, the greater the number of lines linking two items the greater the association.

A brand concept map is created in a three-step process: elicitation, mapping, and aggregation. Each of these steps is discussed in the context of developing a brand concept map for the Mayo Clinic.

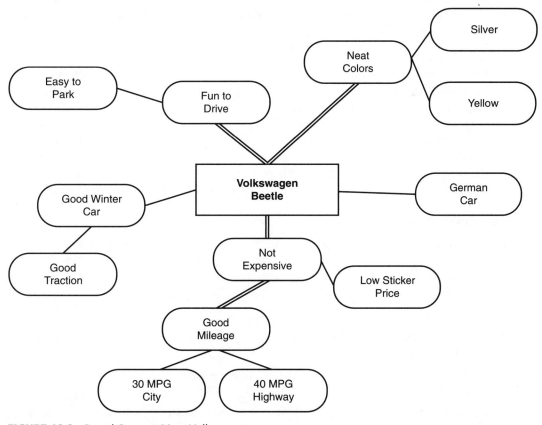

FIGURE 18.8 Brand Concept Map: Volkswagen

Elicitation

The *elicitation step* is where researchers identify the most important brand associations. These associations can be obtained qualitatively through focus groups or through quantitative surveys. Regardless of the approach used, a researcher must be certain to adhere to four criteria:

> First, data used to identify salient associations should be gathered from the same consumer population as the one being used in the mapping stage. Second, data used to identify salient associations should be based on consumer responses to open-ended questions (e.g., "When you think of [brand], what comes to mind?"). Open-ended questions allow consumers to voice whatever brand associations are most accessible and important to them in their own words. Third, the most frequently mentioned brand associations should be selected to form the final set. [A level of 50% or more is acceptable.] Fourth, in selecting the exact phrasing for salient brand associations, it is important to retain wording that the consumers use rather than wording that researchers or managers more commonly use.

Mapping

Mapping collects brand association data from consumers where each frequently mentioned association from the prior step is placed on an index card, and the entire deck is shuffled and given to a consumer. Next,

> respondents are asked to select any of the pre-made cards that reflect their feelings about the brand. As a check to ensure that all salient brand associations have been included on the cards, blank cards are made available for respondents who want to add additional associations to the set. Then, respondents are shown an example of a BCM [brand concept map] and are given instructions on building their own brand map. Respondents use the brand associations they have selected and connect them to one another and to the brand, using another set of cards with different types of lines (single, double, or triple) to signify the strength of the connection between associations.

Aggregation

The final step is *aggregation* where a researcher codes the maps created by each individual respondent and then, based on the data obtained, uses a set of decision rules to combine the individual maps into one master exemplar map. Coding is a two-step process. First, each attribute appearing on an individual map is coded in four ways,

1. whether the attribute was or was not present,
2. the type of line (single, double, or triple) connecting each association to the target brand or to another attribute,
3. the level at which the association appears on the map (e.g., Level 1 = connected to brand, Level 2 = connected under a Level 1 association), and
4. which brand associations were linked above and below each association on the map.

These codes are then aggregated into summary measures. These summary measures, which guide the creation of the exemplar map, are shown in Figure 18.9 and are described below.

- "Frequency of Mention" is the number of times that a brand association occurs across maps. In Figure 18.9, for example, "expert in treating serious illnesses" was the most frequently mentioned association.

- "Number of Interconnections" reports the number of times that a brand association is connected to other brand associations. An "expert in treating serious illnesses," for example, had the most interconnections to other brand associations (see Figure 18.9). (With regard to this and the prior measure, note that frequently mentioned associations with many interconnections are the strongest candidates for being chosen as "core" brand associations on the exemplar brand map.)

- "Frequency of First-Order Mentions" counts of the number of times that a brand association is directly linked to the brand across individual maps. In Figure 18.9, for example, "leader in medical research" was the association most frequently connected in a direct way to the Mayo Clinic brand.

- "Ratio of First-Order Mentions" reports the percentage of times that a brand association is linked directly to the brand when it is included on an individual brand map. In Figure 18.9, for example, 75.9% of patients who included "leader in medical research" on their brand maps placed this association as a direct link to the Mayo Clinic brand.

- "Type of Interconnections" indicates how frequently a brand association is placed above other associations (superordinate) or below other associations (subordinate) across maps. As Figure 18.9 shows, patients frequently mentioned "latest medical equipment and technology" but placed it more often in a subordinate versus superordinate position. (With regard to this and the prior two measures, note that associations linked directly to the brand on a frequent basis with more superordinate than subordinate connections are strong candidates for being directly connected to the brand in the exemplar brand map.)

As mentioned earlier, a set of decision rules governs how the coded data is translated into an exemplar brand concept map. The set of decision rules is provided in Figure 18.10, while Figure 18.11 describes the detailed steps John et al.[7] used to apply the decision rules to create the consensus brand map.

The final brand map is provided in Figure 18.12. Note that as in the Volkswagen map, the greater the number of lines linking two attributes the greater the association. Additionally, a solid-line circle indicates a core association while a dashed-line circle signifies a non-core association.

Application to Advertising Decision Making

John et al.[8] point out that brand concept maps offer

a picture of how consumers think about brands, with a visual format that makes it easy for managers to see important brand associations and how they are connected in the consumer's mind. In particular, one of the most important

Brand Associations	Core Associations		First-Order Associations			
	Frequency of Mention	Number of Inter-connections	Frequency of First-Order Mention	Ratio of First-Order Mention (%)	Subordinate Connections	Super-ordinate Connections
Expert in treating serious illness	64	75	34	53.1	30	45
Latest medical equipment & technology	60	62	22	36.7	38	24
Leader in medical research	54	60	41	75.9	13	44
Known worldwide	54	57	37	68.5	17	27
Top-notch surgery & treatment	53	44	21	39.6	32	22
Best doctors in the world	51	54	29	56.9	22	52
World leader in new medical treatments	51	74	23	45.1	28	41
Can be trusted to do right by patients	51	69	22	43.1	29	25
Doctors work as a team	50	54	20	40.0	30	34
Best patient care available	49	64	33	67.3	16	45
Treats rare and complex illnesses	49	61	23	46.9	26	18
Can figure out what's wrong when others can't	49	44	15	30.6	35	22
Publishes information to help you stay well	44	57	19	43.2	25	9
Approachable, friendly doctors	44	34	15	34.1	29	2
Caring & compassionate	42	50	19	45.2	23	19
Treats famous people from around the world	38	42	13	34.2	25	0
Comforting to know Mayo exists if I need it	36	25	19	52.8	18	15
People I know recommend Mayo	30	33	19	63.3	11	4
Leader in cancer research & treatment	29	15	11	37.9	18	5
Cares more about people than money	27	23	14	51.9	13	7
Court of last resort	12	20	5	41.7	7	1
Hard to get into unless very sick or famous	5	8	1	20.0	4	1
Very big & intimidating	3	5	3	100.0	0	4
Expensive	3	4	1	33.3	2	1
Uses its reputation to make money	3	3	1	.0	2	1

NOTE: Core brand associations are in bold type; first-order brand associations are in bold italics.

FIGURE 18.9 Attribute Coding for Brand Concept Map

Step	Measures	Rules
1. Select core brand associations	Frequency of mention Number of interconnections	Select brand associations that are included on: • At least 50% of maps. • 45%–49% of maps if the number of interconnections was equal to or higher than that of other core brand associations.
2. Select first-order brand associations	Frequency of first-order mentions Ratio of first-order mentions Type of interconnections	Select core brand associations that have: • A ratio of first-order mentions to total mentions of at least 50%. • More superordinate than subordinate interconnections.
3. Select core brand association links	Frequencies for association links	Select core brand association links by: • Finding inflection point on frequency plot (where inflection point equals target number). • Including all association links that appear on or above the target number of maps.
4. Select non-core brand association links	Frequencies for association links	Select non-core brand association links that are • Linked to a core brand association. • Linked on or above the target number of maps.
5. Select number of connecting lines	Mean number of lines used per link	Select single, double, or triple lines for each brand association by: • Determining the mean number of lines used per link. • Rounding up or down to the next integer number

FIGURE 18.10 Brand Concept Map Decision-Rules

features highlighted in brand maps is the core brand associations, the most important set of brand associations that drive the brand's image. Although consumers may identify many things with a brand, it is the core brand associations, especially those linked directly to the brand, that should be the focus of management efforts to build, leverage, and protect brands.

Advertisers can use the information provided in a brand concept map in a number of ways.

Advertisers may find themselves in the pleasant situation where their desired positioning is the same as the positioning assigned by consumers. Advertisers in this circumstance tend to defend and reinforce their positioning, paying particular attention to the attributes most closely associated with the brand. In the case of the Mayo Clinic

management would need to ensure that these associations and any associations connected to them continue to resonate with consumers. For example, to maintain the perception that the Mayo Clinic has the "best doctors in the world," branding efforts could be aimed at making this association salient in

We used a five-step process to develop a consensus brand map.

In the first step, we identified the core brand associations that would be placed on the map. We used two measures for this purpose: frequency of mention and number of interconnections. We identified associations that were included on at least 50% of the maps as core brand associations. . . . We also included associations with borderline frequencies (45%–49%) if the number of interconnections was equal to or higher than that of other core brand associations, consistent with the idea that high interconnectivity signals the centrality of associations or beliefs. Applying these rules, we found 12 core brand associations for Mayo Clinic patients [see items in bold type in Figure 18.9].

In the second step, we began the process of building the consensus map by identifying which core brand associations should be linked directly to the Mayo brand. We identified these core brand associations (first-order associations) using three measures [see Figure 18.9]: frequency of first-order mentions, ratio of first-order mentions, and type of interconnections. We selected associations with ratios of first-order mentions to total mentions of at least 50%, with more superordinate than subordinate connections, as first-order associations. Applying these rules to the patient data, we selected six core brand associations as first-order associations, which appear as direct links to the Mayo Clinic brand in the consensus brand map [see items in bold and italics in Figure 18.9].

In the third step, we placed the remaining core brand associations on the map. They needed to be linked to at least one of the first-order brand associations; important links between the 12 core brand associations also needed to be placed on the consensus map. To do so, we first counted how frequently links between specific associations occurred across maps. We then compiled a frequency count of how many different association links were noted on one map, two maps, three maps, and so on. . . . We used these frequencies to select which association links would be included in the consensus map.

In the fourth step, we added important links between core and non-core brand associations to the consensus map. Several of the frequently mentioned links were between core and non-core brand associations. Although the consensus brand map could be restricted to core brand associations, it is often important for managers to see associations that drive consumer perceptions of the core brand associations. We added these links to the consensus map; we represented the non-core brand associations with dotted lines to distinguish them from the more important core brand associations.

In the fifth step, we placed lines (single, double, or triple) on the map to signify the intensity of the connection between associations. For each association link, we computed the mean number of lines respondents used and rounded up or down to the nearest integer (e.g., 2.3 = 2) to determine how many lines to use on the consensus brand map.

FIGURE 18.11 Application of Decision-Rules for Brand Concept Map

communications. In addition, communications could stress that "doctors work as a team" and that the Mayo Clinic has "approachable, friendly doctors," because these associations are linked with "best doctors in the world."

Of equal importance, the core brand associations should be protected from erosion or dilution. For example, to protect an association such as "leader in medical research" from eroding, the organization needs to affirm its commitment to medical research through funding, staff, and publicity. An important way that the Mayo Clinic could accomplish this would be to continue to commit to being the "leader in cancer research" and to continue to "publish health information." Activities that are incongruent with the core brand associations need to be questioned for the possibility of diluting

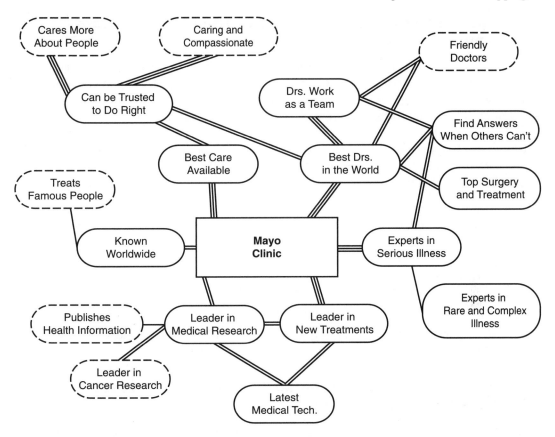

FIGURE 18.12 Brand Concept Map: Mayo Clinic

important brand associations or adding new brand associations that are inconsistent with the image. For example, if the Mayo Clinic opened cosmetic skin care salons, this would certainly be inconsistent with existing associations, such as "world leader in medical treatments" and "expert in treating serious illnesses."

It may also be the case that consumers associate attributes with a brand in a way that runs counter to the advertisers' wishes or goals. In these cases, it is often useful for the advertiser to use judgment to generate the brand's "ideal" map, which can then be compared to the exemplar brand concept map to determine areas of future strategic and advertising focus.

ADDITIONAL CONSIDERATIONS IN THE USE OF PERCEPTUAL, CORRESPONDENCE, AND CONCEPT MAPS

Each of the prior three maps—perceptual, correspondence and concept—provides different but complimentary insights into how consumers perceive a target brand and competitive brands. In doing so, two additional considerations in the use of these techniques need to be noted.

Perceptual Maps for the Same Brands Often Change Across Different Consumer Segments

The prior chapter discussed segmentation, where a large group of consumers is divided into relatively smaller consumer segments. It is often beneficial to use perceptual maps to see how different segments of consumers differ with regard to the value they place on different dimensions and where they place brands on those dimensions.

Consider the two perceptual maps shown in Figures 18.13a and 18.13b. The map in Figure 18.13a represents the placement of automotive brands by 18–24 year olds, while the map in Figure 18.13b represents placement by 45–54 year olds.[9] Note the two important differences between the two maps:

- The Ideal brand is in a different position on the two maps. The placement of this brand indicates that while 18–24 year olds value both "dependability" and "style," the latter dimension is much more important to this group. Conversely, the older group places much more value on "dependability," with the "style" dimension being only of moderate importance.

- Brand placement on the two maps is very different, both in terms of competitive sets and with regard to the brands believed to be closest to the Ideal.

As a result, very different marketing strategies would need to be developed to reach members of each age group.

Comparing Current and Potential Customers Contributes to Strategic Decision Making

The prior example showed how brand and category perceptions differed across consumer segments. Advertisers can take this comparative approach one step further by comparing brand associations of current brand users to other groups defined by brand usage, for example, non-users, infrequent users, and current users. The correspondence map shown in Figure 18.14 provides these three groups' placement of "Healthy Choice Frozen Dinners." The map illustrates the each group associates the brand with a different set of attributes. It is clear that different groups have different perceptions of and associations with the brand. Using this information, the advertiser would need to determine which target group should be the primary target, and how addressing this target affects the perceptions of other groups.

Before and after Maps Can Track Advertising Impact

Brand maps, similar to surveys, provide a "point in time" snapshot of consumers' perceptions. These maps also have the potential to help assess the impact of advertising on consumers' perceptions. In these cases, a brand map drawn prior to the initiation of advertising can be compared to maps taken at a point after advertising exposure.

The advertising agency D'Arcy Masius Benton & Bowles, for example, asked respondents to rate 12 automobile manufacturers on 15 attributes (such as quality, sporty, and technologically advanced).[10] The results of these initial ratings are shown on the pre-exposure perceptual map in Figure 18.15a. The perceptual map shows that, before

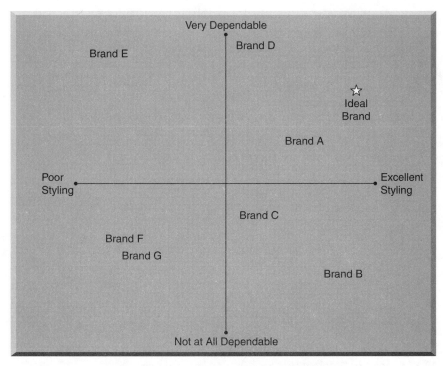

FIGURE 18.13a   Perceptual Map of Automotive Brands: 18 to 24 Year Olds

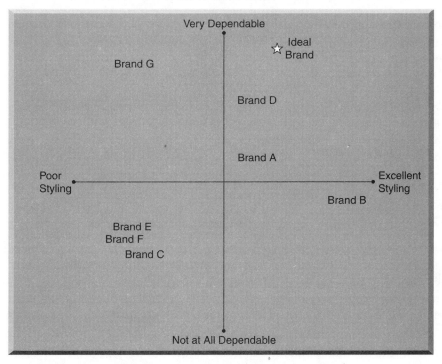

FIGURE 18.13b   Perceptual Map of Automotive Brands: 45 to 54 Year Olds

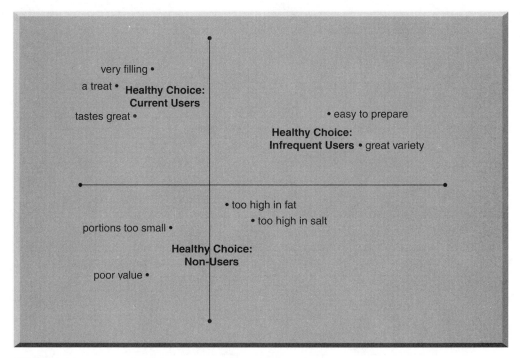

FIGURE 18.14   Impact of Different User Segments on Brand Placement

advertising exposure, consumers used two dimensions to distinguish among car manu-facturers. One dimension related to age of driver and affordability. This dimension was anchored by "affordable, young person's car" and "luxurious, comfortable, older person's car". The second dimension related to car characteristics and is anchored by "a family car" and "high-quality, technologically advanced car,"

Following this initial rating, respondents were exposed to multiple pieces of adver-tising. Each respondent viewed six television commercials and read two print ads for each automobile manufacturer evaluated in the initial ratings. After the viewing, respondents again rated each manufacturer on the same attributes used in the pre-exposure ratings. The perceptual map that resulted from this second set of ratings was different from the pre-exposure map (see post-exposure perceptual map in Figure 18.15b). The post-exposure map showed four ways by which the advertising affected consumers' percep-tions of both the automotive category and individual automotive brands:

1. The advertising appeared to have changed the dimensions with which consumers evaluate and distinguish among automobile manufacturers. One end of the dimension displayed on the vertical axis changed from "high quality, technologi-cally advanced car" to "exciting, powerful fun car." This suggests that the advertis-ing changed the criteria by which consumers distinguish among car brands.

2. It is this new dimension, "family car—exciting, powerful fun car," that most differ-entiates car manufacturers. Manufacturers on the pre-exposure perceptual map were dispersed along both dimensions with many manufacturers at the extremes. The post-exposure perceptual map shows less differentiation along the horizontal

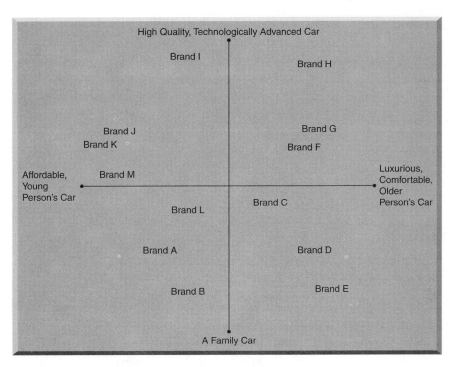

FIGURE 18.15a Pre-Advertising Exposure Perceptual Map

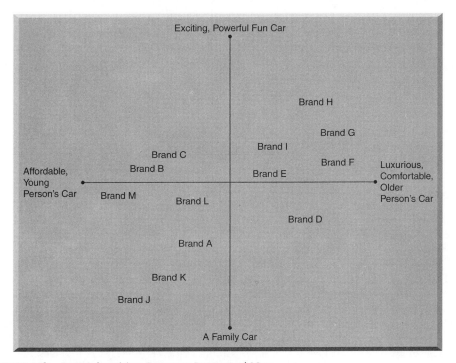

FIGURE 18.15b Post-Advertising Exposure Perceptual Map

axis (more brands now appear near the center) and more differentiation on the vertical axis.

3. Advertising appeared to affect manufacturer image. While some manufacturers' images (such as A, D, F, G, H) were constant, other manufacturers showed great change in image. Consumers changed their perceptions of manufacturers J and K, for example, from a "high-quality, technologically advanced car" to "a family car."

4. Competitive sets appear to have changed for some manufacturers. Brand I, for example, which had no close competitors on the pre-exposure map, appears to compete with a number of manufacturers on the post-exposure map. Similarly, manufacturers B and C, which were far apart on the pre-exposure map, are seen as very close competitors on the post-exposure map.

SUMMARY

Brand maps translate consumers' brand and product perceptions into visual displays that help advertisers better understand

- the number of dimensions consumers use to distinguish between brands and products,
- the nature and characteristics of these dimensions, and
- the location of actual brands, as well as the Ideal brand, on these dimensions.

There are three primary types of brand maps: perceptual, correspondence, and concept. Perceptual maps plot brands along labeled dimensions (which are built from an analysis of individual attributes). Correspondence maps do not use dimensions, but rather plot both brands and individual attributes together in the same map space. Both perceptual and correspondence maps allow for multiple brand comparisons and are interpreted in a similar way: the closer two objects are on the map the greater their perceived similarity or association. Brand concept maps allow for the in-depth exploration and visualization of consumers' perceptions of a single brand. All three types of maps allow advertisers to better understand how their brands are currently perceived and, in response, identify and evaluate alternative strategic decisions for brand advertising and positioning.

Review Questions

1. What are the three primary types of brand maps?
2. What types of information are provided by a perceptual map?
3. When thinking of perceptual maps, what is the relationship between attributes and dimensions?
4. Why do perceptual maps plot the Ideal brand?
5. What is an *eigenvalue*? What is its role in the creation of a perceptual map?
6. How does a researcher determine the number of dimensions consumers use to evaluate brands?
7. How are brands placed on a perceptual map?

8. What is the main difference between correspondence maps and perceptual maps?
9. How does a researcher interpret a correspondence map?
10. What is the primary difference between a perceptual map and a brand concept map?
11. What are the three stages in the construction of a brand concept map? Briefly describe what happens at each stage.
12. Briefly describe the ways in which brand maps help advertisers make better informed decisions.

13. Why is it often important to segment a target audience prior to the development of brand maps?

14. Can brand maps show advertising's impact on consumer perceptions? If so, how is this done?

Application Exercises

1. Your client, Verizon, wishes to determine the dimensions consumers use to evaluate cell phone providers and its position versus the competition on these dimensions. You decide that the construction of an attribute-based perceptual map is an appropriate response to this information need. Sony agrees. Prepare a questionnaire that permits you to collect the appropriate data. Evaluate your questionnaire for thoroughness and completeness.

2. Exchange the questionnaire you developed for the prior exercise with two others in your class. Compare the questionnaires' wording and the lists of product attributes shown in each questionnaire. To what extent are the differences in content significant? How will these differences affect the types of information provided by the perceptual map? Address these two questions and then revise your questionnaire to reflect your conclusions.

3. You have just received the print-out for the initial factor analysis of a study of fast food restaurants. The eigenvalues, as well as other data, for each of the factors are shown below. Which factors would you select for subsequent analyses and construction of the perceptual map? Explain your decision.

Factor	Eigenvalue	Percent of Variance
1	4.29	39.0
2	3.41	31.0
3	2.99	27.2
4	.13	1.2
5	.06	.5
6	.04	.4
7	.03	.2
8	.02	.2
9	.01	.1
10	.01	.1
11	.01	.1
		100.0%

4. You are conducting a perceptual mapping study of consumers' reactions to Internet clothing merchants' sites such as Land's End and L. L. Bean. The data is shown in Figure 18.16. The specific attributes studied are shown in the first column. Given that this particular piece of research identified three key dimensions, each attributes' loading on each of the three dimensions (factors) is shown in the remaining columns. Your client, Sam's Internet Clothes, asks for your point of view on what the dimensions mean. Name each dimension and explain what each dimension represents. Be certain to fully explain and provide support for your answer. In naming each dimension, be specific and be certain to avoid gross generalities in labeling the dimensions.

5. (This is a continuation of the prior exercise.) The table shown at the end of this exercise provides the average dimension (factor) scores for each of the Internet merchants' Web sites measured in the research as well as for the

Attribute	Factor 1	Factor 2	Factor 3
Presents pricing specials that are not available through catalog, telephone, or stores	+.789	−.025	+.026
It's easy to find what I am looking for	−.001	+.879	−.111
It's easy to find my way around the site	+.002	+.895	+.127
The site's sections are marked and labeled very well	+.211	+.789	+.334
I get frustrated and give up shopping	−.112	−.966	+.544
Presents merchandise that is not available through catalog, telephone or stores	+.788	−.022	+.111
There is always a fun contest or game going on	+.669	−.011	+.025
I feel good when I shop at the site	+.222	+.125	+.879
There is very seldom a really good reason to visit	−.987	+.022	+.499
The site's personalization makes me feel special	+.111	−.210	+.758
I'm proud to be a registered shopper at the site	−.105	+.102	+.689
On-site search engine is very effective	−.022	+.799	+.068
Check-out is very often a very difficult and time-consuming process	+.500	−.729	+.125

FIGURE 18.16   Data for Application Exercise 4

"Ideal" merchant. The scale for each dimension is from −3 to +3. The dimensions correspond to the dimensions shown in the Application Exercise 4. Prepare an analysis of this data for your client, Sam's Internet Clothes. Be certain to focus your discussion on micro-issues (based on your examination of each of the appropriate perceptual maps) as well as broader category issues (based on your analysis of the trends exhibited across all three maps simultaneously). What specific insights and recommendations do you have for Sam's (and have you justified these recommendations by

reference to the maps and data)? What specific insights as to the category structure itself do you have for Sam's (and have you justified these recommendations by reference to the maps and data)? Your discussion, which should be about three to four typed pages, should discuss both the findings (what the data "says") and the implications (what the data "means"). Be certain to present specific recommendations (justified by the data) for future Sam's Internet Clothes actions with regard to the structure, form, and content of its Web site as well as for any marketing/advertising efforts.

Brand	Dimension 1	Dimension 2	Dimension 3
A	+1.9	+2.1	+1.1
B	+1.4	+0.3	+0.1
Sam's Internet Clothes	−1.3	+2.5	−1.7
D	−1.6	+0.3	+0.5
E	−2.2	−0.0	−0.1
F	+.2	0.1	−0.5
G	−1.5	−1.6	+0.5
H	+2.1	+1.2	−1.7
I	−1.6	+1.5	+0.1
J	−2.6	+.1	+0.5
Ideal	+1.9	+.4	+2.5

Endnotes

1. Dimensions are also sometimes referred to as "factors." This chapter uses the two terms interchangeably.

2. All placement and discussion of social networking sites is hypothetical and for illustrative purposes only. Maps and discussion do not reflect actual research data.

3. The attributes, data, and outcomes discussed in this section are based on Noam Tractinsky and Oded Lowengart (2003). "E-retailers Competitive Intensity: A Positioning Mapping Analysis." *Journal of Targeting, Measurement and Analysis for Marketing* 12 (2): 114–136. The data shown in this section has, however, been altered, abridged, and simplified and is not representative of the data reported by Tractinsky and Lowengart. Additionally, Tractinsky and Lowengart did not report specific brand placement, and as a result, brand placement in this discussion is hypothetical and for illustrative purposes only.

4. For a discussion of variance and standard deviation, see Chapter 16.

5. Researchers try to keep the number of dimensions low because the more dimensions selected, the more maps we need to create. Note that since each map represents the inter-

action of two dimensions, the total number of maps needed to present the results will increase as the number of dimensions increases. Two dimensions will require only one map, which would show Dimension 1 and Dimension 2. Three dimensions require three maps: Dimension 1 with Dimension 2 (map 1), Dimension 1 with Dimension 3 (map 2), and Dimension 2 with Dimension 3 (map 3).

6. This section draws on the work of Deborah John et al. (2006). "Brand Concept Maps: A Methodology for Identifying Brand Association Networks" *Journal of Marketing Research* 53 (4): 549–563. All data and figures regarding brand concept maps are from this source. All quotes and figures are from this source and are reproduced with permission of the American Marketing Association.

7. John et al., op. cit.

8. John et al., op. cit.

9. This data, as well as the following Healthy Choice data, is fictitious and used for illustrative purposes only.

10. Charles Stannard (1990). "Perceptual Mapping and Cluster Analysis: Some Problems and Solutions." *Quirk's Marketing Research Review* (March): 12–22.

CHAPTER 19

Advertising Testing: Concept and Communications Tests

The prior two chapters described research that lays the foundation for successful advertising communications: segmentation provides important insights into potential target audiences, while perceptual mapping helps advertisers understand their competitive position. The next step in the advertising development process applies insights from this and other research to the creation of the advertising itself. This creation process typically consists of two phases. The first phase explores advertising content and creative options (and is the topic of this chapter). The second phase selects and evaluates the finished advertising (and is the topic of the next chapter).

This chapter explores concept and communications tests. Concept tests allow advertisers to explore consumers' reactions to different advertising messages, identifying the strengths and weaknesses of each message. Once a message is selected, communication tests allow advertisers to explore consumers' reactions to different executional approaches that might be used to communicate the selected message, again identifying the strengths and weaknesses of each approach.

***

When you are done reading this chapter, you should have a better understanding of the contribution of concept and communications tests to the advertising development process as well as how to:

- prepare stimulus materials for use in concept and communications tests
- identify the relative advantages and disadvantages of qualitative and quantitative approaches to concept and communication testing

- identify the key areas of measurement in concept and communications tests and prepare a questionnaire for quantitative tests and a discussion guide for qualitative tests
- analyze and present the results of quantitative concept and communication tests.

Concept and communication tests occur during the early stages of the advertising development process. The tests differ in that concept tests focus exclusively on messages and message evaluation, while communication tests focus on message communication within the context of alternative executions. Nevertheless, the two tests share one important characteristic. Concept and communication tests are both diagnostic in approach, designed to identify strengths and weaknesses rather than select a "winner." This chapter begins with a discussion of concept and communications test characteristics, noting how to create stimulus materials for each type of test. This is followed by a discussion of the key measures used in both types of research. The chapter concludes with a comparison of qualitative and quantitative approaches to data collection in concept and communication tests, considerations in the development of data collection instruments, and a discussion of approaches to data analysis.

CONCEPT TESTS

Early in the advertising planning process, advertisers must determine the message that should be selected and communicated. This is often a difficult decision as more than one message may be relevant and motivating to the target audience. Concept tests help guide this decision by identifying the relative strengths and weaknesses of alternative messages, allowing advertisers to subsequently craft a message that capitalizes on identified strengths and eliminates identified weaknesses. Two concepts designed to prevent sleepy driving are presented in Figure 19.1. Note how the concepts differ in orientation (the headline and first paragraph) but are similar in provided suggestions (the bullet points).[1]

The concepts shown in Figure 19.1 illustrate the characteristics of a concept. A concept is a simple, written expression of a positioning, benefit, reason for being, or unique communication proposition. A concept clearly and realistically communicates without exaggeration, salesmanship, or advertising puffery. Concepts are therefore distinct from advertisements. An advertisement is designed to sell and, consequently, must accomplish multiple goals. An advertisement must break through clutter and attract attention, be memorable and remembered by the target audience, and persuasively communicate the selling proposition. A concept, on the other hand, is designed to communicate. The most important task of a concept is to present the core idea simply and realistically so that consumers' comprehension is maximized and response to the core idea can be confidently assessed.

Product and Non-Product Focused Concept Tests

Concept tests explore alternative approaches to communicating benefits or related propositions.[2] Here, visuals (if used) are kept constant across concepts as different message approaches are explored. Concept tests can be used for both product- and non-product related communications.[3]

Concept 1: Sleep Education

Headline: *IT'S YOU AGAINST THE FORCES OF DARKNESS*

Concept:

Being a shift worker is hard work. On and off the job. You work unusual hours that run counter to your body's natural sleep cycle. This makes it especially difficult to get quality sleep. Especially quality sleep on a consistent basis. But there is something that you can do. There are steps you can take to help improve your sleep. And improving your sleep will help you on and off the job. You can, for example,

- avoid stimulants, such as caffeine and nicotine, several hours before bedtime. If you are working nights and need to sleep from morning until afternoon, try to avoid caffeine after midnight.
- arrange to sleep uninterrupted in a quiet, dark room. This means you may have to turn off or unplug your phone, hang darkening curtains on the windows or wear a sleep eye mask, make appointments outside of your sleep period, and train your family and friends to leave you alone while you sleep. Make your sleep time sacred.
- develop and follow a sleep routine. It's best if you go to sleep and wake up at the same time every day. Try not to vary this too much on weekends. Your body likes routine.
- take extra care to make healthy choices. You may be tempted to reach for unhealthy foods or nicotine to stay awake or alcohol to try to sleep. But ultimately these choices are more harmful than helpful.

This will assist you in your regular routines, as well as ensuring a safer drive to and from work.

Concept 2: Consequences of Drowsy Driving

Headline: *YOU ARE GETTING SLEEPY. VERY SLEEPY. AT THE COUNT OF THREE, YOU WILL NOT WAKE UP.*

Concept:

Being a shift worker is hard. You work long nighttime hours and often leave work tired and sleepy. You're often tired on the drive home. It's important to remember that drowsy drivers run a very high risk of being involved in a fall-asleep crash. In fact, The National Highway Traffic Safety Administration estimates that 100,000 car crashes per year and at least 1,500 deaths per year can be attributed to driver drowsiness. You don't want to be a statistic. One way to avoid a drowsy driver accident or fatality is to make certain that you get a good, sound sleep when you get home. Here are some things that you can do:

- Avoid stimulants, such as caffeine and nicotine, several hours before bedtime. If you are working nights and need to sleep from morning until afternoon, try to avoid caffeine after midnight.
- Arrange to sleep uninterrupted in a quiet, dark room. This means you may have to turn off or unplug your phone, hang darkening curtains on the windows or wear a sleep eye mask, make appointments outside of your sleep period, and train your family and friends to leave you alone while you sleep. Make your sleep time sacred.
- Develop and follow a sleep routine. It's best if you go to sleep and wake up at the same time every day. Try not to vary this too much on weekends. Your body likes routine.
- Take extra care to make healthy choices. You may be tempted to reach for unhealthy foods or nicotine to stay awake or alcohol to try to sleep. But ultimately these choices are more harmful than helpful.

This will assist you in your regular routines, as well as ensuring a safer drive to and from work.

FIGURE 19.1 Concepts for Sleepy Driver Prevention

PRODUCT-RELATED TESTS.   Many concept tests explore messages that relate to the product's positioning, which represents its "niche" in the consumer's mind. This niche, in turn, reflects the product's emphasized benefits. At this stage of the advertising development process, advertisers use product-related concept tests in one of two ways to help refine a product's positioning.

• First, concept tests can be used to identify and then compare the strengths and weaknesses of alternative benefits or positionings. Examples of alternative benefit positionings for a woman's perm-sensitive shampoo are shown in Figure 19.2. Note how the concepts only differ with regard to specific elements of the body copy. The body copy in both messages contains identical introductions and descriptions of product formulation. Beyond these shared elements, the headline and benefit-specific body copy shown in Version A presents the shampoo's benefit as "makes your perm last longer, saving you time and money," while the copy in Version B presents the shampoo's benefit as "keeps your perm healthy." The consistency across concepts makes it easy for respondents to focus on the important differences in the message copy.

Version A: "Lasts longer, saves you money"

Dansk Hair Treatments presents PermaPerm. A shampoo that helps your perm last longer, saving you money.

PermaPerm is specially formulated for permed hair. Its formula is so unique that it is patented. PermaPerm's enhancing shampoo for permed hair is formulated with coconut oil, nettle extract, panthenol, and other natural and organic ingredients for mild, gentle cleaning.

PermaPerm washes out dirt but leaves your perm intact. Independent, clinical tests have shown that, on average, perms shampooed with PermaPerm last three weeks longer than perms shampooed with other leading shampoo brands. When your perm lasts longer, you need to visit your stylist less often. So PermaPerm actually saves you time and money.

A 16-ounce bottle of PermaPerm retails for $3.99 and is available at leading grocery and drug stores.

Version B: "Healthy perm"

Dansk Hair Treatments presents PermaPerm. A shampoo that helps keep your perm healthy.

PermaPerm is specially formulated for permed hair. Its formula is so unique that it is patented. PermaPerm's enhancing shampoo for permed hair is formulated with coconut oil, nettle extract, panthenol, and other natural and organic ingredients for mild, gentle cleaning.

PermaPerm washes out dirt but leaves your perm healthy and manageable. PermaPerm makes permed hair look and feel healthy. Its unique formula fights frizz and dryness. It helps curls stay curly and bouncy. It makes permed hair feel silky and soft. Independent clinical tests show that women prefer the feel and look of their hair after a PermaPerm shampoo, versus the leading brands, by a margin of nearly 2 to 1.

A 16-ounce bottle of PermaPerm retails for $3.99 and is available at leading grocery and drug stores.

FIGURE 19.2   Alternative Benefit Concepts for Product-Related Concept Test

- Second, once a positioning is selected, concept tests can be used to identify the strengths and weaknesses of alternative approaches to communicating the positioning. Once one of the concepts shown in Figure 19.2 was selected for use in the brand's communications, alternative creative could be compared and contrasted.

NON-PRODUCT RELATED TESTS. A great deal of advertising is not product-related, for example, drug and smoking prevention, obesity prevention, energy conservation, and wildlife protection.[4] Concept tests are also used to select messages for these types of advertising campaigns. The goals are the same as in product-related tests: to identify the strengths and weaknesses of alternative message strategies and the strengths and weaknesses of alternative ways to communicate a selected message. The two message concepts shown in Figure 19.3 illustrate this type of message concept test. Both messages are designed to encourage recycling and, similar to the prior product-related example, differ

---

Concept 1: Positive Outcomes

Trash, garbage, and solid waste are all terms used to describe the tons of material that are discarded every day. In fact, the average person generates 4.6 pounds of waste every day. Waste that is headed for a landfill.

Recycling is one way to reduce this amount of waste. And, although significant progress has been made with regard to recycling, there is much more work to be done! Think about what can be accomplished if we all recycle just a little bit more . . .

- *Recycling creates jobs!* More than 56,000 recycling and reuse enterprises employ more than 1.1 million people across the United States. Recycling is a $236 billion dollar industry over a one year period.
- *Recycling is good for the environment!* Recycling reduces the need for raw materials, uses less energy to produce, and keeps products out of landfills!
- *Recycling saves energy!* Recycling aluminum uses 95% less energy than producing new virgin aluminum. One recycled aluminum can saves enough energy to power a television for three hours.

Concept 2: Reduction of Negative Outcomes

Trash, garbage, and solid waste are all terms used to describe the tons of material that is discarded every day. In fact, the average person generates 4.6 pounds of waste every day. Waste that is headed for a landfill.

Recycling is one way to reduce this amount of waste. And, although significant progress has been made with regard to recycling, there is much more work to be done! Think about what can be accomplished if we all recycle just a little bit more . . .

- *Recycling helps prevent global warming!* Recycling produces considerably less carbon than making new materials. In 2000, 32.9 million metric tons of carbon was kept from the air, just from recycling!
- *Recycling reduces water pollution!* Making glass from recycled materials can cut water pollution by 50%. There is also a shortage of drinking water in certain countries, and even certain states nationally. By recycling, we are helping to provide clean water for people.
- *Recycling prevents wildlife and habitat destruction!* By recycling, we reduce the need to destroy habitats for animals, including forests, rivers, wetlands, and swamps. Recycling one Sunday newspaper can save up to one tree!

FIGURE 19.3 Alternative Concepts for Non-Product Related Concept Test

only in the message itself, with one message focusing on positive outcomes while the other focuses on reducing of negative outcomes.[5] The introductory paragraph is consistent across both concepts.

PREPARING STIMULUS MATERIALS FOR A CONCEPT TEST

Special care is needed in the development of materials for a concept test. In addition to body copy, concepts *may* also contain a headline, an illustration, and a tagline. The goal is to put these elements together in a way that communicates without distraction. The following are recommendations for how to create each of these elements.

BODY COPY. At minimum, all concepts need clearly written, focused body copy. Short paragraphs consisting of active, declarative statements communicate better than longer paragraphs composed of passive sentences or sentence fragments. In addition, concept body copy should avoid "advertisingese" as it is important to communicate without embellishment or puffery. Body copy should avoid jargon or industry terminology that is unfamiliar and likely to confuse the reader. Finally, the overall length of concept body copy should be short. Overwritten or overly long concepts have the potential to negatively affect consumer response by boring respondents or causing them to lose focus on the core idea. When this occurs, responses to the core idea may be distorted. A negative response to the concept may reflect the influence of body copy characteristics as opposed to negative responses to the core idea or benefit itself.

Body copy should also be single-minded, or at minimum all individual ideas should be related to a single approach. The rule of "one idea-one concept" is important because it reduces ambiguity in data interpretation. Successful concept test research allows one to determine the relationship between the core idea expressed in the concept and consumer response. When the concept body copy single-mindedly focuses on one core idea, positive or negative consumer response can reasonably be attributed to the relative appeal of the concept's core idea and expressed product benefit. On the other hand, placing multiple ideas or benefits in the concept's body copy confuses the interpretation of the results. An overall neutral response to the concept might reflect an overall blasé consumer response, or it might reflect the average of two extremes—a strong positive response to one core idea and a strong negative response to a second core idea in the same concept.

HEADLINES. A concept test headline succinctly summarizes the main communication idea and provides an explicit lead-in to the body copy. Well-written concept test headlines provide a clear summary and introduction to the ideas that will be discussed later in the concept. In this regard, it is important to remember that concept test headlines are not advertising headlines. As opposed to advertising headlines that may use sentence fragments, questions, or catchy phrases, concept test headlines are best presented as simple declarative statements. This is because simple, straightforward declarative statements generally best communicate the intended message by being very easy to understand.

TAG LINES.   A tagline is a highly focused and brief phrase that clearly crystallizes the essence of the message being communicated. Successful concept test taglines are typically short, specific, believable, single-minded, and directly related to the core communication idea. Taglines in concept tests generally appear after the main body copy.

VISUALS.   Concept tests focus on message communication, and as a result, pictures or other visuals should be used cautiously. Visuals should only be used either when they are an essential part of the communication or when they are needed for brand, service, or other identification purposes. Beyond these two situations, visuals have the potential to make interpretation difficult because it is often impossible to separate reactions to the visual from reactions to the message—one tends to influence the other even when respondents claim that this is not the case.

COMMUNICATION TESTS

Communication testing (also known as copy development research) typically follows concept testing. As noted earlier, communication testing's goal is to evaluate consumers' reactions to different ways of communicating the selected message, thereby identifying the strengths and weaknesses of proposed executional approaches or advertisements.[6] Communication test results help client and agency personnel better understand how to revise an advertisement so that the finished ad maximizes strengths and minimizes weaknesses. Thus, similar to concept tests, communication testing is diagnostic in nature.

The executional approaches shown in Figures 19.4 and 19.5 illustrate the types of materials used in a communication test, in this case alternative print approaches to communicating a message designed to encourage safe food handling. Note that while the approaches differ across the two alternatives, the core message and visuals remain the same.[7]

Reasons for Communication Research

Creative judgment and skill are wonderful gifts. Talented creatives have the ability to translate a strategic plan's essential message and benefit statement into compelling, distinctive, motivating advertising. However, advertisers know that there is considerable risk in relying entirely on creative judgment and taking a proposed advertisement directly into production without any indication of how consumers respond to the ad. Once an ad is produced, the potential for alternation—either to increase strengths or to minimize weaknesses—is greatly reduced. Advertisers therefore use communication research to reduce their risk. Communication research permits advertisers, early in the development process, to examine proposed advertising from the consumers' perspective and to make appropriate changes before production, thus increasing the potential success of the finished advertisement.

The goal of communication research is to complement, not replace creative judgment. The design and presentation of communication research must therefore make certain that information collected during the research contributes to an understanding of the advertising creative. The research should help individuals at the agency understand how consumers are reacting to the advertising and why these reactions are taking place. With this understanding, the creative team can then determine how an advertisement can be revised and strengthened before production.

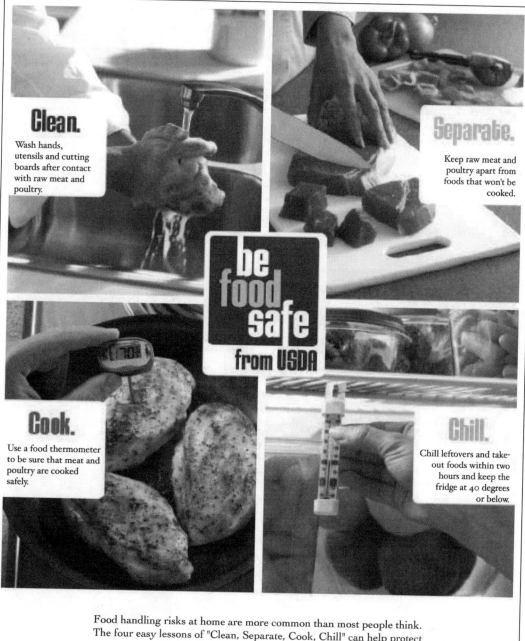

FIGURE 19.4 Alternative Executional Approaches for Communication Test: Option 1

Wash hands, utensils and cutting boards after contact with raw meat and poultry.

Keep raw meat and poultry apart from foods that won't be cooked.

Use a food thermometer to be sure that meat and poultry are cooked safely.

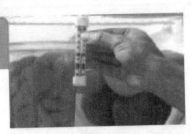

Chill leftovers and takeout foods within two hours and keep the fridge at 40 degrees or below.

Food handling risks at home are more common than most people think. The four easy lessons of "Clean, Separate, Cook, Chill" can help protect your family and keep bacteria from spreading.

Be Food Safe - from USDA!

For more information about food safety visit befoodsage.gov.

FIGURE 19.5 Alternative Executional Approaches for Communication Test: Option 2

PREPARING STIMULUS MATERIALS FOR A COMMUNICATION TEST

Advertisements in communication research are tested in "rough" stages of development. Production values need only give the respondent a reasonably good idea of what the final advertisement will look like. The physical characteristics and level of finish of the test advertisements depend on the advertising medium for which an ad is intended:

- Print ads should be actual size. In terms of level of finish, however, communication testing only requires that the test print ad resemble the finished ad. It is entirely permissible to use drawings instead of photographs and to use simple type styles rather than the intended style that will be used in the final ad.

- Radio ads can be "scratch" tracks.

- Television ads can be tested in one of three formats: storyboards, animatics, or photomatics. Storyboards are the easiest and least expensive form in which to test a proposed television ad. However, in spite of their efficiency, we recommend against their use. Most consumers have difficulty visualizing a finished commercial from a storyboard. As a result, we recommend that proposed television ads be tested in either animatic or photomatic form. An animatic is a storyboard on film or tape accompanied by a rough soundtrack. A photomatic is similar to an animatic except that photographs are used instead of drawings. (Photomatics are most appropriate when a drawing is an inadequate visual representation, for example, when showing an appetizing food shot.) Both animatics and photomatics use camera movement to simulate movements and actions that will appear in the finished commercial.[8]

Finally, regardless of the advertising medium, the written or verbal copy in all tests ads should be identical to the copy that is proposed for the finished ad. The results of a communication test are irrelevant and misleading if this is not the case. Remember, the goal of communication testing is to provide a reliable estimate of how consumers will respond to the finished ad. Thus, it is important that the tested execution reflect the appearance and contain the content of the proposed finished ad.

APPROACHES TO DATA COLLECTION

Concept and communication tests can be conducted using either qualitative or quantitative methodology. The decision on which approach is "best" in a given situation reflects the types of information and insights that need to be obtained as well as timing and cost considerations. Regardless of the approach selected, however, it is critical that respondents are properly screened to ensure that they are members of the advertising's target audience.

Qualitative concept and communication testing is the more commonly used approach. Here, multiple concepts or executions are shown to focus groups for reaction and evaluation, typically after discussion of related topics has taken place. When this approach is used, the following should be kept in mind:[9]

- Individuals in group settings are typically reluctant to admit liking advertising. As a result, negative reactions to concepts and executions need to be probed to distinguish true unfavorable responses from "knee-jerk" negative responses.

- Complex concepts and executions take time to process, especially in group settings. The more complex the stimulus, the greater the amount of time that should be allowed for reflection prior to response.

- "Group-think" can be a problem particularly when the focus is an advertising concept or execution. Initial negative responses can bias the entire group. As a result, it is often useful to have group members write down their initial reactions prior to the start of group discussion.

- Group members may have a tendency to "speak first" and then post-rationalize their comments. As a result, respondents should be given time to think and formulate the rationale for their comments before the start of discussion.

- The presentation of multiple concepts or executions runs a risk of bias, where reactions to the initial stimuli influence reactions to later stimuli. Within any group, participants should be encouraged to respond to each stimulus individually noting its own unique strengths and weaknesses. Discussion of comparative reactions should be avoided until each concept or execution has had a chance to be discussed individually. When presenting multiple stimuli, the order of presentation should be varied across groups to reduce bias due to order effects.

Quantitative concept and communication testing is most commonly performed via one-on-one mall-intercept interviews or through online exposure and data collection. In both situations, respondents are typically exposed to only one concept or execution after which reactions are collected.

Custom or Syndicated Options

Regardless of the methodology selected, advertisers have the option of planning and conducting the research themselves, or they may hire a research company that specializes in this type of research. Both approaches collect the same core set of information, although syndicated services may supplement these measures with their own proprietary measurements (see Figure 19.6 for a description of Gallup & Robinson's approach to concept and communication testing).[10]

MEASUREMENT IN MESSAGE CONCEPT AND COMMUNICATION TESTS

A core set of questions comprises both message concept and communication tests. The manner in which these questions are expressed, however, differs in qualitative and quantitative approaches. The remainder of this section discusses the primary question types used in concept and communication tests, using a concept test of proposed messages for a campaign designed to encourage recycling. (Imagine that the concepts used in this research are similar to those shown in Figure 19.3.) Figure 19.7 (pages 558

Gallup & Robinson Advertising Pre-testing

Concepts can be executed in a number of ways and advertisers need to sort out the most promising creative approaches before incurring the cost of final production in print or TV. Pre-testing of preliminary executions in rough form is a quick and inexpensive means of identifying the winner among the also-rans and in providing insights for further improvement.

G&R is experienced in pre-testing ads for both consumer and B2B target audiences, revealing their strengths and weaknesses and pointing the way to improvements that can make all the difference between success and failure in the marketplace.

With today's technologies, preliminary advertising can be produced that is perfectly adequate for use in measuring potential consumer reaction to the finished product. G&R's flexible pre-testing services can evaluate more communication forms, including print ads, TV and radio commercials, online ads, outdoor ads, POS ads and materials, Web site, direct mail, logos, taglines, and FSI's. We are able to assess ads by themselves, as part of a medium campaign and across media.

G&R offers several services that are ideal for pre-testing preliminary advertising. All offer fast turnaround of results with experienced analysis and actionable recommendations.

Quantitative: WebSelect is an online, non-monadic system for sorting through alternatives quickly and efficiently within a quantitative framework. WebCheck can be used for consumers or specialized B2B samples. For example, Physician WebCheck enables pharmaceutical and medical devices companies to test ads and other marketing materials among online panels of physicians. FasTrac presents test stimuli in the same physical form as consumers will experience in the real world and gathers data through individual face-to-face interviews.

Qualitative: Individual Depth Interviews permit drilling down to core issues when sensitivity and group bias are concerns. Focus Groups conducted by trained moderators experienced in advertising development allow for open-ended probing for insights. Online Focus Groups permit the inclusion of more respondents, eliminate interpersonal bias and can include instantly coded surveys for group discussion.

FIGURE 19.6 Gallup & Robinson's Approach to Concept and Communication Testing

and 559) illustrates how key questions are incorporated into a discussion guide, while Figure 19.8 (pages 560 to 562) displays a quantitative approach to these same question types, in this case using an online survey.[11] Figure 19.9 (pages 563 to 567) illustrates the skip patterns used in the online survey. Beyond the questions themselves, note how diagnostic information is collected differently in each approach. Focus groups allow for interaction and probing, while the survey uses combinations of closed and open-ended questions to collect deeper insights into respondents' thoughts and feelings.

Introduction: Setting the Stage

Respondents are unlikely to have been exposed to message concepts or advertisements in less than finished form, particularly storyboards and animatics. As a result, it is important to begin the research with an explanation of the task and stimulus materials. The

---

Recycling Concepts Focus Groups
Discussion Guide

[Introductory sections of discussion guide are not shown]

What you are about to see are some messages that might be used in an advertising campaign designed to encourage individuals to recycle. We'd like to know how you feel about each message, as your opinions will help us better understand each message's strengths and weaknesses. There are, of course, no right or wrong answers . . . we just want to learn what you think. We'll look at and discuss each message one at a time.

1. In front of each of you is a pad of paper. As I read this first idea, please write down whatever thoughts or feelings are going through your mind as you listen.

Place Concept One on easel. Read Concept. Allow time when done reading for respondents to complete recording their thoughts and feelings.

Let's discuss what you wrote down.

Remove concept from view. Probe for similarities and differences across respondents.

2. What do you think was the main idea of the message?

Probe for additional ideas.

3. Do you recall the name of the organization that sponsored the communication? If so, which organization was the sponsor?

4. Now I'd like you to focus on your reactions to the message. How many of you thought the message was important? How many thought the message was not important?

Probe for reasons. Ask for specifics.

5. Still thinking about the message, how many of you thought that the message was relevant to you personally? How many thought the message was not relevant to you personally?

Probe for reasons. Probe for relevance to other types of individuals.

6. How believable or unbelievable did you find the message?

Probe for reasons. Ask for specifics.

7. Did you find the message unique?

Probe for reasons. Ask for specifics.

8. Was there anything confusing or hard to understand about the message?

Probe for reasons. Ask for specifics.

9. You've already mentioned some things that you like and dislike about the message? I'd like to pursue this a bit further. First, let me give each of you a copy of the message and a red and blue pen. Can you please circle in blue anything you particularly liked and circle in red anything you particularly disliked.

FIGURE 19.7 Discussion Guide for Recycling Concept Test

Allow time to complete.

Let's talk about your likes first. What are some of the things that you circled in blue.

Make certain that all respondents contribute. Compare and contrast responses.

Now, what are some of the things that you circled in red?

Make certain that all respondents contribute. Compare and contrast responses.

Are there any other likes and dislikes that we should discuss that go beyond the words and ideas themselves?

Probe for tone, approach, etc.

Ask Questions 10 and 11 only if these issues have not already been discussed.

10. The individuals who wrote this message have asked me to explore your reactions to two specific aspects of the message. First, what do you think about the spokesperson used in the commercial?

Probe for likes/dislikes, appropriateness, etc.

11. What do you think about the examples used in the message?

Probe for relevance, significance, believability, etc.

12. I'd like to understand how this message might or might not have influenced your attitudes toward recycling. On the pad of paper in front of you, please write down if you think your attitude toward recycling has stayed the same, improved or weakened as a result of what this message had to say?

Probe for reasons for attitude change.

13. Would you say that you are more likely, less likely or unchanged with regard to recycling in the future as a result of hearing this message? Again, please write down your thoughts on the pad of paper.

Probe for reasons for change in behavioral intention.

When done, repeat question sequence for Concept Two.

[Concluding sections of discussion guide are not shown]

FIGURE 19.7   (Continued)

introductory statements in Figures 19.7 and 19.8 illustrate how concepts would be explained and introduced. A similar approach would be used for the introduction of rough executions or animatics, for example:

> What you are about the see is an *idea* for a television commercial that would be part of an advertising campaign designed to encourage individuals to recycle. Because we're interested in your reactions to the commercial's idea and approach prior to finishing the commercial, the commercial you'll see is in rough rather than finished form. Pictures are used to represent key scenes, and the actor's movements are quite basic. As you watch the commercial, please keep in mind that the finished commercial will be a "real-life" commercial like the ones you are used to seeing. It will be filmed with real actors and will look just like a typical commercial. No drawings or animation will be used.

Recycling Concept Test

Thank you for participating in our survey.

What you are about to see is a message that might be used in an advertising campaign designed to encourage individuals to recycle. We'd like to know how you feel about this message, as your opinions will help us better understand its strengths and weaknesses. There are, of course, no right or wrong answers . . . we just want to learn what you think.

Please press the link below to see the message, which will open in a new window. When you are done reading, press the "Return" button beneath the message to close this window and return to this survey.

<u>Click here to see the message.</u>

1)   What thoughts or feelings were going through your mind as you read through the message?

(**1000** characters remaining)

2)   What was the main idea of the message?

3)   What was the name of the message's sponsor?

Please click on the link below to see the recycling message one more time. A new window will open. When you are done reading, press the "Return" button beneath the message to close the window and return to this survey.

<u>Click here to see the message</u>

*4)   How important or unimportant did you find the message?

○ Extremely important
○ Slightly important
○ Slightly unimportant
○ Extremely unimportant

5)   Why did you rate the message as unimportant?

(**1000** characters remaining)

*6)   How much do you agree or disagree with the statement: "The message was personally relevant to me"?

○ Strongly agree
○ Slightly agree
○ Slightly disagree
○ Strongly disagree

FIGURE 19.8   Online Survey for Recycling Concept Test

7) Why do you believe that the message is not relevant to you personally?

(**1000** characters remaining)

*8) How believable or unbelievable do you feel the message was?
- ○ Extremely believable
- ○ Slightly believable
- ○ Slightly unbelievable
- ○ Extremely unbelievable

9) Why do you think the message was not believable?

(**1000** characters remaining)

*10) How much would you agree or disagree with the statement: "The message was unique"?
- ○ Strongly agree
- ○ Slightly agree
- ○ Slightly disagree
- ○ Strongly disagree

11) Why do you think the message was not unique?

*12) How much would you agree or disagree with the statement "The message was easy to understand"?
- ○ Strongly agree
- ○ Slightly agree
- ○ Slightly disagree
- ○ Strongly disagree

13) What about the message was confusing or hard to understand?

(**1000** characters remaining)

*14) How much did you like or dislike the message?
- ○ Strongly liked
- ○ Slightly liked
- ○ Slightly disliked
- ○ Strongly disliked

15) What in particular did you like?

FIGURE 19.8 (Continued)

*16) Was there anything you disliked?

   ○ Yes
   ○ No

17) What in particular did you dislike?

[   ]

*18) Please click either option below to continue.

   ○ Continue
   ○ Continue

19) What in particular did you dislike?

[   ]

*20) Was there anything that you liked?

   ○ Yes
   ○ No

21) What in particular did you like?

[   ]

22) What are your particular thoughts and feelings regarding the spokesperson used to communicate the message?

[   ]

(**1000** characters remaining)

23) What are your thoughts and feelings regarding the recycling examples used in the message?

[   ]

(**1000** characters remaining)

24) How much, if at all, do you think your attitude toward recycling has changed after reading the message?

   ○ More positive
   ○ About the same – unchanged
   ○ More negative

25) How much, if at all, do you think your actual recycling behaviors will change as a result of reading this message?

   ○ I'll recycle more
   ○ I'll recycle about the same
   ○ I'll recycle less

Please click on "Submit".

(Submit)

powered by www.psychdata.com

FIGURE 19.8 (Continued)

Wednesday, November 25, 2009

Recycling Concept Test

[Descriptive Text]

Thank you for participating in our survey.

What you are about to see is a message that might be used in an advertising campaign designed to encourage individuals to recycle. We'd like to know how you feel about this message, as your opinions will help us better understand its strengths and weaknesses. There are, of course, no right or wrong answers . . . we just want to learn what you think.

Please press the link below to see the message, which will open in a new window. When you are done reading, press the "Return" button beneath the message to close this window and return to this survey.

<u>Click here to see the message.</u>

1) [Free Response: Multiple Line Answer (1000 character limit)]
   What thoughts or feelings were going through your mind as you read through the message?

2) [Free Response: One Line Answer (100 character limit)]
   What was the main idea of the message?

3) [Free Response: One Line Answer (100 character limit)]
   What was the name of the message's sponsor?

[Descriptive Text]

Please click on the link below to see the recycling message one more time. A new window will open. When you are done reading, press the "Return" button beneath the message to close the window and return to this survey.

<u>Click here to see the message</u>

*4) [Multiple Choice: Single Select (vertical)]
   How important or unimportant did you find the message?
       Extremely important

           Logic
           If [Extremely important] is selected, then skip to question [#6]
       Slightly important

           Logic
           If [Slightly important] is selected, then skip to question [#6]
       Slightly unimportant

           Logic
           If [Slightly unimportant] is selected, then skip to question [#5]

FIGURE 19.9 Online Recycling Concept Test Survey Skip Patterns

Extremely unimportant

> **Logic**
> If [Extremely unimportant] is selected, then skip to question [#5]

5) [Free Response: Multiple Line Answer (1000 character limit)]
Why did you rate the message as unimportant?

*6) [Multiple Choice: Single Select (vertical)]
How much do you agree or disagree with the statement: "The message was personally relevant to me"?

Strongly agree

> **Logic**
> If [Strongly agree] is selected, then skip to question [#8]

Slightly agree

> **Logic**
> If [Slightly agree] is selected, then skip to question [#8]

Slightly disagree

> **Logic**
> If [Slightly disagree] is selected, then skip to question [#7]

Strongly disagree

> **Logic**
> If [Strongly disagree] is selected, then skip to question [#7]

7) [Free Response: Multiple Line Answer (1000 character limit)]
Why do you believe that the message is not relevant to you personally?

*8) [Multiple Choice: Single Select (vertical)]
How believable or unbelievable do you feel the message was?

Extremely believable

> **Logic**
> If [Extremely believable] is selected, then skip to question [#10]

Slightly believable

> **Logic**
> If [Slightly believable] is selected, then skip to question [#10]

Slightly unbelievable

> **Logic**
> If [Slightly unbelievable] is selected, then skip to question [#9]

Extremely unbelievable

> **Logic**
> If [Extremely unbelievable] is selected, then skip to question [#9]

9) [Free Response: Multiple Line Answer (1000 character limit)]
Why do you think the message was not believable?

*10) [Multiple Choice: Single Select (vertical)]
How much would you agree or disagree with the statement: "The message was unique"?

Strongly agree

> **Logic**
> If [Strongly agree] is selected, then skip to question [#12]

FIGURE 19.9 (Continued)

Slightly agree

    Logic

    If [Slightly agree] is selected, then skip to question [#12]

Slightly disagree

    Logic

    If [Slightly disagree] is selected, then skip to question [#11]

Strongly disagree

    Logic

    If [Strongly disagree] is selected, then skip to question [#11]

11) [Free Response: One Line Answer (100 character limit)]
Why do you think the message was not unique?

*12) [Multiple Choice: Single Select (vertical)]
How much would you agree or disagree with the statement "The message was easy to understand"?

Strongly agree

    Logic

    If [Strongly agree] is selected, then skip to question [#14]

Slightly agree

    Logic

    If [Slightly agree] is selected, then skip to question [#14]

Slightly disagree

    Logic

    If [Slightly disagree] is selected, then skip to question [#13]

Strongly disagree

    Logic

    If [Strongly disagree] is selected, then skip to question [#13]

13) [Free Response: Multiple Line Answer (1000 character limit)]
What about the message was confusing or hard to understand?

*14) [Multiple Choice: Single Select (vertical)]
How much did you like or dislike the message?

Strongly liked

    Logic

    If [Strongly liked] is selected, then skip to question [#15]

Slightly liked

    Logic

    If [Slightly liked] is selected, then skip to question [#15]

Slightly disliked

    Logic

    If [Slightly disliked] is selected, then skip to question [#19]

Strongly disliked

    Logic

    If [Strongly disliked] is selected, then skip to question [#19]

FIGURE 19.9 (Continued)

15) [Free Response: One Line Answer (100 character limit)]
What in particular did you like?

*16) [Multiple Choice: Single Select (vertical)]
Was there anything you disliked?

Yes

Logic
If [Yes] is selected, then skip to question [#17]

No

Logic
If [No] is selected, then skip to question [#22]

17) [Free Response: One Line Answer (100 character limit)]
What in particular did you dislike?

*18) [Multiple Choice: Single Select (vertical)]
Please click either option below to continue.

Continue

Logic
If [Continue] is selected, then skip to question [#22]

Continue

Logic
If [Continue] is selected, then skip to question [#22]

19) [Free Response: One Line Answer (100 character limit)]
What in particular did you dislike?

*20) [Multiple Choice: Single Select (vertical)]
Was there anything that you liked?

Yes

Logic
If [Yes] is selected, then skip to question [#21]

No

Logic
If [No] is selected, then skip to question [#22]

21) [Free Response: One Line Answer (100 character limit)]
What in particular did you like?

22) [Free Response: Multiple Line Answer (1000 character limit)]
What are your particular thoughts and feelings regarding the spokesperson used to communicate the message?

23) [Free Response: Multiple Line Answer (1000 character limit)]
What are your thoughts and feelings regarding the recycling examples used in the message?

FIGURE 19.9 (Continued)

24) [Multiple Choice: Single Select (vertical)]
How much, if at all, do you think your attitude toward recycling has changed after reading the message?

> More positive
>
> About the same—unchanged
>
> More negative

25) [Multiple Choice: Single Select (vertical)]
How much, if at all, do you think your actual recycling behaviors will change as a result of reading this message?

> I'll recycle more
>
> I'll recycle about the same
>
> I'll recycle less

FIGURE 19.9 (Continued)

Show Concept or Execution

The introduction is followed by exposure to the concept or execution. In focus groups, the moderator typically presents and reads the concept or shows the execution, which is often placed on a large board to allow group members to read along. Surveys also show the concept or execution at this point, allowing respondents as much time as desired to read and process the stimulus.

Spontaneous Initial Reactions

Data collection begins by encouraging respondents to talk about the concept or execution in the absence of specific direction. As a result, both qualitative and quantitative approaches begin with an open-ended question (see Question 1 in Figures 19.7 and 19.8).[12] Initiating the interview with this type of question works well for two reasons: it begins the interview in a nonthreatening way, and it provides a respondent with the opportunity to describe in his or her own words the thoughts and feelings associated with the stimulus before the moderator or questionnaire more narrowly focuses the interview. Since the topics mentioned by respondents are those most "top of mind," issues raised here tend to significant.

It is important that a respondent answers this and the following two questions from memory. These initial questions are designed to collect information relative to respondent thoughts, feelings, and recall, all of which can potentially be biased if the respondent has the opportunity to "look up the answer" by reexamining the advertising. This is why the discussion guide instructs the moderator to remove the test advertisement from view and why the online survey continues without allowing reference back to the test ad.

Essential Message

Questions 2 and 3 in the discussion guide and survey probe message and brand name/ sponsor communication.[13] Similar to the prior question, these areas are assessed with open-ended questions asked in the absence of the concept or execution. Open- rather than closed-ended questions are used because we do not want to "prime" the respondent by allowing him or her to choose from a limited list of choices. Additionally, a closed-ended list would also discourage respondents (even with an "other" choice) from volunteering answers not listed, thereby significantly reducing the ability to uncover and probe unintended communications. Note also that Question 2 asks "What was the main idea?" as opposed to "What did the commercial say?" This distinction is important. Concept and communication research are not interested in simply testing the consumer's memory (as is done when you ask "What did it say?") but seeks to determine how the consumer has interpreted and internalized the commercial message (as is done when you ask "What was main idea?")[14]

Reactions to the Message

The concept or advertisement is typically reintroduced at this point, and respondents are given the opportunity to review it a second time. Personal reactions to the message are then explored (see Questions 4 and 5 in Figure 19.7 and Questions 4 through 7 in Figure 19.8). These questions ask respondents to indicate the extent to which they personally feel the message is important and relevant. The approach taken to probe these areas differs across methodologies.

- Qualitative research uses open-ended questions to explore respondents' opinions.
- Quantitative research uses a combination of closed- and open-ended questions specifically designed to focus on negative or unfavorable reactions. Questions 4 and 6 (in Figure 19.8) use rating scales to obtain initial responses. After each scale question, only those respondents who provide an unfavorable rating are asked the follow-up open-ended question. The sequence of a scale followed by an open-ended question provides important diagnostic information and helps advertisers better understand the underlying reasons of negative consumer response to the concept or execution.

Reactions to the message itself are explored next (see Questions 6 to 8 in Figure 19.7 and Questions 8 through 13 in Figure 19.8). These questions ask respondents to indicate the extent to which they feel the message is believable, unique, and easy to understand. As with the prior set of questions, the approach taken to probe these areas differs across methodologies.

- Qualitative research uses open-ended questions to explore respondents' opinions.
- Quantitative research continues to use a combination of closed- and open-ended questions where only those respondents who provide an unfavorable rating are asked the appropriate follow-up open-ended question.

Affective Reactions

This sequence of questions moves the discussion from the prior rational assessment of the message to more emotional reactions to the message. Qualitative research uses a single open-ended question to explore this area (see Question 9 in Figure 19.7), while quantitative research uses a series of closed- and open-ended questions (see Questions 14 through 21 in Figure 19.8). The like/dislike questions on the quantitative survey are sequenced so that Question 14, the scale question, serves as the basis for a skip pattern appropriate to the respondent's attitude. A respondent who indicates that he or she liked the message is immediately asked what he or she liked (Question 15), and is then given the opportunity to state what, if anything, he or she did not like (Questions 16 and 17). "Dummy" Question 18 allows this respondent to skip to Question 22. Similarly, a respondent who indicates that he or she disliked the message in Question 14 is immediately asked what he or she disliked (Question 19), and is then given the opportunity to state what, if anything, he or she liked (Questions 20 and 21), after which the respondent continues with Question 22. In both cases, the pattern of relating the first open-ended question to the respondent's attitude makes the question sequence intuitively reasonable and makes it easier for the respondent to answer.

Message or Execution Specific Issues

Every concept or execution raises some concerns that are unique: Is the spokesperson appropriate? Is the music too loud? Is the pace too quick? Is the situation appropriate? This segment of the questionnaire (see Questions 10 and 11 in Figure 19.7 and Questions 22 and 23 in Figure 19.8) probes unique areas of concern. Open-ended questions are used so that respondents' answers are not constrained or biased by predetermined response categories. The total number of questions asked in this portion of the research depends upon the number of specific concerns.

Attitudinal and Behavioral Impact

Concept and communication research have the option of ending with attitude change or behavioral intention questions. These questions (open-ended in qualitative research and closed-ended in quantitative research) seek to determine the extent to which exposure to the concept or execution has moved the respondent in the right direction.

Questions 12 and 13 in Figure 19.7 and Questions 24 and 25 in Figure 19.8 illustrate one approach to these types of questions. Both sets of questions are designed to determine the extent to which exposure to the concept resulted in the respondent adopting more positive attitudes toward recycling and the likelihood of changing his or her recycling behaviors. Note that these questions are comparative, asking respondents to compare their post-exposure attitudes and intentions to those held prior to exposure.

ANALYSIS OF CONCEPT AND COMMUNICATION TEST DATA

Qualitative research findings are analyzed and presented using the techniques described in Chapter 7. Quantitative findings require the successful completion of the following two tasks:

- *Data summarization* is the most straightforward of the two tasks. Descriptive statistics are commonly used to describe the pattern of response while cross-tabulations and statistical significance are used to provide deeper insights into the data and to provide greater confidence in the conclusions drawn from the data. This section describes considerations in this aspect of analysis.

- The *uncovering of underlying relationships* between measures tends to be the more difficult of the two tasks. While some techniques such as chi-square and correlation can help, this task nevertheless requires researcher creativity. Only through uncovering the relationship among measures can research users best understand the true strengths and weaknesses of the tested stimuli and make informed judgments regarding how to maximize strengths and eliminate weaknesses. The next section illustrates how this can be accomplished.

Data Summarization

Data summarization in concept and communication tests requires an analysis of total sample responses as well as analysis of similarities and differences in responses among important subgroups of respondents, where subgroups are most commonly defined in terms of demographic, attitudinal, or behavioral characteristics.

TOTAL SAMPLE RESPONSES.   The responses of the total sample are always an important starting point for data summarization. One approach is to present the responses to each open- and closed-ended question in an individual table or graph, for example:

Response Options	Total Sample ($n = 200$)
Extremely believable (1)	50%
Somewhat believable (2)	20
Somewhat unbelievable (3)	10
Extremely unbelievable (4)	20
Mean	**2.0**

Alternatively, the responses to related questions can be combined into a single table or graph:

Type of Response	Rating of Message	
	Believability ($n = 200$)	Uniqueness ($n = 200$)
Extremely positive (1)	50%	30%
Somewhat positive (2)	20	20
Somewhat negative (3)	10	20
Extremely negative (4)	20	30
Mean	**2.0**	**2.5**

The analysis of smaller subgroups begins after the data for the total sample has been examined.

DIFFERENCES AND SIMILARITIES IN DEMOGRAPHIC GROUPS.   An understanding of demographic variation in response to a concept or execution response is often of great value. Here, it is important to determine whether responses to the concept or execution were consistent across key demographic groups or whether levels of response varied as a function of demographic characteristics. To determine consistency or variation in response, descriptive statistics such as means or frequency distributions (depending on the level of measurement) are reported for key measures for key demographic groups. The responses of the sample as a whole may also be included to provide a point of reference.

Table organization and data analysis are straightforward when a single concept or execution is tested, or when one concept is examined independently of other concepts or executions. The following table, for example, provides detailed information on two demographic groups' response to a single measure, in this case respondents' ratings of concept message believability.

| | | Women With | |
| | | Children Aged | Children Aged |
Response Options	**Total Sample** (*n* = 200)	**3 to 7** (*n* = 100)	**8 to 12** (*n* = 100)
Extremely believable (1)	50%	75%	25%
Somewhat believable (2)	20	20	20
Somewhat unbelievable (3)	10	5	15
Extremely unbelievable (4)	20	0	40
Mean	**2.0**	**1.3**[*]	**2.7**[*]

*significant at p < .001

Note how the measure's frequency distribution and overall mean as well as demographic group distributions, means, and tests of significance have all been incorporated into a single table. Also note an important insight provided by this analysis: while the majority of the total sample found the concept believable, this was almost entirely due to the positive response among women with children aged three to seven. Significantly fewer mothers of older children found the concept believable.

When several concepts are tested at the same time or when it is necessary to compare concepts tested at difference points in time, analyses require that multiple comparisons be conducted. These comparisons require two approaches to data organization and analysis. First, the data must be organized and presented so that responses to each individual concept or execution can be clearly seen and understood. *Here, data presentation and analysis hold the concept constant and then determines if individuals in different demographic groups reacted similarly or differently.* Depending upon the number of concepts tested, tables can present each concept independently or a single table can simultaneously present data relevant to two or more concepts, for example:

| | Concept A | | | | Concept B | | |
| | Women With | | | | Women With | | |
Response Option	Total Sample (*n* = 200)	Children Aged 3 to 7 (*n* = 100)	Children Aged 8 to 12 (*n* = 100)	Total Sample (*n* = 200)	Children Aged 3 to 7 (*n* = 100)	Children Aged 8 to 12 (*n* = 100)
Extremely believable (1)	50%	25%	75%	50%	70%	30%
Somewhat believable (2)	20	40	0	20	30	10
Somewhat unbelievable (3)	20	30	10	20	0	40
Extremely unbelievable (4)	10	5	15	10	0	20
Mean	**1.9**	**2.1***	**1.7***	**1.9**	**1.3****	**2.5****

*significant at $p = .03$

**significant at $p = .01$

The prior table presents a large amount of data, and therefore runs the risk of confusion. As a result, an alternative approach organizes the data so that differences can be more easily seen. *Here, data presentation and analysis hold the demographic group constant and then determines the extent to which a particular demographic group's reactions were similar or different across concepts.* Data organization for this type of analysis is shown in the following table, which makes it much easier to see that women with younger children find Concept B more believable while women with older children find Concept A more believable.

| | Women with Children Aged 3 to 7 | | Women with Children Aged 7 to 12 | |
Response Option	Concept A (*n* = 100)	Concept B (*n* = 100)	Concept A (*n* = 100)	Concept B (*n* = 100)
Extremely believable (1)	25%	70%	75%	30%
Somewhat believable (2)	40	30	0	10
Somewhat unbelievable (3)	30	0	10	40
Extremely unbelievable (4)	5	0	15	20
Mean	**2.1***	**1.3***	**1.7****	**2.5****

*significant at $p < .001$

**significant at $p < .01$

DIFFERENCES AND SIMILARITIES AMONG ATTITUDE AND BEHAVIORAL GROUPS. Analysis of primary study measures by attitude groups provides important insights into why consumers reacted to the concept or execution as they did. This analysis permits one to determine whether positive attitude change after exposure to the concept or communication is, for example, related to message believability, uniqueness, or the presence/absence of elements communicated to the consumer. Two types of analyses are possible. First, if the measures permit, attitude change can be correlated to other key measures. An example of this approach is illustrated in the correlations (below), where it can be seen that attitude change rises along with individuals' assessment of message believability, importance, and relevance. Ratings of message uniqueness do not appear to be related to attitude change.[15]

	Attitude Change
Believability	.56
Importance	.77
Relevance	.86
Uniqueness	−.03

All correlations greater than .55 are significant at $p < .01$

Once correlations are calculated, statistically significant correlations can then be explored in greater detail through appropriate cross-tabulations. The following table illustrates this approach by cross-tabulating two closed-ended questions, in this case ratings of message importance and attitude change after reading the concept.

		Attitude Change Group	
Response Option	**Total Sample** **(n = 200)**	**Positive** **Change** **(n = 80)**	**Negative** **Change** **(n = 120)**
Extremely important (1)	55%	87.5%	33.3%
Somewhat important (2)	15	6.3	20.8
Somewhat unimportant (3)	10	6.3	12.5
Extremely unimportant (4)	20	0.0	33.3
Mean	**2.0**	**1.2**[*]	**2.5**[*]

*significant at $p < .001$

The table provides important detail to supplement the correlational findings. The data show that almost all individuals with positive attitude change thought the concept's message was extremely important, while those with negative attitude change were much less impressed with the importance of the message, with about even numbers of these individuals believing the message was and was not important.

Additional insights can be obtained by cross-tabulating open-ended questions by attitude group. The following table illustrates this type of analysis and displays the results of the open-ended likes/dislikes question cross-tabulated by type of attitude change.[16]

Open Ended Response	Total Sample (*n* = 200)	Attitude Change Group	
		Positive	**Negative**
		Change (*n* = 80)	Change (*n* = 120)
Any like (net)	**80%**	**80.0%**	**80.0%**
Spokesperson	60%	95.0	36.7
Description of child	30	30.0	30.0
Positive outlook	20	22.5	18.3
Any dislike (net)	**30%**	**32.5%**	**28.3%**
Spokesperson	25	6.3	37.5
Use of fear	13	12.5	13.3
Over-exaggeration	8	7.5	8.3

The data in the table indicates that the concept was well liked. The percentage of individuals in both attitude groups who liked the concept is generally equivalent, and more individuals in both the positive and negative attitude change groups mentioned liking versus disliking some element of the concept. The pattern in these two groups differed in one important respect, however. The positive attitude change group was quite positive toward the spokesperson—almost all were positive and few were negative. The negative attitude change group disliked the spokesperson. Significantly fewer individuals in this group versus the positive attitude group liked the spokesperson, and as many individuals in this group liked as disliked the spokesperson. Other specific likes and dislikes were generally equivalent across the two groups. Thus, the spokesperson used in the concept would need to be re-examined (and perhaps retested or replaced) prior to final selection as this was the single like/dislike that distinguished individuals in the positive and negative attitude change groups.[17]

Finding Relationships Among Measures

The prior section illustrated how data from a quantitative concept or communication test can be analyzed to determine differences in response across different demographic, attitudinal, or behavioral intention groups. Similar types of analyses can be conducted to provide even deeper insights into the pattern of response. Here, the responses to one survey question are examined in the context of responses to a second survey question. Four different types of approaches are possible.

RELATING SKIP SCALE QUESTIONS TO OPEN-ENDED RESPONSES.   Questions 6 and 7 in Figure 19.8 probe reactions to message importance. Question 6, the scale question, asks all respondents to rate message relevance, while Question 7, an open-ended question, is asked only of those respondents who *disagreed* that the message was relevant. The following table relates the responses to these two questions.

Reason(s) for Rating	Individuals Who Rate Message as "Not Relevant" (*n* = 150)
Examples are too weird	83%
Language used is too odd	63
Insulting	30
Doesn't apply to people who already recycle	28
Don't have experiences like the ones described	21

Table base is 150 respondents (75% of sample) who disagreed that the message was relevant.

The data in the table indicate that most individuals (75%) did not find the message personally relevant (see note at bottom of table). Moreover, the lack of relevance appears to arise from the concept's approach. Negative reactions to both the examples and language used in the concept appear to be the primary reasons for the perceived lack of relevance. These high percentages, taken together, would indicate that this is a significant weakness of the concept being tested.

COMPARING THE RESPONSES TO OPEN-ENDED QUESTIONS WITH SCALE QUESTIONS.   The prior example examined the responses to an open-ended question in the context of an intentionally related scale question. This approach can be expanded to the examination of *any* open-ended question in light of the responses to *any* scale question. Given the unlimited number of possible combinations, however, it is important that a researcher not approach this task (and the tasks described in the following sections) haphazardly. Rather every analysis should be designed to answer a specific, pre-identified research question.

Earlier, we illustrated how identified concept likes and dislikes can be examined in terms of different attitudinal groups, specifically those whose attitudes showed positive and negative change after concept exposure. This same type of analysis can be expanded to other combinations of measures. A researcher might ask, for example, "What were the specific likes and dislikes of those who found the message either important or unimportant?" The following table provides the data to answer this question.

Open-Ended Responses	Total Sample (*n* = 200)	"Importance" Rating Group	
		Message Important (*n* = 135)	Message Unimportant (*n* = 65)
Any like (net)	**80%**	**97.7%**	**42.6%**
Spokesperson	60%	80.0	18.5
Description of child	30	40.7	7.8
Positive outlook	20	26.7	6.2
Any dislike (net)	**30%**	**4.4%**	**83.1%**
Spokesperson	25	3.8	69.2
Use of fear	13	2.2	35.4
Over-exaggeration	8	1.5	21.5

The table indicates that those who found the message important liked many elements of the concept, particularly the spokesperson, description of the child, and the positive outlook. Very few in this group disliked anything about the concept. Conversely, those who found the message unimportant liked very few things about the concept and indicated a broad range of things that were disliked, particularly the spokesperson and the approach taken by the message.

Beyond this type of single scale question analysis, multiple scale questions can be examined simultaneously. Here, for example, a researcher might ask: "Are initial thoughts and feelings different or similar for those who found the concept either confusing, not important or not believable?" The following table provides the data to answer this question.

	Type of Message Rating		
Open-Ended Responses	**Message Confusing** (*n* = 40)	**Message Unimportant** (*n* = 65)	**Message Unbelievable** (*n* = 75)
Any positive mention (net)	**30.0%**	**7.7%**	**26.7%**
Made me feel good about myself	10.0	6.2	14.7
Made me proud	7.5	6.2	20.0
People need to hear this	12.5	4.6	13.3
A motivating message	5.0	9.2	14.7
My kids need to hear this	2.5	3.8	4.0
Any negative mention (net)	**95.0%**	**96.7%**	**93.3%**
Too scary	82.5	6.2	10.6
Too many details	90.0	15.4	13.3
Insulting	20.0	89.2	12.0
Hate spokesman	17.5	12.4	90.1
Too emotionally manipulative	17.5	8.4	92.0

The table makes it easy to compare and contrast the underlying pattern of responses across the three groups. On the one hand, individuals in the three groups show a similar overall pattern of response. Few individuals in each group mentioned liking something in the concept, while almost all in each group mentioned disliking something. On the other hand, the specific dislikes varied considerably across the three groups. Those who found the concept confusing disliked the concept's scare approach and use of too many details, those who found the concept unimportant found the concept insulting, while those who found the concept unbelievable focused on their dislike to the spokesman and the concept's perceived emotional manipulation. These types of diagnostic insights would provide direction for future concept revision.

Both of the prior examples used the scale question as the classification variable. This does not have to be the case, however. A researcher might ask, for example: "How do reactions to the message differ among those who liked and disliked the spokesperson?" In this case, the mean scores on the reactions to the message scale measures might be computed for each group, as shown in the following table.

| Scale Question | Mentions of Spokesperson | |
	Positive (n = 133)	Negative (n = 67)
Important*	1.2	4.1
Relevant*	1.4	3.8
Believable*	1.6	3.9
Unique	2.2	2.4
Easy to Understand	3.2	3.1

*Differences in these means between the two groups are significant at p < .001

The data in the table provides complimentary insights to the prior table. Here, where lower numbers indicate more positive scores, the data indicates that reactions to the spokesperson are strongly related to ratings of message importance, relevance, and believability but not ratings of message uniqueness or ease of understanding. This diagnostic insight into the role of the spokesperson becomes an important consideration as the concept's approach is evaluated for underlying strengths and weaknesses.

COMPARING THE RESPONSES TO TWO SCALE QUESTIONS. The relationship between *any* two scale questions can be explored similarly to the approach taken to examine the relationship between attitude change and reactions to the message. A correlation i s computed first, after which cross-tabulations are used to explore the underlying distributions.

COMPARING THE RESPONSES TO TWO OPEN-ENDED QUESTIONS. Finally, responses to two open-ended questions can be examined. The procedure is the same as that described for using an open-ended question as the classification variable for analysis of responses to a scale question, except that here, one open-ended question is used to as the classification variable for an examination of responses to another open-ended question. A researcher might ask for example: "What are the other initial reactions of those who found the concept insulting?" The following table provides the data to answer this question.

Open-Ended Response	Respondents Who Found Concept "Insulting" (*n* = 58)
Any positive mention (net)	**6.9%**
Made me feel good about myself	1.7
Made me proud	1.7
People need to hear this	3.4
A motivating message	1.7
My kids need to hear this	0.0
Any negative mention (net)	**100.0%**
Too scary	8.6
Too many details	75.8
Insulting	100.0
Hate spokesman	82.7
Too emotionally manipulative	79.3

The data indicates that those who found the concept insulting also hated the spokesperson and found the concept too emotionally manipulative. As with the insights provided by the prior analyses, this data would be used to identify necessary changes should the concept be taken forward.

APPLYING CHAPTER CONCEPTS

Health Canada[18] is responsible for helping Canadians maintain and improve their health. Health Canada uses multiple media and creative approaches to communicate with Canadians about health-related issues. In order to ensure that its communications are as effective as possible, communication tests are often conducted to identify *from the target audience's perspective* the strengths and weaknesses of potential creative approaches. The communication tests conducted by Health Canada are identical in their goals and very similar in approach to the communication tests described in this chapter. The online supplemental readings provide two communication test research studies conducted by Health Canada. The first study relies on focus groups to explore reactions to potential television advertisements designed to encourage healthy eating. The second study uses a combination of quantitative and qualitative research to explore reactions to multimedia communications designed to inform individuals about the dangers of secondhand smoke.[19]

Healthy Eating

Health Canada describes the rationale and goals for this research as follows:

Each year in Canada, more than 75% of deaths result from four groups of noncommunicable diseases: cardiovascular, some forms of cancer, diabetes and osteoporosis. An unhealthy diet is a preventable risk factor in all of these illnesses. To address this issue, Health Canada has expanded the content on its website to include tips and tools about health eating, launched a mandatory nutrition labelling program for food packaging (2005), as well as updated and expanded Canada's Food Guide. In February 2007, television ads that focused on nutritional messages were aired to promote the new Food Guide. As a follow-up, Health Canada is designing a second phase of healthy eating ads that require testing.[20]

Three second phase ads were designed and tested in eight focus groups consisting primarily of women, where all participants (both men and women) were parents of children aged 2 to 12. As with all communication tests, the research was diagnostic in orientation, with three specific goals:

- To evaluate and determine whether the new healthy eating creative concepts are:
  - clear, credible, and relevant to the segmented audiences;
  - appealing and appropriate to the cultural and emotional sensitivities of the audience;
  - memorable in the minds of the audience;
  - able to motivate the audience to take appropriate actions; and
  - capable of mobilizing public support behind government action with the designated target audience;
- To determine which of the healthy eating concepts is most effective at reaching the target audience; and
- To elicit suggestions for potential changes to make the concepts more effective at reaching the target audience.

Descriptions of the three tested television advertisements are provided in Figure 19.10. An edited version of the full report is provided in the online supplemental readings.

Secondhand Smoke

Secondhand smoke, also known as passive smoking, is a real and continuing problem that threatens the health of nonsmokers.[21] Health Canada recognized this problem and planned a communications campaign designed to inform both smokers and nonsmokers of the dangers associated with secondhand smoke.[22] Communications testing was recommended to evaluate consumers' responses to proposed creative approaches prior to producing the campaign. The specific goals of the communication test were to identify execution strengths and weaknesses with regard to:

- effectiveness, fit, and appeal
- credibility and believability
- relevance
- clarity and understandability
- sensitivity to the needs of the target audience

"Road"

In this animated spot, members of an animated family are shown riding their bikes along a road that is also a rainbow. The perspective broadens to show that the rainbow represents the Food Guide, and giant versions of different kinds of food are displayed (e.g., bread, milk). The family stops to examine the nutrition label on a carton of milk. The spot ends by showing the mom holding a copy of the Food Guide and the family sitting and eating at a dining room table together. The visuals transition from animation to a shot of the "real" family.

"Kids in the Kitchen"

In this spot, three kids from different ethnic backgrounds are shown having fun while preparing various types of foods in a kitchen. At the outset of the ad, a father figure is shown opening a cupboard, and then leaving the kitchen. The kids dance and move in choreographed sequences while they cook. They prepare food and drink a smoothie. Near the end of the spot, one of the kids throws an apple to another one; this shot transitions to show the kids outside playing catch. The apple morphs into a baseball that is caught by the girl with a glove. Her father is standing behind and is also holding a baseball glove.

"Mom & Company"

This spot opens with an image of a mom and a daughter shopping in a grocery store. The camera perspective shows the daughter in the full frame. The upper half of the mom, including her face, is not shown (as if the images are from the child's point of view). Both the mom and the daughter are pushing grocery carts (the daughter is pushing a child-sized one). Throughout the spot, the mom and the daughter perform the same actions, including examining the nutrition label on a carton of milk, squeezing a melon, and choosing between two brands of oatmeal. The scene then switches to images of a father and young son pushing grocery carts. A child's voice speaks the tagline "Healthy eating. It's for life." The final live image shows the girl in the backseat of a car pretending to feed a carrot to her stuffed kangaroo.

FIGURE 19.10   Concepts Tested in Healthy Eating Communication Test

Note how this chapter earlier identified these areas as important in communications testing.

Heath Canada also recognized that since qualitative and quantitative research often compliment each other in terms of insights provided, a mixed-methods approach might be best for providing the detailed insights required for evaluation of the proposed communications. As a result, the research consisted of

- six focus groups held in Halifax, Montreal, and Toronto. In each city, one group was held with nonsmokers who have a smoker in the household and one group was held with smokers. All participants were parents between the ages of 20 and 55.

- an online quantitative survey of 737 Canadian smokers, nonsmokers, and nonsmokers who live with smokers. Similar to the focus groups, all respondents were parents between the ages of 20 and 55.

An edited version of the full report is presented in the online supplemental readings.

SUMMARY

Concept and communication tests occur during the early stages of the advertising development process. The tests differ in that concept tests focus exclusively on messages and message evaluation, while communication tests focus on message communication within the context of alternative executions. The two tests, however, share one important characteristic. Concept and communication tests are both diagnostic in approach, designed to identify strengths and weaknesses rather than select a "winner."

Concept tests explore individuals' reactions to alternative approaches to communicating a positioning, benefit, reason for being, or unique communication proposition. A concept expresses its idea simply and without exaggeration, salesmanship, or advertising puffery. The most important task of a concept is to present the core idea simply and realistically so that consumers' comprehension is maximized and response to the core idea can be confidently assessed. Concept tests can be either product or non-product focused. Communication tests typically follow the administration of a concept test. Communication testing's goal is to evaluate consumers' reactions to different ways of communicating the selected message, thereby identifying the strengths and weaknesses of proposed executional approaches.

Concept and communication tests can be conducted using either qualitative or quantitative methodology. Although qualitative approaches are more common, the final decision on which approach is "best" in a given situation reflects the types of information and insights that need to be obtained as well as timing and cost considerations. Regardless of the approach taken, core measures in concept and communication research are the same in both approaches and typically include:

- Spontaneous initial reactions
- Message communication
- Personal reactions to the message, concept, or execution
- Affective reactions to the message, concept, or execution
- Message, concept, or execution specific issues

Qualitative research findings from both concept and communication tests are analyzed following the procedures discussed in Chapter 7. Quantitative findings require both data summarization and the uncovering of underlying relationships between measures.

- Data summarization requires an analysis of total sample responses as well as analysis of similarities and differences in responses among important subgroups of respondents, where subgroups are most commonly defined in terms of demographic, attitudinal, or behavioral characteristics.
- Uncovering underlying relationships across measures requires that one question (or set of questions) be examined in light of the response to other questions. Four different types of approaches are possible: relating skip scale questions to open-ended responses, comparing responses to open-ended questions with scale questions, comparing the responses of two scale questions, and comparing the responses to two open-ended questions.

Review Questions

1. In what ways are concept and communication tests similar? In what ways are they different?
2. What is meant by "concept and communication tests are diagnostic?"
3. When are concept tests most appropriately used?
4. What are the characteristics of a well-written concept?
5. How do product-related concept tests help inform advertiser decision making?
6. What are the guidelines for writing concept test body copy?
7. What are the characteristics of concept headlines and taglines?
8. When should visuals be used in a concept test?
9. What is a communication test?
10. How does a communication test inform advertiser decision making?
11. What level of execution finish is required for a communication test?
12. What are the options for testing television commercials in a communication test?
13. What are the special considerations for qualitative concept and communication tests?
14. What are the primary measures used in concept and communication tests?
15. What two tasks are required for the complete analysis of quantitative concept and communication test findings?
16. What types of data summarization analyses are valuable in the examination of quantitative concept and communication test findings?
17. What is meant by "finding relationships among measures?"
18. What are the four ways in which one can find relationships among measures in the examination of quantitative concept and communication test findings?

Application Exercises[23]

Application exercises 1 through 4 reflect chapter content and discussion.

1. Your client, Reebok, has developed the technology for a new type of running shoe. The client and your agency both agree that a concept test be conducted to assess consumers' reactions to this new shoe before committing funds for manufacturing, distribution, and advertising. Reebok has provided the agency with following briefing on this shoe:
   - Combines technologies of GraphLite™, THE PUMP™, and HEXALITE™.
   - Shoe is named THE PUMP GraphLite™.
   - Graphite makes things lightweight while permanently retaining shape.
   - THE PUMP GraphLite™ has a radically designed underfoot arch bridge that offers exceptional support to the serious runner.
   - The bridge retains shape no matter how much one pronates or supinates and dramatically reduces weight of sole (by 20%) without sacrificing support.
   - Incorporation of THE PUMP™ technology in the collar of the shoe provides each wearer with customized heel fit. Just four or five pumps completely cradle the heel in a cushion of air, allowing all individual runners to adapt their shoe to their own personal foot profile and thus, giving each foot a superior, unsurpassed fit.

    • For years, runners have looked for a way to overcome the contradiction of a well-cushioned, lightweight shoe. Now they can stop looking. HEXALITE™ is one of the first foot protection systems that successfully incorporates lightweight technology with superior cushioning. Located in the midsole, HEXALITE™ gives THE PUMP GraphLite™ all the critical cushioning and support necessary to protect runners' feet from the severe shocks their body endures while running.
   - THE PUMP GraphLite™ carries a suggested retail price of $209 and is available wherever fine running shoes are sold.
   - The target audience for this shoe consists of men and women who consider themselves a serious runner.

   Take this information and prepare a concept that can be used to assess target audience consumers' reactions to this new shoe.

2. Prepare the discussion guide and quantitative questionnaire that could be used to explore reactions to the concept developed for the prior application exercise.

3. Agency creatives have been given the assignment to prepare two concepts for the Fuji THRILL all terrain bicycle (ATB). One concept should communicate the principal benefit of "durability without sacrificing responsiveness," while the second concept should communicate "best value for the money." The target audience consists of serious riders who are sophisticated, informed purchasers of mountain bikes. The creatives prepare the headline and body copy for the "durability without sacrificing responsiveness" concept. They show you the copy (shown next). Do you approve the copy as written? If not, what suggestions would you recommend for copy revision?

Headline: There is only one place you won't want to take Your Fuji THRILL: Back in the garage.

Copy: No matter how far off the road you go (or even if you never leave the street) the Fuji THRILL ATB not only endures punishment, its superior performance and handling also inspire you to bring it back for more. From Chrome-moly tubing and Araya silver alloy rims to competition style thumb shifters and 21-speed Shimano Hyperglide components, the THRILL comes equipped with full-fledged mountain bike features at less than a mountainous price. In fact, you can comparison shop from now until the mountains freeze over and you won't find a better value. And like all Fuji ATBs, the THRILL is engineered for optimum durability on the trail-without sacrificing responsiveness and lightness of weight.

4. Six focus groups were held to determine consumers' perceptions of and attitudes toward packaged spaghetti/pasta side-dishes and dinners. Leading brands in this category are Noodle Roni and Golden Saute.

Three focus groups were held with current, regular users of these products (where regular was defined as usage of at least once a week). A principal goal of these groups was the identification of problems and dissatisfactions with currently available packaged spaghetti/pasta side-dishes and dinners. Consumers in these groups indicated a broad range of problems with packaged pasta side-dishes and dinners. Frequently mentioned problems included poor pasta quality, not enough pasta, and too expensive. One problem area, however, was consensually identified as the most significant: a lack of flexibility in preparing the pasta. Each packaged product provides only one sauce flavor. Moreover, directions need to be followed exactly and cannot be customized. As a result, variety in flavors can only be obtained if multiple boxes of different flavors were purchased.

Three focus groups were held with category nonusers, defined as individuals who have not used these products within the past 12 months. An important goal of these groups was the identification of barriers preventing these consumers from purchasing and using these products. While a wide range of barriers were mentioned (e.g., too expensive, poor value, "boxy"/artificial taste), the most significant barrier related to preparation. Consumers did not buy these products because of a perceived lack of flexibility. They like to prepare their own recipes and, whenever possible, customize the preparation of prepared foods.

In response to these groups and other research, Katy Kitchens determined that it would develop a new product designed to respond to both users' and nonusers' attitudes. As part of the advertising development process for this product, named Versagetti, quantitative concept tests were conducted via an online survey. One of the concepts tested is shown in Figure 19.11.

SAMPLE

Versagetti was developed to appeal to two groups of consumers. Group membership reflected the extent of category usage. One group consisted of consumers who currently purchase and use packaged pasta side-dishes and dinners at least once per week (labeled current, regular users). The second group consisted of those consumers who never use these products (labeled noncategory users). All study participants (200 in total), regardless of category usage, were the primary or shared decision maker within their household for main

Introducing Versagetti.
A new line of versatile pasta side-dishes and dinners.

There is a problem with typical pasta side-dishes and dinners like Noodle Roni and Golden Saute. You have no flexibility. You make it their way. Everytime!

When you make these dishes you must exactly follow the manufacturer's directions.

Any attempt to customize the sauce may ruin the meal. So, you can't make it exactly the way you like it.

This lack of flexibility also means a lack of variety. You can only get different sauces and flavors if you buy multiple boxes of several different flavors.

Versagetti solves these problems.

Versagetti is a dried pasta sauce and comes in a 22-ounce container. Versagetti contains only the freshest and most natural ingredients.

Each canister of Versagetti makes ten servings. Each serving makes enough sauce to cover 16 ounces of pasta. But, what makes Versagetti different is that you can customize the flavorings so that one package can produce ten of the same dish or ten different dishes. You can customize the flavoring using your own preferences or by following the on-box suggestions. The choice is yours.

Versagetti, priced at $2.29 per container, comes in two basic flavors: Italian and American.

Versagetti: Maximum Flexibility

FIGURE 19.11   Concept for Application Exercise 4

course and side-dish selection. Furthermore, all participants had to eat pasta or spaghetti at home at least occasionally (defined as at least once per month). Since the study was interested in the reactions of the decision maker, no quotas were established for sex, age, income, or other demographics.

- Of the total study sample, 100 individuals were current category users. These individuals, in addition to satisfying the prior requirements, purchased and used a packaged pasta side-dish or main course at least once per week (on average).

- Of the total study sample, 100 individuals were noncategory participants. These individuals, in addition to satisfying general study requirements, had not used any packaged pasta side-dish or main course in the past year.

ANALYSIS

Key data tables are shown in Figure 19.12 (pages 585 to 589). Examine the tables and then answer the questions on page 590.

Table A. Initial Thoughts and Feelings (Multiple Mentions)

Response	Total Sample ($n = 200$)	Category Users ($n = 100$)	Category Nonusers ($n = 100$)
Any positive (net)	**60%**	**90%**	**30%**
Nice ability to customize	50	80	20
Kids would like	50	76	24
Would add variety	50	50	50
A money stretcher	45	60	30
Would taste good	40	80	0
Would make life easier	30	60	0
Any negative (net)	**65**	**30**	**100**
Wouldn't taste good	55	10	100
Too much work	35	0	70
How is this different?	30	5	55
Silly name	25	20	30

Table B. Main Idea Communication (Multiple Mentions)

Response	Total Sample ($n = 200$)	Category Users ($n = 100$)	Category Nonusers ($n = 100$)
Product flexibility (net)	**74%**	**76%**	**72%**
More flavors	50	49	51
Can customize taste	45	47	43
Can use own pasta	12	11	12
Improved/better taste (net)	**72**	**77**	**67**
Fresher taste	45	42	48
Better taste	40	43	37
More economical	20	20	20
Longer shelf-life	15	14	16

Table C. Brand Name Recall

Response	Total Sample ($n = 200$)	Category Users ($n = 100$)	Category Nonusers ($n = 100$)
Versagetti	90%	94%	86%
Versaspaghetti	3	3	4
Versatile Spaghetti	2	1	3
Spaghetti Versatility	2	1	3
Other	3	1	4

FIGURE 19.12 Results of Quantitative Concept Test for Application Exercise 4

Table D. Ratings of Message Importance (4-point scale; lower numbers are more positive)

Response Options	Total Sample ($n = 200$)	Category Users ($n = 100$)	Category Nonusers ($n = 100$)
Very important (1)	33%	58%	8%
Slightly important (2)	22	33	11
Slightly unimportant (3)	38	8	68
Very unimportant (4)	7	1	13
Mean	**2.2**	**1.5***	**2.9***

*significant at p < .001

Table E. Ratings of Message Relevance (4-point scale; lower numbers are more positive)

Response Options	Total Sample ($n = 200$)	Category Users ($n = 100$)	Category Nonusers ($n = 100$)
The message was relevant . . .			
Strongly agree (1)	39%	72%	6%
Slightly agree (2)	13	16	10
Slightly disagree (3)	10	10	10
Strongly disagree (4)	38	2	74
Mean	**2.4**	**1.4***	**3.5***

*significant at p < .001

Table F. Ratings of Message Believability (4-point scale; lower numbers are more positive)

Response Options	Total Sample ($n = 200$)	Category Users ($n = 100$)	Category Nonusers ($n = 100$)
Very believable (1)	65%	67%	63%
Slightly believable (2)	23	20	26
Slightly unbelievable (3)	12	13	11
Very unbelievable (4)	0	0	0
Mean	**1.5**	**1.5**	**1.5**

FIGURE 19.12   (Continued)

Table G. Ratings of Message Uniqueness (4-point scale; lower numbers are more positive)

Response Options	Total Sample (*n* = 200)	Category Users (*n* = 100)	Category Nonusers (*n* = 100)
The message was unique . . .			
Strongly agree (1)	36%	72%	0%
Slightly agree (2)	13	22	4
Slightly disagree (3)	18	6	30
Strongly disagree (4)	33	0	66
Mean	**2.5**	**1.3***	**3.5***

*significant at p < .001

Table H. Ratings of Message Clarity (4-point scale; lower numbers are more positive)

Response Options	Total Sample (*n* = 200)	Category Users (*n* = 100)	Category Nonusers (*n* = 100)
The message was easy to understand . . .			
Strongly agree (1)	80%	78%	82%
Slightly agree (2)	5	7	3
Slightly disagree (3)	5	4	6
Strongly disagree (4)	10	11	9
Mean	**1.5**	**1.5**	**1.4**

Table I. Initial Like/Dislike Ratings (4-point scale; lower numbers are more positive)

Response Options	Total Sample (*n* = 200)	Category Users (*n* = 100)	Category Nonusers (*n* = 100)
Strongly liked (1)	45%	85%	5%
Slightly liked (2)	20	15	25
Slightly disliked (3)	10	0	20
Strongly disliked (4)	25	0	50
Mean	**2.4**	**1.2***	**3.6***

*significant at p < .001

FIGURE 19.12 (Continued)

Table J. Specific Likes and Dislikes (Multiple Mentions)

Response	Initial Rating of Message	
	Liked (n = 130)	Disliked (n = 70)
Positives		
Easy to understand	85%	93%
Good variety	52	83
Like cooking from scratch	39	14
Better taste than other box pasta	38	10
Good flavors	34	12
Easy for when in a hurry	32	7
Negatives		
No better than other box pasta	8%	100%
Wouldn't taste as good as promised	0	97
Too many options	4	46
Silly name	6	96
Weird	0	92
Why bother, too much work	2	89
Easier to make from scratch	0	89
Why not just open a bottle of sauce	4	92

Table K. Purchase Intent (4-point scale; lower numbers are more positive)

Response Options	Total Sample (n = 200)	Category Users (n = 100)	Category Nonusers (n = 100)
Very likely to buy (1)	40%	76%	4%
Slightly likely to buy (2)	10	14	6
Slightly unlikely to buy (3)	40	5	75
Strongly unlikely to buy (4)	10	5	15
Mean	2.2	1.4*	3.0*

*significant at $p < .001$

Table L. Purchase Intent (4-point scale; lower numbers are more positive)

Response Options	Total Category Users (n = 100)	Noodle Roni Users (n = 25)	Golden Grain Users (n = 25)
Very likely to buy (1)	76%	80%	72%
Slightly likely to buy (2)	14	10	18
Slightly unlikely to buy (3)	5	5	5
Strongly unlikely to buy (4)	5	5	5
Mean	1.4	1.4	1.4

FIGURE 19.12 (Continued)

Table M. Purchase Intent (4-point scale; lower numbers are more positive)

Response Options	Type of Category User		
	Heavy (n = 25)	Medium (n = 50)	Light (n = 25)
Very likely to buy (1)	88%	80%	50%
Slightly likely to buy (2)	12	4	18
Slightly unlikely to buy (3)	0	4	22
Strongly unlikely to buy (4)	0	12	10
Mean	**1.1***	**1.4**	**1.6***

significant at p = .05

Table N. Anticipated Purchase Frequency

Response Options	Total Category Users (n = 100)	Noodle Roni Users (n = 25)	Golden Grain Users (n = 25)
More often than current brand	76%	88%	64%
Same as current brand	18	8	28
Less than current brand	6	4	8

Table O. Formulation Appeal (10-point scale; lower numbers are more positive)

Response Options	Type of Category User		
	Heavy (n = 25)	Medium (n = 50)	Light (n = 25)
Italian (mean appeal score)	**1.2**	**1.3**	**1.5**
American (mean appeal score)	4.7	4.9	5.1

all Italian appeal ratings are significantly more positive versus American appeal ratings

Table O. Formulation Appeal (10-point scale; lower numbers are more positive)

Response Options	Type of Category User		
	Heavy (n = 25)	Medium (n = 50)	Light (n = 25)
Italian (mean appeal score)	**1.4**	**1.7**	**1.6**
American (mean appeal score)	5.2	4.9	5.3

all Italian appeal ratings are significantly more positive versus American appeal ratings

FIGURE 19.12   (Continued)

A. What are the strengths and weaknesses of the Versagetti concept?

B. What are the strengths and weaknesses of the Versagetti message with regard to current category users and nonusers?

C. What are the strengths and weaknesses of the Versagetti message with regard to users of competitive brands?

D. Which benefit shows the greatest strength? Which shows the greatest weakness?

Application exercises 5 to 10 refer to the Healthy Eating communication test in the online supplemental readings.

5. The focus groups began with a discussion of perceived challenges to eating healthy food (see Moderator's Guide). Prepare a short paper that presents your point of view regarding the decision to hold this discussion prior to obtaining reactions to the television advertisements. Do you feel that this discussion was appropriate and had the potential to provide important context for interpreting reactions to the advertising, or do you feel that this initial discussion had the potential to bias responses to the advertising? Be specific in support of your point of view.

6. The focus group showed each television advertisement one at a time with discussion occurring after each presentation. Prior to the start of each discussion, the moderator asked individuals to rate the commercials and write down message communication and reactions. What are this technique's advantages in a focus group setting? What are its disadvantages? When used, should the ratings forms be handed out before or after the first commercial is shown? Does this technique provide valid (unbiased) responses for all commercials shown in the focus group or only the first one? Prepare a short paper presenting your point of view regarding the advantages and disadvantages of this technique and your recommendation for its most appropriate use.

7. The Healthy Eating report does not provide any storyboards for the three television commercials. Select one of the commercials. Then, using the original descriptions shown in Figure 19.10 and the Healthy Eating report, prepare a storyboard for the revised commercial. Accompany the storyboard with a short paper that describes your revised approach.

8. Review the Moderator's Guide for the focus groups. Are there any areas of discussion you would add to the guide? Are there any areas that you would eliminate? Prepare a short paper that presents your point of view, and then modify the discussion guide accordingly.

9. Assume that your budget for the focus groups was doubled, and that as a result you could hold eight additional groups. Would you conduct more groups with the same target audience, or is there an additional target that you would choose? If the latter, would the group be described by demographics or psychographics? Prepare a short paper presenting your point of view, and if you do choose an additional target, be certain to fully describe the target's characteristics.

10. Imagine that Health Canada wants to expand the Healthy Eating campaign into magazines and radio. Based on the research findings, create one example of a print and radio ad. Prepare a short paper that explains your creative strategy and approach. Be certain to explain your creative in light of research findings presented in the Healthy Eating report.

Application exercises 11 to 16 refer to the Secondhand Smoke communication test in the online supplemental readings.

11. Focus group participants discussed the creative materials sequentially; that is, the television advertisement was viewed and discussed, then the print ads, etc. An alternative would be to present all creative materials at once, discuss overall campaign reactions, and then go back to discuss each creative element individually. Prepare a short paper that presents the strengths and weaknesses of each approach.

12. As indicated in the discussion guide, focus group respondents were asked to numerically rate the television commercial and to write down the main message prior to discussion. Do you agree or disagree with this approach? What are the advantages and disadvantages of starting with a numeric rating rather than an open-ended question such as "Write down your initial thoughts and feelings toward the commercial"? Prepare a short paper that presents your point of view.

13. Imagine that you are a consultant to Health Canada, which is contemplating the initiation of

a new communication campaign designed to promote adult physical activity. The Health Canada research committee consists of three individuals: John believes that only qualitative research is necessary to test proposed communication materials, Mandy believes that only quantitative research should be used, and Sally believes that a mixed-methods (combined) approach would provide the most valuable insights. Review the Secondhand Smoke report, and then decide, based on this insights provided by the qualitative and quantitative sections, which individual you most agree with. Prepare a short paper (using the Secondhand Smoke report as the case example) that presents and supports your point of view regarding which individual you think has the strongest position.

14. The Secondhand Smoke report presents the initial creative materials tested online and in the groups. Based on the research findings,

prepare revised creative materials. Place these revised materials in a short paper that presents your rationale for the changes.

15. Review the online questionnaire. Prepare a short paper that presents your point of view regarding the questionnaire's strengths and weaknesses. What additions or modifications would you make to improve the questionnaire? Revise the questionnaire to reflect your analysis.

16. The online questionnaire asked each individual to respond to all creative materials. As a result, due to time limitations, the number of questions asked about each individual piece of creative was limited. An alternative approach would have been to explore each piece of creative in depth with each respondent evaluating only one piece of creative. Which approach do you think is the strongest? Prepare a short paper that presents and provides specific detail to support your point of view.

Endnotes

1. The specific suggestions in the concepts are from Mayo Clinic (2009) at http://www.mayoclinic.com/health/shift-work/AN01616.

2. This chapter focuses on concept tests that explore reactions to potential advertising messages. An alternative type of concept test, typically conducted by brand managers, is the *new product* concept test. Here, marketers may have a number of ideas for new products. These ideas may come from their own internal brand and research/development staff or from consumer research. A new product idea may develop a completely new product category, reflect a line extension, or describe an entry into an existing product category. All new product ideas, however, are not equally appealing to the target consumer. Simply because a marketer can make a product or consumers indicate in prior research that they might have a need or desire for the product does not necessarily mean that consumers will want to buy the product should it become available and/or once they fully understand the product's characteristics. Marketers need to systematically screen new product ideas to identify those that have the greatest potential for marketplace success. It is much more cost-efficient to find out that consumers reject the idea

of a new product rather than the manufactured product itself. A marketer administers a new product concept test to identify, from the consumer's perspective, the new product ideas that have merit and therefore be refined and pursued.

3. Concepts tests are very flexible. While this chapter focuses on concept tests designed to assess reactions to alternative messages, concept tests can also be used to test other message-related components of a communication such as alternative taglines and headlines. The procedures for conducting these types of more narrowly focused tests are very similar to that described for message-focused tests. Additionally, concept tests can be used to explore reactions to alternative visuals that might be used to illustrate a message. These latter concept tests hold the message constant while manipulating the visuals paired with the message. As with tests of taglines or headlines, the approach to this type of concept test is very similar to that of message-focused concept tests.

4. For examples of these and similar types of non-product related advertising, see The Ad Council at http://www.adcouncil.org/default.aspx?id=15.

5. The concepts' content is adapted from GreenSimmons (undated). "Top Ten Reasons to Recycle" at http://green.simmons.edu/news/entries/2008/04/top_ten_reasons.php and Webnation (2008). "Recycling Statistics for the United States" at http://www.altfuelsnow.com/conservation/recycling-statistics,

6. Communication tests thus differ from concept tests in that communication tests are most interested in identifying the strengths and weaknesses of different executional approaches.

7. The source for Figures 19.5 and 19.6 is USDA (2006). "United States Department of Agriculture Focus Group Report on Creative Concept Testing For Food Safety Mass Media Campaign" at http://www.fsis.usda.gov/PDF/BFS_Report.pdf.

8. Examples of storyboards, animatics, and photomatics can be found at hi road productions (http://www.hiroadproductions.com) and Brain Forest Digital Animatics (http://www.brain4est.com/bfd/home.htm).

9. Adapted from Iqbal Mohammad (2008). "Predictive Pre-Testing: An Outline for an Ad Pre-Testing Model Based on Prediction Markets" at http://papers.ssrn.com/sol3/papers.cfm?abstract_id=1265089.

10. The sources for Figure 19.6 are http://www.gallup-robinson.com/concepttesting.html and http://www.gallup-robinson.com/adpretesting.html.

11. Two things are noteworthy regarding the discussion guide shown in Figure 19.7. First, questions are numbered to allow easier reference in the text's discussion. In practice, no numbers would be used. Second, the moderator's instructions provide the flexibility to pursue the questions in whatever order works best given how the group's discussion processes. Beyond the discussion guide, also note how the number of concepts explored varies across methodology. Focus groups allow for the collection of reactions to multiple concepts within a single group, while the quantitative survey focuses on a single concept. In cases where more than one concept or execution is explored quantitatively, multiple groups are used where each group sees only one concept or execution. The materials shown in Figures 19.8 and 19.9 were generated at PsychData (http://www.psychdata.com).

12. The wording for this and other questions is the same in a communication test except that rough "advertisement" or "execution" is substituted for "concept."

13. The concept being explored in this example is non-product-specific and, as a result, Question 3 probes recall of the concept sponsor. In the cases of product-specific concepts and advertising, the question would ask about product name recall.

14. An alternative way to assess message communication is: "Imagine that you needed to tell a friend about what you just saw and heard. What would you tell this friend?"

15. Keep in mind that correlation indicates the relationship between two measures, but does not imply causation. We cannot claim, in this instance, that increasing believability will *cause* a rise in positive attitude change.

16. The percentages in tables reporting open-ended responses do not add to 100% because multiple responses are possible. One individual, for example, could like or dislike more than one aspect of the concept or execution.

17. The examples in this section illustrate how different attitude groups can be examined. The procedure is the same for behavior intention groups, where positive and negative intention groups would be compared and contrasted. In addition, responses can be analyzed by actual behavior groups, for example, comparing the responses of those engaged in the target behavior to those not engaged. In the case of a product-related test, for example, the responses of individuals who currently purchase the product can be compared with those who do not purchase.

18. Health Canada's Web site is http://www.hc-sc.gc.ca.

19. Note that although the titles of both reports refer to "concept tests," the research described is closer what this chapter described as communication tests.

20. All quotes and research materials are from the Health Canada report "2007 Healthy Eating Qualitative Concept Test."

21. See, for example, National Cancer Institute (undated). "Secondhand Smoke: Questions and Answers" at http://www.cancer.gov/cancertopics/factsheet/Tobacco/ETS.

22. The full report is Health Canada (2006). "Second-Hand Smoke: Testing of TV and Print Concepts."

23. Brand names are used for illustrative purposes only.

CHAPTER 20

Post-Production Advertising Testing and Optimization

The research process does not end once an advertisement is produced, an e-mail is sent, or a Web site is launched. Research continues to inform advertisers' judgment so that increasingly more efficient and effective decisions can be made during the next round of strategic and creative discussion. Four types of advertising research follow final production. Copy testing *research evaluates finished advertisements to determine whether or not they should be placed in media and used in the campaign.* Split-run and A/B tests *are related research techniques that allow advertisers to compare a current approach to advertising with one or more potential alternatives.* Full factorial and multivariate techniques *allow advertisers to determine how manipulations of the advertising or other communication stimuli affect consumer response. Finally,* campaign evaluation research *helps advertisers determine the effectiveness of the communication campaign once it has been placed in media and shown to the target audience.*

***

When you are done reading this chapter, you should have a better understanding of:

- how research contributes to improved advertising decision making after communications are produced and aired
- the situations in which each of the four main types of post-production research is most appropriate
- the strengths and limitations of each type of post-production research
- how copy testing is used to determine advertising deceptiveness.

COPY TESTING RESEARCH

Communication research, discussed in the prior chapter, is designed to identify an advertisement's strengths and weaknesses prior to production. Communication testing is therefore diagnostic in orientation. Once an advertisement is produced, copy testing research is conducted to determine whether or not that advertisement should be placed in media and used in the campaign. Copy testing is therefore evaluative in orientation and is used to make "go–no go" decisions about a particular advertisement. Copy testing is most commonly performed on television advertising, although magazine and radio ads may also be copy tested.

This section discusses copy testing methods with a focus on television advertising.[1] The chapter addendum presents a discussion of copy testing from a legal perspective, with particular emphasis on how copy testing is used by advertisers to respond to deceptive advertising challenges from the Federal Trade Commission.

Copy Testing Television Advertising

Unlike concept or communications tests that may be conducted by the advertising agency, client, or outside research company, copy testing is almost always conducted by independent research companies. While all these companies share the goal of separating weak from strong advertisements, the companies nevertheless vary in their approach across the following four dimensions:

- *The naturalness of the viewing situation.* Research companies generally take one of two approaches to advertising exposure. Some companies expose respondents to the test commercial in the context of an actual television broadcast. Other companies provide respondents with a VHS tape or DVD that contains a prerecorded television program in which the test commercial has been inserted.

- *The number of advertising exposures.* Data collection can take place after one or more exposures to the advertising.

- *The timing of data collection.* Companies vary with regard to the amount of time elapsed between commercial exposure and data collection. Some approaches collect data immediately after commercial exposure, while other may wait one or more days.

- *The types of data collected.* Available measures vary among copy testing companies. For any particular copy testing company, normative measures can include one or more of the following: advertising recall, message communication, brand attitude shift, buying intention, pre-post brand preference, attitudes toward the advertising, attitude toward the message.

Differences in approaches to television copy testing are illustrated in the methodologies used by Gallup & Robinson and Mapes and Ross.[2] The following two sections describe these companies' approaches.

GALLUP & ROBINSON INTELETEST.   Gallup & Robinson's InTeleTest assesses consumers' reactions to television commercials when they appear in the context of a prerecorded television program. The program is distributed to respondents via a VHS tape or DVD.

The sample for a typical InTeleTest survey is typically 150 men or 150 women aged 18 and older chosen from 10 geographically dispersed metropolitan areas. Respondents are personally recruited at their homes under the guise of a study to measure television viewing habits. Each respondent is given a VHS cassette or DVD, is instructed to watch it that day, and is told that a follow-up telephone interview will take place the following day. The next day respondents are contacted by telephone and interviewed on InTeleTest's core metrics of intrusiveness (recall), persuasion, brand rating, and commercial reactions. All respondents are then asked to view the test commercial again and are taken through a standardized diagnostic battery that may also include custom questions. InTeleTest's primary measures are operationalized as follows:

- *Intrusiveness* is defined as a commercial's ability to break through the clutter and communicate an advertiser or brand name. InTeleTest measures three levels of intrusiveness: (1) Unaided Recall is the percentage of viewers who, when prompted by the product or subject category, claim to have seen the commercial and correctly identify the sponsor or brand name; (2) Proved Unaided Recall is the subset of the prior group who are also able to accurately describe the commercial; and (3) Proved Brand Aided Recall is the percentage of viewers who, aided by a company or brand name cue, can prove recall of the commercial. As noted earlier, recall measures are obtained after a single commercial viewing.

- *Persuasion* and *brand ratings* measure a commercial's ability to foster favorable attitudes toward the advertised product. InTeleTest measures two levels of persuasion: (1) Favorable Buying Attitude measures purchase intent after a single exposure and reflects the percent of the sample who said that their interest in purchasing the product increased somewhat or considerably; and (2) Brand Rating is the percent of the sample who rate the brand excellent or very good.

- *Commercial reactions* measure two aspects of consumers' affective responses to the commercial. Commercial Liking is measured on a five-point scale (with end points of "I liked it very much" to "I disliked it very much"). Commercial Excellence uses a four-point agree-disagree scale to measure agreement with the statement: "This commercial is one of the best I've seen recently."

Norms are available for all of the previously mentioned standard InTeleTest measures.[3]

MAPES AND ROSS NATURAL EXPOSURE.   Mapes and Ross' Natural Exposure exposes respondents to the test advertisement in the context of an on-air program. The company recruits a sample of between 150 and 200 individuals to view a specific television program under the guise of television program evaluation. Respondents are told that their reactions to the program are the focus of the research.

Mapes and Ross' methodology allows data to be collected across a wide range of commercial response, in particular, persuasion (the primary metric), recall, main idea communication, and detailed diagnostics that measure, for example, how well the sales ideas are communicated in a likeable manner. Each of Mapes and Ross' key measures is operationalized as follows:

- *Persuasion* (the principal metric) measures the ability of the advertisement to change or maintain preference and interest toward the advertised brand.

- *Unaided recall* measures respondents' ability to link the advertised brand to the commercial from a category description, for example, "brands of automobiles." *Proven recall* measures respondents' ability to remember and describe specific and/or unique elements and ideas from the commercial.

- *Idea communication* is measured by asking respondents to describe what they saw and heard to determine how well visual elements attract attention. Consumers are also asked about what they believe is the main idea of the commercial and to rate the importance of the main idea. They are finally asked to what extent the commercial has altered their interest in buying the advertised brand.

Recruited respondents are those who are in the advertisement's target audience. These individuals are generally defined on the basis of demographics and category/brand-usage behaviors. At the time of recruitment, Mapes and Ross obtains brand preferences in six product categories (including the category of the test commercial) using open-ended questioning. Open-ended, nondirective questions in a range of categories are used to reduce any potential respondent sensitization to the test product or test commercial. The test commercial appears during the program the respondents are instructed to watch.

The day following commercial exposure, each respondent is contacted by telephone and, after confirming program viewership, post-exposure brand preferences are collected. The percentage shift from pre- to post-exposure levels of brand preference is interpreted to represent a commercial's persuasiveness. (Thus, persuasiveness is evaluated the day-after a single exposure.) In general, greater shifts in purchase intent from pre- to post-exposure indicate greater levels of persuasiveness.[4] Following preference questions, recall levels are obtained in response to category and brand prompts. All respondents who claim recall are questioned to determine the specific content of their recall. Norms are available to help benchmark persuasion levels and levels of recall and likeability.

An example of the type of data and topline report provided by Mapes and Ross is provided in this chapter's online supplemental readings. A full report, with greater detail, is provided to the client one to two weeks later. Page 16 in the topline report outlines the additional information that a client receives in the full report.

Evaluating Alternative Copy Testing Methodologies

Advertisers have a number of different copy testing options. Each option has its own set of proponents, and each has its own unique set of strengths and weaknesses. However, when evaluating the relative appropriateness of alternative copy testing methodologies, we recommend that the following be kept in mind:[5]

- The closer a methodology is to "real world" exposure, the more accurately the results will reflect "real world" advertising performance and consumer response.

- Respondents are more likely to provide "real world" responses to commercials when they are not aware that they are participating in copy testing research.

- Multiple measures and diagnostics provide a multifaceted look at commercial performance. Therefore, methodologies that provide multiple measures are generally more informative and useful to an advertiser versus those that provide a single measure.

- Among copy testing methodologies, measures with the same name may not have the same underlying data collection methodology. Thus, it is important to be aware of the methodology underlying the collection of data for a specific measure. Different methodologies, for example, measure persuasion very differently. The preferred methodology for any particular copy test is the one whose approach to measurement best corresponds to the advertiser's view of how the commercial is intended to affect the target consumer.

Finally, preferred copy testing methodologies provide norms and evidence of validation. *Norms* allow advertisers to compare reactions to their test commercial to an objective, external criterion. It is important, however, that norms are current, reflect a sample of adequate size, and are appropriate to the product and product category shown in the commercial.[6] An advertiser should never "make do" with norms that are either outdated or not directly related to the advertised product. With regard to validation, only those copy testing methodologies that can empirically demonstrate acceptable levels of reliability and validity should be considered. In addition, key measures should have undergone systematic validation. A description of Mapes and Ross' validation of its persuasion measure is provided in Figure 20.1.

SPLIT-RUN TESTS

Split-run and A/B tests refer to similar types of research. Both approaches permit an advertiser to compare a current approach to advertising to one or more potential alternatives. "Split-run" is the label given to this test when conducted in print media, while "A/B test" is the label given to this test when conducted in an online environment.[7]

Split-Run Test Design

The print yellow pages and magazines are two media in which split-run tests are typically conducted. In both cases, advertisers conducting a split-run test evaluate how well a potential new ad performs when compared against their current ad or a control ad. The name "split-run" refers to the fact that the publisher splits the run (or placement) of the test ads within the advertising medium. A yellow pages publisher, for example, would conduct a split-run test in a particular city by printing an advertiser's current ad in half of the directories and that advertiser's alternative test ad in the remaining half of the directories. The directories would then be distributed as they normally would. Thus, two neighbors who receive their city's yellow pages directory might receive different versions of the advertiser's yellow pages ad. One neighbor would receive the directory with

natural exposure℠ validation

case history one

*A time-series study was conducted to determine to what extent **Brand Preference Change** in Mapes and Ross Natural Exposure℠ tests related to subsequent purchase behavior. The results of this research were published in the <u>Journal of Advertising Research</u> and later reprinted in the <u>Journal of Advertising Research Classics: Eight Key Articles That Have Led Our Thinking</u>.*

JOURNAL OF ADVERTISING RESEARCH

JAR Published Study

- All commercials tested in the *Natural Exposure*℠ system over a five-month period were included, except for new brands, out-of-season products and considered-purchase items.
- The sample of tests covered 55 product categories, with 142 different commercials.
- In total, there were 2,241 respondents, representing 7,283 commercial exposure/product-category purchase opportunities.

The goal of the study was to measure the extent to which respondent brand preference changes are validated by changes in a test brand's share. Two weeks after each *Natural Exposure*℠ commercial test, respondents were re-contacted by telephone. In this unrelated interview, the same individuals were questioned on an unaided basis about category and brand purchases during the two-week period since the advertising exposure. Brand share was measured among those who made a category purchase.

The results of this follow up buying-behavior study were then matched to the responses of the same persons in the copy-test interview. Actual purchase levels were compared to different levels of response to the test commercials. For each commercial exposure/purchase opportunity, three types of respondent classification were possible:

Preferred Pre: Respondent preferred the test brand pre-exposure - not eligible for positive change.

Persuaded: Respondent did not prefer the test brand at the pre-exposure stage but changed to the test brand in the day-after exposure callback.

Not Persuaded: Respondent did not prefer the test brand pre-exposure and did not change preference to the test brand in the day-after exposure callback.

Among those who bought in the product category, purchases of the test brands were an average of 3.3 times greater for those who changed their preference to those brands in the copy tests versus those who did not (42.8% versus 12.8%). Control sample data confirmed that this difference was the result of advertising exposure.

The results clearly show that Mapes and Ross' persuasion measure predicts significant changes in actual purchase behavior.

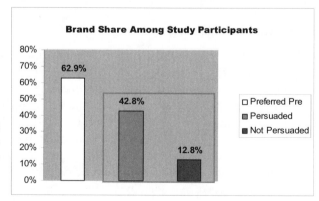

FIGURE 20.1 Validity of Mapes and Ross Persuasion Measure

the current ad, and the other would receive the directory with the test ad. Similarly, a magazine publisher could divide a particular issue of the magazine into two groups, with the test ad being printed in one group and the control ad being printed in the second group. A split-run test, as illustrated below, is therefore a variation of the post-test only research design where data from two randomly selected groups is collected after advertising exposure.

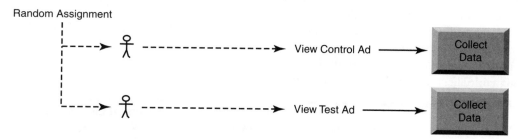

An advertiser faces two important tasks with regard to a split-run test. First, "better" must be operationalized; that is, the advertiser must determine the criteria by which the two advertisements will be compared and the "better" ad identified. In the case of a yellow pages split-run test, "better" might be operationalized as the number of telephone calls generated by each ad. In the case of magazine ad designed to motivate readers to visit the brand's Web site, "better" might be operationalized as the number of Web site visits generated by each ad. Second, once the advertiser has operationalized "better," the ads must be coded in a way that allows the accurate collection of the required data. This would work as follows for a yellow pages split-run test.

> Each yellow pages ad in a split-run test would contain a telephone number unique to that ad; that is, the telephone number appearing in the ad would not be available from any other source. The unique telephone number in each ad is then monitored by a specialized research company hired by the directory publisher or advertiser. When a consumer places a call (using the special number in the yellow pages ad), the call is seamlessly transferred to the regular business number of the advertiser, and is handled in the usual way. Neither the consumer calling in nor the person at the business answering the call is aware that the call is being measured. However, in the process of transferring the call, call-specific information is recorded and compiled with regard to: (a) time of the call, (b) length of the call, (c) time the call ended, and (d) where available, the name and address of the caller. The actual conversation that takes place remains private.[8]

The following might be the approach taken for a magazine split-run test.

> Two magazine ads may both have the goal of motivating visits to the advertiser's Web site. Similar to the approach used in the yellow pages split-run test, a unique URL would be placed in each ad. Visitors using each URL would be counted and then immediately forwarded to the advertiser's Web site.

Split-Run Test Data Analysis

Once data is collected, statistical tests are used to compare the performance of the test ad to the control ad. Imagine, for example, that two different versions of a magazine ad for Dove body wash are tested. Both ads are consistent with Dove's Campaign for Real Beauty. The control ad is simply a new execution with creative tone, manner, and visual style consistent with the campaign. The test ad's message is also consistent with the campaign, but this ad uses a radically different visual approach: the visuals are much more stylized and the overall style is more abstract. Each ad contains a unique URL for those who want to visit the Dove site after reading the ad. The URLs are trackable so that the number of visits generated by each ad can be monitored. The data shown in the following table illustrates the results of the split-run test:

Ad Type	Circulation	Number of Site Visits	Percent of Circulation Visiting Site
Control	2,500,000	425,329	17.0
Test	2,500,000	283,037	**11.3**

Statistical tests compare the number of visits generated by the test ad to the number of visits generated by the control ad. In this case, the level of significance is less than .001, indicating the number of references generated by the control ad was significantly higher than the number generated by the test ad. Given the advertiser's objective and operationalization of "better," the test ad would not be used in the future.

A/B TESTS

An A/B test takes the same general approach as a split-run test and, as a result, is also a variation of the post-test only research design.[9] A/B tests, however, are more flexible versus split-run tests. While split-run tests generally test one advertisement against another, A/B tests can test any control stimulus against a test counterpart, for example:

- A proposed banner advertisement can be tested against the current banner ad.
- A proposed wording change in a Google Adwords ad can be tested against the wording appearing in the current ad.
- The current Web site landing page can be tested against a proposed revised page.
- A new e-mail subject line can be tested against the subject line used in current e-mailings.
- A revised "Purchase Now" button can be tested against the button currently used.
- A two-step checkout procedure can be tested against the current three-step procedure.

The approach and outcome of an actual A/B test is provided in Figure 20.2.

Regardless of the specific stimuli being tested, the same two decisions required for split-run tests must be made for A/B tests: advertisers must first operationalize "better" and then must create a way to collect the data appropriate for this operationalized measure. Some instances, such as that described in Figure 20.2, require only a single measure

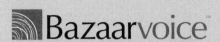

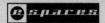

A/B test proves reviews drive up to 14.2% conversion increase

July 14, 2009

eSpares is the UK's largest spare parts retailer, specializing in accessories and consumables for electric home appliances. They offer more than 400,000 different products from over 500 manufacturers. They recently ran an A/B test to conclusively prove whether reviews increase conversion on their Web site.

A/B test solidly proves impact

While other testing methodologies can suggest a strong correlation between an increase in conversion and the addition of Ratings & Reviews, A/B tests more conclusively prove results. An A/B test looks at increases in conversion rates on the same products during the same time-frame, which effectively eliminates all other factors, such as product popularity or seasonality, to conclusively represent correlations.

How they did it

To exclude possible biases, eSpares randomly selected three products within their extensive product catalog with a significant amount of reviews and similar ratings. Then, for five months, they randomly served site visitors either product information that contained review content or product information without review content. The test was run until there was a statistically accurate sample size for all products, and no promotions were run during testing period.

For each product, eSpares measured the relative increase in conversion rates for the visitors who were served Ratings & Reviews content versus those who were not. They then tested to see how confident they were that the results were not due to chance.

Reviews drive up to 14.2% increase in conversion

eSpares reports that each product experienced between a 6.3% and 14.2% increase in conversion for visitors served Ratings & Reviews content. This means that visitors who viewed product information containing review content converted from visitors to buyers between 6.3% and 14.2% more often than persons who did not receive copy containing reviews.

For their two products with relative increases in conversion of 6.3% and 6.6%, eSpares is 80% confident that the increases did not occur due to chance. For their product with the largest relative conversion increase (14.2%), they are more than 95% confident.

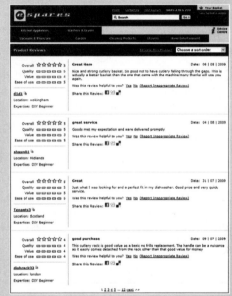

The bottom line

Once again, customer reviews are shown to drive sales conversion. In this case, eSpares found that, when everything else was controlled, visitors viewing the same products with Ratings & Reviews converted between 6.3% and 14.2% more often.

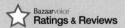

+44 (0)203 178 5763 | europe@bazaarvoice.com
Read more at www.bazaarvoice.co.uk/casestudies

FIGURE 20.2 eSpares: Bazaarvoice Case Study

to operationalize "better." In other instances, it is often in an advertiser's best interest to select several measures.

A/B Test Data Analysis

Consider, for example, the case of testing two Google Adwords ads where the current ad (the "A" ad) uses the word "free" without the mention of brand names while the second ad (the "B" ad) does not use "free" but rather mentions three brand names. Google will rotate the ads so that they have equivalent exposure to randomly selected respondents. One way to evaluate "better" is to track the percentage of exposed individuals who click-through each ad. This data is shown in the table below.

Ad Type	Number of Exposures	Number of Clicks	Percent Clicks
A–Current	275,000	23,989	8.7
B–Test	275,000	16,738	6.1

A statistical test of the data shown in the table indicates that click-through is statistically higher for the current ad versus the test ad.[10] Based solely on this measure, an advertiser might conclude that the test ad is a weaker approach and that the current approach should be maintained. However, imagine that the advertiser has also decided to track sales after click-through, specifically the number of individuals making a purchase and the amount spent on the sale. The data associated with these two measures has been added to the following table.

Ad Type	Number of Exposures	Number of Clicks	Percent Clicks	Percent Buying	Average Sale	Total Sales
A–Current	275,000	23,989	8.7	2.1	$16.27	$ 93,959.25
B–Test	275,000	16,738	6.1	4.8	$21.98	$290,136.00

Note how this additional data leads to a different conclusion regarding the "better" ad. While the percent of individuals clicking-through is greater for the current ad, individuals clicking-through from the test ad are much better customers. Statistical tests of the percentage of individuals making a purchase after click-through and the total revenue generated by purchasers show that test ad is significantly "better" than the control ad: more individuals make a purchase, and these individuals make a larger average purchase thereby generating greater revenue. Based on these latter two measures, the advertiser would likely select the test ad for further use.

Additional A/B Test Considerations

Beyond decisions related to operationalization of "better," advertisers engaged in A/B tests are faced with three additional decisions: the length of the test, the exposure/rotation of current/control and test stimuli, and the characteristics of the current/control and test stimuli.

LENGTH OF TEST. The length of an A/B test should reflect the amount of time required for participants to take action and the amount of time required for a sufficient sample size to be obtained. The following two scenarios illustrate the decision-making process.[11]

- Macy's keeps in contact with its customers via e-mail. The company decides to conduct an A/B test of two e-mail approaches and sends the test and control e-mail to 10,000 consumers randomly selected from its list of registered customers. (Thus, the total sample size for the test is 20,000.) The top chart shown in Figure 20.3 shows the cumulative percentage of e-mail "opens" within two weeks after the initial e-mail, while the bottom chart translates this percentage into the actual number of people opening an e-mail. Given the trends in both charts, a test period of six days is reasonable. By the end of six days, there is more than sufficient sample size and response rate. After this date, very few incremental e-mail openings take place. Note that four days after mailing would have been too soon to end the test. While the

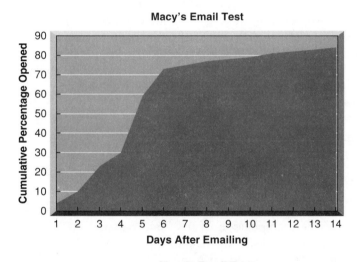

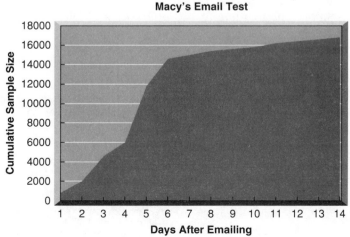

FIGURE 20.3 Considerations in Length of A/B Test

sample size after four days is acceptable, the percentage of opened e-mails (and thus the response rate) was too low. Stopping the test at this point would have increased the risk of nonresponse bias.

- ALLaboutLANGUAGE is an educational company with a Web site that sells self-study materials for foreign language learning. The company offers a free introductory lesson to those who register. Current site traffic is about 1,000 visitors per day with about five people per day registering. The company wants to use A/B testing to compare the effectiveness of a new registration process to the current process. The test would need to run for several months in order for a sufficient sample size to be obtained.

EXPOSURE ROTATION.   There is always the risk in A/B testing that the test stimulus will perform more poorly than the control stimulus. Given this risk, exposing equal numbers of individuals to the test and control ads may have a serious negative impact on the advertiser's business. As a result, advertisers using A/B testing typically expose a relatively low percentage of their total audience to the test ad and then run the test longer in order to acquire sufficient sample size. An advertiser testing two different landing pages, for example, might randomly send 80% of Web site visitors to the current page and the remaining 20% to the test page. The important consideration here is that random assignment must be used to determine which page is seen. It would be disastrous to the test, for example, to have all morning and evening visitors sent to the current page with all afternoon visitors sent to the test page.

CHARACTERISTICS OF CONTROL AND TEST STIMULI.   An advertiser has two options with regard to the characteristics of the test stimuli. An advertiser wanting to compare the effectiveness of a new advertisement versus the current ad would take one of two approaches.

- *The test ad can be created through incremental changes to the control ad.* This approach is illustrated in A/B test illustrated on the top of Figure 20.4, which displays two Google Adwords ads. This A/B test keeps the control and test ad identical except for the manipulation of the benefit expressed in the second line. The control ad uses the phrase "No maintenance or inactivity fees," while the test ad uses the phrase "Guaranteed customer satisfaction." This approach works well when it is important to identify the effect of a single change to the current

---

Single Change: Control Versus Test Ad

Stock Broker	*Stock Broker*
Commission-Free Trades For 30 Days. No Maintenance or Inactivity Fees. YourTradingPartners.com	Commission-Free Trades For 30 Days. Guaranteed Customer Satisfaction. YourTradingPartners.com

Multiple Changes: Control Versus Test Ad

Stock Broker	*100 No-Commission Trades*
Commission-Free Trades For 30 Days. No Maintenance or Inactivity Fees. YourTradingPartners.com	More Than Just a Discount Broker. Open an Account Today and See Why! YourTradingPartners.com

FIGURE 20.4   Control and Test Options for A/B Test

approach. The disadvantage of this approach is that it takes multiple, sequential A/B tests to determine the impact of several proposed changes.

- *An entirely new advertisement could be created and tested.* This is shown on the bottom of Figure 20.4. The advantage of this approach is that it does not restrict the test ad to single or incremental modifications of the current ad. The disadvantage of this approach is that the results are difficult to interpret. While the research might indicate the test ad is "better" than the control ad, it is very difficult if not impossible to isolate the specific reasons why the ad performed as it did.

Given the complimentary strengths and weaknesses of the prior two options, the method ultimately selected should reflect the advertiser's goals, the types of stimuli being tested, and the effectiveness of the stimuli being used as the current/control frame of reference.

Limitations of A/B Testing

A/B testing provides advertisers with an important tool for optimizing the effectiveness of their communication efforts. Nevertheless, as evidenced in the prior discussion, A/B testing has significant limitations. When single changes are instituted sequentially, A/B testing takes a significant amount of time in order to continuously test and compare modified ads to the current "best" ad. When multiple changes are made all at once, it is impossible to say which specific changes affected the outcome. The next two sections discuss procedures that address and resolve these limitations.

FULL FACTORIAL DESIGNS

Full factorial designs are appropriate whenever an advertiser needs to determine the simultaneous effect of relatively few manipulations that have multiple levels (or aspects) of each manipulation. The situations shown in Figure 20.5 have several things in common that illustrate the appropriate use of full factorial designs:

- The total number of manipulations is low, all of the situations have only two or three manipulations.
- The total number of cells is less than 12. Since stimulus materials need to be created for each cell, 10 to 12 cells is generally the upper practical limit.[12]

The advantage of the full factorial design lies in its ability to isolate the effects of each manipulation independently as well as the interaction between factors.[13] This is illustrated in the following situation.[14]

> Imagine that Chevron Oil wants to air an advertising campaign that describes Chevron's commitment to the environment. The goal of the campaign is to improve attitudes toward Chevron. Chevron is unsure, however, how to approach the campaign. The company has identified four possible foci for the messages: the company's recycling efforts, the company's commitment to habitat preservation, the company's donations to Nongovernmental (NGO) environmental organizations, and the company's commitment to elementary school environmental education. In addition, Chevron is unsure as to how to describe this commitment. One option discusses donations in terms of a percentage of sales, while a second option names a specific monetary amount. A full factorial test is recommended where eight different ads

Situation 1	
Research Question:	How do the characteristics of the music used in radio advertisements affect attitudes toward the brand?
Manipulations:	The research manipulates two factors: the genre of the music and the familiarity of the performer. "Genre of Music" has three manipulations: oldies, classical and rap. "Artist Familiarity" has two manipulations: familiar and unfamiliar.
Number of Cells:	The research is a 3 × 2 design resulting in six cells.
Situation 2	
Research Question:	How do the characteristics of comparative advertising affect consumers' attitudes toward the advertised and competitive brand?
Manipulations:	The research manipulates three factors: the tone of the advertisement, the availability of pricing information, and the order in which brands are mentioned. "Tone" has two manipulations: humorous and serious. "Pricing" has two manipulations: price differential between brands mentioned, price differential not mentioned. "Order" has two manipulations: sponsor's brand mentioned first, competitive brand mentioned first.
Number of Cells:	The research is a 2 × 2 × 2 design resulting in eight cells.
Situation 3	
Research Question:	How do the characteristics of banner ads affect click-through rates?
Manipulations:	The research manipulates two factors: ad placement on the page and ad shape. "Placement" has three manipulations: absolute top of page above all content, integrated with content in center of page, standing alone on right-hand side of page. "Shape" has three manipulations: rectangular, small square and large square.
Number of Cells:	The research is a 3 × 3 design resulting in nine cells.

FIGURE 20.5   Examples of Full Factorial Designs

would need to be created. This is because the full factorial design has eight cells (the results of four message strategies and two donation options). The following table illustrates all eight combinations and the names given to each combination.

Combination	Message Focus	Donation Type	Name
1	Recycling	Sales	Recycle Sales
2	Habitat Preservation	Sales	Habitat Sales
3	NGO Donation	Sales	NGO Sales
4	Elementary Education	Sales	Education Sales
5	Recycling	Set amount	Recycle Set Amount
6	Habitat Preservation	Set amount	Habitat Set Amount
7	NGO Donation	Set amount	NGO Set Amount
8	Elementary Education	Set amount	Education Set Amount

Individuals comprising the sample are randomly selected from the appropriate target audience. Each individual is then randomly assigned to one of the eight conditions and shown the appropriate advertisement for the condition to which he or she was assigned. After viewing the ad, each respondent completes a survey that asks for agreement/disagreement with eight statements designed to elicit attitudes toward Chevron. The key outcome measure is the average of these scales where higher numbers indicate more positive brand image.[15]

The first step in the analysis calculates the averages for each factor independently and for each combination of factors. The outcome of these calculations is shown in the following table.

Measure: Attitude Toward Chevron	Average Rating
Message Focus	
Recycling	3.9
Habitat Preservation	4.2
NGO Donation	3.8
Elementary Education	3.9
Type of Donation	
Sales	3.2
Set Amount	4.7
Individual Approaches	
Recycle Sales	3.4
Habitat Sales	2.7
NGO Sales	3.3
Education Sales	3.5
Recycle Set Amount	4.5
Habitat Set Amount	5.6
NGO Set Amount	4.3
Education Set Amount	4.4

The F-values and levels of significance computed for each factor and for the interaction between the two factors are shown in the following table.[16]

Factors Evaluated	F	Level of Significance
Donation Type	56.16	<.001
Message Focus	1.20	.32
Donation x Message Interaction	10.24	<.001

The prior two charts are interpreted as follows:

- Message focus as a main effect exerted no independent influence on attitudes toward Chevron (α is greater than .05).

- There was a significant interaction between the two factors as the level of significance for the interaction is less than .05. This indicates that an examination of each individual approach is warranted.

- Type of Donation as a main effect exerted a significant, independent influence on attitudes toward Chevron (α is less than .05). The mean scores indicate that attitudes toward Chevron were significantly more positive when the donation type was a straight donation rather than a percentage of sales. However, the significant interaction term indicates that it is necessary to examine the scores of the individual ads prior to drawing a final conclusion. When this is done, it can be seen that the combination of habitat and set amount had the most positive impact on attitudes while he combination of habitat and sales had the most negative impact on attitudes.

Understanding the interaction between the main factors, as well as the influence of each factor individually, helps Chevron identify the strongest approach for future advertising. The findings indicate that the best approach for the campaign would be the Habitat Set Amount approach.

MULTIVARIATE TESTING

Full factorial designs have practical limits. While this approach works well for situations in which there are few factors and very limited numbers of manipulations per factor (e.g., in a 2 × 2 or 3 × 3 design), as the number of factors and levels increase so do the methodological demands. It would be nearly impossible, for example, to execute a full factorial design for six factors with multiple levels per factors. A six factor design of the form 3 × 3 × 5 × 2 × 5 × 4 would require 1,800 different stimuli and a sample size of 180,000 with only 100 individuals per cell. Clearly, such research is impossible from a practical perspective.

Multivariate testing, which is applicable to advertising and other communication materials in both traditional and new media, provides a solution to situations in which full factorial designs are not practical due to a large number of factors and levels. Multivariate testing uses a subset of all possible combinations in order to estimate the effects of all combinations. The next section uses an e-mail example to explain the logic and approach of multivariate testing.

An E-mail Multivariate Test[17]

Imagine that the American Savings Association (ASA) wants to improve the efficiency of its e-mail campaigns. "Click-through" from an e-mail to the ASA Web site will be the measure by which efficiency will be measured. The ASA identified five areas of manipulation for the e-mail test with two options for each level, as shown in the table below:

Version	Recipient Personalization	Image	Subject Line	From Address	Length
1	yes	no	long	ASA	short
2	no	no	long	ASA	long
3	yes	yes	long	personalized	long
4	no	yes	long	personalized	short
5	yes	no	short	personalized	long
6	no	no	short	personalized	short
7	yes	yes	short	ASA	short
8	no	yes	short	ASA	long

Note that only 8 combinations are required for this test versus the 32 combinations required by a full factorial design.[18]

The eight combinations used for this multivariate test are not chosen randomly. Rather, they were created systematically.[19] First, within each of the five factors, each level (or alternative) appears with equal frequency. Four of the combinations, for example, contain images, while four do not. Similarly, four of the combinations have been personalized for the recipient, while four combinations have no recipient personalization. Second, there are repeated pairing combinations of the two manipulations of highest interest to the ASA. Of the eight combinations, there are two each of

- no recipient personalization and images present;
- no recipient personalization and no images present;
- recipient personalization and images present; and
- recipient personalization and no images present.

Once all combinations have been selected, an e-mail representing each combination is written and sent to a random sample of individuals on the ASA e-mail list. The click-throughs from each e-mail are monitored, and data collection concludes one week after the initial mailing. The percentage of respondents who clicked-through from each e-mail is shown in the following table.

Version	Recipient Personalization	Image	Subject Line	From Address	Length	% Click-Through
1	present	no	long	ASA	short	14.8%
2	absent	no	long	ASA	long	11.5
3	present	yes	long	personalized	long	14.5
4	absent	yes	long	personalized	short	12.9
5	present	no	short	personalized	long	14.7
6	absent	no	short	personalized	short	13.0
7	present	yes	short	ASA	short	15.9
8	absent	yes	short	ASA	long	12.6

The click-through rates indicate that there are significant differences across combinations. Version 7 generates the highest click-through, while Version 2 is very weak. Thus, this initial analysis of the data informs the ASA as to the strongest of the combinations tested.

The next step determines the underlying reasons why some combinations of attributes performed better than others. This is accomplished by mathematically estimating the relative influence of the five factors. The following table provides the relevant data.

	Recipient Personalization	Images	Subject Line	From Address	Length
Positive Contribution	(present) +7.6%	(yes) +3.4%	(short) +2.2%	(personalized) +.2%	(short) +2.9%
Negative Contribution	(absent) −10.2%	(no) −.2%	(long) −2.2%	(ASA) −.1%	(long) −3.1%

The table is interpreted as follows: Each of the five factors appears as column headings. Each factor's two levels are shown in the column beneath the factor label. The first factor "Recipient Personalization," for example, has two levels: personalization is either present or absent. Similarly, the third factor "Subject Line" has two levels: short and long. Associated with each level of each factor is a number. The number associated with the presence of recipient personalization is +7.6%, while the number associated with the absence of recipient personalization is −10.2%. These numbers represent the percentage difference from the overall average when recipient personalization is present or absent. The presence of recipient personalization increases click-through by 7.6%, while the absence of personalization decreases click-through by 10.2%. Looking across the "Positive Contribution" rows, the data indicates that the presence of "Recipient Personalization" has the relatively greatest impact on click-through (since it is the largest number in the row), while the use of a personalized "From Address" has almost no impact. Similarly, looking across the "Negative Contribution Rows," the data indicates that the absence of recipient personalization has the greatest detrimental effect on click-through, while the absence of images and the ASA from address have almost no impact. (Given that both numbers in the "From Address" column are close to zero, this factor has very little impact and can be eliminated as a concern in future e-mailings.)

The data in the prior table allows ASA to estimate the performance of all 32 possible combinations from the data generated from only 8 combinations. The relative strength of each combination is estimated by substituting and then by adding the numeric values for each level of each factor. Version 1, for example, would have a relative strength score of +8.0% calculated by adding the appropriate values for each of its characteristics (i.e., 7.6 − .2 − 2.2 − .1 + 2.9). The +8.0% is interpreted to mean that this combination of attributes results in an e-mail that is 8% more likely then the overall average to have click-through. The table shown in Figure 20.6 provides the relative strength scores for each of the 8 tested combinations (shown in bold) as well as for each of the remaining 24 combinations where all of the combinations have been ordered from best to worst with regard to their relative strength scores. The ASA would use this data to identify the combinations of characteristics that have the highest likelihood of fostering click-through in future e-mailings. Note that the strongest combination is one that was not tested in the original research.

Advantages and Limitations of Multivariate Testing

Multivariate testing has several advantages over A/B and full factorial designs. First, multiple changes in communication stimuli can be tested and evaluated all at once, reducing the amount of time and cost associated with other approaches. Second, when stimuli are systematically created, a significant amount of learning regarding a broad range of characteristics can be obtained from testing very few stimuli. In fact, when there are just two levels of each characteristic (as in the prior ASA example), the number of actual combinations needed to be tested is only one more than the total number of characteristics being manipulated. As a result, an advertiser can test 7 characteristics with 8 stimuli, 15 characteristics with 16 stimuli, etc. Third, when applied to Web pages, technology now makes it possible to create required versions of test pages "on the fly," thereby reducing the need

Recipient Personalization	Images	Subject Line	From Address	Length	Relative Strength
present	yes	short	personalized	short	16.3
present	**yes**	**short**	**ASA**	**short**	**16.0**
present	no	short	personalized	short	12.7
present	no	short	ASA	short	12.4
present	yes	long	personalized	short	11.9
present	yes	long	ASA	short	11.6
present	yes	short	personalized	long	10.3
present	yes	short	ASA	long	10.0
present	no	long	personalized	short	8.3
present	**no**	**long**	**ASA**	**short**	**8.0**
present	**no**	**short**	**personalized**	**long**	**6.7**
present	no	short	ASA	long	6.4
present	**yes**	**long**	**personalized**	**long**	**5.9**
present	yes	long	ASA	long	5.6
present	no	long	personalized	long	2.3
present	no	long	ASA	long	2.0
absent	yes	short	personalized	short	−1.5
absent	yes	short	ASA	short	−1.8
absent	**no**	**short**	**personalized**	**short**	**−5.1**
absent	no	short	ASA	short	−5.4
absent	**yes**	**long**	**personalized**	**short**	**−5.9**
absent	yes	long	ASA	short	−6.2
absent	yes	short	personalized	long	−7.5
absent	**yes**	**short**	**ASA**	**long**	**−7.8**
absent	no	long	personalized	short	−9.5
absent	no	long	ASA	short	−9.8
absent	no	short	personalized	long	−11.1
absent	no	short	ASA	long	−11.4
absent	yes	long	personalized	long	−11.9
absent	yes	long	ASA	long	−12.2
absent	no	long	personalized	long	−15.5
absent	**no**	**long**	**ASA**	**long**	**−15.8**

Note: "Relative Strength" indicates the percent above or below the overall average a combination is expected to perform.

FIGURE 20.6   ASA Multivariate Testing: Estimating Relative Strength of all Combinations

to physically create and hard-code individual pages. This allows advertisers to test a nearly unlimited number of page characteristic combinations.

There are two limitations to multivariate testing. First, multivariate testing is most efficiently used when there are only two levels for each characteristic being tested, as in the prior ASA example. Multivariate testing becomes significantly more complex when the number of levels per characteristic is three or more. Second, depending upon how the test stimuli are selected, only a very few interactions can be examined.[20]

CAMPAIGN EVALUATION

The contribution of research to decision making does not end once a campaign begins and consumers begin to see the advertising. Advertisers need to know how well the campaign is accomplishing its goals so that future campaigns can capitalize on the current campaign's strengths and reduce or eliminate its weaknesses. Two types of campaign evaluation typically take place:

- *Concurrent evaluation* is most common for advertising placed in media where continuous data collection is possible. Data gathered in concurrent evaluations is typically behavioral and is collected throughout the campaign. Concurrent evaluation, for example, might monitor and collect data on the number of Web site visits generated by a campaign, track the number of banner ad click-throughs, or monitor the number of "forwards" of the viral videos comprising a communication campaign. After a predetermined amount of time, this data is examined to determine whether key measures have met expectations. Automated observational data collection procedures of the type described in Chapter 8 are typically used for concurrent evaluations. The *Reducing Violence Against Women* campaign provided in the Chapter 8 online supplemental readings is an example of a communication campaign that uses concurrent evaluation.
- *Tracking evaluation* is a "point-in-time" evaluation of advertising effects for advertising typically placed in traditional media. Data gathered in tracking evaluations commonly focus on the target audiences' attitudes, beliefs, and behaviors. Data collection takes place a predetermined amount of time after the start of the campaign.[21]

Considerations in Campaign Evaluation

Concurrent and tracking evaluations differ with regard to the time at which data is collected and the types of data collected. Nevertheless, advertisers who participate in these types of research face similar questions, specifically:

- What data should be collected?
- When should the final evaluation take place?
- Are reference groups necessary for data interpretation?[22]

WHAT DATA SHOULD BE COLLECTED?   A critical step in the campaign evaluation process is the specification of the types of data that should be collected. Data specification should always reflect the objectives set for the campaign. Thus, for example, a campaign designed to generate awareness should not measure behavioral change (as this is not a campaign objective). Similarly, a campaign designed to generate awareness and increase brand purchase behaviors should collect data relevant to both goals. Thus, a clear specification of campaign goals and objectives is a prerequisite to the creation of the campaign evaluation questionnaire or the collection of observational data.

WHEN SHOULD THE EVALUATION TAKE PLACE?   Although concurrent evaluations collect data throughout the campaign and tracking evaluations collect data at a single point in time, both types of evaluation must nevertheless answer the same question with regard to data collection timing: "How long does the campaign need to run until we have reliable data on campaign effects?"

- Concurrent evaluations typically answer this question by examining the assumptions made regarding the way in which the campaign is intended to affect/influence the target audience and the need for acceptable sample size. An online banner campaign designed to foster immediate contact with the advertiser's Web site would need a shorter time frame for evaluation versus a campaign designed to influence purchase, especially if the purchase cycle and amount of time needed for decision making is longer.

- Tracking evaluations for ongoing campaigns typically assume that a campaign needs a minimum of 6 to 12 months to exert its influence on the target audience. As a result, tracking evaluations for continuous campaigns generally take place every 6 to 12 months with 12 months being the most common interval. The annual review of the continuous National Youth Anti-Drug Advertising Campaign is an example of this type of tracking evaluation. Other campaigns are finite in their duration; for example, Colorado's tourist advertising only runs during the winter months. In these cases, tracking evaluations take place immediately after the end of the campaign.

ARE REFERENCE GROUPS NECESSARY FOR DATA INTERPRETATION?   A reference or control group provides a context for interpreting data findings and trends. Concurrent evaluations typically do not use reference groups of individuals; instead, this type of campaign evaluation compares observed data to prespecified campaign objectives. An online advertising campaign might decide that "success" is a click-through rate of 4% or greater with at least 50% of those clicking-through completing registration at the Web site. These objectives become the reference against which the campaign is evaluated.

Tracking evaluations typically require two reference groups of individuals. Imagine, for example, that an antismoking campaign is designed to increase negative attitudes toward secondhand smoke and reduce the incidence of smoking around nonsmokers. Tracking data on campaign awareness, attitudes toward secondhand smoke, and incidence of secondhand smoking is collected one year after the start of the campaign. The evaluation finds that among the surveyed random sample of smokers, 85% were aware of the campaign, attitudes toward the danger of secondhand smoke averaged 4.2 (on a 10-point scale where 1.0 is the most unfavorable), and 35% of smokers had reduced their smoking around nonsmokers. The data is certainly impressive, but on the basis of this data, can the advertiser conclude that the campaign is a success? The answer is "no."

The first required reference group for tracking evaluation provides baseline data that helps an advertiser understand attitudes and behaviors prior to the start of the campaign.

A comparison of post- to pre-campaign levels indicates changes occurring over the course of the campaign. Consider the two scenarios shown in the following table.

	Attitudes Toward Secondhand Smoke (Lower Numbers Are More Negative)	Percent of Smokers Who Reduced Smoking Around Nonsmokers
Scenario 1		
Pre-Campaign	6.2	15%
Post-Campaign	4.2	35
Scenario 2		
Pre-Campaign	4.3	34%
Post-Campaign	4.2	35

The two scenarios both report the same post-campaign levels, and in the absence of pre-campaign data the measures appear to be very positive. However, only Scenario 1 provides evidence that the campaign might actually be working. The increase in negative attitudes and reduction in smoking around nonsmokers occurs only in this scenario. Scenario 2, with the same post-campaign measures, shows no impact of the campaign as the pre- and post-measures are nearly identical. Thus, only with a pre-campaign reference group can these two outcomes be distinguished.

At this point, an advertiser still cannot be certain that positive changes on these measures can be confidently attributed to the campaign. After all, multiple other factors might have contributed to the trends seen in Scenario 1. There may have been news programs or other events that showed the dangers of secondhand smoke. A second reference group is needed to determine whether observed trends can confidently be attributed to campaign effects. Typically, this second group consists of those unaware of the campaign, whose attitudes, beliefs, and behaviors are contrasted with those aware of the campaign.[23] Imagine that the trends observed in Scenario 1 occurred. The next step would be to separate the post-campaign attitudes and behaviors of those aware of the campaign from those unaware. The two possible outcomes are shown in the following table.

	Attitudes Toward Secondhand Smoke (Lower Numbers Are More Negative)		Percent of Smokers Who Reduced Smoking Around Nonsmokers	
	Aware	Unaware	Aware	Unaware
Scenario A				
Pre-Campaign	6.2	6.2	15%	15%
Post-Campaign	2.2	6.2	55	15
Scenario B				
Pre-Campaign	6.2	6.2	15%	15%
Post-Campaign	4.2	4.2	35	35

Notice how the comparison of aware and unaware individuals allows the advertiser to understand campaign impact. Scenario A shows aware and unaware individuals starting at the same points: both groups had equivalent attitudes toward secondhand smoke, and equal numbers of both groups were reducing their smoking around nonsmokers. Exposure to the campaign then resulted in significant differences between the two groups. Those aware of the campaign showed movement in the desired direction, while those unaware showed no movement. Thus, positive effects of the campaign can be inferred. This is in contrast to Scenario B. Here, both groups again started at the same point. However, since the overall trends in behavior were the same for both groups, exposure to the campaign cannot be used as the explanation for the observed positive trends. In this situation, other reasons must be found to explain the trend.

APPLYING CHAPTER CONCEPTS

This chapter discussed the ways in which post-production advertising research contributes to advertising planning. Two online supplemental readings provide examples of testing performed at both ends of the post-production continuum: copy testing and campaign tracking evaluation research.

Mapes and Ross Natural Exposure Copy Test

As discussed earlier in this chapter, a copy test must satisfy several criteria in order to be useful to an advertiser. The test must have a sound, validated methodology and appropriate norms. Additionally, the results must be reported in a way that allows the advertiser to clearly see the implications of the findings for decision making. The Mapes and Ross copy test topline report provided in the online supplemental readings satisfies all these criteria. The report presents the results of a copy test of the General Electric (GE) television advertisement "GE Reveal® - Light Bulb." Note how the organization of the report addresses key research-related issues discussed in Chapter 1: the rationale for the research is explicitly stated, key evaluative measures are identified, the methodology is described in sufficient detail, sample characteristics are noted, and the results and their implications are clearly communicated.

The topline report's detailed findings (report pages 9 through 13) illustrate the contribution of copy testing to decisions regarding whether or not to air a particular commercial.

- *Persuasion* (the primary metric) is addressed on page 9, where two types of analyses are presented. First, the test commercial's persuasion score is compared to two of Mapes and Ross' overall norms, in this case the norm for comparative products (consumer packaged goods miscellaneous products) and the overall all products norm. Second, the commercial's persuasiveness among important subgroups is noted. In all cases, the test commercial's persuasion score significantly exceeded the norms.

- Aspects of commercial recall are addressed on pages 10 through 12. *Proven Recall* reflects the percentage of individuals who were able to spontaneously mention a unique visual or textual component of the commercial. *Unaided Brand Name*

Recall reflects the percentage of individuals who were able (without prompting) to recall the GE brand name after commercial viewing. Note how in both cases comparisons are made to overall norms for both the total sample and for key subgroups. *Visual Element Recall* provides insight into which commercial components or ideas were more attention-getting or memorable, as higher scores indicate a greater percentage of individuals mentioning the specific aspect of the commercial.

- Prior to copy testing an advertisement, it is important to identify the commercial's intended communication. This allows the copy testing methodology to determine the extent to which this intended communication was actually communicated to the target audience. The analysis of *Main Idea Communication* is presented on page 13, where the report notes overall communication of the intended main idea and then compares this level to relevant norms.

As you read through the findings, keep in mind that while each individual measure is important, the final decision on commercial airing typically is based on the overall pattern of response. While all measures in this case are quite high, imagine a case where persuasion is high but recall is low, or recall is high but persuasion is low. It is the overall pattern of response, especially responses among key subgroups that lead the decision making process.

Finally, it is important to remember that it is the copy testing company's responsibility to provide a detailed and objective analysis narrowly focused on the research results. It is the advertiser's responsibility to bring an independent point of view to the report, detailing areas in which he or she agrees or disagrees and providing deeper background with regard to data interpretation. GE might, for example, place the interpretation of the persuasion scores in the context of its market share. GE might note that:

> General Electric has the dominant share of the light bulb category. As a result, most consumers are either already positive toward GE or are GE light bulb purchasers. As a result, the group of individuals available to switch to GE is relatively small. Understanding this, it was GE's mandate to develop an ad that not only helped promote the new light bulb "Reveal" in such a way that it was both persuasive and memorable, but also to convey the message of pure clean light. Despite its strong market dominance, GE's creativity worked hard and achieved this by exceeding the applicable Mapes and Ross norms for commercial persuasiveness.

National Tobacco Youth Campaign Evaluation

The Australian Department of Health and Ageing has the goal of helping all Australians achieve better health throughout their lifespan. The Department achieves this goal through strengthened evidence-based policy advising; improved program management; research; regulation; and partnerships with other government agencies, consumers, and stakeholders. In this context, a specific focus is on the encouragement of healthy lifestyles and the prevention or reduction of unhealthy lifestyles.[24]

The National Tobacco Youth Campaign (NTYC) is one specific way in which the Department of Health and Ageing attempts to encourage healthy lifestyles. The NTYC was a national, multimedia campaign that aimed to reduce the initiation and prevalence of smoking among young Australians. The campaign's primary goal was to encourage youth aged 12 to 24 years to reject smoking. The secondary goal of the campaign was to encourage parents to quit smoking in order to discourage their children from smoking.[25]

Tracking evaluation research was used to determine campaign effectiveness. Baseline data was collected before the campaign ran (November/December, 2006), and post-exposure data was collected after the campaign had run (April/May, 2007). Both surveys measured the target audience's knowledge, attitudes, intentions, and behaviors with respect to tobacco smoking as well as their awareness of the NTYC campaign and messages. The total sample size was nearly 3,000.

The full campaign evaluation report is provided in the online supplemental readings. The research reported in the report is a superior example of well-designed tracking research. Note how the use of the baseline sample allows one to clearly assess campaign impact and how the areas explored are explicitly defined and directly related to the campaign's goals and objectives. Beyond the research itself, the report is a model of excellence in data presentation. The report is organized to allow the reader to move through a significant amount of data in a way that fosters understanding. In spite of the amount of data presented, the reader is never overwhelmed by the detail. Finally, note how the data was collected. Questionnaire pre-testing was used to make certain that there were no problems with questionnaire flow or wording and the questionnaire itself (provided in the report's appendices) illustrate many of the guidelines discussed in Chapters 12 and 13.

SUMMARY

Four types of research contribute to advertising decision making after an advertisement or other communication stimulus is produced.

Copy testing research evaluates finished advertisements to determine whether or not they should be placed in media and used in a communications campaign. Copy testing methodologies typically vary the naturalness of the viewing situation, the number of advertising exposures, the timing of data collection, and the specific types of data collected. Two approaches to television copy testing are Gallup & Robinson's InTeleTest and Mapes and Ross' Natural Exposure.

Split-run and A/B tests are related research techniques that allow advertisers to compare a current approach to advertising with one or more potential alternatives. Split-run is the label given to this test when conducted in print media, while A/B test is the label for when conducted in an online environment. Advertisers using both tests must make two important decisions. First, the advertiser must operationalize "better" with regard to ad performance. Second, the advertiser must code each ad so that data relevant to the operationalization can be collected. Beyond decisions related to operationaization, advertisers using A/B testing must make decisions with regard to the length of the test, exposure rotation of the test and control stimuli, and the characteristics of the test and control stimuli.

Full factorial and multivariate techniques allow advertisers to determine how manipulations of the advertising or other communication stimuli affect consumer response. Full factorial designs are most appropriate when the total number of manipulations is low and the total number of cells is less than 10 or 12. The advantage of full factorial designs lies in its ability to isolate the effects of each manipulation independently as well as the interaction between manipulations. Full factorial designs require that stimulus materials be created for each cell in the design. Multivariate testing is an alternative to full factorial designs and is appropriate whenever an advertiser wants to simultaneously manipulate many changes to an advertisement or other communication stimulus. Here, a subset of all possible combinations can be tested and used to infer the effect of all possible combinations.

Multivariate testing has several advantages over A/B and full factorial designs: multiple changes can be tested and evaluated all at once, reducing the amount of time and cost associated with other approaches; relatively few actual stimuli need to be created; and when applied to Web pages, technology now makes it possible to create required versions of test pages "on the fly," thereby reducing the need to physically create and hard-code individual pages.

There are two limitations to multivariate testing: multivariate testing is most efficiently used when there are only two levels for each characteristic being tested, and multivariate testing becomes significantly more complex when the number of levels per characteristic is three or more.

Campaign evaluation research helps advertisers determine the effectiveness of the communication campaign once it has been shown to the target audience. Concurrent evaluation is most common for advertising placed in media where continuous data collection is possible. Data gathered in concurrent evaluations is typically behavioral and is collected throughout the campaign. Tracking evaluation is a "point-in-time" evaluation of advertising effects for advertising typically placed in traditional media. Data gathered in tracking evaluations commonly focus on the target audiences' attitudes, beliefs, and behaviors. Concurrent and tracking evaluations differ with regard to the time at which data is collected and the types of data collected. Nevertheless, advertisers who participate in these types of research face similar questions, specifically: what data should be collected, when should the final evaluation take place, and are reference groups necessary for data interpretation?

Review Questions

1. What four types of advertising research are conducted after an advertisement or other communication stimulus has been produced?
2. How does copy testing differ from communication testing?
3. What four dimensions differentiate approaches to copy testing?
4. What are the key differences between the InTeleTest and Natural Exposure copy testing methodologies?
5. What are the considerations for evaluating the "goodness" of copy testing methodologies?

6. In what ways are split-run and A/B tests similar? In what ways do they differ?
7. What are the most appropriate uses for split-run and A/B tests?
8. What two important issues need to be addressed before conducting a split-run or A/B test?
9. In what circumstances is a single measure appropriate for the evaluation of a split-run or A/B test? What are the advantages of using multiple measures?
10. How does an advertiser determine the length of an A/B test?

11. What are the considerations in determining the relative exposure of the test and control stimuli in an A/B test?

12. What are an advertiser's two options for creating test stimuli in an A/B test? What are the relative advantages and disadvantages of each option?

13. What are the limitations of A/B testing?

14. In what circumstances is a full factorial design most appropriate?

15. What are the primary differences between full factorial designs and multivariate testing?

16. In what circumstances is multivariate testing most appropriate?

17. What are the defining characteristics of multivariate testing?

18. What are the advantages and limitations of multivariate testing?

19. Why do advertisers conduct campaign evaluations?

20. What are the characteristics of the two types of campaign evaluations?

21. Why are reference groups important when conducting tracking campaign evaluations?

Application Exercises[26]

Application exercises 1 through 5 reflect chapter content and discussion.

1. This exercise will help you better understand how differences in copy testing methodologies affect consumers' response. In preparation for the exercise, you will need to (a) ask 20 individuals to participate, (b) preselect a television program, (c) record the selected program, and (d) copy the selected program onto VHS or DVD. Tell all of the participants that you are conducting research to explore their reactions to a particular television program. Here is what to do with the participants.

Ask 10 of the participants to watch the program at the time it airs (no Tivo or delayed viewing). Twenty-four hours after the program airs, use the questionnaire shown in Figure 20.7 to explore responses to both the program and the test commercial. (The questions related to the program are distracter questions). Record their responses as indicated in the questionnaire.

Provide the remaining 10 participants with the program recording and ask them to watch it within the next four hours. Then, the next day (about 24 hours later) use the questionnaire shown in Figure 20.7 to explore their responses to both the program and the test commercial. Record their responses as indicated in the questionnaire.

Ignoring the program-related questions, analyze the data collected for commercial recall separately for each group. Then, prepare a paper that provides the results of your research. Be certain to note how the groups differed with regard to each of the key measures. Conclude your paper with a point of view regarding which approach you feel provides the best data.

2. Visit Amazon's home page. Identify one aspect of the page that in your opinion could be improved. Prepare a paper that describes the steps you would take to test the current page versus your revised page in an A/B test. Be certain to address issues of sample, timing, key measures, and data collection.

3. Imagine that Progressive Insurance wants to increase the percentage of people who request a quote through its Web site. As a first step, the company is considering revising its home page. Visit Progressive Insurance's home page (http://www.progressive.com) and identify six types of changes you would like to explore using multivariate testing. For each change, specify two alternatives that could be tested. Finally, construct a table similar to that shown on page 609 that lists the combinations you would test. Explain how you arrived at these combinations.

4. Imagine that Netflix has explored alternative approaches to its online advertising. Five changes to its current approach are being considered. A multivariate test has been selected

1. Can you please confirm that you watched [INSERT NAME OF PROGRAM].

     Yes, watched program   ☐ → CONTINUE WITH QUESTION 2
     No, did not watch program   ☐ → DISCONTINUE

2. Using a scale of "1" to "10" where "10" represents "Extremely liked" and "1" represents "Extremely disliked" what number between 1 and 10 best represents your reactions to [INSERT NAME OF PROGRAM]?

     _____ [FILL IN RESPONSE]

3. In a four week period, how many times would you say that you watch [INSERT NAME OF PROGRAM]?

     _____ [FILL IN RESPONSE]

4. While watching [INSERT NAME OF PROGRAM] did you happen to see any commercials?

     Yes   ☐ → CONTINUE WITH QUESTION 5
     No   ☐ → DISCONTINUE

5. Can you tell me the names of brands or products you remember seeing advertised in [INSERT NAME OF PROGRAM]? DO NOT PROMPT.

     TARGET BRAND MENTIONED: Yes ☐ → CONTINUE WITH QUESTION 9
                                             No ☐ → CONTINUE WITH QUESTION 6

6. Do you recall seeing a commercial for [NAME OF TARGET BRAND PRODUCT CATEGORY]?

     Yes   ☐ → CONTINUE WITH QUESTION 7
     No   ☐ → CONTINUE WITH QUESTION 8

7. What was the name, or what were the names, of the brands or products advertised in [NAME OF TARGET BRAND PRODUCT CATEGORY]?

     TARGET BRAND MENTIONED: Yes ☐ → CONTINUE WITH QUESTION 9
                                             No ☐ → CONTINUE WITH QUESTION 8

8. Do you recall seeing a commercial for [INSERT NAME OF BRAND]?

     Yes   ☐ → CONTINUE WITH QUESTION 9
     No   ☐ → DISCONTINUE

9. What, if anything, can you remember about the [NAME OF BRAND] commercial?

10. What else, if anything, did the commercial say or show?

FIGURE 20.7 Questionnaire for Application Exercise 1

as the methodology to explore how these changes affect click-through. The combinations tested as well as the results are shown in Figure 20.8. Using this data, prepare a short paper that summarizes the results of the test. Be certain to provide a recommendation for the final creative approach to be used in future advertising.

5. *This exercise is to be completed after reading the chapter addendum.* Between 1985 and 1987, Kraft aired a series of cheese commercials that addressed the issue of calcium in real

versus imitation cheese. Following is the disputed copy in the "Skimp" execution:

I admit it. I thought of skimping. Could you look into those big blue eyes and skimp on her? So I buy Kraft Singles. Imitation slices use hardly any milk. But Kraft has five ounces per slice. Five ounces. So her little bones get the calcium they need to grow. No, she doesn't know what that big Kraft means. Good thing I do. (This audio was accompanied

Combinations Tested

Version	Size	Pricing	"Free Trial"	Movies Shown	Netflix Logo
1	large	mentioned	mentioned	upcoming release	large
2	large	mentioned	absent	recent release	small
3	large	absent	absent	upcoming release	large
4	large	absent	mentioned	recent release	small
5	small	mentioned	mentioned	upcoming release	small
6	small	mentioned	absent	recent release	large
7	small	absent	absent	upcoming release	small
8	small	absent	mentioned	recent release	large

Results

	Size	Pricing	"Free Trial"	Movies Shown	Netflix Logo
Positive	(small)	(absent)	(mentioned)	(upcoming release)	(small)
Contribution	+6.6%	+4.4%	+8.9%	+5.8%	+.2%
Negative	(large)	(mentioned)	(absent)	(recent release)	(large)
Contribution	−1.2%	−3.3%	−11.2%	−.3%	−.1%

FIGURE 20.8   Multivariate Test Results for Application Exercise 4

by a visual of milk pouring into a glass until it reaches a mark labeled "five ounces." The commercial also shows milk pouring into a glass that shows the phrase "5 oz. milk slice.")

The FTC complaint against this commercial claimed two misrepresentations (both of which were implicit rather than explicit in the advertising):

a. That a slice of Kraft Singles contained the same amount of calcium as five ounces of milk.

b. That Kraft Singles contained more calcium than most imitation cheese slices.

If, in fact, these messages were communicated by the advertising, they would be false because

a. a slice of Kraft cheeses contains only 70% the calcium of five ounces of milk, and

b. most imitation cheese slices sold in the United States contain about the same amount of calcium as is contained in Kraft Singles.

Two copy tests were conducted to determine whether the two disputed claims were communicated and, if so, whether they were material. The survey designed and conducted on behalf of Kraft is shown in Figure 20.9. The survey designed and conducted on behalf of the FTC is shown in Figure 20.10.[27] Prepare a paper that compares and contrasts the surveys with regard to the following:

• *Sample universe.* Use each questionnaire's screener to determine the characteristics of the sample in each copy test. In what ways are the two samples similar? In what ways are they different? Present a point of view on the acceptability of each sample for the copy test of the "Skimp" ad. Be certain to address how the responses to the main questionnaire in each test may be influenced by sample characteristics.

• *Questions asked.* Evaluate each questionnaire for specific content. To what extent do the questions on each questionnaire address similar issues? To what extent do they address different issues? To what extent (and how acceptably) does each questionnaire probe communication in the disputed areas and the materiality of the communication?

• *Question format.* Evaluate the strengths and weaknesses of the questions asked on each survey. Which questions are acceptable as written? Which questions do you find problematic? For each problematic question, identify the source of the problem (i.e., bias,

Kraft Survey: Screener Questionnaire

The Screener questionnaire began: "Just so that I can be sure that I'm speaking to the right person, are you the one in your household who is most responsible for your household's food shopping?" After a series of questions to determine age, amount of television watched per week, whether anyone in the household was employed in a sensitive industry (e.g., "by a manufacturer or distributor food or a store that sells food"), and whether the person had participated in a survey during the prior three months that asked about food products, the Screener continued with the following:

E. Today I'd like to talk to you about various types of cheeses. As you know, cheese products that are sold in food stores are packaged in a number of different ways. Some cheese, like cottage cheese, is usually sold in a tub or a container from which you spoon out as much as you want. Other cheeses come as solid pieces or chunks, and it's up to you to cut off as much as you want at any one time. Then there are some cheese products that come individually wrapped in cellophane as ready-to-use single slices. I'd like to know about the types of cheeses you buy. Which, if any, of the following types of cheese have you bought in the past three months, either for yourself or for other members of your household? Did you buy any . . . cheeses packaged in tubs or containers; solid pieces or chunks of cheese; cheese products that come individually wrapped in cellophane as ready-to-use single slices? IF "NO" TO "CHEESE PRODUCTS THAT COME INDIVIDUALLY WRAPPED IN CELLOPHANE AS READY-TO USE SLICES," TERMINATE.

F. ASK FOR EACH PRODUCT BOUGHT IN Q.E. Now, what about eating cheese: Over the past three months, did you eat any [of each of the three types of cheeses]?

G1. The few questions that I have deal with prepackaged sliced cheese products sold in packages of 8, 12, 16 slices, and so on, where each slice comes individually wrapped in its own sheet of cellophane. Which brand or brands of ready-to-use single cheese products have you bought within the past year?

G2. (FOR EACH BRAND NOT MENTIONED IN Q. G1. ASK:) Within the past year have you bought (BRAND)? IF KRAFT IS NOT MENTIONED EITHER IN Q'S G1 OR G2, TERMINATE.

Kraft Survey: Main Questionnaire

Q1a. People buy cheese for a number of different reasons. What are the reasons that you buy cheese? Why else?

Q1b. What are the reasons for your buying individually wrapped cheese food slices?

Q1c. Now I'd like you to think only about "Kraft Singles" Cheese food slices. Please tell me all the reasons that you can think of as to why you buy Kraft Singles individually wrapped cheese food slices? (PROBE:) Any other reasons?

Q2. Now I'm going to mention a number of things that Kraft Singles may or may not contain. For each item that I mention, please tell me if Kraft Singles do contain, do not contain, or you don't know if they contain this item. Do they or don't they contain . . . Protein; Vitamin C; Milk; Riboflavin; Vitamin A; Vegetable oil; Calcium?

Q3. I'm going to read a short list of characteristics about cheese. As I read each one, please tell me how important that characteristic is to you in your decision to buy Kraft Singles. Let's start with . . . Would you say is extremely important, very important, somewhat important or not at all important?

- Has real cheese flavor
- Has consistent quality
- Is good tasting
- Made by a company you can trust
- Is reasonably priced
- Is a source of calcium
- Is convenient to use
- Is individually wrapped so it stays fresh
- Is a source of Vitamin C

Q4. (Asked only of respondents who gave an "extremely" or "very" response in Q3.) Since you said that calcium is important to you in your decision to buy Kraft Single Slices, I'd like to ask you a few questions about it. Do you have any idea as to how much calcium is contained in one slice of Kraft Singles?

Q4b. (For those answering yes to Q4a., ask:) How much calcium is there in one slice of Kraft Singles?

FIGURE 20.9   Kraft Questionnaire

Q5a. As you may or may not know, although each slice of Kraft Singles is made from five ounces of whole milk, it does not contain as much calcium as five ounces of milk. One slice of Kraft Singles actually contains 70% of the calcium in five ounces of milk. Now that I've told you this, I'd like to know whether this difference in calcium matters to you. More specifically, (READ BOTH CHOICES BEFORE RESPONDENT ANSWERS) . . .

- Would you buy Kraft Singles slices even though each slice contains 70% of the calcium in five ounces of milk; or
- Would you stop buying Kraft Singles slices because each slice doesn't contain the same amount of calcium as five ounces of milk? Q5b. Would this difference in the amount of calcium be enough to affect the way in which you use Kraft Singles slices?

Q5c. (For those answering "yes" to Q5b, ask:) In what way or ways would it affect how you use Kraft Singles slices?

Q6a. By the way, do you have any idea as to how much calcium is contained in five ounces of milk?

Q6b. (For those answering "Yes" to Q6a, ask:) How much calcium is there in five ounces of milk?

FIGURE 20.9 (Continued)

FTC Survey: Screener

Q1. Are you the principal food shopper in your household?

Q2. Are you over 18 years of age?

Q3. Do you have children living at home who are under 18 years of age?

Q4. Do you, or does anyone in your household, work for an advertising agency, a marketing research firm, or a company that manufactures or distributes grocery or dairy products?

Q5. Have you purchased any of the following products in the past three months: Cheese or Cheese Products? Deodorant (Anti-Perspirant)? Laundry Detergent?

FTC Survey: Main Questionnaire

Q1. Do you remember seeing an advertisement for cheese slices?

Q2. What brand was being advertised? (If other than Kraft, Terminate)

Q3. Do you remember seeing an ad for Kraft Singles? (If "Don't Know:" Terminate)

Q4. What points does the Kraft ad make about the product? (PROBE:) What else?

Q4a. Is there anything else about the Kraft ad that stands out in your mind? (PROBE:) Is there something else?

Q5a. Does the ad give you any reasons why you should buy Kraft Singles?

Q6. Does the ad say or suggest anything about the nutritional value of Kraft Singles, or about how healthy or good they are for you?

Q7. You said the Kraft Singles ad mentioned (nutrition, healthy, is good for you). What does the ad say or suggest that makes you think they are --?

Q8. Does the ad say or suggest anything about the milk content of Kraft Singles? (If milk mentioned in Q8, ask Q9; otherwise skip to Q10)

Q9. You said the ad mentioned the milk content of Kraft Singles. What does the milk content of Kraft Singles mean to you?

Q10. Does the ad say or suggest anything about the calcium in Kraft Singles?

Q11. Does this ad say or suggest anything about the amount of calcium in a slice of Kraft Singles compared to the amount of calcium in five ounces of milk? (If "no", skip to Q12).

Q11a. Based on this ad, do you think that a slice of Kraft Singles has more calcium than five ounces of milk, the same amount of calcium, or less calcium than five ounces of milk?

Q12. Does this ad compare Kraft Singles to imitation cheese slices?

Q13. Does this ad make any direct comparisons between Kraft Singles and other cheese slices?

Q14. Based on this ad, do you think Kraft Singles have more calcium, the same amount of calcium, or less calcium than those cheese slices they are being compared to?

FIGURE 20.10 FTC Questionnaire

leading, incomplete response options, etc.) and provide a recommendation for correcting the problem.

Finally, based on your observations and analysis, write a complete questionnaire (including a screener) that you feel best addresses the issues underlying testing of the disputed advertisement.

Application Exercises 6 through 8 refer to the Mapes and Ross copy test report provided in the online supplemental readings.

6. Review the methodology for Mapes and Ross Natural Exposure. Write a telephone questionnaire that will collect the information required for this testing procedure.

7. The report provides subgroup analyses by gender (men and women) and purchase behaviors (GE and non-GE buyers). Identify at least two additional subgroups of individuals that you think merit examination, regardless of whether they were included in the initial sample. Prepare a short paper that clearly describes the subgroups and provides a rationale for their selection.

8. While both men and women showed positive responses to the commercial, women were relatively more positive versus men. Do you think that this is or is not a problem? Prepare a short paper that addresses this issue. Be certain to review the script of the commercial on report page 17 prior to beginning your paper.

Application Exercises 9 through 14 refer to the National Tobacco Youth Campaign provided in the online supplemental readings.

9. Using the findings from the evaluation report as your foundation, prepare a paper that presents your recommendations for the strategic, media, and creative direction for the new campaign. Specifically, what do the findings imply with regard to the strengths and limitations of the initial campaign, and how should these factors be addressed in the new campaign?

10. Imagine that the new tobacco prevention campaign will expand the media in which the message will appear. The new campaign will utilize mobile marketing, guerilla marketing, and social media. Revise the current questionnaire to specifically evaluate the impact of these new

media outlets on the targets' awareness and reactions to the campaign as well as message communication.

11. The primary goal of the NTYC was to encourage youth to reject smoking. Pages 20 to 37 of the report address this aspect of the campaign. Read through this section of the report paying particular attention to the measures that were used. Prepare a short paper that: (a) evaluates the strengths and limitations of the measures used and (b) presents alternative measures that might be used to evaluate campaign impact in this area. Assume that data collection will again be done via telephone interviews. Be certain to provide a rationale for your alternative approaches.[28]

12. The NTYC evaluation report provides a detailed analysis of campaign impact on key target audiences. No report, however, can conduct data analyses for *all* subgroups of interest. Identify three subgroups of individuals for which the report did not provide specific data analyses. Prepare a short paper that describes the characteristics of each group and provides a rationale for why you feel a detailed examination of that group is warranted. Your groups can be defined on the basis of any of the questions (or combination of questions) asked on the questionnaire.

13. Data collection for the NTYC evaluation was conducted by telephone. Prepare a point of view that contrasts the strengths and weaknesses of telephone versus online data collection. Be certain to address how each data collection method influences sampling and the format of key questions. Conclude your paper with a recommendation and rationale for the preferred data collection method.

14. The questionnaire shown in the appendix of the report is designed to be used with members of the youth target. Using one of the online survey companies (see Chapter 13), translate the telephone survey into an online questionnaire. Print the completed questionnaire in a way that makes the response options and skip patterns explicit. Then, attach the questionnaire to a paper that describes the specific questions that needed to be changed or modified in making the transition from telephone to online. Provide a rationale for your changes.

Copy Testing from a Legal Perspective[29]

The Federal Trade Commission (FTC) is taking a more active role in monitoring and challenging advertising claims believed to be legally deceptive. According to the FTC, an advertisement is legally deceptive when it displays the following three characteristics:

1. The ad makes a representation, has an omission, or uses a practice that is likely to mislead the consumer. The representation, omission, or practice may be explicit or implied in the advertising. Additionally, the ability of an ad to mislead a consumer does not have to be directly attributable to specific elements in the ad. A consumer can be misled by the overall net impression left by an ad.

2. The representation, omission, or practice is misleading when examined from the perspective of a reasonable consumer.

3. The representation, omission, or practice is "material." The FTC evaluates the extent to which the representation, omission, or practice influences consumer behavior or purchasing patterns. A representation, omission, or practice is material when behaviors or purchasing patterns are affected.[30]

In this context, advertising copy tests represent an important form of evidence offered in support of or in opposition to FTC claims of deceptiveness. The FTC has utilized its own copy tests to assess the validity of its challenges to particular advertisements. Advertisers have used copy tests to counter FTC challenges.[31] Both advertisers and the FTC use copy tests because copy test data responds to an FTC preference for objective, external data. The FTC has stated that:

> The extrinsic evidence we prefer to use and to which we give great weight is direct evidence of what consumers actually thought upon reading the advertisement in question. Such evidence will be in the form of consumer survey research for widely distributed ads.[32]

However, while the FTC has shown a predisposition to rely on copy test data in support of an argument or position, it has also shown a great willingness to discard and ignore copy test findings that result from research that is deficient in methodological planning, execution, or data reporting. An FTC evaluation of the soundness of a copy test addresses the following areas:

- universe definition and sample selection
- research design and use of control groups
- questionnaire design and question formats
- interviewer qualifications, training, and techniques
- data analysis and presentation
- research project administration

The remainder of this chapter addendum presents guidelines for copy test planning and administration in each of these areas. Adherence to these guidelines can substantially increase the likelihood of FTC acceptance of copy test findings.[33]

UNIVERSE DEFINITION AND SAMPLE SELECTION

Copy test research findings are only acceptable when they reflect the opinions and behaviors of appropriate individuals, typically defined as individuals who are relevant to the advertising's underlying strategy, objectives, and target audience. The FTC has criticized and rejected research that included respondents who should not have been included in the sample frame and/or that failed to sample from the universe of all relevant consumers. This is because "the central question in any deceptive advertising matter is: What percent of the relevant population have been misled? When members of the relevant population have been excluded, and persons who are not members of that population included, this all important question cannot be answered."[34] Thus, the psychographic, demographic, and behavioral characteristics of the advertising's target definition must all be reflected in the copy test universe sample definition.

Once the sample universe has been defined, individuals from that universe must be identified and recruited in a methodologically sound and defensible manner. Care must be taken to ensure the following:

- *The sample size is reasonable given the required degree of accuracy.* Sample sizes of about 100 individuals per test condition are generally acceptable.

- *The sampling plan does not appear to be biased toward any viewpoint or opinion group.* Imagine, for example, an appropriate sample universe definition of "purchasers of Brand X within the past 30 days." It would be inappropriate to sample from a list of past 30-day purchasers who were dissatisfied with the product and who used the product guarantee to return the product for a refund. These individuals are clearly biased against the product and are not representative of all product purchasers. A sample of these individuals would result in a biased sample that is not generalizable to the population specified in the sample universe definition and is therefore likely to be rejected.[35]

- *The sampling is reasonable and meets accepted industry practice.* While probability sampling is always preferable over convenience sampling, the FTC has shown a willingness to accept the results of copy tests conducted among individuals recruited by mall-intercept interviews provided that the distribution and location of the malls are reasonable given product distribution and advertising scheduling. The malls must be located where the advertising has run.

RESEARCH DESIGN AND USE OF CONTROL GROUPS

As discussed earlier, the FTC makes a determination of deception based on what consumers "take away" from an advertisement (i.e., the messages consumers explicitly or implicitly receive) and the materiality of the communication. Consequently, one crucial goal of a copy test performed in the context of an FTC challenge is the accurate determination of what is communicated by an ad and the importance of that communication in affecting consumer brand preference or brand choice.

Consumers, however, are not "blank slates." They bring a broad array of preexisting knowledge and attitudes to the advertising viewing situation. Consequently, a copy test must be designed in a way that permits one to distinguish what consumers already think and feel from what they *specifically learned* from an advertisement.

The FTC has responded favorably to copy test designs that use control groups to help distinguish prior knowledge from knowledge acquired as the direct result of advertising exposure. Typically, a post-test only with control group design is used because a pretest design has the potential to sensitize respondents and thus bias how they view the advertising and answer post-exposure questions. An advertiser has several options as to the nature of the control group within the post-test only with control group design.

One option is to define the control group as a nonexposure group. Here, the control group does not see any advertising, while the test group is exposed to the disputed advertising. Data analysis in this design assumes that given random assignment to control and experimental groups, differences in knowledge and attitudes between the control and test group can be directly related to the independent variable, the contested advertising.

The no exposure control group approach works well when the advertising has had limited marketplace exposure. However, when the disputed ad has had significant exposure, the problem of distinguishing communication *from the advertising* versus *from existing attitudes* becomes more complex. The beliefs expressed by individuals in the no exposure group may have been influenced by their having already seen the advertising. Thus, if no differences are observed between the control and exposure groups, it is unclear whether this absence of difference is due to a lack of communication by the test ad or due to the fact that prior exposure to the advertising has caused individuals in both the control and test groups to have acquired the same knowledge and attitudes, resulting in little incremental effect from additional exposure to the advertising.[36]

There are three methods for distinguishing existing knowledge and attitudes from knowledge and attitudes formed after exposure to an advertisement in situations where the advertising has had substantial exposure before the copy test.

One approach uses an experimental design in which one group is exposed to the advertising with the potentially deceptive elements and a second group is exposed to the same advertising in which the potentially deceptive elements have been eliminated. Differences in outcomes between groups are attributed to the presence or absence of the identified and manipulated commercial elements. This approach works well when the deceptive practice or claim can be attributed to only a few specific elements in the ad. However, in situations in which almost everything in the ad is part of a challenged claim, a revised "cleansed" ad would be difficult to use because it would require the deletion of almost all the ad elements. When this occurs, it could be argued that resulting executional differences between the two ads were the primary reason for observed differences.[37]

A second approach exposes a test group to the disputed advertising and a control group to a modified version of the disputed ad. Differences in outcomes between the test and control groups are attributed to the difference between exposure to the original versus modified advertising claim. Russo, Metcalf, and Stephens, who proposed this design, argue that this approach works best in cases where advertisers appear to be exploiting consumers preexisting beliefs toward a particular brand or product.[38]

A third approach exposes a test group to the disputed advertising and a control group to other similar, but nondisputed, advertising for the brand. The ideal control ad is an ad from a different campaign that displays executional similarities to the test ad. This approach is suggested whenever it is believed that significant exposure to the disputed advertising (before the copy test) has the potential to result in a "halo" effect, that is, when consumers are likely to attribute information obtained from prior viewing of the disputed ad to a modified version of that ad. As with the prior design, differences in outcomes between test and control groups are attributed to the exposure to the potentially deceptive elements.

The FTC, in a test of Kraft Singles cheese advertising, used a combination of these approaches. The FTC challenged Kraft Singles cheese advertising that stated that one slice of cheese was made from five glasses of milk. The FTC challenged the ad because it believed that the ad implied that one slice of cheese had the same calcium content as five glasses of milk, which it did not. (One slice of cheese has only 70% the calcium content of five ounces of milk.) The FTC copy test used five cells and was structured to account for extensive advertising exposure before the copy test.

> Cells one and two were exposed to the TV versions of "Skimp" (the contested ad). The only difference was the presence of wording superimposed on commercial 2: "Milk amounts based on cheese content. One three ounce slice has 70% of the calcium of five ounces of milk." Cell 3 (TV-control) viewed another Kraft Singles TV commercial that said nothing about milk or calcium and was not in dispute. Respondents exposed to the Skimp print advertisement (Cell 4) were contrasted to a control group (Cell 5) exposed to another Kraft print advertisement that did not mention milk or calcium. Respondents in each cell followed identical patterns of advertising exposure and responded to identical interview protocols. In terms of the television commercials, a comparison of Cells 1 and 2 indicated the effects of modifying the disputed claim while a comparison of Cells 1 and 3 indicated responses to the disputed versus a nondisputed ad for the same product.[39]

In sum, the presence of a control group greatly increases the strength of copy test results. However, given the options for control group designs, a researcher must be able to justify the characteristics of the control group, that is, whether the control group is not exposed to any advertising, exposed to a modified version of the disputed ad, or exposed to a similar (but not disputed) ad for the same product.

Finally, it is important to note that even the use of a control group cannot redeem a copy test viewed as using a contrived or deceptive research design. Research perceived in this way, in which the results are considered an artifact of the research design, is not only ignored, but is often held against the individuals or company offering the research.[40]

QUESTIONNAIRE DESIGN AND QUESTION FORMATS

The legitimacy and acceptability of copy test data is dependent on the survey methods used to collect that data. Copy test findings that report data collected by faulty questionnaires or flawed individual survey questions are quickly rejected. A researcher must make certain that questionnaire design and question wording are beyond reproach.

Questionnaire design and content should follow the generally accepted principles of survey research discussed throughout this text, and especially in Chapters 12 and 13. At minimum, the questionnaire should

- *avoid biasing questions asked later in the survey by earlier questions.* This can often be accomplished by grouping questions on the same topic together and by completing one topic before moving onto another.

- *proceed, within any specific topic, from the most general questions to the most specific.* This is typically accomplished by using open-ended questions to begin a topic and then moving to a series of more focused closed-ended questions. This form of question progression works well because it permits respondents to provide "top-of-mind" answers without having been sensitized by the response options contained in later closed-ended questions.

- *reflect accepted industry procedures with regard to question sequence.* The Kraft cheese copy test used by the FTC measured "claimed recall" using a generally accepted sequence of product and brand cues:

    Do you remember seeing an advertisement for cheese slices?

    What brand was being advertised?

    Do you remember seeing an advertisement for Kraft singles?

- *be complete.* A survey that narrowly focuses on isolated parts of the advertising is likely to be rejected.

Once the design and content of the questionnaire have been determined, then it is necessary to make certain that the questions themselves are written without bias. Maronick has observed that "probably the single greatest source of conflict in copy test research for litigation is whether individual questions are properly drafted to elicit rather than suggest answers."[41] Adherence to the guidelines presented in Chapters 12 and 13 can greatly reduce or prevent wording-related bias, especially with regard to the most frequently occurring problems where

- *the question lead-in may bias the respondent by not explicitly stating alternative response options.* Asking "How much better or worse . . ." is less biased than asking "How much better . . . "

- *closed-ended questions do not contain an appropriate set of response options.* A set of response options that does not permit respondents to express their true opinion is likely to be rejected. Respondents in American Home v. Johnson & Johnson were shown an advertisement and then asked, using a closed-ended question, to pick which of five options best reflected what they thought was communicated in the ad. The question was rejected because none of the options reflected the literal meaning of the advertisement and two of the remaining options were clearly false. Additionally, a closed-ended question is likely to be found unacceptable if the available choices do not include options that a consumer would find reasonable.

- *closed-ended questions do not contain the full range of response options.* It is important that the set of response options permits respondents to clearly state their opinion, rather than forcing them to choose from a restricted set of options. For example, in seeking to determine purchase intention, instead of asking whether the respondent intends to "continue buying" or "stop buying," one should assess the degree of intention by using a range of options such as "stop buying completely," "continue buying, but purchase significantly less," and "continue buying but purchase less."[42]

INTERVIEWER QUALIFICATIONS, TRAINING, AND TECHNIQUES

The professionalism of the individuals who conduct the interviews and record respondents' comments and responses affects the integrity of copy test data. Real or perceived problems with the individuals who collect the data can cause the entire copy test to be discounted. It is important to demonstrate that interviewers have properly followed reasonable data collection procedures without error or bias. The problem of error can be minimized by

- providing interviewers with formal, systematic training in the procedures underlying the collection of data for the specific copy test.
- supporting training with written documentation.
- systematically monitoring the quality of interviews and correcting problems as soon as they are noted.

Problems of bias can be eliminated by making certain that

- interviewers do not know the name of the organization sponsoring the copy test or the purpose of the research project.
- interviewers are independent of all participants involved in the case.
- interviewer discretion and independent decision making are kept to a minimum. Interviewers should be given passive roles in the data collection process. Interviewer activities initiated at their discretion (e.g., clarifying question wording or question intent, engaging in casual small talk between questions, etc.) may be seen as providing the interviewer with the opportunity to lead, mislead, or bias respondents.

DATA ANALYSIS AND PRESENTATION

The procedures for data reporting discussed in the next chapter apply to the presentation of copy test data. Data must be analyzed and presented in a fair, objective manner where assumptions underlying analytical techniques, decisions, and interpretations are obvious and justifiable. Standards for the analysis and reporting of closed-ended questions are so well established that problems with this type of data are almost always instantly recognizable, for example, when inappropriate manipulations of the data have been performed or when data reporting is selective or incomplete. More ambiguity exists in the treatment of responses to open-ended questions.

The FTC scrutinizes the treatment of responses to open-ended questions and is quick to reject treatments of these responses that appear inherently biased, self-serving, or arbitrary. The likelihood of these negative perceptions occurring can be reduced by

- providing an explicit description of the rules governing verbatim coding.
- developing coding categories and labels that in an unbiased manner reflect the true nature of consumers' responses.
- coding and reporting all verbatims. Any appearance of bias due to selection must be avoided.
- distinguishing between first versus subsequent responses to each open-ended question.
- providing a complete, unedited transcript of all verbatims (to facilitate a determination of the appropriateness and completeness of coding).

RESEARCH PROJECT ADMINISTRATION

The value and acceptability of copy test research findings are always evaluated in light of the experience and expertise of the individuals and companies who planned, conducted, and analyzed the research. Experience and competence count in all aspects of the copy test. Thus, it is recommended that

- the individual responsible for study design and administration be recognized as an expert in survey research in general and advertising copy research in particular. This expertise should be the result of practical experience. The FTC has shown a tendency to criticize an academic witness or consultant when that individual has lacked practical experience in conducting advertising or copy research outside the classroom.
- the companies responsible for data collection have extensive experience and industry recognized expertise in the collection of survey information in general and copy testing information in particular.
- the individuals responsible for survey administration have demonstrated experience in the collection of survey data.
- the individuals responsible for data coding and analysis have demonstrated experience and expertise in these areas.

The presence of experience and expertise is a necessary, but not sufficient basis for copy test acceptance. It must be demonstrated that this expertise was used to design and supervise a copy test that is without internal bias or error. Consequently, it is recommended that the individual responsible for the design and administration of the research

- continuously and closely monitor all steps in the research project.
- act without interference or direction from attorneys. The involvement of attorneys in the design of a copy test or other research study is almost always viewed with a great deal of suspicion.

Endnotes

1. The chapter focuses on copy testing approaches that use questionnaires to collect data. Review Chapter 9 for biometric approaches to advertising testing.

2. Gallup & Robinson's Web site is http://www.gallup-robinson.com. Mapes and Ross' Web site is http://www.mapesandross.com.

3. Norms are an important aspect of copy testing. Most leading copy testing companies have tested thousands of commercials. The data from these commercial tests is used to create norms, which serve as unbiased benchmarks against which a test commercial's performance can be evaluated. Commercials that test above norm are considered to the stronger than commercials that test at or below norm.

4. Positive shifts in pre- to post-brand preference are generally interpreted to indicate positive commercial impact. However, there are instances where maintaining levels of interest can also be interpreted as a positive commercial outcome. This typically occurs for brands that have a dominant share within their category, for example, Campbell's Soup.

5. Several of these guidelines are adapted from Joel Axelrod (1986). *Choosing the Best Advertising Alternative: A Management Guide to Identifying the Most Effective Copy Testing Technique* (New York, NY: Association of National Advertisers and PACT (1982). "Positioning Advertising Copy Testing."

6. Mapes and Ross' normative base, for example, reflects nearly 30,000 commercial tests.

7. As discussed later in this chapter, split-run tests typically compare the relative effectiveness of different advertisements. A/B tests are more flexible and permit an advertiser to evaluate the relative effectiveness of a broad range of advertising-related stimuli.

8. Telemetrics is an example of a research company that assists advertisers with this type of research. The Telemetrics Web site is http://www.telmetrics.com.

9. The letters A and B refer to the two stimuli used in the test where A typically refers to the control or current stimulus and B refers to the test stimulus. While it is most common to use just two stimuli in an A/B test, there is no methodological reason why this must always be the case. An advertiser can, for example, test two new ads against the current ad, which would be labeled an A/B/C test.

10. Review Chapter 16 for the discussion of statistical testing. For additional insights, see J. Farmer (2008). "Statistical Analysis and A/B Testing" at http://20bits.com/articles/statistical-analysis-and-ab-testing.

11. Both situations and data are fictitious and for illustrative purposes only.

12. The number of cells is the result of multiplying the number of levels associated with each manipulation. Thus, the first situation shown in Figure 20.5 has eight cells, calculated as $2 \times 2 \times 2$ (representing the two levels associated with each of the three manipulations). The second situation also has eight cells (calculated as 4×2), while the last situation has nine cells (calculated as 3×3).

13. An interaction occurs when the simultaneous effect of the manipulations is different from the effect of each manipulation independently. Chapter 16 provides a detailed discussion of the analysis and interpretation of factorial designs, including main effects and interactions.

14. The situation and data are fictitious and are intended for illustrative purposes only.

15. Note that this is a post-test only design. Random assignment allows the researchers to assume that initial attitudes toward Chevron will be equivalent across the eight groups.

16. Review Chapter 16 for how to interpret the F-value.

17. This discussion draws on Sunil Gupta (2008). "The Advantages of Multivariate Testing" at http://publications.autonomy.com/pdfs/Optimost/White%20Papers/wp-Advantages-Multivariable-Testing.pdf.

18. The 32 combinations required for the full factorial design are calculated as the product of $2 \times 2 \times 2 \times 2 \times 2$.

19. For more detailed discussion of how to select the best combinations of characteristics for a multivariate test, see Sunil Gupta (2008). "Understanding the Essentials of Multivariate Testing: Volume 2: Counting Effects" at http://publications.autonomy.com/pdfs/Optimost/White%20Papers/wp_optimost_counting_effects.pdf.

20. Beyond the discussed strengths and weaknesses versus A/B and full factorial designs, there are different conceptual approaches to multivariate testing itself, with each approach having its own unique set of strengths and weaknesses. For a detailed discussion, see Sunil Gupta (2008). "Understanding the Essentials of Multivariate Testing: Volume 1: Comparing Multivariate Testing Approaches" at http://publications.autonomy.com/pdfs/ Optimost/White%20Papers/wp_optimost_comparing_testing_approaches.pdf.

21. Examples of tracking campaigns are: Evaluation of the National Youth Anti-Drug Advertising Campaign (http://www.drugabuse.gov/about/ organization/despr/westat/#reports); Expect Respect Television Advertising Evaluation Report (http://epubs.scu.edu.au/cgi/viewcontent.cgi?article=1155&context=educ_pubs); Resist Meth Social Marketing Campaign (http://www.sfhiv. org/files/campaigns/SFMethEvaluation.pdf); and Healthy Living (http://www.infoscotland.com/ infoscotland/95.26.28.html).

22. These questions are in addition to issues related to all research such as sampling, questionnaire design, etc.

23. Individuals defined as "unaware of the campaign" can be identified in one of two ways. First, they can live in the markets in which the campaign aired but are screened for the lack of awareness. Second, they can live in markets in which the campaign had not aired, thus having little if any chance to see the campaign. The second approach requires that other characteristics be similar across the two markets.

24. The Department of Health and Ageing main Web site is http://www.health.gov.au. Additional information on the Department's role can be found at http://www.health.gov.au/internet/ main/publishing.nsf/Content/health-overview. htm.

25. Examples of advertising and other campaign materials can be found at http://www.quitnow. info.au/internet/quitnow/publishing.nsf/Content/ youth-campaign-material.

26. All exercises and data are fictitious. Brand names are used for illustrative purposes only.

27. The Kraft and FTC questionnaires were reported in Appendix A and Appendix B of Jacob Jacoby and George J. Szybillo (1991). "Consumer Research in FTC Versus Kraft (1991): A Case of Heads We Win, Tails You Lose?" *Journal of Public Policy & Marketing* 14: 1–14.

28. A review of concept operationalization (see Chapter 11) will assist in responding to this exercise.

29. For simplicity, we discuss copy test design in the context of an FTC challenge. However, the discussion applies not only to FTC challenges, but also to state advertising challenges and Lanham Act challenges (where one advertiser directly sues another advertiser.)

30. Federal Trade Commission (1982). "Policy Statement on Deception" at http://www.ftc.gov/ oia/assistance/consumerprotection/advertising/ policy_deception.pdf.

31. Copy tests conducted by advertisers are generally designed to address the first and third characteristics of deceptiveness, that is, to demonstrate that the representation, omission, or practice is not misleading, and/or that even if it is misleading, it is not material.

32. Federal Trade Commission v. Thompson Medical Co. Inc., 104 FTC 648, Affirmed 791 P2d 189 (D.C. Circ 1986).

33. This section discusses methodological issues in the context of copy test research. However, these methodological guidelines can be generalized to apply to all research conducted in response to regulatory or legal challenges. The discussion in this section draws from the following sources: Jacoby and Szybillo, op. cit.; David W. Stewart (1995). "Deception, Materiality, and Survey Research: Some Lessons Prom Kraft." *Journal of Public Policy & Marketing* 14: 15–28; J. Craig Andrews and Thomas J. Maronick (1995). "Advertising Research Issues From FTC Versus Stouffer Foods Corporation." *Journal of Public Policy & Marketing* 14: 301–27; Ivan L. Preston (1992). "The Scandalous Record of Avoidable Errors in Expert Evidence Offered in FTC and Lanham Act Deceptiveness Cases." *Journal of Public Policy & Marketing* 11: 57–67; Thomas J. Maronick (1991). "Copy Tests in FTC Deception Cases: Guidelines for Researchers." *Journal of Advertising Research* 31: 9–17; Fred Morgan (1990). "Judicial Standards for Survey Research: An Update and Guidelines." *Journal of Marketing* 54: 59–70.

34. Jacoby and Szybillo, op. cit.

35. This example is based on Smith v. Strum, Ruger & Co. Inc., 39 Washington App. 740, 695 P. 2d 600 (1985). 16 The FTC in Thompson Medical (1984, CD at p. 794-795) noted that the use of mall-intercept designs is acceptable because this type of sampling is a generally accepted method for advertising copy test research. In addition, the use of forced exposure in a mall setting has also been accepted because it directly focuses consumers' attention on the advertising's explicit and implicit messages. [Bristol-Myers Co., 85 FTC 1975].

36. The FTC has explicitly taken the position that a "no exposure" condition is inappropriate when the advertising has had significant exposure prior to the copy test. It has stated that the comparison of nonexposure and test group responses is impractical in cases where "a limited number of consumers in the universe [are] not . . . previously exposed to the challenged ads." See Kraft, Inc., IDF 149.

37. Andrews and Maronick, op. cit.

38. Edward J. Russo, Barbara L. Metcalf, and Debra Stephens (1981). "Identifying Misleading Advertising." *Journal of Consumer Research* 8: 119–31.

39. Jacoby and Szybillo, op. cit.

40. Preston, op. cit. provides an example of a biased research design: "Sears, Roebuck and Co., advertised that its dishwasher could clean the dirtiest dishes, and pots and pans, with no prerinsing or prescraping . . . In its tests, Sears used hotter water . . . than most home water heaters can supply. It used more detergent than its instruction book told consumers to use. It rigged wash cycles to run longer than those on units sold to the public . . . It used lighter loads . . . including laying dishes flat . . . [and it) . . . did some tests with foods that are easy to clean, although the claims had been about foods that are the most difficult to clean." The FTC found the data obtained in this research worthless. For additional information, see Sears Roebuck, 49 FTC 263 1980.

41. Maronick, op. cit.

42. See Jacoby and Szybillo, op. cit.

CHAPTER 21

Reporting Research

It is a waste of time, effort, and money to conduct research if decision makers cannot understand the results. As a result, the effective presentation of findings and implications is an extremely important step in the research process. An excellent presentation gives decision makers the information and insights they need to evaluate alternative courses of action and to better understand the consumer and the marketplace. A poor research presentation greatly diminishes the usefulness of the research and has the potential to lead to detrimental decisions. Advertising researchers must therefore strive for excellence not only in research design and analysis, but also in the presentation of research findings. This chapter discusses considerations that apply to research reporting.

***

When you are done reading this chapter, you should have a better understanding of:

- the characteristics of good report writing
- the components of the written report
- special considerations for the oral research report
- special considerations for the reporting of quantitative and qualitative findings.

Thistory chapter focuses on the reporting of research findings and is divided into three main sections. The first two sections apply to all research. The chapter begins with a discussion of the characteristics of good report writing. The second section provides guidelines for the preparation of written and oral reports. The chapter concludes with a discussion of special considerations for the presentation of quantitative and qualitative data.

CHARACTERISTICS OF GOOD REPORT WRITING

An excellent research report successfully communicates the research project's goals, objectives, methodology, key findings, and implications. Excellence in research presentation can be achieved if you are clear, concise, complete, coherent, and careful in the preparation of all areas of the report.

Clarity and Conciseness

Clarity and *conciseness* are important attributes of a well-prepared research report. A report must clearly communicate the project's methodology, findings, implications, and recommendations in a way that is immediately understandable by the end users of the research. Clarity permits the audience to focus on what has been discovered and the implications of these discoveries. Conciseness saves the audience time and energy. The clarity and conciseness of a research report are improved when you keep the following in mind when preparing the report's narrative.

ELIMINATE UNNECESSARY WORDS.   Many reports take 10 or 12 words to say what could be said in 1 or 2. For example,

eliminate . . .	in favor of . . .
it is important to note that	importantly
due to the fact that	because
in view of the foregoing analysis	therefore, in light of
a supplemental review of the data	additional analyses

USE COMMON WORDS AND SIMPLE PHRASING; DON'T TALK LIKE A LAWYER, RATHER WRITE LIKE YOU TALK.   Researchers often think that a report requires formal, stiff language. This is not true. A report is clear and concise when it avoids popular but meaningless "buzzwords" (e.g., parameter, interface, prioritize, strategize, conceptualize, and scenario) and complex, convoluted phrasing, for example:

eliminate . . .	in favor of . . .
as previously alluded to	earlier
in accordance with the preponderance of the analytical results	the results indicate
a factor that exerts significance influence	an influential factor
in terms of the forthcoming data presentation	now

It is apparent that there needs to
    be a recommendation made, that
    based on the research, management
    consider a reprioritization of the
    benefits that are to be emphasized
    and communicated in the upcoming
    advertising campaign.

The research indicates that the relative
    emphasis given each product benefit
    be reevaluated prior to the develop-
    ment of next year's advertising
    campaign.

MINIMIZE THE USE OF TECHNICAL JARGON, AND USE VOCABULARY THAT MATCHES THAT OF THE READER OR LISTENER. Technical jargon helps individuals who share a common outlook and training quickly communicate with each other. Jargon and technical terminology hinder communication when they are used with audiences who are not specialists and who therefore do not understand what the terms mean.

Most individuals in a research report's audience are not trained researchers and, as a consequence, jargon and highly technical research terminology should be avoided. Leave the technical jargon for the appendices. This does not mean, however, that the concepts underlying technical terminology are inappropriate for a research report. Rather, it is the concept that should be explained and used rather than the technical term. However, when the use of technical terminology or jargon is absolutely needed, make certain that it is clearly explained at the point where it is introduced into the report.

AVOID LONG RUN-ON SENTENCES. Run-on sentences tend to bore and confuse an audience. Consider this statement:

There are many unresolved questions regarding the use of humor in advertising, in general, and within the context of Xerox advertising in particular, and as a consequence the client has requested research designed to help us more thoroughly understand the effect of humor on television commercial main message communication and brand perceptions within the context of Xerox advertising.

This single sentence should be broken down into a series of shorter sentences, presenting just the most important information. For example:

The agency is currently using humor in Xerox advertising but is unsure how it affects the target audience. No Xerox-specific research has been performed and other research investigating the effects of humor in advertising has shown conflicting results. Research is needed to determine the extent to which humor in Xerox television commercials affects message communication and perceptions of the Xerox brand.

USE ACTIVE VERSUS PASSIVE VOICE. The active voice adds interest, brevity, and clarity to the research report, for example:

Passive	**Active**
In the course of my analysis it became apparent that	The analysis shows
There were three reasons for this trend in response.	There were three reasons for this trend.

The option of checking as many or as few of the choices on the checklist was given to each respondent.	Respondents could check as many or as few items as they wanted.

Clarity and conciseness also apply to any visual aids, such as tables and charts, used in the report. Every visual aid should have a specific purpose and should facilitate communication and insights. Finally, clarity and conciseness can also be improved through the physical organization and presentation of the report. Informative section labels can summarize key findings, and bullet points can isolate and highlight key points.

Completeness

A complete report provides details at the necessary level of depth. A well-written research report provides all the detail necessary to help the reader or listener completely understand the research and its implications, but not so much detail that he or she is overwhelmed. The report writer can evaluate the breadth and depth of reported information by objectively reading the report and then asking: "Can my audience fully understand the research findings and *independently* evaluate the appropriateness of conclusions and recommendations without being distracted by irrelevant information?" If the answer is "yes," then the report is likely complete and written at the proper level of detail. This is not to suggest that a report provide a less than complete reporting of results, but rather, that the writer use the report's appendix to present relatively less important detail.

Coherence

Coherence refers to the smooth flow of thoughts in the presentation of findings. A research report is coherent when

- there are smooth transitions between thoughts.
- related pieces of information are grouped and presented together.
- topics are logically arranged and follow each other in an intuitively reasonable way.
- a clear, explicit presentation of findings serves as the direct basis for conclusions, implications, and recommendations.

Care

If you do not care about the correctness of your report, then it is safe to assume that your audience will not care about you or your findings. Nothing deflates a researcher's credibility faster than problems with information content, grammar, and spelling.

- *Information content.* Information presented must be without error. Tables and charts, for example, must be double-checked for accuracy, columns must total to the appropriate number, and table and chart labels must be correct. In addition, it is crucial that what is presented in the text be internally consistent *and* consistent with the information presented in tables and graphs. Errors in any aspect of data presentation, no matter how insignificant in the "big picture," lead to a reduction in the audience's view of the overall research project's and researcher's credibility. After all, if the researcher cannot get the details correct, how can anyone be sure that the design, conduct, and analysis of the research were handled properly?

• *Grammar and spelling.* The correct use of language, grammar, and spelling is also extremely important. Incorrect grammar and spelling get in the way of clear, direct communication of research results. Moreover, grammatical and spelling errors significantly lessen the audience's view of a researcher's competence and professionalism.

The Need for Review

No one has ever written a perfect research report in the first draft. All reports improve with review and revision. Remember,

> the last stage of report preparation, rough-draft revision, is just as important as [the initial writing], but it is the one most scorned by inexperienced writers. Revising a draft is comparable to painting a house: the appearance is improved without influencing the structure. But a report's "appearance" (readability) may determine whether or not it is read.
>
> Before you can revise your rough draft, you must recognize that it is not perfect. Approach it with a critical attitude. This can best be done by setting the draft aside for a few days, or at least overnight. This time lag should give you a fresh viewpoint and allow you to change to the role of a reader. This change in roles is most important because you must try to see what is actually written rather than what you think you wrote.
>
> Successful writers use a wide variety of methods to review and revise. One of the best involves three separate reviews of the report:
>
> **1.** The first review is of the material in the report. In this check, ask yourself these questions: Are the conclusions valid? Is sufficient information given to support the conclusions? Is enough background information given to explain the results? Have all irrelevant ideas been deleted? Are the illustrations pertinent and necessary?
>
> **2.** The second review is of the mechanics and organization. Are the subject and purpose clearly stated? Does the report flow smoothly from topic to topic? Are the relations between topics clear? Is each illustration clear and properly labeled? Are all required parts of the report included?
>
> **3.** The third review is of spelling, grammar, and sentence structure. Is each sentence written effectively? Are the sentences varied in length and complexity to avoid monotony? Are the words specific rather than vague? Have all unnecessary words been deleted?
>
> Make sure that you can truly answer "yes" to all of these questions before you consider your draft finished. Do not try to make one review do the work of three. Trying to cover too many categories in one review usually results in oversights and errors.[1]

THE WRITTEN RESEARCH REPORT

The content and organization of a written research report varies as a function of the report's audience and topic. However, most reports, regardless of whether they are presenting qualitative or quantitative data, will contain the following elements:

- title page
- table of contents and list of illustrations/figures
- executive summary
- background
- description of the methodology
- findings
- conclusions
- recommendations and next steps
- appendices

The remainder of this section discusses each of these components.

Title Page

The title page is the report's first or cover page. While the visual format of title pages shows great variation across reports, most title pages contain the same core set of information, specifically:

- the title of the research project
- the date the report was prepared
- the account or group for which the study was conducted
- internal agency job or control number (if applicable)
- the names of the principal agency researchers involved in the planning, conduct, and analysis of the research
- any restrictions related to distribution or confidentiality

A title page can be straightforward text, as shown in Figure 21.1, or it can incorporate graphics, as shown in Figure 21.2.

Table of Contents and List of Illustrations/Figures

All but the shortest research reports require a table of contents. The table of contents should list the page numbers of major sections and subsections as well as items placed in the report appendix. If the report contains illustrations, charts, or figures, a listing of these should follow the table of contents. The format of the table of contents and list of illustrations should reflect their purpose—to help the reader obtain an overview of the report contents and flow.

ADVERTISING ASSOCIATES, INC.
RESEARCH → INSIGHTS

Research Report:

Youth Prevention Anti-Smoking Advertising Test

September 14, 2009

Prepared for:
Tennessee Department of Education and Prevention Services

Lead Author: McKenna Elyse
Advertising Associates, Inc.
32568 G Street
North Ramonial, Maine 04110
207.555.1234
research@arassociates.com

FIGURE 21.1   Text Based Report Title Page

Executive Summary

The executive summary is the most important part of the research report. It contains a clear and concise *summary* of the information which will be presented in more detail later in the report. A useful executive summary presents information related to:

- *Study background and purpose.* What motivated the research and how will the information be used?

- *Methodology.* How was the information collected?

- *Main findings.* What was learned?

- *Conclusions (with any appropriate limitations) and recommendations.* How does the research impact key decisions? What should be done now that the research is complete?

**Fast Food Advertising and
Childrens' Preference for Fast Food**

Focus Group Findings
September, 2009

Prepared for: Fast Food Advertising Bureau

Prepared by: Martin Michaels
                       O'Connell Agency
                       347 Trade
                       Winds, Ohio 55434
                       555.444.1234
                       oconnell@oca.com

FIGURE 21.2   Graphics Based Report Title Page

The executive summary should be written so that it stands alone. It is common for the executive summary to be the only part of the full research report that is read and for it to be reproduced and distributed by itself without the full report attached. Thus, it is very important that the executive summary provide enough information to permit anyone who reads *only* this portion of the full report to understand what was learned and the basis for conclusions and recommendations. The press release provided in Figure 21.3 is an excellent example of an executive summary.

Background

The background section provides a context for approaching and using the information gathered by the research. It presents the background, research objectives, and rationale for the research project in greater detail than that presented in the executive summary. An example background description is shown below:

> For a number of years the Maine Department of Environmental Protection has provided outreach to educate the general public about the effect of soil erosion on water quality and it has assisted with the implementation of steps to reduce soil erosion. Soil erosion is, in fact, the single largest contributor to water pollution. Unfortunately, past surveys have shown that most of the public has little or no knowledge that soil erosion is an important pollutant.
>
> In order to assess the opportunity to increase the level of the educational effort and change these perceptions, the Maine Department of Environmental Protection engaged Market Decisions and Burgess Advertising to conduct a "test market" to assess the effectiveness of a communication campaign. Research was first conducted to assist in the development of the campaign. This qualitative research explored and identified ways to speak to the public about the negative effects of soil erosion. Based on the results of this research, communications materials were developed and then placed in selected Maine geographic areas. This report presents the results of campaign assessment. Specifically, in order to determine the effects of the advertising campaign, a telephone survey was conducted immediately following the end of the campaign. The survey, consisting of approximately 20 questions, addressed aided and unaided awareness of sources of pollution, aided and unaided awareness of advertising, and unaided awareness of the most important causes of water pollution.
>
> All steps in the research were conducted with the active participation and input from the Maine Department of Environmental Protection staff. This includes development of the focus group discussion guide; review of the focus groups; selection of the test markets; development of the campaign logo and tag line; and development of the radio, newspaper, and direct mail ads.[2]

Highly Influential "Connectors" Pay More Attention To and Engage With Brands More Often In Online Video Than General Viewing Population

NEW YORK, NY (October 8, 2008)—When it comes to advertising, not all online video viewers are created equal, according to a new commissioned study conducted by Forrester Consulting on behalf of Veoh Networks. Released today, "Watching The Web: How Online Video Engages Audiences" reveals that while some online video viewers still only "snack" on short clips, there exists a large audience of young, influential, engaged viewers who watch a great deal of long-form online video and pay attention to the brand messages delivered to them in online video environments.

The study found that Engaged Viewers (viewers who watch more than an hour of online video a week) make up nearly 40% of all online video viewers and watch nearly 75% of all online video. Of these Engaged Viewers, those who spend the most time consuming and sharing long-form content

• are more likely to watch videos all the way through;
• pay more attention to online video more than they do TV;
• interact with and rate the videos they watch more frequently;
• are twice as likely to recall in-video ads and post-rolls than non-Engaged Viewers;
• agree more readily that advertising is fair and helps pay for their free experience; and
• consider banner ads and ads that come in between videos (mid-rolls) most effective.

Who is the Engaged Online Video Viewer?

For Engaged Viewers, online video viewing is not a fad but rather a growing consumer habit: 61% of Engaged Viewers expect to spend significantly more time watching online video in the next year. The study also found that Engaged Viewers are young: while 13- to 24-year-olds make up only 15% of the online population, they represent more than 35% of Engaged online video viewers. In addition, Engaged Viewers watch an average of six kinds of video content—from animation to TV shows to movie trailers—during the course of a month.

The study further segmented Engaged Viewers into three sub-groups based on time spent watching video, types of videos watched, comfort level managing the video viewing experience, propensity to share videos, and amount of attention paid to online video compared to TV:

• Watchers, those who spend just over an hour watching video each week but, besides showing up to watch, don't engage the experience deeply by controlling playback or sharing videos.
• Controllers, those who go one step further; these younger viewers take an active role in controlling their video experiences and feel that online video is important to their lives.
• Connectors, though just 7% of online viewers, consume 20% of all online video and do 42% of all online video sharing.

Connectors and Controllers are especially valuable because they not only watch more online video than others, but they are shaping what others watch through their sharing.

Long Form Video Matters

The most desirable viewers—Connectors and Controllers—watch long-form video more often than Watchers do, so sites that offer a great deal of long-form video are the ideal places to reach them. Long-form video sites not only attract these viewers, but they also foster an environment that secures more viewer attention and engagement with advertising.

FIGURE 21.3 Executive Summary

Given that both Connectors and Controllers spend more time on long-form video sites, they are more apt to feel that advertising is a fair trade off to pay for online video services. Even more important, Connectors are significantly more likely to notice brands and feel ads are useful when presented with products they are interested in.

Implications for Advertisers

As online video viewing matures, advertisers can take advantage of the unique opportunity to reach valuable Engaged Viewers by starting with the following:

1. Think Advertainment, not Advertisement. Engaged video viewers are more open to enjoying the advertising they watch giving marketers an opportunity to create ads that are as entertaining as the video clips they are paired with. Make the advertising a part of this engaging environment by telling compelling stories rather than consistently repeating the same 30-second spot.

2. Active mindset = greater action. Engaged video viewers are more involved in every aspect of the viewing experience, including the advertising. In contrast, watchers who sit down to watch a one-minute user-generated clip come to the screen with very different mindsets. Consider having multiple creative units depending on the mindset d propensity to engage with the medium.

3. Think about all the ad units on the page as a team. All viewers feel advertising can be annoying. But none of them said it had to be annoying. Engaged viewers respond to ad formats that don't intrude unfairly. Their preference for banner ads supports this. But banner ads can be supported by a comprehensive ad experience that ties display ads, sponsorships, and in-video ads together into a coherent package.

4. Target it and they will come. As more viewers spend more than an hour a week viewing online video, it's time for advertisers and the sites that enable them to start matching ads to viewers more intelligently. The easiest place to do this is with long-form content, where the choice of programming—an episode of one's favorite tv show—says more about a viewer than a short clip about a dog on a skateboard ever can.

Methodology

Forrester Consulting conducted this study with more than 1,013 people who watch online video at least an hour each week. These responses were calibrated against Forrester's ongoing Consumer Technographics research to ensure response validity. Building on this insight, a sub-sample of 10 individuals who completed the online survey and gave explicit permission to be contacted for a follow-up interview were recruited to participate in 10 one-hour, phone-based in-depth interviews to discuss their experience with online video more fully. The combination of rigorous quantitative measures and qualitative insight paint a picture of today's engaged online video viewer.

FIGURE 21.3   (Continued)

Methodology

This section *summarizes* the specific decisions related to sampling and data collection. There should be a description of: who participated in the research, why these individuals were selected for participation, key questions asked, how the data was collected, and when the research took place. Remember, however, that this section's goal is a methodological summary. Technical details of the research as well as supporting materials such as questionnaires or interview guides should be placed in the report's appendix.

Findings

The findings section typically constitutes the major portion of a research report, and it is here that the audience is exposed to the results. A well-prepared findings section does the following:

- *It organizes the findings around core topics and presents these topics in logical order.* A report of a test of advertising creative may, for example, organize the findings around the following topics: reactions to the message, reactions to the creative approach, changes in brand attitudes, and purchase intent. A topic-based organization of the findings helps the audience completely understand the findings in one area prior to the discussion of findings from other areas.

  The presentation of results by topic area often requires the integration of findings from questions appearing in different parts of the questionnaire. As a result, we recommend against the use of the question-and-answer format for the presentation of the research results. The question-and-answer format occurs when the results are presented question by question following their order on the survey or questionnaire; that is, the results of Question 1 are presented, followed by the results of Question 2, Question 3, etc. We believe that the question-and-answer format should be avoided for several reasons. First, questions are sequenced in a questionnaire to facilitate the interview process. They are placed in a particular order so that the most insightful, meaningful information can be collected from a respondent. Survey questionnaire order is not in any way influenced by the reasonableness of presentation order in a research report. Thus, presenting findings question by question to reflect their order on the survey typically has no underlying rationale. Second, and perhaps more important, even if the question sequence does lend itself to the presentation sequence, this approach typically prevents the audience from seeing the "big picture." The presentation of results question by question makes it very difficult to discern overall trends and the interrelationships between survey questions.

- *It presents only those findings that are important.* A research study collects a great deal of information. After an examination of all of the findings, a researcher must decide which of the findings provide important insights and which are merely interesting. The former should be in the findings section; the latter should be placed in the appendix.

- *It presents all findings needed to support forthcoming conclusions and recommendations.* Conclusions and recommendations are more likely to be believed and accepted if their basis in the research results is direct and explicit.

The prior guidelines for the findings section of the research report apply to both quantitative and qualitative research. The specific content and approach to presentation varies considerably, however, depending upon whether the data is quantitative or qualitative. As a result, specific guidance for presenting numeric findings from quantitative research and more textual based results from qualitative research are presented later in this chapter.

Conclusions

This section draws conclusions from the findings presented in the prior section. While the findings section presents *what* was learned, the conclusions section tells the audience what the data *means*. This is a critically important section as it lays the foundation for the next section: recommendations and next steps.

Recommendations and Next Steps

Conclusions are a researcher's synthesis of what the research uncovered. They represent deductions drawn from an examination of the pattern of research findings and opinions as to what steps should be taken based on the findings and conclusions. Research reports without recommendations are incomplete and lack closure. Thus, all research reports should contain recommendations for action and next steps.

Appendices

The appendices to the full research report contain material that is too complex, too detailed, or otherwise inappropriate for the prior sections of the report. Materials placed in the appendix might include: the questionnaire used in the survey, findings that are not relevant to the discussion in the findings section, and sampling detail Appendices are very important. They provide a place to present important supporting information without interrupting the flow of the main report.

THE ORAL RESEARCH PRESENTATION

With few exceptions, every research project should be reported in written form, as described in the prior section. In addition, the results of many research studies are also reported in an oral presentation. This format has several benefits:

- It ensures that appropriate individuals have been exposed to the research findings, recommendations, and conclusions. There is never any guarantee that an individual will completely read the written report.
- It provides an opportunity to clarify any questions or problems associated with the written report or that have arisen since the report was issued.
- It provides an opportunity to expand on and extend discussions not addressed in the written report.

Many of the guidelines and recommendations presented for written reports also hold true for oral reports. The oral report must be clear, concise, complete, coherent, and produced with care. However, the differences between oral and written communication require some departure from the specific characteristics of written reports discussed earlier. Since PowerPoint is now the primary medium for oral presentation, the next section provides guidance for increasing the effectiveness of a PowerPoint or similar slide-based research presentation.

Improving PowerPoint or Similar Slide-Based Presentations

A PowerPoint presentation is not the same as or a substitute for the written report. Lawley notes that "attempting to have slides serve both as projected visuals and as stand-alone handouts makes for bad visuals and bad documentation . . . PowerPoint is a tool for displaying visual information, information that helps you tell your story, make your case, or prove your point. PowerPoint is a terrible tool for making written documents, that's what word processors are for."[3] This is because:

- *PowerPoint slides are talking points, not the conversation itself.* PowerPoint slides should help organize and illustrate what the speaker is saying. They are the jumping-off point for more detail and should not be viewed as the complete communication.

- *PowerPoint slides are not self-evident.* Since slides provide the mere skeleton of an argument, not its actual content, people who have read the slides but not heard the presentation normally cannot figure out what the speaker is trying to say.

- *PowerPoint compels the most superficial reconsideration of your own position.* While PowerPoint forces you to organize your thoughts to some degree, it does not ignite a reconsideration of your own argument the way a written document does. PowerPoint provides a thumbnail sketch of what you might say; written documents make you actually say it. Not surprisingly, authors of written documents find themselves altering their opinions as they write.[4]

Understanding PowerPoint's limitations is the first step in the development of a successful oral presentation. With these limitations in mind, the chance for success increases when you next address two critical steps: "The first step in creating a presentation is to decide what the main points are that you wish to communicate and just what you want the audience to remember. The next step is to decide what data you will need to show to support those points. Only after you have accomplished these two steps should you begin to work on the slides themselves."[5] The following suggestions will help you create more effective slides.[6]

- *Think in terms of ideas, not information.* The goal of each slide is the communication of a single, focused idea. When creating a slide, ask "What is the main idea I want someone to remember after seeing this slide?" instead of "What detailed information should I communicate?" Thinking in terms of ideas encourages you to be selective with regard to the information presented in support of the main idea. Thinking in terms of ideas will also help you to avoid information-dense slides. When individuals leave your presentation is not important that they remember each and every individual fact, but it is important that they remember the main ideas. Cluttered, information-dense slides that focus on facts are likely to be a barrier to the communication of ideas.

- *Communicate with both pictures and words.* Pictures can be powerful communication elements when used appropriately. Use these elements only when they can make a significant contribution to communication. Furthermore, avoid "cutesy" stock cartoon images as these tend to distract the audience and reduce your credibility.

- *Use slides as the prompt . . . fill in detail orally.* There is no reason for you to personally be presenting the research findings if all information is contained in and communicated by the slides. In these circumstances, the audience can simply read the slides by themselves. Presentations are much more effective, and audience interest is maintained better, if the slides only contain words, phrases, or pictures that are used as the jumping-off point for a more detailed oral communication.

- *Select no more than three easy-to-read fonts, and be consistent in their use.* There is no practical limit to the number of different fonts that can be used in any presentation. The use of multiple fonts, especially when used on the same slide, tends to be distracting and increases the cognitive workload of the audience. Beyond consistency in font use, make certain that all fonts selected are easy to read (especially with the slide background) and are large enough to be read easily by those some distance from the screen.

- *Think beyond the preformatted slide, using variety in layout to avoid predictability.* You maintain interest in your presentation when you go beyond relying entirely on PowerPoint's preformatted slides. Here, we are not suggesting that every slide needs to look different (you do need a sense of internal consistency) but we are suggesting that having some slides that deviate from the expected will help keep reduce audience boredom. Make certain that even when all slides use the preformatted function, you do not have slide after slide using the same format (e.g., 6 to 10 slides in a row all in the same bullet point format).

- *Maintain a visual focus; avoid too many bullet points on a single slide.* Each slide should have a visual focus that leads the audiences' eyes to one starting point. Additional information should flow from this point. Slides that are cluttered, especially slides with multiple bullet points, just overwhelm and cause the audience to tune-out.

- *Use animation or the "build" function to control information flow and to focus attention. But, avoid gratuitous, overdone transitions on every slide.* The build function for the presentation of bullet points is a powerful means of controlling information flow and maintaining audience attention. Imagine that you have a slide with three bullet points. If, for example, you show a slide with all three points at once, the audience will both read ahead (causing you to lose control over information flow) and will lose their visual focus. Instead, present just one point at a time, using PowerPoint's build function to present each point at the appropriate time. Similarly, if you have charts or tables to present, you can (selectively) build the chart over several slides, focusing each slide on the points on which you want the audience to focus. This provides several advantages over presenting the chart all at once: you control the information flow, audience members can ask questions specific to one aspect of the chart at the appropriate time, and audience members can better understand how individual data points in the chart are interrelated.

The Researcher As Presenter

Presenter skills greatly affect the success of any presentation. As you think about your role as a presenter, remember the following:[7]

- *Pace your presentation for the audience, not yourself.* Do not be afraid to deviate from your initial presentation plan. Instead, adapt your pace and material to meet audience needs. If it is clear that the audience understands your point, you may want to eliminate overheads that provide further explanation. If your audience appears to be befuddled, slow down and provide more explanation than initially planned.

- *Encourage participation but do not lose control of the presentation.* If your presentation is really interesting, your audience will want to discuss the findings and implications. If your presentation is really dull and uninsightful, your audience may be distracted, and discussion may gravitate to other issues. It is your responsibility as the presenter to control the discussion and to make certain that the presentation does not get off track. You must step in if side or other discussions get out of hand.

- *Show respect for your audience.* Do not talk down to your audience or try to show them how smart you are. You demonstrate respect for your audience by
  - beginning and staying positive. Do not begin, for example, by apologizing for the length of the presentation. It is also important to receive both positive and negative feedback in a professional manner; and
  - being prepared and knowing your material. The easiest way to show a lack of respect for members of your audience is to waste their time.

- *Be aware of nonverbal signals.* Your audience will react to what you say, how you say it, and the nonverbal signals sent as part of the oral communication process. You can improve the nonverbal signals you send by doing the following:
  - Maintain eye contact with your audience and do not talk to the screen.
  - Talk to the entire audience, not just senior management or those on one side of the room.
  - Maintain good body language.
  - Dress appropriately, select clothing that is appropriate for the setting and audience.

HANDLING QUESTIONS.[8]   It's not enough that you made it through your talk. Now you must subject yourself to cross-examination and do so while thinking on your feet. You can and must control the exchanges. Experienced speakers offer the following thoughts to help you avoid or defuse awkward situations, keep the questions on track and enable you to maintain your poise, dignity and control of the session.

- *To encourage your audience to ask questions, call for them in a way that suggests you expect and want them.* "What questions do you have?" is an active solicitation, whereas "Any questions?" is rather unconvincing. Remember that the audience needs a moment or two to make the transition from listening to speaking, to formulate their questions and, in some cases, to get up the courage to ask a question before the audience. Wait a minute or so and if no one asks a question, ask one yourself. That will generally get things rolling.

- *Respond simply and directly.* Don't allow yourself to get sidetracked or to ramble as both behaviors give the impression that you are not entirely sure of the answer.

- *Don't bluff.* If you do not have the answer, say so. Then promise to provide the information after time for reflection and further inquiry.

- *Don't lose your cool.* Never respond defensively, with irritation or with anger. These responses show that you have lost control of yourself and your presentation. Train yourself to resist the impulse to fight back or put down the questioner with a snappy reply when you are asked a hostile, negative, or belligerent question. If the question can be restated positively, do so, answer it, and move on. Otherwise, firmly, yet diplomatically, state that this is not the time or place for that debate, but offer to discuss it after your formal presentation concludes. Then move on.

- *If someone asks about something explicitly covered earlier in your presentation, answer anyway.* Perhaps you did not make the point clearly enough. This time, try another approach. If, for example, you covered the point in your talk with graphs and charts, respond to the question with a summary of the most important data covered in the visual material. If your talk progressed step-by-step to a conclusion, in response to a question you might begin with the conclusion and then provide supporting detail.

USING TABLES AND CHARTS EFFECTIVELY

This section provides guidance for the graphic presentation of quantitative data. We begin by presenting general considerations that apply to all tables and charts. This is followed by a discussion of four main types of tables and charts: numeric tables, bar, pie, and line charts.[9] We conclude with a discussion of the software options for creating tables and charts.

Considerations for all Tables and Charts

Tables and charts should add to, not detract from, your research report or presentation. To maximize the effective use of tables and charts, keep the following in mind:

- *Be certain that the table or chart compliments or extends the narrative presentation.* "Start by asking yourself if you really need [a chart]. Perhaps a statistical measure is good enough, perhaps you should use a table. If your job is to find patterns in a data set and build shared knowledge about it, what really matters is how efficiently the message is sent, and how efficiently it is received by the audience."[10] Make certain that your tables and charts maximize communication efficiency.

- *Keep tables and graphs simple.* Each table or chart should clearly focus on the one main idea you want to communicate. Use multiple charts to communicate multiple ideas rather than trying to fit everything into one visual.

- *Make certain that the table or chart is well integrated and consistent with the narrative portion of the report.* A collection of tables placed at the end of a report tends to decrease comprehension when (and if) it is referred to by making the reader jump from one part of the report to another. It is much better to interweave text, tables, and charts. This can be done by placing narrative, tables, and charts on the same page and referring to these items in the narrative. Finally, as discussed earlier, make certain that the points and conclusions presented in the text are the same as those made by the charts.

- *Use tables and charts to present the data. Use narrative to interpret the data.* Merely describing or reiterating what can readily be seen in the table or graph is boring, wastes time, and insults the audience's intelligence. The narrative should point out the significance of the information contained within the table or chart and how this information provides a foundation for later conclusions and recommendations.

- *Be careful and selective in the use of color.* If you use color in your charts or graphs, make certain that any differences marked by color are still apparent if the chart is copied in black and white. Try to avoid odd and distracting colors. Beyond these considerations, XL Cubed provides the following suggestions for the use of color:[11]

  - If you want different objects of the same color in a table or graph to look the same, make sure that the background—the color that surrounds them—is consistent.
  - If you want objects in a table or graph to be easily seen, use a background color that contrasts sufficiently with the object.
  - Use color only when needed to serve a particular communication goal. Don't use color to decorate the display. Dressing up a graph might serve a purpose in advertising, but it only distracts people from what's important—the data—in an information display.
  - Use different colors only when they correspond to differences of meaning in the data.
  - Use soft, natural colors to display most information and bright and/or dark colors to highlight information that requires greater attention.
  - To guarantee that most people who are colorblind can distinguish groups of data that are color coded, avoid using a combination of red and green in the same display.

- *Be careful and selective in your use of fonts.* Make certain that your type is easy to read, especially if the table or chart is reduced from its original size.

- *Don't confuse useful with pretty.* Making a chart prettier or having more of the "wow" factor doesn't make it a better chart. "Many marketers and graphic designers fail to understand this . . . The dominant view among visualization experts (namely Tufte and Few) is that 'form follows function': every ornament in a graph should be eliminated, every object must serve a clear purpose, efficiency should be maximized . . . Beauty should always follow function"

- *Avoid junk charts or just because you can do it doesn't mean you should do it.* Microsoft Excel is one of the most commonly used charting programs, and is quite powerful in the range of charts that it can produce. Keep in mind that many of these charts are totally inappropriate for use in business or research presentations. These charts place a high cognitive demand on the reader and as a result severely hamper the communication of findings and insights. Examples of these types of "junk" charts are shown in Figure 21.4.[12]

Finally, remember the guidelines for the ethical data presentation discussed in Chapter 2. You must make very certain that charts and tables clearly and without deception communicate appropriate trends and conclusions.

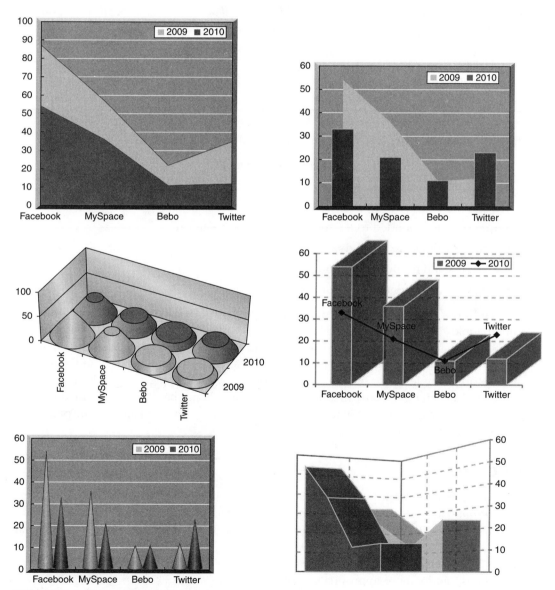

FIGURE 21.4   Examples of Junk Charts

Numeric Tables

Numeric tables are most appropriate for providing exact figures on either a single topic or multiple related topics. The following table, for example, displays consumers' product purchase intent after viewing one of three commercials.

Purchase Intent After Commercial Viewing (Total Sample)

	Commercial A	Commercial B	Commercial C
Purchase Intent Scale	*(Base = 140)*	*(Base = 140)*	*(Base = 140)*
Extremely likely	50.0%	14.2%	7.8%
Slightly likely	21.6	14.2	44.2
Slightly unlikely	14.2	50.0	26.4
Extremely unlikely	14.2	21.6	21.6
Total	100.0%	100.0%	100.0%

This table illustrates the key components of a well-constructed table:

- a descriptive title appears on the top of the table
- columns are clearly labeled
- the number of respondents in each group is shown
- numbers are rounded to a reasonable level of precision
- decimal points are aligned
- columns add to the appropriate total
- fonts are consistent and not distracting

The prior table successfully presents reactions to each commercial and illustrates how multiple sets of data can be clearly arranged to facilitate communication. It is possible, however, to pack tables with too much data, making it very difficult for audience members or readers to understand and interpret the data. The table shown in Figure 21.5 provides an example of this type of overloaded and overly complex table. The problem of too much data can be fixed by first deciding the single point that needs to be made by the table and then creating the table accordingly. The tables shown in Figure 21.6 (page 656) illustrate potential solutions.

Bar Charts

Bar charts are appropriate whenever the goal is to compare quantities or amounts at *one point in time* or to *compare changes over time*. Regardless of your goal for bar chart use, all well-constructed bar charts satisfy a common set of criteria. The before and after bar charts shown in Figures 21.7a and 21.7b illustrate these criteria. The chart shown in Figure 21.7b versus 21.7a has a more informative title, labeled horizontal and vertical dimensions, and a more appropriate vertical scale.

	Number of Commercials	Percent of all Commercials
Average Number of Commercials Reported Seen Per Day By Television Daypart, Gender and Outlet		
Early morning	15	13.4%
Men	7	6.3
Network	4	3.6
Nonnetwork	3	2.7
Women	8	7.1
Network	4	3.6
Nonnetwork	4	3.6
Daytime	34	30.4
Men	20	17.9
Network	11	9.8
Nonnetwork	9	8.0
Women	14	12.5
Network	7	6.3
Nonnetwork	7	6.3
Prime Time	46	41.1
Men	12	10.8
Network	0	0.0
Nonnetwork	12	10.8
Women	34	30.4
Network	20	17.9
Nonnetwork	14	12.5
Late Night	17	15.2
Men	10	8.9
Network	5	4.5
Nonnetwork	5	4.5
Women	7	6.3
Network	5	4.5
Nonnetwork	2	1.8

Source: MNHY 2010 Tracking Study
Base: 50 Men and 50 Women aged 25–54

FIGURE 21.5 Overloaded Numeric Table

ONE POINT IN TIME. The bar charts in Figures 21.8a and 21.8b both display the number of hours individuals aged 18 to 24 spent on various social networking activities.[13] The vertical axis labels each activity, and the height of each bar represents the number of hours spent on each activity. When using bar charts in this way, you should always be sensitive to how the bars are ordered. The chart in Figure 21.8a orders the categories as

**Average Number of Commercials Reported Seen
By Television Daypart: Men Vs. Women**

	Number of Commercials		Percent of Commercials	
	Men	**Women**	**Men**	**Women**
Early morning	7	8	14.2%	12.7%
Daytime	20	14	40.9	22.2
Prime Time	12	34	24.5	54.0
Late Night	10	7	20.4	11.1
Total	**49**	**63**	**100.0**	**100.0**

Source: MNHY 2010 Tracking Study
Base: 50 Men and 50 Women aged 25–54

**Average Number of Commercials Reported Seen
By Television Daypart and Source: Women**

	Number of Commercials		Percent of Commercials	
	Network	**Nonnetwork**	**Network**	**Nonnetwork**
Early morning	4	4	11.1%	14.8%
Daytime	7	7	19.4	25.9
Prime Time	20	14	55.6	51.9
Late Night	5	2	13.9	7.4
Total	**36**	**27**	**100.0**	**100.0**

Source: MNHY 2010 Tracking Study
Base: 50 Men and Women age 25–54

FIGURE 21.6   Examples of Focused Data Tables

they were asked in the survey question. Ordering data in this way, however, is often not the best decision, as it does not allow for a visual focus and makes comparisons as well as the overall trend difficult to see. As a result, when you use a bar chart to present nominal or ordinal level data, it is typically best to order the bars from either lowest to highest or highest to lowest (see chart in Figure 21.8b).

CHANGES OVER TIME.   Bar charts also work well to communicate changes over time, but when used in this way, you have to be selective in the data you choose to present. The charts shown in Figures 21.9a through 21.9c illustrate this use and accompanying considerations. The chart in Figure 21.9a compares the change in social networking activities between 2008 and 2010. Note that the lack of ordering hinders communication. The charts in Figures 21.9b and 21.9c solve this problem. The former chart orders the data by the amount of time spent on each activity in 2008, while the latter chart orders the data by the amount of time spent on each activity in 2010.

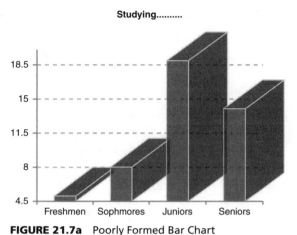

FIGURE 21.7a   Poorly Formed Bar Chart

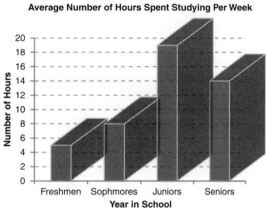

FIGURE 21.7b   Well-Formed Bar Chart

Pie Charts

Pie charts, similar to bar charts, allow you to compare quantities or amounts at one point in time. However, unlike bar charts, pie charts should not be used to show changes over time. Pie charts are the better choice versus bar charts whenever you need to visually represent *a share or segment of the whole*, for example, a proportion or a percentage. The pie represents 100% of the total, and each segment of the pie represents a share of the total. The pie chart shown in Figure 21.10 illustrates a well-constructed pie chart. Note that the chart is appropriately titled, segments are shaded to visually communicate differences, and each segment is completely labeled.

Figure 21.10 (page 659) illustrates a common type of pie chart. This *unexploded* chart displays the sample's age distribution without emphasizing any one of the age segments. When the segments are to receive emphasis, a *fully exploded* chart (see Figure 21.11, page 659) can be used.

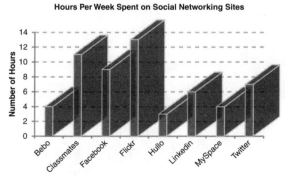

FIGURE 21.8a   Unordered Bar Chart

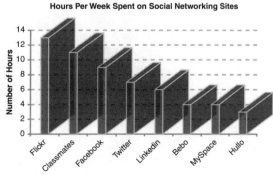

FIGURE 21.8b   Ordered Bar Chart

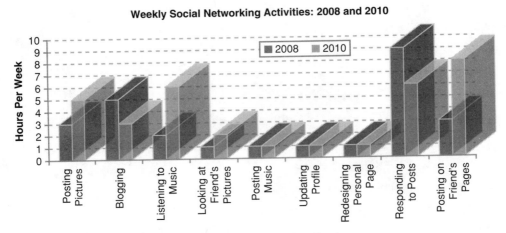

FIGURE 21.9a Visually Complex Multiple Points in Time Bar Chart

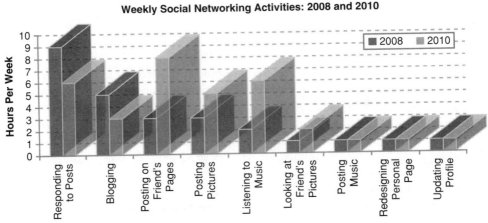

FIGURE 21.9b Ordered and Simplified Multiple Points in Time Bar Chart: Focus on Common Activities

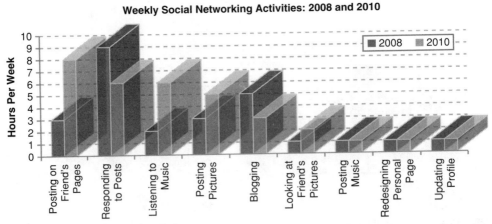

FIGURE 21.9c Ordered and Simplified Multiple Points in Time Bar Chart: Focus on Largest Change

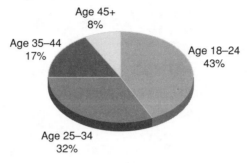

FIGURE 21.10 Well-Formed Pie Chart

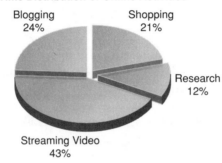

FIGURE 21.11 Fully Exploded Pie Chart

Line Charts

Line charts are appropriate for displaying data trends, especially trends over time. The chart in Figure 21.12, for example, shows the trend in advertising awareness for three

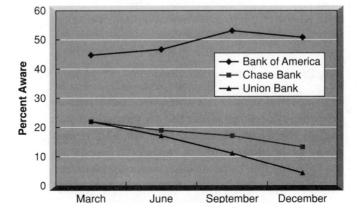

FIGURE 21.12 Line Chart Displaying Trend Data

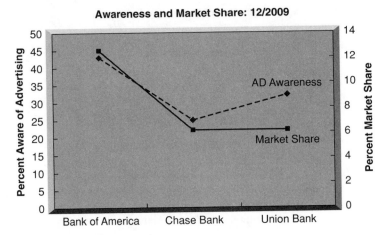

FIGURE 21.13   Line Chart With Dual Axes

brands during 2009. The line chart makes it easy to see which brands are increasing or decreasing in terms of this measure. The chart shown in Figure 21.12 also illustrates the characteristics of well-constructed line charts: the title is descriptive and meaningful, both axes are meaningfully labeled, the visual representation of each line is distinct and easy to see, and the "awareness" axis starts at zero and has reasonable spacing.

Except in well-justified and specialized circumstances, we do not recommend the use of multiple line graphs where the two vertical axes represent different measures and each line is read against a different axis. This type of line chart (Figure 21.13) is often very confusing and difficult to understand.

Software Options for Chart Creation

STATIC CHARTS.   Microsoft Excel is probably the most common software program used for static table and chart creation. Given its popularity, it is not surprising that a great number of individuals have provided tips and techniques for using Excel's charting functions more successfully. Some of these guides can be found at: Peltier Technical Services, About.com: Spreadsheets, Microsoft, LabRight Resources, and The Spreadsheet Page.[14]

A number of programs have been developed to move transform Excel data into more visually appealing charts. While different in cost and approach, all are designed to seamlessly work with Excel for chart creation. Examples of programs that take this approach are: Tableau (http://www.tableausoftware.com/excel-charts-graphs) and DPlot (http://dplot.com/index.htm). Similarly, Analyze-It (http://www.analyse-it.com/products/standard/) is designed to work with Excel to permit both statistical analysis and charting abilities.

Finally, there are software programs that provide alternatives to Excel. These stand-alone programs, such as Smart Draw (http://www.smartdraw.com/exp/cht/), allow you to use import Excel data to create visually distinct tables and charts. We suggest you visit the Smart Draw Web site to obtain a trial version as well as download their whitepaper "Creating Persuasive Charts."[15]

FLASH FOR INTRA- OR INTERNET PRESENTATION.   It is certainly the case that any chart created by Excel or other charting program can be used for internal communication on a company intranet or for external audiences over the Internet. These charts will appear as static images when used in these environments. An alternative to this approach is the use of Flash-based applications to create dynamic (as opposed to static), animated tables and charts. Fusion Charts and XML/SWF Charts are examples of this latter approach.

Fusion Charts and XML/SWF Charts are two programs that use XML to create Flash animated charts for use in Web and desktop presentations. Both programs offer multiple types of 2D/3D charts including line, area, bar, column, pie, doughnut (donut), combination, scatter, bubble, and scroll charts, and both allow the functional and cosmetic aspects of each chart to be extensively customized. It is important to note that while the tables and charts produced by Fusion Charts and XML/SWF Charts can be animated for use online, all can be exported as static images for use in written and oral reports.[16]

SPECIAL CONSIDERATIONS FOR PRESENTING QUALITATIVE DATA

Numeric tables and charts provide the detail in quantitative reports. This detail increases the credibility of the analysis and provides support for subsequent recommendations and conclusions. Qualitative research uses summaries of consensus and quotations rather than numbers to accomplish these outcomes.

Summaries of consensus in a qualitative report indicate the extent to which members of the sample agreed or disagreed with regard to a particular point. However, because qualitative samples tend to be small, numeric descriptors have the potential to inappropriately bias the reader and lead the reader to draw incorrect conclusions. Consider a focus group, for example, for which the report writer provides the following summary:

> 90% of the group were positive toward Concept A, while 70% were positive toward Concept B.

One would rightfully conclude from this statement that Concept A was the much stronger concept; after all, 90% is much higher than 70%. But, in reality, the difference between the two concepts represented the opinions of *just two people*. As a result, we recommend that qualitative summaries use vague quantifiers to describe group size, for example: "all respondents," "the vast majority," "the majority," "a few," and "almost no one." These quantifiers allow the report reader to understand the size of various groups without the bias associated with describing group size numerically. Thus, the prior statement might be better presented as:

> Almost all respondents were positive toward Concept A, while slightly fewer were positive toward Concept B.

Quotations provide the detail in a qualitative report. As such, they should be used whenever there is a need to provide substantive depth to the discussion. Quotations can, for example, be used to support a conclusion, to exemplify a trend, or to compare and contrast alternative points of view. (See the online supplemental readings for Chapters 7 and 19 for examples.) Quotations are only useful, however, if the report reader can quickly identify the quote and successfully relate it to appropriate report content. As a result, the qualitative report should take care to offset and highlight the quotations used in the report. This can be accomplished through the use of indentation and changes in font size, type, or color.

Quotations should be accompanied by source information, but only to the extent to which that information is relevant to the current discussion. Consider the following quotation:

> *"Concept A is the most honest of all the concepts. This one really talks to my heart."*
>
> —A Married Female, Chicago Groups, Aged 53

If this quote was being used to illustrate the differences between men and women, then only the gender descriptor would be required; if the quote was being used to illustrate the differences between younger and older respondents, then only the age descriptor would be required. Finally, with regard to quote identification, actual respondent names should never be used.

APPLYING CHAPTER CONCEPTS

The research reports and presentations shown in other chapter's online supplemental readings illustrate the principles discussed throughout this chapter and serve as examples of excellence in the analysis and reporting of research findings. This chapter's online supplemental reading provides one additional example of superior research and reporting.

Feed Company helps major U.S. brand advertisers maximize the placement and viewing of their online videos. The company states, "We employ innovative marketing tactics to get your brand videos exposed to popular blogs, video sites, and social networks. Our ability to feed engagement makes us the first choice for companies who want to make sure their videos are being watched online."[17] In order to better understand advertisers' perspective on its core business—viral video use and placement—Feed Company conducted an online survey of 40 executives at top U.S. creative ad agencies and media buying firms. The result of the research, the Viral Video Marketing Survey, is provided as this chapter's online supplemental reading.

The Viral Video Marketing Survey is an example of timely research that provides important business insights to Feed Company and a frame of reference for advertisers considering the use of viral video for brand promotion. As discussed earlier in this chapter, however, even the best designed research is of little value if the findings are presented poorly. Fortunately, the Viral Video Marketing Survey does not suffer from this problem. On the contrary, the report is an excellent model for the presentation of research findings:

- a significant amount of information is presented very concisely;
- the visual organization and layout facilitates information acquisition;
- the use of headings to summarize the findings (rather than report specific pieces of data) makes it easy to quickly understand key results and their implications;
- appropriate graphs and charts are integrated with the text-based explanations;

- open-ended comments are integrated with the numeric data to provide deeper insights into findings and implications;
- the single page Executive Summary is clear, concise and works extremely well both to summarize the findings and to encourage the reader to continue reading the full report.

In sum, the Feed Company Viral Video Marketing Survey is an excellent model for research reporting.

SUMMARY

The results and implications of advertising research are presented in oral and written form. Effective presentation is a critical final step in the research process. Research that is well designed, conducted, and analyzed, but poorly presented, is generally research that fails to contribute to the decision making process.

The written and oral presentation of findings and implications can be improved when attention is given to both the narrative and graphic elements of the report. Excellence in research presentation can be achieved when a researcher is clear, concise, complete, coherent, and careful in the preparation of all areas of the report. Report quality is also increased when there are multiple reviews and revisions of the report. The graphic portion of a quantitative report is improved when the researcher prepares and uses the appropriate form of a numeric table, bar, pie, or line graph. The detailed portion of a qualitative report is improved when the researcher takes care in the selection and presentation of respondents' quotations.

A written report generally consists of nine elements: title page, table of contents, executive summary, background, methodology, findings, conclusion, recommendations/next steps, and appendices. While each of these sections is important, the executive summary is the most important, as this section of the report may be the only portion read by decision makers.

An oral research report is not simply the written report condensed or translated onto slides. The quality and value of an oral reports increases when the researcher thinks in terms of ideas (not information), communicates with both pictures and words, uses slides as the prompt (and fills in the detail orally), and takes care in the selection of fonts and layout. When conducting an oral presentation of research results, the researcher should remember to pace the presentation for the audience, encourage participation, and show respect for the audience.

Review Questions

1. What five researcher characteristics are required for excellence in report preparation?
2. List and provide examples of five ways to increase a research report's clarity and conciseness.
3. How can you tell if a research report is complete?

4. How can you tell if a research report is coherent?
5. What are the three steps in report review?
6. What are the components of the written research report?
7. What are the typical elements of a title page?

8. What are the components of an executive summary? What content does each component address?

9. What information is presented in the research report's background section?

10. What information is contained in the research report's methodology section?

11. What are the characteristics of a well-prepared findings section?

12. What is the function of the report appendix?

13. How can a researcher overcome the limitations of PowerPoint in an oral presentation?

14. What guidelines help researchers improve their presentation skills?

15. What guidelines help a researcher better respond to questions?

16. When should numeric tables be used?

17. What are the characteristics of a well-created numeric table?

18. When should bar charts be used?

19. What are the characteristics of a well-created bar chart?

20. When should pie charts be used?

21. What are the characteristics of a well-created pie chart?

22. When should line charts be used?

23. What are the characteristics of a well-created line chart?

24. How should group size and group consensus be described in a qualitative report?

25. What are considerations in the use of quotations in a qualitative report?

Application Exercises

Application exercises 1 through 4 refer to chapter content and discussion.

1. Read and then revise each of the following paragraphs to improve clarity, conciseness, correctness, and coherency.

> Every respondent who participated in the study was exposed to one and only one of the three test commercials. The commercials were named "Going Home," "Heart," and "Fathers Day." Respondents saw the commercial that they were assigned: viewed and then completed a 15-minute self-administered questionnaire. It was believed by the research staff that a self-administered questionnaire was the best venue for data collection. Each commercial lasted 30 seconds. When the self-administered questionnaire was completed, a trained interviewer checked the respondent's responses for accuracy and completeness. It was then decided by the interviewer whether clarification was needed or if the respondent could be excused.

> Each interviewed respondent was requested to provide his or her perceptions of the quality and value of Vita Corporation's shampoos and conditioners so that this recent data could be compared with data from the prior year in order to determine the trend, if any, and the significance of the trend, if any, in changes in the nature of consumer' perceptions of the Corporation's shampoos and conditioners.

> Consumers in the advertising target audience were assessed with regard to their affective and cognitive responses to the advertising. Affective responses represent subjective, nonrational, and emotional responses while cognitive responses, for the purposes of this study, were defined as logical, rational responses without an overlay of affect. Respondents' scores on the total set of scales were calculated, and then a series of subtest scores were calculated in order to develop a respondent profile This profile then lets us determine the breadth and depth of affective and cognitive rresponse to the advertising.

> The decision whether or not to purchase the product appears to be generally related to three factors. First, there is the factor of advertising awareness. While we cannot postulate a causal relationship, we can state with a high degree of certainty that individuals who are more aware of the advertising tend to be more likely to purchase the product. Keep in mind that all three factors are all important. The second, middle factor, relates to disposable income. One is more likely to purchase the product when he or she has more disposable income. This is important and reasonable. Third, but also important, is the factor of geography. Consumers in urban

areas versus suburban and rural areas are more likely to purchase the product.

2. Select an article from either the *Journal of Advertising Research* or the *Journal of Advertising* for which you feel the clarity, conciseness, correctness, and coherency of the methodology or results section could be improved. Revise and improve the writing.

3. Select an article from either the *Journal of Advertising Research* or the *Journal of Advertising* for which you feel the visual presentation of the findings could be improved. Revise and improve the visual aspects of data presentation.

4. Visit Slideshare at http://www.slideshare.net and download a research-oriented presentation on a topic of your choice. Make certain that the presentation is in PowerPoint and not in PDF format. Prepare a critique of the presentation, noting its specific strengths and weaknesses. Redo the presentation in a way that maintains its strengths and reduces or eliminates its weaknesses.

Application Exercises 5 through 7 refer to this and prior chapters' online supplemental readings.

5. Imagine that your supervisor has asked you to prepare a memo summarizing the key findings and insights from two of the following reports/presentations discussed in prior chapters. This memo would be the equivalent of an executive summary. Prepare this memo choosing from:

Sleepy Driver Focus Groups (Chapter 6)

Video Consumer Mapping Study (Chapter 8)

Razorfish Digital Brand Experience (Chapter 12)

Cossette 2009 Social Media Study (Chapter 12)

Massive Jumper In-Game Advertising Report (Chapter 14)

Healthy Eating Communication Test (Chapter 19)

Second-Hand Smoke Communication Test (Chapter 19)

6. You have been asked to turn a PowerPoint presentation into a stand-alone research report. Choose one of the presentations below, and prepare a complete written research report. Be certain that your report includes both text and appropriate graphs, charts, or other visual aids. You can choose from:

Social Media Trends (Chapter 3)

Video Consumer Mapping Study (Chapter 8)

Cossette 2009 Social Media Study (Chapter 12)

Massive Jumper In-Game Advertising Report (Chapter 14)

Generation C (Chapter 17)

7. You have been asked to turn a written report into a PowerPoint (or similar) presentation. Chose one of the following reports, and prepare the presentation slides. Be certain that your report includes text, graphs, charts, or other visual aids as appropriate. You can choose from:

Sleepy Driver Focus Groups (Chapter 6)

One to One: Emotion, Engagement, and Internet Video (Chapter 9)

Tobii Case Studies (Chapter 9)

Razorfish Digital Brand Experience/2009 (Chapter 12)

IAB Online Advertising Effectiveness Research (Chapter 14)

Healthy Eating Communication Test (Chapter 19)

Second-Hand Smoke Communication Test (Chapter 19)

Endnotes

1. NASA(undated). "Chapter 1—Stages of Report Writing" at http://grcpublishing.grc.nasa.gov/editing/CHP1.CFM.

2. Maine Department of Environmental Protection (2001). "Soil Erosion Advertising Test" at http://www.epa.gov/nps/toolbox/surveys/mainepilotreport.pdf.

3. Elizabeth Lawley (2005). "The Culture of 'the Deck'" at http://mamamusings.net/archives/2005/11/19/the_culture_of_the_deck.php.

4. Tom Grant (2006). "Death by Powerpoint" at http://armsandinfluence.typepad.com/armsandinfluence/2006/08/death_by_powerp.html.

5. Terly R. Roper and Read G. Gilgen (undated). "Improving Powerpoint Presentations" at http://www.ashs.org/index.php?option=com_content&view=article&id=167%3Aimproving-powerpoint-presentations&Itemid=80.

6. This section draws on Roper and Gilgen op. cit. as well as Andy Goodman and Cause Communications (2006). *Why Bad Presentations Happen to Good Causes, and How to Ensure They Won't Happen to Yours* at http://www.agoodmanonline.com/publications/how_bad_presentations_happen/index.htm. For additional insights, see Cliff Atkinson (2005). *Beyond Bullet Points: Using Microsoft PowerPoint to Create Presentations That Inform, Motivate, and Inspire* (Redmond, WA: Microsoft Press); and Edward Tufte (2006). "The Cognitive Style of Powerpoint" at http://www.edwardtufte.com/tufte/powerpoint. Finally, for illustrations of all points presented in this section, see the following presentations, all available from Slideshare (http://www.slideshare.net): "How to Torture Your Students Using Powerpoint, Problems with Powerpoint (and Student Presentations)," "Ten Mistakes in Powerpoint Presentation," and "Death by Powerpoint."

7. For additional insight into presentation skills, see "Killer Presentation Skills" at http://www.youtube.com/watch?v=whTwjG4ZIJg.

8. This section is abridged from Office of Naval Affairs (2004). "Tips for Preparing Scientific Presentations—Delivery" at http://www.onr.navy.mil/about/speaking_tips/delivery.asp#qa.

9. The discussion in this chapter focuses on the most common ways research data is presented. However, we strongly encourage a visit to "A Period Table of Visualization Methods" at http://www.visual-literacy.org/periodic_table/periodic_table.html#) and "Data Visualization: Modern Approaches" at http://www.smashingmagazine.com/2007/08/02/data-visualization-modern-approaches/ to see the full range of how numeric information can be presented. In addition, all data presented is fictitious and for illustrative purposes only.

10. Jorge Camoes (2009). "14 Misconceptions about Charts and Graphs" at http://charts.jorge camoes.com/. This Web site is an excellent source for further reading about chart and table construction.

11. Steven Few (2008). "Practical Rules for Using Color in Tables and Graphs" at http://www.bonavistasystems.com/Download2/Practical%20Rules%20for%20Using%20Color%20in%20Charts.pdf.

12. See Jorge Camoes (2008). "Excel Chart Gallery: A Difficult Equilibrium" at http://charts.jorge camoes.com/excel-chart-gallery-a-difficult-equilibrium/ for an extended discussion and additional examples of this topic.

13. All data presented in this and following figures are fictitious and for illustrative purposes only.

14. The locations for these resources are: Peltier Technical Services at http://peltiertech.com/Excel/Charts/); About.com: Spreadsheets at http://spreadsheets.about.com/od/excelcharts/A_Guide_to_Creating_and_Formatting_Excel_Charts.htm; Microsoft at http://office.microsoft.com/en-us/excel/HA010841581033.aspx; LabRight Resources at http://ncsu.edu/lab write/res/gt/gt-bar-home.html); and The Spreadsheet Page at http://spreadsheetpage.com/index.php/tip/C16/.

15. The whitepaper can be downloaded from http://www.smartdraw.com/solutions/whitepapers/Creating_Persuasive_Charts.pdf.

16. Fusion Charts' home page is http://www.fusioncharts.com. XML/SWF Charts' home page is http://www.maani.us/xml_charts/index.php?menu=Introduction. Examples of tables and charts developed with Fusion Charts can be seen at http://www.fusioncharts.com/Gallery/Default.asp, while examples of XML/SWF Charts can be seen at http://www.maani.us/xml_charts/index.php?menu=Gallery Note that neither program is browser or operating system specific, and a user (fortunately) does not need to know anything about Flash in order to create charts with either program. Both programs offer a free downloadable copy, and we recommend that you try each. Single and corporate licenses for both programs are very inexpensive.

17. Feed Company is at http://feedcompany.com.

INDEX